Benedict Arnold

Benedict Arnold

PATRIOT AND TRAITOR

Willard Sterne Randall

QUILL/WILLIAM MORROW
NEW YORK

Recognizing the importance of preserving what has been written, it is the policy of William Morrow and Company, Inc., and its imprints and affiliates to have the books it publishes printed on acid-free paper, and we exert our best efforts to that end.

Library of Congress Cataloging-in-Publication Data

Randall, Willard Sterne.
    Benedict Arnold : patriot and traitor / Willard Sterne Randall.
      p.   cm.
    Includes bibliographical references.
    ISBN 0-688-10968-3
    1. Arnold, Benedict, 1741–1801.   2. American loyalists—Biography.
    3. Generals—United States—Biography.   4. United States.
    Continental Army—Biography.   I. Title.
    E278.A7R36 1990
    973.3'82'092—dc20
    [B]   90-5656
                                                                  CIP

Printed in the United States of America

First Quill Edition

1   2   3   4   5   6   7   8   9   10

DESIGNED BY BARBARA MARKS GRAPHIC DESIGN

To Nan

ACKNOWLEDGMENTS

From the outset of writing this book, I have had the unwavering encouragement of my editors, my literary agent, and my wife. Alan D. Williams, my editor at Arbor House, was generous with his time and with every form of support. His patience and his delicate proddings helped to keep me researching, writing, and rewriting through five years. Taking over the manuscript during a difficult transition, Maria Guarnaschelli, my editor at William Morrow, gave prodigiously of her talents and her insights. Once again, my courageous friend and agent, Ray Lincoln, deserves my gratitude more than I can say. So many times, a talk with Ray raised my spirits. Her good sense has helped me inestimably. And my patient, wise, and irreverent wife, Nancy A. Nahra, has given me the benefits of her poet's ear, her understanding of the eighteenth century.

There are no great collections of the papers of the most famous American traitor, and I owe thanks to many people who helped me to ferret out widely scattered letters and documents. I owe an enormous debt to the editors of the Program for Loyalist Studies and Publications, Robert A. East, James E. Mooney, and Herbert Leventhal, whose years of patient scholarship have helped to make possible a reexamination of the American Revolution. To Dr. Mooney, my first critic on a paper on the Loyalists so long ago, I owe a great deal of thanks for his meticulous and exacting reading of my nine-hundred-page manuscript of this book. I am also indebted to the editors and researchers of the *Naval Documents of the American Revolution* series, whose two-decade effort revealed an untapped vein of Arnold materials. To Galen R. Wilson, then curator of manuscripts at the William L. Clements Library at the University of Michigan at Ann Arbor, I owe special thanks for guiding me to unpublished letters by the British general Benedict Arnold, and when a precious notebook containing weeks of work was lost in Paris, for helping me to find those same letters over again.

7

For years of cooperation, support and friendship, I wish to pay especial thanks to James H. Overfield, chairperson of the History Department at the University of Vermont. At every stage of the research, I had the invaluable assistance of the staff of the Bailey/Howe Library at the University of Vermont, especially Bonnie and Joe Ryan. Personal thanks go to my unflinching friend Wolfe W. Schmokel, to Thomas Visser at Vermont, and to M. Jerome Diamond. Nicholas Westbrook, director of the Fort Ticonderoga Museum, has been generous with his time and the collections in his care. James E. Mooney, librarian of the New-York Historical Society, was especially helpful with his suggestions, as was Esmond Wright, professor emeritus at the Institute of United States Studies of the University of London.

Persistence is the hallmark of a good researcher, and I have had the help of four of them. Lorna Hutchinson helped me uncover traces of the Arnolds' years in Canada in the archives of the New Brunswick Museum at St. John, New Brunswick. Clare Lise Cavicchi and Ryan Madden, both products of the graduate program in history at the University of Vermont, also proved diligent and creative research assistants. And once again my son, Christopher Fairbanks Randall, a keen student of the American Revolution, provided timely assistance. Ann Van Arsdale at the Firestone Library of Princeton University was, as usual, cheerful and helpful. I also wish to thank the University of Michigan for according me visiting scholar status and aiding me with many volumes that would otherwise have been difficult to obtain.

And for the many months of tedious and meticulous labor involved in organizing and preparing the various drafts of the manuscript, I want to thank my copy editor Ted Johnson, and typists, Bridget Butler, Cynthia Markham, and especially Diann Varricchione, as well as my research assistant in France, Mitzi Markese, and Bruce Hattendorf at William Morrow for his editorial assistance.

For help with preparing the illustrations, my thanks to Bill Di Lillo and Sally McCay in Media Photography at the University of Vermont.

For permission to quote from papers in their collections, I am grateful to the Historical Society of Pennsylvania, the Archives Department of the Pennsylvania Historical and Museum Commission, the James Copley Library, Fort Ticonderoga Museum, New-York Historical Society, New Brunswick Museum, Princeton University Library, Special Collections of Bailey/Howe Library, University of Vermont, New York Public Library, New Haven Colony Historical Society, William L. Clements Library of the University of Michigan, Ann Arbor, and Provincial Archives of Canada.

CONTENTS

*Such a dirty, mercenary spirit
pervades the whole [American
Revolution] that I should not be
surprised at any disaster that may
happen.*

George Washington to Joseph Reed, November 18, 1775

BOOK ONE

---★---

"A
VENERATION
BORDERING
ON
IDOLATRY"

---★---

1

"YOU ARE
ACCOUNTABLE TO GOD"

God seems to be saying to
all children, be ye ready.
Pray improve your time,
or death may overtake you
unprepared.

Hannah Arnold to her twelve-year-old son Benedict, 1754

Benedict Arnold was born a Saint, the son of Saints. He was taught by his mother, herself a born Puritan from a devout Connecticut family, that he belonged to God's predestined elect and that if he followed the beliefs of the Puritan covenant with God, nothing he could ever do would deprive him of everlasting paradise. Arnold's mother's family had helped to found Norwich Town, Connecticut, and when the family went to church several times a week, they were conspicuous, having a front-row pew. From his father, a fourth-generation New Englander, Benedict learned, and it was important to him, that the name of Arnold had long been respected in the American colonies. The first Arnold in America had helped Roger Williams to found Rhode Island; his son, the first Benedict Arnold, had been ten times elected governor of Rhode Island, serving for fifteen years, longest tenure of any of the colony's governors.

The fortunes of the Arnold family rose and fell with the tides of war and peace that swept over the Atlantic frontier in the century leading up to the American Revolution. Governor Arnold, great-grandfather of an infamous namesake, died a rich man, but his son lived long enough to spend all the family's money, sell off the family's property, and die in genteel poverty. By the time the governor's grandson came of age, he had to be bound out as an apprentice cooper to learn the trade of barrel-making, which would always provide a living as long as there were ships. Even then, to find a niche in which to ply his craft was not easy: this third Benedict Arnold had to leave his family and friends in Rhode Island, emigrate to the nearest frontier boom town in the neighboring province of Connecticut. In 1730, he lugged his belongings aboard a sloop bound across Narragansett Bay and up the narrow Thames River to the burgeoning new port of Norwich Town.

But the bloodline of Benedict Arnold was almost always enterprising, opportunistic. The young cooper admired the sloop and its captain, Absalom King, and struck up an acquaintance with him. Soon Arnold was selling barrel hoops and staves hammered out and warped and sweated in his shop on Chelsea Wharf to Captain King and his friends. Then Benedict III became Captain Arnold. He sailed Absalom King's ships across Long Island Sound, south along the seacoast to the isles of the Caribbean, decks stacked with lumber, holds crammed with barrels of salt pork and beef and bales of staves to make more barrels to fill with molasses and rum to transport to England. Then, in 1732, while Arnold and King were coming home from a voyage to Ireland, Captain King died at sea. Captain Arnold brought the sad news to Hannah, King's pretty, blond, round-eyed, and now wealthy widow. Little more than a year later, he married Hannah Waterman King and came into control of King's ships, shipyard, wharf, warehouse, house, his wife's fortune. Only three years had elapsed since he had come threadbare to Connecticut. Rapidly now, Captain Arnold expanded his business, built a large new gambrel-roofed white clapboard house on the outskirts of town set back under tall elm trees on a five-acre lot, a house with a dozen ample rooms and eight fireplaces, a house that was testament to his expansiveness. Affable, well-liked Captain Arnold was frequently elected a town official, sometimes against his wishes: surveyor, collector, assessor, then selectman. By the time his son, the infamous Benedict Arnold, was born on January 14, 1741, Captain Arnold was one of the most respected and prosperous merchant shipowners in Connecticut.

There were three measures of social standing in a Puritan town in Connecticut: riches, a long career in either community or church service, or descent from one of the town's original settlers. This trinity of standards was most visibly applied in the Congregational meetinghouse, where pews were assigned according to rank in the community. To their son, Benedict, Captain Arnold and his wife gave all three as his birthrights. This first-family status entitled the Arnolds to their front-row pew in church, which was the heart of the town's religious, political, and social life. His mother, Hannah, was celebrated by other Puritans for her piety, and she turned more and more to her Bible and her prayers as her relatives and friends, her first husband, and her children died. She had had two babies with Absalom King, and they both died in infancy. Then Absalom himself had died. For nearly five years after she remarried, she tried to have Captain Arnold's child, only to have their firstborn, Benedict IV, die at eight months. A second son, Benedict V, replaced him. He was given his firstborn brother's name, not a name of his own, a not uncommon practice among the Puritans of New England. Born in the coldest winter in a century, this Benedict Arnold proved to be hardier. Nearly three years later, Hannah Arnold had another child, a daughter, named after her. But then she had six *more* children. One lived eight years, another four, but all six died. Nine of Hannah Waterman Arnold's eleven children died young, a grim toll even for those times.

Early one autumn morning in 1740, a messenger urged his horse east along the Post Road toward New London and the turnpike to Norwich Town. Following the rutted road through fields of stacked hay, past sere pastures of browsing sheep, he called out to the farmers as he hurried by. For more than a month now, since George Whitefield had landed in America, thousands of the God-fearing and the simply curious had been thronging to hear this young, white-robed evangelist with his powerful, quivering voice. Wherever Whitefield and his entourage had ridden that summer, from Newport, Rhode Island, to Savannah, Georgia, he had packed the churches, the crowds overflowing into fields and onto village greens. In Philadelphia, young journalist Benjamin Franklin estimated that more than twice the population of the town had crowded in from the countryside. In Boston, so many people had jammed one church that its packed gallery tore away, crushing to death five of the faithful. And now he was coming down the Connecticut Valley.

When the dust-coated courier pelted past Nathan Cole's farm, midway between Middletown and Norwich Town, shortly after eight on the hot, dry morning of October 23, 1740, the young farmer was bringing in his harvest, a scant one in this year of severe drought. Cole was fairly typical of Connecticut's backsliding Puritans who turned out to hear Whitefield preach that day. Nothing, he said, had ever impressed him so much before, and he began to keep a spiritual diary that day. In it, Nathan Cole left a rare trace of how the prolonged religious revival called the Great Awakening rocked New England, disturbing the staid old Puritan social order that was by now more than a century old and splitting churches and communities like Norwich Town at the time of Benedict Arnold's birth with a fervor that reverberated all through his childhood.

"I was born," Nathan Cole wrote simply, "and born again." When the rider rode past him, "I was in my field at work. . . . I dropped my tool that I had in my hand and ran home to my wife, telling her to make ready quickly to go and hear Mr. Whitefield." Then Nathan Cole ran to his pasture for his horse "with all my might, fearing that I should be too late." He slid on the tack and mounted, urging the horse toward the house. As soon as his wife came out, he hoisted her up behind him and rode off "as fast as I thought the horse could bear. . . . When my horse got much out of breath, I would get down." Cole's wife then slid forward into the saddle and Cole ran alongside "until I was much out of breath and then mounted my horse again." Running "as if we were fleeing for our lives," Cole and his overburdened horse covered twelve miles in little more than an hour. All along the road, Cole noticed, "no man was at work in his field, but all seemed to be gone."

As they came to a rise overlooking the Connecticut River, Cole and his dun-covered wife looked down in wonder. "On high land, I saw before me a cloud of fog arising. I first thought it came from the great river. But as I came nearer the river road, I heard a noise of horses' feet." The cloud rose and towered above the river and the dry flanking bluffs, shrouding spruce and black walnut trees. "I could see men and horses slipping along in the cloud like shadows. As I drew nearer, it seemed like a steady stream of horses and their riders. Scarcely a horse was more than his length behind another, all of a lather and foam with sweat, their breath rolling out of their nostrils every jump. Every horse seemed to go with all his might to carry his rider to hear news from heaven. It made me tremble to see the sight. How the world was in struggle!"

When they finally got to the outskirts of Middletown, Cole's wife objected to going to a sermon covered with dirt. They rode down to a creek and washed. Then Cole marched his horse and his wife into town. He got as close to the tall, white-spired Congregational meetinghouse as he could. Crushing around it were "three or four thousand people." For a colonial Connecticut farmer it was an astonishing sight. From the riverbank, Cole watched ferryboats "running swift backward and forward, bringing over loads of people, and the oars rowed nimble and quick." Everything, men, women, horses, and boats, "seemed to be struggling for life. The land and banks over the river looked black with people and horses."

The crowd settled down as soon as the Reverend Mr. Whitefield, slender, youthful, pale, almost wraithlike in his flowing white surplice and long blond curls, stepped out onto a makeshift scaffold in front of the meetinghouse, raised his arms, began to preach. "He looked almost angelical," Cole remembered. The words of the Great Awakening echoed out over the Connecticut Valley, and farmers, shopkeepers, and their wives began to sway. Their lives would never be so simple again, and, as Cole put it, "it put me into a trembling fear."[1] The sparks of religious controversy that now flared into angry confrontation had been smoldering in Norwich Town for many years and were to color nearly every facet of Benedict Arnold's early life.

From its founding in 1660 as a Puritan bastion in the Connecticut wilderness, Norwich Town had also been a stronghold of religious conservatism that refused to conform to the standards of other Puritan towns and distinguished itself by being notably intolerant of any religious innovations. When a small group of Quakers from nearby New London began to preach in neighboring towns in the early 1720s, the Norwich Town minister, the Reverend Benjamin Lord, and his deacons, who held sway over the local magistrate, got him to refuse to allow the Quakers to pass through Norwich Town on the Sabbath. The Quakers persisted. On their next visit, they chastised Dr. Lord, a dapper little man who always wore silver buckles on his shoes and knee breeches, for covering his head with a curled white wig in the sight of God. The minister informed the magistrate that the Quakers were violating sabbatarian law by walking on the highway. This time, they were taken to the jailyard and, men and women, stripped and severely flogged. Yet by this time, when Hannah Waterman was a teenage girl, few people went to church on Sundays, and while Norwich Town was becoming the second-largest town in New England, its meetinghouse had been all but empty when Dr. Lord had been called as the new minister fresh out of Yale College. The first thing that Lord noticed when he looked down from the pulpit for the first time was that all of the thirty-odd heads in the pews in front of him were white-haired.

All over New England from 1725 on, as fewer young people joined the church, incipient religious revivals swirled in Connecticut, small at first, mostly in the countryside, leaving Norwich Town virtually untouched. The first sizable revival had taken place at Northampton, Massachusetts, far up the Connecticut River, but printing presses quickly spread sermons among avid Puritan readers of religious tracts in Norwich Town. In 1735, another revival began in Northampton, this time preached by brilliant young Jonathan Edwards, who injected strong doses of fire and brimstone into the usual hell and damnation oratory. Intrigued, Lord rode all the way up from Norwich Town to Northampton on horseback to study Edwards's theology. Lord decided that the revival was a good thing after all and went back to tell the white heads that he thought so. They remained indifferent to his news, but many of the people in Norwich Town who usually avoided church began to trickle in to hear his animated sermons until Lord had a revival movement of his own. In the years of his ministry, Lord multiplied the membership twelvefold. A local historian noted that his services, faithfully attended for more than forty years by Hannah Waterman Arnold and for nearly twenty years by her son, Benedict, were "always impressive. . . . He seemed to have an inexhaustible fund of proper words, pointed sense and devout affection."[2] Another church historian singled Dr. Lord out as an "example of dignity, affability, affection and stability."[3] He also seemed to have an open mind, a rare thing in Norwich Town in those days. In the wake of George Whitefield's 1740 revival, as half a dozen lesser evangelists crisscrossed New England, Lord invited them into his church to preach while many others barred their doors.

Affidavits gathered by an archconservative Boston Puritan minister, who was trying to quash the Great Awakening, show that these revivals followed a familiar pattern. The preaching

seems not so much to inform men's judgments as to terrify and affright their imaginations and, by awful words and frightful representations, to let the congregation into hideous shrieks and outcries. . . . In every place where they come, they represent that God is doing extraordinary things in other places and that they are some of the last hardened wretches that stand out; that this is the last call they are likely to have, that they are now hanging over the pit of eternal damnation and just ready this moment to fall into it, that hell fire now flashes in their faces and that the Devil now stands just ready to seize them and carry them to Hell. They often times repeat the awful words, "Damned! Damned! Damned! Damned!" This frequently frightens their tender mothers and sets them to screaming, and by degrees spreads over a great part of the congrega-

tion, and forty, fifty or one hundred of them all screaming together makes such an awful and hideous noise as will make a man's hair stand on end. Some will faint away, some will fall upon the floor, wallow and foam. Some women will rend off their caps, handkerchiefs and other clothes, tear their hair down about their ears and seem perfectly bereaved of their reason.[4]

The Great Awakening was eventually suppressed, but not before it cleaved Norwich Town along religious and political lines that left it divided right down to the Revolution. All through his childhood, Benedict Arnold was surrounded by strife, much of it religious, despite his mother's efforts to insulate him from it. There had been those who favored allowing in new ideas from the outside, but the conservative minority in Norwich Town's meetinghouse had also grown in reaction to the revival, and they closed ranks to protect established institutions such as the church from a perceived threat from dissenters of all classes. But even wealthy conservatives in Norwich Town, as well as all over New England, had been polarized, and they could not abide Dr. Lord's insistence on moderation and compromise. At the height of the controversy, he played host to clergymen from twelve Connecticut towns "to acknowledge the goodness of God in this revival." Lord agreed with the revivalists that people needed to return to the devout, rigorous religion of their saintly forefathers.[5]

In 1744, the awakened dissenters of the town broke away, led by several elders of the Congregational Church and backed by some of its wealthiest families. They demanded their own separatist church, one that would have nothing more to do with other towns or their churches. Even more shocking, they refused to go on paying church taxes for Dr. Lord's salary. When the New Lights, as the separatists called themselves, moved into the dilapidated old meetinghouse atop Fort Hill looking down on the town, Dr. Lord and his loyalists appealed to the provincial legislature at New Haven to pass a law to enforce Norwich Town's church taxes. The legislature upheld him. One separatist lay preacher was arrested and jailed for twenty days. When his mother, a widow in her eighties, refused to pay, she, too, was imprisoned until her tax was paid, over her protest, by her son-in-law, the town magistrate, who went on paying it for twenty-five years until she finally died. That same year, when Benedict Arnold was twelve years old, forty separatists, including all their leaders and many of the town's most influential citizens, were imprisoned. According to the town's leading historian, "there was perhaps no town in the colony where the conflict between the standing order, supported by civil authority, and the Separatists was more vehement and protracted than at Norwich."6

In the first major revolt against the established order in New England, three hundred new separatist churches were formed by people who dared not only to resist paying church taxes but to support each other's dissent from law. The Great Awakening had begun with a massive effusion of pent-up religious fervor; it ended with repressive laws. When George Whitefield rode down the Connecticut Valley for the first time, tens of thousands turned out in peaceful awe. When his disciple, James Davenport, came the last time, he was jailed and a riot ensued. Quiet, sullen crowds were now refusing to be cowed by magistrates. The sheriff of Hartford had to release Davenport and his followers to preach in the streets before his deputies dared to enforce a deportation order. The Great Awakening, America's first youth movement, was driven underground, suppressed by clergy and politicians worried by their disregard for their traditional powers. Resenting the heavy-handed repression, older, more established citizens joined the young. Only the intervention of another imperial war may have postponed a civil and religious war.

Benedict Arnold was born, and lived most of his life, in a world where his mother country, England, was perennially at war with the hated French. Three times since the town had been founded, the king's recruiters had strutted into Norwich Town with fifes and drums to entice young men to march off to war: in 1689, in 1715, and now in 1740, when an American regiment was formed to fight the Spanish in the Caribbean after a typically minor yet emotionally charged incident. A dubious character named Robert Jenkins, an English sea captain, had presented himself at the bar of the House of Commons in London and brandished a bottle which contained a pickled ear he insisted was his own, declaring that the Spanish coast guard had severed it in a raid on his ship off South America. Europe was already convulsed by war: Frederick the Great of Prussia was on the march, seizing Silesia from the Austrians, England's ally. Thousands of British shipyard workers were unemployed. War was good for the British economy. Now an indignant Parliament had a pretext for making the conflagration general, and England and Austria faced France, Prussia, and Spain. The early news was all bad for the English and for their colonists, as they lost a long series of battles against the Spanish in Florida, the West Indies, and Central America. An expedition was mounted by the British with the aid of her American colonies to attack Havana; in New England, militiamen drilled on village greens. Shipowners like Captain Arnold fitted out their vessels with cannon to prey as privateers on the French and the Spanish.

When Benedict was five, French-led Indians attacked settlements as near as the coast of southern Maine, while Spanish privateers raided plantations within forty miles of Philadelphia. Indians forayed from Canada and from French fortresses at the mouth of Lake Champlain into adjoining New York province in bloody attacks that alarmed all of defenseless New England. From the northeastern shore of Lake Champlain, Abenaki Indians staged their perennial raids on western Massachusetts and present-day Vermont, Maine, and the Connecticut Valley. By the time Benedict was old enough to play with a toy gun, all of New England was astir with the fervor of a crusade against the Catholic French in Canada who had for a half century led Indians against the English settlements. When Benedict was four, Norwich Town troops joined the great New England expedition against the French bastion of Louisbourg in the Acadian Highlands and, with the support of a British fleet, captured it in June 1745. Within months, the French and their Indian auxiliaries counterattacked, burning Saratoga, New York, and attacking the rich fur-trading center at Albany. To live in New England in these times was to be in almost constant expectation of an Indian attack, and Benedict Arnold's childhood was full of martial excitement.

For his father, there was also money to be made. Coastal waterfronts like Norwich Town boomed as the young men who had been idlers during peacetime, out of work and drifting and drinking until their fathers died and they came into their inheritances, now either found jobs in the shipyards or went off to fight in the militia or seek riches on the decks of privateering ships. At first, there was plenty of cash for anyone willing to work, as British subsidies commingled with colonial levies and investors speculated heavily on privateering expeditions. The town, its taverns, and its wharves abounded with the signs of prosperity. Men whose pockets had been empty now paid with gold and silver. Captain Arnold evidently was one of those who felt confident enough not to question whether this was a bubble that could burst. He built ships and furnished his new house handsomely, and Hannah had the help of servants while she trained her son and daughters how to be good Puritans.

Quick, strong, able to rivet other little boys with his dark-eyed gaze, Benedict very early became a leader of Norwich Town's children in the games they played on the green and at Mystic Cove. In the long winters, he wore the scarlet cloak his mother made him as he skated for hours on the frozen river, developing powerful legs and a rugged constitution that was inured to harsh winter weather.

Local historian Francis Manwaring Caulkins records that he was a show-off at ice skating. When it was time for him to go to school, something that only the rich could afford for their children, Benedict's mother enrolled him in Dr. Jewett's one-room school in the Montville section of town. There he imbibed *Dilworth's Grammar* and *Cocker's Arithmetic* and learned to write in a strong, assertive hand. As the religious fervor and wave of arrests in Norwich Town worsened and trade with the Caribbean was interrupted by the protracted intercolonial war, young Benedict's schooling was bound to be affected, as was his life at home. Captain Arnold had overextended his business into the very areas most vulnerable to enemy actions at sea, and he sank slowly into debt, hounded relentlessly by his creditors. As his empty ships rotted at their moorings off Chelsea wharf, Captain Arnold began to spend more and more of his time consoling himself over tankards of Jamaica rum at Peck's Tavern on the village green. His patient, pious wife worried that the uproar over the Great Awakening coupled with her husband's drunkenness would damage their only son.

Fifteen miles north along the Quinnebaug River lay the farm town of Canterbury, dominated by an austere Congregationalist meetinghouse under the pastorate of Hannah's kinsman Dr. James Cogswell, a distinguished young scholar and preacher. A Yale divine who had opposed the Great Awakening and maintained a hard-line conservative Puritanism, he was renowned as a teacher of logic and a graceful orator. Like many college-educated Puritan ministers, he supplemented his small salary (much of it paid in firewood, food, and housing) by taking in boarding students and running a small school. Specializing in educating the sons of "gentlemen of trade,"[7] he included among his students a future president of Yale and the forebears of Nathan Hale and of President Grover Cleveland. On Sundays, he impressed parents as well as students with thunderous sermons that lasted up to three hours. While Benedict's father was rarely sober enough to worry about providing an education for his only son, Hannah scrimped to see that Benedict got the best schooling available at the time. She packed off eleven-year-old Benedict to Canterbury in the autumn of 1752 and told her cousin Cogswell he was not to spare the rod and spoil her son. Benedict took along his new homemade school uniform, a long blue coat and white ruffled shirt. Benedict studied English, mathematics, the Bible, and the laws of a Puritan God, as well as the language, history, and logic of the ancient Greeks and Romans, a classical education of the standard form used at scores of similar small New England private schools. Most of all, he was supposed to imbibe discipline, tradition, and respect for authority, to believe in the power of the word, written and spoken, and the necessity of order. He excelled in Latin and math—these he loved—but there was little place for leisure, play, individuality.

In his two years at Canterbury, Benedict benefited from Cogswell's mild temper and friendly manner. He saw his father only in the summertime, when he made trading voyages with him across the Sound and to the Caribbean. Captain Arnold was sailing less now and drinking more heavily as his debts multiplied. Only letters from Benedict's mother survive. Rarely does his father emerge from her shadow. Benedict was as negligent about letters home as any boy away at school, even when his mother prodded him: "Beg will you write us. . . . I have sent you one pound chocolate."[8] At fourteen, he was writing home for more money. Hannah Arnold probably dug down into her private hoard of hard money to pay Benedict's room and board; what little pocket money he received came erratically from his father. Mostly, his mother's letters are melancholy, filled with the sad news of death and dying. The years Benedict was away at school included one of the worst outbreaks of yellow fever, which recurrently ravaged swampy, coastal Norwich Town. In the miasmic summer of 1753, when Benedict was back at school, the entire Arnold family was stricken. As soon as she could, Hannah wrote to Benedict:

My dear child through ye goodness of god we arre sturring and something comfortable at present but deths are multiplied all round us and more daly expected and how soon our time will come we know not. Pray my dear whatever you neglect do not neglect your precious soal which once lost can never be regained your uncle Zion Arnold is dead. He left time ye 5 of this instant. . . . Give sarvis to Mr. Cogshall and lady and dear Mrs. Hannah.

> *From your affectionate mother,*
> *Hannah Arnold*

There was a brutal, brief postscript: "Captain Bill has lost all his sons. John Post has lost his wife. John Lathrop and his son Barnabas are dead."[9] For years now, Hannah had been warning Benedict to be prepared to "step off the banks of time," and the boy must have been rendered apprehensive. That summer, her grim notes from home brought to life all her gloomy predictions. Two weeks later, she wrote:

I but wright to let you know that your poor sisters are yet in ye land of living. But for 3 or 4 days past we looked on Mary as one just stepping off ye banks of time, and to all appearances, Hannah just behind. But to ye surprise of all beholder, Mary is something revived, but I am afraid what ye event will be. Hannah is waxing weak and weaker, hath not got up one hour this seven days past, and her distemper increasing. What God is about to do with us I know not. Your father is very poor. Aunt Hyde is sick and I myself had a touch of ye distemper, but of divine goodness it is passed off light with me.

My dear, god seems to be saying to all children, Be ye also ready. Pray take ye exhortation, for ye call to ye is very striking: that God should smite your sisters and spare you as yet. Pray improve your time and beg of God to grant his spirit, or death may overtake you unprepared. For his commission seems sealed for a great many, and, for aught you know, you may be one of them. My dear, fly to Christ. If ye don't know ye way, tell him. He is guidance of ye Holy Spirit to guide you to that only shelter from death eternal. For, death temporal we all must try, sooner or later. Farewell.

Your distressed mother,
Hannah Arnold

Hannah Arnold, like anyone else in the eighteenth century, could not know that it was mosquitoes in undrained coastal swamps which determined who lived and who died of yellow fever. To her, it was a great mystery why her son was spared while her daughters, friends, and relatives were stricken, but Benedict should not be smug about his escape. "God may meet you with this disease wherever you be, for it is his servant." That she made him stay away in the dry hills of Canterbury probably saved his life: "I must not have you come home for fear that should be presumption. My love to you."[10]

In her dour way, Hannah Arnold loved her son and her daughters, and it must have pained her terribly that her son was away when his eight-year-old sister, Mary, died. Benedict's father recovered, though, and so did Hannah, and gave birth again. This baby, too, took the name of a dead sister, but then a short time later she too died.

There is not another letter from Hannah Arnold to her son for over six months, until April 1754, when Dr. Cogswell wrote Hannah about Benedict's behavior. Benedict had recently horrified the headmaster when, during a barn fire, he appeared in the smoke on the blazing building's ridgepole, balancing high above the flames, and walked from end to end. Dr. Cogswell wrote to Hannah with considerable understatement that Benedict was a bright boy, "so full of pranks and plays."[11] His long-suffering mother wrote Benedict, strangely avoiding a direct reprimand:

Dear child:
Pray, my dear, let your first concern be to make your peace with God, as it is of all concerns of ye greatest importance. Keep a steady watch over your thoughts, words and actions. Be dutiful to your superiors, obliging to equals and affable to inferiors, if any such there be. Always choose that your companions be your betters, that their good examples you may earn.

From your affectionate
Hannah Arnold

By spring 1754, two of Benedict's three little sisters were dead, and there was no more mention of them. The bereaved Hannah was struggling to keep her house together, her boy in school. Captain Arnold's business had foundered in the long postwar depression. Yet Hannah tried to put on a brave face. "I have sent you fifty shillings. Use it prudently, as you are accountable to God and your father. You father puts in twenty more."[12]

His father's illness, slide into alcoholism, and death dragged on through that winter, however, and his financial failure made it expedient for him to absent himself from Norwich Town the following summer, possibly to try to borrow money in New York City. On August 9, 1754, Benedict, who had not gone home that summer to sail with his father, received a cryptic note at school from his mother:

My dear:
I write to let you know ye situation of our family. Your father is in a poor state of health but designs, if able, to set out for New York on August 23, and if I can, I shall journey with him, and if Providence shall permit, we shall be back by ye middle September when I shall send for you home. My dear . . . make ye Lord ye dwelling place and try and trust his care. We have a very uncertain stay in this world. . . . We have an interest in Christ without which we must be eternally miserable. Your sister Hannah is poor but gives love to you. . . .

Your tender and distressed mother,
Hannah Arnold[13]

Wracked by uncertainty, debt, and death, Hannah Arnold finally had to pull her son out of school. It must have been a terrible blow to her and to Benedict, especially since, from all indications, the boy was thriving. But there was no more money. The striking thing is that Benedict Arnold evidently treasured these letters. No others, none from his father, survive from his childhood. Despite all his later vicissitudes, despite moving all he owned across the Atlantic five times in three wars, he apparently clung to these letters from his mother. They are all that remains of the world he grew up in.

When Benedict was thirteen, his father's business, which had teetered for a decade, finally collapsed. Worse, he was wanted for arrest on the grounds of evading his creditors, and only the intercession of Hannah's relatives kept him out of jail. Benedict Arnold had been the well-off son of a rich merchant just long enough to miss all that he now lost. That autumn, home from school and idle, he grew restless. Even though their money was gone, the Arnolds clung to their big house, where they settled into genteel poverty, still trudging down the aisle to their front-row pew on church days even as their clothes grew obviously older, as Benedict's father looked more and more dissipated. There was, it was true, plenty for a boy to do around Norwich Town, with its sparsely populated 2,700-acre Mohegan Indian settlement amid twin rings of rock-castellated hills where young Arnold learned Indian ways from the last remnants of the tribe. There Chief Benjamin Uncas, fat old son of the great warrior Uncas, presided over some two hundred Mohegans, who taught Arnold to fish, paddle a canoe, and stalk deer. Young Arnold learned, too, to slip into Indian garb and adopt their habits. On steamy summer days, he and his Indian friends went swimming in the great pool below the falls and diving from the sterns of ships riding at anchor along the waterfront, fishing in the river, hunting and trapping and horseback riding in the nearby fields and woods, looting birds' nests, and snatching apples from the orchards. Then Benedict fell in with a new group of Norwich Town boys. They staked out the old meetinghouse atop Fort Hill and from it imitated the Indian raids that they had heard about from their parents. The hill had once held the last Mohegan Indian fort, and from it Uncas and his warriors had aided the whites during King Philip's War. Benedict and his friends staged mock battles up and down the hill. They also prowled the Chelsea Landing waterfront, its weathered wharves and warehouses, ropewalk and sail lofts. Before his father had lost his ships, Benedict had loved those summer voyages learning the sea: all his life he would prefer the danger and freedom of shipboard life. Benedict was growing fearless as he crept aboard a neighbor's ship, climbed hand over hand to the masthead, swung out to a stay, and slithered down to thump on deck and dive overboard for the swim to shore before he could be caught. But according to the local legends, Benedict Arnold grew even bolder that summer, braver, as if trying to prove his courage. Years later, Dr. Benjamin Rush of Philadelphia wrote that Arnold had told him that he had been "a coward till I was fifteen."[14] He seemed to be trying to prove himself, to demonstrate his courage, as if the family's honor were on the line more now as his father lost his position in the town and the respect of his neighbors. Resentment at the sudden change in his family's status may have accounted for a series of skirmishes with local authorities.

No one had objected when, probably on a dare, Benedict jumped onto the revolving blades of a waterwheel at the mill above the falls and held on as the wheel plunged down underwater, dragging Benedict under, then came back up slowly. If the boy wanted to drown himself, then so be it. Everybody knew about his stunts: he frequently tried to impress other boys by making running jumps over loaded wagons on the town's main street. But he went too far when he organized a gang of sorts with whom, on Thanksgiving Day, when the townspeople gathered for a baked-bean dinner and a modest bonfire of celebration atop Bean Hill, he stole barrels of tar from the waterfront and ignited a blaze the likes of which Norwich Town had never seen before. As the town constable and his assistants huffed up the hill, shouting and brandishing their staffs, Benedict, providing a rear guard for his friends to escape, turned, tore off his coat, and threatened to thrash the burly constable, swinging and screaming until he himself was subdued.

At thirteen, Benedict Arnold was a leader of boys and a fighter, but he was not a bully. He was tall for the times, five feet nine when the average height was three or four inches less, and he was muscular, broad-shouldered, and strong of leg, partly from shimmying up the ratlines and hauling on shrouds aboard his father's sloop. But by this time, his bold actions were just one more embarrassment to his mother, who apparently had taken over his upbringing as her husband slipped deeper into his bottle. The episode with the constable, all too public, coupled with the family's deepening debt prompted her to find a new home for her only son, one where he would be bound by a master as well as fed and clothed by him. Among Hannah Arnold's relatives was another distinguished Yale graduate, Dr. Daniel Lathrop, trained as a physician in London but an apothecary by profession, indeed the only one between Boston and New York City and, as a consequence, quite rich. Hannah Arnold decided to apprentice Benedict to the Lathrops to learn a trade. At least for

the next eight years and probably all his life as a result, Benedict
Arnold was to be consigned to a world of herbs, poultices, and powders. Late in 1754, just after Captain Arnold was finally arrested for
debt,[15] he and Hannah signed Benedict's articles of apprenticeship
and the boy moved down Washington Street to the Lathrops'
riverfront mansion. Legally, he was now their servant for eight
years, until he turned twenty-one.

There were few finer houses in Connecticut than Benedict's new
home, a sprawling white house just north of the fork of Town and
Washington streets with its face to the village green and its back
giving out onto gracious gardens and a long view of ships' masts in
the river. Its owner, Dr. Lathrop, was a distinguished veteran who
had led Connecticut's regiment in the last war, riding at its head on
the long march to Louisbourg. Now there was a new war looming
between England and her ally, Germany, against France and her
ally, Spain, and Lathrop had been given the contract to supply surgical instruments and medical supplies to the British Northern
Army. Consequently, he needed two more apprentices to help with
the additional orders. Young Arnold stepped through the neat white
picket fence and was given a room up under the eaves of the
Lathrop mansion and soon saw for himself the liveried servants, the
handsomely furnished rooms, the long, low yellow carriage that
made this one of the most opulent families in Connecticut. Arnold's
world was circumscribed by the Lathrops once he entered the barn-
like shop across the street from the house and became fascinated by
all the goods imported from England, Europe, and the Indies for
sale: in addition to drugs, there were wines, fabrics, dried fruits,
condiments, perfumes, powders, musk, and embalming fluids smuggled in by way of French ports in the Caribbean. There were obvious
rewards from learning such a business, and Benedict was to have a
good teacher. Daniel Lathrop and his brother, Joshua, had been
partners in the business since graduating from Yale College in 1733.
Daniel had gone to London to study medicine, then returned with a
luxurious assortment of goods to set up his apothecary shop. A
shrewd Yankee even by Connecticut standards, he had gotten himself appointed colonel of militia and then received contracts to supply British troops from New York to Boston, growing ever richer
and better known in the bargain. A local ditty sung to the tune of
"Yankee Doodle" celebrated his business acumen:

> Colonel Lathrop, staunch and true,
> Was never known to balk it;
> And when he was engaged in trade
> He always filled his pocket.[16]

Colonel Lathrop, an expert at buying, selling, and breeding horses, was also the man who taught Benedict Arnold how to be a trader and who must have given him his masterful knowledge of horse trading.

The person who turned him into a gentleman was Lathrop's wife, Jerusha. Another of the wards Jerusha Lathrop took in and raised was Lydia Huntley Sigourney, daughter of her gardener, who became Connecticut's leading woman writer of the nineteenth century, leaving fifty-nine lachrymose novels. One of them, *Letters of Life,* gives a vivid picture of Jerusha Lathrop and of life in her house. She described Mrs. Lathrop as fair-skinned, open, with expressive blue eyes and fine features. She was tall and graceful, dignified yet playful, quick to smile, proverbially generous; she opposed religious strife and said that the spirit of controversy should be subjugated. Daughter of a governor, she had lost her parents early. Mistress of a house full of slaves and servants, she quickly adopted Benedict as if he were the son she never had: all three of her children had died in a single year in infancy from yellow fever. For nearly fifty years, she "adopted" a series of nephews, nieces, and the orphans of her servants.

The heart of Jerusha Lathrop's world was a large, low-browed parlor with a great fireplace burning hickory logs. The bull's-eye windows were draped with crimson curtains, and polished wainscot darkened and preserved the walls. In a corner opposite the fire, Jerusha Lathrop presided from her rocking chair, governing according to the gilded tall case clock and looking out over her favorite possession, an ebony-framed mirror that her family had brought from England. There was always a favorite cat on a green cushion at one elbow, a Bible and a copy of Edward Young's melancholy graveyard poem *The Complaint, or Night Thoughts on Life, Death, and Immortality* on a small round table. Here she knitted one of the twenty pairs of socks she allowed her family for winter as her husband, Daniel, cast up accounts at a high desk in an adjoining room with a succession of bright young clerks, including Benedict Arnold.

On warm days, Jerusha took Benedict to the gardens and taught him horticulture: flowers, vegetables, and herbs brightened her life and yielded much of her husband's profits. From his first visit, Benedict had been struck by their beauty, and he would imitate much of what he saw when he planted his own gardens. In Jerusha Lathrop's parlor, Benedict Arnold imbibed many of his notions of a gentlemanly way of life.

In 1754, shortly after Benedict's apprenticeship began, the French and Indian War broke out in the Ohio River Valley with George Washington's defeat at Fort Necessity. The fighting lasted for nearly ten years. All America became aware how vulnerable the British army was the next year when an expeditionary force under General Edward Braddock was ambushed and slaughtered near Fort Duquesne in western Pennsylvania. The Appalachian back country from present-day Maine to Georgia lay exposed to attacks by Indians loyal to the French, who carried out skillful diplomacy and encouraged raids from the safety of their citadel at Quebec. Scalpings and burnings of English settlements all along the frontier in this war triggered a general conflict in Europe and in the colonies of the European powers as England and France vied for control of territories and trade all over the world.

A scrappy young man could hardly have been expected to remain content among the pill bottles of Norwich: Benedict Arnold itched to fight the French. All through his youth he had been taught that they were the hated enemy, the murderers of babies and women. However, there was a law in Connecticut forbidding apprentices or servants bound to their masters to enlist. In 1757, Benedict's opportunity came when the French-led Indians invaded the Champlain Valley between New York and present-day Vermont and raided south, assailing Fort William Henry on Lake George, capturing and massacring its garrison of fifteen hundred. New England lay exposed to Indian attack, and Dr. Lathrop gave his permission to the sixteen-year-old to accompany Norwich troops to Fort William. The alarm was over by the time Benedict arrived after marching for a week, and he turned back without seeing any action. But he'd had a first taste of army life and found it far more exciting than an apothecary's. For the next year, he grew more restless at each new account of distant battles.

It was the early spring of 1758 when Benedict left Dr. Lathrop's house one morning and kept walking down the Post Road, all the way to Westchester County, New York. There no one knew he was a servant; moreover, there was a higher enlistment bonus in New York. On March 30, 1758, he joined Captain Reuben Lockwood's company of Westchester militia on its march up the Hudson River to take part in the British attack on Fort Ticonderoga, the main French bastion on the New York–Canadian frontier. When Hannah Arnold learned that Benedict had run away to join the army, she was distraught. She went to Dr. Lord, a man of considerable influence, who arranged to have young Arnold brought back against his will on the grounds that his mother was ill and his father unable to help her care for his younger sister, Hannah. Terribly embarrassed, Benedict returned to Norwich Town and his chores in Dr. Lathrop's shop. A year later, he escaped again. This time it was Dr. Lathrop who had him hauled back after he placed an ad in the *New York Gazette* offering a forty-shilling reward. This third attempt to join up was more successful. In the spring of 1759, the call for volunteers went out for the climactic campaign of the last French and Indian War. British armies were striking north and west across New York and south along the St. Lawrence to besiege Quebec and Montreal. Convincing his mother that he should enlist, he again hurried across the New York line to sign up in the militia company of Captain James Holmes, his old platoon leader. Finally, he got an honest look at a soldier's life: it was hard and boring. His company marched north to Albany, where Benedict fell in with his friends as they drilled and trained for the expedition against the great French fortresses at the headwaters of Lake Champlain. Benedict impressed his messmates with his ability to shoot, to jump over ammunition wagons, to wrestle, to march long distances without apparent fatigue. His strength and endurance at feats of derring-do were more famous than his ability to withstand the monotony of rear-area military routines: drilling, clearing forest roads, building stockades, digging trenches.

He was also worried about his mother. In camp, he learned she was gravely ill. He did not wait to receive permission to go home, which probably would have been denied anyway. He left camp one night, just as he had once left Norwich Town. Absent without leave in modern military terms, he could have been arrested and treated as a deserter. That Benedict Arnold risked death as a deserter to visit his mother is open to question, however. While desertion has never been a light offense even in times of peace, as military historian Willard M. Wallace points out, a firm military tradition had not been worked out yet in the American colonies. Desertion from colonial armies and from colonial forces in the American Revolution was a fairly common occurrence and not regarded by society quite as it is in recent times. Yet men were hanged or shot for deserting from time to time, and only the fact that Arnold was actually going to his mother's bedside and undoubtedly meant to return to his unit mitigated his offense. Moreover, he probably could not have obtained a furlough had he waited, because the campaign against the French was about to begin in earnest. Hitching rides with farmers and sleeping in haylofts, he no doubt lied that he was on a furlough home. He was taking a great risk to be at her bedside, nonetheless, for there was a forty-shilling reward for his arrest as a deserter. A notice in the May 21, 1759, *New York Gazette* described him as "18 years old, dark complexion, light eyes and dark hair." When British recruiters came through Norwich Town again early that summer of

1759, his mother hid him in her house and then had him moved from house to house among sympathetic neighbors.

Hannah Arnold died, at age fifty-two, on August 15 of that summer. Benedict probably handled all the details of burying her, even if it meant exposing himself to arrest or imprisonment. That he had to do everything himself, arrange a funeral, provide for his fifteen-year-old sister, pretty, blond, blue-eyed Hannah, see that she could take care of their alcoholic father, is beyond doubt. He probably even wrote his mother's epitaph: the task must have been beyond his father, who had become the town drunk. On Hannah Waterman Arnold's headstone, a sad moon face rises on an angel's wings, and between delicate vinelike tracery is her memorial: "She was a pattern of piety, patience, and virtue."[17]

Flouting the law to help his family may have done a great deal for Benedict Arnold's reputation in Norwich Town, especially with the Lathrops. He had loved and respected his mother, and these qualities endeared him to Jerusha Lathrop, who more than ever became his protector and surrogate mother. She was a sensitive, cultivated woman, and it was probably her intercession on more than one occasion that kept young Arnold out of jail. She helped him with his mother's funeral and the support of his father and beautiful blond sister. The Arnolds had no money left. Apprentices made nothing. Although Benedict could have argued that his father was no longer legally competent and that his house and property should pass to him to manage, he still was not legally of age for another year. Grieving for his mother, still bound to the Lathrops, he apparently turned to Mrs. Lathrop for guidance. In any case, he left his father in the care of his sister Hannah and, evidently with the blessing of Mrs. Lathrop and the colonel, returned to his militia unit without punishment on March 26, 1760. He had been absent without leave for a full year. He had missed most of the excitement of the grand English campaign to wrest Canada from the French: the Union Jack now flapped over Montreal, Quebec, all of eastern Canada, northern New York, present-day Vermont and New Hampshire, the Ohio and Mississippi valleys, and all the lands west of the Appalachian mountains for the first time. The great French fortresses at Louisbourg, Ticonderoga, and Crown Point had been blasted into rubble: the French themselves had burned and destroyed many of their forts and villages as they retreated. No longer was there the hereditary threat against New England. Only the tedium of garrison life remained until Benedict Arnold was mustered out and sent home. In four forays to the army, Benedict Arnold had never seen action. But he had come to know its discipline, its camaraderie.

By winter 1760, he was back in Norwich Town in time to face the final humiliation of his father's long descent into disgrace. For years, the old sea captain had become drunk each day in the local taverns, then staggered the mile or two home to the catcalls and jeers of men who had once worked for him. All too often, it had been Benedict who had to go find and fetch him. Benedict Arnold acquired his lifelong hatred of drunkenness. His badly wounded pride also apparently taught him to hate Norwich Town and some of its more exalted citizens. On May 26, 1760, shortly before Benedict returned from the army, his father, who had been drinking even more heavily since his wife's death, was arrested by Justice of the Peace Isaac Huntington on a warrant that said he "was drunken in said Norwich so that he was disabled in ye use of understanding and reason, appearing in his speech, posture and behavior, which is against the Peace of Our Lord, ye King and the laws of this colony."[18]

Young Arnold was away when his father died. There was nothing left for his son to inherit: he had long since sold off his pastureland to his neighbors and relatives to help pay his debts. To keep him from debtor's prison, Dr. Lathrop had put up £300 and taken back a mortgage on Captain Arnold's house.[19] On his return from the army, Benedict had left Norwich Town once again, this time for the final phase of his training by the generous Dr. Lathrop. Shipping aboard a Lathrop vessel as supercargo, he learned the fundamentals of trading in the Caribbean. Soon he was doing business for the Lathrops in the West Indies, in Canada, and as far away as London. Someone who had known Benedict Arnold at thirteen would not have recognized him at twenty. The troublemaking boy had turned into the responsible chief clerk of Norwich Town's principal business. Only Dr. Lathrop, shrewd judge of horseflesh, had seen his talents in time to help him. Benedict was working hard now as Dr. Lathrop's assistant to prepare himself to open his own apothecary shop somewhere outside Norwich Town.

Within months of Benedict Arnold's coming of age in January 1762, his father died. Once again, the Lathrops were generous, giving him a large cash gift to help him set up in business. Technically, they owed an apprentice only two suits of clothes (and these could be secondhand) and a pocketful of change when he completed his seven-year term of servitude. Instead, they gave him £500, a small fortune for the time, the equivalent to minister Lord's salary for ten years! One year later, Dr. Lathrop also deeded over to young Benedict his father's house and grounds, clearing it of the £300 mortgage.[20] The colonel also gave him letters of introduction and recommendation after Benedict turned down his invitation to stay on, with the implicit promise of a share of the business someday. To leave the Lathrops must have been a painful decision: Jerusha had been so kind, the colonel so generous, so much more a father than Benedict's own. But the young Arnold yearned to be independent, to get away from Norwich Town. Moving to New Haven, he left the valley of his birth behind as quickly as he could. Except for short visits, he never returned.

2

"A FAIR PROSPECT
OF IMPROVING!"

*Smuggling is rivetted in the
constitution of the
inhabitants of Connecticut
as much as superstition
and religion and their
province is a storehouse
for the smugglers of the
neighboring colonies.*

The Reverend Samuel Peters, *General History of Connecticut,*
1784

In the spring of 1762, with letters
from the Lathrops to introduce him to London merchants, Benedict
Arnold sailed at age twenty-one to England to buy stock for his own
apothecary shop. He bowed and charmed his way through the shops
of Charing Cross and the Strand and came back to Connecticut
laden with goods bought on credit eagerly extended him, thanks to
the Lathrops' backing. His new home, New Haven, was the fastest-
growing seaport on Long Island Sound, already the third-largest
town in Connecticut. As the colony's eastern capital, it was the site

of a new statehouse building and the colony's center for litigation. A town of only eight thousand people, it nonetheless boasted three large brick churches on the eastern end of its green opposite Yale College's single massive brick building. Farther southwest was the seaport, a collection of wharves, warehouses, and no fewer than fifteen taverns. New Haven was ideally positioned for trade: raw materials and farm goods from the interior were bartered for finished goods and luxuries from England and Europe, many of them smuggled through the Caribbean.

In a rented store on Chapel Street between the green and the waterfront, Benedict Arnold hung out a black sign with gilt letters which proclaimed:

B. Arnold Druggist
Bookseller & c.
From London
Sibi Totique[1]

Arnold was proud of his Latin motto, "For Himself and for Everybody," and since ladies of means would only respect a merchant who knew the tastes of London, Arnold shaded the truth about his provenance, preferring to be called Dr. Arnold from London. His was more a department store than an apothecary, and fancier than a general store, a hybrid in the style of the Lathrops' Norwich emporium. The only store of its kind in New Haven, it offered the usual herbs and medicines (dock, essence of balm gilead, Bateman's Pectoral Drops, aphrodisiacs such as tincture of valerian, and Francis's Female Elixir and other bracing notions for the ladies), but it specialized in luxuries: Arnold recognized that the tastes of Puritan New Englanders were changing. He stocked all the latest cosmetics from London (rose water, cold cream, ladies' court plasters), necklaces, earrings, buckles and buttons, "a very elegant assortment of mezzotint pictures, prints, maps, stationery ware and paperhangings for rooms."[2]

Like his mentor Lathrop, he sold medical books and surgical instruments. For students across the green at Yale, he offered a rich assortment of books. From his own reading and schooling at Canterbury and from studying his market, he blended the wares of college, capital, and seaport town, creating the sort of place where people were likely to spend money. Dr. Arnold's shop was a showcase as much for his own wide readings as for his tastes in merchandise. If Benedict Arnold read half the books he sold (and there is evidence from his writings that indeed he did), he was as lettered as any young man who had the good fortune to go to Yale. Literate, charming, a man with a knack for selling things, he soon moved to better quarters on Church Street and then to a large storefront on Water Street, along the harbor. Although his business thrived, he yearned to go to sea. Not only was there more profit for the middleman-merchant than for the retail seller of imported goods, but Arnold loved the life on a ship. He wanted to buy a sloop and trade in the Caribbean and in Canada, now that there was peace in America and the French had been driven out.

Benedict Arnold had a strong physical appearance: a distinctive nose, a high forehead suggesting intelligence, a prominent chin, and gray piercing eyes. He was handsome in a way that made people notice him, so much so that many thought this powerful, confident man was arrogant before they even heard his words delivered with a strong voice backed by a quick mind. It may have helped give him a certain charm that a succession of beautiful women had doted on him since boyhood: his pretty, patient mother, his adoring younger sister, the indulgent Jerusha Lathrop all persuaded Benedict Arnold that women appreciated him. Consequently, he apparently always thought he could successfully besiege whatever woman he chose. If he had romances with women before his first marriage at twenty-six, it was undoubtedly at a discreet distance from prim and proper New Haven, most likely during island-hopping cruises in the Caribbean.

Single men were distrusted in Puritan New England and in many places paid a special bachelor tax. Arnold, while he was still single, kept up the semblance of a family home after 1764, with his sister, Hannah, living in their parents' house in Norwich Town. Indeed, he seems to have been jealous of any man who dared to approach Hannah. One incident with a potential suitor demonstrates how close the two were and how hot-tempered Arnold could be if he thought his authority was being challenged. On one of his visits back to Norwich after the end of the French and Indian War in 1763, Arnold discovered that a young French dueling master was seriously courting Hannah, who was then nineteen and under Benedict's guardianship. The man was hardly to blame: Hannah was tall, graceful, witty, pretty like her mother, if not quite beautiful, and a favorite in Norwich Town society. She also obviously came from one of Norwich Town's first families. This Frenchman must have been a patient man, because Hannah was forever talking about another man, the brother to whom she was so devoted. Benedict, however, was less than charming to the Frenchman, who only months before had been considered an enemy who could have been killed for coming to a Puritan stronghold like Norwich Town. A product of a New England which had been trained to hate the French in particular and Catholics in general, Benedict reacted hotly when the Frenchman ignored his warning and continued to call on his sister. Moreover, he considered the Frenchman's unchaperoned visits to his sister improper. Even worse, Hannah ignored his demands that she discourage her suitor.

One evening, Benedict arrived in Norwich Town after the long ride from New Haven with one of his friends and could see, through a parlor window, the Frenchman alone with his sister in the candlelight. Anger pulsing through him, Arnold asked his friend to go to the front door and knock and enter as if he were Benedict coming home alone. Meanwhile, Arnold concealed himself. When his friend knocked, the Frenchman threw open a window and jumped out, and Benedict fired. Fortunately for the Frenchman, either the light was bad or Arnold, a crack shot, deliberately aimed high to warn him off. If he only intended to frighten the man, he certainly succeeded. The Frenchman left Norwich Town. One unsubstantiated story is that the two men later met in the West Indies and Arnold, still seething with resentment that the Frenchman had risked compromising his sister in Puritan Norwich Town, accepted the Frenchman's challenge to a duel and severely wounded him.

Hannah Arnold certainly never saw her suitor again, but she still worshiped her brother and talked too much about him for most men to stand when they came to call. One historian has sagely observed that, virile and proud and independent as he was, Benedict Arnold paid women the compliment of needing them. Indeed, all the women he loved—Hannah, his mother, his two wives—responded by needing him, even if, as in Hannah's case, there may have been times when they were aware of his shortcomings. Proud Hannah had every reason to refuse to help Benedict, but she was to prove over and over again that she was deeply loyal to him no matter what he did. Shortly after firing at the Frenchman, Benedict paid off his father's £300 note on the family home and sold it, forcing his sister to leave the house where she had always lived and using the money to buy a sloop and then moving Hannah to New Haven, where she knew no one, to mind his house and his store while he sailed the Caribbean.[3] By eighteenth-century standards, he was not only well within his rights but generous to her, always providing for her and even entrusting her more and more with his business affairs. This was much more than he had to do: he could have forced her to marry someone he chose or even bound her out as a servant. And if Hannah ever resented Benedict's spending the money he made by uprooting her, she nonetheless swallowed her pride and went along to New Haven with him. She never married: perhaps she was too proud ever again to ask or require her brother's approval. Perhaps, too, she was afraid of his volcanic temper and settled for the role of business and household manager, a better fate than a woman without a dowry could expect at the time.

A British victory in the Seven Years War in 1763 brought an end to a century and a half of commercial rivalry and intermittent warfare between the French and the English in North America. It should have brought a massive expansion of trade by English colonists into the void left by expulsion of the French. For many Americans, however, and eventually for Benedict Arnold himself, peace produced a long depression. The sudden end of British wartime subsidies to colonial governments to pay their militias and the drying-up of wartime contracts to feed, house, and transport British armies led to a collapse of colonial economies. Moreover, a new British currency act forbade the printing of colonial paper money at the very time the British were redoubling efforts to tax American trade to pay for American defense. The new taxes had to be paid in silver or gold. Thus the first serious attempts to regulate American trade and enforce customs duties further shocked colonial markets.

For Benedict Arnold, peace meant an end to the threat of seizure by the French during expeditions around the Caribbean and along the Canadian coast. With the £700 proceeds from selling his father's house, Arnold bought a forty-ton sloop, which he named the *Fortune*. Advertising in the *Connecticut Gazette* for "large, fat, genteel horses,"[4] barrels of pork, bales of hay, and bags of oats, he crowded every inch of his holds and strapped lumber on his decks and set sail south toward the Caribbean and St. Kitts, Martinique, and the Bay of Honduras or north, running down east to Nova Scotia, Newfoundland, the St. Lawrence, Quebec, and Montreal, cities he would come to know not only as a sailor but also as a soldier. Exchanging livestock and lumber for Spanish gold or valuable cargoes of salt and cotton, which were in short supply in New Haven, he traded shrewdly and expanded carefully. But when other men could not pay him, he lost 50 percent on two voyages in 1764. As he waited "sometimes three years to be paid," his "every bill [of exchange] was protested."[5] At twenty-four, he was nearly ruined. But he refused to trim his sails, and by 1766, only twenty-five, he had three ships in trade and his apothecary was flourishing.

*   *   *

Finding itself with a far-flung empire acquired in only a few years, the British government undertook a thorough review of American policy and taxes. After the French surrender, the British became the overlords of all the Indians between the Appalachian Mountains and the Mississippi River, now the western boundary of British territory. By proclamation, the British forbade settlement west of the Appalachians: what had been so hard won by British and American colonial troops became a huge Indian reserve. Settlers already west of the mountains were ordered to leave, and British troops were sent in to police the settlers as much as the Indians. Someone would have to pay the soldiers, and the new Treasury lord, George Grenville, expected the Americans to help. A look at the English national debt in 1763 was enough to make any minister look for new answers: as of January 5, 1763, according to the Exchequer, the funded debt stood at £122 million, a staggering sum that carried annual interest of £4.4 million. For three years, the debt grew annually by £7 million because of the costs of maintaining the new empire. Financing the debt absorbed more and more ministerial time and turned English attention increasingly to America, which, in European eyes, already possessed wealth. In truth, this wealth was more legendary than real.

Relatively little can be known about Benedict Arnold's activities as a trader in the ten years preceding the American Revolution, because, like so many American merchants at the time, he was involved in smuggling. Every Connecticut and Rhode Island shipper who dealt with the French and Spanish in the Caribbean in the molasses trade between 1733 and 1765 was a smuggler, according to Colonial Office records in London. *Nothing* was credited for the two colonies in an "account of all the duties collected under the Molasses Act," even while "of all the northern provinces their industries were most dependent on the French sugar islands."[6] Benedict Arnold's business was secret by definition. To keep accurate records would have been self-destructive, yet not to engage to some degree of smuggling was all but impossible if such a business was to survive increasingly stringent British trade policies. Moreover, many of New England's most prominent citizens—the Hancocks of Boston, the Trumbulls of Connecticut, the Browns of Rhode Island—built their family fortunes on evasion of the welter of contradictory trade laws that had grown up over a century. Smuggling, in fact, had become an economic necessity on which depended the welfare not only of shipowners but of farmers and merchants and virtually anyone else doing business in colonial America. British governments had understood the economics of winking at trade laws for a century, but at exactly the time when young Arnold bought his first sloop and headed south, the British began tinkering with their trade laws as one inept aristocratic amateur after another tried to make sense out of the administration of the new British Empire.

A clever and careful status quo had existed almost since the settling of the first British colonies in North America. British colonies in the West Indies depended on the mainland North American colonies for materials such as food, livestock, lumber, barrel staves, naval stores, even ships; in exchange, they provided sugar and molasses to make rum. But they could not produce enough of these, their two basic commodities, to keep pace with mainland colonial growth. British officials for generations had turned a blind eye as North America obtained the shortfall from illicit trade with the islands controlled by rival Spanish, Dutch, and French empires. In peacetime, goods flowed freely between the West Indies and American mainland ports, and the British home government was content to have made trade profits from manufactured goods—furniture, glass, fine clothing, good wines, carriages—exported to the colonies by English merchants. These laissez-faire practices made up a British colonial policy of what was considered "salutary neglect" until the 1730s, when the British government, pressured by West Indian merchants who sat in Parliament and wanted a monopoly on the rich sugar trade, forced through the Molasses Act at about the same time Benedict Arnold's father was sailing Absalom King's ships to the Caribbean. The new duty was high: sixpence to the gallon. This was too much for mainland merchants, so they simply began to evade the duty by the systematic smuggling that two generations of Benedict Arnolds engaged in.

Several practices were quickly worked out to circumvent the Molasses Act. Foreign sugar and molasses could either be brought from French or Spanish ports directly to the mainland or bought by cynical British West Indian merchants unable to meet the voracious demands of their illegal northern customers. These cargoes could then either be landed clandestinely along thousands of miles of American seacoast—and whole towns sprang up to handle the illicit trade—or part could be landed surreptitiously at one destination while duties were paid on the rest, the stated cargo, as false papers (secured from Caribbean customs officials) were presented to customs officers. Even without false papers, mainland customs collectors could be bribed to overlook part of the shipment. If all perfectly corrupt, it was considered perfectly legal, and there might have been less provocation for the American Revolution if the British had not tried to tinker with a system that was working so handsomely to everyone's benefit. By the time the last French and Indian War began in 1756, however, trading with the enemy was so widespread that some British officials began to chafe. In actuality, even the proclamation of war had only made such trade a misdemeanor.

At the end of the war, in 1763, a new government came to power in London that took the view that America was paying far too little of the costs of administering its government and its defenses. Although the French had been defeated in a series of smashing British victories, there still were thousands of miles of frontiers, with forts to be garrisoned and supplied. The new British administration expected the Americans to pay not all of the costs for the requisite twenty thousand redcoats, but certainly a major share. For forty years, revenues from the Molasses Act hadn't even covered the expenses of collection. A far more stringent set of duties was introduced immediately after the war ended.

Away from New Haven during the early antitax protests, Benedict Arnold was busy making the reputation that made men fear him even if they didn't always respect him. A man who went to sea was always accorded respect on account of the danger and difficulty of his way of life. A ship's officer had to be a man's man, since no man would follow the orders of a man he did not fear at sea, where everything depended on a strict code of discipline. Among gentlemen in general, and ship's officers in particular, the ultimate sanction for violations of the code of honor was the duel. One incident shows just how far Benedict Arnold was willing to go if he felt his honor insulted and explains why sailing men in New Haven were willing to follow him when he was scarcely twenty-five, even if he had never been an officer in the anti-French wars. Among the protocols between ship's captains was a tradition that whenever ships of the same nationality or from the same home port came across each other in a foreign harbor, there was a formalized round of visiting toasts, in which the younger captains were invited for drinks by the oldest captain or the captain of the largest ship. On a voyage to the Bay of Honduras in his sloop, *Sally,* young Captain Arnold was invited to join several British and American colonial captains aboard the vessel of the senior British shipper for an evening's festivities. But Benedict was apparently too busy getting his papers in order to clear for sailing the next day, and because he needed every man to help load his ship, he could spare no one to row over to Captain Croskie's ship with his apologies. The next morning, however, before he sailed, he went in person to extend his apologies. But

Croskie was a prickly Englishman, and what ensued was one of those exchanges which helps to explain why so many Americans hated their British overlords by 1776 and why so many Englishmen despised the upstart Americans. Croskie was probably still suffering from a rum-induced hangover when young, bright-eyed Arnold came bounding aboard his ship. "You damned Yankee," Croskie bellowed at Arnold in front of their men. "Have you no manners?" Flushing angrily, young Captain Arnold on the spot challenged the senior man to a duel. Quietly, he took off his glove and handed it to the man. Croskie accepted.

On a small island in the bay, the two men, their seconds, and a surgeon were supposed to meet at sunrise the next day. Arnold, his seconds, and the surgeon were there at the appointed hour as the morning mist began to burn off. Croskie was late. It appeared he had decided against the duel. Arnold was about to leave when one of his seconds spotted a boat approaching loaded not only with Croskie and his seconds but a half-dozen burly natives. Suspicious, Arnold cocked his pistols and leveled them at the boat and forbade the Indians to come any closer or he would shoot them. He then demanded an explanation from Croskie, who only mumbled some reply and, believing Arnold meant his threat, waved off the boatload of men and stepped ashore with his seconds. Obviously rattled, Croskie took the first shot, as the challenged party, but missed. Then Arnold aimed and fired at him. His bullet creased Croskie's arm. There was a brief respite as the surgeon bandaged the wound. Then the two men resumed their positions thirty yards apart as their seconds reloaded their pistols. Arnold turned to Croskie and shouted at him: "I give you notice! If you miss this time, I shall kill you!"[7] By this time, Croskie believed that Arnold would do whatever he said. The English officer apologized for insulting Arnold. His honor satisfied, Arnold shook hands with the man, accepted, rowed back to his ship, and sailed home to New Haven.

With postwar trade depressed in Britain, levying new taxes or increasing existing ones was not a popular solution. The ordinary Englishman was growing restless under the burdens of paying for a bloated government and even a victorious war. As prime minister, Grenville stuck to his guns on the need for new taxes to pay for garrisoning the new American conquests. He did not ask the Americans to pay any of the interest on the huge war debt that had helped liberate them from perennial fear of the French, but he was adamant that they pay a part of the £350,000 annual bill for twenty battalions—roughly ten thousand troops—billeted on the mainland. He talked Parliament into *reducing* the tax on molasses from sixpence to threepence (producing revenue equal to a mere one-third of the cost of billeting troops), but in return he insisted on efficient collection of that share.

The Sugar Act of 1764, as it was called, enumerated a list of goods which could only be shipped to England itself and not to Europe or the West Indies. The act banned import of non-British rums and wines and created or raised taxes on a wide variety of consumer goods. It set double duties on foreign goods and required that raw materials such as iron, hides, whale fins, raw silk, and potash from the colonies be first shipped to England before they could be reexported either as finished goods or as raw materials to European markets. But the provisions for enforcement were what produced outrage in America. Merchants and ship captains would now have to be more careful to prepare a proper manifest of the cargo in their holds, in all cases obtaining papers before they loaded and unloaded. This all but eliminated the traditional arrangements with customs inspectors. To police the new laws, not pliable customs clerks but British navy officers were assigned to crack down on smugglers, using warships stationed in every major port.

The British government's timing could not have been worse. One part of the problem was that very few Americans, in a barter-and-credit economy, had any gold or silver or cash of any kind to pay for anything, let alone higher taxes. Each colony had tried to create new paper currencies, some of them based on America's most plentiful and valuable commodity, land, but the king's Board of Trade had vetoed them. Merchants such as Benedict Arnold had trouble collecting on their customers' accounts and in turn they could not pay their debts in London, where suppliers had continued to advance them credit because they needed America's market for Britain's goods. But America was broke. One sharp-eyed British visitor noted in a letter home to England that he "would not give £800 for the whole province" of Connecticut. He had been "all over it," including New Haven's largely idled waterfront, and came away convinced that "they are all mortgaged to the full to the Bostonians and New Yorkers."[8] High unemployment and high debts fueled American resentment of British trade policies and made even more detested any English efforts at cracking down on smugglers.

What brought Benedict Arnold out into the open as a leader in American resistance to the new British laws, however, was not the crackdown on his covert trading activities but a second set of British taxes imposed hard on the heels of the first. The Sugar Act was, as

Arnold's young friend the New Haven lawyer Jared Ingersoll wrote to a treasury official in London, like "burning a barn to roast an egg." In any case, smuggling was so widespread that the British could only hope to catch "one vessel in a hundred."9 Even so, the prospect of new revenues from sugar did not satisfy the new British ministry, which by 1764 was also enacting new post-office regulations for America to collect a tax on all stamped paper. Long collected in England, the stamp tax was designed to raise £60,000 a year, which, together with the expected yield from Sugar Act imports, would have made up two-thirds of the cost of maintaining the British military establishment in the colonies. Actually, only one-third of the British troops were within mainland American colonies or along the frontier at this time, and two-thirds were in the Caribbean, so the levies fell disproportionately on the Americans. Henceforth, Americans would be required to purchase, with gold or silver, tax stamps to be affixed to newspapers, almanacs, pamphlets, broadsides, insurance policies, ship's papers (a tax on a tax), even playing cards and dice. All legal documents, licenses, and diplomas were to be printed on paper embossed with the royal stamp.

In an attempt to appease the Americans, the ministry appointed only Americans to be the stamp agents. Merchants such as Benedict Arnold were divided as to what action they should take. Many, like Benjamin Franklin in Philadelphia, believed that Parliament would not do anything to impair English business, since "its loss in point of commerce is infinitely more than its gain in taxes."10 Many merchants also undoubtedly expected that the old arrangements with customs collectors would still work, no matter what Parliament did. But these merchants were surprised to find a new and inflexible breed of customs agents operating within a reformed system. For decades, the customs agency had been run by absentee political appointees in England who farmed out the actual collecting to hired deputies who went to America and remitted only a portion of their harvest to their British employers. The Grenville ministry dashed this system by requiring all customs agents to move to their posts in America. A wave of resignations ensued, making way for appointment of a zealous new breed of collector. Another major shift was that the Customs Service for a century had operated from its own revenue cutters offshore. Now it moved onshore, where it could more closely scrutinize incoming cargo and be more available to informants. What Americans could now expect was shown quickly in Rhode Island in December 1764, when a British navy boarding party followed up a tip from an informant and tried to search a smuggling ship. A melee ensued, an American soldier attacked the

British sailors with a broadax, and the British lieutenant in charge
ran him through with his sword. Incidents of this sort made the
work of smugglers harder and more dangerous: now they had to
sneak into caves on moonless nights and off-load cargoes into small
boats and transport them at great expense and risk overland in carts
to the nearest city. Many men had to be paid off in gold and then
trusted. There was often an informer skulking about who, either for
reward money or to settle an old score, would pinch on the smugglers. That same month at the end of 1764, a New York mob
showed what an informer could expect. When George Spencer told
customs agents about contraband cargo, wealthy and powerful merchants had him arrested for debt. Then, as he was paraded through
the city on the way to jail, he was pelted with the filth of the streets.
He was left in jail until he promised to leave the city.

As the depression deepened, announcement of the stamp tax levies
set off a new round of riotous protests from Boston to Charleston.
In New Haven, Benedict Arnold, whenever he was home, attended
the rallies and meetings, aligning himself with a radical group of
merchants and shipowners that gradually became determined to take
steps to prevent the imposition of new taxes in Connecticut. Arnold's friend Jared Ingersoll warned a British friend of theirs in the
Treasury in London that merchants were unanimously opposed to
the new taxes, that there was not a single merchant "with the most
distant intention to pay the duties."[11] The people of New Haven
were deeply divided: the old, established families at the First Congregational Church and most of the faculty and students of Yale
College were against any form of open opposition to England. All
around New Haven, the controversy swirled. Jared Ingersoll was
only one of the men from the most venerable Connecticut families
who were ambivalent about the tax: while he protested it, he was
eager, for financial reasons, to be appointed distributor of the
stamped parchment. Opposition came from unpredictable quarters.
In Stratford, Connecticut, Anglican priest William Samuel Johnson
gloomily told Yale professor Ezra Stiles, "From this time, date the
slavery of the colonies."[12] The *Connecticut Gazette* asked "whether
Americans were going to be bondsmen." The New Haven newspaper ominously printed the names of all thirteen stamp commissioners in America and called them "mean, mercenary hirelings,
parricides among yourselves, who for a little filthy lucre would at
any time betray every right, liberty and privilege of their fellow subjects."[13]

Reading, listening, speaking against the taxes, Benedict Arnold decided to throw in with a secret group calling itself the Sons of Liberty, pledging to resist new British measures and to take any step, even if it meant violence, necessary to prevent the enforcement of the Stamp Act. They were determined to seize and destroy the stamped paper and to force the resignation of all stamp commissioners. Before the crisis was over, the Sons of Liberty numbered as many as ten thousand members in Connecticut alone. In New Jersey, a mob of eight hundred pressured the lawyers who were not already in their ranks to boycott and close the courts. In Boston, the stamp commissioner was mobbed, pursued, and beaten twice before he finally resigned. On August 21, 1765, the new stamp commissioner for Connecticut was burned in effigy at Norwich Town, and again the next day in New London. The ceremony was precise and elaborate, and was reported in detail by the *Connecticut Gazette*. At six o'clock the evening of August 22, 1765, there appeared on New London's gallows an effigy of Jared Ingersoll "with a boat placed a little back of his right shoulder wherein was concealed a young imp of the Devil peeping out of the same in order to whisper in his ear." On the breast of the effigy was a copy of the Stamp Act and an inscription in praise of liberty. A crowd assembled, pulled the effigy from the gallows, mounted it on a pole, and carried it through town "attended by the people of all professions and denominations." There was music, guns fired in the air, drums beaten, cheering crowds. A tall elm tree was designated as the Liberty Tree. "Arriving at the place of assignation," the *Gazette* continued, "a halter was placed around the neck of the effigy, which was again suspended in the air on the gallows and, a bonfire being erected under it . . . was consumed."[14] All through the hanging and burning, the cannon in the town's fort kept up a steady tattoo while children chanted.

The objections of many Americans to British intrusions cut across class lines. The members of mobs were drawn from all social classes. When a customs informer was tarred and feathered in Norfolk, Virginia, "all the principal gentlemen in town" were present. Indeed, as the protest widened, respectable members of the community organized and led the mobs. In Boston, the effigies that signaled mob violence were prepared by the "Loyal Nine," a social club of leading merchants and tradesmen. They included the publisher of the *Boston Gazette,* one Harvard-educated merchant, and two distillers.

Royal officials in every colony now feared that mob violence was leading to anarchy as they found themselves powerless to act. With no police forces and British troops stationed in only a few major towns, several governors tried to keep the hated stamps out of their

colonies entirely. New Jersey governor William Franklin, son of the
leading Philadelphia politician, did not feel that his father's mantle
of prestige would reach far enough to protect him. He asked the
captain of the British ship delivering the stamps to New York City to
keep them there, as did the governor of Connecticut. But New York
City was no safer now. There were royal troops stationed at Fort
George on the Battery, and mob leaders believed that the royal governor intended to use them to enforce the Stamp Act. It did not help
to cool passions when Major Thomas James of the royal artillery
boasted that he would cram the stamps down New Yorkers' throats
with the help of a handful of men. Major James's house was the last
in a series of buildings demolished by parties of rioters led by sea
captains and organized by the Sons of Liberty.

On the night of September 10, 1765, the Stamp Act rioting spread to
New Haven. There is little question that Benedict Arnold was at
least somewhere on the edge of the crowd. Although his leadership
cannot be proved at this early date, he was a respected figure in the
town's resistance movement by this time. Early that evening a crowd
gathered in West Haven after New Hampshire's stamp commissioner
had been frightened into resigning by the ominous warning that
"your person and estate will be greatly endangered if you continue
in this office." According to the *Connecticut Gazette,* they marched
past Ingersoll's house with

*a horrible monster or male giant twelve feet high whose terrible
head was internally illuminated. He was mounted on a generous
horse groaning under the enormous weight. This giant seemed to
threaten destruction to every person or thing around him, which
raised the resentment of a number of stout fellows who constantly
pelted him with stones till he fled. The assailants pursued and soon
took him captive, and triumphantly drove him about a mile in the
town, attended with the discordant noise of drums, fiddles and
taunting huzzahs. The people then directed their course toward a hill
called Mount Misery. There the giant was accused, fairly tried and
condemned by a special jury as an unjust intruder, a patron of ignorance, a foe of English freedom, and was sentenced to be burnt . . .
amidst the joyous acclamations of near three hundred libertines,
men, women, and children. It should be mentioned that through the
whole of this rare show, no unlawful disorder happened.*[15]

It was important in each newspaper account to point out the or-
derliness of the mob, as if to insist that it was in the care of the

better sort. Connecticut was among the slowest colonies to react to the Stamp Act, one possible reason being the apparent determination of leading officials not to dignify the proceedings with a response. Governor Thomas Fitch refused the crowds' demands to call a special session of the legislature, as Virginia had done. When a mob finally paid a visit to Jared Ingersoll in New Haven and threatened to tear down his house unless he resigned, he was able to come outside and persuade them that he couldn't resign until the colony took some official action in the matter. He said he would be glad to put in a good word for them to the governor, and if the evil stamps could not be kept out of the colony and should happen to appear at his house, he would gladly throw open its doors to the public so the people could make a bonfire of them.

Sons of Liberty like Arnold, who wanted action, who wanted Ingersoll to resign immediately, were frustrated by the conservatism of even some of their own leaders. Another three weeks passed before Governor Fitch decided to call the assembly. Meanwhile, admiration grew for the stout Ingersoll for refusing to be cowed. Finally it was arranged that Ingersoll would ride to Hartford, where the assembly was sitting, to meet the mob that demanded his resignation. At the southern edge of Wethersfield, the main body of five hundred mounted Sons of Liberty, every man carrying a "stout, clean shaven willow wand," advanced in perfect military formation toward Ingersoll and his legal associate, Major Elihu Hall of Wallingford. Without a word, the entire formation opened, allowing Ingersoll and his friend to pass, then just as silently wheeled about and escorted them to a large elm tree on the east side of the village green. The men dismounted and formed a great circle around Ingersoll. They shouted for him to resign. He balked. He'd given his word and bond; he wouldn't resign until he could get "the sense of the government." At that point the crowd's leader, Major John Durkee of Norwich Town, veteran of the French and Indian War, answered, "Here is the sense of the government. No man shall exercise that office." When Ingersoll again argued, he was threatened by the mob. The moderate Durkee tried to take matters indoors to a tavern, and the riders began to move that way, but Ingersoll boldly tried to go on to the capital. Someone seized his horse's bridle: "You shan't go two rods from this spot before you have resigned." He was hurried inside and held a virtual prisoner by a committee negotiating with him. Later, as the crowd grew restless, he drew up his own resignation and went out to read it to the crowd, ending by throwing his hat in the air and leading three cheers for "Liberty and Property."[16] Amid handshakes all around, Ingersoll and the crowd's leaders went off to dinner together, then rode off at the head of at least one thousand men to read his resignation to the assembly. The protesters, trumpets blaring, marched around the statehouse as its occupants fled. Again, Ingersoll had to read his resignation from the steps of a tavern, this time throwing hat and wig in the air. Then the protesters rode home. When Ingersoll finally read his resignation before the assembly a few days later, it was repudiated and the governor issued a proclamation to suppress all further riotous proceedings.

Benedict Arnold was at sea through much of that winter as delegates of nine colonies met in New York City for their first congress on the tax crisis. One upshot was passage of an agreement banning the purchase of all English goods until the Stamp Act was repealed and the Sugar Act modified. Almost all legal American trade with England was suspended even as smuggling increased. Courthouses, vital for the recording of sales of property, land deeds, and debts, were shut down by lawyers' boycotts. British exports to America dropped off so significantly that American agents asked some thirty English towns engaged in the American trade and now suffering from its loss to support their movement in Parliament to repeal the Stamp Act.

In the next two years, Arnold ran up £16,000 in back bills with six London suppliers, and they began pressuring him for payment. Coming home to New Haven late in 1765, Arnold slipped past British customs cutters in Long Island Sound and unloaded enough illicit cargo to keep his business solvent through another winter. Nevertheless, he was worried. His London debts were sizable, even by the standards of Connecticut merchants. He had plenty of reason to resent the recent customs crackdown. How was he supposed to pay off his British creditors if the British government made it impossible to turn a dollar in trade? To keep his ships at sea, to lay out money for horses and feed and lumber to sell in the islands, to pay his officers and crews and pay off the necessary officials in the West Indies—all these things required cash from his customers on Water Street, and they, of course, were running behind in their payments to him. He was in a bind. To ease his reliance on the dicey Caribbean trade, Arnold had branched out north and west, cramming the holds of his brigs with horses and barrels of beef and pork and his decks with lumber, sailing six months out of twelve. First he would head south to the Caribbean to sell these cargoes for cash, then buy up European manufactured goods and rum, sugar, and molasses. Trading as he went, he stopped off long enough in New Haven to go over his accounts with Hannah while he reloaded with woolens and cheese that would fetch a high price to the north. Then he followed the Sound again, sometimes to the Hudson River and days of tacking up to the Dutch patroons' settlements, swinging wide at the great bend of the river at West Point and running down the prevailing summer winds as far as the big fur-trading center at Albany. His cargoes more valuable as the season progressed, he raced back to New Haven in time to take on another load, this time bound for Canada, down east along the coast quickly to the Gaspé, then up the St. Lawrence to Quebec, or a few days' good sailing farther upriver to Montreal, where he could barter for luxury goods just over from England. By the time a thousand men from his native northeastern Connecticut were circling the statehouse with Jared Ingersoll in tow, Benedict Arnold was back in New Haven, his temper toward British sympathizers growing shorter by the month.

On his return to New Haven, Arnold learned of a fresh threat. British merchants had hired a lawyer and began to menace him with threats of seizing his ships for nonpayment of debts. He in turn began to sue his debtors. As one New York creditor threatened him and spread rumors of his insolvency, Arnold wrote angrily: "I assure you that it is with the utmost indifference I observe the unjust and false aspersions your malice could invent."[17] But Arnold clearly was growing frustrated by the worsening cash bind. Arnold's letters to the *Connecticut Gazette* over the next few months demonstrate his resentment at the treatment Americans were receiving from their British masters and his amazement at the timorousness of New Haven neighbors in the face of the British. He considered his community endangered by a crisis over who should lead them, the hard-driving new men like himself who were taking such a financial beating at the hands of faraway British administrators, or entrenched conservatives centered on First Church, exerting control through the age-old alliance of Connecticut's church, state, and landed gentry, who branded anyone like himself an interloper. The rich landlords still controlled New Haven through its town meeting, and they were opposed to any changes. By 1765, these established families made up only 3 percent of the population, amounting to about 250 people who dominated the town meeting, appointed all local officials, sent representatives to the assembly, and controlled the militia. The new people like Arnold numbered nearly 7,750, but many were disenfranchised and without effective voice.

Until the Great Awakening of the 1740s, a majority of Connecticut residents had no voice in secular or church government. A shrinking percentage of Congregationalists, usually propertied descendants of the founding Puritan families of each town, made their wishes known through their church elders and ministers and then through the ministerial associations, which influenced the general assembly, which passed and enforced laws. Individual dissent was all but useless and political parties were nonexistent in a system which invoked the authority of God and state. But the Great Awakening was a social as well as a religious revolution which quickly led to major political changes as well. When the awakened, many of them young and from the lower and middle classes, broke with officially established congregations to form separatist churches and called themselves New Lights, conservative congregationalists such as the Arnolds of Norwich Town became known as Old Lights, and were proud of it. Everyone in a town, and eventually in the colony, knew who went to which church and which side of the great rift everyone else was on.

Reasserting themselves, the Old Lights had attempted to outlaw the Great Awakening by passing and rigorously enforcing laws against itinerant preachers such as George Whitefield. This touched a nerve among some of the elders: to ban the use of churches for revivals and to arrest preachers sounded like persecution. Increasingly, when sheriffs and magistrates did the bidding of Old Light ministers and enforced the anti-itinerant preaching law, angry crowds intervened. When Old Lights in Norwich Town forced the issue of collecting taxes from everyone to support the minister, New Lights began to protest that church and state were too closely connected. It was the first widespread tax resistance in America, fully ten years before the Stamp Act crisis. Old Lights purged New Lights from pulpits, firing even the famous Jonathan Edwards. Many of the elite began to withdraw from Congregational churches and join the New Lights. Open resistance to anti-itinerant laws shocked Old Lights, who rightly sensed that the spirit of rebelliousness went beyond a specific statute. Old Lights castigated New Lights as enemies of order and government who were plotting "a great change in the civil government."[18] The religious revolution took on more overt political form by the 1750s. The New Lights, who believed that to fight their religious revival was to fight against God, insisted that the real issue had become religious toleration. Gradually, an opposition political party composed of New Lights grew up in the Connecticut assembly, and it began to object to every bill that represented the commingling of church and state. Becoming known as the New Light Party, it now included men from distinguished families. By the 1760s, New Lights controlled the Connecticut assembly and were leading opposition to the Stamp Act, enforcing their opposition through the activities of the Sons of Liberty.

The changes the New Lights demanded in government were as

fundamental as those they had demanded in religion. The Old Light Party of the early 1760s wanted colonial government to become more responsive to the economic needs of the people through established channels with England, thus giving the people a stronger reason to obey and respect authority; the fundamentalist New Lights rejected this appeal to rational self-interest and insisted that nothing short of a complete conversion experience similar to what they required in church should take place in government, with repentance for past political sins and a new and inspirited political life as well as spiritual devotion to purging and rectifying the flaws of government and society. The Great Awakening and the Stamp Act protests were linked in a twenty-five-year process that led up to the American Revolution. Many of the awakened churchgoers who had never had a role in church or state had found a voice in government by the end of the Stamp Act crisis, joining protests against the new British tax policies and against the conservatives who supported the British.

The political shakeup went as high as the statehouse, where Governor Fitch was called to account by the New Lights for refusing to convene the assembly to discuss the Stamp Act. In the first elections after the Stamp Act crisis, Fitch and his Old Lights were defeated and New Light leader Jonathan Trumbull became lieutenant governor; three years later, he was elected governor, the first New Light to hold the office. The New Light victory was complete and enduring. Trumbull remained in office throughout the long revolutionary era. The New Light movement and the Stamp Act crisis combined to produce new leaders who could mobilize men for political action. By October 1765, wrote Ezra Stiles, professor of moral philosophy at Yale, three-fourths of the men in Connecticut were "ready to take up arms for their liberties." They numbered "very boys as well as the hardy rustic" and they were "full of fire and ready to fight."[19] One estimate is that upward of ten thousand men had joined the Sons of Liberty, although conservatives were able to point at some questionable figures among them. Dr. Benjamin Gale, himself a founder of the Sons of Liberty, said that the assemblage at one of their conventions was a "babel" and included "several pimps and smugglers."[20] Soon the Sons' influence began to sweep from eastern seaport towns most directly affected by the depression into the western counties.

Benedict Arnold had stayed out of the New Light–Old Light struggle through the Stamp Act crisis, but in February 1766, according to his own account in the *Connecticut Gazette* on February 21, he took part in a riot that finally pitted him against Old Light authorities in

New Haven and brought him into the open as a leader of the Sons of Liberty and adherent to the New Light Party. Arnold wrote in the *Gazette* that the riot was the result of a misunderstanding between Arnold and Peter Boles, who had "been on a voyage with me in which he was used with the greatest humanity, on our return was paid his wages to his full satisfaction and informed me of his intention to leave the town that day, wished me well and departed the town, as I imagined." Boles gave a slightly different version. After a single cruise with Arnold aboard *Fortune,* he said, when he asked Arnold for more money, Arnold, who undoubtedly had been smuggling contraband goods, said he considered the request blackmail and suggested the man get out of town at once. Instead, Boles went to the New Haven customs house on January 24 to inform the king's agents that Arnold was a smuggler and, he hoped, to receive a reward, a percentage of the goods and prize money to be realized when a smuggler's ship was seized and sold at auction. Unfortunately for Boles, the customs commissioner, David Wooster, was not in: it was the Sabbath and the staunchly Puritan customs collector had the day off. Instead, Boles talked to an assistant, one Sanford, asking him what share of a cargo seized by the crown would be given to an informer. When Sanford did not tell him—either he couldn't or he wouldn't—Boles refused to give any further information until the collector returned the following Monday. In small-town New Haven, a sailor going into the customs house on the Sabbath was conspicuous. Moreover, so few ships were clearing the port or discharging cargo in the dead of that winter of depression and trade boycott that it wouldn't have taken much sleuthing on the part of customs officials to guess exactly which ship Boles had in mind.

Two days later, Benedict Arnold learned of Boles's first visit and his intention to return later that day. A man with considerable property and upper-class connections by this time, Arnold was also aggressive and decisive, and he could see quickly that his chances for the fortune he so badly wanted were in jeopardy. He roared off to the tavern where he knew he could find most of his crew. He told them Boles was trying to inform on them. He had to say no more. In a matter of minutes they had located Boles in another tavern and dragged him out and, in Arnold's own words, published for all Connecticut to see, "gave him a little chastisement." In other words, they beat him up, "on which he left the town."

But Peter Boles did not stay away. On Wednesday, January 28, he returned to New Haven to enlist the aid of more conservative merchants and to get their protection as he testified against Arnold.

Boles went to the home of Captain Beecher, a wealthy ship's captain, a business rival of Arnold's, and a man aligned with the Old Lights. There, at seven o'clock the next evening, Benedict Arnold and several other Sons of Liberty paid a visit on Boles and forced him to sign an extraordinary sworn statement that Arnold had prepared for him:

I, Peter Boles, not having the fear of God before my eyes, but being instigated by the Devil, did on the 24th instant, make information or endeavor to do the same, to one of the Custom House Officers for the port of New Haven, against Benedict Arnold, for importing contraband goods, do hereby acknowledge I justly deserve a halter for my malicious and cruel intentions. I do solemnly swear I will never hereafter make information, directly or indirectly, or cause the same to be done, against any person or persons whatever, for importing contraband or other goods into this Colony or any part of America, and that I will immediately leave New Haven and never enter the same again. So help me God.

For his part, Arnold, after making it quite clear to Boles that he thought he should be hanged for endangering his fellow crewmen and captain, promised "not to inform the sailors of his being in town," provided Boles would leave it immediately "according to our agreement."

But Boles did not leave town. He felt safe enough to stay at Beecher's house while Arnold, believing the man had left, went home and went to bed. Shortly before midnight, Arnold said, "I heard a noise in the street and a person informed me the sailors were at Mr. Beecher's. On enquiry, I found the fellow had not left town." Arnold now undoubtedly told his sailors that Boles was hiding at Beecher's. A few minutes later, as the shouting woke the town, a large crowd hurried toward the commons and the gallows beside the courthouse. "I then made myself one of the party," Arnold later admitted publicly, "that took him to the whipping post." There they tied up Boles and in the January cold ripped off his shirt and bared his back. While Benedict Arnold and the crowd, by now including many other Sons of Liberty, watched, one of *Fortune's* crewmen used a short piece of rope to lash Peter Boles "near forty times," according to Arnold's own count. Then, as Arnold put it, Boles was "conducted out of town," probably astraddle a split rail. This time, the informer did not return.[21]

*   *   *

Four months earlier, in September 1765, when mounted mobs had forced Ingersoll to resign and demanded that Governor Fitch call a special session of the assembly, New Haven's freemen had met to elect deputies to the legislature. The townsmen present had been unanimous that the Stamp Act must be repealed. New Haven's delegates carried to Hartford instructions adopted by the September town meeting, protesting that the tax had been imposed "without their consent by themselves or representatives" and that in the act "the colonists are distinguished from their fellow subjects in Great Britain." The townsmen resented the fact that they had "readily and cheerfully"[22] fought as Englishmen against the French only a few years before.

By the following February 3, as they filed into the courthouse on New Haven Green, the county court had not been able to do business in four months—no judges were sitting, no criminals being prosecuted, no debts being collected—and many of the town's leading citizens thought that things were going too far when Benedict Arnold enforced the will of the rabble with a length of rope. The town's resolve against the Stamp Act was still virtually unanimous: 273 out of 274 men at the town meeting voted for continued opposition. The main item on the agenda was whether the Stamp Act should just be ignored and business continued as usual, or whether there should be active opposition. There was also considerable tension about the legality of documents not bearing the hated stamps and what to do about accepting them:

We hear that a person in a neighboring government lately refusing to pay a debt for which he was attached, because the writ was not on stamped paper . . . The populace immediately passed the three following votes, and resolve, namely Vote 1. That this man is not a Christian. Vote 2. That he ought to be of some religion. Therefore, thirdly, Voted, that he be a Jew. Whereupon, resolved, that he be circumcised. This resolution so terrified the poor creature, that he begged for forgiveness for his improvidence.[23]

Benedict Arnold and his friends in New Haven's Sons of Liberty did not want such confusion to continue, if it could be averted without backing down on their demand that the tax be repealed. Overwhelming their opponents in the town meeting, they easily passed a resolution by 226 to 48 votes to go ahead with business without stamps. To continue a complete shutdown of the courts and trade would "involve the people in great difficulties." The officers of the courts were requested to carry on "the usual business in such courts in the usual and accustomed manner," i.e., without stamps. They also voted for a resolution to restore order in the town, pledging to be "especially watchful and painful in bringing to proper punishment all such disorders" such as the Boles riot. It was clear that civil authority had ceased to exist unless it was with the cooperation of the Sons of Liberty, who now solemnly promised that "we will mutually assist one another and particularly the civil authority."[24]

When the county court reopened, one of its first actions was prosecution of the Boles rioters. The town's conservatives were not willing to let the radicals take over the town or administer justice by mob rule. Two conservatives on the grand jury indignantly insisted that Justice of the Peace Roger Sherman bind Arnold and nine of his men over for a trial. The next day, a crowd paraded through the streets, supporting Arnold and his men and burning the effigies of the two grand jurors. Under pressure from both sides, Sherman issued arrest warrants charging Arnold and his men with beating Boles "in a shocking, cruel and dangerous manner,"[25] but Sherman did not preside over the trial or appear in court. Nor did Benedict Arnold, on the advice of Jared Ingersoll, who suggested Arnold be out of town and let him coolly argue the case in court. Ingersoll charged Arnold only £7 5s. for his defense and that of his crewmen. The appearance of a man who was the king's attorney, a justice of the peace, and a former stamp commissioner certainly helped to get Arnold and his men off lightly.

Perversely, Arnold decided to appeal over the heads of the magistrates to the people through the medium of the *Connecticut Gazette.* Boldly, he admitted his guilt; "I was a party concerned in whipping the informer the other day." Then he launched into an attack on Boles in print: "He is clearly seen through the grass, but the weather is too cold for him to bite." Then Arnold gave his own detailed account of the Boles beating and whipping, ending with a plea for public support:

Query: Is it good policy, or would so great a number of people in any trading town or any other on the Continent (New Haven excepted) vindicate, protect and caress an informer, a character, particularly at this alarming time, so justly odious to the public? Every such information seems to suppress our trade, so advantageous to the colony and to almost every individual both here and in Great Britain, which is nearly ruined by the late detestable Stamp and other oppressive Acts which we have so severely felt, so loudly complained of, and so earnestly remonstrated against that one would imagine every sensible man would strive to encourage trade and discountenance such useless, such infamous informers.

Arnold's honest, angry salvo had many effects in the long run, but its first was to convince the court to come down squarely on both sides of the case. Magistrates David Wooster and Enos Allen convicted Arnold and his men of disorderly conduct, but instead of imprisoning them or having them whipped, fined Arnold only fifty shillings, awarding the money to Peter Boles for the damage to his reputation, and then ordered him to leave town. As Arnold summed it up, "Colonel Wooster and another gentleman were of opinion that the fellow was not whipped too much, and gave him 50 shillings, damages only, citing the infamous nature of Boles's offense and its tendency to injure the community by casting suspicion upon honest dealers and obstructing the point of trade."[26]

Benedict Arnold's nighttime dash to the whipping post had been a plunge into revolutionary politics. The fact that the British repealed the offensive Stamp Act in March 1766 temporarily and slightly calmed anti-British tempers. The ban on printing paper money and the tightened enforcement of the Sugar Act still remained major irritants. The issue, Arnold argued in a second article of the *Gazette,* was much deeper than a specific piece of legislation: it was whether England had any right at all to pass laws for the colonies or repeal laws passed by the colonies themselves. In a third article in the *Connecticut Gazette* on February 21, 1766, Arnold argued that the new British trade policy as well as the Stamp Act itself denied the liberties granted every freeborn Englishman by Magna Carta. By this time, Arnold was talking and corresponding with leaders of the resistance from other colonies, including John Dickinson in faraway Philadelphia, and David Wooster, one of the magistrates who had fined him in the Boles case. At twenty-five, Benedict Arnold emerged from the Stamp Act crisis a vocal and popular hero in New Haven and a conspicuous political figure.

3

"ARE THE
AMERICANS ALL ASLEEP?"

*When the present necessary war
against Great Britain commenced, I
was in easy circumstances. I was
happy in domestic connections and
blessed with a rising family. I
sacrificed domestic ease and
happiness and a great part of a
handsome fortune.*

Benedict Arnold before a court-martial, December 1779

Benedict Arnold at twenty-five was typical of many American gentlemen trying to live like English gentry on the edge of a wild continent. At home in New Haven, he wore fine clothing and white satin stockings, sipped tea, and made his way in society. Away from his drawing room, he was an aggressive ship's captain fast becoming Connecticut's most successful smuggler. He took pains to keep the two roles distinct, which may explain how a man who fought duels and supervised whippings could successfully seek the hand of the daughter of one of New Haven's oldest families. Sometime before the winter of Stamp Act rioting, Benedict Arnold began to pay court to Margaret Mansfield, daughter of Samuel Mansfield, high sheriff of New Haven County.

Little is known about the sheriff's daughter except that she was a lifelong member of the conservative First Church on the green and, according to local tradition, was a handsome, aloof, painfully shy woman who steadfastly refused to answer Benedict Arnold's letters even as she agreed to marry him. Arnold may have met her through his growing acquaintance with her father, a wealthy merchant who had inherited the post of high sheriff from his father. Both Mansfield and Arnold were members of New Haven's small Masonic lodge, which was enough to make them close friends and confidants with all the bonds of a select secret society. In New Haven as elsewhere in the colonies, Freemasonry was flourishing as the Age of Enlightenment succeeded the Great Awakening. In Pennsylvania, Benjamin Franklin joined; in Virginia, George Washington. Benedict Arnold joined other men who were embracing Freemasonry because it mixed conviviality with a sense of brotherhood and stressed fortitude, temperance, prudence, and justice, encouraging belief in God but also emphasizing the Golden Rule. Also, to be sure, to join was to be admitted to the upper echelon of society in New Haven. Benedict and Margaret also attended the same church. In matters of church politics, Arnold appears to have attempted to remain neutral. As leader of the Sons of Liberty, he was definitely aligned with the New Lights, but when he went to church, it was to an Old Light church, no doubt because of Margaret's family's membership.

Certainly one of the more eligible young men in New Haven, Benedict Arnold easily won his suit for Margaret Mansfield's hand, and it must have made him a little bit proud that he cut out a long line of suitors. On February 22, 1767, only a year after being arrested in the Boles affair, he married Margaret Mansfield, age twenty-two, in the aisle of First Church. From his letters to her, it is plain that he married her because he was in love with her more than because of any dowry she brought with her, and that he delighted in lavishing on her the goods he gained by legal as well as illegal means. Soon after she moved into the modest house on Water Street, they began to have children: three sons, a small family for the times. The oldest, of course named Benedict, was born on February 14, 1768, then Richard on August 22, 1769, and Henry, on September 19, 1772. Arnold's sister, Hannah, still single, helped Margaret with the children, for it became evident after only a few years that her health was not strong, and that she was as gloomy as Arnold's mother had been, only more silent and uncommunicative. When he was home from sea, the house was filled with the noise of children, lodgers (mostly his wife's relatives), and household chores, but also with a growing sadness and loneliness emanating from a wife who grew more passive and melancholy each year. His letters from sea are filled with two major themes: not to let the creditors bother her, as all would be well when he returned from this voyage, and why do you not write? From the days of their courtship, his was always a one-sided correspondence. "I have now been in the West Indies seven weeks and not heard one syllable from you since I left home," he wrote Margaret from St. Croix in May 1766. "Dear girl, it seems a whole age since I left you."[1] But he ignored her unresponsiveness and married his Peggy, as he affectionately called her, anyway. A few months after their first child was born, he had to go off to sea again, and still she wrote him none of the news: "I have not had the pleasure to receive any letters from you, though there has been several vessels from New Haven. I hope a few days, every one of which seems an age, will make me happy with you and my friends in New Haven."[2] When another ship came with still not a word from her, Arnold wrote again five days later: "I assure you I think it hard you have wrote me only once when there has been so many opportunities. You cannot imagine the trouble and fatigue I have gone through since here."[3] His business affairs had grown more difficult and dangerous than ever, and he felt increasingly alone because of his wife's refusal to correspond with him. In 1773, two sailors informed on him, and he nearly lost a vessel. As soon as he escaped this scrape, probably by paying off some customs officials with his last remaining cash, he was arrested on the complaint of the same New York merchant Arnold had threatened so long ago. To avoid the legal expenses of a long lawsuit, he promised to pay the man and posted a bond. He was supposed to sail at once to Barbados, but he was broke and desperate, and, he wrote Margaret, he would wait for the next post "and shall be very unhappy if I have not the pleasure of hearing you and our dear ones are well." As if it were not plain enough, he added that the mail had now come and he had discovered with an "anxious and aching heart"[4] that there was no letter.

The passage of time did not improve their relationship, if Arnold's letters to Peggy are any indication. After seven years of pleading for an occasional line, Arnold wrote from Quebec on October 5, 1773, "I am now under the greatest anxiety and suspense, not knowing whether I write to the dead or the living, not having heard the least syllable from you this last four months. I have wrote you almost every post . . . have this three posts expected answers and been disappointed. I am now loaded and am set to sail tomorrow for

Barbados." But he continued to wait. Two days later, he still had not sailed, hoping against hope for word from her before more weeks and months at sea. On October 7, he wrote once more before embarking: "With an aching and anxious heart, I resume my pen. The post arrived yesterday and no letters. This I cannot account for, as I wrote you eight weeks past, and the post is generally only four or five going and returning. I have now given over any thoughts of hearing from you until I get to the West Indies. . . . I sail this afternoon." He would be home "with all dispatch"[5] by December.

Arnold attempted to escape the silence of their relationship at home by seeking the solitude of a ship captain's life at sea. At sea he expressed himself perhaps more clearly, pouring out his feelings in letters more than he could talk to her at home. Not that he was romantic, especially about the sea. Such language would have been alien to his time, as his journal often shows: "Fresh breeze until 6 p.m. The remainder of the day blows excessively hard in squalls from south to west, and plenty rain. Large sea."[6] He kept abreast of news from New Haven from other captains, even if he could obtain none directly from his wife. Arnold wanted his seagoing life and its financial rewards, but he missed his wife and children terribly. He had a knack for putting himself on the fringe of a society and then complaining about it. He sent letter after letter of affectionate prose to her, interspersed with news of his travels and pleadings for scraps about "our dear little prattlers."[7]

Yet she must have worried, for his letters were punctuated with a "things will get better" motif. Indeed, Arnold may have been overly sensitive to his wife's reactions to his occasional business difficulties because of his own father's business failure. In fact, each year Arnold tried to give Peggy a bigger share in his business activities, which now were intertwined with those of her father. Samuel Mansfield was so impressed with his son-in-law's business acumen that he had become Benedict's business partner, running the stores and the warehouse and the wharf while Arnold ran their affairs at sea. It was a mercantile marriage of convenience for both men, the sheriff who bought and sold, all open and aboveboard, the rum that the ship's captain procured by smuggling; the debtor shipowner mariner protected, at least tacitly, from arrest and prosecution by his father-in-law, the high sheriff. A letter Benedict sent Margaret on January 21, 1774, gives a hint of the financial pressures put on both of them by the creaky colonial mercantile system:

Dear Peggy:
Inclosed is Captain Sage's remit for ten joannes Portuguese gold

coins, and Jon Barrett's, which he is to sell in Turk's Island and remit you the proceeds, which I expect will be about six joannes more.* This is all I could possibly send you at present. I hope those people I owe will rest easy until I return, when they may all depend on being immediately paid. . . . I a few days since heard of the death of Mrs. Babcock and Polly Austin, which surprise me much. They were in the prime of life and as likely to live as any of us. How uncertain is life, how certain is death. May their loud and affecting calls awaken us to prepare for our own exit, whenever it shall happen. My dear Life, pray by no means neglect the education of our dear boys. It is of infinite concern what habits and principles they imbibe when young. I hope this will find you all well, and that the Almighty may preserve you in health and happiness is the sincere prayer of, dear Peggy,

Your loving husband,
Benedict Arnold[8]

How much these letters resembled those Arnold's mother had once sent him at school! But Margaret Arnold was clearly less the unchallenged mistress of her house than either Hannah Arnold or Jerusha Lathrop had been. Arnold's sister always asserted more authority over servants, children, and in-laws than the two *matresfamilias* Arnold had known. Poor Hannah, without a house, home, or husband of her own, was more pushy than her mother had ever been, and poor Peggy's home was run by a domineering sister-in-law who only took orders from her brother when he was home occasionally. Perhaps unconsciously, Benedict Arnold patterned his married life with Peggy after a curious blend of his perception of his proud pious mother and his accomplished adoptive mother. His idea of what a man should do for a woman was to take care of her, as his father had never been able to do, and then be devoted to, and shower with luxuries, the pampered woman this produced.

As long as a year before their marriage, Arnold had begun a long struggle for survival in his business. British merchants had grown tired of delays in payments from American debtors and were hiring American lawyers to sue recalcitrant merchants. Hard on the heels of the Boles affair, Benedict had to hire his lawyer friend Jared Ingersoll to defend him against a monumental lawsuit for debt. On July 7, 1766, six London merchants led by publisher Thomas Longmans hired Annapolis, Maryland, collection lawyer Bernard Lintot to sue Arnold for £1,700 in old debts and seize his ships and cargoes

---

* One Portugese joanne, or joe, was worth about £5 sterling.

to satisfy them. The brilliant Ingersoll, by now the king's attorney
for New Haven, concocted an agreement that pleased everyone. He
drew up an indenture that conveyed title to one of Arnold's brigs,
the *Sally,* and her cargo for the security and payment of "the one
half of the demands of the said merchants of London against the
said Arnold, being £850 12s. 8d." According to the agreement, it
was up to Ingersoll to decide what other security Arnold should post
"in case his trip is not sufficiently successful and he desires to make
another," but Arnold was to be free to go on sailing the *Sally* while
he worked off the debt, and he was to have a "reasonable time"[9]
that was unspecified to do it. Arnold signed the indenture on May 9,
1767; Ingersoll and a leader of the Sons of Liberty witnessed the
document. Then Arnold sailed off for a successful smuggling voyage
to the Caribbean, returning to pay off a third of the debt with contraband rum and goods. At about this time, Arnold branched out
into a new, legal, and lucrative business, importing vast amounts of
Honduras mahogany for the New York furniture and paneling trade.
By 1772, Arnold needed another wharf for his expanding operations: he paid £16 16s. for a waterfront lot.[10] Arnold had paid off
his debts and amassed enough wealth to build a fine new house
overlooking the harbor for his growing family, and some of his imported mahogany went into building it. The white clapboard house
had two great chimneys, a portico and pillars, marble fireplaces, and
unusually large closets, since Arnold and his wife had large ward-
robes. The meticulous Arnolds had a large shoebox built into a side
entryway just off the main hallway to house their collection of fashionable boots. It was a house in the very latest English style, with a
center hallway, gambrel roof, and pediments over the windows, and
rich, mahogany paneling. In the basement, there were large wine
racks built into the arched support vaults of the chimneys. There
was also a hint of Arnold's double life: a secret staircase led from a
first-floor closet to the basement. From the outside, the house
seemed serene, surrounded by formal gardens with graveled walk-
ways leading through rows of elms and maples to the orchard,
where Arnold planted a cash crop of one hundred "thrifty"[11] fruit
trees. There was also a two-bay carriagehouse and stables for a
dozen horses. All in all, the three-acre waterfront estate was summed
up by historian Samuel Peters as "by far the grandest in New
Haven."[12]

In the winter of 1770, Benedict Arnold returned from the Caribbean
to find his reputation besmirched and his wife refusing to let him
touch her. Once again, the duels of the Caribbean came back to

haunt him. A ship's captain named Fobes, a friend of one Brookman, who had challenged Arnold to a duel to avenge the humiliation of *his* friend Croskie, had spread rumors that what Brookman and Arnold had been dueling over was a whore who had been given to Arnold as the prize for curing Brookman of a dose of venereal disease. Arnold had enemies in New Haven who spread the story while he was away, and Peggy believed Benedict's enemies more than she believed him. Denied her bed, Arnold sued Captain Fobes for slander. His lawyer, Ingersoll, sent a young associate, Elihu Hall, to the islands at Arnold's expense to gather evidence for the trial. The charge that he had contracted venereal disease hurt Arnold in the Puritan town of New Haven. The allegation, Arnold wrote to his colleagues in the Caribbean, "has hurt my character here very much and given my family and friends much uneasiness." He asked them to attest to "my being in perfect health all the time I was in the Bay." In those days, the only treatment for gonorrhea, probably the malady in question, was a long feverish and painful confinement in bed with heavy doses of mercury and alcohol, which would have made Arnold conspicuously absent from business. Arnold reminded his colleagues that they had been aboard his ship daily. "I shall take it as a particular favor if you'd give Hall your deposition in regard to my character in the Bay, my manner of living, with regard to drinks when at your house and the company I kept, which I believe no one can say was of bad character, consisting of but the most reputable people." He also had Hall seek depositions about the true character of his troubles with Brookman and Croskie, which made the duels common knowledge in New Haven perhaps for the first time by spreading them on the court record.[13]

As Arnold prospered and cut a more public figure, he naturally attracted jealousy. He responded aggressively to challenges with Puritan self-righteousness wrapped in a code of honor that required vengeance. Few men risked confronting such a man in person, so his enemies constantly circulated rumors. Arnold could never simply shrug off all the mud. He had to pitch it back, as in the Fobes slander case, embroiling himself in chronic controversy. Yet there were some charges he had to fight legally, and his only recourse was to rely on business associates who also had dealings with his enemies. He would not have dared to put them on the spot if he *had* contracted the disease, and could not have risked putting them on the court record if he feared they could be successfully challenged. Once he received the depositions he needed, Arnold was satisfied to circulate copies around town and let the matter drop short of an embarrassing courtroom trial. Apparently, so was his wife, for when he returned from sea the next winter, they conceived their third and last child, Henry, who was born in the summer of 1772.

For several years after he married, Benedict Arnold had confined himself mostly to his business, paying his debts and establishing his family in New Haven, but like most leading citizens he was involved in the smoldering colonial crisis with England. In March 1766, the Stamp Act had been repealed, but Parliament had passed a troublesome Declaratory Act in its place, claiming it had jurisdiction over the colonies "in all cases whatsoever." Parliament also renewed a Quartering Act which required all colonies in which British troops were garrisoned to furnish them with supplies. The colonies were not asked whether their legislatures approved of extending this wartime measure into peacetime; they were simply required to come up with the money. Parliament also imposed additional restrictions on colonial trade. As England encroached further on colonial charter rights and customs officials ransacked warehouses and holds for smuggled goods, Benedict Arnold channeled his energy into eluding them and hampering their searches.

In March 1770, after four regiments of British regulars were shifted from frontier outposts to Boston to discourage dissent, a series of clashes between soldiers and civilians culminated in the so-called Boston Massacre. The news of dead Americans lying in the snow in Boston reached Arnold in the Caribbean. For now he put aside material strivings and wrote hotly back from St. George's Cay to New Haven how "shocked" he was at "the most cruel, wanton and inhuman murders." He had been as much wrapped up in his own business affairs as any colonial merchant, but this was too much to bear in silence. "Good God!" he wrote to merchant friend Benjamin Douglas on June 9, 1770. "Are Americans all asleep and tamely giving up their glorious liberties, or are they all turned philosophers that they don't take vengeance on such miscreants? I am afraid of the latter and that we shall all soon see ourselves as poor and as much oppressed as ever heathen philosopher was."[14] No longer content with legal disputations, Arnold craved action. Whenever he was home now, he organized and honed his Sons of Liberty as they enforced a second boycott of British goods that brought about the repeal of all the Townshend duties except a trifling threepence in the pound on tea. In June 1772, as Arnold cruised the Caribbean and Margaret awaited the birth of their third child, the British customs schooner Gaspée ran aground on Namquit Point, seven miles below Providence, Rhode Island, while pursuing a smuggling vessel. After dark, eight boatloads of men attacked the schooner. Lieutenant Dudington, in command, was seriously wounded. He and his crew were put ashore as the *Gaspée* was burned to the waterline. The British offered a £500 reward and sent in an investigating commission made up of royal governors and chief justices to identify the rioters and send them to England to stand trial for treason, but no witnesses came forward and the commissioners had to leave town. As the crown order in the *Gaspée* affair was read in newspapers by angry men all over America, committees of correspondence were set up to coordinate colonial protest to the British innovations endangering American civil liberties, such as the right to a speedy trial by a jury of one's own peers guaranteed by Magna Carta. Against this backdrop, Parliament passed the Tea Act of 1773 to enable the British East India Company to increase revenues from tea duties, authorizing the company, a royal monopoly whose stockholders included many key British officials, to ship tea directly to the colonies. As East India men sailed toward America, radical leaders tried to force the company's agents to resign. When the radicals protested in vain in Boston that the tea should be returned to Great Britain without paying the tea duty, Governor Thomas Hutchinson refused. One thousand men disguised as Mohawk Indians crowded aboard the *Dartmouth,* pried open 342 lacquered tea chests, and dumped them into the bay.

In January 1774, immediately after the Boston Tea Party, Arnold asserted himself in New Haven politics. With his Sons of Liberty, he set out to stifle all opposition in Connecticut. When the Reverend Samuel Peters rose in the town meeting of the Connecticut Valley town of Hebron on August 29, 1774, to oppose a motion which branded the British reprisals unconstitutional, he faced a roomful of anti-British neighbors, who were nonetheless conservative about the colonial crisis and not convinced that their more anarchic neighbors to the east in towns such as Boston had not gone too far. Peters, a fitting antagonist for the Sons of Liberty, demanded that copies of the Boston Port Act and Magna Carta be read to the town meeting before a vote was taken "to inform us what is constitutional and what is not." Hebron's local Sons of Liberty were caught off guard; nonetheless, they proposed that the town contribute to the relief of poor people behind British lines in blockaded Boston, where there already was a shortage of food. Peters objected. All over New England, he said, Sons of Liberty were harassing their opposition, the party loyal to British authority. Men had already been brutally tarred and feathered. Peters insisted that a man should neither "be marked as a Tory nor liable to tar and feathers" simply because he refused to "give to the Boston poor." He was against relief because "should this town vote to give to the poor of Boston, the very record will be an everlasting proof against us, that we are rebels to the law of the kingdom." Furthermore, Boston deserved "the rod for their riotous conduct," and Hebron shouldn't "meddle in other men's matters. . . . We may with as much propriety vote convicts free." In an uproar, the town meeting broke up without reaching a decision.

All over New England that weekend, rumors flew of a British invasion, reaching Hebron on Sunday morning, September 4, as Peters's parishioners filed into services at the Anglican church. Fighting had broken out, a messenger shouted outside the church. The British commander, General Thomas Gage, was slaughtering old men and babies. Peters tried to calm his parishioners. "Keep your seats. The report is not true. General Gage is a good man who would not hurt old men and babes nor fire on the town of Boston. . . . Even if fighting broke out," the Church of England priest exhorted them, "you must not take up arms against General Gage. It is high treason to levy war against him."

In Hebron as in the once solidly Congregational colony of Connecticut generally, the Church of England had grown steadily for half a century. Its original members, like the New Light separatists, had been fined heavily and imprisoned for refusing to pay taxes to support Connecticut's established state church. Anglicanism became even more popular when its clergy denounced the wave of religious enthusiasm of the Great Revival. The New Lights detested Anglicanism's Roman Catholic-like vestments and rituals and its forgiving theology, and the Old Lights resented the Church of England's success in attracting conservative members. Thus both factions were united in opposing the establishment of Anglican bishops in America. As the wave of terror that marked the onset of the Revolution intensified, Anglican priests, such visible symbols of England, bore the brunt of popular resentment to British policies. In some churches they brought pistols to the pulpit to protect themselves as they preached submission to king and Parliament as well as God. In colonies such as Connecticut where there were almost no royal officials to attack, and where New Light government officials were pushing the colony into the Revolution, an Anglican priest, especially such an outspoken critic of the radicals as the Reverend Samuel Peters, was an obvious scapegoat for unpopular British policies.

Later that Sunday, September 4, 1774, a large body of men left Hebron without the Anglicans. The next day, they were back in town: the rumors of fighting had been false, as Peters had told his parishioners. But before he could congratulate himself, the frustrated marchers joined a mob of several hundred armed men from towns as far away as New Haven. Traveling more than sixty miles on horseback, the New Haven and New London Sons of Liberty went about chastising the Anglican vicar for encouraging his flock to dissent from the resistance movement.

Probably the only lengthy account of the Sons of Liberty raid on Hebron was by Peters himself, and it is as highly partisan as the rest of his so-called history of Connecticut, but he positively, unequivocally, and erroneously identified Arnold as the leader of the men who led the "violent affray" outside his house in the darkness that night. Pushing, shoving, and shouting as Peters bellowed back at them, a handful of Sons of Liberty crowded into his house, forcing the priest to come out and face the crowd. Meanwhile, Peters's papers were searched for copies of letters he had written "unfriendly to the rights and privileges of this colony." Although Peters had written many letters opposing the radicals, none could be found. They did, however, find a series of resolves Peters had framed endorsing the Tea Act and condemning nearby towns for rioting. A committee drew up charges against Peters and read them to him when he came out to face the crowd in the darkness. Their indictment charged him with writing articles for a New London newspaper that preached "a doctrine destructive to the liberties of America," with using his position to influence the Hebron town meeting to thwart support for the people of Boston, and, worst, telling people the day before in church that it was treason to resist "good man" Gage. These were sentiments "contrary to the general opinion" and "inimical to our liberties both civil and religious."

Peters did not hesitate to admit the charges, but the crowd wanted more. There were shouts that Peters was "a Tory rebel, a Roman Catholic, a tool of tyranny." He should be hanged in effigy at a liberty pole. No, he should be tarred and feathered. They grabbed Peters and put him on a horse and forced him to ride to the village green. There he felt compelled to sign a statement that George III had "forfeited his Kingdom," that the prime minister, Gage, and the Anglican bishops were "tyrants," and that, in America, "only the voice of the people" could govern men's liberty. As he stood in the midst of an angry mob that night, the words "the voice of the people" must have seemed ironic to Peters. He finally signed the paper, and then there were shouts from the crowd: "Liberty! Liberty! Destroy the badge of Babylon! Damnation to the church! The King is a fool. The King is a Roman devil!" But Peters was not that easily silenced. "You have done enough. You have forfeited your lives and property to the laws of God and man." A Son of

Liberty from the town of Lebanon who was a neighbor of New Light Governor Trumbull shouted back, "Damn your soul!" Governor Trumbull himself, he said, "told us this day to come and give it to you. So he will not help you."[15]

After Samuel Peters was escorted back to his house, the Sons of Liberty rode out of Hebron, content that they had silenced the only Anglican priest in Connecticut who was speaking out publicly against the radicals. A few days later, Peters eluded Sons of Liberty surveillance on his house and patrols on the roads, slipped out of Hebron, and rode to New Haven, where the Sons of Liberty paid him another, less peaceful visit.

In late August 1774, Connecticut's delegates to the first Continental Congress, called as a direct result of British closing of the Port of Boston, gathered at New Haven for the hard 160-mile journey by carriage to Philadelphia. Connecticut remained deeply divided, with conservative lawyer Jared Ingersoll campaigning hard against Connecticut's sending any delegates to Philadelphia. Of nine delegates elected by the assembly's Committee of Correspondence, only three eventually were willing to take their seats in the Congress: among those who declined, two backed out, claiming ill health, and a third, the Reverend William Samuel Johnson, claimed "previous engagements." Of the first five nominated, only two, New Haven merchant Silas Deane and Colonel Eliphalet Dyer of Windham, accepted. Any three delegates could attend, but Deane, a close friend of neighbor Benedict Arnold, wanted to take advantage of the conservatives' reluctance to attend the Congress and send an expanded and more radical coterie. With the aid of the governor's son, Captain Joseph Trumbull, and New London radical Samuel Holden Parsons, they rallied support for two more delegates. The nominating committee this time split east-west: western Connecticut was far cooler to risking British reprisals than the eastern towns, which actually were closer to British raiding parties. The compromise added to the delegation the moderate merchant-magistrate Roger Sherman of New Haven, the judge who had once indicted Benedict Arnold for flogging an informer. Deane was dealing with both sides, at the same time nominating the radical Trumbull and coaxing Dr. Johnson to go to Philadelphia with him. According to John Adams of Massachusetts, Deane had intrigued mightily in the affair, and "under the pretext of avoiding to commit the legislature of the state in any act of rebellion, got a committee appointed with some discretionary powers, under which they undertook to appoint the members to Congress."[16]

It was an odd threesome that gathered in New Haven for the journey south. The pious Puritan magistrate Sherman had been trained as a cobbler and had prospered both as a merchant and as a multiple officeholder: the only delegate not a Yale graduate, he had nonetheless been the college's treasurer for a decade. Deane, born the son of a blacksmith, had graduated from Yale and married well twice, becoming a rich merchant connected to the best families in the colony. Dyer, also a Yale graduate, at fifty-two was chief justice of the colony's superior court, of which Sherman was also a member.

The trip started out auspiciously enough, the carriage escorted to lodgings by crowds in each town. By August 25, dust-covered from the road, they were accompanied to a great ceremonial dinner in New York City. But three days later, Sherman was objecting to sending their carriage over the ferry to Perth Amboy, New Jersey, the evening of August 28, "because it is Sunday." Deane continued to pour out his resentment to his wife, Elizabeth. They had baked and been mosquito-bitten for four hours of an "excessive hot day" and then "part of us, not myself for one, assisted in rowing over." Deane was having a hard time controlling his dysentery—"I never underwent more to keep up my part of the conversation"—but the rest of the company had a high time, as Dyer remembered it. Deane did little to help his illness at their next stop, a tavern in Frankford, Pennsylvania, where he slaked his thirst with several orders of excellent bottled cider. While Arnold, Dyer, and Sherman feasted on chicken Samuel Blachley Webb had killed, the homesick Deane complained to his wife about the bad food, bad roads, bad houses he had seen. At five the next morning, they were off to Philadelphia, where they alighted at Biddle's Tavern. In a letter to his wife, Deane wrote that "Mr. Arnold and myself are the lodgers." They spent the day visiting other delegates "and find them in high spirits."

That night, thirty of them had coffee together to talk over "preliminaries" and agreed to wait to begin their proceedings until the following Monday. The Connecticut delegates went sightseeing on Friday and Saturday—the famous Jersey covered markets on High Street, the insane asylum in the barred basement of the stately Pennsylvania Hospital, where Dr. William Shippen regaled them with case histories and showed them the latest anatomical drawings from London. All day Sunday, they went to church services, three in all. That same day, the New York delegates arrived, and Connecticut's delegates huddled with them and with Sons of Liberty leaders. They decided that they must mount a Connecticut-based expedition to silence the most influential pro-British newspaper in America, James

Rivington's *New York Gazette* of New York City. Deane, while "waiting for my barber," wrote to his wife to pass the word to Sons of Liberty leader Joseph Webb of Wethersfield that they had agreed that Rivington's paper was "to be stopped" and that "a great number of the gentlemen of this city" were subscribing money to "promote the same" raid "throughout Connecticut" and that Webb was "to put it forward."[17] The Tory paper, which carried the royal coat of arms on its masthead, printed attacks on the Continental Congress and, in November 1775, was destroyed in a raid by 150 Sons of Liberty from Connecticut. Deane was accompanied by his young protégé, Benedict Arnold, to a series of political caucuses and dinners. Arnold no doubt helped to plan this latest suppression of antirevolutionary dissent. Behind the scrim of gathering to protest British oppression, the Sons of Liberty from a dozen colonies discussed the elimination of opposition.

Much of the advance planning for the First Continental Congress was done at an endless round of dinners, luncheons, coffees, and teas in the week before the formal sessions began. Leading Philadelphians hosted these gatherings, which were attended by men who had corresponded with one another and read one another's writings but had never met. One family, the Shippens, stands out for its hospitality. Many revolutionary leaders argued their views at Judge Edward Shippen's dinner table. Shippen was proud to introduce his three beautiful daughters—his youngest, the dainty and precocious Peggy, although only fourteen was already one of the city's more popular debutantes. She was flirtatious and quick-witted, was already steeped in her father's business, and could talk confidently with men about politics and trade. Benedict Arnold met her for the first time at dinner that September.

By the end of that first weekend of September 1774, delegates from all mainland colonies except Quebec had arrived in Philadelphia for the Congress. Few, if any, foresaw a war of revolution against the mother country; many expected to conciliate their complaints with Parliament peacefully. But the most radical among them were seething. John Adams of the Massachusetts delegation summed up their complaints after having breakfast at the home of Dr. William Shippen with Richard Henry Lee of Virginia: "Lee is for making the repeal of every revenue law, the Boston Port Bill, the bill for altering the Massachusetts Constitution, the Quebec Bill and the removal of all the troops the *end* of Congress and abstinence from all dutied articles the *means*—rum, molasses, sugar, tea, wine, fruits, etc."[18]

Of all the colonies in America, Pennsylvania was the most evenly divided: the majority of its populace was made up of pacifist Quakers and more than 250 German pietist sects, but there was also a strong party loyal to the British, who ruled the colony for the Penn family. Governor John Penn had even refused to call a special assembly after the closing of the Port of Boston, maintaining there was no emergency. That steamy September, Philadelphians agonized over the course of the New England radicals as post riders, delegates, militiamen, and redcoats came and went down the broad cobbled streets, all of them making it increasingly difficult to remain neutral. The Pennsylvania government was such a symbol of pro-British conservatism that revoluntionary leaders from New England, Virginia, and Pennsylvania had decided not to convene their convention in the opulent statehouse (now called Independence Hall) but to meet in a union hall nearby. Thus when the delegates finally assembled, they walked to Carpenters' Hall, a small, handsome building with a good meeting room and library for committee meetings down a quiet alley and away from prying Tory eyes. The choice of the union hall also was deeply galling to more conservative political leaders, who were appalled that mechanics and carpenters were allowed to be identified so closely with the leaders of the protests against England: the choice of Carpenters' Hall, according to Silas Deane, was "mortifying to the last degree" to the Penn party, which boycotted the convention's opening.

By the time the first meeting was called to order on Monday, September 5, there had been a weekend of tension in the city that underscored the precarious nature of the long-smoldering crisis with England. The next day, Deane wrote to his wife that "this city is in the utmost confusion, all the bells toll muffled and the most unfeigned marks of sorrow appear in every countenance."[19] The reason was the news from Boston. Rumors of British invasion of Massachusetts had arrived in Philadelphia, carried by Connecticut militia leader Israel Putnam. The British seizure of gunpowder at Medford magnified into the shelling and burning of Boston. In the ensuing panic, Pennsylvania militiamen drilled and marched through the streets of Philadelphia even as the last redcoated British regiment in the middle colonies, the Royal Irish, strode down Arch Street to the waterfront and boarded troop transports taking them north to reinforce Boston.

One young British officer who could have joined them had only arrived in Philadelphia aboard the British vessel *St. George* on September 2, two days after Benedict Arnold pulled his portmanteau from atop Silas Deane's carriage and began to look up old Philadelphia friends. The British officer was Second Lieutenant John André of the 7th Foot, the Royal Welsh Fusiliers, sent out from England to join his regiment at Quebec. An officer for five years, he had never fought a battle, but instead had pursued the life of dilettante poet, playwright, and artist; he was a fixture in England's literary society who had recently been jilted after a long and celebrated love affair. From the safety of England, André had taken the unrest in America lightly, but upon arrival he found Philadelphia in the grip of anti-British frenzy. Ordinarily, it would have been André's inclination to linger in Philadelphia, meet its leading artists and poets. He had hardly left his ship on the sail-crowded Delaware River and been rowed ashore when Putnam spread the rumor about British bombardment of Boston. Suddenly the streets of Philadelphia were filled with armed and angry men. It was not a safe place for a young, solitary British officer. Oddly, André decided not to travel aboard a British warship, but to travel alone north to New York City, then sail up the Hudson to Albany, traveling on foot and hunting small game as he made his way to Lake Champlain. Stopping off at dilapidated British posts along the way at Ticonderoga and Crown Point, he sailed down the St. Lawrence to Quebec on a schooner, wrapped in a bearskin robe. "We had scarce any provisions on board," he wrote to his sister in England of his first encounters in this hostile new world, "and were clustered up, by way of keeping out of the cold, with a black woman, an Indian squaw in a blanket, an Indian boy and the sailors round a stove."[20] It was the first of John André's strange journeys through an America he would never understand.

Benedict Arnold returned to New Haven late in the autumn of 1774 and plunged into the resistance to British policies and the obliterating of opposition to the radical movement. The Coercive Acts against Massachusetts consolidated efforts by the New Light Party to draw Connecticut into united opposition to British reform measures when Connecticut's general assembly immediately denounced them and asserted the right of the American colonies to be governed by their own assemblies in taxing and policing themselves. Many town meetings echoed this doctrine and condemned Parliament, pledging to supply the people of Boston despite the blockade, and in many towns such as New Haven set up their own committees of correspondence to coordinate anti-British resistance. One town, Farmington, burned the Boston Port Act before a Liberty Pole forty feet high. And there were the signs of incipient revolt: a Tory who signed an address praising Massachusetts governor Hutchinson on his departure into exile in England was mobbed at Windham and again at Norwich Town. When he sought help from Norwich Town magistrate Samuel Huntington, he was refused on the basis that Hutchinson had been the "principle agent"[21] in bringing on the present punitive measures by Parliament. In early August, three hundred men from Litchfield County joined a mob in Great Barrington, Massachusetts, which obstructed court sessions in the Berkshires and kidnapped Jared Ingersoll's Tory cousin.

The Sons of Liberty were also becoming more violent: for years, their terror tactics had been limited to intimidation, with Arnold's flogging of Boles a rare exception. Increasingly, they resorted to tarring and feathering, followed by a painful ride on a rail that, to the naked passenger, had especially painful consequences. One Tory newspaper in New York City, the *Mercury,* recounted how Dr. Joseph Clarke "was seized in the township of Hartford" and "to the indelible disgrace of their police carried upon a rail about the parish."[22] The sharp-edged rail slashed and chafed the doctor's genitals and groin, his ride jouncing and bruising him so painfully that he fainted several times. Another doctor examined him later and found him badly injured.

Shortly after Benedict Arnold returned from Philadelphia, he learned that the Reverend Samuel Peters and his family, after fleeing Hebron, had taken refuge with Tory friends in New Haven. Arnold and his Sons of Liberty, about three hundred of them according to Peters, surrounded the house where they were hiding. Years later, from his exile in England, Peters wrote that Arnold and his "intoxicated ruffians" savagely attacked his family that night, dragging them to the Liberty Tree on the green. Some were only roughed up. "Others were covered with filth and marked with the sign of the cross by a mop filled with excrements in token of their loyalty to a King who designed to crucify all the good people of America. . . . Even women were hung by the heels, tarred and feathered."[23] Peters's gown and suit were torn from him. His mother, daughter, two brothers, and servants were beaten up. One brother died soon afterward. Peters and his family fled New Haven the next day, crossing the British lines into Boston, then sailing for England. From the safety of exile, Peters identified the leader of the New Haven mob as Benedict Arnold.

The only force in Connecticut that could be relied on by late 1774 was the powerful and by now quite public Sons of Liberty, which increasingly was taking over and filling the ranks of the Connecticut militia. The militia theoretically included all adult males in the colony, and an entire generation of Yankees had been trained by the

British and fought alongside them little more than a decade ago. They were the part-time volunteer soldiers of their colony and were legal in the eyes of the British, but their top commands were now being taken over by radicals and they were being mobilized by the radical governor and the New Light majority in the assembly to oppose the British.

When General Gage's troops had marched out of Boston in September 1774 to seize the Medford, Massachusetts, munitions depot, New England had mobilized spontaneously, with many militiamen and farmers marching one hundred miles and more, only to turn back when they learned that the British had shed no blood. But the turnout of forty thousand militia against him had persuaded the cautious British commander, Gage, to fortify the land approach to Boston. Gage, a veteran of the French war, knew that he faced thousands of veterans itching to fight his own raw troops.

In December 1774, the Connecticut general assembly commissioned two independent military companies, organized two new militia regiments, and ordered an array of artillery. Unwilling to wait for the Continental Congress in Philadelphia to write petitions to king and Parliament for redress of colonial grievances, the Connecticut assembly authorized unprecedented military preparations, ordering the militia to train for twelve days before May 1, 1775, double the normal rate, and approved a high pay rate of six shillings a day for private soldiers, double the wages of a day laborer at the time. Four more regiments of militia were organized, for a total of six regiments—upward of six thousand men in peacetime in a colony of only one hundred thousand. Fast ships were dispatched to obtain weapons and gunpowder from the West Indies. Three months later, in March 1775, a virtual purge of officers of old militia regiments took place. Officers suspected of disloyalty to the radical cause were forced out when the assembly went back into session and investigated charges against allegedly disloyal officers. In addition, a dozen top militia officers resigned quietly. They were replaced by radicals, often leaders of the Sons of Liberty.

As militia companies sprang up all over America, a group of sixty-five "gentlemen of influence and high respectability" gathered in December 1774 in New Haven to sign articles of agreement for an independent New Haven militia company. It is probable that Arnold drafted the document, which outlined the proper conduct for a member of the militia, forbidding drunkenness, gambling, profanity, and corporal punishment by officers. Having an instructor to teach them "the military exercise"[24] (again probably Arnold himself) and agreeing that each member equip and arm himself, the group petitioned the general assembly to be constituted the Governor's Second Company of Foot. Granted a charter in March 1775, the guardsmen began drilling at the lower end of the New Haven Green in their brilliant scarlet coats trimmed with buff facings, white breeches and stockings, and black half-leggings. The election of officers took place March 15, and Arnold, who had been the unit's organizer, was chosen captain, the highest rank. It was a prestigious office at the head of an elite group, and it recognized Arnold's rising influence in the colony as well as his ability as a leader. Once a week, Arnold strapped on his dress sword and assembled his men and trained them in military discipline, marksmanship, and the manual of arms. Using as their headquarters Hunt's Tavern on the lower green, the guardsmen prepared for the confrontation everyone, radical and Tory, was awaiting.

On April 14, 1775, General Gage received a long letter of instruction from Lord Dartmouth, the colonial secretary. Gage was a sober, persistent man known as Honest Tom by his troops in the French and Indian War, a tall, slender lady's man who had dealt with the Americans for more than twenty years. Leader of colonial troops throughout the Indian war, he had been wounded in the disastrous attack on Fort Ticonderoga in 1758. He had distinguished himself for caution, unwilling to fight unless he had superior force. As the military governor in Montreal after the war, he had won friends for the British conquerors among French Catholics by his strong sense of fair play and justice and his good-humored relations with aristocratic French families. Commander in chief in America since the French surrender, Gage had pulled in troops from the frontier outposts to build up the Boston garrison in 1768. He had been caught off base in 1773 during the Boston Tea Party: he had gone home on leave to England with his family because the political crises seemed to have eased. Returning to Boston with the Port Act in his hand, he was the first of several British commanders to attempt to rule with a sword and an olive branch, acting both as civilian governor seeking a political solution and as commander of professional soldiers enforcing his own edicts.

Gage advocated a tough line in his dispatches back to authorities in England: both Connecticut and Massachusetts should be stripped of their charters, and Boston's radical leaders should be rounded up and shipped in irons to London to be tried for high treason. He advocated using force and offered sound advice to the British officials under pressure to ease trade restrictions: "If you will resist and not yield, that resistance must be effectual at the beginning. If you think ten thousand men sufficient, send twenty. A large force will terrify, and engage many to join you; a middling one will encourage resistance, and gain no friends." Married to the daughter of a prominent Tory, he wished to encourage conservative Americans to resist the Sons of Liberty by offering them military protection: in the spring of 1775, more than one thousand Tories had fled for protection through the British lines into Boston as the last radicals escaped the city.

Formulating his own plan to break up radical resistance, Gage had written to London in December 1774 as petitions from the First Continental Congress reached British rulers: "I hope you will be firm," Gage counseled, "and send me a sufficient force to command the Country by marching into it and sending off large detachments to secure obedience through every part of it." In February 1775, he reiterated, "To keep quiet in the Town of Boston only, will not terminate affairs. The troops must march into the Country." He shrewdly sized up the crisis in America as militia units drilled on village greens and congressmen debated: "The eyes of all are turned upon Great Britain, waiting for her determination." The determination came in a series of Parliamentary actions. A conciliatory movement to remove troops from Boston was crushed in the House of Lords by sixty-eight votes to eighteen. Merchants' petitions were pigeonholed. A plan for negotiating a settlement was defeated in the Lords after a bitter debate. The anti-American ministry of Lord North, on the other hand, rammed through both houses a joint address to the king declaring the Americans in rebellion. Then North further restrained New England trade, cutting off the Yankees from their traditional fisheries. On April 14, 1775, news of all these measures reached Gage along with authorization to subdue the countryside and to arrest and punish the "ringleaders of the riots at Boston" as well as "the destroyers of the tea."[25]

At three o'clock the morning of April 19, 1775, seven hundred handpicked British light infantry and grenadiers stepped off, without rations or bedrolls, for what they expected to be a quick fifteen-mile foray to Lexington, where the Massachusetts revolutionaries were known to be storing munitions. At first light, Major John Pitcairn and the British advance guard turned a bend in the Great Road where it approached Lexington Green and spotted the roughly formed ranks of minutemen, summoned by express riders who were rousing the countryside. The Lexington minutemen under Captain John Parker had their instructions. They were to stand their ground, not fire unless fired upon. But Major Pitcairn of the Royal Marines gave these British subjects other orders as his 180-man vanguard halted only thirty paces away on the green: "Disperse, ye rebels! Lay down your arms!"[26] Captain Parker, cautioning his men not to fire, passed the word for them to disband, and the minutemen began to melt away as they had on other nights. But then a shot rang out, nobody could remember from where or from whom, followed rapidly by a British volley, then another and another, none of them ordered by an officer, many of them hitting the Americans in their backs as they fled. When the blue smoke cleared, eight minutemen lay dead, ten more were being dragged off wounded.

Unscathed, the British regulars reformed ranks, cleaned their bayonets, gave a cheer, marched on. The revolutionaries had moved their supplies to Concord, and the British quick-stepped after them. As they marched in glimmering red ranks, hundreds of minutemen slipped up behind walls on both sides of the road, fidgeting, waiting tensely for orders. In Concord, the redcoats were again unable to find the munitions, instead burning some twenty barrels of flour and a few gun carriages and carriage wheels before regrouping at North Bridge. Here the minutemen made a stand and opened fire. The first British casualty of the American Revolution dropped, dead. As the firing increased, the British began to retreat, dropping back toward Lexington under a galling crossfire that now came from behind walls and fences and from houses and woods. The British suffered 273 dead or wounded by the time a relief force came to their rescue and counterattacked the Americans at Lexington. On the march back to Boston, the British set fire to dozens of houses from which snipers supposedly had fired on them. Some Americans, including women and children, were shot through house windows or died in the flames. In all, there were about one hundred American casualties. For Massachusetts revolutionaries such as Samuel Adams, it was a "glorious morning"; for the British, a debacle.

Even as the fighting continued, the Massachusetts Committee of Correspondence summoned post riders to Watertown, where revolutionary leaders had fled from Lexington. By ten o'clock, Colonel Joseph Palmer handed his most trusted rider, Israel Bissell, this message:

> *Wednesday Morning near 10 of the Clock*
> *Watertown*
>   *To all friends of American liberty: let it be known that this morning before break of day a British brigade consisting of about 1000 or 1200 men landed at Phips farm at Cambridge and marched to Lexington where they found a company of our colony militia in*

*arms, upon whom they fired without any provocation and killed six
men and wounded four others. By an express from Boston we find
another brigade are now upon their march from Boston supposed to
be about 1000. The bearer, Israel Bissell, is charged to alarm the
country quite to Connecticut, and all persons are desired to furnish
him with fresh horses, as they may be needed. I have spoken with
several who have seen the dead and wounded.*[27]

Bissell carried word to committees of correspondence as far as New
York City. The news stunned New Haven. Next night, the townspeople crowded into the Middle Brick Church, bastion of the Old
Lights, for an emergency town meeting. The conservatives lost the
first round when radical Roger Sherman was elected moderator by a
single vote. The conservatives were then joined by more moderate
prorevolutionaries in voting against sending armed aid to the rebels.
Instead, a moderate committee of selectmen was appointed to run
the town's affairs and leave military matters to the colony and the
king. But as they went home, they had to dodge runners Arnold had
sent out to gather the Sons of Liberty, any interested college students
as well as Arnold's Foot Guards, whom he called to a meeting to
support the Massachusetts radicals. Before the night's secret deliberations were over, sixty-three men, including several Yale students,
had vowed to join Arnold the next day, ignore the town selectmen,
and march to Boston to reinforce the American army forming there.

    For Benedict Arnold it was a night of departure from a way of
life, and he may well have wondered how long it would be before
his comfortable routines returned. He spent most of his last night at
home awake and busy. From his porch that night, Arnold could
look out over the prosperous setting he had made for himself and his
family. By many accounts the richest man in Connecticut's eastern
capital, he had ships, wharves, a new store, stables of fine horses and
carriages, and slaves and servants. He was not eager to leave his wife
and his three little boys, now seven, six, and two, for what could be
the last time. It took many more hours to arrange things for them, to
go over the business with his father-in-law, wife, and sister, who
would now have to run it. Thank God he had cleared his debts! To
be sure, he now had more than he could have imagined when he
arrived in New Haven, thirteen years before. Only four years later,
he would stand before a court-martial and muse about this day.
"When the present necessary war against Great Britain commenced," he would tell his fellow officers, "I was in easy circumstances. I was happy in domestic connections and blessed with a

rising family. I sacrificed domestic ease and happiness, and a great part of a handsome fortune."[28]

On the morning of Friday, April 21, 1775, Arnold, his wife, Hannah, and the boys were up early. Clad in his new gold-braided red uniform, Arnold strapped on his saber. Then they all walked together over to the green, where his men were assembling and a large crowd gathering. Captain Arnold inspected his men. Then the men stood at ease as a New Light minister, the Reverend Jonathan Edwards, son of the great revivalist who had done spiritual battle with the Old Lights until he had dropped dead, now called down the blessings of Providence on Arnold and his men.

When the brief service was over, Arnold, mounted on his best sorrel, led his men in formation across the green, battle flag flying as the crowd cheered, to Hunt's Tavern, where the town's selectmen were meeting. Deploying his men around the inn, flintlocks at the ready, Arnold called for the town's leaders to come out. The selectmen prevailed on one of their number, Colonel Wooster, to go out and try to calm Arnold down. Wooster, head of the colony's militia, stepped outside and reminded Arnold and his men that the town had voted neutrality the night before. Arnold had little patience for Wooster. He gave Wooster five minutes to turn over the keys to the town's powder magazine so that he and his sixty men could get gunpowder and march north. Wooster tried to stall Arnold.

"This is colony property," Wooster said. "We cannot give it up without regular orders from those in authority."

"Regular orders be damned," Arnold shouted back. "Our friends and neighbors are being mowed down by redcoats. Give us the powder or we will take it."

When Wooster objected once more, Arnold said that if he were not given the keys at once, he and his men would tear down the doors of the powder magazine and take what they needed. "None but Almighty God shall prevent my marching!"[29] he roared.

Wooster handed him the keys.

4

"THE GREATEST
CONFUSION AND ANARCHY"

Some persons have determined to

injure me in your esteem by

misrepresenting matters of fact.

Benedict Arnold to Dr. Joseph Warren, May 1775

Leading his column of scarlet-coated Foot Guards—a slash of color against the pale green of a Connecticut spring—Captain Benedict Arnold marched north toward Hartford on the Friday morning of April 21, 1775. Arnold and his men left the wealthy town of New Haven without subsidy from the town fathers. Each volunteer had to bring along what food or money he could scratch together. Arnold brought his own cache of gold coins, but he also had to borrow from friends: a recently discovered promissory note shows that he borrowed £20 to help feed his men in taverns along the road.[1] They had scarcely left New Haven behind when Colonel Parsons overtook them on the road on his way to meet other revolutionary leaders who were gathering for an emergency meeting in Hartford. Parsons, colonel of the New London militia, as well as a member of Silas Deane's revolutionary clique, had led his regiment toward the fighting at the first Lexington alarm and had seen firsthand the conditions around Boston, where more than twenty thousand ill-prepared militia were attempting to besiege the British. Despite the enthusiastic turnout, Parsons told

Captain Arnold, the Patriot army had no supplies. The makeshift army needed food, blankets, ammunition, and, most of all, cannon. Without artillery, it would be impossible to bottle up the heavily armed British or even to defend American positions.

For nearly twenty years now, Benedict Arnold had been traveling all over colonial America, from northern Canada to the southern Caribbean, on foot, on horseback, by sloop and brig, and by stagecoach learning its harbors, roads and fortifications. Three times as a young man he had marched to the Hudson River–Lake Champlain line of old French forts which had been conquered by the British and their American auxiliaries. In recent years, on trading voyages, he had observed their deterioration after the British shifted their redcoat garrisons to riot-prone Boston. At two forts in particular, Arnold pointed out to Colonel Parsons, Fort Ticonderoga and Crown Point at the southern tip of Lake Champlain, there were hundreds of good cannon for the taking. A few hundred men could overpower the corporal's guards in these old forts, then drag the guns to Boston to bombard the British.

Colonel Parsons shrugged off young Arnold's suggestion when they parted at Hartford, and the New Haven men headed east, but Arnold kept thinking about those guns and forts, and when he reached the town of Pomfret near the Rhode Island line, he mentioned them again, this time to General Israel Putnam, a famed Indian fighter who had just been placed in charge of Connecticut's troops and was on his way to Patriot headquarters at Cambridge.

Striding into the ragtag American camp at Cambridge eight days after Lexington, Arnold's Foot Guards cut such figures that they were immediately singled out to escort the body of a British officer mortally wounded at Concord through the lines to British headquarters in Boston. It was the first time the British saw the spit-and-polish Arnold. Back in camp, Arnold was introduced on April 30 to the Massachusetts Committee of Safety. The Continental Congress was to debate for nearly two more months before sending George Washington to take over the army; meanwhile, Massachusetts radicals Samuel Adams and Dr. Joseph Warren and other committee members were being bombarded with schemes to fight the British. Arnold was ushered into a meeting and described the ruined condition of the two frontier fortresses and their feeble garrisons and scores of usable cannons.

Arnold's analysis of British unpreparedness was dead accurate. Built in 1755 by the French as their principal fortress in New York, the massive Fort Ticonderoga had been so well designed that its guns had repulsed a vastly superior British army in 1758, only to be

abandoned and blown up by the retreating French. Rebuilt along
with its smaller sister at Crown Point by the British at enormous
cost, it had since been allowed to molder, its intended walls cracking
under the frost heaves and thaws of a dozen brutal northern winters
until even its gates could not line up well enough to close. It was
held by only forty redcoats.

The ground for approval of Arnold's plan to seize Ticonderoga
had already been fertilized. Radical leaders had already concluded
that they must act quickly to prevent a British attack from their rear.
Two months earlier, they had commissioned a Pittsfield attorney,
John Brown, to travel north to Montreal as their secret emissary to
radical merchants in Montreal. Brown not only set up a route for
intelligence about the British buildup to reach Massachusetts, but
impressed on both Montreal and Massachusetts radicals the importance of Fort Ticonderoga. After their meeting with Arnold on April
30, Dr. Warren asked Arnold to submit a written proposal. Arnold
was brief:

> *Gentlemen:*
> *You have desired me to state the number of cannon, etc. at Ti-*
> *conderoga. I have certain information that there are at Ticonderoga*
> *eighty pieces of heavy cannon, twenty brass guns, from four to eigh-*
> *teen pounders, and ten to twelve large mortars. At Skenesboro, on*
> *the south bay, there are three or four brass cannon. The Fort Ticon-*
> *deroga is in a ruinous condition and has not more than fifty men at*
> *the most. There are large numbers of small arms and considerable*
> *stores and a British sloop of seventy or eighty tons on the Lake. The*
> *place could not hold out an hour against a vigorous onset.*[2]

Two days later, the Massachusetts committee sent a subcommittee headed by Dr. Warren to confer with General Artemus Ward, the
heavy, plodding descendant of Puritans who was commanding the
American troops besieging Boston. Ward was easily persuaded by
the subcommittee's enthusiastic report. Warren and Ward struck a
bargain: the Massachusetts provincial congress was to give Arnold
£100 in cash, and Ward would supply him with ten horses, two
hundred pounds of gunpowder, two hundred pounds of lead, and a
thousand flints, all that he could spare. Arnold was commissioned a
colonel, appointed "to a secret service,"[3] and allowed to select two
captains to help with the recruiting. The next day, May 3, the
provincial congress approved Arnold's mission. That night, he and
his aides rode west with their pack train.

* * *

When Benedict Arnold had left Samuel Holden Parsons at Hartford on April 23 and marched on toward Boston, Parsons could not stop thinking about Arnold's suggestion that artillery from the poorly defended Lake Champlain forts could be hauled east. Not only had he seen the primitive state of the volunteer New England army around Boston but he knew how very few heavy guns there were to guard Connecticut's ports and arm her ships. At a hastily summoned secret conference of the Connecticut Committee of Correspondence, Parsons proposed that Connecticut revolutionaries organize an attack on the two fortresses before New York or Massachusetts could take the initiative. Governor Trumbull had not called the assembly into session and was not likely to do so because of strong sentiment running against becoming embroiled in what was widely perceived as a Massachusetts quarrel with the British administration. Also, with no legislature in session, the Connecticut Committee of Correspondence had almost unlimited power. Yet, to authorize a military expedition into another British province—especially without British approval— was an illegal act of war. To use public funds to support such an enterprise was also illegal, but the Connecticut revolutionaries were already committed to the common cause with Massachusetts radicals, so they brushed aside the lawbooks and "borrowed" £300 in tax money from the provincial treasury on their personal security. They sent £100 of it west with six recruiters under the command of a retired military engineer, Captain Bernard Romans of Wethersfield, to prepare Connecticut's speedy and totally illegal invasion of New York. The next day, they dispatched two other veterans, Captains Edward Mott and Noah Phelps, with five more men to overtake Romans and rouse the Green Mountain Boys in the New Hampshire Grants, present-day Vermont.

To radicals in New England, it appeared not only that the old British forts in upstate New York were ripe for the plucking, but that they must be seized and held to keep them from being reinforced by redcoats from Canada or loyal militia that could be called up any day by the British royal governor. Indeed, one leading Loyalist, Colonel Philip Skene, a Scottish veteran of the French and Indian War who had staked out a thirty-thousand-acre plantation at the southern end of Lake Champlain and defended it with cannon, a ship, and a blockhouse, had recently sailed to England to receive his appointment as royal governor of the new province of Ticonderoga and Crown Point. At the time of Arnold's mission, Governor Skene was on the high seas with instructions to raise a regiment of Loyalist troops to hold the forts for the British. Had his ship put in to New

York City instead of Philadelphia, where he was seized and jailed only a few weeks later, the outcome of the revolution might have been somewhat different. As it was, in all of New York province, there were only 150 British troops to resist a revolution.

It took less than three days for Arnold and his subalterns to lead the heavily laden supply horses the 110 miles over sodden roads from Cambridge to Williamstown, high in the Berkshire Mountains of northwestern Massachusetts, but the journey must have seemed maddeningly slow to Colonel Benedict Arnold, eager to prove himself in his first command. By nightfall of May 6, he arrived on the Massachusetts-Vermont border, only to learn that Colonel Commandant Ethan Allen had received a conflicting command from Connecticut revolutionaries acting on the information he had given Samuel Holden Parsons two weeks earlier. Arnold was furious at this opportunistic challenge to Massachusetts's—and his own—authority, but he let none of his anger show as he sat down the next morning to write a recently discovered letter to the Albany Committee of Safety:

> Gentlemen
> Being appointed by the Congress of the Province of Massachusetts Bay commander of a number of troops now on their march for the reduction of the fort at Ticonderoga and having directions and authority from the Committee of Safety to supply the troops with provisions, [to] draw for the same, I now take the liberty to request you to forward [to] Lake George twenty barrels pork, forty hundred good biscuits. If not to be procured immediately, flour in lieu thereof, also, one hogshead rum, and that you will give directions in case we succeed in the reduction of the place to have a sufficient number of carriages ready at Fort George to transport thirty pieces of cannon of 18 lbs. and 24 lbs. to Albany, which will be of the utmost consequence to the army at Cambridge, and for which I have the General's particular authority.
>
> > I have the Honor to be
> > Gentlemen
> > Your most Hmbl. Servt.
> > BENEDICT ARNOLD, Colonel[4]

Having ordered provisions for ten days, Arnold left behind his recruiting officers and, on Tuesday night, May 3, rode northwest to overtake Ethan Allen.

*   *   *

By the time Arnold had reached Williamstown, recruiting in western Massachusetts was all but finished, and forty-five Pittsfield men had ridden north to Vermont to join Ethan Allen's attack. The Pittsfield contingent, as Committee of Safety member Thomas Allen wrote to revolutionary leaders in eastern Massachusetts, "expected to be reinforced by a thousand men" from Vermont. The plan for the attack on Ticonderoga, they had been told, was to be carried out "with the greatest secrecy" and had been "concocted at Hartford"[5] while Massachusetts' leading revolutionaries, Samuel Adams, John Hancock, and the governor and council of Connecticut, had been present. This was not true. The Massachusetts revolutionaries had only been passing through Hartford on their way south to the Continental Congress in Philadelphia: if the governor and council of Connecticut had lent their official sanction, there is no record of it. Apparently, Ethan Allen's brother, Heman, had misrepresented his authority for raising troops in Massachusetts as he headed north to join his brothers and the Boys. In fact, the Allens had never been able to raise more than two hundred Vermonters, not the thousand Heman claimed, and were at this moment heading toward Lake Champlain with only 130 men to begin the attack without waiting for biscuits and salt pork Ethan Allen had ordered from Williamstown. Benedict Arnold had learned of Allen's shortage of supplies and knew that without food or gunpowder, the Boys could not begin their attack. Confident he could overtake the Allens, Arnold covered the fifteen miles to Bennington in a breakneck ride. There, he had been told, in a ramshackle tavern with a stuffed mountain lion on a pole out front he would find the headquarters of the Green Mountain Boys. The ride, through deep mud over the mountains, ruined Arnold's sorrel: he later billed the Massachusetts Provincial Congress £16 for it.[6]

Ever since word of Lexington had reached Bennington, the leaders of nearby towns and officers of the Green Mountain Boys had been assembling there. They had turned the Catamount Tavern into the capital of the new state of Vermont, and a crude carved plank sign over the door now proclaimed the barroom the "Council Room." As these rough-cut veterans in fringed buckskin hunting shirts and high boots drank rum and argued about politics, they had stacked their flintlock muskets. When the red-uniformed Colonel Benedict Arnold clambered up the front steps and pushed open the door, men who had been swearing about redcoats suddenly saw one, started, and scrambled for their weapons. Soon there were muskets cocked and pointed at Arnold, who hastened to identify himself and produce his papers. Arnold explained in clipped tones that he had been em- powered by the Massachusetts provincial congress to take over their command and lead them in the attack. The gun barrels now came down and the Boys began to hoot and jeer and mimic Arnold and jump up and dance on the tables. All of them had fought under British officers who looked like this ramrod-straight officer, but they had never seen such an elegant American, especially one accom- panied by an orderly. There was something chillingly authoritative about his tone and bearing, however, and pretty soon the catcalls subsided and a number of their leaders came forward and identified themselves. They explained that they had met as long ago as a week before, had constituted themselves a Council of War, and held elec- tions for officers, with ranks of officers decided by the number of men they had raised. Ethan Allen had, of course, been unanimously elected colonel-commandant, James Easton of Pittsfield a second colonel, lawyer John Brown, also of Pittsfield, a major, and Mott a captain. The council, he admitted, had no legal authority from Mas- sachusetts or Connecticut, but its men would only follow the orders of their own elected officers. When Arnold pressed his orders on them, emphasizing that General Ward himself had commissioned Arnold, the council began to waver. If Arnold hurried, he could still overtake Allen at Castleton, fifty miles north, where he had gone to await salt pork, beans, gunpowder, boats, and his Boys, now being rounded up by couriers in the hills of Vermont. Mott reiterated that the men, some of whom may have suffered under harsh British disci- pline in the French and Indian War, had been promised that they would be commanded by their own officers.

Early the next morning, May 8, Arnold and his orderly hurried off to Castleton, where he learned that the Committee of War was meeting before setting out to join Allen, who had already ridden farther north to Shoreham, jumping-off point for the attack across Lake Champlain. Once again presenting his credentials, Arnold claimed command. The men he faced across a tavern table at Cas- tleton were grimly determined not to accede to Arnold. As Captain Mott explained two days later in a letter to the Massachusetts provincial congress, he, Mott, considered that the idea to take the fortress was his own and that he had been given authority by the "principal men of the Assembly at Hartford" to join Captain Noah Phelps of Connecticut and military engineer Bernard Romans to go north and spy on Fort Ticonderoga. Phelps, who now coolly identi- fied himself to Arnold, said he had gone to the fort, much of the Connecticut money still in his saddlebags, and passed himself off as a fur trapper who needed a haircut and shave from the fort's barber. In conversations inside the fort, he had verified how weak its garrison was but learned that reinforcements were expected any day. The rest, including the ruined walls and the open gates, he had seen for himself. Colonel Easton had meanwhile ridden north to Jericho, Vermont, to recruit while a party of thirty Vermonters set out to attack a plantation at the southern tip of the lake and take into custody a Loyalist, Major John Skene. They were to seize Skene's schooner, the *Katherine,* and his small boats and bring them up the lake the twelve miles to Hand's Cove at Shoreham, on the Vermont shore one mile up the lake from Ticonderoga, to rendezvous with Ethan Allen and 140 of his best Boys.

"After we had generously told [Arnold] our whole plan," Captain Mott reported to Hartford, he "insisted that he had a right to command them and all their officers, which bred such a mutiny among the soldiers [that] nearly frustrated our whole design."[7] When Arnold could not wrest control of the expedition away from Mott and his council he rode off again in pursuit of Allen, this time overtaking him twenty-five miles farther on, in an open field at Shoreham. As Arnold in his fresh scarlet uniform and his orderly approached Allen, Captain Mott and his council rode closely behind Arnold, apparently worried that Allen might relent without their support: they had refused to ride beside Arnold or give any appearance of supporting his authority. As it turned out, they were right to worry. At first, the massive green-uniformed Allen with his oversized epaulets and shiny brass buttons seemed to cave in before the trim, professional-looking officer in red. There was something inborn and recognizable in Arnold's whipsaw air of authority, and Ethan Allen was one of the first to defer to it. Furthermore, Arnold's credentials were all in order, clearly indicating a higher authority than the oral orders of the Boys' self-appointed council meeting in a frontier barroom. Now that Arnold had challenged him, Allen realized he had no authority other than that conferred by the fact that the men and guns around them answered to his orders.

At first, Allen appeared to cave in, announcing that Colonel Benedict Arnold would henceforth lead the expedition. But the men sensed something in his unusually clipped tones. As if at a signal, they silently walked to the edges of the field and stacked their guns as several of them announced they would club their firelocks over their shoulders and walk home before they would serve under anyone but Allen. Benedict Arnold was outraged, but there was little he could do except rely on his firm belief in order and discipline. He could not condone such insubordination to an officer's orders. He had been a ship's captain too long to fold in the face of incipient mutiny. Coolly, bravely, surrounded by two hundred angry veterans, Arnold negotiated with Allen until he was ready to accept a compromise. Allen was to lead his Green Mountain Boys as well as the sixteen Connecticut men sent over by Parsons while Benedict Arnold, exercising his valid Massachusetts commission, would lead all Massachusetts troops. Side by side, in a joint command, they would lead the first American offensive of the Revolution early the next morning. As a token of conciliation, Allen gave Arnold a short blunderbuss to carry into battle; Arnold had arrived with only his saber and pistols.

The target of the joint New England attack was colonial America's most strategic stronghold, lying midway on a line of fortified lakes and rivers that ran from New York City to Quebec. To the south of Fort Ticonderoga there was another pair of forts at either end of the evergreen-rimmed bowl of Lake George, just to the north of the vital artery, the Hudson River, that is navigable all the way to New York City. Above Ticonderoga, Lake Champlain surges northward 110 miles into Canada, where its waters flow into the Richelieu and then the St. Lawrence and on to Montreal and Quebec. The keys to this line of fortified lakes and rivers connecting New York City with Quebec were the fortresses of Ticonderoga and, twelve miles farther north on Lake Champlain, Fort Amherst at Crown Point. On the evening of May 9, Benedict Arnold, Ethan Allen, and about 250 men marched north silently along the old Crown Point Military Road, their movements shielded by the dense forest as they passed within a mile of Ticonderoga's sentries.

What made the attack on Fort Ticonderoga such a blow to the British was not only that they had spent nearly £2 million to rebuild and garrison its works but that so many thousands of British soldiers had died to conquer it: on July 4, 1758, the mightiest military force thus far assembled in the New World had marched through the woods to attack the French in the great star-shaped fortress. But the French had entrenched the land approach behind a three-quartermile row of earthworks across the entire Ticonderoga peninsula and rimmed it with cannon. In front of them, a one-hundred-foot-wide trench had been dug and filled with an abatis made of felled trees with sharpened branches that slashed attackers while the French fired down nearly point-blank at them. For seven hours, another British assault was unleashed hourly into the bloody tangle until two thousand redcoats had been killed. Four thousand Frenchmen had been able to hold the fort against a British army five times more numerous in what one military historian has called "one of the most incredible incidents of bravery and stupidity in the annals of the British Army."[8]

The British never did succeed in taking Fort Carillon. When the French withdrew to Canada in 1759, they blew it up along with Fort St. Frederic at Crown Point. At enormous cost, the British had rebuilt and renamed them both. Now Fort Ticonderoga was occupied by only forty-six British soldiers under two officers and their wives and children, who could sleep securely although there was an enemy force less than a mile away because they still had not learned of the fighting at Lexington and Concord three weeks earlier. Even if they had, they had little reason to expect an attack. Not only was the invasion an illegal act of intrusion by Massachusetts and Connecticut, but New York's government had officially and expressly forbidden such a raid, since partisans on both sides of the imperial struggle in New York still hoped for reconciliation. The Continental Congress in Philadelphia had resolved that on no account should New York revolutionaries try to molest the redcoats, who should be allowed to enter and occupy barracks but not be allowed to construct any new fortifications or impede the free passage of citizens. Most of all, force of arms should be exercised only if the British troops violated the people's rights in Massachusetts. Clearly, this had not happened at Ticonderoga. New York's revolutionary leaders interpreted this to mean that on no account should the people take the law into their own hands and confiscate military property belonging to the British crown. Furthermore, there had been no declaration of war. As late as May 16, six days after the attack, the politicians in Philadelphia were declaring that "this Congress has nothing more in view than the defense of the Colonies."[9] Only after the attack did Congress form a committee, with Colonel George Washington of Virginia as chairman, "to consider what posts are necessary to be occupied in New York."[10] Washington's committee later passed an after-the-fact resolution to justify the seizure of Fort Ticonderoga, citing "indisputable evidence that a design is formed by the British Ministry of making a cruel invasion from the province of Quebec."[11]

Just how much the British garrison knew of the planned attack was unclear to Benedict Arnold, who fully expected sharp resistance and who must have grown more apprehensive as the hour for the attack approached and one thing after another went wrong. The key to Ethan Allen's plan was the raiding party he had dispatched to Skenesboro at the southern end of the lake to round up boats. By dark, there were 230 men assembled along the eastern shore of Lake Champlain at Hand's Cove, safely screened from view by headlands. There, in a darkened spruce grove, they waited silently, anxiously.

By one-thirty in the morning, six hours later, with barely enough time to ferry the men across before daylight, there were still no boats. What neither Allen nor Arnold learned for several more days was that the raiding party had been distracted by a cellar stocked with "choice liquors,"[12] according to Major Skene, some of which they consumed on the spot, others along the road back to Vermont. The raiders could not find Skene's schooner, which was cruising far to the north, but finally a single thirty-three-foot-long bateau, scow-rigged with a lugsail, bumped ashore at Hand's Cove. It was three o'clock in the morning and Allen and Arnold were huddling in the rain, trying to decide whether to postpone the attack, when the scow finally ground ashore. Already the sky was turning gray against the black silhouette of hills to the east. Even before the scow arrived, the two commanders agreed that they must attack with as many picked men as they could get across in the next hour. As it set out on its first crossing, forty men and their supplies weighted down the scow nearly to sinking. As it was rowed across the squall-whipped waters, whitecaps broke over the boat's gunwales and soaked the men. Arnold, straight and rigid, stood obstinately in the bow, wrapped in a cape against the cold as Allen, Easton, and Brown held on in the stern. The boat took a nerve-racking ninety minutes to cross and recross one mile of heaving water and then, when there were eighty-three men deposited only a quarter mile east of the fort, the little army—scarcely a company of men—picked their way up the steep outer slope of fortifications to begin the attack. Four years later, Ethan Allen published a memoir in which he claimed that as the men reached the far side of the lake just north of a jutting piece of land known as Willow Point, he had formed his troops into three neat ranks facing the shore and harangued them with a speech calculated to inspirit them for the attack:

Friends and fellow soldiers: You have, for a number of years past been a scourge and terror to arbitrary power. Your valor has been famed abroad. . . . I now propose to advance before you and, personally, conduct you through the wicket gate: for we must this morning either quit our pretensions to valor, or possess ourselves of this fortress in a few minutes: and, inasmuch, as it is a desperate attempt, which none but the bravest of men dare undertake, I do not urge it on any contrary to his will. You that will undertake voluntarily, pose your firelocks.[13]

Even if Allen had scribbled down these noble sentiments, he had little chance to read them. It was dead quiet where the men were clambering ashore only a musket shot away from the eastern redoubt that protected the boat landing. Only the utmost surprise could now salvage the expedition. Leading their men, Allen and Arnold slipped silently past the unguarded redoubt, hugging the towering northeast ramparts as they hurried up the steep slope two hundred yards toward the looming granite walls of the main fort.

At four o'clock, with only a third of their men and none of their food across the lake, Arnold and Allen and their veterans were picking their way toward the main gate, which would no longer close. Just outside the gate was a smaller wicket gate and sentry box. Despite General Gage's written warning sent from Boston on March 8, there was only a single redcoat guard, and he was dozing. Arnold, on the left, and Allen, on the right, later both claimed that they rushed the man simultaneously, but other witnesses said that only one man could squeeze through at a time and that as they charged, the faster Arnold raced ahead. The startled sentry aimed and fired. Fortunately for Arnold, the guard had been asleep on a damp night. His gun misfired, the hammer snapping harmlessly in the pan before the man threw it down and ran toward the barracks, the Green Mountain Boys chasing after him. As they surged through a casement under the east wall, a second sentry appeared. This time, Ethan Allen reached him first. The redcoat fired high and rushed with his bayonet: Allen sidestepped and swung at his head with his heavy saber. His blow could have decapitated the man had it not struck a comb in the English sentry's carefully coiffed and powdered white hair. Deflected, the stroke only staggered the man. (Allen later claimed he had altered the sword's sweep out of humaneness.) As his men surrounded the guard and pulled him to his feet, Allen demanded he lead them to the commandant's quarters. Amazingly, no one knew the fort's precise layout despite the reconnaissance of the Green Mountain Boys. Benedict Arnold knew where the main barracks were, however, and could see that the muskets were neatly stacked out front. He quickly deployed his men to rush into the barracks, ordering each man to wake a redcoat in bed at gunpoint and keep him prisoner while their weapons were removed to the other side of the fort. Meanwhile, Arnold, Allen, and a half-dozen men ran across the parade ground to the west wall and hurried up a stone stairway to the officers' quarters shouting, "No quarter, no quarter."

In the officers' quarters, Lieutenant Jocelyn Feltham jumped up and ran, undressed, to the commandant's door to wake Captain Delaplace "and receive his orders." The commandant didn't answer.

The young subaltern rushed back to his room, pulled on a coat, and, still naked from the waist down, ran toward the din, his breeches in his hand, hoping that his visible symbols of authority would help him rouse the garrison. More men were racing up the stairs. "With great difficulty I got into Delaplace's room," Feltham later reported. While Delaplace coolly dressed and put on his sword, the young officer opened a side door and ran downstairs. Stalling, Feltham asked the two men poised now just below him "by what authority they entered His Majesty's fort." Ethan Allen, brandishing his saber, retorted, "In the name of the great Jehovah and the Continental Congress," though neither, in fact, had asked Allen's intercession. While Allen waved his sword over Feltham's head and his men pointed their flintlocks at him, Arnold showed him his orders. Allen then warned Feltham "that if there was a single gun fired, neither man, woman or child should be left alive in the fort." There were approximately forty women and children, dependents of the soldiers, in the fort. "Mr. Arnold begged it in a more genteel manner," Feltham later reported. "It was owing to him they were prevented getting into Captain Delaplace's room." Finally, Captain Delaplace, fully dressed, came out and surrendered his sword and pistols.

While the British officers were placed under guard, the redcoats were drawn up in ranks on the parade ground inside the fort. More American militia continued to pour into the fort until there were about four hundred Vermonters who, according to the British lieutenant, "came now to join in the plunder which was most rigidly performed as to liquors, provisions, etc. whether belonging to his Majesty or private property."14 One of the first discoveries by Allen's Boys was a wardroom cellar under the officers' quarters housing ninety gallons of rum, enough liquor to slake the thirsts of the Boys and their friends for three days. Soon there was, as Benedict Arnold informed the Massachusetts Committee of Safety, "the greatest confusion and anarchy, destroying and plundering private property, committing every enormity and paying no attention to public service." Arnold tried to get the men to help with the official business of stripping the fort of its cannon and gunpowder to get them moving south to Lake George and on their way to Boston, but the Boys instead got roaring drunk and began to loot the barracks. Arnold repeatedly tried to wrestle stolen property out of their hands. At one point, he had a tug-of-war with a Vermonter over a sewing table that a crying woman begged him to save. Arnold's insistence that there be no further looting only infuriated Ethan Allen. Arnold wrote the next morning to Dr. Warren and his Massachusetts committee:

On and before our taking possession here I had agreed with Colonel Allen to issue further orders jointly, until I could raise a sufficient number of men to relieve his people, on which plan we proceeded . . . since which, Colonel Allen, finding he had the ascendancy over his people, positively insisted I should have no command, as I had forbid the soldiers plundering and destroying private property. The power is now taken out of my hands and I am no longer consulted.[15]

Colonel Allen not only refused to order his men to stop looting the private property of prisoners, but stripped Arnold of his joint command at gunpoint. The Boys, as they roared around the fort ransacking it, took to firing off guns: two shots were directed at Benedict Arnold, but their unsteady marksmen missed him. When Arnold still insisted on an end to the looting, over and over again reciting military law to the looters, one of them leveled his musket, rested its muzzle against Arnold's chest, and cocked it, saying he would kill Arnold if he interfered. Arnold leveled his steely grayish-blue eyes and stared the man down. After a few tense minutes, the man lowered his gun and went reeling off.

When Silas Deane's brother, Barnabas, arrived at the fort to inspect Connecticut's troops and the uses of the province's money on the expedition, he reported back that but for Arnold's efforts, "no man's person would be safe who was not of the Green Mountain Party."[16] Deane also asserted that there was a war within a war at Ticonderoga: Ethan Allen and his land-speculating mountain men from Vermont were persecuting New Yorkers now in their power and were planning, by taking and holding the area, to force their land claims on New York. Disgusted, Arnold confined himself to the officers' quarters, waiting for more of his own recruits to arrive from western Massachusetts. He continued to write his report to the Massachusetts provincial congress. The plan was falling apart, he wrote: Allen and his henchmen were "governing by whim and caprice." The party Arnold had dispatched to seize the other key fort, at Crown Point, had returned after meeting headwinds on the lake: "That expedition and taking the sloop is entirely laid aside." The ten-gun British sloop-of-war *George* could control all shipping on Lake Champlain. In the mayhem around him, he wrote, one hundred British troops could retake the fort "and there seems no prospect of things being in a better situation." Arnold offered to resign his command if Warren wanted to relieve him, but he would not resign to Ethan Allen: "Colonel Allen is a proper man to head his own wild people, but entirely unacquainted with military service. As

I am the only person who has been legally authorized to take possession of this place, I am determined to insist on my right. . . . I think it my duty to remain here against all opposition until I have further orders." There was no hint of fear, only determination in his tone— and pride at what he felt he had accomplished despite Allen: "As I have, in consequence of my orders from you, gentlemen, been the first person who entered and took possession of the fort, I shall keep it at every hazard."[17] He began to keep a terse regimental memorandum book. Under May 10, he entered: "Mr. Allen, finding he had a strong party and being impatient of control and taking umbrage at my forbidding to plunder, assumed the entire command and I was not consulted. . . ."[18] Publicly unfazed, Arnold also used the enforced idleness to study the fort and take a thorough inventory of its guns with Bernard Romans, who had just arrived at Ticonderoga after leading a successful attack on Fort George at the southern end of Lake George. Romans had broken with the other officers sent from Hartford and had gone off with sixteen new recruits to attack the old fort, held only by two retired British officers. Now he reported to Arnold and, after protesting the looting to Allen, joined Arnold as he poked through the ruins. The hoard of cannon was far greater than Arnold had first told the Massachusetts revolutionaries, he wrote to Dr. Warren at Watertown, but most of the prized cannon that had prompted the invasion were in wretched condition: "It is impossible to advise you how many cannon are here and at Crown Point, as many of them are buried in the ruins." A large number were "lying on the edge of the lake." Since the lake was high with spring runoff, many were covered with water. "The confusion we have been in"[19] prevented Arnold from organizing men to get the cannon moving toward Boston: Arnold urged engineer Romans to go to the Massachusetts authorities to tell them of his dilemma and seek their help. Eventually, weeks later, the newly created chief of artillery of the American army, Colonel Henry Knox, was dispatched to transport the cannon to the heights overlooking Boston, where they brought about the British withdrawal from the city nearly a year later. Meanwhile, the guns continued to rust. As he waited for his own men to arrive, he could see the numbers of Allen's men constantly diminishing. Once the rum and booty were gone, the Boys melted back into the hills, unable to stay away from their hardscrabble farms too long, unwilling to undergo the work and the tedium of garrison duty, much less risk a British counterattack.

While Arnold stalked the walls of the fort, fired off letters, and jotted down memos, Ethan Allen was busy writing, too. His version not only assured his place in history but served to help his friends and harm his rival, Arnold. His accounts varied from day to day. For four years he continued to embellish them, ultimately publishing an unabashedly purple memoir. "The sun seemed to rise that morning with a superior lustre," he said of the day of the attack, and was only occasionally and inadvertently truthful, as when he spoke of his men as "conquerors who tossed about the flowing bowl." He had apparently been tossing about the bowl a bit when he wrote his first account to the Massachusetts congress, which not only did not mention Benedict Arnold—"I took the fortress at Ticonderoga by storm"—but said that Allen's crony, Pittsfield tavernkeeper James Easton, had led Arnold's fifty Massachusetts troops "with great zeal and fortitude." Arnold later charged that Easton had cowered down by the boats along the lake, pretending to dry his musket until the attack was over. Allen also gave a slap on the back to his lawyer friend John Brown, already well known to Massachusetts authorities, stating that he had been "personally in the attack,"[20] when actually he had been in a tavern across the lake helping to draft ex post facto orders for Ethan Allen.

The self-constituted "Committee of War of Ticonderoga"— Easton, Noah Phelps, Epaphras Bull, and Edward Mott—plotted and schemed with Allen to discredit Arnold and deprive him of any credit in the victory. They certified to the Massachusetts congress that they had "given the command thereof into the hands of colonel Ethan Allen and said Arnold refused to give up his command, which causes much difficulty, said Arnold not having enlisted one man neither do we know that he has it or can do it. . . . We think Arnold's farther procedure in this matter highly inexpedient. . . ."[21] To make sure that his first version of history went unchallenged, Allen sent Easton to Cambridge, Massachusetts, with the report. Easton also apparently took along Arnold's version of events, which disappeared. Ethan Allen also gave Easton yet another version of events, this time to take to the Albany Committee of Safety on his way to Philadelphia to inform the Continental Congress of its still-unwanted and unauthorized conquest. Allen's May 11 version to the Albany committee is the only document over his name which mentions Arnold: "I took the fortress of Ticonderoga with about one hundred and thirty Green Mountain Boys [actually, the best count is about eighty-two] . . . Colonel Easton with about forty-seven veteran soldiers distinguished themselves in the action. Colonel Arnold entered the fortress with me side by side." On the 12th, to Governor Trumbull in Connecticut, Allen penned a somewhat different account. Boastfully, Allen prophesied that within ten days, he would seize the king's much larger sloop-of-war out on the lake and make "Lake Champlain and the fortifications thereon . . . subject to the Colonies."[22] The two men who carried Allen's falsified reports both harbored grudges against Arnold. John Brown had worked in Arnold's cousin Oliver's law office in Rhode Island and was bitter toward the Arnold family after being fired. Tavernkeeper Easton, like Brown, was a self-styled militia colonel who thought that he, not Arnold, should have been commissioned to lead the Massachusetts troops and now was working hard to discredit Arnold and gain Arnold's colonelcy.

It was another week before Arnold wrote Cambridge his final report, and by then he had learned of Allen, Easton, and Brown's duplicity. To his friend Dr. Warren, he wrote angrily, underscoring every word:

Beg leave to observe, I have had intimation given me, that some persons had determined to apply to you and the Provincial Congress, to injure me in your esteem by misrepresenting matters of fact. I know of no other motive they can have only my refusing them commission from the very simple reason that I did not think them qualified. However, gentlemen, I have the satisfaction of imagining I am employed by gentlemen of so much candor that my conduct will not be condemned until I have the opportunity of being heard.[23]

He had begun to work around Allen, sending off his own men as they arrived on missions with those of Allen's officers he believed he could trust. He found he had much in common with Bernard Romans, the military engineer Connecticut had sent on the expedition. Romans had apparently fallen out with Mott and the council of war over irregularities in orders, especially on looting. Romans had helped Mott and Phelps spy out the defenses at Ticonderoga before the attack. Indeed, he was one of the few qualified engineers in the American colonies. Dutch-born, Romans had been trained as a civil engineer in England and had served with the British in the French and Indian War as a military engineer and cartographer. He had mapped much of the Caribbean, including the Bahamas and all of Florida, where he had also gathered specimens and drawn plants as a botanist. His maps were used by the British and the Americans in the Revolution, and he went on to design the first fortifications at West Point. He had come north to publish his works on Florida, and was living in Wethersfield when the fighting broke out. But Romans was accustomed to military discipline, and he quickly broke ranks with Allen's supporters, who began to bad-mouth him in their reports. Benedict Arnold asked him to help him appraise the condition of the forts, and together the two men examined walls, cannon, supplies. By the third day after the attack, Romans was writing back to Hartford about the "feeble state"[24] of the men and provisions at Ticonderoga. Arnold also joined forces with Captain Seth Warner, Allen's number-three officer, a capable man who helped him to organize the capture of Fort Amherst at Crown Point with its nine-man garrison.

When more of Arnold's men arrived, he dispatched them to Skenesboro to fetch Skene's schooner, the *Katherine*. On Sunday afternoon, May 14, the fast little schooner arrived, docking at the old boatyard across the neck of water east of the fort at the foot of Mount Independence. A jubilant Arnold later noted in his regimental memorandum book, "We immediately fixed her with four carriage guns and six swivel guns."[25] He instructed his men how to pierce the schooner's sides for gunports, how to lash down the guns and run them out with blocks and tackle. As soon as the vessel was provisioned with food and rum, shot and shell, Arnold boarded *Katherine* and renamed her *Liberty*. Then he fired off his last report to Massachusetts before sailing.

To Dr. Warren, he wrote, "I intend setting out in *Liberty* directly, with a bateau and fifty men to take possession of the British sloop [the largest ship on the lake, the *George*]. We are advised this morning by the post [that the *George*] is at St. John's [St. Jean, or St. Johns, Quebec], loaded with provisions and waiting a wind for this place." If the warship was allowed to sail south with a cargo of redcoats, Ticonderoga might once again fly a British flag. As he wrote, Arnold was confident that the number of his troops was growing even as Allen's men faded back into the forests. He reported that he did not like the way things had been going with Ethan Allen: "The dispute between us is subsiding. . . . I am extremely sorry matters have not been transacted with more prudence and judgment. I have done everything in my power, and put up with many insults to preserve peace and serve the public."[26] But now he had a more dangerous fight on his hands.

Leaving behind Allen and his dwindling garrison, Colonel Arnold and his little squadron sailed out onto Lake Champlain, towing with them the only other sizable boats, two thirty-three-foot bateaux which Arnold had armed with bow guns. Safely away on his first naval expedition, Arnold stopped off briefly at Crown Point, now controlled by revolutionaries, to inspect its ruined works and guns with engineer Romans, whom he then dispatched with his report. And then, with Benedict Arnold at the tiller, *Liberty* set sail for Canada.

5

"WE ARE
MASTERS OF THE LAKE"

*The American colonies are in danger
from Canada, whether in the hands
of the British or restored to the
French.*

Benedict Arnold to Continental Congress, June 15, 1775

As the schooner *Liberty* glided out
onto Lake Champlain, Benedict Arnold set in motion his audacious
plan for capturing or destroying the *George*. He knew the importance of the northern forts: without them, the Americans would be
exposed to invasion from advanced British bases in Canada. Even
without control of Lake Champlain itself, the British, with Indian
allies, could harass the Vermont and New York shores and eventually surround and cut off Fort Ticonderoga and Crown Point. As
Ethan Allen and his mountain men watched from the shore, *Liberty*
disappeared up the lake. Allen was embarrassed and angry. He was
not about to allow Benedict Arnold to steal any of the glory, much
less the prize money for a captured British warship. Calling for his
men to abandon whatever they had been doing at the fort, he ordered them to crowd into four bateaux, row after Arnold, and race
him to St. Jean. At first Arnold and his men were actually at a disad-
vantage. Arnold's newly appointed aide-de-camp, twenty-year-old
Eleazar Oswald, noted in his journal that "contrary winds retarded
our voyage."[1] Allen at least had oars.

All day Monday, Arnold chafed as the wind died. By Tuesday morning, May 16, he was able to give orders to cast off again. As he set a course for Canada, *Liberty* heeled over and raced into the wind, this time with room to maneuver. By nightfall they had reached Split Rock, thirty-five miles to the north. The next day, Wednesday, *Liberty* coursed a remarkable sixty-five miles. By dusk, *Liberty* dropped anchor at the Canadian frontier at Point au Fer after a magnificent day's sail that left Ethan Allen far behind.

Arnold's luck changed with the wind the next morning, the 18th. All day long, within sight of the Canadian shore, Arnold and his men sat nervously, their boats again becalmed. Arnold used this time to send out a scout to infiltrate the British lines to St. Jean, thirty miles downriver: Lake Champlain emptied into the narrow fast Richelieu River here, carrying a man in a canoe swiftly north. By dark, the scout was back. The *George* was anchored at its wharf. The British knew that Ticonderoga and Crown Point had fallen. Hundreds of redcoats were on their way from Montreal to reinforce St. Jean and sail on the *George* to recapture the lake forts. The Caughnawaga Indians of Canada had taken up the hatchet to join the British attack, and their support was encouraged with presents sent daily by the British governor, General Guy Carleton. In addition, there were more British ships on the stocks at St. Jean.

Benedict Arnold knew he must attack, wind or no wind. They would row with the current in the two bateaux all night and hit before the British reinforcements arrived, and before the big British sloop could sail out onto the lake. With the *Liberty* and a captured sloop-of-war, Arnold felt he could hold the lake and forestall the inevitable British counterattack.

Leaving a crew of fifteen behind to guard *Liberty,* Arnold divided his remaining men, with Captain Oswald at the helm of the second boat. Each boat was armed with swivel and bow guns. With thirty-five men in two open boats, the man who had conceived and helped to lead the first American offensive by invading another sovereign province only a week later now led the first naval attack in American history. It was also the first American invasion of a foreign country and an act which committed the Continental Congress to extend the revolution to Canada, an enormously ambitious step. But to Benedict Arnold, it was all part of his original orders from the Massachusetts Committee of Safety to secure and protect the Lake Champlain region. He led his little squadron indefatigably through a wilderness all night, his men rowing without respite until they had covered the miles down the Richelieu by dawn. Hiding his boats and men half a mile upriver from the small fort, Arnold sent a scout ahead. At sunrise, Arnold and his men were still waiting impatiently "in a small creek infested with numberless swarms of gnats and mosquitoes." The scout was back in half an hour. The British were "unapprised of our coming." Shoving their boats back out into the Richelieu's rapid current, they "directly pushed for shore," landing about one hundred yards from the British barracks.

On Thursday morning, May 19, 1775, at six o'clock, Arnold personally led a charge on foot against the British outpost. Captain Oswald, at Arnold's side during the attack, recorded that a British sergeant had turned out his squad of thirteen redcoats at a sentry's warning of Arnold's approach. But the spectacle of three times their number, "briskly marching up in their faces," overwhelmed the British soldiers. "The men had their arms," Oswald noted with some amazement, but as Arnold, saber drawn, and his men rushed at them, "they returned within the barracks, left their arms, and resigned themselves into our hands."[2] Arnold left a handful of his men to guard them. Still, there had not been a shot, and he hoped to keep the surprise as he led the bulk of his men quickly down to the waterfront. In a few minutes, Arnold and his best men were swarming over the sides of the *George,* waking the seven-man crew with the loud banging of gun butts on cabin doors and hatch covers. His bloodless capture of a British man-of-war and fort was over in a few minutes. Now Arnold could survey his prize. He wrote to the Massachusetts congress that he had taken "the King's sloop of about 70 tons with two brass six-pounders and seven men without any loss on either side."

From his prisoners, Arnold learned that the captain of the post "was gone to Montreal and hourly expected with a large detachment for Ticonderoga." Arnold was still stunned by his luck when he wrote the next day: "It seemed to be a mere interposition of Providence that we arrived in so fortunate an hour." Arnold also learned that another captain and forty men were "expected there every minute" from the British fort at the Falls of Chambly, twelve miles to the north. Hurriedly, Arnold set about stripping St. Jean of anything that could help his force or hinder the British. For two hours, his men crammed the sloop with guns, gunpowder, food, uniforms, blankets, rum—"such stores as were valuable"—including two fine brass field pieces. He manned four large British bateaux and sank five more. Then, "the wind proving favorable," he led his small navy of eight vessels—now the first American navy—running downwind up the Richelieu and out into Lake Champlain again. His first military victory had been swift and important, and he was exultant as he strode the deck of the fine British sloop, which he now commanded and renamed the *Enterprise.*

*   *   *

Only fifteen miles south of the Canadian border, near Isle La Motte, the triumphant Benedict Arnold saw a sight which must have made him rub his eyes in disbelief. There, with four open boats full of drooping Green Mountain Boys, was Ethan Allen. Incredibly, they had rowed four days and nights to overtake Arnold and beat him to the attack on St. Jean. Now they were exhausted and famished: in his enthusiasm to outstrip Arnold, Ethan Allen had not provided them with food or blankets. The sight of them after a hundred miles of rowing softened Arnold toward the flamboyant Allen. As he told it to Dr. Warren and his committee, "I must, in justice to Colonel Allen, observe that he left Crown Point soon after me for [St. Jean] with 150 men and on my return I met him five leagues this side and supplied him with provisions, his men being in a starving condition."[3] In fact, Arnold fired off a salute to the Green Mountain Boys from *Enterprise*'s cannon and then opened up his holds to feed and warm the men and gave them all several drinks of rum. As Arnold toasted Allen and Allen toasted Arnold and everyone toasted congress—Allen years later still warmly recalled "several loyal Congress healths"[4]—they fired off their muskets and put aside their jealousies of the past ten days. But then Ethan Allen insisted that he and his Boys go on and row to St. Jean and retake it and hold it. Arnold told them about the approaching British forces, but Allen was steadfast. "It appeared to me a wild, impractical scheme," Arnold told Dr. Warren, "and provided it could be carried into execution, of no consequence, so long as we are masters of the lake, and of that I make no doubt."[5] Still, Allen went ahead, and Arnold, in a show of goodwill, fully supplied him. He watched affectionately as the "mad fellows" rowed off toward Canada and then he sailed back toward Ticonderoga, filling many hours of a long day on the lake writing letters in the captain's cabin, composing a report to Massachusetts, and then, as he had done years ago amid the controversy over the Stamp Act, abstracting it in a "Letter from Crown Point" that appeared in Philadelphia in the *Pennsylvania Packet* on July 5, right under the noses of the Continental Congress. Late the next afternoon, after sailing one hundred miles in thirty-three hours, the *Enterprise* sailed up to Fort Ticonderoga "and having saluted the fort, came to anchor."[6]

Riding down to the Skenesboro sawmills to buy planks for boatbuilding and gun carriages, Arnold was busy arming the sloop and the schooner with heavier guns. He had just sent off his trusted seconds-in-command, Captain Oswald to Connecticut, Captain

Jonathan Brown to Cambridge, with news of his victory and a detailed inventory of the guns and ships he had so far captured. Peace had all but returned to Ticonderoga by May 21 when Ethan Allen and his men came splashing down the lake again as if they were chased by the devil. No doubt sheepishly, Allen told Arnold that he had indeed approached St. Jean on the 19th. Arnold reported to Dr. Warren by express rider that Allen and his Boys had planned an ambush but "his people being so much fatigued thought proper to retreat and crossed the river where they continued the night . . . At dawn the next day they were, when asleep, saluted with a discharge of grapeshot from six field pieces and discharge of small arms from about two hundred regulars. They made a precipitate retreat and left behind three men." Once again, Allen and his men, not being able to overtake Arnold's ships, had rowed the entire one-hundred-mile length of the lake without provisions. To his memo book, Arnold confided the fiasco "did not in the least surprise me as it happened as I expected."[7] What Arnold also now expected was a British attack. Benedict Arnold wrote two drafts of this May 23 letter, in the first reporting that he had captured £160 in the cabin of a sloop-of-war. He omitted it from the second draft; "as it was the property of the captain, I don't choose to make use of it at present."[8]

The news that the British were on the march and had the support of thousands of Indians forced Arnold and Allen to have a council of war. They agreed on one major point: their fear of British attack. They decided to divide their forces, Arnold taking command on the lake and at Crown Point, Allen at Ticonderoga. Obviously, Ticonderoga could not be repaired in time to serve as the main line of defense, and while old Fort Amherst at Crown Point was in little better condition than Ticonderoga, if the British were able to take it, they would have a staging area from which to attack Ticonderoga and move quickly south. Ticonderoga's walls were too badly breached for Arnold and his men to repair, and too many of its cannon were useless, but at Fort Amherst, the walls at least were in better condition, and in the ruins of a fire that had swept the fort a few years earlier, there were one hundred cannon worth salvaging at all costs, if only to keep them out of British hands. Arnold would take his ships to Crown Point and prepare its defense. His recruiting officers, trading on the news of his early victories, were already filling the ranks of his men. By the time Arnold left for Crown Point on May 22, he had 150 men, while Allen had fewer than one hundred men left at Ticonderoga, because of the disheartening debacle at St. Jean. Effectively, Arnold controlled the entire region now, from Fort

George in the south to the Canadian frontier, 110 miles north. With this small number of troops, he needed to concentrate his strength, so he took eighty men with him to reinforce Crown Point.

By Tuesday, May 23, as he noted in his records, "all hands" were "employed in fixing the sloop and schooner and putting them in the best posture for defense." His makeshift navy was to make the lake its first line of defense. About noon on the 23rd, one of Allen's men who had been captured at St. Jean and had managed to escape arrived and said that there were three hundred British regulars at St. Jean—about 40 percent of all British troops in Canada—along with an undetermined number of French Canadians "making all possible preparation for crossing the lake."[9] At this intelligence, Arnold sent off express riders to Fort George, Skenesboro, and as far south as Saratoga, one hundred miles away, "for the people to muster and join us."[10] He also sent an express rider to Philadelphia. However, the intelligence from St. Jean proved to be unreliable. A British ship's carpenter named Samuel Adams who had defected from St. Jean to join Arnold was next to arrive. He told Arnold that only 120 British and Canadians had routed Ethan Allen's sleeping soldiers, and that most of them had immediately marched back up north to the fort at the Falls of Chambly to repair its works.

On May 24, when a Connecticut revolutionary committee of inspection arrived in response to Bernard Romans's plea for help, Arnold welcomed the "sundry gentlemen"[11] (including Silas Deane's brother, Barnabas) and was proud to show them his post, but most of all he was pleased that they brought sixteen able-bodied seamen with them, as well as £500 to begin feeding the men and paying them their back pay. He turned over the sloop *Enterprise* to Captain John Prout Sloan and eight veteran sailors and officers, then assigned eight inexperienced men and fifteen handpicked soldiers as marines, supplying them all with blankets and new uniforms, and paid them their back pay. He appointed Captain Isaac Mathues and a core of seasoned marines to the *Liberty*. Arnold's expense account has recently come to light in the manuscript archives of Princeton University. The Connecticut money did not go very far. As the expense records indicate, Arnold personally paid £1,388 1s. 3d. to recruit, outfit, and feed his own men, and to build up his little navy and defend Crown Point and its New York neighbors once he had spent the £100 the tight-fisted Massachusetts treasurer had advanced him.

A study of his expense records indicates much more than the day-to-day details of financing a regiment, however. It reveals that Arnold had been given broad powers for his secret mission by Mas-

sachusetts revolutionaries, which included seizing or building
enough ships to control Lake Champlain and thus temporarily protect the entire New England backcountry. When Arnold finally submitted his expense accounting, he reported paying Captain Sloan
and his men from May 3. Evidently, he had sent a recruiter to Connecticut from Watertown even as he rode after Ethan Allen so that
he would have experienced sailors ready to man his ships once he
could capture them. It was one of the more brilliant aspects of his
1775 summer campaign that by May 24, less than a week after his
first raid on Canada, and exactly two weeks after taking Ticonderoga, he had seaworthy ships and crews ready to block the British
counterattack.

After seeing off Barnabas Deane and Colonel Charles Webb of
the Connecticut militia, who departed on May 25 for an inspection
of Ticonderoga, Arnold went back to work, "getting down some
cannon, mortars, etc. from the walls of the fort . . . clearing out the
northeast redoubt and arming the vessels."[12] For the next ten days,
his soldiers, with the assistance of Colonel Skene's seized slaves, dug
out fifty-eight heavy guns, which he loaded on the ships or mounted
onto carriages to be sent overland to Fort George at the southern
end of Lake George and thence to Boston. Together, men and oxen
wrested more than one hundred guns from Crown Point's ruins. Arnold also ingeniously set fifteen men to digging out a ton of lead and
iron cannonballs from the ruins of Fort St. Frederic, the old French
fort nearby which had been blown up as it was evacuated fifteen
years earlier. As he wrote to the Albany committee, he was desperately short of shot and shell for his ships and would take all contributions.

By the end of May, Arnold's recruiters, who could point to his
successful attack on Canada, were able to send him an increasing
number of men, but still it was only a dribble compared to the two
thousand he needed to hold the northern frontier. His regimental
records tell the story: "May 31st. 30 men of Captain Nathaniel
Buell's New York company . . . June 1st. Arrived here part of Captain James Wells Company of 20 men from Cambridge. . . . 20 men
sent by Committee of Safety at Albany."[13] In all, according to Arnold's records, he mustered between three and four hundred men,
including six companies and the crews of the two ships which he
paid himself. To consolidate his regiment, he appointed capable
young Eleazar Oswald as lieutenant colonel and commissioned
Jonathan Brown as major. Arnold and his undermanned regiment
managed to safeguard 110 miles of frontier from Fort George north
to the Canadian border for two months. After the Connecticut com-

missioners inspected Ticonderoga and interviewed dozens of participants in the campaign, they pulled Connecticut's last remaining troops out of Ticonderoga, men who had marched with Ethan Allen and his Boys, and turned them over to Arnold at Crown Point. Then they insisted that since Ethan Allen had no more Boys on hand to command—he had transferred his last twenty Vermonters to Arnold on May 27—he relinquish command of Ticonderoga to Arnold as well. Allen complied, but, strangely, he lingered at Ticonderoga.

Benedict Arnold had little time to worry about Ethan Allen. He built up the defenses, doubled the guards at night, and reconstructed the Crown Point fortifications. Soon he had rounded up skilled carpenters and wheelwrights and was buying boards and planks from a nearby sawmill to build barracks for his men, then a guardhouse and blockhouse. He found a grist mill across the lake on the Vermont shore and laid out £33 to buy wheat to bake bread. While boards were cut to build more boats and gun carriages, Arnold bought up all the oars he could find—927 feet of them from one Jesse Doud for £13 14s.

Some of his outlays were for less prosaic purposes. He hired an Indian interpreter, Winthrop Hoit, who had been kidnapped as a child in a raid by Caughnawaga Indians. Hoit had returned to the white settlements, but he could easily slip into Canadian Indian settlements on scouting missions. It was Hoit who had guided John Brown to Montreal the preceding spring to gather intelligence for the Massachusetts Committee of Safety. Arnold put him on the books as Indian interpreter and sent him off on a twenty-day spying mission through British lines to Montreal with a band of Stockbridge Indians Arnold had recruited in Massachusetts. He also formed a company of rangers, all veterans of the French and Indian War, and dispatched them on a reconnaissance mission to St. Jean to obtain more accurate information of British reinforcements and intentions.

By June 2, Arnold's seamen had finished making sails for his bateaux and for *Liberty*, which he was rerigging, and eight carpenters were busy repairing the barracks. Arnold had enough boards and nails left over to send to Ticonderoga to repair the barracks there. On the same bateaux with the lumber was Ethan Allen, who had come to Crown Point to plead for men and supplies: Allen had written to the Continental Congress to urge another invasion of Canada. Arnold understandably put him off, since he was about to sail toward Canada again himself and he was too busy stocking his ships with salt pork, rum, and flour as well as hiring a ship's surgeon and a surgeon's mate, against the expectation of sharper fighting.

It had now been ten days since Arnold had written to Dr. War-ren that he was "determined to make a stand" against the expected British attack at Crown Point "to secure the cannon,"[14] but so many recruits were pouring in now that he considered the fort se-cure. On Sunday, June 4, a fresh wind "sprang up," at ten in the morning. Arnold ordered the entire Crown Point garrison paraded and, after a rousing speech, asked for forty volunteers to serve as marines—the first American marines—for his ships. Ready at last to carry out a reconnaissance in force to ascertain British strength, he "immediately embarked" 155 men on board Liberty, Enterprise, and three armed bateaux. At three in the afternoon, he noted, the ships "weighed anchor and proceeded down the lake with a small breeze." At the last minute, he had sent ashore a precious quarter cask of gunpowder to be divided among the new recruits. In all his ships, he now had only 150 pounds of gunpowder. By nightfall, he dropped anchor at Buttonmould Bay, ten miles from Crown Point on the Vermont shore, "where we lay all night."[15] Arnold learned that the Indians he had sent to Canada had been captured. The Stockbridge party had insisted on stopping off at St. Jean, even though Hoit had been "fearful of being taken prisoner." There they were captured by British soldiers and taken north by boat to Montreal, where Governor Carleton ordered them jailed. He or-dered a search made for Hoit, who had managed to reach the Caughnawagas alone. "He narrowly escaped being taken," Arnold noted, "and says the French informed him the Stockbridge Indians [had been] imprisoned at Montreal but, on the intercession of the other Indians, had been set at liberty." Arnold also learned that Carleton "had threatened the inhabitants of Montreal that unless the English merchants would defend the place [against the Amer-icans], he would burn it and retire to Quebec." Hoit also reported that "the Canadians and Indians utterly refused joining the King's troops." Moreover, three hundred British regulars were entrenching St. Jean. Arnold must have been excited by the news. He knew from documents he had taken from prisoners of his first raid on St. Jean that there had been only 717 British regulars in all of Canada, and he had captured seventy of them in all. That meant that if Hoit's information was accurate, fully half the British troops in Canada now were dug in and facing him at St. Jean. To attack and defeat them would so weaken Montreal and Quebec that all of Canada might easily fall to an American attack. He had to strike before Brit-ish reinforcements arrived from England.

The next morning at four o'clock, June 6, Arnold ordered his squadron to weigh anchor. By eight, they had reached Point au Fer, on the west shore of the lake where it narrows into the Richelieu, three miles south of the Canadian border. By ten, he had sailed his ships into Canada and halfway downriver to Hospital Point, where he peeled off three bateaux. Each boat was armed with a single bow cannon and grapeshot-firing swivel guns and bore twenty men who were to act as his advance guard. After the reconnaissance party left, Arnold sent off a four-man party to bake bread and another scouting party by canoe down the Richelieu to "discover the motions of the enemy." By four that afternoon, the three bateaux and the small canoe got close enough to St. Jean to confirm that there were indeed what appeared to be three hundred British there. They were spotted by a British guard boat that opened fire and chased them. From one of the parties, Arnold received a report that "the regulars were determined to pay us a visit the next day." Still, Arnold was unwilling to withdraw from Canada to a safer position on Lake Champlain. He sent a small yawl downstream to St. Jean that night; it returned by morning, reporting that "about two hundred men were entrenching." When they were spotted at dawn by a British patrol, the redcoats fired two cannon shots at them. The Americans returned the fire, keeping up "a continual fire for some time."[16]

Arnold's reconnaissance brought him the intelligence he needed, but the British regulars were heartened by the fact that they were able to hold off the Americans. "We begin to have some notion of the enemy," young John André wrote home to England, "and I am happy to say that they do not appear in a very formidable light." As Arnold camped at Isle aux Noix, his men probed the British outpost and sniped at the regulars, but, under orders from Arnold, refused to come out into the open and fight. They "infest the woods," André wrote, "firing from the bushes on our bateaux, which are constantly moving up and down the river to watch their motions. We have daily expeditions to the woods. I had this duty yesterday, and though I am not particularly keen after the pleasure of being shot at, had almost as leave as met the Yankees as been baked in the sun for the mosquitoes' dinner."[17]

By the night of June 8, Arnold was confident that he had enough men and heavy enough guns on his ships to risk an attack on St. Jean. All he needed was a favorable wind, but for three days now, there had been a strong north wind. The river was too narrow for tacking upwind. He would either have to wait for a south wind or row his ships. Some of his men continued to bake bread to eat on the return crossing of Lake Champlain. Others began to cut down slender trees to fashion oars. Now, however, Arnold changed his mind and decided to dash to Crown Point and pick up enough troops to return and attack St. Jean. If the British were entrenching at St. Jean, he did not have to worry about their attacking Crown Point. He would be back in a matter of days, this time to fight a British army on Canadian soil. With his fastest and largest boats— *Enterprise, Liberty,* and two bateaux—he weighed anchor for Crown Point at five on the morning of June 9. By late the afternoon of the 10th, thanks to a "fair wind," he had run downwind one hundred miles, dropping anchor at five o'clock at Crown Point.[18]

Arnold had thought himself compelled to move quickly to blunt the expected British counterattack from Canada, and as a result he had all but outrun his communications with the revolutionary leaders. He was abruptly overtaken by politics as he sailed back to Crown Point. Near Burlington, Vermont, he met a bateau carrying thirteen men from Saratoga en route to join his squadron and his third-in-command, Major Jonathan Brown, who gave him the latest conflicting instructions from politicians.

The electrifying news that the British fortresses had fallen without a single casualty to a few hundred frontiersmen had caused euphoria immediately followed by consternation. Many American politicians had not been ready for the provocative step of seizing British forts and confiscating British property. The news had reached Philadelphia on May 17, a week after the initial attack, in the saddlebags of Ethan Allen's friend John Brown of Pittsfield. By the time he finished speaking, delegates were writing home of Ethan Allen as the "hero" of Ticonderoga, the first of the Revolution. The next morning, Brown was ushered into Carpenters' Hall. He gave not only his version of the attack but his own analysis of the conditions in Canada he had observed during his mission to Montreal for Massachusetts the past March.

Congress reacted strongly, legitimizing the seizures by a resolution which cited "indubitable evidence that a design is formed by the British Ministry of making a cruel invasion" from Quebec province. The first congressmen sidestepped any jurisdictional squabbles by claiming that "several inhabitants of the northern colonies residing in the vicinity of Ticonderoga" who were "exposed to Canadian incursions"[19] had taken the post. The Continental Congress was still in its formative stage, had not anticipated the outbreak of fighting, had no army of its own, and, indeed, was deeply divided even on the issue of defense. Probably half the delegates, especially those from New York, were opposed to inflammatory measures and, along with the other Middle Atlantic colonies, favored negotiation and reconciliation. At the same time that Arnold and Allen were storming Ticonderoga, Congress was passing a resolution calling for purely defensive measures. But Arnold's continued military actions on Lake Champlain were overtaking cautious congressional military policy.

The Congress set up a committee on New York military affairs headed by the tall, somber forty-three-year-old Colonel George Washington, delegate from Virginia and the only member to attend consistently in uniform. Washington must have known more about the strategic importance of Ticonderoga and Crown Point, but some congressmen had never heard of them and didn't know where they were. Others, such as Washington's fellow Virginian Richard Henry Lee, were elated by the news: "We know the plan of Ministry is to bring Canadians and Indians down upon us," Lee wrote to his brother, Francis Lightfoot Lee. "For this reason, the provincial troops of Connecticut and Massachusetts have wisely taken, by a brave coup de main, possession of the forts at Ticonderoga and Crown Point." But delegate Lee was under the impression that there were two hundred usable cannon at Ticonderoga, and he reported the Congress's first decision on the matter the very day the news arrived: to remove the guns and ammunition to the south end of Lake George, build a fort there, evacuate Crown Point and Ticonderoga, and, from a new base at Lake George, "intercept the communication and march of Canadian and Indian forces"[20] into New York and New England. Just how the guns were to be hauled away and who was to build a new fortress on Lake George on such short notice was left unclear.

Meanwhile, Allen and Arnold were instructed to take a complete inventory of everything taken from the king's fort and be prepared to return it if peace negotiations were successful. Obviously, Congress did not know of the looting of Ticonderoga or Skenesboro. By the May 18 resolution, Congress also urged the New York provincial congress to ask New Hampshire, Massachusetts, and Connecticut to send in reinforcements. The request touched off more controversy. New York, split over taking any part in what was widely viewed as a Massachusetts-bred revolt, had been officially ignoring all requests for aid by Allen and Arnold. But now, for the first time, the Albany Committee of Safety joined with New England in opposing the Continental Congress's recommendation that Ticonderoga and Crown Point be evacuated, leaving the New England and New York frontiers undefended. The Massachusetts Committee of Safety, which had, until then, not publicly acknowledged Arnold's role in the campaign, now praised his efforts. The committee, wrote its chairman, Dr. Warren, "highly approved" his conquests and had learned that Connecticut and New York were making "ample provisions" to reinforce him. Between the lines, Arnold could read that therefore Massachusetts would not. But Dr. Warren said that he and the committee were chagrined to hear that the command dispute with Allen had soured him to the extent that, in three consecutive letters to them, Arnold had asked to be relieved. The committee assured Arnold that it placed the "greatest confidence" in his "fidelity, knowledge, courage and good conduct"; they asked that he "at present dismiss the thoughts of quitting your important command." The letter, spread over the minutes of the Massachusetts congress, clearly restated Arnold's overall command of revolutionary forces on the frontier, especially in the absence of any conflicting commission from another colony's congress. It was these orders that Arnold had carried with him as he had sailed toward Canada. But the Massachusetts committee inserted some disquieting language. Arnold was not to think about resigning "at present." He was to stay on at least until New York or Connecticut took on the tasks of maintaining and perhaps even commanding the Lake Champlain forces "agreeable to an order of the Continental Congress."[21]

But which order by the Continental Congress? While New York, Connecticut, and Massachusetts committees and congresses were all busy passing the buck, none of them overly eager for the responsibility of seizing the king's forts despite the popularity of the attack among frontiersmen, the Continental Congress contradicted its May 18 resolution on an almost weekly basis. Arnold could not be sure how accurately the Continental Congress had been informed of his actions. He wrote to Philadelphia "as commanding officer here" as soon as the May 18 resolution reached Crown Point. Had Congress not been told by the Massachusetts Committee of Safety either of his appointment or his instructions? He enclosed copies. Then he delineated Ethan Allen's activities and his own. They had, he added, "agreed we should take a joint command" and he related his side of their dispute. For the first time, he publicly accused Allen of "preventing my carrying my orders into execution" for nearly a week until his own troops had arrived.

His letter went on to give precise and accurate information about Canada and the lake based on his intelligence-gathering efforts, including how many guns he had placed on what ships and how many he had managed to send south to Lake George. He went on to protest Congress's May 18 directive: ". . . the report of Ticonderoga's being abandoned has thrown the inhabitants here into the greatest consternation," he wrote. "There is about five hundred families to the northward of Ticonderoga who, if it is evacuated, will be left at the mercy of the King's troops and Indians and who have, part of them, joined the army and cannot now remain neuter." To remove his forces would be "entire ruin, as they have large families and no dependence but a promising crop in the ground." Moreover, he tried to persuade Congress that "Ticonderoga is the key to this extensive country and, if abandoned, leaves a very extensive frontier open to the ravages of the enemy." Mustering troops against "continual alarms" would "probably cost more than the expense of repairing any garrisoning it."[22] Arnold's letter did not reach Congress for eleven days.

Ethan Allen and Benedict Arnold, after a council of war on Arnold's flagship on May 27, agreed on the necessity of attacking Canada while holding the lake. Allen wrote the same day to the Continental Congress, outlining a proposal to attack Montreal or, at least, draw a line of defense *north* of Vermont. If the cannon and the troops were withdrawn to Lake George, as Congress had resolved on May 18, all of settled Vermont lands to the east of the Green Mountains and all of the lands west of the mountains to Lake Champlain would have to be evacuated and left open to British and Indian attack.

By the time the Continental Congress's May 18 resolution reached the Connecticut Committee of Safety in Hartford five days later, revolutionary leaders there had just learned of Arnold's successful—and Ethan Allen's unsuccessful—attack on St. Jean. "The first we greatly rejoice in," William Williams wrote back to Connecticut's delegates in Philadelphia. "As to the latter, we wish it had never been attempted for many reasons. . . . It seems to us and everyone here that it would be of vast importance to retain that important key of Ticonderoga."[23] Connecticut asked "the venerable Congress" in Philadelphia, "our at-present superior legislature,"[24] to reconsider giving up the forts.

Four days later, Major Brown, Arnold's aide, met at Hartford with an emissary from the Massachusetts congress to the Connecticut congress. Colonel Joseph Henshaw sent a now thirdhand communication to Arnold that Connecticut was about to send one thousand militia to reinforce Ticonderoga—under the command of a Connecticut militia officer, Colonel Benjamin Hinman, who was also to command four companies of New York artisans in rebuilding the fort at Ticonderoga. Henshaw's letter, given to Arnold aboard the *Enterprise* on June 9, added that Arnold was "expected to continue with Colonel Allen and put the place in the best posture of defense you are able." Arnold was to be, therefore, in a three-way command with Hinman and Allen, until he "receive[d] further instructions from the Massachusetts Congress."[25] Henshaw had been originally intended to go to Ticonderoga himself, but he was anxious to return to Watertown. Not only had he failed to untangle the confusion over command, but he had disregarded a vital piece of a May 27 resolution by the Massachusetts Committee of Safety, which directed that if Connecticut sent men to garrison Ticonderoga, Massachusetts's Colonel Arnold was to pull out and return to Watertown to "render accounts of his expenses in that expedition in order that he may be honorably discharged."[26]

While Massachusetts back-pedaled and Connecticut pledged to "exert every nerve"[27] to preserve the outposts, the Continental Congress debated northern frontier defense on May 31. Arnold's victory at St. Jean "altered the opinion of Congress," just as Arnold's terse communiqué of May 23 that there were four hundred British regulars at St. Jean "making all possible preparations to cross the lake and expected to be joined by a number of Indians" had led to this emergency debate. Rescinding its May 18 resolution, Congress, worried that New York "may be too slow in raising men,"[28] asked Connecticut to send in the thousand reinforcements. Massachusetts had already begged off, saying that all its available troops were committed to the siege of Boston.

It was this resolution from the Continental Congress that awaited Arnold on June 9 as he sailed south on Lake Champlain to marshal his forces to again assault St. Jean. Congress left it to Connecticut without consultation by New York or Massachusetts to decide the command of the new troops, a fact which must have alarmed Benedict Arnold, especially since the news reached him at the same time as the conflicting June 1 resolution of the Massachusetts provincial congress asking Arnold not to quit.

In the same breath as asking Arnold not to quit and instructing him to finish raising the four hundred men prescribed in his commission to form a regiment, the committee appointed by the provincial congress to oversee the Champlain theater of the war sent off a dispatch to the Connecticut house of assembly that "we have postponed sending further assistance to Captain Arnold."[29] The designation "captain" effectively denied Arnold's commission as colonel by Massachusetts and thereby the legitimacy of his regiment. To Arnold, had he seen it, its meaning would have been clear enough: Massachusetts was washing its hands of the Champlain campaign and Arnold was supposed to revert to the rank of a Connecticut captain. Arnold also did not know that his friend and protector Dr. Warren would no longer be overseeing Arnold's frontier campaign.

On May 20, Dr. Warren, who had until then apparently not specifically outlined Arnold's secret mission to the provincial congress, became its president, and turned the Committee of Safety's affairs over to a new chairman, Dr. Benjamin Church.

One of the highest-ranking Massachusetts revolutionaries, Church was even more important now that the Adamses and John Hancock had gone to Philadelphia to the Continental Congress. Son of the deacon of First Church of Boston, grandson of a famous Indian fighter who had hunted down King Philip while Arnold's great-grandfather presided over Rhode Island, Church seemed as irreproachable as his credentials were impeccable. Educated at Boston Latin and Harvard, where he was classically trained to debate any question dispassionately from either side, he had studied medicine in London and had returned to Boston with an English wife. A gifted man who early became prominent in revolutionary politics, he led a double life. He was one of the civic leaders protesting the Boston Massacre in 1770 and gave a physician's expert deposition after examining the body of Crispus Attucks, the first black casualty of the American Revolution. A member of the Boston Committee of Correspondence, he delivered several key orations. At the same time, however, he is said to have contributed articles to the Loyalist newspaper the *Censor:* his brother-in-law by a second marriage was John Fleming, the pro-British printer. Some other Patriots, such as Paul Revere, suspected that the high-living and adulterous Church, who maintained a mistress in the rooming house where he had lived since the provincial congress had moved out of Boston, had been the informer who furnished the royal governor, Hutchinson, with information from a secret meeting in 1774. But most Patriots continued to trust him, and he served as a delegate to the provincial congress in 1774. He may also have furnished the vital intelligence to the British commander, General Gage, that resulted in the British march to Lexington and Concord in April 1775, for by this time he was evidently on Gage's payroll as an informer. He continued to rise in revolutionary ranks, serving on the province's Committee of Safety, where he was in a position to know of all military espionage and political activities.

On May 16, one month before the Battle of Bunker Hill, Church was chosen by Massachusetts congressional president Warren to take secret correspondence to the Continental Congress, asking the Philadelphia convention to assume control and support of the Massachusetts army. For nearly three months now, Church had been sending Gage letters, some of them in bad French, which gave the enemy the most secret military and political secrets—and his correspondence was so expertly concealed that much of it was not discovered until Gage's papers were opened and studied in the twentieth century. He was sent as a courier to the Continental Congress and was still in Philadelphia, sitting with the Massachusetts delegation, when Congress deliberated what to do about the Lake Champlain problem. When he returned to Massachusetts, he assumed his new duties at the helm of the Committee of Safety. Its former chairman, Dr. Warren, was no longer overseeing Arnold's mission and apparently did not have time to outline to the entire provincial congress just what it was that Arnold was supposed to be doing out on the frontier at the head of a Massachusetts regiment. The energetic Dr. Warren had taken his new office, where he would have been in a position to buttress Arnold's activities had he not also taken over the committee to reorganize the entire American army besieging Boston. Then, on June 14, only a few days after Arnold's return to Crown Point, Dr. Warren also was appointed major general of the Massachusetts militia, which was preparing to entrench and fortify Breed's Hill overlooking the town of Boston, a move that was sure to provoke a British attack. Four days after Arnold dropped anchor at Crown Point, his friend and protector Dr. Warren was preoccupied with moving men and guns to Breed's Hill even as Dr. Church presided over a meeting of the Committee of Safety at Watertown.

While the Continental Congress and three provinces were deliberating on a northern strategy, Ethan Allen and his friends had been taking advantage of the confusion to reassert themselves. While Allen had publicly relinquished command at Ticonderoga on May 27 after all his Boys had returned home, the return of his friend Colonel Easton from Massachusetts with news of the challenge to Arnold's authority apparently rekindled Allen's pretensions to command. Ethan Allen was determined to invade Canada. He had begun hinting, first to Massachusetts, then to the Continental Congress, that if he had two or three thousand men, he could take Montreal. Easton had been hard at work building up Allen's stock in Massachusetts and denigrating Arnold. An article appearing in the May 18 issue of the *New England Chronicle,* datelined Cambridge, tells the tale. "Yesterday Colonel Easton arrived at the Provincial Congress in Watertown from Ticonderoga and brings the glorious news of the taking that place. . . . About 240 men from Connecticut and this province under Colonel Allen and Colonel Easton" had taken the fort. Easton not only took credit for leading Massachusetts troops but described, in the newspaper circulated before the provincial con-

gress and the entire American army, how the men had fought a battle with cutlasses and bayonets and wounded several British soldiers
(he did not mention that most of the garrison were invalids, women,
and children). In Easton's account, "The commanding officer soon
came forth, Colonel Easton clasped him on the shoulder, told him he
was his prisoner and demanded an instant surrender."[30] As the article proceeded, there was no further mention of Ethan Allen and
none of Arnold. There was a long, fictitious dialogue between
Easton and the British commandant, repeatedly mentioning Colonel
Easton, who supposedly had then sent off detachments to capture
Crown Point and Skenesboro and then counted up the cannons he
would send to the rescue of the *Chronicle*'s readers. Easton had also
gotten to tell his story before the provincial congress—just before it
stopped referring to Benedict Arnold as colonel.

Arnold had returned to Crown Point already frustrated by the
Continental Congress's less-than-clearcut orders, but since he had
not received an incontrovertible order *not* to maintain his forward
position on the Canadian frontier, he planned to march every man
he could spare aboard ships for a quick return to the north. At
Crown Point, however, he found that there was an unauthorized
council of war taking place in his office without him—one called by
Ethan Allen at the urging of Colonel Easton. The day before, Allen
had, quite publicly, made known his plan to attack Canada at the
head of any army (whose was unclear) and had dispatched one of
Arnold's soldiers to the Massachusetts congress, requesting two or
three thousand men to be led by "intrepid commanders"—he hinted
that he and Easton would fit that billing. He also pointed out that
his attack would act as a diversion to draw off British troops from
Boston and have the "unspeakable advantage in directing the war
into Canada." His scheme, he contended, would be nicely rewarded
"by gaining the sovereignty of Canada." Allen had also, without
authorization by Arnold, been sending messages to Montreal,
appealing to pro-American English merchants there to send him,
personally, munitions and money to help him mount a campaign.

Late in the afternoon of June 10, as Arnold sailed into the narrows approaching Crown Point, Allen, to the amazement of Arnold's garrison, had summoned the council of war, the prerogative
only of a commanding officer. Eighteen officers were present: Ethan
Allen, his brother, Ira, and his cousin, Captain Remember Baker,
Easton, Major Samuel Elmore of Connecticut, Seth Warner, Captain
James Noble (the man Arnold had left in charge at Crown Point),
and a dozen of Arnold's company commanders, lieutenants, and
commissaries. Allen had persuaded Major Elmore, the ranking of-

ficer present, to convene and preside over the meeting. After laying out his plan of attack, Allen then convinced the officers that they should send him at the head of a delegation to the Continental Congress. The resolution Allen had drafted declared him and the other officers present "in possession of Ticonderoga and Crown Point." Allen's wording was, at the least, deceptive: he claimed that three hundred British regulars were "entrenching upon the Grants near this place." Supposedly, this meant on the Vermont shore, but in fact no one had found redcoats nearer than St. Jean, more than one hundred miles away. Allen wanted to put five hundred of his Boys on someone's payroll, and even he must have blushed at his third-person nomination. "Colonel Allen has behaved, in this affair, very singularly remarkable for his courage, and we must, in duty, recommend him to you and the whole continent."[31]

Benedict Arnold arrived near the end of the meeting and evidently did not interrupt it, but he was furious. Allen and Easton had actually gone on record as "in possession" of the forts. Once again as they had before attacking Ticonderoga, they had trumped up a council to write them orders, and then had sent off the proceedings to the Continental Congress! Arnold tensely summarized his reaction to the episode in the regimental memorandum book:

Colonel Allen, Col. Easton and Major Elmore had called a council of their officers and others not belonging to my regiment. I sent for Major Elmore, who excused himself. On which I wrote the council that I could not, consistently with my duty, suffer any illegal councils, meetings, etc., as they tended to raise a mutiny. That I was at present the only legal commanding officer and should not suffer my commands to be disputed, but would willingly give up the command whenever anyone appeared with proper authority to take it. This had the desired effect and they gave up their expectation of commanding.

Arnold rowed out to the *Enterprise* that night. He did not run the risk of being seized by Allen and his men. Because he was the only skilled gunner, and his ship's officers were all accustomed to naval discipline, they remained loyal to him. The next morning, Sunday, June 11, 1775, Arnold "went on shore early and gave orders to have the guards doubled to prevent any mutiny or disorder." The would-be mutiny had collapsed, and Ethan Allen was only interested in getting away from Crown Point as quickly as he could, without giving up his pretensions. The next morning, Allen, Major Elmore, Easton, and several officers of the Boys climbed into a bateau and "attempted passing the sloop without showing their pass"—a pass signed by Arnold. This was a calculated slap at Arnold, who was on the deck of the *Enterprise*. Captain Sloan of the *Enterprise* responded by ordering Allen's boat to come about and return to shore until it showed the proper paper. Arnold was insisting on his orders. He returned to the fort and had Major Elmore brought to him for a "private discourse." Elmore quickly explained that he had been sent by Connecticut with four hundred troops to reinforce Ticonderoga and that Ethan Allen was trying to commandeer them to lead on an attack on Canada. At this point, as Elmore explained what had happened, Easton brushed past the guard on Arnold's door and stalked into Arnold's office. It was a serious breach of military decorum, but, more than that, it deeply offended Arnold that this coarse, loud-mouthed tavernkeeper should barge in on a private conversation between two officers and then go so far as to insult Arnold in front of a fellow officer. There is no record of what Easton said. It probably had something to do with Arnold's refusing to let them leave the base, but whatever it was, all Arnold's anger at Ethan Allen and frustration over the past month's provocations brimmed over. As he put it in his memo book, "I took the liberty of breaking his head." Not quite literally, but evidently Arnold, completely losing his temper, drew his sword and cracked Easton over the head with the flat of its blade, demanding that Easton, whom he considered a coward, fight a duel with him. "On refusing to draw like a gentleman, he having a hanger [sword] by his side and cases of loaded pistols in his pockets, I kicked him very heartily and ordered him from the Point."[32]

The weeks of strain were clearly showing as Arnold, however understandably, threw away his usual composure and himself committed a serious breach of decorum and military propriety by striking an officer in the presence of subordinates. But Arnold himself remained unrepentant about the incident and wrote that it was to "the satisfaction of a number of gentlemen present." Later, when Arnold was shown the *Chronicle* crediting Easton with the capture of the lake forts, Arnold sent off a letter to the *Chronicle* signed "Veritas" which exposed Easton's part in the expedition as grossly exaggerated, accused him of cowering in the bushes at Ticonderoga until the danger had passed, and said he had often been heard abusing Arnold behind his back "in a base and cowardly manner" while, to Arnold's face, he was "always very complaisant."[33]

To make matters worse for Arnold, not only had he lost control in front of several officers, but his plan to return to the Canadian frontier was all but dashed by the interference of yet another political committee, the Albany Committee of Safety. Supine and unwilling to help for a month, the Albany revolutionaries had, at this critical moment, decided to pull back their men to Ticonderoga, in effect reviving Ethan Allen's commission. With Allen and the New Yorkers leaving on the same day for Ticonderoga, it appeared that there was a connection between Arnold's treatment of Easton and the withdrawal of the New York troops. In fact, the Albany committee was still following the Continental Congress's advice of May 18 and was pulling back all of its men from Crown Point and Ticonderoga to Fort George. More bad news came the next day, even as Arnold faced the fact that, temporarily, at least, he could not return to St. Jean. As he sent off a five-man scout to the north and put his men to work on extending the earthworks, another letter arrived from the Albany committee, pulling out a second company of men.

Since it was obvious that only the Continental Congress could countermand its own orders, Arnold decided to send Lieutenant Colonel Oswald to Philadelphia with a detailed summary of intelligence he had gathered and his own analysis and suggestions for a northern strategy that included an attack in force into Canada before massive reinforcements could arrive from Boston or England. It was also the first time Arnold revealed how broadly he had interpreted his secret orders, especially using Indians to find out the intentions of Canadian tribes. Shrewdly, Arnold led off with good news. The Caughnawagas, according to his Indian interpreter, Hoit, had consulted "with some gentlemen of my acquaintance" in Montreal. "The Indians are determined not to assist the King's troops against us," Arnold assured Congress, "and have made a law that, if any one of their tribe shall take up arms for that purpose, he shall immediately be put to death. This is confirmed by five of their chief men, who are now here with their wives and children and press very hard for our army to march into Canada, being much disgusted with the British regulars." It was the first time Arnold revealed outside the Lake Champlain region the extent of his secret negotiations with the Indians. "Three Stockbridge Indians, whom I lately sent to them with a belt of wampum and speech, confirm the above."

Arnold had established contact with an American merchant in Montreal who had written Arnold that the Indians were remaining neutral and that, moreover, "great numbers" of Canadians "are very impatient" for an American expedition into Canada. "They are determined to join us whenever we appear in the country with a proper force to support them." Arnold reported that during his incursion to Isle aux Noix, he had talked to many Canadians eager to join him if he attacked *quickly*. "Governor Carleton, by every artifice, has been able to raise only about twenty Canadians," and these were the old French gentry, "those of the noblesse who are in expectation of places of honor." Many other Canadians feared provoking the Americans or were sympathetic to their cause. According to Arnold, Carleton "is now in Montreal and has threatened the English merchants that if they will not defend it in case of an attack, he will set fire to the city and retreat to Quebec." Arnold also gave Congress a detailed breakdown of British forces in Canada obtained by interception of a British dispatch boat: only 370 redcoats were between him and Quebec.

"From my personal knowledge of the country" and from the "disposition of the Canadians," Arnold assured Congress that if it decided to "take possession of Montreal and Quebec," all of Canada would fall to two thousand well-armed and disciplined Americans. Boldly, he laid out a plan of attack. With seventeen hundred men he would sail for St. Jean, landing one thousand men to cut off communications while seven hundred held the lake. The gates of Montreal would be opened by friends of America. To take Canada, Arnold urged Congress, would discourage Tories from carrying on a civil war, because they could not expect British reinforcements from the north and would have no haven to escape to. Because there were large quantities of arms and supplies already in Canada, an invasion actually was economical, as it would cost less than repairing the single fort of Ticonderoga, which it would make unnecessary. Furthermore, it would make warfare more difficult and expensive for England, which had come to depend on the half million bushels of cheap wheat exported from Canada to the British Isles every year, and it would also deprive England of the lucrative fur trade. In a final paragraph listing the supplies and men he would need for the expedition, Arnold added: "no Green Mountain Boys." Although often tactless, in this case Arnold took pains not to tread on the delicate prerogative of the Continental Congress: "I hope the exigency of the times, and my zeal in the service of my country, will apologize for the liberty of giving my sentiments so freely, on a subject which the Honorable Congress are doubtless the best judges of, but which they in their hurry may not have paid that attention to which the matter requires." Only haste could explain to Arnold Congress's foolhardy recommendation to give up Lake Champlain.

Arnold's plan was clear, detailed, and based on generally accurate intelligence. Its success depended, unfortunately, on a prompt and forceful decision from the Continental Congress. If Congress had moved at once and authorized Arnold to strike before Quebec's Governor Carleton could be reinforced, Arnold's plan to conquer all

of Canada with a few thousand men very likely would have succeeded. As it was, Congress was divided on defensive versus offensive war and chronically distracted. As Arnold's aide arrived in
Philadelphia, news of a bloody battle outside Boston had just arrived. Three precious months were lost before Congress, without acknowledging Arnold's authorship, fully adopted his plan. In offering
his services at the head of the invasion force, Arnold was so confident that he was right and that the Continental Congress would
agree that he had gone ahead and given Oswald a list of supplies he
would need to take to Canada. He ended his long letter to Congress
with an impassioned plea which sets forth some of his long-range
thinking:

*The American colonies in general are equally in danger from Can-
ada, whether it remain in the hands of the English under the present
form of its government or should be restored to the French, which
many suspect is intended by the Ministry in England. But, should
Canada be placed under a free government agreeable to the English
Constitution, like the other colonies, we should forever after be secure from any danger that way.[34]*

Along with this bold plan, Arnold sent a second document to the
Continental Congress which shows not only his broad-based support among New Yorkers he was protecting, but his own ideology
and character as a young revolutionary. Long lost, it was recently
discovered in the archives of Fort Ticonderoga. Arnold's Declaration
of Principles antedated the Declaration of Independence by more
than a year. It was signed inside the rebuilt fort at Crown Point on
June 15, 1775, by thirty-two leading "freeholders, freemen and inhabitants of the province of New York," including the owner of a
thirty-thousand-acre wilderness estate, the captains of Arnold's New
York militia companies, a boatwright, a ship's carpenter, an Albany
revolutionary committeeman, and, first to sign, its author himself,
Benedict Arnold. Arnold's 236-word declaration did not call for independence from England but indicated that New Yorkers were
holding the cannon captured at the forts as a precaution against
their use by the British, just as seizure of the forts was intended to
protect the inhabitants from depredations in the area by British soldiers and their Indian allies. The declaration petitioned Congress for
reconciliation with the mother country, once the British learned that
their American colonists were determined "never to become slaves."
The keynote of Arnold's declaration was that the "salvation of the
rights and liberties of America depends, under God, on the firm

union of its inhabitants in a vigorous prosecution of the measures necessary for its safety." Arnold and his fellow declaimants were also "convinced of the necessity of preventing the anarchy and confusion which attend a dissolution of the powers of governments" as much as they were "alarmed at the avowed design of the British Ministry to raise a revenue in America." Orderly American legislatures should govern the American colonies themselves without encroachment by the British Parliament and its taxgatherers. Forming a general association "under all the ties of religion, honor and love to our country," the freemen at Crown Point swore to adopt and uphold any measures recommended by the Continental Congress or the New York provincial congress "for the purpose of preserving our Constitution"—and by this they meant the English Constitution—by opposing "the execution of the several arbitrary and oppressive acts of the British Parliament." They vowed to fight on "until a reconciliation between Great Britain and America on Constitutional principles."[35]

On June 15, 1775, Arnold sent Lieutenant Colonel Oswald off to Philadelphia with his plan to attack Canada and the declaration. That very day, the Continental Congress appointed George Washington of Virginia as commander in chief of the American army and sent him north toward Boston. It would be months before Washington, building an army from the chaos he found in Massachusetts in the aftermath of the bloody battle of Breed's Hill, could turn his attention to Canada, the northern frontier, or Benedict Arnold.

Despite the June 1 plea of the Massachusetts provincial congress that Arnold banish any thought of resigning his command, its Committee of Safety, under its new chairman, Dr. Church, was busily undermining Arnold's position in a series of actions that had begun with the dispatch of Colonel Henshaw to Connecticut. If Connecticut's house of assembly was ready to take over the forts, Henshaw was to proceed to Ticonderoga and advise Arnold to turn over his command to Trumbull's designee. Henshaw's orders were complicated and contingent, perhaps even calculated to create confusion. Dr. Church may have known that Trumbull and Parsons were committed to Ethan Allen and his faction and were extremely unlikely to appoint Allen's rival to permanent command. Henshaw was told that if the Connecticut assembly had not sent officers and men to Ticonderoga, he was to tell Arnold to stay on. Meeting with Connecticut leaders, Henshaw learned that Trumbull had opened up a third possibility by sending a delegation to Albany, to ask New York's revolutionaries to assume responsibility for its own forts. The confusion was only compounded by Arnold's abortive May 23 warning that the British were about to attack down the lake. New York was less than thrilled at the prospect of having to assume responsibility for the Massachusetts-Connecticut attack on royal forts or its territory and only wanted to make sure that the cannon and supplies remained in New York and were not sent on to Boston. Colonel Henshaw simply sent a note off to Arnold with his aide, Major Jonathan Brown, and rode back to Massachusetts. Major Brown delivered Henshaw's letter to Arnold aboard *Enterprise* on June 9. Arnold was to continue "guarding against any surprise from the enemy." He would later "receive further directions from the Congress."[36] To Arnold, Henshaw's note could only have meant, in the light of all other conflicting orders and recommendations from all directions, that he had not, for the moment at least, been superseded. Henshaw gave no hint that an investigative committee had been formed and was on its way to Crown Point, if indeed he knew it. He probably also had left Hartford before he learned that Massachusetts had formally bailed out of the frontier war with an apology to New York and turned over its soldiers to the only colony that seemed willing to fight in the backcountry—Connecticut.

On June 4, Henshaw was back in Watertown, Massachusetts, with word that one thousand Connecticut troops were on the march to Ticonderoga. That same day, Ethan Allen's initial version of his seizure of Ticonderoga a month earlier was brought before his committee by Dr. Church, along with Easton's various accounts and his petition to be made colonel over all Massachusetts troops on the frontier. Church could point to Henshaw's news that Colonel Benjamin Hinman, appointed by General David Wooster, Arnold's nemesis from New Haven, had been commissioned by Connecticut to lead Connecticut militia to Ticonderoga as if it were Connecticut's decision to replace Arnold with Hinman. In fact, Connecticut's Governor Trumbull only intended Hinman and his troops to serve *alongside* Arnold and the Massachusetts troops until the Continental Congress appointed an overall commander. But the clever Dr. Church apparently convinced the beleaguered Massachusetts congress that Trumbull wanted his own appointee in command. Many Massachusetts revolutionaries considered the Ticonderoga campaign an embarrassing and bothersome sideshow. With Dr. Warren preoccupied with preparing for what was an imminent battle at Boston, Dr. Church had a clear field for intrigue. By June 12, acting on a recommendation from Dr. Church's Committee of Safety, the full Massachusetts congress had been persuaded to elect an investigative committee "to repair to the fortress of Ticonderoga" with sweeping authority not only to "carefully observe" how Benedict Arnold "has executed his Commission and instructions," but to give him "such orders as to you shall seem meet." In other words, a civilian committee of the provincial congress was to take virtual command *over* Arnold after he turned over his post to "such chief officer as is or shall be appointed by Connecticut." Further, the three elected revolutionary politicians—Walter Spooner, Jedediah Foster, and James Sullivan—were authorized to decide if Arnold was to be allowed to continue in Massachusetts's pay based on their investigation into his "spirit, capacity and conduct," and if they decided, they could act as a tribunal that could "discharge the said Arnold" and "direct him to return to this colony and render his account."[37] Lastly, the committee had the power to appoint replacements for Arnold or any uncooperative officers. The committee's orders, to be shown to Arnold, read like an indictment.

Benedict Arnold, waiting for clearance from the Continental Congress to invade Canada, still had no hint of the precariousness of his position. He was preoccupied with the latest reports from St. Jean and from Montreal and worried that precious days were being lost as the British entrenched and negotiated with the Indians and French Canadians, making attack more difficult and potentially freeing British troops to attack Crown Point and also Ticonderoga. On June 20, Arnold recorded, "This day lined out an entrenchment across the Point where I propose mounting fifteen nine-pounders, which secured the redoubt and an encampment for two thousand men." The old fort was abuzz with construction, as Arnold's high-spirited men worked on fortifications, ships, a new guardhouse, barracks, wheels for cannon. On June 21, three Connecticut companies arrived to reinforce Crown Point. The next day, Arnold noted, "Arrived here three gentlemen from the Provincial Congress of Massachusetts Bay."[38]

Arnold's first hint that his command was being challenged had come abruptly a few days before when six hundred more reinforcements from Connecticut had arrived in response to his warning of an imminent British attack. On Friday, June 16, Connecticut's Colonel Hinman arrived at Crown Point and was rowed out to the *Enterprise,* where he was presented to Arnold, who was taken aback by Hinman's matter-of-fact demand that Arnold turn over the command of the lake and all its forts and ships to him. When Arnold recovered himself, he brushed aside Hinman's orders, arguing that they merely paralleled his own, and that Hinman was only in charge of his own troops and subservient to him, Arnold, as overall commander by virtue of his being the senior officer by date of commission on the scene and also by virtue of the fact that Arnold had received no positive order from Massachusetts to turn over the command. Hinman, no expert in the military law that Arnold invoked, quietly left the ship. Arnold no doubt learned at this time that Hinman's commission came from the man Governor Trumbull had appointed as Connecticut's brigadier general with overall responsibility for the frontier troops, David Wooster of New Haven, the very man Benedict Arnold had confronted over the keys to the powder magazine little more than two months earlier.

On Thursday, June 22, the three Massachusetts investigators arrived at Crown Point. To Arnold, it was just another delegation of politicians visiting the troops, possibly bringing some money for back pay. Nothing prepared him for the confrontation aboard *Enterprise*. Arnold was told to step down at once as commander and informed that if he wished to remain in charge of the Massachusetts militia, it would have to be as second-in-command to Hinman of Connecticut. Arnold flatly refused. He would resign first, Arnold told them. There was no attempt at negotiation between the red-faced Arnold and the tight-lipped representatives from Watertown. Later that same day, Arnold received a brief note from Walter Spooner, committee chairman: "It is the expectation of the provincial Congress that the chief officer of the Connecticut forces at these stations will command. . . . You will conform yourself to the directions of said Congress." He was to turn his troops over to Hinman and then—the final slap—"lay an account of your disbursements before the Provincial Congress."[39]

Still, Arnold had not formally resigned. He ordered the committee off his ship and retired to his cabin. It was obvious he could not accept the terms of the committee, that not only his own but all the commissions of his officers would be subverted by the utter disregard for rank and seniority implicit in his new orders. That night, with the detailed indictment of the Massachusetts congress before him, he drafted a long letter to the Massachusetts committee. To "examine my conduct," in such a forum, without a hearing or court-martial proceeding, especially at that time and under those conditions, he considered "unprecedented." The committee's instruction from the congress, moreover, contained "a very plain intimation that the Congress are dubious of my rectitude or abilities, which is a sufficient inducement for me to decline serving them longer." But beyond his command, Arnold found it deeply insulting that "the Congress have authorized you to judge my spirit, capacity and conduct." The time to judge if an officer was fit was *before* he was commissioned, he urged, and not afterward, and then not by such a committee. And then to appoint a junior officer over him after all that he had conquered "plainly indicates the loss of Congress's confidence." The whole manner of the drumhead proceeding was "a most disgraceful reflection on him and the body of troops he commands" and was "a sufficient inducement to resign."

In addition, a careful reading of the congressional instruction indicated to Arnold that only troops still fit for duty were to be transferred to Connecticut's muster rolls and paid off by Massachusetts. There had been "very great hardships" among his men, digging and hauling and rowing and fighting in the hot, bug-infested valley for nearly two months. "By sickness or hard labor, they are reduced and not fit for service and of course do not pass muster." Were they now to lose "their former time and service and be reduced to the distress of begging their bread until they can get home to their friends?" It was on this note, the failure of Massachusetts to discharge its obligations honorably to him as well as to his men, that Arnold finished his letter of resignation. He had asked the Congress for money and had received only £100 to keep an army in the field for two months. He had advanced another £1,000 of his own cash and borrowed money on his word to pay his men when it became necessary. This had put him in a terrible financial bind. "My own credit is at stake and I am reduced to the necessity of leaving the place with dishonor or wait until I can send home and discharge those debts out of my private purse, which I am determined to do."[40]

Benedict Arnold not only disbanded his regiment on June 24, 1775—six weeks after storming Ticonderoga—but he resigned his Massachusetts commission. Had he not, all of his officers and men would have been put under the command of not only the timid Hinman but the new colonel of the Massachusetts regiment that Spooner and company had waiting in the wings: Colonel James Easton, the boastful tavernkeeper, with his friend Squire Brown of Pittsfield as second-in-command.

To Benedict Arnold's growing disgust, many of his recruits, faced with the alternatives of being mustered into Colonel Easton's reformed regiment or being left penniless hundreds of miles from home, reenlisted under Easton. The gloomy Arnold went aboard the sloop *Enterprise* at noon and went to his cabin to dine and then gather his books and papers and make a final entry in the memo book of his disbanded regiment. It was the longest entry and most abject:

Applied to the committee from the Massachusetts Bay for cash to pay off the regiment, which they refused. I am reduced to great extremity, not being able to pay off the people who are in great want of necessary's, and much in debt. This gives me much trouble to pacify them to prevent disorders.

Soon he was interrupted: a minority of his men, he was informed by Captain Sloan of *Enterprise,* including the officers and crews of his ships, refused to submit to Hinman and Easton and demanded to be paid off. This was not just a threat. They would simply up anchor and return the ships to their former owners—the British. When Arnold told the men he could not pay them, the men locked him in his cabin. They were apologetic but explained they must be paid and, while they meant him no harm, they did not want him to interfere. Then, according to Arnold's record of this incipient mutiny, they "sent a boat after the Committee from the Congress, who had left this place for Ticonderoga about three hours before."[41]

At four that afternoon, a boat arrived from Ticonderoga with five barrels of pork and five of flour for the mutineers, an attempt by the committee to pacify them. They were to be allowed to cook meat and bake bread to take on the long trudge home. That evening, two Connecticut militia officers, Captains Sheldon and Bigelow, came on board *Enterprise* with the sobering news that thousands of colonists had been killed in a battle at Breed's Hill near Boston. New York and Connecticut magistrates friendly to Arnold joined the Massachusetts committeemen and also came aboard late that night to talk to the mutineers. A compromise was negotiated. The Massachusetts committee pledged that their congress would honor all claims for back pay after a formal hearing in Watertown. In the meanwhile, Benedict Arnold issued his own promissory notes for the men's back pay and out-of-pocket expenses until he could travel to Massachusetts to confront Dr. Church's committee.

As events in the next several months proved, Benedict Arnold had been successful far beyond his own expectations. He had at age thirty-four—only a year older than Thomas Jefferson and ten years younger than Washington—emerged in the opening weeks of the war as a skillful and bold officer who led his men by his own courageous example. He was already the best field commander in the war on either side, and he knew it; he was able to fight on land or sea, able to plan strategy, logistics, fortifications, gather intelligence. He had helped to take two of Britain's most valuable fortresses, capture and arm a flotilla, deprive the British of communications or control of a vast frontier region, pin down half the troops in Canada, neutralize Indian adversaries. Only three days after Arnold resigned, the Continental Congress, clearly influenced by Arnold's proposals on Canada, authorized Major General Philip Schuyler to put together a northern army and, recognizing the importance of the Canadian frontier war, created a separate Northern Department under this rich and influential New Yorker.

As former Colonel Arnold passed through Albany, Schuyler welcomed him and treated him with deference, asking him to take the time to sit down and write his own analysis of conditions around Lake Champlain for the Continental Congress. The tall, regal Schuyler, head of one of New York's great landowning families, impressed Arnold with his understanding of the importance of order and discipline in time of war. Schuyler's New York constituents were shocked by Arnold's removal. Five hundred of them had signed an address of appreciation for Arnold's military efforts and for his protection of their homes and property from the British, the Indians, and the Green Mountain Boys, sending it off to the Continental Congress. Arnold's terse summary, written at Albany on July 11, spurred Congress to act:

When I left Crown Point, there were at that post near three hundred men, without employ, having received no orders to fortify. . . . At Ticonderoga, about six hundred in the same state. . . . At Fort George, upwards of three hundred men, some few employed in building bateaux and on scouting parties. Very little provision. . . . None made for the sick, which are daily increasing . . . only five hundred weight of gunpowder . . . no engineer or gunner. . . . Great want of discipline and regularity among the troops. . . . On the other hand, the enemy of St. [Jean] indefatigable in fortifying and collecting timber for building vessels.[42]

General Schuyler was so impressed by Arnold that he asked Arnold to serve as adjutant general for the new Northern Department of the Army.

But Arnold wanted to go home, straighten out his financial affairs, put together his records, and go to Massachusetts to clear his name of the Spooner committee's ugly implications. He knew he had loyal supporters—Schuyler, Silas Deane, his own officers and men, the people around Crown Point—but he could not stand the idea, even, that there were people laughing, and lying, about him. He did not yet know of Dr. Church's treachery nor that his friend and protector Dr. Warren was dead, shot in the face as he led the Massachusetts rear guard out of a deathtrap of a fort atop Breed's Hill during the Battle of Bunker Hill on June 17. Tired, broke, suffering from an acute attack of gout in his right foot, Arnold received one more blow, the news that on June 19, as a cold north wind had lashed his ships on Lake Champlain and a Massachusetts committee rode west to fire him, his thirty-year-old wife, Margaret Mansfield Arnold, had died suddenly and without any known cause. Even as word reached New Haven that the war was far from over and was indeed worsening, Arnold, left with three boys under the age of eight and his personal life in ruins, rode home to Connecticut.

6

"THE CANADIANS WILL BE PLEASED"

Come then, ye generous citizens,
range yourselves under the standard
of General Liberty, against which all
the force and artifice of tyranny will
never be able to prevail.

General George Washington's Manifesto to the Inhabitants
of Canada, September 1775

The summer of 1775 had turned into a grim interlude in the life of Benedict Arnold, his first command ending in shambles, his first wife, so long disapproving and incommunicative, dying, his business career interrupted by a war that made his enterprises almost impossible. When Arnold returned home, he found that his sister, Hannah, had already stepped in as the head of his house in his absence, helping to bury his wife, solacing the grieving Mansfields next door, uncomplainingly assuming all the burdens of running Arnold's big house, and, most of all, taking charge of raising his three sons, aged seven, six, and three.

Within four days of Margaret Arnold's death, Hannah had enrolled the two older boys, Benedict and Richard, in a school in New Haven and was turning her hand to salvaging her brother's business affairs. One West India brig was groaning at its moorings off Water

Street wharf with no cargo and no crew. Hannah lined up the sale of sixty thousand barrel hoops and staves and had them ready for her brother to purchase as soon as he arrived home. It was a wise choice of cargo, one that would fetch badly needed cash and could not be seized for smuggling. Only weeks before the outbreak of fighting, Arnold had dispatched one brig, the *Polly*, with a cargo of lumber to Barbados, giving its captain orders to "buy rum or get cash—I would prefer the latter."[1] Another of Arnold's brigs, the *Peggy*, was probably already lost to the British: it had been on its way to Quebec when the fighting broke out and no doubt was seized by the British authorities there when they discovered that its owner was the man who had been seizing their ships.

All that Benedict Arnold could do at first was to listen gratefully to Hannah as he sat numb and aching and looked out over the harbor. In addition to gout, his malaria from the West Indies had flared up again in the swamps of the Champlain Valley. Yet by July 26, less than three weeks after he had returned home, Arnold said goodbye to Hannah and the boys and rode north again to face the Massachusetts congress and then get back into the war. The invasion of Canada was *his* idea, and even if Massachusetts had forced him to resign and the Continental Congress had given the Northern Army to Philip Schuyler, he was not about to be kept away. Schuyler had kindly offered him the post of adjutant general. But Arnold did not want a desk job. He wanted a fresh commission in the field. Furthermore, he had found a copy of a British army engineer's journal and his map and was outlining a plan to slip into Canada and surprise the British. He was on his way to Cambridge to tell George Washington about it.

Just when it was that Benedict Arnold first heard of John Montresor's 1760 march from Quebec to the coast of Maine is a matter for speculation, but it may have been as long before as the event itself. Arnold had made his first trip to Quebec in 1759 to take a shipload of medical supplies to the British army besieging Quebec for his employer, Dr. Lathrop, who had the surgical-supplies franchise for the British. He had also sailed along the coast of Maine just about every year to the St. Lawrence, and it is easy to picture him looking into the mouth of the Kennebec River and wishing there were a shortcut. People in Maine had known about the old Indian route up the Kennebec and down the Chaudière River to within four miles of Quebec since the French Jesuits had used it a century earlier, and French-led Abenaki Indians had followed it in their birchbark canoes in the late seventeenth century to strike the English settlements around Penobscot Bay. Arnold knew Abenakis who had made the journey, and he might have known a young military engineer named Montresor who had been at the British siege of Quebec. Arnold had gotten to know many of the British establishment in America during his travels, and at some point he had obtained a copy of Montresor's handwritten journal of two trips through the wilderness from Quebec to the Maine coast and back. When Arnold arrived in Cambridge in early August, he reported to Washington's headquarters and was ushered into the office of the new adjutant general, Horatio Gates. Arnold told Gates that he had come to offer his services and had a plan of the utmost secrecy that he wished to present to General Washington. It seems that Arnold didn't tell Gates or anyone else his idea for an attack on Quebec until he told Washington about August 15.

Soon Gates was ushering Arnold in to see tall, stoop-shouldered George Washington, who had arrived to take command at Cambridge only a month earlier and found a ragtag army living in terrible conditions, with about seventeen thousand men (nobody knew exactly how many) living in shanty towns of huts made of sod, planks, and fencerails or tents made of linen or sailcloth. Most men wore the clothes they had on when they left home, homespun breeches, rough linen shirts, and leather vests. They carried the family firelock, and were as worried about food for their families back home as about fighting the British. All of his time Washington had spent in throwing up defenses: where scores of men had been digging trenches and earthworks, hauling timbers, and planting pointed trees at the enemy, thousands were now put to work. There were no trained sergeants and few experienced officers to teach his troops the myriad details and routines of military life and to impose discipline and order. Washington not only ordered his officers to crack down on unsoldierly practices but made courts-martial, cashierings, drummings out of camp, and floggings the grim commonplaces of daily life until he had purged from the camps all officers and men he considered unsoldierly. Washington had been shocked to find British and American officers and soldiers talking to each other on the lines, shocked at instances of cowardice by American officers under fire in the Battle of Bunker Hill, of insubordination. He insisted on precise discipline, forbade cursing, swearing, and drunkenness, required punctual attendance at daily worship, neatness among unlisted men and officers, the best possible sanitation. He imposed severe sanctions for infractions, especially for theft and straggling from camp. Each day, the men were formed up to witness floggings of wrongdoers, from a commonplace thirty-nine lashes to as many as five hundred.

The greatest problem facing Washington was finding officers to lead his men. As he had told the Massachusetts congress even before seeing his army, he firmly believed that all the deficiencies of his troops could be made up by the activity and zeal of his officers. Washington was already struggling to put together a continental general staff to replace the haphazard militia system. The officers closest to him were of the patrician breed he knew and trusted. Washington immediately had run into serious difficulties with the New England officers he and his staff had superseded. A Virginia aristocrat, he saw New England's spirit of leveling democracy as part of the difficulty. He found "an unaccountable kind of stupidity in the lower class of these people" which "prevails but too generally among the officers."[2] Washington saw himself, and the British saw him, as the Oliver Cromwell of the American Revolution. Like Cromwell, he saw the struggle as a civil war with the virtuous American colonies oppressed by a corrupt ministry in the service of an errant king. He was a member of the aggrieved squirearchy, like Cromwell, and also of the Continental Congress, which, like Cromwell's Parliament, opposed the ministry and its army by putting its own powerful army in the field to force reforms. But also, like Cromwell, Washington saw that the army, including its generals, must be subservient to the wishes of the elected politicians: the people voted for the congressional delegates, not for him as general. As one of those representatives he had helped to create Congress's Continental Army, and he never failed to remember his own subordination to that Congress.

Washington and Arnold had much in common. Classically educated, both men had made a thorough study of modern European warfare. They had observed the British army at close range and understood its weaknesses in fighting a war thousands of transatlantic miles from supply bases in an age of wooden ships, slow communications, widespread political corruption, and erratic logistics. They displayed familiarity with the latest European battle theories, which called for rigid discipline that enabled the use of massed firepower at close range. Both understood, too, the relationship of the highest technology to the aristocratic code of their times, a patrician order governed by the elite, ruled in war by an officer class which insisted on rank, order, and discipline and emphasized leadership by personal example. Most of all, they were daring soldiers by inclination, and they sensed and admired this trait in others.

For several days, Arnold briefed Washington on conditions on the southern border of Quebec Province as he had left it. He told him of the eagerness of Montreal merchants to cooperate in an

American invasion that would help them to oust Carleton and the French seigneurs from power. He stressed that the French Canadians wanted to join the Americans but dared not until there was an American army inside Canada to protect them from the British. Time was the most urgent consideration: unless the Americans moved quickly, they risked not only the arrival of a massive British reinforcement but the disenchantment of the French habitants. Arnold also underscored the fact that Governor Carleton was down to six hundred redcoats in all of Canada, and had shifted at least half of them to St. Jean. In addition, another one-fourth of the regulars had been shifted south to the string of French posts at Montreal, at Sorel where the Richelieu River empties into the St. Lawrence, and at Chambly, twelve miles north of St. Jean. This meant that only a few dozen redcoats could be left at Quebec, the capital city and the key to all of Canada. A quick thrust at Quebec from the *north* not only would force Carleton to draw off men from St. Jean and Montreal but could bring about the surrender of Quebec without a fight. Arnold had in mind an attack on Quebec with a thousand picked men: men who were trained to handle boats to get them up the Kennebec, down the Chaudière, and across the St. Lawrence, men who were used to fighting in the woods, to moving quickly, and, most of all, to following orders. A thousand shock troops appearing suddenly outside an undefended Quebec far behind the British lines at St. Jean would encourage the already sympathetic inhabitants to surrender. If Arnold had succeeded, he would have made Canada the fourteenth American state. Arnold and Washington agreed on the importance of seizing and neutralizing Canada before it could serve for the British as it always had for the French, as a staging area for invasions down river valleys and lakes into New England and New York. Both leaders could also see that to add Quebec Province to the rebellious colonies—an area at that time containing one-third of modern-day Canada as well as the present states of Illinois, Ohio, Indiana, Wisconsin, and Michigan—would be to more than double the land area of the new American nation.

Arnold's bold plan called for a surprise attack on Quebec through a pathless wilderness where only a few men in canoes had ever been before. And, Arnold assured him, there was still time to strike before the early Canadian winter set in. The lateness of the season was even an advantage. It would dissuade the British from attempting to send reinforcements on ships that could become icebound. By August 20, Washington had endorsed Arnold's diversion in force, appointed him a colonel in the Continental Army to remove him from the vagaries of provincial politics, offered him his pick of one thousand men from the Continental forces blockading Boston, and told Gates to give him whatever he needed.

Washington made only three stipulations. Canadians must be treated as fellow Americans making a common cause against British oppressors. Arnold must clear himself of the charges against him and account to the Massachusetts provincial congress so that he would leave Massachusetts's service with a clean slate. And if Arnold succeeded in linking forces with Schuyler's army, moving up from the south, he was to put aside his own independent command and subordinate himself in the chain of command under Schuyler. For this last reason, Washington would not authorize and approve Arnold's mission until Schuyler approved it in writing. Since Washington had already been authorized by Congress to launch an attack against Canada if the Canadians wanted it, he did not again specifically ask Congress's permission for Arnold's attack. To ask Congress would risk rejection of a plan already covered by Washington's general authority from Congress, could add weeks of delay, and would take the risk that spies in Philadelphia would inform the British. Washington wanted to draft a proclamation to the citizens of Canada for Arnold to take with him and distribute. And while Arnold was appearing before Dr. Church's committee, Washington was to write a letter to Philip Schuyler at Ticonderoga informing him of their new plans for Canada. Neither Washington nor Arnold foresaw that it would take a month, a crucial month at the end of a Canadian summer, before Philip Schuyler replied.

If he had not already been given an independent command to attack the largest city in Canada, Benedict Arnold might have been disappointed to have to go before Dr. Church's committee and answer for spending his own money to maintain an army and a small navy on Lake Champlain for most of the summer. He found the Massachusetts committee eager to take him on. Why was he weeks late? As Dr. Church flipped through his receipts, Arnold informed the committee that far from his owing Massachusetts any money as the committee contended, Massachusetts owed him a great deal. The committeemen had heard all sorts of reports about Arnold—from his enemies Easton and Brown, from Spooner and his investigators on the frontier—but they were evidently not prepared for Arnold to confront them and straightforwardly claim that they owed him nearly £1,000.

The day-long hearing was as fierce a fight as any on the battlefield. Arnold resented the insinuations of the committeemen. Why did they doubt his veracity when he said he had to spend his own money after the meager £100 they had given him to pay for an entire regiment had run out? He presented each committee with copies of a set of ledger sheets itemizing all his expenses, listing pay for entire companies, for carpenters and a shipwright, for lumber, for milling grain, and for much more. But why, the committee wanted to know, had Arnold not obtained proper receipts for each expenditure? Arnold insisted that as the man on the scene for Massachusetts, he had to make countless decisions on behalf of the province and pay prevailing prices and wages. He had spent what he considered appropriate to maintain his men. Now was not the time for civilians to second-guess a field commander operating under primitive and difficult conditions. The Church committee, in its turn, took special umbrage at the number of personal charges Arnold had levied against the public account. Even before the hearing, the committee had refused to pay bills of credit drawn by Arnold on Massachusetts until it issued its report on his account.

All day long, the argument raged, as quills scratched "disallowed" beside ledger line items. The first target was Arnold's horse, which, he maintained, he had purchased on the authorization of the provincial congress before he had ridden west to Ticonderoga. In his summary of disallowances, Arnold was later to write, "1 Sorrel Horse rec'd by order of the Committee—valued at Cost when bought £16."[3] The committee only allowed him £3. The committee also struck out £38 4s. 9d. for the wages of a wheelwright Arnold had hired to build gun carriages to transport cannon. Arnold was supposed to pay troops and use them as carpenters, not hire carpenters, no matter how skilled they were. Arnold's openhanded policy of paying well for workers and skilled mariners did not go down easily in Massachusetts, where it was viewed as driving up the cost of war. The accusations ranged from the petty—paying out £3 15s. for an officer's out-of-pocket expenses for two months without obtaining a proper receipt—to much more serious charges. They objected that he had acted as his own commissary and then charged a broker's fee; they refused to pay for livestock Arnold had bought from Colonel Easton until Arnold produced a receipt and disbelieved Arnold's claim that Easton would not cooperate by giving him one now. They demanded to know what had happened to the £160 reportedly found aboard the captured British sloop. Dr. Church's committee apparently presumed that Arnold had pocketed the money as a prize of war and they therefore disallowed £163 from his expenses for soldiers' pay. Since Arnold had not attached the company's pay table, Dr. Church would not accept Arnold's word of honor that he had ever paid the company of men before he disbanded them and the men went home. Finally, Dr. Church's committee disallowed £100 Arnold said he had paid the crew of the sloop *Enterprise* and insisted on paying the happy crewmen—the very men who had mutinied and locked Arnold up—another £100.

When the hearing was over, the committee reserved judgment until a later date. After two months it released its findings and repaid Arnold £757, only 65 percent of the money he said he had spent in the name of the Massachusetts congress. It was six more months before Washington and Silas Deane finally prevailed on the Continental Congress to order him reimbursed in full by Massachusetts. Fortunately for Arnold, his old friend Deane had been in Cambridge on a congressional tour of inspection of the American army when the hearing took place. When he saw how angry and humiliated Arnold was by the proceedings, Deane sent a letter to Philip Schuyler two days later reminding Schuyler that he had once considered Arnold for his adjutant general: "If the post is not filled, wish you to remember him, as I think he has deserved much and received little, or less than nothing."4

On August 20, 1775, Washington formally approved Benedict Arnold's expedition against Quebec. To Schuyler, Washington wrote on that date "express to communicate to you a plan of an expedition which has engaged my thoughts for several days. It is to penetrate into Canada by way of Kennebec River." Washington assured Schuyler that "I can very well spare a detachment of one thousand or twelve hundred men." If Schuyler still planned to invade Canada from the south, he was immediately to inform Washington when and with how many men. He was also to update intelligence on the "sentiments of the inhabitants as well as those of the Indians."5 Arnold's trusted friend Eleazar Oswald took Deane's and Washington's letters and rode to Ticonderoga. He too would be marching to Quebec as soon as he could bring back Schuyler's authorization. Because he had resigned when Arnold had disbanded his regiment, Oswald was once more a civilian. Arnold could not obtain a commission for Oswald, who volunteered to march along anyway, without rank, as Arnold's private secretary. Arnold agreed to pay him out of his own pocket.

The American invasion of Canada began on August 30, 1775—more than three months after Benedict Arnold's and Ethan Allen's first raids into Canada. The main attack, under the command of the ailing Philip Schuyler, began amid high winds and rains on Lake Champlain that further delayed the invasion. The invasion fleet consisted of Arnold's old flagship, *Enterprise,* the schooner *Liberty,* three gondolas, and two new row galleys (each carrying two hundred men from Colonel David Waterbury's 5th Connecticut Regiment) and a few score bateaux. The expedition's Puritan chaplain, the Reverend Benjamin Trumbull, eldest son of the governor of Connecticut, sat under a flat broad-brimmed black hat and described the fleet of darting, straining vessels as an eager congregation hurrying to church. There were already hints of autumn color in the maple forests flanking either shore. The flash of brilliant red and gold foreshadowed for Trumbull the fires of hell flaring up at the arrogant, sinful British and their painted Indian allies which the godly Puritans around him were going north to cast into hellfire.

It was early September by the time the Puritan army disembarked on Canadian soil and waited for General Schuyler, who had been ill for nearly a month, suffering intense pain from a severe case of rheumatic gout, to come north and take command. Wrapped in his cloak against the chilly morning air, Schuyler left Fort Ticonderoga to lead the second wave: artillerymen with their cannon in big bateaux, five hundred more of Hinman's Connecticut troops, three hundred New York Dutchmen.[5]

Schuyler had run into a quagmire of delays that began as soon as Arnold left him at Albany and headed north in early July as the new commander of the Northern Army. Schuyler reached Fort Gage at the northern tip of Lake George at ten one night in mid-July. Schuyler and his staff found everyone asleep with only nodding sentries guarding the vital portage to Lake Champlain. When he reached Ticonderoga, he was again dismayed. Hinman's Connecticut regiment was down to thirteen hundred men, idle, squabbling, insisting that they would follow only their own generals, no Dutchmen, no Yorkers. The flagship *Enterprise,* far from patrolling the lake to warn of British incursions, was sagging at anchor, sails furled, crewless. Schuyler was forced to wait for a regiment of Green Mountain Boys he had been promised. Schuyler set about disciplining his troops, making sentries stay awake at night, forbidding drunkenness, preaching obedience even as he made scores of enemies among the New Englanders by putting New York officers over them.

Sending Major Jonathan Brown north to Montreal on another intelligence mission with Ethan Allen as his guide, Schuyler learned that General Carleton had heavily reinforced St. Jean and was fortifying it and building invasion craft for a counterinvasion, now that he was winning the support of the Indians. The possibility of Indian warfare was a major issue in the early planning of the Revolution on both sides. Stockbridge Indians, who dressed and lived like white men, had fought on the American side at Bunker Hill, giving the

British a precedent for the use of Indians in their ranks throughout the war. But on the northern frontier, Arnold had asked the Canadian Indians based at Caughnawaga to stand aside and let the white men fight each other.

In August, the prospect of all-out Indian war had loomed nearer when gunfire broke out just north of the Canadian border. Canadian militia Captain François de Lorimier, with five Caughnawaga scouts, had spied an empty bateau tied in a clump of alders near the head of the Richelieu. After taking it in tow with their canoe, they were hailed by a party of Vermonters, who claimed the boat. When de Lorimier refused to return it, the leader of the American patrol, Ethan Allen's cousin, Captain Remember Baker, opened fire on the Indians from behind trees. The Indians fired back. When the Vermonters stopped firing, the Indians streaked north, returning the next day with a large number of reinforcements. In the underbrush, they found Captain Baker's corpse. He had been shot through the head. They beheaded him. In his pockets they found letters proving he had been corresponding with a leading English merchant in Montreal and with a Caughnawaga chief. When Schuyler heard about the first casualty of the Canadian invasion, he was furious at the Vermonters. Schuyler wrote Washington that he still believed that "the Canadians and Indians will be friendly to us, unless for the impudence of a Captain Baker who, without my leave, went upon a scout and, contrary to the most pointed and express orders," had fired on Indians. He promptly sent an apology through the Iroquois of New York for the incident that could have set off a chain reaction on both sides of the border. Later in August, Schuyler met with Six Nations leaders in the old Dutch church in Albany, where seven hundred tribesmen dressed in lace-trimmed hats, ruffled shirts, and blankets decorated with wampum sat cross-legged in the churchyard and agreed to "keep the hatchet buried deep."[6]

Schuyler still had trouble raising New Yorkers to join his invasion force. It was late August before four companies of the 1st New York Regiment—Dutch troops from in and around New York City—finally reached Ticonderoga. Schuyler, meanwhile, had ordered more boats built to transport his men and refused to embark, despite the passage of precious weeks, until enough tents arrived. Schuyler had been ill through most of August, in so much pain that he had not written Washington for three weeks by the time Benedict Arnold's secretary, Eleazar Oswald, arrived at Ticonderoga. Schuyler was grateful Washington had honored him by asking his approval of Arnold's plan. He knew Washington could have gone ahead and attacked Quebec on his own authority. He was relieved that Arnold and his troops would supplement his own "weak and ill-appointed" force. Schuyler's seventeen-hundred-man army was "insufficient to attempt Quebec." But with all his men concentrated on the posts between Lake Champlain and Montreal, "should Arnold's detachment penetrate into Canada and we meet with success, Quebec must inevitably fall into our hands." Arnold's scheme was just the stimulus Schuyler needed, and he left to rejoin his army and press the attack on St. Jean that night. Yet he closed his letter of approval with one sour note: he had heard much about Arnold and the hubbub over his command, and he wanted Washington to put Arnold on notice. "Your Excellency will be pleased to be particular in your orders to the officer that may command the detachment that there may be no clashing over command should we join."[7]

Early in June, as the Continental Congress had first deliberated Benedict Arnold's proposal to invade Canada, John Adams had written to fellow Bay Colony politician James Warren, "Whether we should march into Canada with an army sufficient to break the power of Governor Carleton, to overawe the Indians and to protect the French has been a great question. It seems to be the general conclusion that it is best to go, if we can be assured that the Canadians will be pleased with it, and join us."[8] That summer of 1775, many Canadians—French Canadians and British settlers alike—were eager to join the Americans, to make a vast area of North America the fourteenth and largest state. That Canada could have been restrained from adding its weight to the spreading rebellion against the British ministry by only six hundred British regulars was the handiwork of an enigmatic royal governor, Brigadier General Guy Carleton, one of the few British officials who refused to flee the revolutionaries. Over the next two years, Carleton would lock in repeated combat with Benedict Arnold. Arnold had first met the "high and mighty" Carleton, as he called him, when he took medical supplies north from Norwich for Dr. Lathrop. Carleton was Wolfe's quartermaster general.

Through the influence of a former student who became Duke of Richmond and secretary of state for the Northern Department, Carleton was appointed as military governor of Quebec because he spoke French and was familiar with Canada. Carleton fought secretly and sometimes vindictively with other British officials to create a colony in which the French were kept peaceful by honoring their traditions, their laws, and even their Roman Catholicism, to the consternation of approximately three thousand New England settlers and traders who flocked in to take over good lands from the

French and the fur trade with the Indians. Carleton despised Yankees and feared their struggle for increasingly radical democracy.

The secret plan for Canadian government which Carleton had written and personally had taken to England to see through Parliament created a vast colony entirely different from any other British American province. It had been passed as the Quebec Act in May 1774, shortly after the Boston Tea Party. Extending Quebec's borders to the Ohio River, deep into territory claimed by Connecticut, Massachusetts, and Virginia and blocking their westward expansion, it had created a single-house legislature appointed by the king to advise the governor, with no lower house elected by the people. French land-tenure law was preserved and British law courts abolished along with habeas corpus and trial by jury. The Quebec Act, widely regarded as a model of the form of government the British wished to impose on their other colonies to the south, also granted "permission to Roman Catholics to enjoy the free exercise of their religion and to their clergy to receive from their parishes their accustomed dues and rights,"[9] noted a Jesuit archivist in Quebec. As Ezra Stiles of Yale College put it, it had established the "Romish Church and IDOLATRY."[10] Established Catholicism meant that for the first time since the Reformation, there were in British territory bishops supported by tithing of the crops and incomes of all citizens.

In Protestant New England, the injection of an explosive religious issue had brought together politicians and clergy, Old Light and New Light, to drum up support for armed resistance to the British reforms. Within a month of the signing of the Quebec Act, the Reverend Peter Whitney, pastor of the Church of Christ in Northborough, Massachusetts, had protested the presence of a popish bishop and Catholic priests in Quebec as "not safe for any Protestant government."[11] The Reverend Samuel Sherwood of Fairfield, Connecticut, had told parishioners that they were on the point of being deprived of "the liberty of our conscience"[12] and that New England should unite against the British government's new policy, burying differences such as the New Light–Old Light split. Such sermons had been printed for wide distribution. Ezra Stiles of Yale called the Quebec Act the outstanding grievance against the British government. Protest against the Quebec Act had been incorporated into the most radical Massachusetts document, the Suffolk County Resolves, drafted by Dr. Joseph Warren. The Resolves called the new Canadian charter "dangerous in an extreme degree to the Protestant religion and to the civil rights and liberties of all America. . . . As men and Protestant Christians, we are indispensably obliged to take all the measures for our security . . . to acquaint ourselves with the art of war as soon as possible."[13] On September 18, 1774, the Continental Congress had endorsed the Suffolk Resolves and ordered them printed and distributed throughout North America and in England.

When it came time for Thomas Jefferson to write the Declaration of Independence in June 1776, in its bill of particular offenses against the American people warranting their break with the mother country, he alluded to the Quebec Act as a primary cause of the Revolution, attacking king-in-Parliament "for abolishing the free system of English laws in a neighboring province, establishing therein an arbitrary government and enlarging its boundaries so as to render it at once an example and fit instrument for introducing the same absolute rule into those colonies."[14]

In the summer of 1775, Washington, an Anglican himself, was acutely aware of the volatility of the religious issue in the Canadian campaign, as he made clear in a proclamation he personally wrote for Arnold and Schuyler to distribute among French Canadians. His manifesto explicitly guaranteed Canadians that "the cause of America and of liberty is the cause of every virtuous American citizen, whatever may be his religion."[15] In his written orders to Arnold, he was quite explicit in insisting on religious toleration:

I also give it in charge to you to avoid all disrespect or contempt of the religion of the country and its ceremonies. Prudence, policy and a true Christian spirit will lead us to look with compassion upon their errors without insulting them. While we are contending for our own liberty, we should be very cautious of violating the rights of conscience in others, ever considering that God alone is the judge of the hearts of men and to him only, in this case, they are answerable.[18]

When Carleton had returned to Canada in February, 1775, to launch the new Canadian government, he had been greeted by the news that a majority of Montreal's English merchants opposed the Quebec Act and moreover they had just sent off a thousand bushels of wheat to help feed the blockaded people of Boston. At the same time, Carleton had learned that they had to dispatch to General Gage in Boston two of the four regiments of redcoats stationed in Canada. Sure that the French would now rally to his standard, Carleton had retained fewer than eight hundred redcoats in Canada. It was to prove one of his costliest blunders. The departure of half the British troops had quickened the pulses of pro-American radicals in Montreal. Montreal was closer to New England than Quebec, and was more responsive to every stage of the American rebellion. Hundreds of its transplanted New Englanders had organized a committee to seek closer ties with Boston radicals and had openly opposed the Quebec Act by sending their own emissary to Parliament. He was the immensely wealthy Thomas Walker, Benedict Arnold's closest friend and best informant in Canada. For his vocal opposition to Carleton's policies, Walker had been visited one night by six men in civilian clothes with blackened faces: undoubtedly British officers, they had cut off one of Walker's ears.

While Carleton had written sunnily to authorities in London that "all ranks of people"[17] applauded the Act, businessmen such as Walker were firing off their own addresses to king and Parliament, demanding repeal. In the capital at Quebec, only twenty-five merchants signed repeal petitions, but in Montreal, 162 merchants, a majority, protested. When the only newspaper in the province, the Quebec *Gazette,* did not dare print the petitions or the Continental Congress's letter to the "Oppressed Inhabitants" for fear of losing its government printing contract, Walker had paid to have them translated into French and had them distributed by businessmen on horse-and-wheat-buying visits to farms. Meanwhile, the Continental Congress fired off another letter opposing the Quebec Act, this time an anti-Catholic diatribe to the British people which dampened Canadian enthusiasm for the revolutionary cause. Written by lawyers John Jay of New York, John Dickinson of Pennsylvania, and Thomas Cushing of Boston and addressed "To the Inhabitants of Great Britain," it protested the establishment of Catholicism on British soil, calling Catholicism "a religion that has deluged [your] island in blood and dispensed impiety, bigotry, persecution, murder and rebellion in every part of the world."[18] When a copy was brought back from England to Carleton, he had turned it over to Quebec Bishop Jean Olivier Briand, who had seminarians translate it into French and send copies to all parish priests to read from their pulpits to prove that "Les Bostonnais" meant to persecute Catholics after they invaded Canada. Carleton had also ordered Congress's letters, one coaxing, the other condemning Catholics, posted side by side in public squares and market places and on church doors.

In February 1775, little more than a month before Lexington, the Massachusetts provincial congress had directed the Boston Committee of Correspondence to send an emissary to Canada. Lawyer John Brown of Pittsfield, soon to clash with Benedict Arnold at Ticonderoga, had carried Sam Adams's letter to the Canadians, inviting them to set up their own committees of correspondence and to send delegates to the Continental Congress. When Brown had reached Montreal on April 9, 1775, Thomas Walker called a meeting of merchants at the Montreal Coffee House. He had begun by reading Adams's letters, then had made a motion to send two delegates to Congress. But many merchants had cooled in response to Congress's intemperate letter to England. If they joined Congress, would they have to comply with Congress's embargo on trade with England? Yes, Brown said. The motion had failed. Then one merchant charged that Massachusetts was threatening an invasion of Canada "if a man of [us] should dare to take up arms against the Bostonians."[19] The merchants could agree on nothing more than setting up a secret committee of correspondence, with Walker its chairman.

On May 1, 1775, the day the Quebec Act officially had taken effect and before news of the fighting in Massachusetts reached Montreal, a crowd gathered in the Place d'Armes at Montreal's center. There King George III's bust had been smeared with a coat of black paint and a rosary of potatoes and a wooden cross draped around its neck. On the cross was the inscription "Behold the Pope of Canada, or the English fool."[20] Thomas Walker had been accused of the desecration, but a young Jewish merchant, David Franks, who would become Benedict Arnold's aide-de-camp, later admitted his handiwork. Indignant British officers had offered a £50 reward for the culprit. The next day, a French merchant told bystanders that the proper punishment for such an insult was hanging. At that, young Franks had punched the Frenchman as another merchant named Salomon shouted that it must have been done by a French Canadian. When a Frenchman retorted it was more likely a Jew, Salomon punched him in the face. Both Franks and Salomon had been dragged off to jail.

On May 25, 1775, news had reached Carleton at Quebec that Ticonderoga had fallen. Taken completely by surprise, Carleton had moved his headquarters to Montreal to prepare for the impending invasion of Canada.

For Lieutenant John André of the 7th Regiment, which accompanied Carleton to Montreal, the outbreak of fighting on the Canadian border had also been a surprise. In a series of letters home to his sister, Mary, André had anticipated a long, leisurely stay in Canada. That spring of 1775, he had expected to move to Montreal, then be transferred deeper into the Canadian interior to a fort on one of the Great Lakes, in Indian country. By May, the snowdrifts had turned to deep mire on the roads as the hooves of horses dragged cannon and supply wagons south: Carleton had decided to make his stand at the string of forts on the Richelieu River between Montreal and Lake Champlain. Lieutenant André's unit had sailed up the St. Lawrence to Montreal, then had disembarked to march closer to the Americans. André's unit was to reinforce St. Jean:

We are to go thirty miles out of town. . . . We are to take humanity a peg lower. . . . In proportion as our beds are bad, we are to fatigue ourselves the more. . . . Today silken dalliance clothes our limbs and we wreathe the bow and wind the dance. Tomorrow, we hut in a style little above the brute.[21]

On the dusty gray Sunday morning of September 3, 1775, the sixteen-thousand-American army besieging Boston formed up for inspection all along the ten-mile cordon of trenches and fortifications that were now investing the British. General Washington with his aides and brigade commanders toured the lines on horseback, accompanied by Benedict Arnold, riding a big chestnut horse and wearing a cockade in his tricorn hat and his red Foot Guards uniform. Freshly commissioned a colonel, Arnold seemed to be studying every man with his sharp gray eyes, and indeed he was: Washington had given him the pick of his entire army for an elite thousand-man regiment for the swift overland attack on Quebec. The Reverend Samuel Spring, who was on review that day with his Massachusetts regiment, vividly remembered that inspection: "The drum beat in every regiment for an instant and a general parade of the whole army, as for review, was ordered. All was bustle. In a very brief space, the whole army was paraded in continued line of companies. With one continued roll of drums, the general-in-chief with his staff passed along the whole line, regiment after regiment, presenting arms."[22]

Many of the men had grown tired of the heat, the boredom, the grind of camp life under the summer sun. The prospect of action, especially in a cooler place, excited men who, at most, had fought only once in nearly five months in the army. When Colonel Arnold reached Spring's camp, he ordered the men formed up: "Officers, to the front, ten paces, march!" Then, in quick succession, "Officers to the center, face! Officers, to the center—march! Form hollow squares." To each square, Arnold read "the secret orders of Congress." The colonel made it plain that he didn't want to take along anyone who didn't want to go. "It was a perilous service, and not compulsory," Arnold warned them. "Volunteers were called for." When an officer intoned the words "Volunteers step one step in advance,"[23] the entire regiment stepped forward. All along the lines that morning, in regiment after regiment, entire units volunteered. By noon, Arnold had five times the number of volunteers Washington had authorized.

For two weeks he had anxiously awaited the return of his young New Haven friend Eleazar Oswald from Ticonderoga with a verdict from General Schuyler. Meantime he busied himself at Washington's headquarters in Cambridge, making a detailed plan of the march up the Kennebec River to fall on Quebec from the rear. During this agonizing wait, Arnold was a lowly captain surrounded by generals, nonetheless enjoying the cordiality of staff officers toward a current favorite. It was several more months before Martha Washington arrived to preside as hostess, but in the meantime the wives of Massachusetts officers, especially Lucy Knox, arranged dinners and teas. At one of these, she apparently introduced Benedict Arnold to young patriot ladies, but Arnold was evidently too gloomy and preoccupied with recouping his money from the provincial congress to warm to any of them. Presently he went off to Watertown to present more documentation for his expense account. Should Schuyler approve, Arnold would need money for Hannah and the boys and for his personal expenses in Canada. As summer ebbed, he faced Dr. Church again at Watertown and still heard nothing from the west. Assured by Gates nearly a week earlier that Washington had already approved the expedition pending Schuyler's agreement, Arnold had evidently rushed preparation of requisitions for troops, supplies, weapons, boats, maps, transportation, all the myriad details necessary to make and move an army. Then he learned that his plans lay stacked in the pile on Gates's desk, where they were to remain until word came from Schuyler. Arnold asked to see Washington the night of August 24, only to be told Washington did not have time to see him again until *after* the courier returned. That summer night, there were some early signs of the hostility between Gates and Arnold that was to grow over the years. Gates appears to have strongly suggested that Arnold not leave camp until Oswald's return, but Arnold left without his permission the next morning to attempt to settle his business in Watertown, four miles west. Gates sent an express rider after him with a paper for Arnold to sign acknowledging receipt of a direct order to return to headquarters. Washington did not want to lose a minute tracking down Arnold once Oswald returned. It must have been obvious to the red-faced Arnold that Washington expected Schuyler's cooperation.

On September 2, Eleazar Oswald returned from Ticonderoga with Schuyler's enthusiastic endorsement for Arnold's diversion in force and news that the main attack had begun on the Richelieu

River. Within three days, Washington not only met with Arnold for a series of conferences but signed his commission as a full colonel in the new regular army, the Continental Line. Thus Arnold was freed from provincial politics and made responsible directly to Washington himself. Exuberant at the large number of men eager to join his expedition, Arnold made his selection by choosing men who were under thirty and taller than average. He asked each man two key questions: "Are you an active woodsman? Are you well acquainted with bateaux?"[24] Between them, Arnold and his adjutant, Captain Christian Febiger, had to decide who were the winners of this liars' contest. Some of the men actually were woodsmen from Maine. Many of the Rhode Island troops and some from Massachusetts and Connecticut were fishermen or sailors who had actually rowed a boat before, but all too many of the men were willing to shade the truth in order to join the expedition and get away from the tedium and the heat of camp life. By nightfall, Arnold and his staff had weeded out all but 747 of the four thousand men, many of them veterans of the Battle of Bunker Hill. With the riflemen, Arnold now had his new regiment of 1,050 men. The next day they assembled again on the Continental Commons to meet their officers and receive their unit assignments. Only two days later, the musketmen, men who had been farmers, fishermen, artisans, shop clerks, and students from all over New England, received orders to join Arnold's regiment and pitch new tents on Cambridge Commons.

The next morning, the riflemen, big, rangy backwoodsmen wearing buckskin and carrying Pennsylvania rifles, formed ranks and arrived at headquarters. Many officers, including Washington, were relieved to see the riflemen go. Since they had arrived in camp a few weeks earlier after marching 650 miles in twenty-one days from their base in Lancaster, Pennsylvania—stopping only twice to tar and feather suspected Tories—they had been robbing farms and fellow soldiers and violating military etiquette by sniping at British officers at long range against Washington's express orders. Their guns, capable of hitting a man in the head at half a mile or in the nose at 150 yards, outraged the British, who were already calling the American riflemen "these shirt-tail men with their cursed twisted guns the worst widow- and orphan-makers in the world."[25] The Virginia riflemen were put under the command of Captain Daniel Morgan, a big, burly man who had been a teamster in the French and Indian Wars and had been given five hundred lashes for punching a British officer. Arnold partitioning his regiment into four battalions, which were called divisions, made Morgan the commander of his first division, the vanguard. As his second-in-command (and commander of the second battalion) he chose Lieutenant Colonel Christopher Greene to head the Rhode Island troops. As head of the third division, he chose Major Return Jonathan Meigs of Connecticut. In charge of the fourth division, the rear guard, he appointed Lieutenant Colonel Roger Enos of Vermont, an expert on supply. Five volunteers, all holding the rank of captain, went along to serve as Arnold's aides; they included Eleazar Oswald and Matthias Ogden and Aaron Burr of New Jersey. Burr, nineteen, always adept at attaching himself to interesting men at critical times, went along without pay and took with him a nineteen-year-old Abenaki Indian princess, Jacatacqua (the men called her Golden Thighs).

As soon as Washington commissioned him, Arnold made two other key appointments. As his adjutant general and military engineer, he named Captain Christian Febiger, an engineering officer in the Royal Danish Army who had emigrated to America five years earlier; his father, a horse trader in the Danish Virgin Islands, was an old friend of Arnold's. As the expedition's chaplain, Benedict Arnold chose six-foot-tall, deep-voiced Samuel Spring, thereby making a rare declaration on religion. Arnold chose Spring not just as a morale officer, but to help him inspire his men at a time when many common soldiers still took religion seriously. Spring was a student of the archconservative Dr. John Witherspoon of Princeton, signer of the Declaration of Independence.

Even before Washington finished penning his orders, Arnold was rushing his regiment's departure. On the same day that Oswald returned from Ticonderoga, Arnold wrote to his friend the wealthy merchant Nathaniel Tracy of Newburyport, thirty miles north of Cambridge, asking him to cooperate in Arnold's effort to gather a small fleet of ships quickly, quietly, and without the notice of British navy coastal patrols to transport his regiment ninety miles northeast to the mouth of the Kennebec. Like Arnold, Washington considered this the most dangerous stage of the expedition. Massachusetts revolutionary William Tudor reported to John Adams "the daily piratical acts of [British Admiral Samuel] Graves's squadron. . . . There is scarce a vessel that escapes the clutches of the cutters and men of war that infest the coast."[26] The week that Arnold's army left for Maine, the British took eleven ships captive to Boston with their cargoes and crews. Somehow, Tracy was able to find and conceal a flotilla until Arnold arrived.

The plan of the expedition was calculated at every step to save time. The army would march overland to Newburyport, then sail to Maine and up the Kennebec River as far north as possible to Gardinerstown, where two hundred shallow-draft bateaux were being

built to carry the men and their supplies all the way to Quebec, with
the exception of a half-dozen portages between the headwaters of
the Kennebec and a chain of ponds that connected it with the Chaudière, which flowed one hundred miles north to Quebec. The only
detailed reports available were Montresor's map and his journal. Arnold did not realize that he had a copy purposely altered by British
army clerks to be deceptive. It was the practice of eighteenth-century
explorers deliberately to alter directions and distances to prevent use
of their documents by an enemy. Arnold had to rely on the map and
on the corroboration of others who had actually taken the route.
Mostly, these were Abenaki Indians, who had no written records,
but there was also a surveyor in Maine who was familiar with the
terrain. As Arnold was preparing his final plans, Adjutant General
Gates introduced him to Major Reuben Colburn, a boatbuilder from
Gardinerstown, Maine, who happened to be at Cambridge and offered his services. Arnold asked Colburn to build bateaux for six or
seven men each that could be paddled, poled, or rowed. In addition,
he offered to introduce Arnold to Samuel Goodrich, a Gardinerstown surveyor and mapmaker who might also be useful to
Arnold, for a price. Arnold asked if he could make Montresor's
journal and map an accurate set of maps of the route, as well as
charts of the river's depth and speed at that time of year, producing
enough copies for each of his divisional commanders. Colburn hurried to Maine and set to work building the boats. He did not tell
Arnold, and indeed he knew it, that Goodwin was the official surveyor for the Plymouth Company, a decidedly Loyalist enterprise.
Goodwin prepared the maps, billed Washington for them, and meticulously misstated routes and distances at every turn.

By the second week of September, delay seemed to be an even
greater enemy than Carleton's redcoats. The next snag was the refusal of a company of Colonel Enos's Connecticut troops to march
unless they received a month's pay in advance. They were worried
about their families, since they would be somewhere in the middle of
the Maine woods when the next pay was due. Arnold saw to it that
they were paid back pay as well as a month's pay in advance before
they left, but days ticked away while the necessary paperwork
wended its way through headquarters. Meanwhile, the men drew
their uniforms.

*Over a pair of boots I draw a pair of woolen trousers of coarse
coating. A short, double-breasted jacket of the same. Over this
comes a short coat, curiously fringed, with a belt as curious. My
blanket slung over my back, as that's a thing I never trust from me.*

To these, add a tomahawk, gun, bayonet and a small round hat with a snap-up brim topped by a large fox tail with a black feather curled up together.[27]

There were still shortages of blankets and equipment when Arnold ordered the troops to muster on Cambridge Commons on September 11 for a final review. Early that morning, he sent off a convoy of supply wagons toward Newburyport.

As he sent off the musketmen on September 14, Arnold had a final round of conferences with his aides at headquarters. An entire month had been lost on politics as Washington waited for Schuyler's approval. Since nothing requiring payment could take place until Washington had signed his commission and fiscal authorizations on September 3, the boatbuilders had not been able to get to work until September 8. As Arnold waited for paperwork and supplies, he had wanted to dispatch Abenaki Indian scouts to reconnoiter the route and mark the trail, but Washington was unalterably opposed to the use of Indians, even though the Abenaki leaders had walked all the way from their Kennebec villages in Maine to Cambridge to volunteer to fight on the American side.

No matter how much time had been lost, Washington was sure that once the army got moving, the men could make it up on the march. Arnold believed they could make the march to Quebec in only twenty days from Gardinerstown. To save time, Washington agreed to send along his manifesto to the Canadians by courier so that Arnold would not have to wait any longer. Indeed, so confident was Washington that the expedition would succeed that when he finally wrote Congress a week later to inform it of Arnold's departure, he underestimated the distance and difficulty of the march enormously so that Arnold's forecast of twenty days en route seemed plausible.

In his written orders, Washington emphasized that the invaders were to "consider yourselves as marching, not through an enemy's country, but that of our friends and brethren, for such the inhabitants of Canada and the Indian nations have approved themselves." He ordered strict "punishment [for] every attempt to plunder or insult any of the inhabitants," warning especially against "violating the rights of conscience in others."[28] Washington agreed with Arnold that the French and Indians should be urged to stand aside while the British and American armies fought over the future of Canada.

*   *   *

By the time Benedict Arnold and his staff rode out of Cambridge at five o'clock on Friday, September 15, his men had been moving northeast for three days. Two hundred fifty-two riflemen in fringed leather leggings, moccasins, and butternut-gray shirts with short capes swung gracefully along, carrying rifles with fifty-eight-inch barrels. The woodsmen were festooned with scalping knives, tomahawks, canteens, and cartridge boxes. They covered thirty miles of dusty roads over rolling hills in less than two days, camping on the banks of the Merrimac River just outside Newburyport by evening of the 12th. The youngest soldier was Cadet John Henry, whose father was a Lancaster, Pennsylvania, rifle maker. Two women marched along with their husbands. Joseph Grier's bride, six feet tall, was described by Henry as a "large, virtuous and respectable woman."[29] Jemima Warner went because she was worried about her husband's health.

By dawn on Wednesday, September 13, ten companies of eighty-four musketmen set out. At the head of one marched Captain Henry Dearborn, twenty-four, with his black Newfoundland dog. Dr. Isaac Senter, the young regimental surgeon, was not used to marching. He trailed the division with his gentleman friends, Aaron Burr, Matthias Ogden, and Chaplain Spring, who wore his black wool canonical suit in the searing late-summer heat. The first day they trudged seven miles, the second day twelve miles, and the last twelve miles to Newburyport the third day. They took comfortable lodgings at Davenport's Inn just as "the rear of the army came up"[30] and filed into temporary billets in the town hall, the Presbyterian church, and the port's two ropewalks. The men found Newburyport hospitable in small welcome ways: expedition surveyor John Pierce "lodged in a good feather bed."[31]

Benedict Arnold, his staff, and the grooms who were to return their horses to Cambridge covered the fifty miles to Newburyport in a single day. While Arnold and his aides ate, Eleazar Oswald rode to the town armory, where he requisitioned 270 blankets from the local Committee of Safety and also obtained two hundred pounds of ginger, which Arnold considered the best cure for the seasickness he expected for so many of his men. The officers rode the last twenty miles to Newburyport and the waterfront mansion of Nathaniel Tracy, the wealthy shipowner who had been rounding up ships, crews, and supplies for Arnold for weeks. To the untrained eye, the eleven boats assembled by Tracy to transport the troops to Kennebec appeared to be dirty little fishing boats. To Arnold, they were an amazing assembly of fast little sloops and topsail schooners. Despite the additional delay, Arnold insisted on sending the three fastest ships out on patrol to make sure the entire expedition did not come to an abrupt end in a British naval trap.

Almost as soon as Arnold arrived in Newburyport, a thick fog set in. While Arnold awaited the return of his patrol boats from scouting in search of British warships, he supervised the loading of the remaining vessels. He gave strict orders that there was to be no looting or harassing of Tories in the town. Most of the men were taking advantage of their last days of liberty for many weeks. Arnold had ordered extra leave for one company of men, who had marched from their homes in Newburyport to Lexington on the first day of fighting five months earlier. He sent them ahead of the troops with the supply wagons and gave them a full week with their families, a move that won him friends in the town. The riflemen and the musketmen packed the taverns and stores and were welcomed into scores of homes, where they were well fed, given round after round of drinks, and in many places shown to the feather beds upstairs.

The soldiers were assembled early Sunday morning, September 17, at the riflemen's camp one mile west of town on the south bank of the Merrimack for a grand review by Colonel Arnold and his staff, then paraded down to the Presbyterian meeting house, a tall, white, high-spired building towering over the ships jamming wharves in front of it. Surveyor Pierce noted in his journal that the fog had cleared and a large crowd was assembled all along the route. Abner Stocking of Connecticut, twenty-two, grumbled that they were "still" in Newburyport but then praised his fellow soldiers: "We passed the review with much honor to ourselves. We went through with the manual exercise with much alacrity." For months, Washington's soldiers had been drilling. "The spectators, who were very numerous, appeared much affected. . . . Many of us should never return to our parents and families."[32] Chaplain Spring, marching with Colonel Arnold at the rear of the column, recorded that the troops swung briskly along, climbing the steps of the meetinghouse amid cheers. "They marched in with colors flying and drums beating and formed two lines which I passed, they presenting arms and the drums rolling until I was seated in the pulpit. Then the soldiers stacked their arms all over the aisles, and I preached to the army and to the citizens, who crowded the galleries, from the text: 'If thy spirit go not with us, carry us not up hence.'"[33] Spring preached without notes, with what many men later recalled as a stream of eloquence. One observer recalled that "the subject of his discourse [was] the marvelous and daring expedition on which they were about to set forth. . . . The profoundest silence fell over the audience."[34] Benedict Arnold, Daniel Morgan, the townspeople never forgot the sermon. What thrilled Spring that day, as many listeners knew, was that "I preached over the grave of Whitefield." The man who had brought the Great Awakening to New England thirty-five years earlier was buried in a crypt directly under Spring's pulpit.

"After the service, the officers gathered around," Spring recounted. "Someone requested a visit to Whitefield's tomb. The sexton was hunted up, the key procured, and we descended to the coffin." Swords and boots clattered on the stone stairs. "Whitefield's body had lain in the tomb six years." As Arnold and his officers "gathered in the dark vault around the tomb" the officers persuaded the sexton to take off the lid of the coffin. "The body had nearly all returned to dust," said Spring. "Some portions of his grave clothes remained. His collar and wristbands, in the best preservation, were taken and carefully cut in little pieces, and divided among them."[35]

7

"BELOVED
BY THE SOLDIERY"

*I sometimes think
that Canada has been* earned by *the
march of
Colonel Arnold.*

Dr. Benjamin Rush to Patrick Henry, July 16, 1776

On their last night ashore, Benedict Arnold and his officers feasted at the Newburyport mansion of his good friend Nathaniel Tracy, the rich shipowner and merchant who had spent £700 of his own money to provide ships and crews for the first leg of the journey to Quebec. While Arnold's picket boats searched the coast for the British, he and his officers enjoyed good food and wines served on white linen with silverware: Arnold and Tracy were good friends. For a few hours, Arnold could forget his apprehension about the slipping-away of time. Meanwhile, Arnold's company commanders were having a hard time keeping the men aboard their ships, where they had been ordered with their gear. Arnold had to excuse himself and give an order that the riflemen were to be placed under guard to prevent them from continuing to loot Tory houses.

The picket boats were back early next morning. The coast was clear. At seven in the morning, Arnold and his staff boarded the topsail schooner *Broad Bay,* his choice as flagship for the run down east to Maine. At nine the tide was full enough for the eleven ships, their decks crowded with soldiers, to cross the harbor bar. "We got underway with a pleasant breeze," wrote Private Abner Stocking, twenty-two, of Connecticut, "our drums beating, fifes playing and colors flying. Many pretty girls stood upon the shore, weeping for the departure of their sweethearts."[1] By noontime, all the vessels but one had glided across the bar. The schooner *Swallow,* overloaded with 250 men and their supplies (although Arnold's orders specified one hundred men to a vessel), ran hard aground on the rocks and stuck fast. For three agonizing hours, as the townspeople watched and the remainder of his ships lay exposed to any British ship happening by, Arnold and his men labored with long lines and rowboats to free the stranded ship. First he ordered the men redistributed among the other ships. Every small boat in the harbor laboriously ferried the men and their supplies from ship to ship. Scott's Connecticut company was rowed over to the schooner *Hannah,* already crowded with men and supplies. But the *Swallow* was still stuck. It was four in the afternoon and the better part of another day had been lost before Arnold left *Swallow* behind and the remaining ten ships began to pick their way east toward Maine, hugging the rockbound shore, following Arnold's flagship, its jib and mainsail straining.

Shortly after dark, the threat of British patrol boats lessened as a brisk west-southwest wind blew up. Arnold ordered a lantern raised to *Broad Bay*'s masthead and four guns fired the signal for individual skippers to "make sail,"[2] each finding his own way. Soon the ships were plowing into the deep swells created by a storm at sea, as lightning flashed and rain poured down. The pitching and rolling of the ships belied sworn statements about years of experience aboard ships. Hundreds of men, as Arnold put it, became "extremely seasick."[3] But it was a fast, following sea rapidly pushing the ships northeast, even though the worsening weather forced hundreds of sick men to crowd into tiny holds belowdecks as heavy rain pelted down and the fog thickened. Arnold and his men had no way of knowing that not only bad weather but internal disputes in the British high command had protected them from the enemy.

To conceal the movement of more than one thousand armed men and all their supplies in an area of Massachusetts with so many Loyalists was a difficult task. Yet somehow Arnold managed to hide his entire flotilla and move it nearly one hundred miles on the open sea when a single British warship could have wrecked his expedition. He did it by a clever ploy. A week before Arnold marched, British commander Gage in Boston had already sent an urgent dispatch to Vice Admiral Graves, in charge of the British fleet in North American waters: "I have certain advice by two deserters that about 1500 men have marched from Cambridge which are said to be gone to Canada and by way of Newburyport."[4]

In any event, Arnold did not try to mask that his men were marching to Canada—he just never told anyone *where* in Canada. Gage called in his chief engineer, John Montresor, who believed that a military expedition up the Kennebec was impossible. Gage was left with only one conclusion, that Arnold was really "intended for Nova Scotia," which lay all but undefended a few days' sail from Newburyport. To Graves, Gage sent a strongly worded message, urging him to move quickly.

I should therefore think it exceedingly necessary some small vessel should be immediately sent to watch their motions and to use every effort to surprise some of the rebel small vessels, which would be very much the best method to get intelligence which, if the officer of the small British warship should think certain, he might give notice to the ships of war in the Bay of Fundy. . . . Intelligence may be sent by land from Annapolis Royal to Halifax. I should hope that the naval force you have in that province would, with timely notice, be able to defeat any attempts the Rebels can make at sea for a descent there.[5]

The tone of the message makes clear that Admiral Graves was proving himself incapable of moving quickly, and that Gage had no authority over him—indeed, Gage had previously warned that the Americans were about to attempt something big in Nova Scotia, which already was teetering on the verge of joining the Revolution. Graves had persisted in fighting a defensive war, using his sizable fleet to seize American shipping and raid coastal islands and towns for firewood, sheep, and cattle to supply British sailors and soldiers at Boston, ignoring Gage's suggestion. Fully nineteen days later, Gage sent Graves a crisp note, once again prodding him to move. He evidently had received another intelligence report that Arnold's force had reached Maine. By October 13, it became apparent that Graves had finally taken action, as six British warships passed present-day Portland, Maine, on their way to Nova Scotia. By this time, Arnold had more than a month's head start. When they were unable to find Arnold, the British returned to Portland, where they shelled and burned the town, infuriated at the people along the Maine coast who had kept Arnold's mission secret for weeks.

On October 7, the captain of the British sloop-of-war *Lively,* which had been guarding British transports hauling firewood from the islands in Penobscot Bay to Boston, wrote excitedly to Graves that he had finally learned from an informer that "1500 men under the command of Colonel Arnold"[6] were going up the Kennebec and were destined for Quebec. But by this time, Arnold's ruse had alarmed all of Nova Scotia: the British governor, Sir Francis Legge, sent a fast dispatch boat to England on October 17, telling his older brother, British secretary of state Lord Dartmouth, that he had declared a state of emergency and imposed martial law. His panicky letter was full of misinformation: a British colonel had arrived at Halifax with word that the American general John Thomas had marched eastward from Boston to invade Nova Scotia, to destroy the vast navy yard at Halifax and "cut off all supply of wood, hay and provisions from the troops at Boston,"[7] and had already burned a fort in present-day Saint John, New Brunswick.

By late October, General Gage read, in a copy of the *Pennsylvania Packet* sent to him by a spy in the Continental Congress, an article about the capture of one of Graves's ships after it ran aground in Brigantine, New Jersey. The ship, carrying British recruiting and training officers, had been bound for Halifax from England to defend Nova Scotia from Arnold when it had been battered and blown off course by a storm in the North Atlantic. According to the ship's officers, General Gage was so concerned about Arnold's invasion that he himself was to sail "in a day or two in a merchant ship of sixteen guns,"[8] having given up on Graves and the Royal Navy. For his part, Graves was sitting smugly aboard his flagship, HMS *Preston,* in Boston Harbor. On October 18, he had turned over all ships in Nova Scotia waters to his man on the scene in Halifax. He also responded to Governor Legge's urgent appeal for aid with a droll comment that "the 1500 men from Newburyport, who were expected to be gone towards Halifax, went up the Kennebec River, and 'tis generally believed are for Quebec, from whence we have lately received very unfavorable accounts."[9] As Arnold's little fleet passed soundlessly nearby, guided only by the lanterns he had ordered set at the masthead, the Royal Navy man-of-war *Lively* was anchored in Penobscot Bay with a fleet of transports, their crews of British seamen sleeping before another hard day of loading firewood for the garrison in Boston.

It was still foggy and raining as Arnold ordered a jack hoisted to *Broad Bay*'s maintop, then fired his signal cannon. A cheer broke out and echoed across the waters of Eels Eddy, just inside the mouth of the Kennebec River, as the little fleet nosed together and dropped anchor. In less than twenty-four hours, Arnold and the eight ships covered one hundred miles. Three ships lost their way, but only for a matter of hours. In the dense fog, two ships, *Conway* and *Abigail,* had wandered through the islands in Sheepscot Bay after overshooting the Kennebec's mouth. Another, the sloop *Hannah,* had run aground but would work itself free shortly. The noise of Arnold's fleet flushed the bird life: crook-necked cormorants beat clumsily into the air, clouds of ducks and Canada geese struggled into ragged V's away from the onset of winter. Aboard his flagship, Arnold noted the signs of approaching winter, the low level of the river, how dry were the leaves of the fiery red maples lining the water's edge, parched and dead from a year of drought in the Kennebec Valley. But Arnold was relieved that not a man had been lost: he had brought an entire fleet through the British naval blockade of Massachusetts "without the least molestation from the enemy,"[10] he promptly reported to Washington, although he confided to his friend Tracy, "Our voyage has been very troublesome indeed."[11]

As the fog momentarily lifted, what was a first glimpse of Maine for most of the men revealed rocky, tall-pine-covered islands in every direction. Slowly, the ships threaded through a reef. Half an hour after sunrise, Dr. Senter, with Aaron Burr aboard the sloop *Sally,* could make out the mouth of the Kennebec and a small, makeshift fort. Maine militiamen lined its parapets, cheering and waving as a pilot boat worked toward *Broad Bay* to guide the fleet to Parker's Flats, nine miles upriver.

A summer-long drought, Arnold now discovered, had left the Kennebec shallow all along its course, its rocks and shoals either exposed or covered in many places by only a few feet of water. Arnold had planned to sail nearly half the length of the river, which flowed almost due south from the highlands on the Canadian border, but, he now learned, he would not only have to work against the current but must contend with rocks and rapids in badly overloaded small boats.

After a rest of only six hours, Arnold ordered the men back on the ships, which were to proceed as best they could the four miles to Georgetown. It would be impossible for the ships to stay in formation because of the thick fog. Arnold plowed ahead, his flagship dropping anchor off the cluster of hamlets loosely called Georgetown. Here a fresh company of Maine volunteers, all able scouts and marksmen, woodsmen familiar with bateaux, joined Arnold. They had been organized by Samuel McCobb, the town clerk of Georgetown, who had recruited a company of troops eight days after Lexington and had fought behind the rail fence at Bunker Hill.

On learning of Arnold's expedition, McCobb had rushed back to Georgetown and raised another company, and now was ready to march to Quebec. Arnold, who spent the night in Georgetown, assigned McCobb to Lieutenant Colonel Enos's division, where men who knew the Kennebec would become vital in keeping his troops supplied.

That night the last of the missing transports overtook Arnold, and at five the next morning, the two vessels began to tack upriver, but the "wind and tide unfavorable."[12] Arnold left the ships behind and hired a carriage to speed him to Gardinerstown, thirty-four miles upriver, where he was to pick up the two hundred bateaux he had ordered. As he drove toward Major Reuben Colburn's shipyard on the eastern edge of Gardinerstown, Arnold could first make out Colburn's house on a bluff set back from the river overlooking a long slope down to the shore, beyond it a cluster of ample houses and gristmills. As Arnold and Oswald drew closer, they could make out the neat rows of bateaux. At first it seemed miraculous that Colburn and his partner, Samuel Agry, could find enough skilled shipwrights and carpenters to produce two hundred bateaux in only two weeks. Arnold had little reason to be euphoric, however, when he got down and began to inspect the boats. As he tried to heft first one boat, then another, he found that they were badly built, made out of heavy, wet green pine planks that would shrink and crack stretched over even heavier oak frames. Many were too small, yet they must have weighed, on average, four hundred pounds each. Arnold had ordered bateaux of uniform length, twenty-five feet long, with flared lap-straked sides and pointed bow and stern to keep the supplies high and dry in rough water: each was to be equipped with two pairs of oars, two paddles, and two long setting poles for pushing through shallow water and was to be able to carry six or seven men and a ton of supplies. At least twenty of the boats were as small as eighteen feet long, far too small for six big men and their guns and gear; the occupants would have no room to move around, let alone do the hard work of poling and paddling through river rapids. The high-sided bateaux were a variety of sizes up to twenty-five feet, but all were badly caulked. The green wood was shrinking as it dried on the riverbank; the boats should have been in the river so the seams could have been swelling shut. On land the planks could be relied on to shrink up to a half inch per plank, leaving seams wide open for water to rush in. Arnold evidently had assumed that Major Colburn would use seasoned wood, which would not shrink. Indeed, there was an ample supply of seasoned wood at Portland, which he had had to pass on his way home to begin work. But Colburn was apparently determined to hold on to as much of his contract money as he could. The result was a meadow full of ill-suited, badly made, undersized, overweight boats to carry Arnold's army through four hundred miles of rough water and portages to Quebec. Arnold was still steaming when he wrote to Washington three days later. "I found the bateaux completed, but many of them smaller than the directions given, and very badly built—of course I have been obliged to order twenty more to bring on the remainder of the provisions. . . . They will be finished in three days."[13]

Arnold did not waste any time squabbling with Colburn. He hired two caulkers to repair the boats and paid Colburn in cash. It had probably been Arnold's idea to use bateaux for this expedition, and he could not change tactics at this point. The only alternative had been birchbark canoes, and it is doubtful that two hundred large enough canoes could have been built so quickly. There had been a simple misunderstanding over the meaning of the word "bateau": what passed for one in Maine was a small, heavy craft used ordinarily for logging on flooded rivers, while Arnold no doubt had in mind the light, long whaleboats used on Long Island Sound. But for the men in the ranks who knew about wild rivers and long portages, the clumsy boats they began to drag down to the waterline must have been an ominous portent. Private George Morison of Hendricks' rifle company wrote, "Could we have come within reach of the villains who constructed these crazy things, they would fully have experienced the effects of our vengeance. Avarice or a desire to destroy us—perhaps both—must have been their motives."[14]

He deployed one hundred more boatmen to steer the acceptable bateaux ten miles upriver to Fort Western. Then he returned to *Broad Bay,* which, because of the shoals and low water, could go no farther upriver. However, for the next three days the ship afforded him the distance and privacy he needed as he began a series of meetings and dictated orders to young Oswald. As each transport arrived, he deployed its men. Some were sent ahead in bateaux, others marched forty-five miles along the dirt road on the east side of the river to Fort Halifax (at present-day Waterville), where they were to form up in divisions and draw their rations. As the ships anchored and discharged their men around him, Arnold talked coolly with Major Colburn, pressing on him the need to finish the new bateaux and repair the worst of those he had purchased.

On Washington's orders, Colburn had sent two scouts ahead to report on the hazards of the route and mark a path. They had returned with alarming news. The British had set up a base on the Chaudière and redcoats were waiting to intercept the Americans.

Norridgewock Indians had taken up the tomahawk, and thousands of them were waiting to ambush the expedition. As Arnold read and listened, he decided that there was more smoke than substance to the report. He did not believe that Carleton could spare any redcoats now that Schuyler's attack on St. Jean was under way. Arnold learned that the source of the entire report was a chief of the Norridgewock tribe named Natanis who had told the scouts that Carleton knew of their expedition and would meet it in force. Accustomed to the tactics of Indians since his childhood days in Norwichtown, Arnold discounted Natanis's information as a bluff that had scared the already nervous woodsmen. To Washington, he wrote that the scouts had actually seen only one Indian, "a noted villain."[15] Colburn's scouts had gone on with their mission for only another day after meeting Natanis, then, their supply of rum apparently exhausted, they had turned back only halfway to Quebec. Arnold decided to ignore their report, send out his own scouts, and, in the meantime, rely on Montresor's journal and the maps drawn up from Montresor's journal by the Loyalist surveyor Goodrich, which had just been handed over to him by Major Colburn.

While he waited for boats, men, and supplies to reach the jumping-off point, an outbreak of stealing swept the Tory houses of Gardinerstown. Arnold ordered public floggings of the thieves, meting out whippings of thirty-three lashes. Three Connecticut men were flogged for insubordination, and a sergeant was publicly stripped of his rank. One thief was drummed out of the army and sent back in disgrace. When one drunken brawl led to the shooting death of a Norwich Town musketman by a Maine woodsman, Arnold convened an all-day court-martial. The man was sentenced to death. Arnold had him led to a gallows with a hangman's noose around his neck but then at the last instant ordered him sent back to Washington with a recommendation that his life be spared. "I wish he may be found a proper object of mercy,"[16] he wrote Washington. He had established that he could be tough yet compassionate.

For the march to Quebec, Benedict Arnold was inventing a new kind of army unit, a light infantry regiment specially adapted to long-range amphibious raids. During the French and Indian Wars, the famous Indian fighters Rogers's Rangers had been used to scout for overland raids and to strike out across lakes and rivers, but these rangers, using canoes and operating in smaller numbers, had been hampered by inability to transport provisions over long distances and were therefore incapable of sustained operations. Arnold's new light infantry unit also outmoded its British counterpart, which was essentially dismounted cavalry that could not move far from transport ships or land bases. Arnold knew his innovation was important, because from September 27 onward he kept his own detailed journal to demonstrate its operation to Washington. He described a regiment composed of fast-moving sharpshooters—the riflemen (being used in large numbers for the first time)—and tall, strong, hard-marching musketmen capable of carrying out conventional open-field or siege warfare against a town, all moved by boats that could conceivably extend their striking distance anywhere across the criss-crossed watercourses of North America.

Arnold had fused infantry, rangers, and vessels into a fast-striking force, and as late as September 27, as he mustered his new regiment and dispatched their bateaux at the rate of one battalion each day, he still was telling Washington that he would be in Quebec in only twenty more days. He had managed to provide every man with enough rations to last forty-five days, long enough, he expected, to put them inside the well-fed, well-armed precincts of the French fortress city.

Arnold's plans hit another obstacle as he prepared to send off the first battalion from Fort Western on September 27. He had detailed companies of riflemen to each battalion to act as their scouts, their officers reporting to each battalion's commanders. Immediately, Daniel Morgan, who had emerged as leader of the riflemen by sheer force of personality, appeared in Arnold's cabin. When angered, Morgan reverted to his teamster's manners. His men had enlisted, he told Arnold, with the understanding that they would follow only their own officers and, he insisted, Washington had approved the arrangement. Perhaps the apparition of another Ethan Allen floated before Arnold's eyes for an instant, but if so, he banished it by compromising. He settled the row by assigning the riflemen as a separate battalion under Morgan's command to act as a vanguard for the army. Instead of acting as scouts for each battalion the riflemen would now leave first, in a body, and mark and clear a road for the portages. They would also act as a buffer in case of Indian attack, a possibility that must have excited them. Making it clear that the arrangement might only be temporary, pending review by Washington, Arnold wrote back to the commander in chief for retroactive permission. For now, he seemed satisfied that he had defused the challenge to his command and dispatched Morgan and his men.

Because he still lacked accurate intelligence and was uncertain about the route ahead, Arnold next sent his own scouts, recruited, from Morgan's division. He placed them under the command of

Pennsylvanian Archibald Steele, who selected his own men, including sixteen-year-old John Henry, three Virginians, and four Pennsylvanians. With two Maine guides, the scouts set out in two canoes on a journey of up to twenty-five miles a day. Arnold also sent ahead another scouting party, led by Lieutenant Church, to mark a trail across the Great Carrying Place between the Kennebec and the Canadian border. They also had orders to kill the Abenaki chief Natanis. It was three weeks before they reported to Arnold again, nearly starving.

On September 27, a courier from Washington arrived with the commander in chief's proclamation to distribute among the French Canadians. Sending off a flurry of last-minute messages—a letter to Hannah, a thank-you note to Nathaniel Tracy, and demands that Lieutenant Colonel Enos hurry up with the rest of the boats, supplies, and men—Arnold ordered "the sick and criminal"[17] aboard *Broad Bay* and sent them back to Cambridge. That day and the next morning, he watched with satisfaction as first Greene's battalion and then Meigs's went off in squads of heavily laden bateaux, each poled and rowed by four men while an equal number, the relief crew, marched along a dirt road on the riverbank. As he fired off his last orders, Meigs's Massachusetts and Connecticut men, including all the best boatmen, worked out into the rough current, their setting poles stabbing the river bottom and paddles biting into the choppy water. The men, all tired of camp life, were in high spirits as they got underway. After the last troops had pulled out of sight, Arnold and his aide, Oswald, went down to the river's edge and stepped into a long birchbark canoe crammed with bearskin-covered bundles of supplies and paddled by hired Abenaki guides. Waiting for them in the bow of a second canoe was Aaron Burr in his new ranger's uniform with the rabbit-trimmed hat. Steadying the boat, her long black hair spreading down the back of her hunting shirt, crouched the beautiful princess of the Swan Island Abenakis, Jacatacqua, part Indian, part French, wholly in love with Burr. Between them sat her hound dog. As two Abenakis steadied the lead canoe, Arnold, clad only in a breechclout, climbed in and knelt down. Quickly, silently, the canoes nosed out into the main channel, rapidly overtaking the main body of bateaux. It was a crystal autumn afternoon. As Arnold watched elm and ash, beech, maple, and oak leaves drop into the churning white water, his canoe darted among the bateaux, to the cheers of the laboring oarsmen and the loaded-down marchers on the shore road. From that moment on, Benedict Arnold, one diarist noted, was "beloved by the soldiery,"[18] and he smiled and waved and called them by name as he rushed toward a Canadian winter.

* * *

The drought of summer had left the Kennebec River by late September, and a long chain of rapids with endless exposed rocks made steering a loaded bateau nightmarish to Connecticut farmboys and tricky even for the most practiced Abenaki Indian guides. After eight miles of battering by the rocks, Arnold's borrowed canoes were "proving very leaky,"[19] and he had to put into Vassalborough, four miles short of Skowhegan, to exchange them for dugout wooden canoes. It was too late to go on to Skowhegan, so he found lodgings for the night. By six o'clock in the morning, Arnold was helping the Indians to carry his canoe and supplies around Three-Mile Falls. By ten o'clock, they had reached the cluster of abandoned blockhouses and barracks at the mouth of the Sebasticook River that marked the western boundary of Maine settlement. That night, Benedict Arnold would begin to sleep, like his men, in a tent.

Half a mile farther upstream, at Ticonic Falls at present-day Skowhegan, Arnold watched as his men unloaded the bateaux, hoisted the heavy boats out of the water, and set them down on their shoulders. He could see that although four men carried each boat, the wet weight dug hard into their weary shoulders and made for slippery footing as the men struggled uphill over the thickly wooded dirt path around the falls. With ropes and shoulders, the men bullied the boats up the three-mile slope as teams of men marched alongside, bent under the weight of barrels and bearskin-wrapped packages of provisions. Some men actually relished the hard work and the camaraderie that came with it. Private Caleb Haskell of Ward's Rhode Island Company wrote tersely, "Now we are learning to be soldiers."[20]

From the Maine coast all the way north to Skowhegan on the Kennebec River, a distance of nearly fifty miles, settlers had overflowed from Massachusetts and filled the river valley with their farms since the end of French and Indian raids only fifteen years earlier. But after Skowhegan, settlement ended and only wilderness remained. Houses, roads, mills, the heartening smoke from chimneys in clearings abruptly disappeared. Ahead of Arnold's army lay nearly three hundred miles of trackless forests, swamps, wild rivers, and lakes. On October 2, the expedition left the settlement at Skowhegan, the farthest point of English expansion into the heart of Maine. Arnold, after luxuriating in a warm bed at Widow Warren's Tavern, hired a wagon to carry him, his aides, and their canoes around five miles of white water to get in front of the army. Then they covered another five miles by canoe, passing through the bateaux of Greene's division in a cold, driving rain. Writing to Washington after watching the men's struggles, Arnold told the commander in chief bluntly, "We have had a very fatiguing time. . . . The men in general, not understanding bateaux, have been obliged to wade and haul them for more than half way up the river." But he still exuded confidence, "as the men are in high spirits." Arnold was already obviously worried about their slow process, however. In a postscript to Washington, he added:

Your excellency may possibly think we have been tardy in our march, as we have gained so little, but when you consider the badness and weight of the bateaux and the large quantity of provisions, etc. we have been obliged to force up against a very rapid stream, where you would have taken the men for amphibious animals, as they were great part of the time under water; add to this the great fatigue in portage, you will think I have pushed the men as fast as could possibly have been. The officers, volunteers and privates have in general acted with the greatest spirit and industry.[21]

To the great fatigue of portage was added a new kind of suffering on October 2, as men who had waded and thrashed through foaming rapids all day and slept on the ground in wet uniforms woke to find that the temperature had suddenly plunged and their clothing was "frozen a pane of glass thick."[22] Abner Stocking complained, "Our fatigue seemed daily to increase, but what we most dreaded was the frost and cold from which we began to suffer considerably."[23]

Striking out ahead of his army that morning, Arnold raced six miles upriver, arriving by ten o'clock just below the elbow-shaped gorge at Norridgewock Falls. Surveying the next difficult portage, Arnold had time to wander through the ruins of the ancient eastern capital of the St. Francis Abenakis and a French Jesuit mission built in the seventeenth century. Arnold noted in his journal: "Here is some small vestiges left of an Indian town [destroyed by the English about ten years since], the foundation of an old church and altar. . . . The founder of the church and the whole tribe are extinct, we are told, except two or three." Arnold was probably told the story by Jacatacqua, nineteen-year-old princess of the Swan Island Abenakis, who was descended from the Norridgewocks. Arnold was taking pains to learn all he could about the Indians and the French, whose relations with his army he considered crucial to the expedition. Arnold's time for musing was short. He rode on along the badly rutted portage road, soon overtaking the lead division,

Morgan's riflemen, "who had just got their baggage over the carrying places."[24] More and more, he had been worried by the slow pace of the expedition: in eight days, the regiment had covered only fifty miles, slowed down by leaky boats and untrained boatmen. The sight of Morgan's men—big, shambling, easygoing, familiar with wild rivers and back-breaking portages—must have reassured him that his men would learn to make better time on the march. That night, Arnold pitched his tent with the riflemen, talking with Morgan and his officers until late into the night. The next morning, October 3, he was down on the riverbank waiting when the first of Meigs's bateaux—carrying the bulk of the army's food—caught up. As Thayer's and Hubbard's companies dragged their boats ashore, they emptied the bales and barrels out over Father de Rasle's grave, spreading out and sorting their waterlogged supplies on their blankets. Hubbard and Thayer were irate about the bateaux. They showed Arnold carelessly nailed, badly caulked floorboards, cracked pine knots, and knees that should never have been used for boatbuilding. Seams in nearly all the boats had opened up too far to be caulked. In all of the badly damaged boats, they found warped green planks. As the boatmen and their officers cursed the boatbuilders, Arnold surveyed the extent of the damage. Hubbard and Thayer had their men tip the split-open barrels so Arnold could see inside. What he saw sickened him. The barrels had leaked brine meant to preserve salted meat and left writhing maggots. Salt fish had been carelessly piled in boats; the salt had washed off and the fish had rotted. Cracked barrels had soaked up river water and burst, turning containers of flour and peas into soggy, moldy putty. Beef put up with salt in the heat of summer was now found to be bad. Much of the expedition's food obviously would have to be jettisoned; precious salt beef and cod, peas, cornmeal, and flour would have to be thrown away, leaving only some salt pork and flour, both already in alarmingly short supply. Arnold said little, only ordering the company of caulkers and carpenters he had providentially brought along to set to work repairing the bateaux and recoopering burst barrels.

Arnold was paying for his eagerness to recruit on such short notice at Cambridge: much of the damage was the fault not merely of the boatwrights but of inexperienced boatmen who had misrepresented their nautical skills and misdirected their setting poles as they pushed them down into the churning river, allowing the boats to yaw across the current and ship water that sloshed around until it found fissures in barrels and bags. All he could do was to stop the expedition long enough for repairs—and to sort out which men could handle boats and which could only be trusted with marching alongside. Eight more days were lost.

As the carpenters worked frantically, the men slept, ate, drank, repaired themselves, but also further depleted the already meager provisions. Arnold packed the men into abandoned French houses and stores at night, then pushed them all day to ferry over the mile-and-a-half uphill portage what supplies they could salvage, dispatching each unit as soon as it had boats and food enough. He trudged from company to company, spending one night in Morgan's camp before sending the riflemen ahead to clear a road and build lean-tos at the next carrying place. He spent a day with Greene's Rhode Islanders before sending them forward. His heart must have sunk when the last battalion brought up the rest of the supplies. In his journal for October 7, Arnold noted tersely, "The last division employed in examining their bread [part of which is wet and unfit for use]."[25] Evidently, he appeared outwardly confident to the officers and men resting at Norridgewock and eating all the fish they could catch. While the noise of splashing, swearing soldiers was obviously frightening away the game, leaving little but tantalizing footprints, fish could not escape, and the soldiers were able to gorge after half an hour's fishing.

By October 8, Enos's rear guard completed the portage—it had taken this last division fully five days to get across. Arnold was more than ready to set out again, but an all-day torrential rainstorm kept him for another restless day until the river subsided. On Monday, October 9, Arnold noted in his journal, "Struck our tents—carried our baggage across the portage."[26]

Early the morning of October 11, after spending the night with the Maine troops of Captain McCobb, Arnold struck out early with his guides and aides, reaching Carratunk Falls by nine. The falls was only fifteen feet high, he noted, but the portage nearly half a mile. Then "we proceeded up the river about five miles against a very rapid stream," his Indian guides sweating and straining silently hour after hour. Suddenly the Kennebec began to narrow into little more than a creek between high hills. "Here the mountains begin to appear, on each side the river, high, and snow on the tops." From a wide river four hundred yards wide "full of a great number of small islands," the Kennebec at its headwaters now became "very rapid and shallow water."[27] After winding its way through the islands for twelve miles against the current, Arnold's advance party was ready to drop.

In a dazzling autumn sunlight the next morning, October 11, still obliviously following Montresor's directions, they reached the portage Montresor had named the Great Carrying Place. Here the army would have to leave the Kennebec and carry everything overland to the Dead River to avoid an unnavigable loop of water at the junction of the two rivers. According to Montresor's journal and Goodrich's maps, there was a twelve-mile series of portages made easier by three ponds where the boats could be refloated. Arnold jumped ashore at the Carrying Place, where dozens of bateaux already lined the river. His party overtook the first and second battalions.

Covered with mud, muscle-weary, Arnold's men laughed when a man slipped, cheered when Arnold hefted his canoe with the others. "We were half leg deep in mud," wrote Private Morison, "stumbling over fallen logs, one leg sinking deeper in the mire than the other. . . . Down goes a boat and the carriers with it. A hearty laugh prevails."[28]

Hemlocks and cedars ringed the first pond, their branches twisting in the hard-blowing wind. The tired and thirsty men who had paddled twelve miles against the current that day on a single meal of salt pork and johnnycake the night before threw themselves on the ground and drank their fill of the brackish pond water. They made it only slightly farther up the path before they became sick. By noontime, the doctor was busy trying to help dozens of retching, writhing men, stretched out for a dozen miles along the river: "Many of us were in a sad plight with the diarrhea." The sick were estimated at one hundred. Arnold had been putting off making a decision about the sick. Dr. Senter suggested building a hospital where the men could rest and recuperate until they were fit to go on or go back. Arnold decided on a log building protected by a blockhouse. He would leave behind Captain Goodrich's company of Maine woodsmen to build them. Senter suggested who should be allowed to stay: Captain Williams of Enos's Connecticut battalion was recovering from a near-fatal bout of dysentery, but he was still too weak to walk, let alone command his company. Ensign Irvin of Morgan's company of Pennsylvania riflemen had been left helpless, his joints stiffened and swollen by acute rheumatoid arthritis from the weeks of wading in icy water and sleeping on the cold wet ground. "His situation is most wretched," Senter told Arnold, "he is overrun with vermin, unable to help himself in the least thing, attended constantly with the most violent pain."[29] A dozen other men were just too played out to go any further. What finally convinced Arnold he must build the hospital was the comment by Senter that it was taking four riflemen to carry Ensign Irvin. Arnold needed every able-bodied man to press on as quickly as possible to Quebec, since his original timetable called for them to be in Quebec by now. He would put Irvin, an officer and a Philadelphia-trained physician, in command, and the sick would nurse one another while the rest of the men continued on.

It took fully five days for Arnold's army to cross the Great Carrying Place. Nights of sleeping on soft beds of blue joint grass and feasts of salmon trout alleviated only slightly the exhaustion of each day's work. It took eight or nine trips to move boats and supplies over each of the four portages. During the five days, Arnold met almost constantly with his officers, visiting each unit and finally calling a council of war to assess the expedition. He and his officers decided that a log storehouse should be built to serve as a supply depot for the remaining food supplies. He sent orders to his commissary, Captain Farnsworth, seventy miles south at Fort Western, to hire some men to send up to the Great Carrying Place the approximately one hundred barrels of provisions that he had left behind to provide a source for resupply if food ran short before the troops reached the French Canadian settlements on the Chaudière or in case retreat became necessary. Apparently his order never reached Farnsworth. Arnold also polled his officers for a tally of men and provisions. He was down to 950 effectives, with twenty-five days' provisions for each man in the first three battalions. With communications with Enos in the rear almost nonexistent, he had no accurate count of men or supplies in the fourth battalion.

Neither Arnold nor his men were discouraged. In a letter to Washington, he described them as "very cheerful" although they were "much fatigued in carrying over their boats, provisions, etc."[30] To Schuyler at Ticonderoga he wrote that he hoped "in a fortnight of having the pleasure of meeting you in Quebec." He deliberately misstated his location as "Dead River, 160 miles from Quebec,"[31] when he was nearly twice that far away. He obviously was trying to mislead not Schuyler but Carleton, should the letter be intercepted. The letter, if captured, would have a shocking effect that could only help Schuyler by forcing Carleton to pull back troops to defend Quebec, thus easing pressure on Schuyler. In another letter addressed to Quebec to merchants he had dealt with and who he knew were sympathetic to the Americans, he deliberately misstated the strength of his troops, claiming to have more than twice the actual number. The letter introduced its three Penobscot Indian couriers, led by one Eneas; it also sought intelligence of the situation in Quebec, asking his merchant friends (whose identities he shaded with false names) to "immediately write me by him of the disposition of the Canadians, the number of troops in Quebec, by whom commanded," as well as "what ships are at Quebec and, in short, what we have to expect from the Canadians and merchants in that city."[32]

In these two letters, Arnold did not primarily intend to proclaim his coming but was only taking pains to intimidate Carleton if his couriers betrayed him or were captured. But in a third and far more important letter he sent by Eneas to Lieutenant Steele at the head of his scouts, he ordered Steele to detail Private John Hall, a British deserter who spoke French, to go to Sartigan on the Chaudière River (present-day St. Georges) with the Indian messengers to gather intelligence. There he was to hire a Frenchman to go to Quebec to deliver this letter to the merchants and get an answer. Arnold enclosed a handsome stipend of £20 in gold as an incentive for the Frenchman. But they were to be silent about their mission: "Desire him to caution the Indians not to let any one know of our march."[33] In spite of Arnold's actual intentions, Eneas and his friends took the letters and the money and paddled off as fast as they could—straight to Quebec Lieutenant Governor Hector Cramahé, warning that Arnold was coming.

Arnold had better luck with his own men. On Thursday, October 12, Lieutenant Steele returned from his three-week reconnaissance mission to the Chaudière River. Arnold noted that Steele, who was half starving and thoroughly exhausted, "says he discovered no Indians," and that the Dead River, their next waterborne leg of the march, he "judges to be 80 miles—most part of the way of fine deep river—the current hardly perceptible." Steele's news cheered Arnold: there would be more portages, but mostly short, the longest four miles, with firm ground underfoot and "plenty of moose and other game on the river." Steele agreed to set out at once, without even taking time to rest, and return to the Chaudière with twenty axmen and a surveyor "to clear the portages and take a survey of the country."[34] Morgan's men brought fresh fish and meat while Steele ate and told Arnold that they had failed in only one part of their mission: they had not managed to catch and kill Natanis. They had surrounded his hut at dawn and had rushed it, but he was gone.

On Sunday, October 15, one long month after Arnold had left Washington's headquarters at Cambridge, Arnold helped push off his canoe into West Carry Pond, last watery link in the Great Carrying Place. The lake was over three miles long and nearly as wide, and there was ice at its edges. By eleven, he was helping to tote his canoe up snow-covered Mount Bigelow. As the men reached the summit, they could see below them what looked like "a beautiful plot of firm ground, level as a bowling green."[35] But the mirage quickly turned into a nightmare of grass-and-moss-covered bog concealing roots and knees and mud a foot deep that tripped and cloyed at the burdened, cursing troops. Morgan and his men had changed into breechclouts and leather leggings. While the riflemen labored to clear away underbrush and provide footing wherever possible, Greene's second battalion made seven or eight passages each way to get their boats and supplies over, then, passing through the rifle companies, took the lead, launching their bateaux down Bog Creek the mile or so to its confluence with the Dead River. Captain William Hendricks of the Pennsylvania riflemen noted that here the river jogged northwest and was deep, dead, "very black."[36] In all, the crossing of the Great Carrying Place had consumed up to a full week for some units such as the riflemen, first to arrive and last to be allowed to move. Private Morison called its fourteen-mile obstacle course "the most prodigious march ever accomplished by man." By now, Morison wrote, his comrades had become "knit together by mutual sufferings and animated by one common cause."[37] When Arnold overtook Greene's battalion, he learned that Greene's supplies were already so low that he had ordered the men put on half rations of pork and flour. After distributing the meat from the butchered oxen, Arnold ordered the daily ration strictly enforced at twelve ounces each of flour and salt pork. For some men, the ox roast in a driving rainstorm was a memorable occasion before even harder times. Arnold meanwhile had sent Greene's second-in-command, Major Bigelow, with three officers, six noncommissioned officers, and eighty-seven men in twelve boats back to Enos's rear battalion to get more provisions. To distract his men until they returned, Arnold ordered the first three battalions to set to work making cartridges. By October 17 the shortage of food had become so critical that as Morgan's riflemen passed through Greene's hungry battalion on its way back into the lead, they stole a cache of food Greene had left unguarded on a small island.

For two days and nights, rain had been falling heavily, turning the portage path to ooze and flooding the Dead River. At four the next morning, Arnold, his aides, and his Indian guides were awakened by the roar of a wall of water rushing through the flat Dead River basin, stirred up by a West Indies hurricane that had been moving slowly northwest across Maine. "Very luckily for us," Arnold wrote, "we had a small hill to retreat to, where we conveyed our baggage and passed the remainder of the night in no very agreeable situation." At dawn, Sunday, October 22, Arnold surveyed "a very disagreeable prospect, the country round entirely overflowed, so that the course of the river, being crooked, could not be discovered." The water had risen, in three days, more than twelve feet and was moving so rapidly that "the current renders it almost impossible for the bateaux to ascend the river. . . . Add to this our provisions being nearly exhausted." Indeed, when Arnold and the vanguard pressed ahead while the rest of the army retrieved and tried to repair its gear—strewn over twelve miles of flooded river— they ran into such "a very rapid stream"[38] and so much floating debris that seven more bateaux overturned. It took nearly two hours to rescue all the men. Seven more boatloads of food, guns, gunpowder, and clothing were lost the next day. At the same time, Meigs's division, marching ahead on shore, took a wrong turn and became lost at a dead-ended stream. All of Arnold's remaining bateaux were needed for a two-hour rescue operation to bring the thoroughly soaked and demoralized men back to the bank of the Dead River. Meanwhile, Captain Thayer and eight of his men had spent all night wading through the raging cold water. "Exhausted with cold and fatigue," he and his men reached their detachment at nine in the morning as "the sun rose with a little rain."[39] The army marched only half a mile that day, then camped at a spot the men named Camp Disaster.

That night, Monday, October 23, 1775, as the men struggled to build fires and sat, teeth chattering, in sodden wool uniforms, Arnold summoned an emergency council of war of officers of the first two battalions to decide whether to go on: if he was going to turn back, it had to be now, while there was food enough to reach the Kennebec. Wrapping a cloak around his soggy red Foot Guards uniform, Arnold knelt sharpshooter-fashion before the headquarters fire where a score of miserable officers were crouching and, as they tried to dry off, rammed home his points, driving his right index finger into the palm of his left hand. In the smoky firelight, Arnold had to raise his voice over the hissing and sputtering of wet firewood and the coughing of his officers. Men keeping diaries remembered how the smoke added to his intense emotions to make Arnold's eyes shine. He left no question where he stood. Arnold did not deny that the expedition had run into greater hardships and losses of supplies than anyone had imagined. They were down to near-starvation rations in some battalions for men who were working hard and needed all they could eat: Dr. Senter had told him that he had seen one man eating a candle that day. All the game they had expected had been driven off by the noise of the army and the hurricane. The storm, hunger, and now the cold were making everyone miserably uncomfortable. The terribly underestimated distance was frustrating, the delay created by these difficulties all the more so. Arnold paused. No one disagreed with him. Then he smiled wryly. But there were some things to be thankful for. The worst of the march had to be over, and only one man had died. Everyone left with the army was still reasonably healthy. The men were uncomfortable and often exhausted, but if the remaining supplies were evenly divided and strictly rationed, they should last until the army reached the French settlements on the Chaudière. The cold would bring an end to the rains and would harden the ground to make marching and hauling supplies easier. Arnold remained convinced that they would still reach their goal and take Quebec.

His Spartan appeal was effective. After only a few questions, his officers, infused with Arnold's indomitable spirit, gave their assent to his plan. Arnold issued a stream of orders. The sick and the weakest men from every division were to be sent back to the rear with four days' rations, enough to get them to Fort Halifax, where there would be plenty more. The remaining rations were to be redistributed. Arnold ordered Greene and Enos to bring up their best men, only as many as they could provide with enough rations to last fifteen days. Furious at the deficiency of their maps, Arnold could only guess how far they were from the Chaudière. To Washington, he wrote that he had finally discovered that both Montresor's maps and the versions he had had drawn from it were frauds. "I have been deceived," he wrote, "in every account of our route, which is longer and has been attended with a thousand difficulties I never apprehended."[40] To reach the French settlements as quickly as possible and bring back more food, Arnold was detaching Captain Oliver Hanchet of Suffield, Connecticut, and fifty picked men. Arnold himself would set out at once with this flying company to procure supplies and clear the route for the main force. Once he found the way, he would send back guides to bring the expedition forward. Meanwhile, the army was to repair its equipment, reload its bateaux, and, when Enos had sent up his excess supplies from the rear, proceed toward the Chaudière. Arnold's letter containing his orders to Enos was detailed and unmistakable. He was to send up his best men, with fifteen days' supplies: it would take fifteen more days, he now estimated, to reach Canada.

The next morning, as Hanchet raced ahead with a dozen boats, two inches of snow fell. Twenty-six men were sent back by Meigs to join forty-eight disabled men from Greene's battalion. After sending his written orders to Enos in the rear, Arnold set off at noon, covering "seven miles very rapid water" and portaging around two waterfalls. With luck, he would arrive in two days at the source of the Canadian river that would speed him toward Quebec. That night, the wind shifted to the north and the rain turned to snow. By dawn October 25, he had left camp with four Indians and twelve woodsmen, rowing and portaging again across marshes, rivulets, and a string of small lakes. Here Arnold's maps failed him again. He must have wondered how his army would fare as he and his Indian guides groped for a channel.

Arnold discovered the next day that he was at last in the Chain of Ponds, actually a stairway of ponds, lakes, and waterfalls that was carrying him higher toward the divide which was the last major physical barrier before the Chaudière. Although Goodrich's maps were worthless, Montresor's descriptions were helpful. On Thursday, October 26, he followed a "narrow and very crooked and rapid brook" about three miles to the first portage of the day. After crossing Lost Pond, "in a few minutes we arrived at another portage," then another lake, then a third and fourth. By four in the afternoon, Arnold was buoyed by the realization, at least if Montresor's diary was accurate on this point, that they had "entered on the great carrying place into Chaudière Pond."[41] For two miles they climbed steadily, bent under the weight of their dugouts. By dusk, they had ascended a four-mile, thirty-five-degree slope. It was midnight before they had gone back down for their gear and climbed up again and could pitch their tents. Arnold had to make a difficult decision. It was obvious that the maps that had failed him would fail his divisional leaders as well. The army following him could become hopelessly lost if it was not guided through the Chaudière Ponds. Yet his sense of time told him that he would scarcely have enough food to save his hungry army even if he personally kept on as fast he could toward the French settlements. He decided he must go on and find food. It was better to risk having his men temporarily lost than to starve. Sending back a Maine guide, Isaac Hull, to bring his soldiers on in his wake, Arnold, dressed in a red Foot Guards uniform and riding in a captured British canoe, plunged on toward Canada.

Far to Arnold's rear, Dr. Senter, attached now to Greene's division, had gone to bed the night before concerned for the men "almost destitute of any eatable whatever except a few candles." He woke on October 25 to find his tent sagging under the weight of six inches of wet snow that had fallen during the night. While they awaited resupply by Colonel Enos's division, Greene had sent an express up the river to describe to Arnold the worsening state of Greene's troops.

At noon on the 25th, Enos and his captains and adjutants arrived at Greene's camp and immediately went into a meeting with Greene, Major Bigelow, and Captains Thayer, Topham, and Ward to decide whether Enos should resupply Arnold or ignore his orders. As the ranking officer and Arnold's second-in-command, Lieutenant Colonel Enos presided. Dr. Senter, who attended the meeting, later recorded that he was surprised that there was any question of following orders, but that he sensed trouble as soon as Enos arrived with his officers. Enos's men wore "melancholy aspects." There were "a number of grimacers." They "had been preaching to their men the doctrine of impenetrability and non-perseverance." It was Enos who had decided "to hold a council of war"[42] to question Arnold's orders: Greene and his officers were reluctant to hold an official council of war without Arnold's knowledge or consent.

According to Thayer, when Greene and his officers voted to advance, "they held a council of war amongst themselves [Enos, McCobb, Williams, and Scott] and unanimously decided that they would return, and not rush into such imminent danger."[43] Senter recorded that the party against going on urged the impossibility of proceeding, "averring the whole provisions, when averaged, would not support the army five days." Enos then insisted that he had lost most of the provisions and had scarcely enough supplies left for his own battalion; furthermore, if they abided by Arnold's orders, there would not be enough food left for the rest of his battalion to retreat to the Kennebec. He was down to his last barrels of pork and flour, he said. To avoid putting more strain on his dwindling food supplies, he urged that his entire battalion return to Cambridge, and he urged Greene and his battalion to join them. Greene listened in disbelief. He reminded Enos and his officers that at the very least, they would be guilty of insubordination if they did not follow Arnold's written orders to join him "with all possible dispatch."[44] What Enos was proposing would have cut Arnold's force nearly in half, surely crippling the expedition. Greene and his staff insisted that only the weak and unfit should be sent home. Evidence in expedition diaries indicates that Enos had at the very least six days of full rations for all four hundred men assigned or attached to his division. If, according to Arnold's orders, Enos had sent back the sick, the carpenters, and the commissaries and his 150 weakest men with three days' half rations, he still could have sent forward his one hundred best men with fifteen days' food and a sizable quantity of flour, meat, and ammunition for Greene's division.

When they voted whether to go ahead or return, the vote was even. At first, Enos voted to go on, but then he shifted at the insistence of his own officers to break the tie. Greene and his men decided to go on with Arnold, Enos to turn back. To Greene's surprise, Enos promised him four barrels of flour and two of pork, but when Greene sent Thayer and Matthias Ogden with a boat to collect them, Enos gave them only two barrels of flour and no meat. Enos kept all his weapons, and all the army's medical supplies.

When word passed up along the river of Enos's defection with roughly one-third of the army and half its supplies, some men were furious, others disheartened: Captain Dearborn was sure the defection of an entire battalion and so many supplies was "very fatal, and mortifying to us all." Dearborn, whose company had been detached from Enos's battalion and was ahead with Greene, was at the carrying place three days later when he heard the news. He worried that they were too feeble "to think of entering such a place as Quebec" and "were sure to die if we attempted to turn back." The bulk of the army was still one hundred miles from the nearest French settlement, three hundred miles from the nearest American settlement in Maine. Dearborn took some heart from this calculation: "We could be in no worse situation if we proceeded on our route."[45] Not so Private Morison, who found Enos's defection "very distressing. . . . We depended much upon this store. . . . We were now reduced to a short allowance of flour only." Yet Morison never considered turning back: "No one thought of returning. We found it best to endure it patiently."[46] Captain Dearborn wrote that night in his diary:

Our men made a general prayer: that Colonel Enos and all his men might die by the way, or meet with some disaster equal to the cowardly, dastardly and unfriendly spirit they discovered in returning back without orders.[47]

It was another three days before Benedict Arnold learned of Roger Enos's treachery. As late as October 27, he had written to him, "I hope to see you soon in Quebec."[48] Arnold was careful not to show his fury among his men. There is not a word of his reaction in his own diary before October 30, when he sent it off to Washington, and he undoubtedly knew of it by then. When he finally wrote Washington about Enos a month later, he had cooled down to the point of commenting that his turning back had been "contrary to my expectations."[49] Enos and his well-fed men reached Cambridge, Massachusetts, on Thanksgiving Day, arriving after "a long and wearisome journey . . . abundantly satisfied."[50] When Washington heard that Enos was in camp, he immediately ordered him arrested and brought before a court-martial made up largely of Enos's friends, presided over by Brigadier General John Sullivan of New

Hampshire. The formal charge was "quitting his commanding officer without leave." All of Enos's officers were present to testify in his favor, but none of Arnold's officers or men could travel from Canada to testify against him. General Sullivan, after admitting on the court record grossly understated estimates of the supplies Enos had on hand at the time of the October 25 council of war, ruled that "the return of the division was prudent and reasonable" and that had he gone on with Arnold "it would have been the means of causing the whole detachment to have perished in the woods for want of sustenance."[51] Enos was acquitted, yet only cold silence awaited him in camp and at headquarters. Eight days later, Enos resigned his commission. He never again served in the Revolution, although he eventually became a major general in the Vermont militia.

Arnold no longer had enough men to take Quebec by storm unless, as he now doubted, he found the enemy "not apprised of our coming."[52] Yet while he did not give up his plan to carry out the attack, he had begun to reconcile himself to the loss of too much time and too many men to do anything more than sever communications between Quebec and Montreal until he could link up with Schuyler's forces. He had just learned from a French Canadian scout that Carleton was making a stand against Schuyler at St. Jean. Bitterly disappointed that Enos's defection had cost him the glory of taking Quebec unassisted, Arnold set about saving the remainder of his army. On October 27, his scouting party, led by Church and Steele, had returned from the French town of Sartigan on the Chaudière. He sent back a dispatch at once "to the field officers and captains . . . to be sent on, that the whole may see it":

Gentlemen—
I have this minute arrived here and met my express from the French inhabitants who, he tells me, are rejoiced to hear we are coming, and that they will gladly supply us with provisions. He says there are few, or no, regulars at Quebec, which may be easily taken. I have just met Lieutenants Steele and Church, and we are determined to proceed as fast as possible with four bateaux and fifteen men to the inhabitants and send back provisions as soon as possible. I hope to be there in three days. . . . I hope in six days time to have provisions halfway up the Chaudière.

He ordered his officers to abandon their bateaux, march around the lakes, "strike off to the right hand" to "escape the low swampy land and save a very great distance." He hoped that by this route they would avoid getting lost in the labyrinth of creeks and lakes of the

Chain of Ponds. He told them that they should ignore their copies of Montresor's map, which omitted Rush Lake, Spider Lake, and the false mouths of Seven Mile Stream (now called Arnold River). That very day, Captain Hanchet's advance guard got lost. Hanchet and sixty men had left the last carrying place with Arnold and had been ordered to follow him by the cautious land route to the east. It was nearly midnight before they were found and retrieved by canoes. The next morning, as Hanchet's exhausted men slept, Arnold sent off Maine guide Isaac Hull "to pilot them up."53 Then in a canoe with Oswald and two Indians, with Steele, Church, and thirteen riflemen following him in four bateaux, Arnold "paddled on briskly," by ten in the morning dashing thirteen miles and reaching Lake Megantic, source of the Chaudière River. Arnold was exuberant, impatient, as he "went ashore, made a fire."54 He had reached Canada, exactly six weeks after leaving Cambridge.

Arnold's cautionary order reached the first division too late. Five companies had already set out into the Chaudière Ponds by the time Arnold's orders reached them. The morning of October 28, Arnold's soldiers had a scant breakfast. In Greene's and Meigs's divisions, all of the remaining flour was divided according to Arnold's estimate that there would be more provisions in seven days. Every man got seven pints of flour for seven days, a gill, or quarter pint, of flour for breakfast, half a pint for the main meal at noontime, a quarter pint for supper. Some of the men cooked up all their flour at once into cakes, mixing flour and water and laying the cakes on hot coals, then carrying along the cakes to munch as they marched without stopping. There was too little pork to divide evenly, less than an ounce a man. The officers decided to forgo their share so their men would each get a morsel that could be cut. Captain Thayer watched as some of his men took raw hides that had lain "for several days in the bottom of their boats, intended to make them shoes or moccasins." Chopping them into pieces and singeing off the hair, they boiled them and "wrung out the juice into their canteens."55

Morgan's officers had been warned by the scouts, Church and Steele, that the mountainous border between Maine and Canada called the Height of Land was "very dangerous."56 Captains Hendricks and Smith decided that they would only partially follow Arnold's directions to get rid of all their boats. They decided to keep one boat per company. Morgan disregarded Arnold entirely and ordered seven boats carried over the mountains. "Our shoulders were so bruised by them that we could not suffer any thing to touch them,"57 wrote Captain Hendricks. Meigs followed Arnold's advice and left behind his bateaux. The men were glad to be rid of the cursed boats: "With inexpressible joy we dropped these grievous burdens,"[58] Private Morison wrote. Meigs was ecstatic to learn that the messenger from the French inhabitants had reached Arnold with gifts of a loaf of bread and some fruit as tokens of friendship and that Schuyler was successfully fighting the British at St. Jean. Cramming their food, gunpowder, and belongings into their knapsacks, the soldiers took up their guns and climbed over the Height of Land.

Very early the morning of the 29th, the men "began descending towards an ocean of swamp." Under an enticing covering of moss, the men found frigid water and ice; "after walking a few hours in the swamp we seemed to have lost all sense of feeling in our feet and ankles." The men "walked in great fear of breaking our bones or dislocating our joints." To stop walking "was sure death."[59] Ahead, many acres of trees had been laid flat, making a straight-line walk impossible. Between these were mire holes where men fell up to their armpits, thickets where dead twigs snapped into their eyes, and on either side of the swamps, precipices and ravines. Despite the grim landscape, Private Morison noted that the army advanced twelve miles that day.

By the time Isaac Hull brought Arnold's warning to keep to the high ground, Morgan had already launched his bateaux into the great swamp and four other companies had waded in on foot, each seeking its own shortcut. It was bitter cold that morning as the men waded into water to their waists. Up front, Captain Dearborn had discovered an Indian canoe and went ahead in it to reconnoiter the web of waterways. At midmorning, he happened upon Goodrich's company stalled at a branch of Seven Mile Stream while Goodrich went in search of the bateau carrying his company's flour supply. Goodrich had planned to bring the boat back and ferry his men across the deep Seven Mile Stream. By late afternoon, as Dearborn brought his own soaked troops up, he decided to search for Goodrich. He heard distress shots fired in the air and found Goodrich and his men stranded on an offshore island, still looking for the bateau. For nearly ten hours, they had been wading in freezing water up to their armpits and still had located neither the boat nor a ford where the soldiers could cross. The men bedded down on a small island only an inch above the waterline, hoping it would not rain overnight. With no food, they spent the night trying to warm themselves by smoky fires fed by branches hacked from knee-deep water. That night, four inches of snow fell.

The Pennsylvania riflemen had followed Captain Smith into the swamp that day, the half-blind drummer boy, John Shaeffer, tripping and falling so many times that the hardboiled riflemen made him their laughingstock. "Shaeffer would frequently, drum and all, tumble into the abyss," wrote John Henry, who pitied his handicapped young fellow townsman and learned to admire him. "This man, blind, starving and almost naked, bore his drum, unharmed by all its jostlings, safely to Quebec, while many hale men died in the wilderness."[60] What made the blind drummer even more wretched that day was that someone had taken his cakes, his ration for the day. John Henry took up a collection of a tin cupful of flour for him. Hoisting his drum and hanging it from his shoulder, John Shaeffer stared ahead and grasped the hand of John Henry as they sloshed through the icy bog, groped through alder thickets, stumbled over roots. In order to keep track of every soldier and keep each company close together, Arnold had ordered each man to stay in his place in line. If he dropped out, he would be missed; if he rejoined his unit, however, it was at the rear of the line. If he was not at the rear of his unit, he was presumed lost. But the unit had to remain intact.

In the same company were the two women, the wives of Private Warner and Sergeant Grier. As they came to the edge of a flooded swamp and began to wade in, someone called out, "Warner is not here." Another reported that he had sat down, sick, under a tree a few miles back. Warner had often lagged behind, Henry reported. "His wife begged us to wait a short time and, with tears of affection in her eyes, ran back to her husband." Finally, the company had to enter the pond, "breaking the ice here and there with the butts of our guns and feet."[61] They were once again waist-deep in water. Here they waited a little longer before Jemima Warner overtook them—alone. She had found her husband sitting against a tree. She cradled him in her arms until he died. The ground was already frozen, she could not bury him, so she quickly covered his body with leaves and twigs. Picking up his rifle, she ran, sobbing, after her company. She trudged on again with her company until they found Captain Dearborn, who had spent the entire day shuttling the stranded soldiers of the low-lying island with his canoe and Goodrich's recovered bateau. Dearborn had ferried across half of what was left of the army. At day's end, he went back to the deserted wigwam to pick up his company's supply of pork and flour, but some of Morgan's riflemen had expropriated it all.

When Isaac Hull finally reached Greene's campfire at the meadow east of Seven Mile Stream on the morning of October 29, he found five companies of troops—Hendricks's riflemen, Greene's three companies, and most of Hanchet's men—still encamped. The men

cheered when Hull told them of Arnold's envoy from the French
habitants, and as they prepared to follow Hull over the high ground,
as Arnold had ordered, some of them gulped down all of their rations, sure that there would soon be plenty more to eat. "This news
put us in high spirits," wrote Captain Hendricks, "but it proved
hurtful to many of us, for we, supposing we were much nearer the
inhabitants than we really were, ate up our bread more lavishly than
otherwise we would have done."[62]

At first Hull kept to the dry ground, bearing northeast, but
slowly, imperceptibly, he began to bear westward. Before long
Greene's battalion was slowing down, crawling through blowdowns,
thrashing through alders, crashing through ice into bogwater. As he
turned eastward, Hull led the way along a stream he was sure would
regain the high ground. Instead, it came out at a spider-shaped lake,
which was not on Greene's copy of Montresor's map. As Hull tried
to extricate the men, more hours were lost. By now, men began to
drop out: Private Samuel Nichols of Topham's company was never
seen again. By dark, everyone, including Captain Thayer, was cursing Isaac Hull: "We find now that the pilot knows no more the way
than the most ignorant of ourselves."[63] That night, as snow fell
heavily, nearly two hundred men, completely cut off from the rest of
the expedition, dropped down at the edge of a vast swamp, kicking
away wet snow to make places for themselves to sleep in soaked
uniforms. Few men had anything to eat. Captain Thayer had shot a
single partridge on the wing and shared the small bird with several
comrades.

On the snowy morning of October 30, 1775, some five hundred
miles due north of Boston, Benedict Arnold's invasion of Canada
was on the edge of doom. Floundering in the swampy headwaters of
the Chaudière River, the first five companies were scattered. After
wandering for two days, they did not know that they were only a
few hundred yards away from the southern tip of Lake Megantic,
the thirteen-mile-long body of water from which the Chaudière falls
100 miles to empty into the St. Lawrence opposite modern-day
Quebec. The rest of the army, following Isaac Hull and more or less
heeding Montresor's map, had stumbled down from the 2,100-foot
Height of Land, descending across Beautiful Meadow. Hull should
have followed the ridge of highland, as Arnold had commanded, and
borne northeast and west around Rush Lake and Spider Lake until
they had reached the shores of Lake Megantic.

Following Hull, they had attempted a shortcut that led them
into a swamp nearly five miles wide, trudging around Rush Lake

and into Spider Lake, neither of them on Montresor's map. There they had collapsed. A third day in the swamps began with a march through Spider Swamp and an attempt to get around the Spider River, too deep to cross. Finally, they found a crossing about four feet deep. Some in their uniforms, others naked and holding their clothes wrapped around their weapons above their heads to keep them dry, they waded across. While the soldiers shivered and dressed, Hull, Greene, and the other officers climbed to the nearest hilltop. Aaron Burr's consort, Jacatacqua, led two Penobscot Abenakis, who had been shadowing the army and had slipped into camp the night before, up the hill after them. She said that they knew the country, since it was their hunting grounds, and they would be willing to lead the army to safety. Greene eagerly accepted. The men were so heartened that they covered fifteen miles. At four that afternoon, a cheer went up as they found footprints—the path followed three days earlier by Arnold's advance party. As they pitched camp, the men could see Lake Megantic, source of the Chaudière, opening out.

The men assigned to Captains Goodrich and Dearborn had been spared three days' slogging. Following Arnold's orders, they kept doggedly to the shoreline of the high ground, meandering from one deep bay with its marshy tip to another. Near the mouth of one deep stream, Dearborn overtook Goodrich to search for his bateau-load of supplies. Goodrich had been "near beat out"[64] by the time Dearborn dragged him into his canoe. Warmed and dried beside a night campfire, the two returned to their men the morning of the 30th. All that day, Dearborn ferried the two companies of men, one man at a time, across the river, then repeated the process at another river less than half a mile's march farther on. Unwittingly, they had crossed the outlet of Spider Lake. On the 31st, they rested as Greene and his five hundred exhausted men overtook them on the shore of Lake Megantic.

The hideous month of October was over as the foot soldiers set off down the Chaudière the next morning. The raging river soon revealed how it had earned its name, French for "caldron." As they marched along the shore, they found debris from ten boats, Morgan's seven and three from Smith's and Hendricks's Pennsylvania companies. While the musketmen had wandered in the swamps, Morgan's rifle companies, all skilled woodsmen, had gone "astray over mountains and through swamps which could scarcely be passed by wild beasts." The northwest wind was freezing the riflemen's buckskins by nightfall, when "we found ourselves within five miles of the place we started from," having "marched fifteen miles in vain." Finding Arnold's path the next day, the riflemen kept to the high ground and launched their remaining boats into the Chaudière on November 1. They began the day "in better spirits than for many days past," the riflemen marching alongshore as the bateaux went ahead. They found, amid the wreckage of Morgan's boats, that the ailing Lieutenant McClellan's boat "had been overset in the river." Captains Smith and Morgan were also thrown into the river by the boiling current. "Captain Smith lost his chest and clothes, with his officers uniform and a considerable sum of money. Captain Morgan also lost his clothes and cash." (Arnold had given each company commander £30 in gold to cover expenses on the road.) "One of his men was drowned."[65] It took two hours to rescue all the men thrown into the frigid rapids.

As the main body of Greene's musketmen caught up with Morgan's advance guard, they found the results of Morgan's refusal to follow Arnold's warning: guns, gunpowder, the last food supplies, and clothing strewn along the banks and dashed against the rocks of the wild river by the swirling rapids, seven boats stove in and jammed into rapids below a waterfall, shattered cargoes lining the river for ten miles. One man had drowned. Rifleman George Innes of Virginia was wedged underwater between two rocks. John Henry had been hobbling along with one moccasin for days. He found the crew of one boat, "having lost all but their lives," huddled around a fire on the sandy shore at the foot of the twenty-foot-high cataract. They had hauled the boat over the mountains as a litter for their pneumonia-stricken platoon leader, Lieutenant McClellan, who would now have to be left behind.

Later that morning, Henry plunked down on a log with some of Thayer's men, knocking over a kettle. As two-thirds of its contents splashed into the sand, a rifleman jumped up and pointed his gun, but another rifleman "soon made up friends." The two men gave Henry a cup of their greenish broth. "They said it was made from the flesh of a boar. From the taste and smell, it was a dog."[66] It was all that remained of Dearborn's Newfoundland. Dearborn was too sick and weak to care when Goodrich came to him and asked if he could butcher his pet dog. "Even the feet and skin" were devoured, Major Meigs noted in his diary.[67]

For two days, most of the army had nothing to eat at all except roots and bark off trees and broth from boiling shoes and cartridge boxes. On November 3, at about noon, Captains Thayer and Topham saw "some men and horses and cattle making towards us." The cattle driver, "sent towards us by Colonel Arnold," offered to butcher the first cow for Thayer and Topham, but they sent it back for their men and marched on for four more hours, finding a group of men "devouring with avidity a calf—we fortunately got some."[68] Private Vining had just feasted on an owl and now drank the broth of the beef and the owl together and waited until the next day to eat the beef.

Dr. Senter, after marching eight miles that morning, stopped and rubbed his eyes at "a vision of horned cattle, four footed beasts." As the animals came closer, "our vision proved real! Exclamations of joy! Echoes of gladness resounded from front to rear, with a Te Deum. Three horned cattle, two horses, eighteen Canadians and one American."[69]

The supplies poured up the river road, dispatched by Arnold with precise instructions for feeding his men. True to his word, it had been exactly six days since he had promised his men relief. The food was to be sent on to the falls of the Chaudière: "Those who have provisions to reach the falls will let this pass on for the rear, and those who want, will take sparingly as possible, that the whole may eat with relief."[70] Arnold kept careful records: "two oxen, 1 cow and 2 sheep, £13.4 . . . bread, £9 . . . 3 bushels potatoes, £6." He paid cash for everything. He had no trouble getting help to drive the livestock up the river road to his starving men. He paid Charles Roderick twelve shillings for "three days' hire"[71] driving livestock he had just purchased from his brother, Pierre. As the livestock reached Dr. Senter, he selected a heifer and meticulously cut it into one-pound rations per man. Soon two birchbark canoes appeared, laden with cornmeal, mutton for the sick, even tobacco. "We sat down, ate our rations, blessed our stars and thought it luxury,"[72] wrote Dr. Senter.

After lunch, the restored army marched nearly twenty miles in a single afternoon, in all covering a remarkable thirty miles that day. At ten-thirty on Friday, November 3, Arnold's army, reeling like drunken men and down to 675 of the 1,080 men who had left Cambridge fifty-one days earlier—40 percent of his army lost by death or desertion—entered Sartigan, the first French settlement, many of the barefoot men leaving bloodstains on the snowy riverbank. Private Morison saw them collapse as they tried to scale the bank of the last barrier, the Famine River; they rolled down helplessly, then groped for their guns in the snow and, catching at twigs and shrubs, pulled themselves upright for the last short trudge into the collection of huts and wigwams clustered around a Catholic church called St.

Georges. Soon the whole army was gorging on roast beef, grouse, chicken, potatoes, vegetables, and bread fresh-baked by the habitants.

For the last two days Arnold had been riding up and down the river, making sure his men got fed. Every few miles, more animals were slaughtered, until every man had eaten meat. Abner Stocking described what the awed French Canadians saw as the soldiers stumbled out of the wilderness: "Our clothes were torn in pieces by the bushes and hung in strings. Few of us had any shoes, but moccasins made of new skins—many of us without hats—and beards long and visages thin and meager. I thought we much resembled the animals which inhabit New Spain called the Ourang-outang."[73] Only Arnold was missing from the feast. He had gone on ahead to round up still more supplies and confer with the Indians. It was several weeks before he had time to write about the expedition to General Schuyler:

In about eight weeks, we completed a march of near six hundred miles . . . the men having with the greatest fortitude and perseverance hauled their bateaux up rapid streams, obliged to wade almost the whole way, near 180 miles, carried them on their shoulders near forty miles over hills, swamps and bogs almost impenetrable, to their knees in mire. . . . Short of provisions, part of the detachment disheartened and gone back, famine staring us in the face, an enemy's country and uncertainty ahead. Notwithstanding all these obstacles, the officers and men, inspired and fired with the love of liberty and their country, pushed on with a fortitude superior to every obstacle—and most of them had not one day's provisions for a week!

There was only praise for his men, no hint of self-praise in Arnold's account, but the fact that only Enos's men had turned back, that every other soldier had either followed him or died in the attempt, attested to Arnold's triumphant leadership. It had been a brilliant military achievement that in only two months had wiped away any doubt of the innate military genius of the self-trained soldier. Arnold did not mention that he had personally covered the distance nearly three times, that he had very nearly been killed when only the capsizing of his canoe in the Chaudière saved him from going over the Great Falls and being dashed to pieces with most of his boats, or that he, too, had emerged weak, thinned, bearded, and half starved after not eating for three days and living on a few hundred calories a day for two weeks. Indeed, he did not dwell on all that had gone wrong: 40 percent of the men lost or deserted, and all but four boats and all weapons, ammunition, and medical supplies lost. All he would say was that there had been "a thousand difficulties I never apprehended."[74]

Washington's reaction to the news that Arnold's army had survived the wilderness march was unconcealed relief and generous praise for Arnold. In a letter to Schuyler, Arnold's commanding officer, Washington said that "the merit of that officer is certainly great, and I heartily wish that fortune may distinguish him as one of your favorites. He will do everything which prudence and valor will suggest." But Washington was equally censorious of Enos for sabotaging the expedition: "In consequence of Enos's return," he wrote Schuyler, "Arnold will not be able to make a successful attack on Quebec without the cooperation of Montgomery."[75] Indeed, Enos's appearance in the camp at Cambridge caused great indignation, veterans testified years later. He was looked upon as a traitor for deserting his companions and endangering the expedition. To Arnold himself, Washington wrote to praise his "enterprising and persevering spirit—it is not in the power of any man to command success, but you have done more, you have earned it."[76] When word of Arnold's march reached the Continental Congress, the overjoyed reaction was quickly spread throughout the colonies by delegates' letters home. "Heaven seems to have interposed in preserving almost miraculously what still remains of the brave little army,"[77] a North Carolina delegation wrote. The march of "that little army,"[78] wrote another delegate, "is thought equal Hannibal's over the Alps."

But the tribute that pleased Arnold the most was the praise of his men, a sample of which survives in their diaries. Young John Henry wrote that he would always remember Arnold as "brave to the point of temerity," a man with "an active spirit."[79] One of Arnold's officers writing from Quebec to a fellow officer a few weeks later called him "a gentleman worthy of trust," a man of "invincible courage, of great prudence: ever serene, he defies the greatest danger—you will find him ever the intrepid hero and the unruffled Christian."[80] Private Stocking summed up how the men felt about the officer who had become "beloved by his soldiers":

Our bold though inexperienced general discovered such firmness and zeal as inspired us with resolution. The hardships and fatigues he encountered, he accounted as nothing in comparison with the salvation of his country.[81]

Arnold displayed his customary reserve when he learned a few weeks later that as he gathered his men to cross the St. Lawrence and storm Quebec, Ethan Allen was on his way to England as a British prisoner of war after prematurely attacking Montreal.

BOOK TWO

"IT
WAS
ARNOLD"

8

"I KNOW NO FEAR"

*My detachments are
as ready as naked men
can be to march
wherever they may be
required.*

Benedict Arnold to George Washington, November 20, 1775

On the afternoon of November 3, 1775, Colonel Benedict Arnold arrived at Ste. Marie on the Chaudière River, thirty miles east of Quebec, and expropriated the Château de Lauzon as his headquarters. Donning his best gold-braided epauletted red Foot Guards regimentals, he prepared speeches for a conference with Indian chiefs from eastern Quebec and Maine while his bedraggled men caught up with him.

The French Canadians all but overwhelmed the *Bostonnais* with their generosity as they staggered into the settlements along the Chaudière. Not only did they agree to sell them livestock, bread, rum, horses, canoes, and anything the Americans needed, but in many cases they would not even accept payment for their labor and food. The French Canadian habitants as far north as the Chaudière had heard of Arnold's unopposed conquest of the great once-French fortress at Ticonderoga, of his victory at St. Jean, of the recent battle at Chambly, where many British prisoners had been taken. But they had another motive for cooperating with the Americans. Carleton's

Quebec Act promised few reforms that would benefit them and, indeed, would only increase the power and influence of oppressive seigneurs by confirming feudal land-tenure rights and taxes and requiring them to work and fight for their British conquerors. Their spirit of incipient rebellion had been fed by pro-American Montreal merchants who pressed American propaganda on them when they made their fall buying trips. In thirty-seven of fifty parishes, a British investigative commission subsequently found the militia officers had actively cooperated with the Americans. At the Château de Lauzon, the habitants had humiliated their seigneur, hiding their guns and attacking British recruiting officers with scythes and pitchforks. Now they were flocking to help Arnold, celebrating their new spirit of rebellion with a feast in the manor house of absent militia Colonel Taschereau. It was snowing heavily as the bedraggled Arnold, his secretary Oswald, a few Indians, and a half-dozen riflemen slid their canoes ashore and the Canadians rushed to help them. The smiles of the Frenchmen turned to awe when they got a better look at these wildmen from the south with their long rifles. The rumor immediately started that they were invincible, that their gray linen shirts and cloaks were made of *tole* (sheet iron), not *toile* (linen). That they could have survived forty days in the wilderness in the winter amazed these experienced *coureurs de bois*. Arnold did not have to do more than suggest what he needed and the Canadians began herding their livestock along the river road, their horses sagging under the sacks of flour.

The next day, Saturday, November 4, was John Henry's seventeenth birthday. Fording the Famine River, he clattered into a house where Arnold's adjutant, Lieutenant Steele, had spread a feast. Henry knew not to overeat: "a Pennsylvania German of our company" ignored his warning and stuffed himself on boiled beef, hot bread, and boiled and roasted potatoes, and he died two days later. "We lost three of our company from imprudence." Young Henry ate a little raw bacon. A few days later, he sat down on a log beside the road as his unit trudged ahead. Arnold, on horseback, saw Henry drop out and hurried over. When Henry told Arnold he couldn't go on, "he dismounted, ran down to the riverside and hailed the owner" of a nearby house. Arnold "put two silver dollars in my hands"[1] as the Frenchmen carried him to his house. (There is no record of the expense: Arnold was ignoring congressional auditors by not getting a receipt.) Henry was one of nearly one hundred stragglers whom Arnold had arranged to be nursed back to health.

All along the one-hundred-mile line of march from the Canadian border to the St. Lawrence, Arnold's men admired the whitewashed houses gathered around Roman Catholic churches, the roadside Calvaries and Virgins. At night they crowded into houses, slept on cornhusk beds between French Canadians who said their rosaries morning and night. Young Dr. Senter wrote of dinners of "boiled potatoes, butter, hot bread," and he was equally impressed by "the politeness and civility with which the poor Canadian peasants received us." His friends Burr, Jacatacqua, and Matthias Ogden had for several days been stopping their canoe at every house, trying to buy rum. They found "a merry old woman at her loom and two or three fine young girls." Burr spoke fluent French. Some eggs, rum, sugar, and sweetmeats made Burr and friends "very happy." When the old woman learned they had marched from Boston, she "immediately fell to singing and dancing Yankee Doodle with the greatest air of good humor."[2]

As Arnold's army had marched through fresh heavy snow into the town of Ste. Marie, the jubilant French Canadians rang the church bells to welcome them. The village was already filling up with Abenaki Indians, some eighty of them with their chieftains, "to know our reasons for coming among them in a hostile manner," wrote Dr. Senter, "pretending they were unacquainted with our intentions."[3] The St. Francis chieftain, Natanis, was waiting as Arnold's aide, Captain Steele, rode into Sartigan. John Henry, who had rejoined his unit, wrote that "Natanis came to him in an abrupt but friendly manner and gave him a cordial shake by the hand, intimating a previous knowledge of him." When Henry and his messmates arrived, Natanis also approached them "and shook hands in the way of an old acquaintance." The riflemen now learned that when their scouting party had first encamped on the Dead River on September 29 seeking the route through the Chaudière Ponds with orders to shoot Natanis on sight, "he lay within view of our camp. Now they learned that it had been Natanis who had paved their road through his tribal hunting grounds, even driving moose within gunshot range, even as they surrounded his hunting lodge and attacked it. When Lieutenant Steele finally asked Natanis, "Why did you not speak to your friends?" Natanis answered simply, "You would have killed me."[4]

Benedict Arnold was surprised, too, when he learned that the chieftain to whom the other Indians were deferring was the man he had called "the noted villain" Natanis. Again he asked the obvious question. Again Natanis answered that he would have been killed. Arnold knew a great deal about Indian ways, but he could not judge

them. He was happy for this opportunity to mend relations with
Natanis and Sabatis, and he was cordial to Paul Higgins, their east-
ern chief, the son of a Massachusetts farmer and an Indian woman.
This was the man who had led his warriors all the way from the
Penobscot Abenaki village on Swan Island, Maine, to Cambridge,
Massachusetts, where his offer to guide Arnold's expedition was refused by Washington. Arnold also was cordial to two other
Abenakis, Eneas and Sabatis, whom he wrongly trusted. He had sent
them ahead to the French settlements and they had kept his gold and
taken his dispatches straight to the British authorities in Quebec.
Now, unknown to Arnold, they were back to spy on him. On Saturday, November 4, when the Indians gathered at Arnold's headquarters at Château du Lauzon, Dr. Senter spotted Eneas and his fellow
courier, Sabatis, and was immediately suspicious. Although Arnold
probably knew he had been betrayed to the British, he apparently
wanted the two informers to carry messages of another kind. Paul
Higgins interpreted as the Indians settled into facing arcs on the
floor of the crowded manor house. According to Dr. Senter,
Natanis, designated the spokesman by the other Indians, spoke
"with all the air and gesture of an accomplished orator." No other
Indian presumed to speak: Natanis was their great man, one of only
three survivors of the Massachusetts raid on Norridgewock as a
small boy and one of the few St. Francis Abenakis to survive extirpa-
tion by Rogers's Rangers in the last French and Indian War.

Benedict Arnold had studied the Mohegans as a young man in
Norwich Town and had traveled among them as a trader in Maine,
New York, and Canada. Now, through his interpreter, he read them
Washington's manifesto and distributed copies of it in French. He
had also prepared his own speech filled with the lies and metaphors
that were the standard fare of Indian conferences on the American
frontier. It was probably the only speech he ever made to Indians,
and Dr. Senter wrote it down:

*Brothers, we are the children of those who have now taken up the
hatchet against us. More than one hundred years ago we were all as
one family. We then differed in our religion, and came over to this
great country by consent of the king. Our fathers bought land of the
savages, and have grown a great people. . . . We have planted the
ground, and by our labor grown rich. Now a new king and his wicked
great men want to take our lands and money without our consent.
This we think unjust. . . . The king would not hear our prayer,
but sent a great army to Boston and endeavored to set our brethren against us in Canada. The king's army at Boston came out*

into the fields and houses, killed a great many women and children while they were peaceably at work. The Bostonians sent to their brethren in the country, and they came in unto their relief, and in six days raised an army of fifty thousand men, and drove the king's troops on board their ships, killed and wounded fifteen hundred of their men. . . . Now we hear the French and Indians in Canada have sent to us that the king's troops oppress them, and make them pay a great price for their rum, etc., press them to take up arms against the Bostonians, their brethren, who have done them no hurt. By the desire of the French and Indians, our brothers, we have come to their assistance, with an intent to drive out the king's soldiers. . . . If the Indians, our brethren, will join us, we will be very much obliged to them, and will give them one Portuguese [joe] per month, two dollars bounty, and find them their provisions, and the liberty to choose their own officers.[5]

Arnold knew that British troops had not killed women and children while they were peaceably at work, and that nowhere near fifty thousand patriots had fought back. He knew the British had not been driven back to their ships, but the phrase had long been a commonplace of Indian speeches—that one day they would drive the English back to the sea. But he also meant to remind them of the colonists' great numbers. They should not imagine that the tattered remains of a regiment they had seen and were now helping to rescue all along the Chaudière was anything like the full might of the Americans, who had grown as numerous as "the stars in the sky." After they had passed around calumets filled with strong Virginia tobacco, they agreed on a treaty. Natanis rose once again to make a final speech, addressing himself to Dark Eagle, the name he had chosen for Arnold. "Dark Eagle," he ended, "will soar aloft to the sun. Yet when he soars the highest, his fall is the more certain."[6] Four months after Indian auxiliaries of the British had slain Remember Baker, Benedict Arnold, acting without Washington's orders and only informing him afterward, signed up Natanis, Sabatis, and fifty of their Abenaki warriors to join his attack on Quebec. It was a crucial reinforcement. He paid the Indians as much as he paid his Continentals. In return, he got Indian scouts, marksmen, and, most important, their canoes, which he would need to cross the St. Lawrence. By now, his advance guard had informed him that Lieutenant Governor Cramahé, a former British army captain, had learned of his intentions and that Cramahé had ordered all boats for fifty miles around burned. Six months ago, Arnold had asked them to remain neutral, to stand aside while the two armies contested for the control of Canada. Now with his army depleted by Enos's desertion and by illness, he made a plea for recruits. Nevertheless, they chose to remain neutral. Before the Americans left Ste. Marie, however, the habitants, over the protests of their priest, insisted on rereading at mass George Washington's manifesto with its explicit guarantee that "the cause of America and of liberty is the cause of every virtuous American citizen, whatever may be his religion."[7]

From his temporary base at Ste. Marie, Arnold dispatched Morgan's riflemen to Point Lévis, seven miles north on the eastern shore of the St. Lawrence and only a mile across the water from Quebec. Arnold also sent off Indian messengers to the south to carry a dispatch to General Schuyler, who had written to Arnold of his anxiety for his safety after so long a silence. Schuyler's message was also Arnold's first news of the campaign on the Richelieu far to the south. Montgomery, who had assumed command, had taken the British fort of Chambly, north of St. Jean, with a large number of British prisoners, weapons, and ammunition and was now investing Carleton's main force at St. Jean. Arnold later gave Montgomery the first details of the Kennebec expedition. Two-thirds of his detachment had arrived safely at the St. Lawrence. He had written to Schuyler, he said, sending messages "by an Indian I thought trusty enclosed to my friend in Quebec. . . . I make no doubt he has betrayed his trust. . . . I find they have been some time apprised of our coming in Quebec and have destroyed all the canoes." Arnold had already obtained more canoes, he told Montgomery. "I propose crossing the St. Lawrence as soon as possible." Arnold detailed all the intelligence he had received about the state of Quebec's defenses. He thought that there were only three hundred defenders. "I shall endeavour to cut off their communication with the country." He would either attack or, if the Quebec garrison was reinforced, "keep them in close quarters until your arrival here."[8] Arnold asked Montgomery to reinforce him with a regiment if St. Jean had not yet fallen.

By two o'clock on November 4, with twenty Indian canoes on their shoulders and Indian recruits marching with them, the first rifle units stepped out in formation after a review by Arnold, Morgan, and their officers. Arnold insisted on a little parade to inspire the French and Indians as they left Ste. Marie, purblind John Shaeffer out in front banging his drum and Caleb Haskell of Rhode Island playing his fife. It had been warm and fair for the last few days as the companies regrouped; now it turned cold, and heavy wet snow began to fall on the muddy road. Four miles above Ste. Marie the route left the Chaudière and the settlements and turned northwest through a forest where the men once again tramped through "snowy mire half-leg deep." To Arnold's calls of "Hurry up, boys! Hurry on!"9 the column in three days reached Point Lévis, emerging from the forest a tantalizing mile of water away from the mightiest fortress in North America. After their seven-week ordeal in the wilderness, the cluster of church spires and turreted palaces behind thick granite walls atop a sheer cliff must have been a stirring sight. Between the Americans and the citadel remained one more barrier, the fast-moving St. Lawrence. Arnold had now scraped together forty canoes. Filled with men and supplies, they would nearly swamp on a calm day, and as Arnold reached the river a northwest wind was rising, whipping the water to whitecapped waves. They would have to wait for a calmer day. Riding at anchor in the river were two British men-of-war, the sloop-of-war *Hunter*, the frigate *Lizard*, and an armed transport, as well as the British longboats plying the channel day and night: their guns could easily sink his canoes.

Arnold immediately deployed his men along the river in the abandoned manor house and mills of Loyalist militia colonel Henry Caldwell, who had raised two hundred men and taken them into the walled city. That afternoon of November 8, a British picket boat approached Point Lévis, sent to retrieve oars from Caldwell's mill. Morgan and his men took cover, but suddenly Morgan decided, without consulting Arnold, to capture the boat crew. At too great range, his men opened fire. The longboat pulled offshore, leaving a midshipman behind. Plunging into the water, he tried to swim after the boat. Morgan ordered his men to fire again. Bullets spattered within inches of the officer's head. Swimming toward shore, he tried to surrender. Sabatis, the brother of Natanis, decided to end the episode with his knife and dived into the water. Morgan jumped in too, reached the officer first, and dragged him to shore. The captive turned out to be the younger brother of *Hunter*'s captain. As Morgan and his men tried to climb the steep riverbank and run toward Arnold's headquarters in Caldwell's house, the man-of-war itself warped close to shore and pelted them with grapeshot. Arnold's presence had been discovered. He would have to attack Quebec without the advantage of surprise.

For five days, Arnold's crossing was prevented by a gale accompanied by heavy snows and by round-the-clock British patrols. Arnold tried to make the most of the delay by sending carpenters to nearby sawmills and forges to make scaling ladders and pikes that would be needed to storm the citadel. He desperately needed information from Schuyler's army to the south. Twice he had sent couriers, twice they had been intercepted. Without heavy reinforcements and artillery, he felt it would be pointless to launch an assault on the city. By now he had learned that Quebec had been reinforced twice by Loyalists, on the 5th by 130 Scottish Highlanders, veterans of the battle-seasoned Black Watch, Campbell's and Fraser's regiments and by twenty-four trained gunners from the two men-of-war, and on the 12th, as he still waited for the storm to subside, by two hundred more Loyalists, also veteran Scottish Highlanders who had emigrated to New York after the French and Indian War. They had first marched, bagpipes skirling, to Montreal, then, after learning his plans, proceeded in forced march along the west side of the St. Lawrence from Montreal, led by Colonel Allen McLean.

Now Arnold faced not the handful of redcoats he had expected but 1,150 defenders, including a battalion of marines formed from veteran crews of British and Loyalist ships, as well as 380 raw French Canadian militia. The weeks lost on the Kennebec with leaky boats and the cowardice and treachery of Enos began to gnaw at Arnold, as his letters to Washington and Schuyler show. He was as near to discouragement as he ever came when he learned that, incredibly, the British could not find the long-unused keys to Porte St. Jean on the land side of the city, so they were forced to leave the gate open, even at night. Arnold decided to cross the river and storm the city without waiting for reinforcements. At a council of war that night, Arnold and Greene agreed to attack, even though a majority of their officers recommended caution.

Arnold waited until the night of the 13th, when heavy cloud cover masked the moonlight. He had kept the canoes hidden at the mouth of the Chaudière and now ordered them brought around after dark. In the meantime, he wrote once more to General Montgomery. He had just learned that the two Indians who had carried Montgomery's October 29 dispatch to him and whom Arnold had sent back with his detailed plan on November 8 had been taken prisoner. From their canoe in the river they had mistaken McLean's Loyalist column for Montgomery's force, put into shore, and been captured. Arnold knew he had to cross quickly. "I have near forty canoes ready, and as the wind has moderated, I design crossing this evening." British ships "lie opposite to prevent us, but make no doubt I shall be able to evade them." Indian scouts had just brought word that Montgomery had captured St. Jean after a fifty-eight-day siege and had "invested Montreal." Arnold also sent off a last-minute dispatch to Washington. He had written the commander in chief at the same time as Montgomery, and this message too had been intercepted by McLean. It was obvious, he wrote Washington, that the city of Quebec was all but his. British civilians were fleeing:

fifteen merchant ships had been "loading day and night and four have already sailed."[10] Quebec's businessmen were leaving before he could capture them. Early that evening, Arnold briefed his captains on his detailed plan. The two British warships had been joined by a third armed sloop and were anchored apart in midriver, with armed patrol boats playing between them every hour. They would have to be evaded, but the cold, the wind, and the darkness should work in the Americans' favor if they remained absolutely silent. If they moved quickly and quietly, timing their crossings every hour between patrols, they should be able to get the entire army across before dawn.

At nine o'clock, Arnold got in the lead canoe with Morgan and gave the order to push off. It was absolutely dark as they bumped out into the river against the choppy current, steering a course between *Hunter* and *Lizard* from Point Lévis to Point Pizéan, just southwest of Quebec. As the first canoes approached *Hunter,* they came so close they could see the grillwork pattern of lights from her cabin. Suddenly, Arnold whispered harshly for the men at the paddles to stop. Peering tensely ahead, he could make out in the darkness a blur of movement near his bow, hear the soft thump of oars on leather tholes, the light splash as they cut the water. But the guardboat crew did not see the line of long, low canoes. Arnold decided to veer off closer to Wolfe's Cove, slightly to the south. This made it necessary to make a signal for the convoy of canoes to use as a beacon. Landing with Morgan and seizing an abandoned smithy, he ordered the canoes back for more troops and helped Morgan build a small signal fire in the forge, telling his oarsmen to steer for the pinprick of light. Posting guards and sending out pickets, Arnold anxiously watched the river. By now, the tide was going out, making the crossing even more perilous. Once again the wind was rising, breaking up the clouds until, occasionally, moonlight shone through. As they recrossed, one dugout broke up, flipping Arnold's aide, Lieutenant Steele, into the frigid river. The rest of his crew was rescued by the nearest canoe, but there was no room for Steele: he clung to its stern as one of his men sat on his arms to keep him from slipping under. Dragged into the forge, he was rubbed down with handfuls of snow to bring back his circulation. To warm him, his men had thrown more wood on the fire, and soon the British patrol boat spotted the fire and swung toward shore. Attempting a ruse, Arnold hailed her, ordered her to heave to. But the crewmen refused. Arnold ordered Morgan's men to fire. Further crossings would have to be delayed, but Arnold had gotten his best five hundred men across the river.

*   *   *

When James Wolfe ended the year-long siege of Quebec in 1759 by finding a goat path up from the river to the Plains of Abraham, his presence the next morning with an army at the gates of Quebec had so stunned its French defenders that they had foolishly come out and fought. Arnold decided to follow the same path—now actually a road—and the same strategy and deploy his men in deserted British barracks in Ste. Foy, two miles southwest of the city, and in houses hastily abandoned by Loyalists who had fled into the city. The next day he would march to the city gates and demand Quebec's surrender. Built on the side of a massive promontory called Cap Diamant (Cape Diamond), the city faced east and had been built behind walls at the narrows where the St. Charles River flows south to mingle with the St. Lawrence. Most of the town had spread beyond the walls, running off down Mountain Road to the Lower Town, which sprawled along a thriving waterfront of docks, warehouses, and handsome narrow streets of elegant century-old stone houses. The city presented its back to the Plains of Abraham to the west, its walls all but blocking any view inside. On the west, newer suburbs, spreading out from Ste. Foy and around to St. Roch, girdled the city, pressing up to the walls, which had fallen into disrepair. What Arnold could not see inside the walls was the activity caused by news of his arrival.

On November 2, the day Arnold's army stumbled into Canada, his secret messages were delivered by the Abenaki Eneas to Quebec's aged lieutenant governor, Hector Theophilus Cramahé. Because of his French background more than his military ability, Governor Carleton had made him his lieutenant governor. Cramahé had done virtually nothing to prepare the city for defense, even after Eneas placed Arnold's letters in his hands. But he did notify Captain Thomas Mackenzie, captain of *Hunter,* who had immediately summoned the captains of all merchantmen and the skipper of *Lizard* to a meeting at Cramahé's palatial office in the turreted Château St. Louis. There they had decided to arm volunteers and set up patrols on the river. Three days later, as Arnold had powwowed with the Indians at Ste. Marie, Captain Colin Campbell, sent by Carleton to recruit Highlanders in Newfoundland, returned on a schooner crowded with more Scottish veterans of the French and Indian Wars. Campbell had offered experienced fighters two hundred acres of land. It had been a bad year in Newfoundland, with the American boycott of British imports and exports and a blockade by American privateers. The generous bounty offer enticed away 20 percent of the island's male population. The first boatload of the self-styled Royal

Highland Emigrants, noted *Hunter*'s captain on November 5, arrived at the same time as a sloopload of volunteers from Prince Edward Island and the frigate *Lizard* from Newfoundland with more recruits and a brig from London with guns and ammunition. The next day, November 6, the schooner *Magdalen* had arrived in Quebec, according to British militia Lieutenant William Lindsay, bringing intelligence of Arnold's expedition all the way from England. That same day, the recruits from the Maritime Provinces, including many carpenters, were put to work building gun platforms on the old earthworks west of the city and "erecting barrier gates on every avenue" into the Lower Town, which wrapped around the foot of the crag 150 feet below the citadel. By November 7, Cramahé reported that he had assembled a council of war at his house, attended by all militia and navy officers. "It was unanimously agreed to defend the city to the last extremity."[11] Immediately, all ships—except for the men-of-war—were ordered stripped of their guns and ammunition, which were sent to the Upper Town. It was this activity which Arnold had mistaken for the evacuation of the town.

Yet the people of Quebec, according to Cramahé, were divided on defense: a number of "bad subjects English as well as French" were refusing to do guard duty and were "endeavoring to poison the minds of their fellow citizens in hopes of persuading them to give up the town." Indeed, on the night of the 11th, rebellious Quebec merchants had held a secret meeting and decided to send a message to tell Arnold that the town was still virtually undefended, one of its main gates open. Overnight, the situation had changed when Colonel McLean marched in with his tough Royal Highland Emigrants on the morning of November 12. That same afternoon, Cramahé and British naval officers were meeting at Prentiss's Tavern on Rue St. Louis, a few blocks inside Porte St. Louis, with the ships' captains, militia officers, and the town mayor. There was a new spirit of resistance in the city since McLean's men had arrived in their kilts, lace-trimmed jackets, feathered bonnets, and sporrans. Cramahé told them that according to his intelligence, the Americans were across the river with two to three times their numbers, and more rebels could be expected if Montreal fell, which seemed imminent. Some in the room were less pessimistic and considered the tired and aged Cramahé part of the problem. Cramahé himself was content to be a bureaucrat and wisely asked Colonel McLean to take over the city's defense.

McLean made it clear that he could brook no further talk of capitulation. He knew that Arnold had lost much of his force and had asked Montgomery for reinforcements. Most important, he knew that Arnold thought there were only three hundred men to defend Quebec. He ordered trenches dug, gun platforms built, artillery mounted.

The gunfire at Wolfe's Cove that killed three men patrolling from the *Lizard* signaled Quebec that Arnold's army had indeed crossed the river. "The people in town are in great confusion," Arnold wrote Captain Hanchet on the eastern shore, informing him that a pro-American merchant had brought him intelligence from inside the city, warning him that Colonel McLean was planning "to pay us a visit this morning with 600 men and field pieces."[12]

Arnold had been putting the finishing touches on a proclamation calling for the immediate surrender of Quebec, citing the "unjust, cruel and tyrannical acts of a viral British parliament" and promising that the property of every citizen would be "secured to him" unless he had to storm the town: then "you may expect every severity practiced on such occasions."[13] Arnold now decided to advance immediately to draw McLean into a confrontation. He ordered his men to march to within half a mile of the city walls, just beyond musket range, in such a fashion that the ends of the line were concealed, giving the illusion of a greater number. In tattered and torn uniforms, their hair and beards grown wild, bristling out beyond the odd hat, their shoes no more than raw hides, Arnold's men filed out in the fresh snow, rifles and muskets shouldered in a line three hundred yards long. Then they turned toward the walls, now lined with civilians, soldiers, Scots, and sailors. From behind the line came Benedict Arnold, raising his arms. As if at a signal, a cheer swept the line, then another and another. It was a wild, sustained cheer for the man who had brought them here against the odds and for the men who had died in the swamps and rapids. From the walls above, there was no sound.

When the sound subsided, Arnold ordered forward his aide, Matthias Ogden, with a drummer under a white flag to deliver his demand of surrender. As Ogden approached Porte St. Jean, a heavy cannon flashed and a twenty-four-pound ball arced toward him, followed by musket balls, which narrowly missed him. The firing, Arnold later complained to Cramahé, was "an insult I could not have expected." Arnold attributed the firing to the "ignorance of the guards,"[14] but in fact McLean had ordered it. Soon other guns opened up, lobbing cannonballs at the American line. Laughing, the Americans ran after them, and carried them back to their formation to use in their own cannon. Only one found its mark, shearing off the leg of one of Morgan's riflemen, who died soon afterward.

Arnold's bluff had failed. Four days later, on November 18, scaling ladders were brought up. Then Arnold made the horrible discovery that he had seriously blundered by not making a thorough inspection before the attack. As he explained in an emergency dispatch to Montgomery, he had not been able to "make an exact scrutiny of the arms and ammunition of my detachment" before that day, and what he found made an immediate attack impossible. Fully one hundred guns were "unfit for service";[15] most of the ammunition had been ruined. There were not five good rounds for each man whose gun would fire, not even enough to fend off an attack. Frustrated and embarrassed, Arnold had to retreat until Montgomery reinforced him. While he waited for aid, all he could hope to do was cut British communication by land.

That night, as quietly as they had come, the Americans marched off, following the river twenty miles to Point aux Trembles, leaving only a rear guard at Quebec. As Arnold marched south, two crowded British warships passed, taking two hundred redcoated reinforcements from Montreal to the capital city. There was little more he could do until his men had warm uniforms, ammunition, medical supplies, siege mortars to throw shells over the thick walls into the town, and field artillery to fend off counterattack. The only optimistic note was the help of the habitants. Not since they had sailed to the Kennebec had Arnold's men been so well fed. In the homes of French Canadians they wolfed down roast beef, pork, potatoes, cabbages, and turnips as they warmed in front of hot cookstoves and watched the snow blanket the village. Until Montgomery's reinforcements arrived, all Arnold could do was sit and worry that the great opportunity was slipping away in the thickening river ice and the swirling gusts of a Canadian winter. To Washington, Arnold wrote that his men were "almost naked and in want of every necessity." Then he added dejectedly, "Had I been ten days sooner, Quebec must inevitably have fallen into our hands, as there was not a man then to oppose us."[16] As Arnold waited for Montgomery, Governor Carleton sailed past Arnold's tattered army to take over the defense of Quebec. Distant booming from a cannon salute proclaimed his arrival in the Canadian capital.

With the quick capture of Quebec now completely out of the question, Arnold concentrated all his energy on helping his men. He had winced as he saw his brave soldiers hobble shoeless along the river. As his commissaries searched for cured leather and his men set to stitching moccasins, Arnold wrote report after report to Washington, Schuyler, and Montgomery, not once showing his utter disappointment at his failure to take Quebec. Fully two more weeks passed before the first reinforcements arrived. On November 27, Arnold received word of the fall of Montreal, as well as the heartening news that a shipload of cannon and ammunition was about to be landed only thirty miles upriver. Sending a detachment to fetch them, Arnold also sent forward Morgan and his riflemen to reconnoiter Carleton's activities at Quebec.

The first reinforcements reached Arnold at Pointe aux Trembles on December 1. Carleton had gotten away from Montreal with one hundred redcoats, but the same high winds that had prevented Arnold's crossing from Point Lévis to Quebec had trapped Carleton's supply ships in the narrow channels of the Berthier Islands at the confluence of the St. Lawrence and Richelieu rivers. Colonel Easton had placed an artillery battery at Sorel that had prevented the British fleet's escape, and Carleton alone escaped, disguising himself as a habitant and slipping past Easton in a skiff.

It was the arrival of a former British officer, Brigadier General Richard Montgomery, conqueror of St. Jean, Chambly, and Montreal, that saved Arnold's army. A veteran of Wolfe's attack on Quebec in the French and Indian Wars, he had married the heiress of a 150,000-acre Hudson River Valley estate. His relative-by-marriage Philip Schuyler had transformed the former British captain into an American general. To the British, he was now a traitor and a deserter. As Colonel Benedict Arnold stood at attention in front of his ragamuffin regiment and saluted this turncoat hero, he not only turned over his troops and his command to Montgomery, but was eclipsed in the eyes of many of his men. One of the first to switch allegiance was Aaron Burr, who asked Arnold for a letter of recommendation so he could leave Arnold and become Montgomery's aide-de-camp. Montgomery announced that every soldier was to receive a bounty of a gold Spanish dollar from the Continental Congress, a new British winter uniform, warm and heavy fur-lined white-belted blanket coat, hat and leggings, shoes and snowshoes, all captured from British transports at Montreal. But Montgomery brought only three hundred reinforcements. Montgomery's manner and his generosity dazzled Arnold's men. Private Morison wrote in his diary that night, "General Montgomery was born to command. His easy and affable condescension to both officers and men, while it forbids an improper familiarity, creates love and esteem. His recent successes give us the highest confidence in him."[17] For his part, Montgomery was full of praise for Arnold's regiment—"an exceeding fine one, inured to fatigue and well accustomed to cannon shot," he wrote to Schuyler. Praising Arnold's superior "style of discipline," he called him "active, intelligent and enterprising."[18]

Amid the compliments, Arnold nevertheless saw the problem: out of three thousand troops who had come with Arnold and Montgomery into Canada, the great pincers movement came down to three hundred of Montgomery's men to augment Arnold's six hundred. Even with the help of some two hundred French Canadians expected any day from Chambly, the Americans were now outnumbered by almost two to one by British and Loyalist forces who had rushed to reinforce Quebec. And the enlistments of many of Arnold's men would expire on December 31.

When he arrived in Quebec on November 19, Governor Carleton took over the defense of the last town in the province still in British hands, establishing his headquarters in the Recollets Convent in the center of Quebec. He had reason to be convinced that the city, surrounded by thick walls at their lowest point thirty-five feet high, could withstand an American siege better than its unpredictable garrison could sustain a battle in the open against Montgomery and Arnold's seasoned veterans. A conventional siege was impossible, as the elaborate system of parallel trenches needed for siege warfare could not be dug in the frozen ground. Further, he knew how puny was the American artillery: no cannon capable of piercing the walls, only a few mortars capable of lobbing shells into the city. An inventory of the city's supplies revealed that there was enough food—large quantities of mussels, eels, and fish—for five thousand to hold out for fully eight months, certainly enough time for reinforcements and resupply from England. That would leave the Americans facing a bitter winter outside the walls with no choice but to storm the city as soon as possible.

To prepare for the inevitable onslaught, Carleton ordered day-and-night preparations. Since the river had not yet frozen solid enough to prevent the passage of ships, Carleton dashed off one last round of dispatches to British officials in London, requesting ten thousand men and a fleet of ships to break the American blockade. He candidly revealed that the greatest problem facing the defenders was the divided loyalties of the citizens. The acting governor, Cramahé, had already reported to London that "no means have been left untried to bring the Canadian peasantry to a sense of their duty" while habitants were flocking to the American army and provisioning the invading Americans. Cramahé had been able to raise only 543 French Canadian militia in Quebec, according to his December 1 census of the city. Nearly one-third of his eighteen-hundred-man garrison he considered untrustworthy and unreliable (the figure included all adult males in the city). Carleton also had his doubts about the four hundred seamen in the garrison, many of them kidnapped by press gangs. Carleton confessed to Lord Dartmouth that he was pessimistic: "Could the people of the town and seamen be depended on, I should flatter myself we might hold out till navigation of St. Lawrence was possible again [next spring]. . . . We have so many enemies within and foolish people, dupes to those traitors . . . that I think our fate extremely doubtful."[19]

Dealing firmly—and with unabashed opportunism—with his political enemies inside the city, Carleton issued an ultimatum that every man in the city had only four days to join the militia and agree to fight, to leave the city, or to be treated as a spy: thus he not only expelled most of the city's opponents to the Quebec Act but an untold number of fence-sitting merchants. John Dyer Mercier, Benedict Arnold's business correspondent, clamped in irons on a British sloop-of-war as an American collaborator, was expelled. Merchants who had organized committees to oppose the Quebec Act and encouraged Arnold's attack by promising to swing open the city's gates were also drummed out at Palace Gate. As the stream of Quebec's leading citizens and their wives and children left the city on December 1 to the slow beat of drums and jeering from the walls, they received cheers of welcome from the American lines. General Montgomery wrote to Schuyler that "the Governor has been so kind as to send out of town many of our friends who refused to do military duty, among them several very intelligent men capable of doing me considerable service. One of them [Edward Antill] I have appointed chief engineer."[20] Montgomery and Arnold found shelter, rations, and staff jobs for many of them.

To deprive the Americans of further support, Carleton enlisted the support of the Roman Catholic Church. Anyone helping or serving with the Americans would be denied the sacraments. They could not be married, baptized, or buried in consecrated ground. It was a severe sanction in an avowedly Catholic society, but the pastoral letter circulated by Quebec's bishop at Carleton's instigation was widely ignored. Fortunate in finding experienced Loyalist officers, Carleton appointed Colonel McLean to command the garrison. He put Colonel Henry Caldwell, his assistant in the last war, in charge of training Loyalist militia. Among the Loyalist volunteers, Carleton found James Thompson, a veteran Scottish military engineer who had served in the French and Indian Wars: he appointed him chief engineer. Taking charge of three companies of skilled carpenters he recruited from the ranks of the Highland Emigrants, Thompson set to work building a six-hundred-yard line of palisades across all the open ground between the Citadel at the south of the city walls and Porte St. Jean to the west. Thousands of yards of stout spars were stripped from merchant ships in the harbor and commandeered from lumberyards. Fourteen carpenters built a new palisade at Palace Gate, the northern entrance to the city, and cut loopholes for muskets. They built a new bastion, a triangle jutting out to protect new outer defenses, and a new blockhouse pierced for cannon. Two companies of Loyalist carpenters newly arrived from Halifax and Newfoundland fashioned pointed palisades around all the open ground on Cap Diamant and erected a large blockhouse just outside Porte St. Louis, the main entry to the city, and another at the foot of Cap Diamant, at the river's edge. As gun platforms were built by Highland carpenters, cannon were hoisted up what is now Mountain Road by pigtailed sailors using blocks and tackles. Every gunport in the city walls was repaired; every waterfront window in the Lower Town boarded up, then slit with gunports in case of an attack over the frozen river. And to light up every ditch and niche in a night attack, hundreds of lanterns and pots of burning oil were mounted on posts atop the walls. All day long, the Scottish carpenters and British sailors labored; every night from nine to dawn, they stood guard duty, peering into the blowing snow.

On December 5, 1775, sentries on the south walls of the city watched apprehensively as a long American column marched into sight. More than one thousand armed men led by a cavalcade of sleigh-riding officers swung ominously toward the city, then divided, its left wing wrapping around to the west and disappearing among the suburbs of St. Roch and St. Jean, the main column halting astraddle the main road into the city, Grand Allée, and dispersing among deserted British barracks and loyalist houses in Ste. Foy, little more than a mile southwest of the city. Nervous Loyalist gunners began firing erratically as rumors spread inside the city that Montgomery had added 4,500 reinforcements to Arnold's army, thought to be about two thousand men. That would mean the Americans outnumbered the British three to one. As American bateaux moved north toward Wolfe's Cove and Captain John Lamb's New York artillery company used ox teams to drag their cannon on sledges across the Plains of Abraham, a British officer caught a glimpse of Montgomery and Arnold's party of officers arriving at a staff meeting at Menut's Tavern in Ste. Foy and ordered his cannon to fire. When the shelling stopped, Montgomery's calèche lay splintered and his horse's head had been shot off. From the west, Morgan's riflemen opened fire from inside houses in St. Roch. Some of them broke into the old Intendant's Palace, once the seat of

French Canadian government, and, climbing to its cupola, began sniping at Loyalist sentries and British gunners atop the walls.

Until Montgomery could build gun emplacements to protect his own forces, however, there was little he could do but conduct a paper war. First he wrote a proclamation addressed to Carleton and the citizens of Quebec, informing Carleton that his forces were "a motley crew of sailors" and "a few of the worst troops who ever styled themselves soldiers." Most of the city, "the greatest part," were friends of the Americans "who wish to see us within their walls." Montgomery warned that he was having trouble restraining his men from "insulting your works" and taking "an ample and just retaliation" for continued hesitation to open the gates and surrender. He urged the governor to reconsider "the absurdity of resistance."[21] Since previous messengers under flags of truce had been fired on, Montgomery, following Arnold's advice, sent an old woman, a noncombatant, to Carleton with the proclamation. Carleton allowed her to be brought before him, but he refused to read the document. Instead, he summoned a drummer boy and told him to take the fireplace tongs and consign it to the flames. Then he ordered the old woman jailed overnight and drummed out of the city the next day. Montgomery's next message, at Arnold's suggestion, was delivered to Quebec merchants by a more direct route. Arnold's Penobscot Indians wrapped copies of a propaganda handbill, which proclaimed that private property had "ever by us been deemed sacred,"[22] around arrows and fired them over the city walls. There is evidence that Carleton at least looked at this missive, for a copy of it can be found in his correspondence to officials in London.

His demands ignored, Montgomery now ordered the city shelled. Under Arnold's direction, the New York artillery built a five-gun mortar battery in St. Roch that kept up a steady cannonade over the north wall for two days, but its fire hit nothing of consequence; its gunners were inexperienced and the guns were of too small a caliber. "The townspeople had conceived that every shell would inevitably kill a dozen or two people and knock down two or three houses," wrote Loyalist militia officer Ainslie, "but after they saw that their bomblettes, as they called them, did no harm, women and children walked the streets laughing at their former fears."[23] Royal Navy gunners meanwhile began firing back, right through the houses that hid the American battery, apparently with such effectiveness that the American mortars were withdrawn. Next, Arnold ordered artillery batteries in Ste. Foy drawn up seven hundred yards from the south wall. French Canadian volunteers had made two thousand bundles of sticks to form gabions and, instead of packing them with earth to make breastworks, he had his men working all one night in bitter wind and snow, mounding up snow around gabions, pouring water over them. They quickly froze into rock-hard forts. From behind these works, Captain Lamb's gunners began a steady cannonade which also failed to do any substantial damage. The British replied with even heavier guns.

Colonel McLean ordered the militia to sally from the gates and demolish houses which were screening his view of the gunners. Instead, they set a blaze that, in the high wind, burned all day and night, destroying many of the houses nearest the city walls. After spreading through St. Roch and St. Jean, the flames threatened to leap the city walls. Now Carleton's gunners silenced Lamb's battery. A great puff of smoke went up as the concerted British fire blew up two gun emplacements, killing three men and wounding several more. By daybreak December 18, only shards of ice and piles of gabions protruded from the snow. There was one more American casualty. As she went to fetch water, a twenty-four-pound British shell sheared off the head of Jemima Warner, who had lost her husband in the Chaudière swamps.

Tempers were flaring on both sides. While American cannonfire had proved little more than a nuisance, Morgan's riflemen had kept up a murderous fire as they sniped at anyone who became even partly visible above the walls. Aiming from chinks in log huts they built in the ruins of St. Roch and from the Intendant's Palace, they were picking off British sentries every day. The rifle, introduced by Morgan's men under direct orders first from Washington, incensed the British. After one sentry was shot through the head at long range, Loyalist Captain Ainslie wrote bitterly of "skulking riflemen. . . . These fellows who call themselves soldiers . . . are worse than savages. They lie in wait to shoot a sentry! A deed worthy of Yankee men of war!"[24] Carleton ordered his gun crews to open fire on the Intendant's Palace. By December 18, the elaborately turreted ninety-year-old French landmark lay in smoking ruins. But as quickly as one American battery was silenced, Arnold opened up from another. Lamb's gunners, probably with Arnold at the linstock, opened fire on the Citadel below from atop Cap Diamant, one hundred feet higher. Next, a battery including the Americans' heaviest gun, a twenty-four-pounder, began hurling shells across the St. Lawrence from old British works at Point Lévis. But the British soon found the range and began killing American gun crews. So deadly, so incessant was British fire that Arnold began to have trouble finding officers who were willing to risk duty at advance posts. Captain Hanchet of Connecticut refused to take up a position within

British cannon range, but Captains Thayer and Topham saluted Arnold and set off with their men. They were soon under such heavy fire that they could not come out of their forward picket post except at night.

Even after the fighting began, Arnold wanted to make one more attempt to enter the city peaceably. He got Montgomery's permission to request personally Carleton's surrender. Montgomery wrote a letter that promised Carleton and Cramahé safe conduct to England if they would strike their colors. Accompanied only by a drummer and Captain John McPherson, one of Montgomery's aides, Arnold, unarmed and wrapped in a white blanket coat, appeared outside Porte St. Jean under a flag of truce and handed Montgomery's letter to a British guard. Minutes went by; still Arnold was not invited in to talk to Carleton. Finally, one of Carleton's aides shouted down to him from the wall that the governor would not treat with rebels, would neither receive them nor read their letters. If Arnold wished to meet with Carleton, he must first beg the king's mercy. Steaming, Arnold turned his back and walked away as Loyalist sentries raised their muskets. Only the bark of a British officer's command to hold their fire prevented Arnold from being shot in the back.

Montgomery's first letter from Quebec recommended Benedict Arnold to the Continental Congress for promotion to a generalship as the man "who has borne the burden of the service here," the man he most respected: "I have paid particular attention to the recommendations of Colonel Arnold." His praise of Arnold was singular in a long report detailing problems he had had with other subordinate officers. After Ethan Allen had bungled the first attack on Montreal and stirred up resistance among French Canadians by looting farms on the Richelieu, Allen's second-in-command among the Green Mountain Boys, Seth Warner, had "refused to march" to follow Montgomery to the relief of Arnold's force near Quebec. Another Allen partisan, Colonel James Easton, who had taken over Arnold's old Massachusetts regiment, had consented to block Carleton's fleet from escaping at Sorel only after a desperate Montgomery gave Easton's "half-naked" men permission "to go beyond the letter of the law" and take the uniforms and, "by way of stimulant," all public property taken on the ten vessels. Unless he caved in, Montgomery told Schuyler, Easton's men "might grow impatient and relinquish the business in hand."[25] Colonel Edward Mott, the erstwhile Council of War chairman who had cut tailor-made orders for Ethan Allen at Ticonderoga and refused to accept Arnold's, had also refused to march with Montgomery to Quebec. What Montgomery may not have known was that he had refused to go any farther north because Mott considered Montgomery's Scottish aide, Colonel Donald Campbell, a former British officer, "very profane—I should be very sorry to inform your honor that there is scarcely a word from headquarters without some oaths and curses."[26] In protest, Colonel Samuel Mott led his Puritan troops home. Puritan militia officers were increasingly being replaced by professional soldiers, many of them former officers in the British army. But swearing had less to do with the army's impatience than homesickness and old provincial rivalries. Chaplain Trumbull had blessed the expedition as it had left Ticonderoga but now cursed it. "There never was a more ill-governed, profane and wicked army," he fulminated into his diary. "We have not had one day of thanksgiving or one of publick prayer,"[27] and once again, the gods of the hills were refusing to serve the gods of the valleys. The Vermont, western Connecticut, and western Massachusetts troops had refused to march with Montgomery any farther and would not come to the rescue of Arnold after his run-in with Ethan Allen. As the Canadian winter worsened, two-thirds of the American army in Canada headed home.

Richard Montgomery was Benedict Arnold's model of what a soldier should be, and in December 1775, the two were like brothers. When he might have been expected to be jealous of Montgomery, who, after all, had superseded him, Arnold instead lionized Montgomery, backing his every decision. Both men chafed for action. As other, more timorous officers plumped for a slow siege of Quebec that could last for months instead of a quick all-out assault, Montgomery agreed with Arnold: "it is of utmost importance to finish it at once."[28]

In his next letter to Schuyler, Montgomery added that a British attack from Quebec was expected. Arnold, he said, was ready and eager to fight, "and his troops wish for it."[29] Arnold basked in Montgomery's recommendation for promotion. In the company of able leaders who appreciated him, like Montgomery, Washington, and Schuyler, Arnold not only never got into trouble but always played the cheerful subordinate. To Montgomery's moodiness, Arnold was the buoyant, irrepressible counter. As Montgomery had sailed toward Quebec from Montreal, he had written to Schuyler, "I must go home." He wanted to "walk by the side of the lake this winter" with his wife, Janet. He was as homesick as any of his men. He hoped that Schuyler would be well enough to come to Montreal and take over Montgomery's command: "I am weary of power and totally want that patience and temper so requisite for such a command."[30] Once he had spent a few days around Arnold, however, he was bullying his old compatriot Carleton and authorizing Arnold's every request to bombard, blockade, spy, attack, storm. He admired Arnold's optimism, and the combination of enthusiasm and discipline he had instilled in his troops.

Since the fall of Montreal, Montgomery had been brooding in letters back to Schuyler at Albany about the rebelliousness of the troops, "who are exceedingly turbulent and indeed mutinous."[13] He had been forced to give in to Colonel Easton on the plundering of Carleton's supply ships and had been impressed by Arnold's refusal to allow his troops to pillage the suburbs of Quebec. On the other hand, Arnold had been having trouble with thievery by Morgan's riflemen ever since leaving Cambridge, and it had come to a head when some of Morgan's riflemen robbed homes in Ste. Foy of food, household goods, and family heirlooms as they waited for Montgomery. Some of Smith's Pennsylvanians broke into Lieutenant Governor Cramahé's country house, stealing blankets, mattresses, cutlery. The Virginians came along next and pilfered anything that was left. Then the Pennsylvanians raided a nearby farm, butchering livestock and riding off with sleighloads of fresh meat. Their depredations violated not only all orders from Congress and Washington but Arnold's own personal instructions, and Arnold was furious at Morgan for exerting so little control over his men. The two quarreled loudly just before Connecticut Captain Oliver Hanchet refused to carry out Arnold's order, on December 2, to convey artillery and munitions to within cannon range of Quebec's walls.

Arnold had considered Oliver Hanchet one of his better officers and he had complimented him by choosing his company to go ahead and mark the trail from the Kennebec to Sartigan and then bring back emergency food supplies. But when Hanchet disregarded Arnold's directions and got lost in the swamps, Arnold loudly rebuked him in front of his men. Hanchet felt he didn't have to listen to his commanding officer. He refused Arnold's direct order to take forward the supplies at Quebec because the danger was too imminent. Arnold could have arrested him for insubordination or cowardice, but instead raged at Hanchet and swore he would arrest him but didn't. Only a week later, Hanchet again refused to follow a direct order because it was too dangerous and again Arnold overlooked it. Arnold could not spare Hanchet's men. At Hanchet's first public dressing-down, his friend Goodrich's company of Maine troops announced they were going home with Hanchet's men, but with threats and promises, Arnold kept both companies from leaving.

* * *

By the time Montgomery called a council of war on December 16, more than a month had passed since Arnold had brought his ragged troops over the St. Lawrence. It was still Montgomery's contention that "to the storming we must come at last."[32] Nothing had changed, nothing was to be gained by waiting, not to mention the December 31 enlistment deadline. Arnold sent in a clever servant who was captured and then escaped by getting his jailer drunk, and by this ruse, Arnold learned that the British now outnumbered the Americans two to one, even if the British thought *they* were badly outnumbered. The Americans had little artillery, while the British had 150 guns, and they were using them with devastating effect. But the British had three miles of walls to protect. Montgomery had hoped to have more reinforcements from Schuyler and from Washington, but Washington would spare no more troops and Schuyler's forces continued to dwindle.

There was also the growing problem of infighting among officers: Hanchet had been joined by two other malcontents, Goodrich and Jonas Hubbard, and they not only were against storming the city but now flatly refused to fight under Arnold. They wanted Montgomery to form a new corps under the command of Arnold's old enemy Major John Brown. Brown had come to Quebec with Montgomery as a staff officer. Arnold later wrote to the Continental Congress that Brown "now assumes and insists on the title of colonel, which he says the general promised him at Montreal." Montgomery had indeed promised Brown promotion to get his men to march to Quebec with him, but that had been before Easton and Brown had incurred Montgomery's wrath at Sorel, where they had looted Carleton's ships. "When Major Brown wrote to remind him of his promise," Arnold reported to Congress, "the General handed me his letter and told me that, as Colonel Easton and Major Brown were publicly impeached for plundering the officers' baggage taken at Sorel, contrary to articles of capitulation and to the great scandal of the American army, he could not, in conscience or honor, promote him [Major Brown] until those matters were cleared up. He then sent for Major Brown and told him his sentiments very freely." Arnold added that because of the scandal, "I believe it would give great disgust to the army in general if those gentlemen were promoted."[33]

Even as Brown petitioned Congress for promotion, Montgomery was beginning to suspect him of plotting with the three recalcitrant Massachusetts captains against Arnold, and, at the very least, stirring up Massachusetts troops until he got command of them away from Arnold. Montgomery had had trouble with Brown from the

start of his command. On December 5, he had put Brown on report
to Schuyler for promising French Canadian militia on the Richelieu
a share of the loot from Fort Chambly. He was forced to make good
the pledge and had to promise the militia the cash value of the munitions which he needed for his army. When Montgomery next wrote
to Schuyler, it was to report that one of his staff officers had spent
the entire day of the 12th in Hanchet's tent. Hanchet, reported
Montgomery, "has made some declarations which I think must
draw upon him the censure of his country if brought to trial. . . .
This dangerous party threatens the ruin of our officers."[34] Arnold
was all for a trial on the spot, but Montgomery did not know if he
could afford the luxury of a court-martial at this time. In his message to Schuyler, he only penciled in the names of the offending
officers so Schuyler could erase them. All he could do at the council
of war was to refuse Hanchet's request for a separate command for
Brown: "This is resentment against Arnold," he wrote to Washington, "and will hurt him so much I do not think I can consent to it."
He also ruled that no man would be expected to join the assault if
he was in the least bit reluctant. Only two men from Hubbard's
company signed up to scale the walls, according to surveyor Pierce,
"two of Goodrich's men and but a few of Hanchet's men, but all
Montgomery's and the majority of the riflemen."[35]

The worst effect of all this plotting, as Montgomery told
Schuyler, was that it forced him to change his plan of attack.
Montgomery and Arnold had planned to attack at night during "the
first strong north-wester,"[36] setting fire to houses in the Lower
Town on the St. Roch's side to destroy the new palisades and draw
off Carleton's troops while the main attack came over the east walls
by scaling ladders. Arnold, according to John Pierce, had obtained
detailed maps of the entire city, and it was here that the walls were
most vulnerable. Arnold still favored such an attack, but he was
overruled by Montgomery, who argued that the desertion of several
men to the British as well as loss of so many Massachusetts troops
left them "too weak."[37] To Schuyler, he wrote that he was determined, despite the "strange divided state of the troops," to "make
the best of it" with only the eight hundred troops he could now rely
on. Dr. Senter thought that Hanchet should be replaced, and he volunteered his services. Arnold answered on the reverse side of his
letter:

Dear Sir:
I am much obliged to you for your offer and glad to see you
spirited, but cannot consent you should take up arms, as you will be

wanted in the way of your profession. You will please to prepare
dressings, etc., and repair to the main guard house at 2 o'clock in
the morning with an assistant.

> *I am in haste, yours.*
> *B. Arnold, Col.*[38]

In the final vote in the council of war among the field officers,
only Major Bigelow voted against scaling the walls. The attack
would come on the first snowy night, when clouds blocked the
moonlight. The men would wear hemlock sprigs in their hat brims
to distinguish them from the enemy, who would be wearing the
same uniforms. And every company would take part in the attack.
To keep the army from being further weakened, Arnold publicly
apologized to Hanchet: "I am a passionate man."[39] After a tense
week of officers' maneuvering, on Christmas evening, Montgomery
and Arnold reviewed their riflemen in a meadow beside the St.
Charles River and distributed an extra ration of rum to the men.
Then Montgomery stepped forward to address them. The riflemen
answered Montgomery with a cheer. Any protest had been drowned
out by Montgomery's Christmas present to his men: "All that get
safe into the city will live well," a recruit quoted him in a letter
home, "for they are allowed to plunder and take what they
please."[40] The cheer at this announcement carried over the city wall.

Since December 23, when an American deserter had informed Carleton of the decision of the American council of war to attack on the
first snowy night, Governor Carleton and his men had been sleeping
fully clothed at the Recollets Convent at Quebec's center. Early the
morning of December 27, a fresh snowstorm blew in, and at two
o'clock the American troops were paraded on review, but before the
army could get into its positions, the night cleared, the snow
stopped, and a break in the clouds appeared. That night a few more
frightened deserters fled into Quebec. Once again Montgomery and
Arnold had to change their plan as forward observers reported tell-
tale enemy movements. All that remained now was to wait. The
latest strategy was for a four-pronged attack. Two detachments were
to attack the west walls at Porte St. Jean and Palace Gate. They were
to set fires to decoy the defenders away from the real attack, to be
made at either end of the Lower Town by Montgomery, leading the
New York troops, and Arnold, leading the men who had come up
the Kennebec with him. All day the 28th the British kept up a heavy
cannonade. That night it was maddeningly clear and mild. The next
day remained clear. Men who were preparing to march home three

days later at the end of their enlistments set about washing their clothes and settling bills they owed one another.

At eight o'clock the night of December 31, 1775, sergeants began to bang on doors in the American billets in Ste. Foy and shout, "Be ready at twelve." The wind had shifted to northeast and was blowing up into a gale. At Morgan's camp beside the St. Charles, men made crude white paper bands and slid them over their caps: "Liberty or Death." At two o'clock, as wet, heavy snow covered their boots, Arnold's men stood at attention outside his headquarters at Scott's Bridge near the General Hospital two miles west of the city while his captains filed up to report their men present. Arnold, in white British uniform except for his own regiment's fur cap, stood under a lean-to as his secretary, Captain Oswald, checked off each unit on a muster roll by lantern light. Captain Lamb reported in, then went off to inspect the harnesses on the side that was to drag the lone cannon, a six-pounder. Arnold came out shortly before four o'clock and went down the street to join his advance storming party of thirty men. With him were his Kennebec veterans Greene and Bigelow, his veteran officers from the Kennebec. His captains— Hubbard, Thayer, Ward—trudged off to line up troops. Two captains were missing. Dearborn was stranded across the St. Charles River by the unusually high tide, and Captain Smith of the riflemen was asleep, drunk, on a table in Morgan's headquarters. Arnold gave his command to Lieutenant Steele.

At four o'clock sharp, one, two, three rockets arced up and burst in darkness: The signal to attack sent a cheer through his men as Arnold dashed out of his command post. Lamb's gunners slipped into their harnesses and followed the advance party. As Arnold and his aides ran by, a picked group of Morgan's riflemen grabbed their scaling ladders and pikes and rushed off after him, single-file, gripping their blanket coats tightly around the firelocks of their rifles to keep the large wet snowflakes from soaking their priming. To the south, on the Plains of Abraham, Major Brown's party of Massachusetts and Connecticut troops picked up their ladders with less enthusiasm and set off toward St. John's Gate with Colonel Henry Livingston and two hundred French Canadians carrying bundles of faggots. They failed to set fire to the gate and palisades as ordered, and as someone ran back to ignite the blaze, British shells began to burst near the rear of the column. In the distance, Brown's men could hear the clang of the cathedral bells and see the city walls light up in the glare of hundreds of flares and fire baskets. Quebec's garrison was awake and waiting.

Inside the walls, Captain Malcolm Fraser of the Highland Emigrants commanded the main guard that night. He had just passed the sentries at Porte St. Louis at four when he saw the signal rockets in the white murk above Cap Diamant. Running down Rue St. Louis toward the Place d'Armes, Fraser yelled, "Turn out! Turn out!" and sent runners off all over the city. His cry brought Governor Carleton down from his emergency headquarters in the Recollets Convent into the square as Fraser ordered the basilica's bell rung and the drums of the city guard to beat "To Arms." American artillery fire added to the din of British gunfire in the center of town, but off at the edges and down along the waterfront, the swirling snow obscured the white flashes over the city, and the outpost guards had no idea the attack had begun.

Two miles from the city, on the Plains of Abraham, General Montgomery had strapped on his short sword shortly before four o'clock and led his column of 350 New Yorkers from his Holland House headquarters through heavy snow to Wolfe's goat path and then down to the St. Lawrence over the very route Arnold had taken six weeks earlier. Hugging the foot of the cliffs for two miles, his column stumbled and slithered, hunched forward into the blinding snow, gradually becoming strung out over several hundred yards. Great chunks of river ice littered the narrow riverbank. Encumbered soldiers had to pick their way around them and then fight for their footing, cursing and swearing in the darkness. By the time Montgomery and his officers reached the first barrier of palisade running from the foot of Cap Diamant to the water's edge, it was already five o'clock and his main force was one hundred yards behind him in the gloom. Montgomery, drawing his sword, ordered carpenters to begin sawing through the timbers of the barricade. He himself pulled them down as the saws bit into them. Looking back and not yet seeing his men, he decided to step through a gap and lead his officers ahead. As he stepped through, he spotted a two-story log blockhouse off to his right. It was silent and it seemed unoccupied. He stepped back through the hole, waving for his officers to hurry up. With fifteen of his officers, he turned and ran toward the second barricade. As he got within forty feet or so of it, three cannon on the second story of the blockhouse opened fire at once amid a volley of musketfire. A shower of lead balls slammed into Montgomery and his men, cutting them down, hitting Montgomery in both thighs, the groin, and his jaw and killing him outright, and slaughtering most of his staff, fourteen officers in all. Aaron Burr, with Montgomery's second-in-command, Colonel Donald Campbell, crawled back through the broken stockade and led a precipitous retreat, never for an instant considering, apparently, the possibility of a second charge that might have dislodged the British. Inside the blockhouse, fifty terrified militia and a handful of British navy gunners were only being kept from running the other way by a ranting Loyalist officer who was threatening to bayonet the first coward to try to get past him.

The snow was falling fast by the time Benedict Arnold and his aides left the shelter of St. Roch and headed across open fields for Palace Gate. Running along the foot of the hill leading up to the walls, they passed between widely spaced warehouses. "In these intervals," reported John Henry, "we received a tremendous fire of musketry from the ramparts above us." It was pointless to fire back, because the British were out of sight. The line snaked along the shore. As John Henry ran hard on the heels of Lieutenant Steele, a hawser from a beached vessel "took me under the chin and cast me head-long" fifteen feet down into a snow-filled pit. His comrades could not stop. Henry thrashed around until he found his gun. Then, one knee injured, he tried to get back into line, only to be shoved aside by men who didn't know him. He stumbled back to the attack under fire from the north wall. By now, Arnold's column was running down Rue St. Paul, about to turn into the narrow, house-lined confines of Sault-au-Matelot. Henry observed that the firing from the walls had slackened: many of the British had been pulled off by Carleton to reinforce the militia at Cap Diamant, "called off to resist Montgomery."[42] The British could not believe that Arnold's single strand of riflemen was the main American attack: it must be coming at Cap Diamant.

At the head of his column, Benedict Arnold dashed out ahead with Morgan and Captain Oswald. Now they were joined by Lamb's gunners. As they ran into Sault-au-Matelot, the snow was knee-deep. Ahead, Arnold could see a log barricade. He had hoped to use Lamb's cannon to shell the barrier before he rushed it, but the cannon had slipped off the road into a snowbank, and all he could do now was charge ahead and fire through the loopholes at the gunners inside. As Morgan and a handful of riflemen shoved their weapons through the slits and fired point-blank at the defenders, British militia opened fire from houses on both sides. As Arnold ordered his men over the barricade, he felt numb in his right leg; when he tried to run on, he couldn't move the leg but pitched forward in the snow. Trying to push himself up, he managed to get onto his other leg and tried to hop along through another and another volley of gunfire, shouting to his men, "Hurry on! Hurry on, boys!" He got to one side of the street and leaned against a wall, waving his sword, urging his men to follow Morgan. He ordered Eleazar Oswald to go with Morgan and take command. Blood was seeping out over the top of his boot now, staining his white leggings. Mathias Ogden and Chaplain Spring ducked the hail of musketfire and tried to carry Arnold to safety. But Arnold refused to let them take him back through the advancing column toward the General Hospital until most of the troops had passed. He was still shouting to his "brave boys," John Henry remembered, "in a cheering voice as we passed, urging us forward," and he added that Arnold's departure "dampened the spirits" of the troops. As he was carried back through the Connecticut line, a chant went through the troops, "We are sold."[42]

It was three days before Benedict Arnold realized what had happened after he was carried into the Catholic hospital on the western edge of St. Roch. Dr. Senter and four nuns cut away his clothing and set to work prying out the lead fragment that had shattered his lower right leg. Dr. Senter wrote that the wounded had been "tumbling in" since the attack began. Senter later wrote that "the ball had probably come in contact with a cannon, rock, stone or the like ere it entered the leg." Whatever the musketball hit "had cleft off nigh a third." The weapon commonly used by the British at this time was a .69-caliber Tower musket. Even with a third shaved off, the slug would have been the size of a modern American .45-caliber bullet, but after hitting another object would have been flattened and sharp. "The other two-thirds entered the outer side of the leg, about midway." Just missing Arnold's boot top, the ricocheting slug had followed "an oblique course" between the shin and the inner bone of his leg, lodging in his Achilles tendon, "where upon examination I easily discovered and extracted it."[43] Dr. Senter told Arnold he would be incapacitated for four to six weeks, though many other surgeons of the time would simply have amputated his leg. But the stubborn Arnold refused to listen to his doctor's urging that he allow himself to be carried out into the countryside, away from the danger of British cannonfire or infantry attack. Instead, Arnold propped himself in his bed, armed with his pistols and sword—and ordered that every other wounded man make sure his gun was ready to fight the British if they came.

As Arnold slipped in and out of consciousness, he dictated letters and interviewed the arriving wounded about what had happened. Later that morning, he sent off his first letter. Begun ten minutes after he reached the hospital, it was to David Wooster, the man who had refused to give him the keys to the colony's powder magazine only eight months earlier. The dissolute, Catholic-hating Wooster was now commandant of the rear-area Montreal garrison. As a brigadier general, he outranked Colonel Arnold, even if command at Quebec, the main target of operations, had devolved on Arnold when Montgomery died with most of his aides.

It was several more days before Arnold could talk to a senior officer who had been on the spot. He learned that Morgan's men had taken a large number of Loyalists prisoner just after Arnold had fallen at the first barricade. The Americans' own rifles were too wet to fire, so Morgan seized the prisoners' guns. Morgan had outrun most of his troops and allowed his junior officers to counsel him to wait for more troops to arrive before they stormed the barrier on the south end of Sault-au-Matelot. It was a crucial mistake. Now that it was getting light, the panic of hundreds of Loyalists was subsiding and they were pouring in around Morgan's men: they knew that Montgomery's attack had been defeated. Colonel McLean and militia Colonel Caldwell had rightly assessed that Morgan's force of roughly five hundred was all that was left of the American force. They sent in reinforcements under their best, most experienced officers. Morgan and his men were forced to take cover in doorways and alleys, a few making it into a two-story tavern on the northwest corner of Rue St. Jacques and Sault-au-Matelot, where they dueled diagonally across the street with Loyalists firing from merchant John Lymeburner's stone mansion.

Slowly, the British surrounded Morgan's troops. Morgan had killed Royal Navy Captain John Anderson in the assault on the first barricade, when his men rushed in, yelling, "Quebec is ours!" But the British had refused to come out and fight and had instead poured an increasingly accurate and deadly fire into Morgan's troops. Now the British were sniping from high windows. A sergeant in Hubbard's company was shot down next to Private Fobes as they advanced; Fobes stopped to turn him over. Then Captain Hubbard, who had schemed to avoid storming the city, slumped against a wall, dying.

As Morgan ordered scaling ladders up and led the charge over the barricades, two of his lieutenants, John Humphries and Samuel Cooper, dropped dead in the street. Others were shot off the ladders. Lieutenant Steele, Arnold's intrepid scout, lost three fingers. Mathias Ogden was shot in the shoulder. Grapeshot tore away artillery Captain Lamb's left eye, his cheek, several teeth. An aide bandaged him with a black handkerchief and dragged him off. Captain Topham had survived a cannonball crashing through his bed a few weeks earlier. Now he was hit.

When Major Meigs tried to bring up Lamb's cannon and two hundred reinforcements, his Indian guides, including the Penobscot Chief Natanis, were shot and wounded. In the swirling blizzard, the cannon foundered in a drift, and Meigs twice missed the street leading to Morgan's trapped riflemen, his ill-trained men becoming hopelessly snarled when they tried to countermarch. Reinforcements, Dearborn's latecomers, were hit hard as Colonel McLean released a sally force of five hundred Emigrants to cut off the Americans from the rear. Surrounded, Dearborn surrendered when his gun misfired. "Neither I nor one in ten of my men could get off our guns, they being so exceedingly wet."

The house-by-house fighting in the Lower Town had gone on for four hours, Arnold learned. Loyalist Captain Nairne led his men up a ladder wrested from Morgan's men and charged in a window with bayonets fixed, driving the Americans from room to room and out into the street. Morgan ordered his men to take cover and fire back at Nairne's storming party. Captain Hendricks was shot dead at a window. More than 150 of Morgan's men were killed or wounded, and most of the others were out of ammunition. Slowly, they filed into the house that Loyalist Captain Nairne had cleared at bayonet point to surrender. Finally, the gate to the second barricade opened and most of the remaining riflemen, including Morgan and all his officers, ran in to surrender to Colonel Caldwell. Morgan was the last. Backed against a wall, he said they would have to shoot him to get his sword. At length, Morgan spotted a black-robed priest in the swarm of troops around him. Was the man a priest? Yes. Then Morgan would give *him* his sword. "No scoundrel of these cowards shall take it out of my hands." In a final engagement, on Carleton's orders, a Loyalist task force attacked St. Roch but was driven back by a single blast from an American six-pounder. The British were temporarily prevented from attacking the suburb where Benedict Arnold waited doggedly if somewhat woozily. As he finished dictating his emergency request to General Wooster for reinforcements, he ordered a musket issued to every patient.

By late the afternoon of January 2, Arnold was coherent enough to meet Major Meigs, who had been sent by Governor Carleton to retrieve the personal belongings of the captured Americans and learn the details of the American defeat. Every field officer except Campbell and Major Brown had been killed, wounded, or captured. Four hundred and twenty-six Americans—including virtually all of the Kennebec marchers—had been taken prisoner. Somewhere between thirty and one hundred had been killed, many buried in the snow. In addition, about one hundred of Montgomery's New Yorkers deserted their posts and headed home. Montgomery's body had been found by a Loyalist drummer boy searching for souvenirs. He found Montgomery's ivory-handled sword and showed it to Captain Thompson, Carleton's engineer, who demanded it for himself and had the boy show him where he got it. Thompson felt sure he had seen that silver dog's head on the sword's pommel before. Nearby was a fur officer's cap with the initials "R.M." A woman tavernkeeper recognized the dueling scar on Montgomery's face. Finally, American prisoners were brought from the Quebec Seminary, where they were being held, to identify him. Meigs had seen the body, he told Arnold. Arnold wept. To Arnold's surprise, Carleton was treating the prisoners, Arnold wrote later, "very humanely,"[44] and Hector Cramahé had paid to bury his old comrade Montgomery in a flannel-lined coffin side by side with his men. When Meigs went back inside the walls with the prisoners' baggage, Arnold handed him a large amount of his own cash to distribute among the officers.

Still no answer had come from Wooster at Montreal, and no reinforcements. In a letter he intended to have copied by Wooster and passed on to Washington and Congress, Arnold pleaded with Wooster, "For God's sake, order as many men down as you can possibly spare, consistent with the safety of Montreal, and all the mortars, howitzers and shells that you can possibly bring." He wanted the New York troops stopped from going home: "I hope you will stop every rascal who has deserted from us and bring him back again." Arnold had no intention of retreating from Quebec and he planned to continue the siege. All that had gone wrong with Montgomery's assault was the cowardice of his own men: "Had he been properly supported by his troops, I make no doubt of our success." Arnold was also angry that Major Brown had refused to carry out his orders to rescue the six siege mortars from St. Roch's right after the battle. Though he had only eight hundred men left, half of them French Canadian militia, he managed to conceal his weakness from Carleton by rotating his troops. To keep up the illusion of strength, he did not tell the French Canadians that Montgomery was dead: he told them Montgomery had gone off into the woods to gather more troops! And he forbade Meigs to tell anyone how many Americans had been lost.

As Arnold slowly recovered, he filled his ranks with hundreds of new Canadian recruits, ordered more ice fortifications built ever closer to Quebec's walls, even resumed sporadic cannonades. He intended to make the British waste their ammunition, he wrote, and he wanted more cannon to keep up the siege. "I am in such excessive pain from my wound," he wrote to Wooster—and here the letter trailed off. He all but admitted he could no longer command. "Many officers here appear dispirited. Your presence will be absolutely necessary."[45] Before the pain once again overcame him, he once again refused to be evacuated. "We entreated Colonel Arnold," wrote Dr. Senter, "for his own safety to be carried back into the country where they could not readily find him, but to no purpose. He would neither be removed nor suffer a man from the hospital to retreat."[46]

By January 4, Arnold finally consented to be moved. Painfully, he was taken by sleigh to Montgomery's old headquarters at Holland House in Ste. Foy, behind the main American lines. Flat on his back, he managed to write to Hannah. He was deeply saddened, he told his sister, by the death of his "truly great and good friend" Montgomery. He told her of his own wound, saying that "the loss of blood rendered me weak." But he managed to reach the hospital "near a mile on foot." He was quite impressed by Carleton's "politeness" to the prisoners; "the prisoners are supplied with everything the garrison affords." Moreover, Carleton was making no further attempt to attack Arnold's scattered forces. He expected Wooster to arrive from Montreal in a few days with reinforcements, and he was already planning a spring offensive:

I have no thoughts of leaving this proud town until I first enter it in triumph. My wound has been exceedingly painful, but is now easy, and the surgeons assure me will be well in eight weeks. I know you will be anxious for me. That Providence which has carried me through so many dangers is still my protection. . . . I know no fear.[47]

But Wooster did not come. Quebec was too close to the fire for him. Eventually, he sent a few New York troops. Arnold borrowed from merchant friends in Montreal to feed a growing number of French Canadians who now joined the regiments, but they came without weapons, uniforms, even snowshoes. By sham and bluff, Arnold kept Quebec under siege until April 1, when Wooster finally came, three months late—to replace him. As news spread south of Arnold's march, Montgomery's death, Arnold's heroic attack and determined siege, he had become one of the first heroes—and to date the only live one—of the Revolution.

Much had happened to clear Arnold's name. Dr. Church's high-level espionage for the British had been discovered in October, while

Arnold was ascending the Kennebec. After Church's arrest, his committee had agreed to pay some of Arnold's claims from the Champlain campaign. The final report said Arnold had misappropriated $86 from a militia company's payroll, but it was probably nothing more than Arnold's bad habit of handing out money to his men without getting a proper receipt. In any case, when the Massachusetts provincial congress agreed to pay only 20 percent of Arnold's accounts, Washington had sent them on to the Continental Congress in Philadelphia, where Arnold's good friend Silas Deane saw to it that the entire debt was paid in full to Hannah Arnold in January. He also nominated Arnold for brigadier general before he sailed to France as America's first envoy to Europe.

The news of his promotion reached Arnold at Quebec in February. As his men shivered and suffered through a Quebec winter, Arnold sent a steady stream of impassioned letters south, begging for reinforcements, food, clothing, cannon. He was completely out of lead and could not resist the slightest enemy counterattack, he wrote Wooster, who remained safe and warm in Montreal all winter. By now, Arnold was convinced that a prolonged siege would be a fatal and futile exercise, that it would take ten thousand men to dislodge Carleton and resist the massive British counterattack he expected in the spring. The death of Montgomery and the sufferings of his men in prison—a plot to escape had been betrayed and all his men were now painfully clamped in long rows of leg irons and chains in the old Quebec jail—was embittering Arnold. He had given up on Wooster and sent his trusted young aide, now Major Mathias Ogden, to describe to Congress his plight and what it would take to keep up the fight for Canada. He had, he informed Congress, found a way to save a vast amount of money and time by having an iron foundry at Trois Rivières furnish shot and shells instead of lugging them all the way from Crown Point. He knew how short of gunpowder the American army remained, and he lured Congress with the prize for continuing to fight for Quebec: inside its powder magazines were three thousand barrels of gunpowder, ten thousand stands of arms, seven thousand uniforms, a vast array of cannonballs, 150 cannon. So far he had received a puny reinforcement of only one hundred men. He had burned all that remained of St. Roch, burned their ships in drydocks to deprive the city of firewood. He was continuing to raise large numbers of French Canadians. Carleton was having "no effect"[48] turning the habitants against the Americans, but Arnold's stubborn stand in a Quebec winter had impressed many of them.

By February 1, Arnold's continued siege was plagued by problems, not the least of which was Major Brown, who now called himself "colonel." Arnold finally wrote to Congress about Brown's pretentions and insubordinations: Brown had been joined by Easton, and both were again insisting on Brown's promotion and an independent command. Arnold sent a trusted aide to Philadelphia with a detailed complaint of their plundering and plottings. In a postscript, he said he did not mind if Easton and Brown knew of his allegation: "The contents of the enclosed letter I do not wish to be kept from the gentlemen. . . . I should despise myself were I capable of asserting a thing in prejudice of any gentleman without sufficient reasons to make it public."[49] By late February, Arnold wrote Washington that Carleton had attacked him once, sending five hundred men out after his field pieces. "But on our troops advancing to attack them, they made a precipitate retreat under cover of their guns." By the last day of February, four hundred fresh troops had arrived and Arnold was feeling stronger and more confident, "able to hobble about my room, though my leg is a little contracted and weak." He would soon be "fit for action," he added. He was preparing to fight off the expected British reinforcements and to assault the city again by scaling its walls. The snow was piled so high an army could walk over the walls in some places on snowshoes. If he received five thousand men in time, he could take the city and "I make no doubt of holding it." But the reluctance of Congress to help with more than reassuring words was all very confusing to him. He complained to Washington about the conditions Congress permitted; "the troops very illy clad and worse paid." His officers "think themselves neglected" while "those who deserted the cause and went home last fall have been promoted."[50]

In his February 27, 1776, letter to George Washington, Benedict Arnold so unburdened himself that he must have given the commander in chief the impression that he was hardly fit to go on: "The choice of difficulties I have had to encounter has rendered it so very perplexing that I have often been at a loss how to conduct matters." He may also have given Washington to believe he was once again considering resigning when he asked for "some experienced officer" to take command; explaining that "the service requires a person of greater abilities and experience than I can pretend to."[51] Washington was in the middle of reforming his command and lengthening enlistments in the Continental Army from a few months to a minimum one-year term to avoid repetitions of the mass expirations that had pressured Montgomery and Arnold to make their ill-fated attack. He was casting about for good generals, and he had few. Charles Lee had gone south to ward off a British invasion in the

Carolinas; Schuyler still was confined to his sickbed; Montgomery was dead; and now Wooster was proving himself capable of causing only confusion wherever he went, which was never into battle.

When Wooster arrived at Quebec early in April, he systematically ignored Arnold, even as he wrote Congress to express amazement at Arnold's tenacious siege: on February 14, Wooster wrote to Philadelphia that "General Arnold has, in a most surprising manner, kept up the blockade of Quebec, and that with half the number of the enemy."[52] Washington was writing to Congress that the blockade "exhibits fresh proofs of Arnold's ability and perseverance in the midst of difficulties."[53] Yet when Wooster rode into the American camp on the Plains of Abraham on April 1, he turned a deaf ear to the opinions and suggestions of the men who had intimidated the city of Quebec all winter with little more than willpower. By April 20, less than three weeks later, Arnold was writing to Philip Schuyler that he had obtained Wooster's permission to leave Quebec and take over Wooster's old post at Montreal. He explained that one day after Wooster arrived, he had been injured again when, during an alarm, he had rushed to mount his horse at an outpost and the horse had lost its balance and fallen right on top of Arnold's wounded leg. For ten days, Arnold again could not move. But his leg hurt far less than being snubbed by the incompetent Wooster: "Had I been able to take an active part, I should by no means have left the camp, but as General Wooster did not think proper to consult me in any of his matters, I was convinced I should be of more service here than in the camp, and he very readily granted me leave of absence until I recovered of my lameness."[54]

By late April, Arnold had come to the conclusion that Quebec could not be taken by siege. The American force was "so very inconsiderable" that he was "very dubious" of success. He had done all he could, he told Schuyler, even opening fire with new artillery batteries within musket range of the walls. But the bombardment was more to impress the French Canadians and reassure American prisoners, since there was far too little shot or shell to do any real damage. He had even built fireships to sail into Quebec's port and burn all enemy ships. There was only enough food left for three weeks, and unless more provisions could be brought all the way from New York with eight or ten thousand reinforcements, he advised Schuyler to allow him to withdraw the army south to the falls of the Richelieu River, between Chambly and St. Jean, above which navigation by a British fleet would be impossible. Here he envisioned an American line of defenses that would protect the Richelieu forts and the Lake Champlain region while leaving a strong American presence in Canada until Congress was ready to send sufficient forces to conquer Quebec. His plan, if approved, called for American batteries and a fleet of small warships to keep small British troop transports from sailing up the Richelieu. Eight small gondolas would be sufficient, as nothing larger could be gotten over the falls. And gondolas would be easy to build: he had already sketched one and sent an officer to Crown Point for cannon. Above all, Arnold was busily taking steps to make sure that if a British counterattack came, the enemy could not get around his lines to the south. But he was pessimistic. Only five hundred men remained at Montreal, half threatening to march home. No matter what bold plans he formulated, "everything is at a standstill for want of resources and, if they are not obtained soon, our affairs in this country will be entirely ruined."[55]

Only a week after his gloomy prognosis, Benedict Arnold received a pleasant surprise. On April 29, a delegation of commissioners from the Continental Congress—Benjamin Franklin, Samuel Chase, and Charles Carroll—arrived in Montreal after a grueling winter journey all the way from Philadelphia. They brought with them gold to help resupply the American army and a printing press to issue propaganda in French. As commissioners to Canada, they gave the American invasion political status: they were authorized by Congress "to promote or to form a union between the United Colonies and the people of Canada."[56] Their first task was to assess military conditions, and the day after they arrived, Arnold summoned a council of war.

Benjamin Franklin, as well as being a Pennsylvania delegate to Congress, was chairman of that colony's Committee of Safety and the man in charge of building river defenses and a navy to protect the American capital from British naval incursions. At his instigation, a huge *chevaux de frise*, a submerged line of pointed timbers to impale enemy ships, was being built by five thousand volunteers to block the channel of the Delaware River. Arnold enthusiastically proposed a similar device across the St. Lawrence. Franklin had also commissioned construction of row galleys. Larger than gondolas, they were long low ships that could be sailed or rowed and were ideal for inland waters, where the oceangoing capabilities of British warships could be turned against them. Franklin upheld Arnold's plans for fortifying the Richelieu. That same day, Arnold wrote Schuyler that the commissioners had agreed to build forts at "two important posts" on the St. Lawrence and build "immediately" four row galleys or gondolas at Chambly "under my direction." Used to building ships, he had already recruited French carpenters and bateaux builders and rounded up materials, requisitioning hawsers and anchors from Ticonderoga, and he now urged Schuyler to send him "fifty or a hundred good seamen with proper officers."[57] The new general was, in his enthusiasm, taking on the sound of a naval officer.

That night, as he often did at a moment of great crisis, Arnold threw a party for the congressmen in the mansion of his one-eared merchant friend Thomas Walker, Arnold's Montreal headquarters. It was a brilliant assemblage in the gloom of a civil war in a Canadian backwater in winter. Benjamin Franklin, just turned seventy years old, undoubtedly the most celebrated American of his age, was there, and Charles Carroll of Maryland, a French-educated Catholic and, as the wealthiest man in America, a symbol of the wealth that backed the American cause, and his cousin John, a Jesuit priest educated in Quebec, French-speaking and familiar with French customs. And there was eloquent, irascible Samuel Chase, a rich Maryland merchant who had formed a firm friendship with Arnold at Montreal. It had been Chase who suggested to John Adams that Congress send political commissioners to strengthen Canadian support. Like Arnold, Chase believed that "the success of the war will, in great measure, depend on securing Canada to our confederation." Chase had wanted the commission to hold a provincial convention as the other colonies had done; there the commissioners would "explain the views and design of Congress and persuade them to send delegates"[58] to Philadelphia. Nothing had come of Chase's idea until Mathias Ogden had arrived from Quebec with Arnold's report on deteriorating conditions in Canada: Arnold told Congress that support for the American cause might grow if some members of Congress came to assure the Canadians of American friendship. If such a mission was not sent, the Canadian campaign was in danger of failing. Arnold's message swayed Adams, who nominated Chase. Also attending the party that night was the new American commander in Canada, Major General John Thomas, promoted over Arnold's head and stopping off on his way to Quebec from Boston, where he had used the cannon Arnold had seized at Ticonderoga to drive the British out of Boston.

The reception which Arnold put together that night even impressed the richest man in America. Charles Carroll described it in a letter to his mother:

We were served with a glass of wine while people were crowding in to pay compliments: which ceremony being over, we were shown

into another apartment, and unexpectantly met in it a large number
of ladies, most of them French. After drinking tea and sitting some
time, we went to an elegant supper, which was followed with the
singing of the ladies.[59]

But there was little time left for Arnold's opulent diplomacy. Arnold
had warned Washington of an outbreak of smallpox among his
troops, but the commander in chief had sent an uninoculated regiment of Massachusetts farmers under Major General Thomas, who
was to replace Wooster as the American commander and who himself had never been exposed to the deadly disease. Thomas's promotion over Arnold's head must have been a jolt to him. It was the first
time he was passed over for promotion, and even if when he had
been wounded he had told Washington he thought someone more
senior than himself was needed to command the respect of his more
troublesome officers, now that he had successfully blockaded
Quebec all winter he expected a promotion in recognition of his
efforts in Canada.

By May 1, when Thomas took over from Wooster at Quebec,
reinforcements were belatedly flooding into Canada: 417 Green
Mountain Boys came from Vermont in sleighs, with whole new regiments from Massachusetts, Connecticut, New Jersey, Pennsylvania,
New Hampshire. Few of the troops had ever been inoculated, and
they also arrived ill-clad and unarmed, and Arnold's scrupulosity
about paying for everything dissolved under the pressure of such
great numbers. Now receipts, not gold, were given for grain and
guns, to be paid off when the campaign ended. Recruiting of French
Canadians had already suffered from Wooster's open anti-Catholi-
cism. He had forbade mass on Christmas Eve, arrested Recollet
brothers for communicating with confrères in Quebec, spied on
curés by planting informers in parishes to report to his officers.
Clergy who preached loyalty to the crown or who denied absolution
to pro-American habitants had also been arrested by Wooster's officers.

Thomas inherited a ragged army and a smoldering civil war, but
he, too, ignored Arnold's counsel. He found only nineteen hundred
men besieging Quebec—and fully half of them were suffering from
smallpox. On Arnold's orders, two hundred men at Montreal inoculated themselves by putting a pinprick of serum from a sore under a
fingernail, a practice first introduced in New England fifty years earlier but still opposed by many Puritans as usurping the power of
God by deliberately giving a disease. On May 16, Arnold gave a
general order for all troops to be inoculated. But Thomas came from

Massachusetts, where in his father's lifetime there had been riots after enlightened doctors and clergy tried to introduce inoculation. Overriding Arnold's objections, Thomas banned further inoculation under penalty of death, refused it himself, and sent all the inoculated soldiers to Arnold at Montreal. That same day, Thomas was infected; in two weeks, he was dead.

While he was still alive, a British ship, the frigate *Surprize,* hove into view off Quebec at six o'clock the morning of May 6. For seven weeks, a convoy of British warships and troop transports had been racing west from England, passing through fields of icebergs until, by mid-April, the fleet dared to break the pack of ice in the Gulf of St. Lawrence, leaving behind a trail of torn copper sheathing from their bottoms. The main convoy of fifteen ships carrying ten thousand redcoats had been stalled by the fog off Anticosti Island; *Surprize* had been sent ahead until she came close enough for her officers to spy the blue pennant over the Union Jack fluttering on a flagpole above Quebec Citadel, Carleton's agreed-upon signal that he still held the city. In a matter of minutes, two hundred redcoats were clambering ashore at Quebec. Carleton personally led eight hundred Highland Emigrants, redcoats, British militia, and French Canadians onto the Plains of Abraham, their bayonets glistening. The Americans, all but two hundred who were too sick to move, began to run. They left everything: local legend has it that British redcoats, cooped up on *Surprize* for several weeks on salted rations, sat down for the noon meal the Americans had obligingly cooked for them. Thomas and the Americans retreated all day, halfway to Montreal. "The army was in such a scattered condition," said Dr. Senter, that it was "impossible to collect them even for a regular retreat. In the most helter skelter manner, we raised the siege, leaving everything. All the camp equipage, ammunition, even our clothing, except what little we happened to have on us."[60] Trudging all night, seizing bateaux to cross spring-flooded streams and creeks, the Americans were pursued by the frigates *Surprize* and *Martin* and raked by their gunfire, and many boatloads of the wounded were overtaken and captured by the British. The army did not halt until Deschambault, the very spot where Arnold had wanted to mount shore batteries on a high bluff overlooking the falls of the Richelieu. General Thomas had vetoed Arnold's plan, but *now* he called a council of war: was it prudent to make a stand? All but three of his officers voted against a fight. Thomas remained with only a small rear guard, ordering the rest to continue to retreat.

It was four days before Arnold, at Montreal, knew of the American rout at Quebec. Arnold also called a council of war, proposing to march to Deschambault to join Thomas and make a stand. He was determined to attempt to stop the British offensive and hold the Richelieu-Champlain region. At first, Arnold was opposed by Congressmen Chase and Carroll (Franklin had already left, seriously ill). Arnold boldly overruled the congressmen and decided to march with virtually his entire force to make a stand at Deschambault, another if necessary at the mouth of the Jacques Cartier. The council of war, including Chase and Carroll, finally voted with Arnold, but the two commissioners had their doubts and sent them to Congress. It was another six days before Arnold could reach Deschambault, where he learned that Thomas had already retreated up the St. Lawrence to Trois Rivières.

With two-thirds of the Montreal garrison seriously ill and his army without food, pay, tents, uniforms, or medicine, Arnold saw that the Canadian adventure would soon be over. On May 31, he sat down to write an extremely frank letter to Major General Horatio Gates on his way from Philadelphia to replace Thomas. (He had worked closely with Gates, Washington's adjutant general, in planning the march to Quebec.)

I shall be ever happy in your friendship and society; and hope, with you, that our next winter-quarters will be more agreeable, though I must doubt it if affairs go as ill with you as here. Neglected by Congress below; pinched with every want here; distressed with the small-pox; want of Generals and discipline in our Army, which may rather be called a great rabble; our late unhappy retreat from Quebec . . . our credit and reputation lost, and great part of the country; and a powerful foreign enemy advancing upon us,—are so many difficulties we cannot surmount them. My whole thoughts are now bent on making a safe retreat out of this country; however, I hope we shall not be obliged to leave it until we have had one bout more for the honour of America. I think we can make a stand at Isle-aux-Noix, and keep the lake this summer from an invasion that way. We have little to fear; but I am heartily chagrined to think we have lost in one month all the immortal Montgomery was a whole campaign in gaining, together with our credit, and many men and an amazing sum of money. The Commissioners from Congress this day leave us, as our good fortune has long since.[61]

Arnold's letter to Gates also gave the first hint of another American debacle, this time as the main British army marched and sailed along the St. Lawrence. A vanguard of Canadians and Indians under

English officers had outrun the main force and, reaching Arnold's outpost at the Cedars, overrun it, capturing five hundred of Arnold's men. Arnold rushed to their rescue, but as he reached the southern tip of Montreal Island, he saw bateaux taking his men away. Arnold could not pursue: he had no boats. He sent a message to the British commander that he would personally hold him accountable with his life if the Indians harmed any of their prisoners. The British replied that if Arnold dared attack, the Indians would slaughter the prisoners. Arnold was "torn by the conflicting passions of rage and humanity. A sufficient force to take ample revenge, raging for action, urged me on one hand, and humanity for five hundred unhappy wretches who were on the point of being sacrificed if our vengeance was not delayed, plead equally strong on the others."[62] Arnold decided he must risk the safety of the prisoners. He led a flotilla of eighteen canoes toward the British camp. Amid a shower of British grapeshot, he ordered his Caughnawaga crew close enough to count the cannon, spot the troop placements. Reluctantly, he had to give the order to his overloaded canoes to retreat. At a hastily summoned council of war, he urged another attack to destroy the enemy and blunt the British advance, even if it meant sacrificing the prisoners. He was opposed by Colonel Hazen, the Chambly squire Arnold had until now trusted to defend the Richelieu River. Hazen was a man who had vacillated between British and American loyalties; but Arnold was not yet aware of this. Both men argued loudly until Arnold was outvoted. Arnold had given Hazen such a tongue-lashing before his staff that he had made a new enemy. The next day, the British commander, to Arnold's surprise, offered to release his prisoners if Arnold would allow him to withdraw his small force of redcoats and Indians and rejoin the main British army. He also required that Congress release an equal number of British prisoners. Arnold conferred with Carroll and Chase and then agreed to the British terms.

Returning to Montreal, Arnold prepared to evacuate the indefensible city: so many French Canadians had now deserted the Americans that he raged at his staff that he was "convinced that they are in general our bitter enemies."[63] Arnold decided to drop all pretense at diplomacy and coerce them: if they molested his troops, he was prepared to burn their town.

While Arnold had all spring cooled his heels in Montreal, trying to clothe and feed his hand-to-mouth army, the three commissioners had helped him in his attempt to procure food and supplies. In a series of meetings, Franklin had urged on Arnold the necessity of seizing provisions, since the Canadians would not accept American currency. To help feed the troops, Franklin lent Arnold, he later said, £343 in gold out of his own pocket. After one meeting on May 15, Arnold had written to Chase:

I believe I know your sentiments in respect to provisions, and shall not let the army suffer. . . . Blankets and coarse linen are exceedingly wanted. . . . Will it not be advisable and justifiable to seize on all such goods in Montreal as we are in absolute necessity for, and pay them the value? The British Government has set us many precedents, and necessity will doubtless justify retaliation. This I submit to your better judgment.[64]

Congressmen Chase and Carroll authorized seizure from Tory merchants, and Arnold reported back to them:

I am making every possible preparation to secure our retreat. I have secured six tons of lead, ball and shot. Merchandise of the inhabitants I have not yet taken hold of: I intend it tomorrow. It is impossible to know one hour beforehand the necessary steps to be taken. Everything is in the greatest confusion. Not one contractor, commissary or quartermaster: I am obliged to do the duty of all.[65]

He obtained from Carroll and Chase permission to seize all Tory property in Montreal that might help his army, paying not with gold but with nearly worthless Continental money. Arnold personally went to warehouses and began to list what was to be requisitioned. Then a rumor swept the city that the British were near; he later swore that he ordered the goods quickly bundled up and the name of each merchant written on the outside. Then he ordered a trusted staff officer to escort the seized goods to St. Jean, where Colonel Hazen was to sign for them and see that they were safely stored. When the goods reached St. Jean, Hazen refused to sign for them, put them in the fort's storerooms, or post a guard. Soon the packages left on the riverbank were looted by Hazen's men. Since there was no record of what was in them, there was no way of knowing how much should be reimbursed for them. Eventually, Arnold brought charges against Hazen. With his usual gusto, Arnold had gone about stripping warehouses and ships to supply his destitute army, at all times keeping Schuyler and Sullivan informed of his actions. "I am now removing a parcel of goods I have seized for the use of the Army,"[66] he wrote Schuyler. "I have received your instructions respecting the Tories and their effects. Most of the former had absconded. Great part of the latter is secured. I have sent to St.

[Jean's] a quantity of goods for the use of the Army—some bought and some seized."67

At St. Jean, when Arnold discovered that the seized goods had been looted, he wrote to Sullivan:

The goods I seized at Montreal and sent to Chambly under the care of Major Scott have been broken open, plundered and huddled together in the greatest confusion. They were taken in such a hurry it was impossible to take a particular account of them. Each man's name was marked on his packages. When Major Scott arrived at Chambly, he received your positive orders to repair to Sorel. The guard was ordered to return, and the goods to be delivered to Colonel Hazen to be stored. He [Hazen] refused receiving or taking care of any of them, by which means . . . the goods have been opened and plundered, I believe to a large amount. It is impossible for me to distinguish each man's or ever settle with the proprietors. . . . This is not the first or last order Colonel Hazen has disobeyed.68

Arnold was now reporting to the latest American commander, John Sullivan of New Hampshire, who had been president of the Enos court-martial and already was an anti-Arnold partisan. Sullivan wanted to make a stand at Montreal despite Arnold's arguing in a council of war that the British would bypass Montreal and march directly to Chambly and St. Jean, cutting off his retreat and trapping the entire American army. Arnold was tired of the inexperienced generals Congress had put over him, and in a letter to Schuyler he blasted Sullivan:

Shall we sacrifice the few men we have by endeavoring to keep possession of a small part of the country which can be of little or no service to us? The junction of the Canadians with the Colonies—an object which brought us into this country—is at an end. Let us quit then and secure our own country before it is too late. There will be more honor in making a safe retreat than hazarding a battle against such superiority which will doubtless be attended with the loss of our men and artillery and the only pass to our country. These arguments are not urged by fear for my personal safety. I am content to be the last man who quits the country and fall, so that my country may rise. But let us not all fall together.69

In the confusion of the American withdrawal, Arnold now emerged as the leader of an orderly retreat that included stripping everything that could be useful to the enemy—horses, wagons, boats, food, grain, cannon—and burning what could not be carried—bridges, barns, ships, crops. Arnold's idea of total defensive warfare excited the officers around him, and in the end, Sullivan retreated to St. Jean as British men-of-war sailed up to Montreal. Arnold was ready to retire quickly and in good order. It took him only two hours to ferry his troops and supplies, with all the sick and wounded, across the St. Lawrence, his men marching smartly only one hour ahead of the British until they overtook Sullivan's disheveled units, half of the men suffering from smallpox, all of them hurrying toward Lake Champlain. As Sullivan burned Chambly and boarded his men into bateaux on the Richelieu, Arnold volunteered to create a rear guard to protect the forlorn fleet of hundreds of bateaux overloaded with eight thousand men drifting slowly toward Crown Point.

As he prepared his own withdrawal from Canada and managed to stay only one hour ahead of the advancing British army, Arnold ordered St. Jean stripped. He even had a British warship on the stocks dismantled quickly, the parts numbered, loaded into bateaux, and taken south. Fort, houses, shipyard, anything that could help the British invasion of America he then ordered set afire. In the firelight, he ordered his own men off in their bateaux, holding back one boat and its crew. By now, the night of June 13, flames were visible miles to the north, guiding the British along the Richelieu. Arnold and his aide Wilkinson rode toward them as his men rowed away. Against the firelight the weary advance guard of British grenadiers recognized Arnold and his horse. Shouting, they rushed toward him. He waited, according to Wilkinson, until the last possible second, until they were within musket shot, and then he turned his horse and spurred it to the water's edge. Then this man who so loved horses drew a pistol and killed his horse with a single shot through the head, insisting that Wilkinson do the same. Then, as the British approached at the double-quick, he gave the order to row for the south end of Lake Champlain. The first American to attack Canada in the summer of 1775 was the last to leave little more than one year later. The Americans had withdrawn, but in good order, offering fierce resistance. A few days later, a triumphant Governor Carleton wrote to London that he had cleared the last American rebel out of Quebec. Back came the response from the new secretary of state: "I am sorry you did not get Arnold, for of all the Americans, he is the most enterprising and dangerous."[70]

9

"FOR THE
HONOR OF AMERICA"

When you ask for a frigate, they give
you a raft. Ask for sailors, they give
you tavern waiters. And if you want
breeches, they give you a vest.

Benedict Arnold to David Hawley, August 1776

In the days immediately following the Declaration of Independence on July 4, 1776, by revolutionary politicians in Philadelphia, the smallpox-ravaged remnants of the American northern army rendezvoused in the ruins of the old British fort at Crown Point. Stripped of most of its usable cannon by Benedict Arnold a year earlier, the vast star-shaped fortress was full of dying soldiers who were being weeded out before they could contaminate any more of the 3,500 survivors of a ten-thousand-man army.

On July 7, the American general officers in charge of defending northern New York and the New England backcountry against certain British invasion rode in to Crown Point from Albany for an emergency council of war. Already, Indians and British light infantry were probing through the forests southward along the lake shores, ambushing American hunting parties and attempting to cut the military road which led south along the Vermont shore toward New York City, east to the New England coast. Unknown to the Americans, the British had divided their Northern Army and were sending a second force, Loyalists and Indians, slashing east from Lake Ontario to attack Ticonderoga from the rear. With the main British army preparing to strike north from New York City, there were *three* British armies invading the new state of New York. The British were certain that before the year 1776 was out, the American rebellion would be over, its armies routed and returned to their proper submission, its leaders bound in irons aboard British ships for treason trials in London.

At the northern tip of the lake, the British were refitting for their summer offensive. They seemed to possess overwhelming advantages. In addition to ten thousand regulars they had two thousand German mercenaries including two hundred professional artillerymen and some seven hundred handpicked crewmen from the Royal Navy fleet anchored at Quebec—tough experienced crews for a fleet to be built and sailed on Lake Champlain, including royal engineers, shipwrights, carpenters, blacksmiths, and career officers who had volunteered to hunt down and destroy the American rebels. They had brought with them from England enough provisions for a year for twelve thousand men. To screen their advance and to scout out the enemy, the British had assembled four thousand Indians, eager to fight. To erect fortifications, to clear forest highways, and to harvest firewood and crops for such an army and navy, Carleton had invoked the emergency powers in the Quebec Act, calling to active duty more than one thousand habitants. In all, some seventeen thousand men were preparing to descend on the Americans' sick and demoralized rear guard at Crown Point. And in the holds and on the decks of the British warships anchored in the St. Lawrence, all cut and numbered, were the planks and masts, guns, rigging, and sails, of twenty-five ships: three large new men-of-war, one heavy artillery ketch, and twenty-one gunboats, an entire fleet made in England for fighting on Lake Champlain, then disassembled and shipped to the mountains of the Canadian-American frontier. Each of the three men-of-war was larger than any vessel that had ever sailed on Lake Champlain.

The British were ready to carry out the ministry's plan to divide and conquer America, snuffing out its year-old rebellion. In a coordinated campaign designed to cleave off radical New England from the supposedly less rebellious middle colonies and prevent reinforcements from the South, Carleton's Northern Army was to plunge down Lake Champlain, down Lake George, and on down the Hudson River to Albany to link up with the main British expeditionary force attacking northward from New York City. On July 4, as the

Continental Congress debated for the last time the resolution that the former British colonies were "and of right ought to be free and independent states," the main British invasion army had sailed into New York Harbor. For two weeks, tall warships glided in and dropped anchor, 479 of them in all, the largest force ever sent out from Europe, carrying 34,000 redcoats and Hessians. With their arrival all hope that Washington could help defend the far northern frontier evaporated.

Riding north to Crown Point with his aristocratic young staff was the American officer charged with defending New York, Major General Philip J. Schuyler. He had been inspecting the fragile line of defenses scattered one hundred miles north from Albany to Crown Point. From the outbreak of fighting in Massachusetts, Schuyler had been both military and political leader of New York's resistance to the British. It was a role that came easily to this hereditary Dutch aristocrat. Manager of lumbering operations and gristmills in the Hudson Valley, owner of a fleet of trading vessels that carried the products of his plantations to England and the West Indies, he had been born to a Dutch merchant and the daughter of another patroon family, the Van Rensselaers, and was related by marriage to the Livingstons. From the earliest rumbling of revolution, Schuyler had come to the forefront to oppose the British, yet he was less than a radical. He never sympathized with the terror tactics of the Sons of Liberty, nor could he condone mob violence, although his faction in New York politics had been involved in both. He had been appointed by the Second Continental Congress as one of the first four major generals under Washington and given command of the Northern Department, which embraced all of New York State. No American officer knew the problems of defending New York better than Schuyler. He knew all of the forts from Ticonderoga four hundred miles west to Niagara, having served the British as a supply officer during the French and Indian War. He was probably more familiar with the intricacies of supply than any other American in the early years of the Revolution. A cautious commander, he preferred a strong defense to taking the offensive.

While he was careful, Schuyler was also sure of himself. He had just rebuffed a direct challenge to his authority from the second-highest-ranking rebel general arriving at Crown Point that day, Horatio Gates. Schuyler was all that Gates wished to be, but Gates was a better politician. In the spring of 1776, Gates's reorganization of Washington's army completed, he had ridden to Philadelphia to lobby before Congress for his own command. The recommendation of Washington had combined with the gratitude of Boston politicians to make Gates a major general and the ideal contender to confront the patriarchal Schuyler in a bruising power struggle.

As they led their entourage north toward Crown Point, Schuyler and Gates inspected Skenesboro, vital for its iron forge, sawmills, and shipyard, all in operation on Schuyler's orders day and night, although its output was severely hampered by shortages of every kind. Worst of all, there was no one in charge who was capable of producing the ships needed to keep the northern front supplied and defended.

When he presented himself to Schuyler a few days earlier, Gates had maintained that Congress had ordered him to take over command of the Canadian army. Schuyler evidently knew little or nothing of Gates's intrigues with Boston politicians; he probably only knew that Gates had acted successfully as Washington's chief of staff for roughly a year. But in Massachusetts, Gates had also been busy developing his own contact in Congress under the guise of keeping Congress informed of the army's activities. Washington appreciated his efficient, European-style staff work, but already tension between Gates and Washington had developed. When Washington had wanted to attack Boston over the ice the preceding winter, Gates had led opposition to the plan in a council of war: outvoted, Washington had abandoned the plan. When Washington moved south and began to fortify New York City, Gates had gone on to Congress in May, criticizing Schuyler and his handling of the Canadian campaign in private conversations. John Adams was especially impressed with Gates: he had first met him when the former British major had come to Philadelphia with Washington to receive his commission from Congress, and Adams had visited Gates at Washington's headquarters in Cambridge as part of a congressional inspection tour.

As early as February 1776, as Arnold's army shivered outside the walls of Quebec, John Adams had begun to involve himself in the northern campaign. An undated memorandum in his hand shows "forces to be raised and maintained in Canada and New York . . . St. Lawrence and Hudson Rivers to be secured" high on his list of important considerations for Congress, higher even than a "declaration of independency." Adams had been on the congressional committee that reported to the full Congress on April 23. On May 25, Congress had appointed a committee, which included Adams, to meet with Washington and Gates on their ideas for "a plan of military operations for the ensuing campaign."[1] By May 30, only five days later, the committee reported its hasty deliberations to the entire Congress "relative to the defense of New York." The report came at a time when delegates were understandably distracted, riding home to seek the authorizations of their individual provincial congresses to support the Declaration of Independence.

Gates had arrived in Philadelphia on May 21, with Washington's qualified letter of recommendation to John Hancock, president of Congress. By the time Washington arrived only two days later, Gates had learned that he had been promoted to major general. How Gates won such precipitate advancement can only be explained by John Adams's powerful influence in Congress. Two months earlier, Gates had begun to write Adams from Boston, describing the American investiture of the city in vivid detail. Even earlier he had also begun writing to other American political and military leaders of his views on the mishandling of the Canadian expedition. Adams apparently overlooked the trait that had given Washington reservations about Gates, his insistence on the defensive. "Our business," Gates had written to Adams, "is to defend the main chance, to attack only by detail, and when a precious advantage offers."[2] Weeks before Gates's arrival in Philadelphia, Adams had written to Gates, "I wish you was a major general. . . . What say you to it?" Gates, of course, was delighted.[3]

As soon as he had attained his new rank, Gates had begun a campaign of criticizing more senior generals, beginning with Washington. Adams wanted to send Gates to Boston to build up its defenses, after Gates had written to him chastising Israel Putnam, the American general left in charge at Boston when the British evacuated the city, for lagging in the rebuilding of its fortifications. But Washington refused on the grounds that Gates himself had predicted that the British would not attack Boston. Gates criticized Washington in a letter to Samuel Adams on June 8, claiming that he had "positive" information that the British would return to Boston.[4] It was clear fabrication on his part. On June 13, Samuel Chase wrote to Gates that the recommendations of the Adamses were about to pay handsome dividends. "A general is to be sent to Canada with the powers of a Roman dictator. Many of the Congress have their eyes upon you."[5] On June 18, as the American invasion force retreated toward Crown Point, John Adams wrote to his wife, Abigail, that Gates was being given the Canadian command. The same day, Adams wrote his friend Gates, "We have ordered you to the post of honour, and made you dictator in Canada for six months."[6]

At Albany, General Schuyler, on hearing of Gates's appointment to head the Canadian army, cordially invited the new major general to stay with him at his manor house. As soon as Gates arrived, Schuyler gave him bad news. There *was* no more Canadian army.

The last American troops had been transported south to Crown Point, and technically, Gates had a command only as long as the Americans were on Canadian soil. When he presented his commission to Schuyler, Gates said that it was obvious that Congress intended him to relieve General Schuyler as commander of the *entire* Northern Army, *wherever* it was. But Schuyler pointed out that since Gates's troops were now under Schuyler in New York, Gates, too, was Schuyler's subordinate. Further, as Schuyler coolly pointed out, he had been created a major general a full year before Gates. In the politics of command, this automatically gave him seniority of rank. Gates agreed to subordinate himself temporarily as Schuyler's second-in-command while he appealed to Congress, but a power struggle had begun that would disturb the American army for years. Schuyler at once sent a dispatch rider to Congress for clarification. In only three days, the answer came back: Schuyler was in charge. As the two generals stopped to inspect Fort Ticonderoga on their way north to Crown Point, Gates wrote to John Adams, "I have been deceived and disappointed."[7]

When the American generals saw the remains of the American army, their disappointment must have bordered on despair. Crown Point juts out like a fishhook into the mouth of Lake Champlain, and on July 7, 1776, the old stone walls were surrounded only by a wooden stockade and earthworks. As the officers rode west around the southern tip of the lake toward the fort, on that hot summer day the stockade loomed above them on a bluff high above the shoreline, which now swarmed with abandoned bateaux. Through the fort's great iron gates, a scene of horror unfolded: thousands of sick and dying men, lying out in the hot noonday sun, others moaning from their makeshift tents. And yet the army was in no worse disrepair than the fort. In December 1773, a cook had accidentally set fire to a kitchen wall that was coated with tar to seal it against the weather. The flames spread quickly through the barracks, where the walls were coated with tar as well. Carried on the winter wind, burning embers soon ignited the dry roofs of other buildings until all of Fort Amherst was aflame. It had smoldered for months until its ruins were reduced to gaping rows of chimneys unable to provide the least shelter. A small corner of one barracks had eventually been repaired to house two dozen British officers, men, women, and children captured by the Americans in May 1775. It was here that Benedict Arnold greeted Schuyler and Gates and their entourages as they arrived the afternoon of July 7. In another corner of the fort was a new cemetery, with three hundred fresh graves.

With Gates came Colonel John Trumbull, son of Connecticut's governor, who found "not an army but a mob, the shattered remains of twelve or fifteen very fine battalions, ruined by sickness, fatigue, and desertion, and void of every idea of discipline or subordination . . . the officers as well as men of one colony insulting another."[8] Ethan Allen's brother-in-law Dr. Lewis Beebe arrived with retreating New Hampshire troops to find "not the least preparation for fortifying the garrison." The soldiers were "either sleeping, swimming, fishing or cursing and swearing." Beebe said Gates "gives universal uneasiness" and feared mass resignations, and "then we shall be in a fine pickle." Chaplain Spring preached a sermon on a theme from the Book of Timothy: "Behave thyself."[9]

While each officer registered his shocked reaction to the scene, five general officers filed into a wardroom and began their council of war. Schuyler presided in an armchair at the head of the table, flanked by Arnold and by gaunt John Sullivan. Gates sat, round-shouldered, to Schuyler's right, in the position of honor. To his right was Wilhelm Frederick, Baron de Woedtke: Congress had appointed him a brigadier general to serve the Canadian expedition, and he had been on his way there when the invasion ended. He died, apparently of smallpox, two weeks after the council of war and was buried with military honors at Ticonderoga. Benedict Arnold, the lowest-ranking officer present, by tradition spoke first and presented his assessment. Fort Amherst could not be held; it faced the wrong way for an attack from the north. Built by the French to thwart British invasion from the south, it was guarded on the south and west by outer works that made attack difficult from all but the north. But any number of ships could sail down the west shore of the lake right under the bluff on which the fort was constructed, and be within point-blank cannon range before they were detected. Furthermore, the fort could not be rebuilt in time. As soon as the British had enough boats for their army, they would attack down the lake from Canada. The only chance to stop them was to delay them until the northern winter could put a temporary halt—at least for another year—to British invasion plans.

The strategy which Arnold proposed seems to have been based on the premise that the cautious Carleton would never have the temerity to lead his troops, many of whom had never faced a harsh northern winter, in the fierce winds and heavy snows of northern New York. During the time that this policy of delay could purchase for the Americans, the United States might expect increased aid from the French, who were already sending in arms, money, and ammunition through their possessions in the Caribbean. Arnold's Connecticut friend and neighbor Silas Deane had already been dispatched by Congress to France to negotiate for aid, and would soon be joined by Benjamin Franklin. Moreover, a season of recruitment and construction of new fortifications at Fort Ticonderoga to the south could slow the British assault on the heavily populated areas of New York and New England even further.

Arnold's plan was to force the British to slow down the invasion by making them build a fleet to protect their barges full of troops. There were no north-south roads through the thick forests and swamps that surrounded the lake, and the entire force would have to come south by water in a hundred small, open, unarmed troop transports. As he retreated, Arnold had seized or destroyed every boat bigger than a canoe. Recent torrential rains in Quebec Province had turned the road south from Quebec to St. Jean into a quagmire. It would be weeks before the British could build at St. Jean or transport overland from Quebec the hundreds of precious flatboats they needed to transport their infantry and artillery south along the lake. Arnold knew that if he built an American fleet that threatened to attack the infantry barges as they came up the lake, or could even threaten to shell the British bases, the cautious Carleton would postpone his expedition until every redcoat and biscuit was thoroughly protected. For every ship that the Americans built, the British would delay until they could build more, even bigger, with superior firepower. If the Americans could build a thirty-six-gun man-of-war, a frigate, it would take the British all summer and fall to build a ship so large. The army which built one would have undeniable control of the lake and its surrounding region—indeed, of the whole New England backcountry. Such a daring race would cost the British a season of war; they would have to remain in Canada another year before they could march south. This would give the Americans time to rally, dig in, rebuild their forts and their army, and defeat the British armies piecemeal.

That Arnold, a brigadier general with no naval rank, could dare to think in such terms only underscored the lack of a regular American navy. There was a naval committee in Congress, but a majority still insisted on the fiction of a defensive war even after the invasion of Canada. To have a continental navy, they reasoned, would be to risk a direct confrontation with the Royal Navy, which supposedly minded less if Americans defended themselves in inshore waters than if they fought on the open sea. Instead, there were eleven state navies. This sort of political reasoning exasperated Benedict Arnold. As soon as he saw the British fleet sailing up the St. Lawrence in May 1776, he saw that Lake Champlain, Lake George, and the

Hudson River lay open to naval as well as army attack, and he had designed a navy for the Northern Department. For more than two months, Arnold had been working on plans for the fleet. In his own hand he had drawn "dimensions for two gondolas to be built at Chambly."[10] The retreat had scotched his plan for a new, smaller, faster, sloop-rigged gondola, forty-eight feet instead of sixty. He had redesigned this boat, until then mostly used to transport supplies and men, as a fighting vessel. It would carry three heavy guns, a twelve-pounder in its bow and two nine-pounders amidships, one firing to port, one to starboard, guns big enough to blow away the rigging, shatter the mast, even pound holes in the hull of larger ships—and absolutely indispensable to counteract British gunboats and armed launches, which were routinely used to escort larger ships in British naval engagements. Bristling with swivel guns that could fire grapeshot just above the water, it could rake open boats with deadly fire. But the Americans should not rely solely on such small craft. They provided no shelter for seamen in the cold winds and waters of a mountain lake, and their powder supplies were exposed, prone to explode. Arnold reported that three of them had been completed and five more were on the way. But as the mainstay of the American fleet, Arnold wanted to propose a ship larger and bolder and capable of firing far more lead than any gondola. He wanted row galleys—long, light, slender ships whose design dated back to the Greeks and the Romans. Arnold's design had two important innovations: the galleys would be seventy-six feet long and heavily armed, with nine-, twelve-, and fifteen-pound guns salvaged from Crown Point and Ticonderoga, and would have two large lateen sails, like Arab pirate ships in the Mediterranean, making them maneuverable in any direction. Perfect for rivers, coves, and shoal-depth waters, row galleys had a shallow draft and could be propelled by their crews hauling away on thirty-six sweep oars even at night or when there was no wind; they were ideally suited for rounding the headlands of Lake Champlain. Low to the water, they were also a difficult target for the high British men-of-war. The British, with little experience in lake sailing, could be counted on to build big, cumbersome ships better suited to the open seas. To swoop out of concealment, fire nearly one hundred pounds of shot in a single broadside, then slide back out of range before a large enemy ship could come about and bring its guns to bear: this was the tantalizing prospect Arnold offered the council of war.

It was a bold scheme, but not farfetched. Connecticut had recently commissioned row galleys to assist in Washington's defense of New York Harbor. Gates had seen row galleys in Philadelphia, commissioned by Franklin; thirteen were being used by the Pennsylvania navy to protect Congress and the capital. Indeed, Arnold must have discussed them with Franklin at Montreal. Virtually all of Congress had taken junkets down the Delaware on the racy, cigar-shaped galleys.

What Arnold wanted, then, was an American fleet consisting of one large ship-of-war, eight to ten row galleys, and eight gondolas, in all twenty ships to face the British and force them to slow their invasion. He would need as many as a thousand workmen, five hundred experienced shipwrights and ship's carpenters, and as many axmen to fell timbers. Most of all, he would need, he had calculated, nine hundred experienced seamen to sail his fleet.

Schuyler and Gates were deeply impressed by Arnold's bold scheme. Before the meeting was over, they had resolved to abandon Crown Point, withdrawing the sick and wounded to hospital camps on Lake George and the fit to Fort Ticonderoga. Schuyler would return to Albany, where he would guard against the attack he predicted from the west and assure the northward flow of men and material. Gates would be in command at Ticonderoga, building up its defenses against attack from the north. His deputy commander was to be Arnold, with the title of Commander of the Lakes. A soldier was to build and command America's first naval fleet. Only one key element of Arnold's plan was rejected. He could build his gondolas and galleys, but not a ship of the line: too many resources would be tied up in such a ship, Schuyler ruled. Arnold was to be left at Crown Point temporarily, in charge of the rear guard, as the main American army retreated south. Within two weeks, however, he was to be on his way to Skenesboro with the powers of a commodore and the unanimous backing of the American command, to build his fleet.

For his part, Gates, his immediate superior, was aware that in New Haven Arnold had been a master sailor whose fast small ships had specialized in the tricky business of transporting horses from Canada to the Caribbean. He also knew that Arnold had thoroughly reconnoitered Lake Champlain and not only knew the enemy positions but had sounded its coves and channels, testing its winds, currents, and safe anchorages. Washington wrote to Gates of his approval for Arnold's plan for defense of the Lake Champlain region: "I trust neither courage nor activity will be wanting in those whom the business is committed." If such a fleet was "assigned to General Arnold, none will doubt of his exertions."[11]

But even before Gates heard from Washington, he was unequivocally supporting Arnold's plan to Congress, writing that "General

Arnold, who is perfectly skilled in naval affairs, has most nobly undertaken to command our fleet upon the lake. With infinite satisfaction, I have committed the whole of that department to his care."[12]

As Benedict Arnold rode south to Skenesboro to speed the building of his fleet, despite his voluble enthusiasm for the task, he must
have known that he was engaged in an uneven contest with British
shipbuilders to the north. The British fleet that had forced him south
from Quebec carried with it seasoned sailors, officers, expect carpenters, and blacksmiths and all of the specialized skills and tools he
would lack in building his makeshift navy. Against these Arnold
had, at first, only house carpenters rushed to him from Albany.

Below Fort Ticonderoga, the waters of Lake Champlain grew sluggish and ever narrower, backing up through forests and swamps to
the head of navigation at Skenesboro. There, in the sweltering heat
of July, hidden away from the British more than one hundred miles
from their lines, Benedict Arnold began to build his navy. He already knew from reconnoitering the lake the year before that British
ships sailing up the lake from Canada toward Lake Champlain's
headwaters would have to pass through narrow, shoaled channels at
either end, squeezing single-file past silted river mouths. Only at the
lake's center, halfway down the lake, did Champlain widen to sixteen miles. In these constricted places, where the British fleet would
have to file by slowly, Arnold wanted to spring a trap. In the meantime, even if they had enough ships to escort their infantry barges
south and made it up the open lake as far as Ticonderoga, the British could easily be shelled by American artillery from nearby hills on
both sides of the lake as it petered out toward southernmost
Skenesboro. So well chosen was this site that to strike at Arnold's
shipbuilding base at the head of navigation would be virtually impossible. The British would have to run a forty-mile gauntlet of
deadly crossfire to reach this base hidden behind an island at the
elbow of swamp where Wood Creek and Lake Champlain merged.
There, in a wide natural harbor flanked by protective high hills and
guarded by blockhouses, Arnold began to forge a beaten army into
an upstart navy.

Temporarily beyond British reach, Arnold began to sort out the
men and equipment he needed. The greatest danger to his men was
not a British army or a fleet, but panic. The memories of brave
stands atop Breed's Hill and in the streets of Quebec seemed to have
been discarded in the months of ignominious retreat. Moreover, his
troops were still being decimated by smallpox. Entire New Hampshire regiments, never before exposed to the disease, were still being

cut down by it. Colonel Trumbull, arriving at Crown Point with Gates, had observed that it was impossible to peer into a single tent or lean-to without seeing someone dead or dying. As convoys of bateaux resumed the dreary evacuation south, Benedict Arnold ordered the living to burn the debris of the dead—tents, shelters, blankets, barracks—then dig up, dismantle, and destroy anything that might be useful to the British. But he was reconsidering abandoning Crown Point. He asked Gates if it would not be wiser to leave an outpost of one regiment at Crown Point to protect its boat landing. This could be the rearguard outpost, the eyes and ears to the north for the army and navy to the south. Without waiting for concurrence, he bivouacked men in barracks he had built the year before outside the walls, then gave orders to put to the torch all that was left inside Crown Point.

Then he catalogued his men according to skills. Within three days of the council of war, Arnold sent Gates his accounting of workmen in the army. Every carpenter, armorer, blacksmith was methodically classified. What he needed was men who knew how to build ships. "The ship carpenters . . . gangs of fifteen each" Arnold shipped off to Skenesboro under officers whom he had taken the responsibility to appoint. This was an irregular step, but Arnold justified it on the grounds that "I believe it will expedite the works."[13] Choosing and commissioning officers was clearly Gates's prerogative, but Arnold brushed aside protocol and sent his own men off to Skenesboro to take over the shipyard. He retained a few score soldiers at Crown Point to unearth cannon and ammunition he had located the year before. They dragged sledges of shot and shell, including seven tons of lead sheets, down to the waterline to bateaux, three tons of lead for Skenesboro, four tons to Gates.

Within a week of the Crown Point strategy meeting, Horatio Gates had taken up Arnold's refrain of naval superiority as if it were his own, but he was using it now as a club to hammer away at the reputation of his antagonist General Schuyler. In his first official communication from Ticonderoga to the Continental Congress, Gates wrote to Hancock that he had concurred with the other generals in resolving "by every means in our power to maintain the naval superiority of Lake Champlain." He painted a picture of official harmony, of traveling south from Crown Point to Fort Ticonderoga with Schuyler to lay out new encampments and "to examine our naval force upon the lake." Here, however, he launched into criticism of Schuyler again, whose overall responsibilities in the Northern Department had, until the council of war, included all shipbuilding.

Indeed, for more than a year, without blueprints, shipwrights, or proper tools, Schuyler had managed to turn out hundred of bateaux and even a few gondolas to ferry men and supplies back and forth to Canada, but Schuyler had seen his objective as providing an army and its supplies, not building ships suitable for naval warfare. Now that his strategy had shifted to meet the British invasion, Schuyler was vulnerable to Gates's hindsight. "The vessels," Gates wrote to Congress, "which should have been constantly armed as vessels of war, have hitherto been solely employed as floating wagons." To Congress, Gates was scathing of Schuyler when he turned to Schuyler's pet, the gondola. The gondolas Schuyler had ordered built at Skenesboro "are nothing but in name. When done, they seem to be vessels very unwieldy to move."[14] Feigning an expert's knowledge of naval affairs to Congress, General Gates got it exactly backward. Schuyler favored gondolas, at least in part, because they were versatile—because they could be used to transport men and munitions as well as to fight. Arnold himself had used them at Quebec and probably was the first to suggest to Schuyler more than a year earlier that they should be the workhorse of the Northern Department. Moreover, the very ship on which Gates lavished so much praise, the schooner *Royal Savage,* had distinguished herself as a remarkably poor sailer, one so temperamental that she could be gotten away from the dock only if the point of wind was perfect. Obviously, Gates didn't know the difference between a warship and a yacht, but then neither did many members of the Congress to which this damaging letter was directed.

Ending his first command report to Congress with the further complaint that Schuyler still maintained that Gates's congressional appointment related *only* to Canada, Gates pointed out that Schuyler had blocked his appointment of Governor Trumbull's youngest son, John, as his deputy adjutant general. This last was certainly calculated to stir up old New York–New England animosities. Finally, Gates asked that any replies from Congress be sent directly to him at Ticonderoga, not through normal channels, which would be through Schuyler's headquarters at Albany. Understandably, he didn't want his commanding officer to read them.

Benedict Arnold apparently knew nothing of this intrigue: he was preoccupied with assembling the tools and supplies to build his ships. While he was surrounded by forests, his most pressing need was wood: planks, dried and cured, for ships' hulls that would be light and tight and would not leak and wallow. He needed boards, and Colonel David Hartley, his aide-de-camp, found thousands of them. Arnold promptly set sail on his own reconnaissance around the lake, sending his newly appointed second-in-command, Brigadier General David Waterbury, off to Skenesboro. Arnold was eager to scout the lake, first up the Vermont shore, then down the New York, taking soundings, observing the way the wind played on headlands, pinpointing protected anchorages.

Mornings on Lake Champlain are still and airless, white heavy morning fogs burning off and wind gathering through the day in warm updrafts that form taut high clouds, piling up on the hillsides until they fairly explode into thunderstorms in late afternoon. Aboard *Enterprise* and followed by *America* and *Liberty,* Arnold ran before the prevailing summer wind north toward Canada. Dropping anchor frequently to row ashore and visit sawmills, Arnold decided which timber piles were worth hauling south to Skenesboro and which should be put to the torch to deprive the British. He had to assume that the Indians and the British light infantry were never far behind him, seeking the same supplies. Once again, from Crown Point fifty miles north, as far as the mills at the mouth of the Onion River which had so recently supplied Montgomery's advance, he left fragrant pyres of lumber, columns of resinous smoke marking his defiance of the enemy. He left nothing usable in his wake as his ships, laden with between twenty and thirty thousand board feet of timber, came about and lumbered south.

Arnold sailed into Skenesboro on July 23, 1776. What he saw and heard as the *Enterprise* made its way down the narrow channel could not have heartened him. Despite the keening of the sawmill and the tangle of timber spewing from it into the harbor's mouth, instead of the expected din of hammers pounding together a fleet he heard only a weak tattoo. Only two gondolas were under construction. Not one row galley was on the stocks, and Skenesboro seemed all confusion. While only a few men were building ships, the rest loitered outside Philip Skene's manor house, which had been made the headquarters and the main barracks for shipyard workers. Skenesboro had been turned into a rear-area rest camp for unemployed militia, not the linchpin of American naval strategy Arnold had intended. All around the harbor, where men were supposed to be building a fleet, they were either building or filling bunks, beds, and barracks.

As soon as *Enterprise* arrived at the long quay in front of Skene House, Arnold stumped angrily up the path to find out why so little had been done. The answer, he quickly learned, was one Captain Jacobus Wynkoop, self-styled Commodore of Lake Champlain. When General Schuyler had belatedly decided in May to make

Skenesboro the Northern Department's shipbuilding base to turn
out large numbers of bateaux to resupply his army in Canada, he
had sent in this corpulent, plodding yet feisty New York militia officer to take over the garrison and oversee the work. By July, even
Gates was growing exasperated with the slow pace of production at
Skenesboro, although his criticism may have been partially motivated by the fact that Wynkoop had been appointed by Schuyler. To
Arnold, Gates had confided on July 17, "I think the Commodore
seems slow, and wish he may retain all that prowess for which he
says he was so famous last war."[15] The pompous Wynkoop was
captivated by his commission as the man in command of whatever
vessels the Americans already possessed on the lake, turning his back
on the preparations at Skenesboro and instead leading a handful of
small boats out on preposterous expeditions down the lake, fleeing
back toward the American lines at any hint of danger. In one such
episode, Wynkoop had mistaken a flock of gulls for the sails of a
British fleet and had beaten a retreat back to the protection of Ticonderoga's guns. Indeed, he had stripped all the guns from his
ships.

Returning to report to Gates at Ticonderoga after his reconnaissance, Arnold found Gates's nervous memo of July 13 on the subject
of Wynkoop: "I labor continually to get the Commodore to Crown
Point with the vessels." Gates had agreed with Arnold that all American vessels should be first used to strip the abandoned fort and
carry south all men and supplies, but Wynkoop had gone to
Skenesboro, certain that the fastest way to please his Dutch master
Schuyler was to ignore Gates and now build the gondolas that
Schuyler preferred. Yet in two months, only one had been completed. While Gates sputtered and Arnold raged, Wynkoop apparently had decided that only one gondola should be built at a time
and all other energies should be poured into building sleeping ac-
commodations for his men, whose indolence was becoming legendary. The plan was to build the larger ships' hulls at Skenesboro, then
row them to Ticonderoga, where, opposite the fort's warehouses,
the masts would be lowered from a bluff of Mount Independence to
be stepped on the decks, then rigged as their sails were fitted out,
their cannon mounted. In addition, one new schooner, the *Revenge,*
was to be built at the Ticonderoga yard. By late July, Gates was
beside himself at the delays: "We shall be happy, or miserable," he
wrote to Arnold, "as we are, or are not, prepared for the enemy."[16]

Commodore Wynkoop stubbornly refused to acknowledge that
he had been superseded not only by Waterbury but by Arnold. A
Yorker, he would not serve under these New England officers. He

pretended to be required only to follow the orders of Schuyler. When Arnold had sent Waterbury to Skenesboro with shipwrights, carpenters, and the lumber brought all the way from St. Jean to build the first row galley, Wynkoop had ignored his orders and taken all but a skeleton crew off shipbuilding. He seemed obsessed with the idea of making Skenesboro another Ticonderoga, a New York base to rival the New England stronghold to the north. All hands sent down from Crown Point had been pressed into felling trees to build blockhouses and stockades, barracks and bunks—innumerable windowless, stagnant, unhealthy barracks where, indeed, Arnold once again found sick men, exhausted from felling trees all day in the sun, who were unable to sleep in the hot summer evenings. Arnold went straight to Waterbury. It wasn't long before Waterbury apprised him of the extent of Wynkoop's intransigence and the precious time and material and men wasted. Fortunately for Wynkoop, he was apparently away on another of his fool's errands to the north.

Cooling down, Arnold inspected the yards. There was little he could do except stockpile lumber and drill the militia until skilled help arrived. Arnold had written to Schuyler and Washington and Governors Trumbull of Connecticut and Cooke of Rhode Island, and Washington had written to Congress. Arnold needed five hundred experienced ship's carpenters and shipwrights: none could be found short of Philadelphia or New London. He had only the handful he had found at Crown Point. Arnold knew there were plenty of shipwrights and carpenters willing to leave their homes and families to trek into the New York wilderness—if the price was right.

When an insufficient number of men answered Arnold's first call for crews to man his fighting ships, Arnold suggested to Gates that the reason was that there was no chance for prize money. On privateer ships, every crewman and officer received a share of the sale price of each captured ship and its cargo. Gates wrote to Congress with Arnold's suggestion of bonuses. The Marine Committee, with the authorization of the full Congress, offered "encouragement" in the form of an eight-shilling-per-month bonus for each noncommissioned officer, seaman, or marine. Governor Cooke of Rhode Island wrote back to Congress with alacrity that his state's quota would now be met and Rhode Islanders would soon be on their way to Skenesboro. On July 23, however, as Arnold headed south to Skenesboro, he must have been surprised when the proffered "encouragement" failed to produce the 348 officers and men he needed at once to man his first crop of ships. Gates's order-of-the-day was clear enough: in order for the Army of the United States to continue to support its naval superi-

ority and command of the waters of Lake Champlain, Congress was
offering untrained militia soldiers at Fort Ticonderoga the same eight-
shilling bonus it was giving salt-seasoned sailors. Still, only seventy
men—one-fifth the men Arnold needed—turned out the next morning to sail with him to Skenesboro.

The failure of this particular recruitment offer led Arnold to
send an express rider to General Schuyler in Albany the next day to
appeal for help. Then he reported the request to Gates. "I have sent
off an express this morning to General Schuyler. . . . Have requested
him to send either to Connecticut, or to General Washington, for
two or three hundred seamen who will be absolutely necessary to
man what craft we shall soon have completed. Without a larger
number of seamen than can be found in the Northern Army, our
navigation will be useless."[17] Arnold also forwarded to Schuyler a
long list of supplies that he had been unable to find at the Ticonderoga storehouses or at Skenesboro. Schuyler turned it over to Captain Richard Varick, his aide-de-camp, authorizing him to strip ships
stranded at the docks in Albany. The Hudson River was already
closed to navigation above New York City by a British blockade.
Oceangoing ships were rotting at their moorings. Owners, including
Schuyler, were to be reimbursed by Congress. What could not be
requisitioned at Albany was to be taken at Poughkeepsie and
Esophus, farther downriver. Blocks, anchors, cables, and a ton of
iron of the proper grade to make nails were to be rushed to Arnold
at Skenesboro. Sails and rope were to be ordered from Connecticut
seaport towns. Once again, Arnold did not wait to work through
proper channels. He sent his own purchasing agent off to Connecticut, only to have him overtaken and superseded by order of
Schuyler.

But the dragnet for men and munitions yielded so slowly that
more and more money had to be offered. As Arnold personally
showed carpenters what he knew about shipbuilding and waited for
experienced shipwrights, he again asked Schuyler to send to Congress in Philadelphia to offer whatever inducement it took. The result was congressional authorization of a pay rate of $32⅔ in new
Continental currency monthly for shipwrights, an astronomical sum
for the times.* In all the state and Continental navies, only one officer was paid more: Commodore Esek Hopkins, head of the Continental Navies himself. The new pay table also offered fourteen
shillings a month for ship's carpenters, more than double what a
soldier or sailor was normally paid and nearly five times what an

---

* There were three Continental dollars in each £1 of English money; both currencies were
in use, as well as a confusing array of state currencies, through much of the war.

artisan could make in Philadelphia in peacetime. In addition, the shipbuilders were offered one and a half the normal rations of food and double rations of rum every day, as well as travel allowances for every day en route to Skenesboro, including time spent on shipboard. Happily, shipwright Thomas Casdrop of Philadelphia, part owner of a shipyard that had produced two row galleys for the Pennsylvania navy, rounded up fifty ship's carpenters, and marched north to the frontier boomtown of Skenesboro.

Benedict Arnold evidently still did not realize how desperate his situation was. For his strategy to succeed, he had relied on massive assistance from the maritime towns of New England, New York, and Pennsylvania. In New England alone, more than seventy thousand men were employed in shipbuilding, five times the number in the army and navies combined, working night and day at high wages to build privately owned ships—privateers—to raid British commerce; captured prize cargoes could be sold at high profits that were divided among officers and crews. In all, Washington, the state governors, and the revolutionary governors signed fully two thousand letters of marque—privateering licenses—each commissioning a marauding ship. While each state had a navy, they were minuscule compared to the private navies under construction or already at sea. Pennsylvania, with only a score of ships in its state navy, alone issued five hundred privateering licenses. Two thousand private ships bristling with eighteen thousand cannon were built for the profitable pursuit of British merchant ships during the Revolution. Even Washington had a vested interest in the new system. By resolution of Congress, the commander in chief received a share of every ship and cargo auctioned off in the ports at which captured ships were sold.

More immediately worrisome to Arnold was that he did not know how rapidly conditions were changing to the south. When he had outlined his bold plan at Crown Point on July 7, it had been based on old news about the British. The only British in North America at the time were on Canadian soil, in Halifax, Quebec, or St. John's. Since then, two more British fleets had arrived, off New York City and off the Carolinas. After the British had landed on Staten Island in early July, the New York provincial congress had abandoned New York City and retreated to White Plains. What militia New York, Connecticut, and Massachusetts could muster were on their way to help Washington fortify western Long Island and southern Manhattan. With good reason, Arnold had written to Gates, in his last letter on July 10, "I am anxious to hear from New York."[18]

True to his word, Washington had written Congress that same

day for reinforcements for the Northern Army: three regiments were detached from the Boston garrison and marched to reinforce Ticonderoga. It was, Washington told Congress, "a matter of the greatest importance to have a sufficient force" on Lake Champlain "to prevent the enemy passing the lake."[19] To help draw a hard line against a northern invasion, Washington had urged Congress to rush the skilled artisans Arnold so desperately needed. Indeed, he assumed that they had already been sent. The Marine Committee of Congress called for help from as far away as Maine. On July 16, Governor Cooke of Rhode Island wrote to John Hancock: "I have appointed Captain Barnard Eddy, a very suitable person, the chief carpenter. He hath already enlisted twenty men, who are to be well provided with tools and arms at the [Marine Committee] rate."[20] From the Connecticut War Office, Governor Trumbull said that his state, too, would spare all the men it could, and he dispatched Captain Jonathan Lester from Arnold's hometown of Norwich Town. Lester had just finished building a row galley, the *Shark,* for the Connecticut navy, and he marched to Skenesboro with twenty-five skilled ship's carpenters. But only a fraction of the men needed were on the march. A month passed before Governor Trumbull wrote to Washington in New York City. "Schuyler has requested that two hundred seamen may be raised in this state to man the vessels on the lake [but] most of our seamen have marched with our militia to join your army."[21] On receiving word that the main British armada had anchored off New York, Trumbull had sent off every experienced seaman he could find aboard two new row galleys to help defend New York Harbor. What few sailors he had left he needed to defend the exposed shipyard at Stonington.

To raise crews in Connecticut, Governor Trumbull had to exceed the generous salaries offered by Congress. Trumbull sent Schuyler a bill on August 13 for a company of sailors raised by Captain Seth Warner, one of the officers Benedict Arnold had specifically requested to serve under him as a ship's captain. Warner informed Trumbull that he could find forty men to march to Skenesboro. But, above and beyond the handsome bonus already authorized by Gates, Trumbull had to agree to a further "bounty" of $20, about $1,200 in 1990 currency! Moreover, each man was to be given a cash "premium" to pay for, or take the place of, a blanket, a gun, a cartridge box, and a knapsack, worth another $800 in 1990 currency, plus "the same allowances and marching money as the other troops in Continental service." This "marching money" amounted to a day's pay for each twenty miles traveled on foot or by ship. Indeed, Trumbull recognized that cash was the only incentive to get men aboard Arnold's fleet in time to meet the British onslaught—not the promise of payment, either, but cash in hand, "the premium and first month's wages to be paid before they begin their march."[22] It was gold, Yankee gold and Yorker gold, which smoothed the ways for the patriots to aid in the war effort.

While Arnold waited impatiently for the crews and carpenters he so relied upon, he set about reorganizing the ragtag militia he had found at Skenesboro. Ignoring Wynkoop for the moment, he decreed that no more gondolas be constructed and that the six underway be rushed. Then he had a new platform erected for the first row galley. He divided his men not into the fifteen-man crews that had poked along but into groups of twenty-five men, each to build a ship. Then he set five hundred men to work felling trees in the forest, cutting down tall pine trees with their axes and dragging them out with oxen. Another one hundred men were divided into shifts to keep up production day and night in the sawmills. Arnold had found another mill at Cheshire, seven miles farther up Wood Creek, to keep Fort Ticonderoga supplied with lumber for its ramparts and barracks, thus freeing the sawmill at Skenesboro for the fleet's use.

Suddenly, Arnold's prospects brightened. On July 24, the first of 150 ship's carpenters marched into Skenesboro, their tool bags slung over their shoulders. An exhilarated Arnold set them to work. By July 31, six row galleys were on the stocks at Skenesboro, and Arnold went off to Ticonderoga to report to Gates. By the end of July, in just three weeks since the emergency council of war, Gates was writing to Washington, exclaiming over Arnold's achievements to date: "General Arnold, ever active and anxious to serve his country, is just returned from Skenesboro, where he has been to give life and spirit to our dockyard."[23]

Everyone but Arnold seemed satisfied at his progress, even smug about American safety. The longer the British did not attack, the more doubt arose that they might not, at least for this year. Well fed and well clothed again, the New England troops at Fort Ticonderoga were like happy children, frolicking along the shores of this beautiful mountain lake, rowing out to fish for the salmon and northern pike that abounded in the deep cool waters. It was all Gates could do to keep enough men or boats on hand to supply Arnold's dockyards, much less submit to the hard work of building fortifications and digging trenches in the summer sun. On July 31, as the exasperated Arnold waited to return to Skenesboro, Gates issued this general order at Ticonderoga:

Fishing in bateaux being prejudicial to the men's health, to the service and the bateaux, it is positively prohibited— The bateaux master will order those bateaux which as not wanted for immediate service to be drawn up and put in proper repair.—Two bateaux are to be delivered to the order of the Commanding officer of each regiment. . . . He is to be answerable for them. The rest of the bateaux are to be immediately collected and placed under the care of the bateaux guard. . . . The Bateau Master is positively forbid to part with any bateaux from the Landing without a signed order from Head Quarters.[24]

Only Arnold, it must have seemed to him, was still worried about the British.

Arnold had half his fleet, but not the half that mattered. The row galleys were at last begun; three row galleys, as he later wrote Gates, "will be superior to our whole naval force."[25] But who would sail them? To Schuyler, just before he had left Skenesboro, Arnold had written confidentially that the first three galleys would splash down the ways into Lake Champlain in three more weeks, but they would "require a much greater number of seamen to navigate them than can be furnished from the Northern Army"; to date only seventy men had accepted the 100 percent bounty, and while carpenters and shipwrights were streaming in, no seamen had arrived from New England or Philadelphia. Arnold needed nearly a thousand sailors and marines, and he had only seventy. Again, the problem, he frankly admitted, was money. Since there were no prizes of cargo or payrolls to be captured, not even "the common premium and ten dollars per month extra wages" could entice them. Unless he could send directly to Connecticut for three hundred seasoned sailors to distribute among his crews of soldiers, unless he could offer still higher bonuses for service on his ships, "our navigation will be useless." He also needed experienced ship's captains. He listed five of them "who are men of spirits." Almost as an afterthought, he added, "We are at a loss for gunners."[26]

It was two more weeks before Arnold received answers to his pleas, and the responses were devastating. All available Connecticut seamen had marched off to New York City to serve as militiamen while British troops landed on Long Island. Three out of five ship's captains, Arnold's old friends, declined to join him. No anchors or cables could be found in the tumult of the New York, Albany, and Hudson River waterfronts. Of the one thousand seamen he needed, only three hundred arrived from all New England to help him protect the New England backcountry, to keep New England from being severed from the United States. As the weeks went by and his shipbuilding crews worked night and day, Arnold sent ever more strident memos to Gates. By late August, as he sailed north on a storm-tossed lake with untrained crews, Arnold begged for "one hundred good seamen as soon as possible." By the time he had sailed, Arnold was willing to settle for a few good men: he would train the rest himself.[27]

With each request, Gates grew more exasperated with his subordinate. He was working "early and late" to fulfill Arnold's requisitions. "Believe me, dear sir, no man alive could be more anxious for the welfare of you and your fleet."[28] To be sure, Gates himself poured out his frustrations, that same day, to his superior, Schuyler, momentarily setting aside their rivalry. "The general [Arnold] makes no doubt the enemy will soon pay him a visit. I hope not before we get the row galleys to his assistance. It is a lamentable case that our galleys must wait for cordage and for guns to be completed." Gates explained to Arnold over and over that one severe shortage was of blacksmiths to assemble gun carriages and make fittings for the ships. There were plenty of cannon, but all the gun carriages had to be made on the spot. Surely blacksmiths could be recruited by Schuyler. More than six weeks had passed since they had met and planned the campaign at Crown Point. Gates presumed that Schuyler was dragging his feet. "The powder, lead and flints I wrote for so long ago is not yet even in part arrived. Pray hurry it up. The moments are precious, and not one of them should be lost."[29] Gates's presumptuous note was carried to Albany by Major Henry B. Livingston. At a hurried meeting the next day, Schuyler ordered another aide to dispatch a boat to Poughkeepsie to seize, if necessary, anchor cables vital to naval gunnery. The next day, three more bateaux were sent off to Poughkeepsie to commandeer "such cables and cordage"[30] as they had. Gates, Schuyler, Trumbull, everyone involved was doing all he could amid the confusion and endless unpredictable shortages of war.

But by October 3, nearly two months after the generals of the Northern Army had embarked on their plan to build a navy, the prognosis was dim. On receiving Arnold's long memo of "articles repeatedly asked for,"[31] Gates at Ticonderoga brushed aside his pile of paperwork and wrote a long letter to Arnold. There was mixed good news: two more row galleys had sailed the day before "with all the seamen to be had here." There were two companies of Connecticut seamen, paid an astonishing forty-eight shillings a month, six times what a soldier was paid, who had been on their way to fight in New York as infantry when Washington sent them north with their officers to sail under Arnold, and Gates added 110 soldiers he had drafted from the garrison at Ticonderoga to add to the combined crews "besides the number you determined upon for the full complement of each row galley." But there was also bad news: "Not one of the two hundred seamen promised from New York have yet arrived here. I now give up the hopes of seeing them for this year." Worse still, even though Gates's commissary, Colonel Trumbull, had crammed the relief ship with enough food for a month and warm uniforms, half the cordage was still missing, and there were no anchor cables. Gates said that Trumbull and his staff had done all they could: "They assure me they have put every article that you demanded in your last letter on board the *Liberty* schooner except what is not to be had here. Where it is not to be had, you and the princes of the earth must go unfurnished." Gates sent Arnold fourteen barrels of rum and some fresh beef, all he could spare, but his overriding message to Arnold was: "Be satisfied."[32]

If Gates was satisfied, Arnold was not. He did not have all the ships he needed, and he could not finish the ships he had. He was short one hundred seamen. His supply of gunpowder was so short that he could not allow gunnery drills. He was disgusted with Congress, with Gates, with Trumbull and the commissaries who were supposed to supply him. "When you ask for a frigate, they give you a raft. As for sailors, they give you tavern waiters. And if you want breeches, they give you a vest."[33] While the spirits of the men around Arnold soared at each new story of American success, Arnold was filled with a growing apprehension. He had not forgotten the army at the other end of the lake, and he felt increasingly powerless to rouse his colleagues to prepare adequately to oppose it.

As Benedict Arnold champed at the bit to sail, he busied himself with a pile of last-minute correspondence in his cabin on *Royal Savage*. There were personal matters to attend to, many of them only now coming to light. At least twice a month he wrote to his sister, Hannah. He apparently had decided, after the shock of the Quebec campaign, to write a last will and testament, and he sent it to her. Hannah alluded to it in a letter she wrote him August 5 from New Haven: "Should heaven in wrath deprive me of you, I shall religiously observe it." Arnold trusted his sister completely and had turned over all his business dealings to her. He evidently sent her his pay, giving her complete discretion to manage his money and property. He seems to have trusted Hannah's judgment more than anyone's. Her letters show her nervous about her new role. Few women had to make such decisions in those times. She had decided to sell off one of his ships, a brigantine: she had consulted with his friends, who had told her the odds of an American ship making a voyage safely through the British blockade were ten to one, and it was impossible to get a crew, there being scarcely enough men left at home to grow food. Hannah had Benedict's three children to feed, and she was selling off his warehoused rum and sugar for cash. She feared the merchandise would depreciate. She invested the £530 proceeds of the sale of the brigantine in annuities in New York. She was also lending out his cash on hand: he had too much cash, she said, some £1,318, so she was lending it out at good interest for three to six months and she had gotten "real security" for it. "The money was lying dead and so much in paper, a great risk, that it was better to put some of it out upon interest. . . . Hope you will not disapprove of what I have done." She was also paying his bills with cash she raised by selling his goods. "I have paid upwards of £1,000 for you in your absence and, if you ever live to return, you will find yourself a broken merchant, as I have sold everything upon hand."[34] And she was trying to find someone to fix the roof—it was leaking worse than ever—but all the roofers were afraid to come to that corner of Connecticut.

Hannah was also her brother's confidante, and his military friends knew it. They stopped by to visit her and passed messages through her that they could not have delivered safely themselves. Major Meigs, captured at Quebec, and Captain Dearborn were released on parole to nearby Middletown on condition they speak to no one about war, politics, or their fellow prisoners. Meigs wanted to go to Lake Champlain to see Arnold personally, as he wrote to him on July 29, but all he could do was visit Hannah and send messages through her. He also gave her news of Eleazar Oswald and the other prisoners still held at Quebec and turned over to her receipts Oswald had obtained for the money Arnold had given Meigs to distribute among his fellow officers in prison.[35] And when he could get no accurate information from Gates at headquarters about the fighting around New York City, it was Hannah who gave him vivid details. "We have had a most bloody battle on Long Island, where 'tis said thousands on both sides have lost their lives," she wrote him on September 1. "Good God! What havoc does ambition make amongst your noblest works—brother slain by the cruel hand of brother, mothers weeping for their darling sons, sisters for affectionate and perhaps only brothers. . . . The dear little boys yet remain . . . blessed in ignorance. . . . Oh, that their future life may be unclouded." She sent him "four waistcoats and three pair stockings" and, in each letter, tidbits of news about his boys. Benedict was in school in Middletown, where Major Meigs had visited him. "Benedict and Richard will write you soon," she promised, and they did. "Little Hal sends a kiss to Pa and says, 'Auntie, tell my Papa he must come home, I want to kiss him.'"[36]

While Benedict Arnold sailed back and forth between boatyards in his enthusiastic drive to build a fighting fleet, his old enemies were busy, too. At this critical moment, Arnold found himself facing a hostile court of inquiry at Fort Ticonderoga investigating charges that he had looted Montreal on his retreat from Canada. It was a serious charge: Canadian merchants and captured British officers had indeed been robbed, and Arnold stood accused by his old nemesis, Colonel John Brown, who had carried his grievances against Arnold to Congress, where a committee had been set up to look into the Canadian debacle. At the head of the court was Colonel Enoch Poor of New Hampshire, a friend of Lieutenant Colonel Enos, who had turned back from the Quebec march. Poor and many of his fellow frontier-bred officers loathed Arnold, whom they considered part of Schuyler's elite New York faction. Dr. Beebe, Poor's brigade surgeon, thought that a court-martial was too good for Arnold: he preferred "to make the sun shine through his head with an ounce ball of lead."[37]

In reporting the looting incident at Montreal to Schuyler in June, Arnold had hinted that he had upbraided Hazen until he had "finally received them and placed sentinels over them," but too late. The goods had been "neglected in such a manner that great part were stolen or plundered. . . . I found the goods broken open, plundered, and mixed together in the greatest confusion, and great part missing."[38] Arnold had sent a copy of this report to Hazen, who demanded a court of inquiry to clear his name. Enoch Poor quickly turned it into a court-martial of Arnold, who was ill-prepared: a letter recently found in Canadian archives shows he was desperately trying to locate Thomas Walker's clerk, who had apparently helped him bundle up the packages but was hard to reach since he had fled Montreal.

The reason that Benedict Arnold had had only five days to whip the base at Skenesboro into productive trim in July 1776 was that he had to return to Fort Ticonderoga to face a court-martial on July 26 on orders from Gates. The court-martial was to drag on for days, raising Arnold's anger to the boiling point as jealous officers junior to him in Canada now gathered around to tear at him like jackals. At first, Arnold would have preferred to produce witnesses to clear his name: he knew that Thomas Walker was in Albany. He wrote to him to ask if his clerk, Shepherd, who was familiar with the inventories of the Montreal warehouses, could come and testify for him. Walker wrote back that he had "no knowledge of the stores in question, having left Montreal three weeks before you did." Moreover, Shepherd said he had worked "only in the back vaults"[39] and did not know about the confiscated goods. Disappointed that neither Walker or Shepherd would appear for him, Arnold took the offensive. He accused Hazen of being responsible for looting and damaging the goods, producing as his prime witness Major Scott. But the court-martial, headed by Colonel Enoch Poor, rejected Scott as "so far interested"[40] as to render his testimony inadmissible. By not spelling out this "interest," the court in effect impugned Major Scott's integrity. After other witnesses testified, Arnold again asked that Scott be allowed as a witness. If his request was denied, Arnold added intemperately, he would enter a formal protest on the court record. His request was again denied. "As the court have refused accepting my principal evidence, Major Scott," Arnold then declared, "after my having declared to them, on honor, that he had punctually obeyed my orders respecting the goods he had in charge from Montreal to Chambly, and of course is not in the least interested in the event of Colonel Hazen's trial, I do solemnly protest against their proceedings and refusal as unprecedented, and I think unjustified."[41] The court's response was to enter in the court records its opinion that Arnold's protest was "illegal, illiberal and ungentlemanlike," and demanded that he apologize for his "error."[42] The court's reply, even more than its refusal to allow his subordinate to testify for him, was unprecedented. Moreover, its wording could only have been interpreted by Arnold as an affront to his highly developed eighteenth-century sense of honor.

On August 1, after a court-martial had dragged on for a precious week, Benedict Arnold sent the court his angry rejoinder. Castigating the officers, especially Colonel Poor, for "ungenteel and indecent reflections on a superior officer," he said he was protesting the proceedings to Congress. "Congress will judge between us." General Gates would see to it that the procedures of the court were sent to Philadelphia. "This I can assure you, I shall ever, in public or private, be ready to support the character of a man of honor. . . . As your very nice and delicate honor, in your apprehension, is injured, you may depend, as soon as this disagreeable hearing is at an end [which God grant may soon be the case], I will by no means withhold from any gentlemen of the court the satisfaction his nice honor may require."[43] Not only did Arnold refuse to apologize, he was challenging each officer on the court-martial to a duel.

Ignoring Arnold's hotheaded challenge, the court demanded that
Gates place Arnold under arrest for adding "insult to injury." Arnold's protest "was not the only injury offered us: the whole of the
General's conduct during the course of the trial was marked with
contempt and disrespect toward the court."[44] Prudently, Gates
passed the buck to Congress, as both Arnold and the court had requested. He refused to arrest his most valuable officer. Instead, he
dissolved the court-martial for showing "too much acrimony." To
Congress, Gates wrote, "The warmth of General Arnold's temper
might possibly lead him a little farther than is marked by the precise
line of decorum," but Arnold could not be spared: "The United
States must not be deprived of that excellent officer's service at this
important moment." Indeed, Gates felt the charges might be base-
less. "Whatever is whispered against General Arnold is the foul
stream of that poisonous fountain, distraction."[45] It is also entirely
possible that Arnold had been talking to Gates, who knew that Arnold was a wealthy man who had no need to loot warehouses and,
in fact, had always dealt harshly with looters in the army.

Despite shortages, sickness, and charges of corruption, Benedict Arnold had put together a navy by early August. Even while he was on
trial, he had seen to it that shipbuilding raced ahead at Skenesboro
and Ticonderoga. Before he had sailed north to Fort Ticonderoga to
testify, Arnold had fired off a note to General Schuyler telling him
that fully two hundred ship's carpenters had by now arrived at
Skenesboro and that four row galleys were already under construction. Philadelphia shipwright Thomas Casdrop had devised a pivot-
ing skid for cannon that made it unnecessary to bring a ship about
before it could bring its guns to bear: Arnold had adapted this for
both row galleys and gondolas, which, he informed Schuyler, would
be "nearly of the construction of those built in Philadelphia."[46]
Heavy guns dug up at Crown Point and Ticonderoga were modified,
allowing them to recoil on wooden tracks after they were fired so
that they would not capsize a small ship and could be rapidly reloaded and then run back out again on their skids and fired. Adapta-
tion of this innovation to small ships such as gondolas and row
galleys, already more maneuverable than larger ships in confined
lake passages, made possible the use of far heavier guns than such
small vessels could ordinarily use. In addition, Arnold had sent off
to a forge at Winston Manor on the Hudson for scores of small new
swiveling cannon known as swivel guns that had only recently been
invented at the Carronade Iron Works in Scotland. Arnold's ships
would fairly bristle with the latest in lethal hardware. By the time

Arnold faced the court-martial at Ticonderoga, he had completed and armed four gondolas that had "gone up to Ticonderoga" for rigging and arming. Two more would be ready in five days, he reported to Schuyler, another four in ten days, and the entire complement of gondolas he had promised Schuyler would be included in his fleet. During the same three-week period, the first two row galleys were to be finished.

Apparently, learning from Gates about the value of propaganda, Arnold also sent off an "Extract of a Letter from Skenesboro" to be published in the *Pennsylvania Gazette*, under the noses of Congress. Using a well-known literary device of the times, he masqueraded as a militiaman in a Pennsylvania regiment assigned to serve on one of Arnold's ships. No other officer or enlisted man at Skenesboro could have dared to mail such information at such a critical time without risking a charge of spying, yet Arnold had evidently decided that good news from the north was the fastest way to attract more recruits. Indeed, Arnold may have wanted British spies to see it, aiming to make Carleton slow down to build more ships.

Within the next five days, the schooner *Liberty* was completely refitted with eight guns at Ticonderoga and two more row galleys skidded down the ways into Wood Creek. In exactly four weeks, Arnold had driven his men to produce four row galleys even as they put the finishing touches on seven gondolas. Arnold and his men achieved a near-miracle of wartime production despite a new round of illness that was spreading rapidly through the barracks at Skenesboro in the muggy August heat. Arnold hinted of this latest illness in a letter to Gates: "I arrived here at ten o'clock last night . . . a little feverish but no ague yet. A dose of physick this afternoon I hope will settle matters in order."[47] Gates already knew of the sickness that posed the latest threat to Arnold's navy and had sent Dr. Jonathan Potts, his chief physician at Ticonderoga, down to Skenesboro. Despite the distraction of the court-martial, Arnold managed to direct the mounting of guns by the blacksmiths, oversee the rigging of lines, sheets, and stays as cordage came from New London and Middletown, and order the cutting of sails as canvas arrived from Albany.

By the time the court-martial disbanded, Arnold was more than ready to sail for Crown Point. On August 15, he received Gates's written orders to take over all American ships on the lake, superseding Commodore Wynkoop. Gates gave Arnold none of the credit for building a squadron of ten ships in five weeks. In a letter to Governor Trumbull dated August 11, he boasted, "Our fleet grows daily more and more powerful. Enclosed is a list of those manned, armed

and ready for action at Crown Point." As soon as five more ships
were rigged at Ticonderoga, they "will this week join those at
Crown Point when General Arnold will sail with the whole down
the Lake—Three fine row galleys will be finished in a fortnight—
This is a naval force when collected that promises to secure the command of Lake Champlain."[48]

When Arnold wrote to Schuyler, he gave proper credit to
Schuyler's aide-de-camp, Captain Varick, who indefatigably ran
down every item Arnold needed. And he lauded the men who had
labored night and day: "The carpenters go on with great spirit."[49]
To Gates, Arnold was more reserved: "I hope to be excused if, with
five hundred men half naked, I should not be able to beat the enemy."[50]

Before he sailed, Arnold went once more to Ticonderoga to receive his sailing orders in writing. Privately, Gates was candid: "I am
entirely unacquainted with naval affairs," he told Arnold. For the
record, he gave Arnold explicit, even if somewhat confused, orders.
Arnold was to take full command of the fleet, superseding Wynkoop, but not attack the enemy unless they sailed south; "should the
enemy come up the lake and attempt to force their way through the
pass you are stationed to defend [that site was left to Arnold], in
that case you will act with such cool, determined valor as will give
them reason to repent their temerity." If the British managed to
force their way to Crown Point, Gates assumed that Arnold would
still be able to "retire with your squadron to Ticonderoga"[51]—in
other words, retreat to defend Fort Ticonderoga.

Not only were Gates's orders ambiguous—a soldier with admit-
tedly no naval knowledge telling Arnold he could not attack but was
only to defend the army—but Arnold was to keep secret the fact
that his hands were tied. Indeed, Arnold was to create the deception
that he was under orders to invade Canada again: "Words occasionally dropped from you, with that prudence which excludes every
sort of affection and which, I believe, you possess, may, together
with all your motion, induce our own people to conclude it is our
real intention to invade the enemy, which, after all, may happen. It
will keep up their spirits without affecting your reputation."[52]

Orders in hand, Arnold returned to his ships and prepared to
sail. He had little more than half the ships and men he had requested, but already Indian and Canadian raiding parties were probing dangerously close to Crown Point. He still had no ship's doctors,
a critical shortage. Earlier attempts to recruit doctors had failed, and
Arnold would settle for a single surgeon's mate. He knew of a surgeon's mate who had a "good box of medicines." He pleaded with

Gates to send him "or someone else who will answer to kill a man *secundum artem* [according to established medical practice]."[53] Finally a single surgeon's mate arrived with rented tools. Arnold's sarcastic humor only thinly masked his bitterness that he had difficulty persuading a single doctor to risk his life by sailing with the first American fleet into battle with the men about to attempt to stave off the British invasion.

Arnold could wait no longer for the rest of his ships: they would have to overtake him. Shortages still plagued the effort. There was no iron for nails to hammer down quarterdecks on the row galleys. The day before he sailed, Arnold wrote Schuyler for six tons of iron "to compleat the galleys."[54] The most recent shipment from Albany had been disappointing: there were bellows and blacksmith tools, but little iron; oakum for coating ropes, but no rope. Arnold tried to send off a regiment of troops from Ticonderoga only to learn that the oars for the bateaux to carry the men south had been pilfered "to carry provisions and baggage"[55] on men's shoulders. Amid preparing for a naval battle, Arnold had to send work crews to fell trees to make more oars. One new ship after another was lining up at Ticonderoga to be fitted out, waiting for desperately needed material. In the end, Schuyler ordered a raid on American shipyards where it was being hoarded. Schuyler himself reprimanded the revolutionary committee at Poughkeepsie, which had refused to cooperate.

Among the numerous shortages, the most critical was the exasperating lack of skilled seamen. There were plenty of New England men rushing to defend Fort Ticonderoga who had spent years at sea, but would rather have a stone fortress around them when the British attacked than face cannon at close range in small wooden ships. As a last resort, Arnold decided to *draft* them. On August 10, with Gates's approval, he ordered twelve subalterns, twelve sergeants, twelve corporals, five drummers, and 259 privates, primarily from two regiments of New Hampshire troops, aboard his fleet.

Forty-eight harassed hours after his court-martial ordeal ended, Benedict Arnold sailed smack into his next crisis of command. At two o'clock on Saturday afternoon, August 17, 1776, he received word from Colonel Hartley that British advance parties including Canadians and Indians were within seven miles of Crown Point and were trying to encircle an American work party Arnold had sent out to make replacement oars for the bateaux. Dispatching Hartley with one hundred troops to protect the withdrawal of the oarmakers, Arnold hastily summoned Captain Isaac Seamon, his senior captain and the skipper of the newly built schooner *Revenge,* and Captain Premier of the schooner *Liberty* to his tent outside the ruined walls of Crown Point. Arnold handed them their written orders: "You will immediately get your vessels under sail and proceed down the lake seven or eight miles. If you make any discovery of the enemy, you will immediately give me notice."[56]

No sooner had Seamon and Premier embarked than a larger American ship, the *Royal Savage,* bore down on them and opened fire, sending cannonballs across their bows. A voice boomed across the open water: "Heave to!" Aghast, Captain Seamon ordered his crew to drop sail and his helmsman to come about, while he swung loose a boat over the side and rowed straight for *Royal Savage.* Puffing and redfaced, he climbed up to confront Captain Jacobus Wynkoop, Commodore of the Lake. Wynkoop demanded to see Seamon's orders, then demanded that he and Premier sail back to Arnold at once. The portly Yorker scribbled out this message for Arnold:

> *On board the* Royal Savage *August 17th*
>
> Sir
>
> *I find by an order you have given out that the schooners are to go down the lake. I know no orders but what shall be given out by me. . . . If an enemy is approaching I am to be acquainted with it and know how to act in my station. I am sir yours.*
>
> *Jacobus Wynkoop*
> *Commander of Lake Champlain*

A year of humiliations and frustrations no doubt added to Arnold's temper as he watched through his spyglass. He may have realized that it was the court-martial that had eroded his authority to this point, that something could and must be done about it at once. Sitting down to dash off a letter to Wynkoop, he calmed himself:

> Sir
>
> *I am surprised you should pretend to contradict my orders. . . . I acquainted you some time since that the Commander in Chief had appointed me to take command of the Navy on the Lakes, had I not received this appointment from my rank in the Army and as commander in chief of this post. . . . It is your duty to obey my orders, which you have received and executed for some time past. You surely must be out of your senses to say no orders shall be obeyed but yours. Do you imagine that Congress have given you a superior*

command over the commander in chief, or that you are not to be under his direction? If you do not suffer his orders to be immediately complied with . . . I shall be under the disagreeable necessity of convincing you of your error by immediately arresting you.

> *B Arnold B Genl & Commr in Chief of*
> *the Fleet on Lake Champlain*[58]

Arnold ordered Seamon and Premier to sail at once back down the lake to cover the withdrawal of the work party even as he sent off a boat with his missive for Wynkoop. The two captains went out to their ships but did not sail. Caught between conflicting orders, they sat on their hands. "I waited some time, expecting the vessels to sail," Arnold reported in a dispatch to Gates later that day, but "finding they did not I went on board the *Royal Savage,* only to find that Wynkoop had issued orders for Seamon and Premiere to sail under *him.* He refuses to be commanded by anyone, and imagines his appointment, which is by General Schuyler, cannot be superseded. I have shown him such parts of your instructions as I thought necessary, which has brought him to reason. He says, if you think proper to turn him out, he will quit the vessel."[59]

Gates responded to Arnold at once: "It is my orders you will instantly put Commodore Wynkoop in arrest and send him prisoner to headquarters at Ticonderoga. You will at the same time acquaint the officers of the fleet that such of them as do not pay an implicit obedience to your commands are instantly to be confined and sent to me for trial."[60] Gates also wrote to Schuyler in Albany: "I dare say you will without scruple forthwith dismiss him the service. . . . He is totally unfit to command a single vessel. . . . The times will not admit of trifling—Decisions alone must govern these occasions."[61] Arnold sent Wynkoop off in chains in a bateaux with a note to Gates. "No other person in the fleet has disputed my orders," he reassured Gates, so there was no further need to deal harshly with Wynkoop, to make any more of an example of him. Arnold could have called for Wynkoop's trial and execution on a charge of gross insubordination under fire. Instead, he magnanimously recommended that "if it can be done with propriety, I wish he may be permitted to return home."[62] Gates reluctantly agreed, passing along Arnold's advice as his own. Schuyler sent Wynkoop to Congress to plead his case in person, as far from Lake Champlain as he could. The American command, alarmed by a British raid so near to Crown Point, finally agreed with Arnold that it was still possible that a battle would take place even so late in the season.

10

"YOUR FRIENDS ARE NOT YOUR COUNTRYMEN"

Is it possible my
countrymen can be
callous to British
wrongs, or hesitate
one moment between
slavery or death?

Benedict Arnold to Horatio Gates, October 7, 1776

Benedict Arnold sailed north from Crown Point on August 24, 1776, leading the first half-completed American navy toward the British lines on the Canadian frontier. The ten small ships snapped to attention around him, their newmade sails fluttering and filling, the sunlight glinting off their barn-red sides, their blunt black cannon. Strung out behind Arnold's flagship, the twelve-gun, two-hundred-ton *Royal Savage,* came the schooner *Revenge,* mounting eight cannon in her ports and ten of the new swivel guns on her gunwales, then the eight-gun schooner *Liberty* and the ten-gun sloop *Enterprise,* the four ships arrayed to protect the smaller, squatter gondolas. Six gondolas were ready: *New Haven, Providence, Boston, New York, Connecticut, Philadelphia,* named for the revolutionary cities that had sent men to build them.

Their single, square-rigged sails unfurling, the gondolas, only fifty-nine feet long yet carrying forty-five men, nosed low into the lake's swells, plodding northward crowded with untrained men, shot and shell, confusion. Not one of the row galleys was ready to join them: four were lined up at the docks at Ticonderoga, still unrigged, and four more were still on the stocks at Skenesboro.

On Lake Champlain in late August, a month-long season of sudden equinoctial storms begins. Winds pinwheel furiously and mount to gale force, fifty miles an hour velocity and more, lashing water into waves up to twenty-five feet from trough to crest. Such swift storms can tear up anchors, swamp and swallow ships, dash them against rocky islands. A week of storms greeted the first American reconnaissance in force, slowing its progress, forcing Arnold to put into protected coves, his seasick crews, landsmen, made more miserable by sodden clothing and the impossibility of keeping cookfires lighted in small brick fireplaces aboard each vessel. Cold soggy bread and colder nights of trying to sleep on heaving hard wet decks provided the backdrop for Arnold's first naval report back to Gates in dry, warm Fort Ticonderoga. The first night out, after strong winds carried his fleet twenty miles north, a "violent storm" hit. Huddling his ships at anchor off Willsboro, New York, Arnold passed the word at two the next afternoon, when the storm had still not abated, to weigh anchor and head back up the lake ten miles to the relative shelter of Buttonmould Bay. There a high headland juts out from the Vermont shore, deflecting the northeast wind and providing protection in its lee. Since he did not have a single spare anchor or anchor cable, Arnold did not dare take needless risks. The storm lashed the lake for fifty miles. Even to this veteran of Caribbean hurricanes, "the hard gale made an amazing sea."[1] Miraculously, no one was hurt and only one supply boat sank.

But the storm did not slow down the first phase of Arnold's mission to gather intelligence of British shipbuilding and troop displacements. Arnold was starved for accurate information on the activities of the British. To gather the knowledge the American command needed to decide whether still to expect an attack over the lake that season or to dig in for a winter's wait behind Ticonderoga's fortifications, Arnold had to rely on a system of spies— trained scouts posing as American deserters—and handsome cash bounties. When his ships finally reached the old French settlement at the northern tip of Isle La Motte, near the Canadian border, Arnold dispatched four parties of scouts, one led by Ethan Allen's younger brother, Ira, to slip through the woods on either side of the lake and infiltrate British lines at the mouth of the Richelieu River. By way of inducement—Arnold believed that it took money to win the advantage in wartime—he offered a £500 hard money reward—the equivalent of $17,500, a fortune at the time—for the best information on the size and character of the forces opposing him. One scouting detail was led by Lieutenant James Whitcomb, a former officer in Rogers's Rangers. With three other former rangers, Whitcomb embarked in a canoe at night from Arnold's flagship anchored off Isle La Motte, making their way along the New York shore toward Isle aux Noix and the main British base twenty miles north at St. Jean. A second party of four, led by Ensign Thomas McCoy and including another former ranger, Sergeant Eli Stiles, was put ashore on the east side of the lake. A lone French Canadian, Antoine Girard, was sent to spy out the British advanced works on Isle aux Noix.

Despite lingering rough weather, Arnold took advantage of the strong south wind to outrun the storm, pushing his untrained crews hard. His little fleet dashed north twenty-three miles in one day. The specter of an American fleet emerging from the gray mist, sailing right up through the British outposts, touched off rumors that Arnold was about to invade Canada again. Several hundred Loyalists and Indians were camping on the shores as Arnold's ships passed by, entering the mouth of the Richelieu River. "The evening after our arrival," Arnold reported, this exposed British force "made a precipitate retreat"[2] down the Richelieu to the British outpost at Isle aux Noix.

As Arnold probed ever closer to the main British force, he wrote to Gates of his intention to deploy parties of spies so that he would "soon have it in my power to send you a very full account of the strength of the enemy by sea and land." His bravado was not unmixed with pique. He had just learned that Congress, at the same time that it was hearing unsubstantiated charges against him about the looting at Montreal, had decided to promote over his head *another* former British officer with less experience. Arnold sent perfunctory congratulations to the newly created Major General Arthur St. Clair, but he was seething when he wrote to Gates that because so much of what he needed to win control of the lake was being denied him, he was certain that he would ultimately be repulsed by the British. When that happened, he, too, would go to Philadelphia to argue his case before Congress. And if they did not right this latest wrong by making him a major general, he would resign, go home. But for the moment, all this to Gates was *"entre nous."*[3]

Despite lack of support, Arnold *was* the man in charge on the front line against the British. On September 12, the first British attack came. A French Canadian, Arnold quickly informed Gates, had come to the water's edge at Wind Mill Point and "desired to be taken on board the *Liberty*." The American captain instantly "suspected him and went near the shore with his boat, stern in, swivel guns pointed and match lighted. . . . When the Frenchman found he could decoy the boat no further, he made a signal to the enemy. . . . Three or four hundred Indians, Canadians and [British] regulars rose up and fired on the boat. They wounded three men. The boat returned the fire with their swivels and small arms." Hurrying up within point-blank range in *Royal Savage,* Arnold "fired several broadsides of grape before they dispersed."[4] The men wounded in the attack, all from New Hampshire, later died.

In the dangerous ebb and flow of maneuvering between the lines, Arnold was also in an ideal position to attract deserters from the British army, always a valuable source of intelligence. That same day three British soldiers made it to Arnold's forces. One was Sergeant Thomas Day, a Yorker who had been captured with Lamb's artillery company in the disastrous attack on Quebec. The British had offered Day the choice of enlistment in the British army or deportation to England in chains. Day enlisted. He was assigned to McLean's Highland Emigrants. He escaped and made his way through the woods to Arnold's ships. Although Arnold had the legal right to hang him, he trusted this man who, regardless of uniforms, had hiked to Quebec and back and still wanted to fight on the side of the Americans. Day brought Arnold the first detailed account of British shipbuilding. There were "two schooners taken to pieces and brought up to St. [Jean] . . . two or three days to cross the lake for Crown Point." Arnold fired off his written report of the interrogation to Ticonderoga with the three deserters. Day confirmed that William Gilliland, proprietor of a great estate on the New York shore, was doubledealing with the British at St. Jean. Gilliland had been the first to sign the petition supporting Arnold in June 1775 and had also signed Arnold's declaration, but Sergeant Day now testified to Arnold in a sworn affidavit that Gilliland had arranged to send a British spy to Crown Point and back to St. Jean. He further swore that he had heard that Gilliland and several of his tenant farmers had secretly armed themselves by illegally buying the weapons of American soldiers retreating from Isle aux Noix to Crown Point "for a mere trifle of rum." The sergeant averred that when he told Gilliland that "he thought it very wrong to buy those articles of the soldiers as it was defrauding the country," Gilliland had answered that, "it was no matter how much they got out of the country, the more the better." Sergeant Day also said that he had been in Gilliland's house when "a number of our officers were passing."

Gilliland observed, "There comes a company of damned beggars."[5] Day's sworn affidavit was enough to convince Arnold that Gilliland was a traitor: he had him arrested and sent to Crown Point in irons.

In mid-September, both combatants were cooled by days of drenching rains and high winds. Shortly after midnight the morning of September 16, under cover of a hard gale, the first of Arnold's spies to return from Canada paddled up to an American boat on guard duty off Isle La Motte. It was Girard, the French Canadian. Girard reported to Arnold that there were fully three thousand British regulars on tiny Isle aux Noix defended by "forty pieces of cannon mounted on the lines" around the half-mile-square island, making the advance base virtually impregnable. At St. Jean, said Girard, there were three thousand more men as well as 150 bateaux. He told Arnold that he had learned from another French Canadian that there were an additional three hundred bateaux assembled farther north at the Falls of Chambly. Moreover, there were two British schooners already completed and manned at St. Jean, one mounting twelve, the other fourteen brass twelve-pounders, as well as four gondolas carrying three guns each, a number of flat-bottomed boats that would carry one heavy gun, a large floating battery, and a two-masted ketch "nearly done" that would carry twenty-four eighteen-pounders and two large mortars. "He imagines the whole will be completed in a fortnight," Arnold wrote to Gates, sending off his warning by fast boat to Ticonderoga.

But Arnold had reason to suspect Girard. He "has brought a safe-conduct pass from the Isle aux Noix, from which, and the distance he had to go, the bad weather and the time he was gone, I believe he has been no farther than the Isle aux Noix, and that he has been enjoined by the British officer there to give the foregoing account. Had not they been convinced he was in their interest, I don't imagine they would have suffered him to return." Arnold was also clearly worried that Girard had compromised his other agents. "I have every reason to think him placed as a spy on us. I have therefore sent him to you to be disposed of as you may think proper."[6] He sent off Girard a prisoner to Ticonderoga.

Two days later, on September 18, Arnold wrote excitedly to Gates that the second of the spies, Lieutenant Whitcomb, had just returned with two British prisoners. Both "seemed cautious of giving any information," but somehow Arnold had extracted a vital piece of information, one that had been omitted by Girard: "There is a ship on the stocks at St. [Jean] designed to mount twenty guns, nine- and twelve-pounders," larger than anything the Americans had, nearly twice as heavily armed as any of Arnold's row galleys. "The ship, the enemy says, will be completed in a fortnight." It was to be manned by experienced British navy seamen and gunners brought from the fleet at Quebec. The British ensign also said "there was talk of crossing the lake soon."[7] Arnold had pleaded for such a ship for his own fleet at the July 7 council of war. Now he reported to Gates that the British had emerged with a clear advantage.

For weeks, Arnold had received conflicting reports, steadily growing more anxious as he awaited the return of the last spying party, led by Ensign McCoy. It had been gone nearly three weeks now, and it was extremely unlikely that it could have gone undetected so long. In fact, McCoy's party was captured two weeks later as it tried to make its way back to the American fleet. Only one man, Sergeant Eli Stiles, escaped. He had left St. Jean with Ensign McCoy and had last seen him at ten the morning before Stiles confirmed that Girard indeed had been fed misinformation deliberately by a British officer and had overstated British strength at the advance base at Isle aux Noix, evidently to ward off attack, and also at St. Jean, where Girard had especially exaggerated the estimated completion times of British ships. Stiles said he personally had counted one hundred tents on Isle aux Noix. Based on the standard of ten British troops to a tent, this meant that there were *one* thousand, not three thousand, troops there. Stiles had then worked his way north through the woods along the Richelieu River as far north as St. Jean, where there were too many tents to count—"he imagines about three hundred"—and saw "34 large birch canoes paddle by him towards Isle aux Noix. . . . Supposed they contained about six hundred Indians and one regular officer—Saw a schooner lay at the wharf with frigate sails which he supposes not completed and was on the stocks planked to her wales." It was "something larger than the other two." This confirmed the British ensign's report of a large new man-of-war. Stiles "saw nothing of any floating batteries" (as Girard said he had seen) and "believes there was none." The British bateaux, Stiles reported, "appear twice as large as ours and carried fifty or sixty men, one of which rowed near by him."[8]

For more than two weeks, Arnold had been working on an even more dangerous operation, one so sensitive that he never revealed the names of all the participants. The mission has remained virtually encoded in letters that passed between Arnold and Gates in August and September 1776. It shows how clandestinely Arnold could operate. The plot had begun in secret correspondence between a congressional committee and agents in Europe nearly a year earlier, and while many of its details can now be reconstructed, some can still only be pieced together as the surviving papers of participants—and these are far from complete—are discovered and published by modern scholars.

In December 1775, even as Benedict Arnold besieged Quebec, the Continental Congress's Committee of Secret Correspondence, headed by Benjamin Franklin, held a series of secret night meetings with an agent sent to Philadelphia by the French foreign minister. As yet, the French government was formally at peace with England and supposedly neutral in the American struggle. But by late December 1775, the agent wrote back to Paris that Congress had made up its mind for independence. At the same time, Franklin wrote to his old friend the French gentleman of letters Charles-Guillaume Frédéric Dumas, at The Hague in the Netherlands, appointing him as the committee's European agent. At this time, for all practical purposes, Franklin *was* the secret committee. He had spent sixteen of the past eighteen years in England as legislative agent for several colonial assemblies, and he had traveled widely in Europe. Franklin had left England precipitately in March 1775 after being fired as deputy British postmaster general for his role in leaking the correspondence of British officials in Massachusetts to the Boston revolutionaries. In his place as colonial agent in London, Franklin had left Arthur Lee. The outbreak of rebellion made all correspondence between Lee and Congress illegal. But while the French agent was carrying word to Paris of America's intention to rebel from Britain, Franklin moved quickly to have Lee commissioned as Congress's diplomatic agent in England, instructing him to find out how foreign powers were disposed to American independence.

When Franklin went to Canada as one of Congress's commissioners in March 1776, he and Arnold discussed the British invasion from the north and how best to counteract it. At the urging of Franklin and Jefferson, Congress had resolved to offer rewards to Hessian deserters who might "choose to accept of lands, liberty, safety, and a communion of good laws and mild government." Congress would grant them American citizenship and "for every such person fifty acres"[9] of virgin land. On August 14, Franklin and a committee appointed to study the Hessian problem urged Congress to raise its offer to Hessian deserters to include generous rewards of land for officers as well as enlisted men. On August 28, Franklin sent Arnold the two congressional resolves translated into German. "Some of them have tobacco marks on the back, so that tobacco, being put up in them in small quantities, as the tobacconists use, and suffered to fall into the hands of these people, they might divide the papers as plunder. . . . If you find it practicable, you may convey them among the Germans that shall come against you."[10] It was up to Arnold to figure out a way to slip them behind enemy lines.

So dangerous was the business of offering bribes to deserters, however, that Arnold was even cautious in communicating with Gates. Gates told Arnold, "Enclosed is a copy of a letter I have just received from Dr. Franklin. The *Tobacco* is not yet come, it will be sent to you in the first row galley."[11] Acknowledging Gates in a long letter about supplies, Arnold replied on September 15: "Cannot a Frenchman or two who is acquainted in Canada and can be depended upon, be sent me with the tobacco?"[12] Less than a week later, Gates replied that Arnold would have to come up with some other way. On September 21, tucked away in another letter, Arnold wrote cryptically, "The tobacco papers were delivered to me. I will endeavor to send them soon."[13] It was another week before Arnold wrote to Gates on September 28 that he had "dispatched into Canada a German, who was mate of the *Revenge,* and a New England man, who speaks French well. . . . They are extremely well acquainted with the country, go in character of deserters." Arnold sent off Sergeant Stiles and a companion to distribute the tobacco papers, *sans* tobacco, among German troops encamped at Isle aux Noix. Each carried the two congressional resolves, "sixteen of each sort sewed up between the soles of their shoes. . . . As they run a great risk, I have promised them in case they succeed five hundred dollars between them."[14] There is still no way of knowing whether the German mate survived to collect his share of the reward, but Sergeant Stiles came back in four days. He reported a British buildup at Isle aux Noix, and more British ships completed. As Stiles paddled south to rejoin Arnold, "he passed Wind Mill Point in the night and believes there was four hundred Indians there, and that on the bay opposite, he saw many lights and fires and supposes the regular troops were encamped there."[15] For nearly a month, Arnold had been sifting the intelligence reports brought back by his intrepid operatives, and was still not satisfied. He put two more scouts ashore on Isle La Motte "to watch the motions of the enemy."[16] By October 1, Arnold wrote to Gates that the British invasion, including ten thousand men, twenty-seven ships and 250 bateaux, and one hundred pieces of field artillery, was about to begin.

As late as August 5, as Gates drew up Arnold's sailing orders, his chief of staff, Colonel James Wilkinson, had written to Schuyler's aide, Captain Varick, making light of the chances of a British attack that year: "Our navy are in great forwardness but I seriously believe we shall have no other use for them than to transport our army to Canada."[17] Arnold's extraordinarily accurate intelligence report jibes in almost every detail with an official report sent on September 18 from Carleton's headquarters at Quebec to the colonial secretary, Lord Germain, at Whitehall in London.[18]

There was snow now on the mountaintops of Vermont at night and frost on Arnold's ill-clad men as they huddled for warmth around the cookfires. For weeks, his men had eaten no fresh provisions, no fresh meat, only potatoes and stale bread. Gates had answered his requisitions with orders to send his men to forage for their own food on the Vermont shore, which, as anyone should have known weeks ago, was filled with Indians: fifteen Americans had already been captured and were on their way to England in irons. When Arnold complained to Gates's commissary about the lack of supplies and the high prices charged by merchants, he was told, "We are glad to get supplies at any rate, and nothing is more natural amongst mankind than to take advantage whenever they can: this seems at least the custom amongst merchants."[19] Firing off one last angry memo to Gates, Arnold ticked off a "Memorandum of Articles which have repeatedly wrote for, and which we are in the extremist want of." It included virtually every type of cannon shot needed for the imminent battle, "musquet ball" for the marines in the topmasts, "all the useless old iron that will do for langridge [shrapnel-like canister shot]." He lacked "buck shot" for the swivel guns, some of which guns he also still lacked, and there were no usable slow matches to fire them: "very little on hand and that exceeding bad." He was still waiting for anchors and anchor cables (he had not one spare anchor in a season of storms), caulking irons, blocks and tackles, sail needles, twine, pitch, tar, grenades, nails, rope. Virtually every item needed to put the finishing touches on his ships and fit them out for fighting was still in desperately short or nonexistent supply as late as ten days before the British attacked. At the bottom of the list were Arnold's most urgent requisitions: "Rum, as much as you please. Clothing, for at least half the men in the fleet who are naked. One hundred seamen (no land lubbers)."[20]

As much as Arnold's strategy of delaying the British by forcing them to stop and build a fleet to contest superiority of the lakes, it was British incompetence coupled with Arnold's scorched-earth policy that had made a British attack impossible before October. Indeed, in the difficulty the British had in obtaining supplies, it is not too great a leap to say that Arnold's dogged winter siege of Quebec helped to contribute to the costly British delays. During five months of scavenging for food and supplies in the Quebec region, Arnold had also cut off resupply of the city and its garrison. When the British raised the siege in May, they found that they immediately had to deplete precious military rations allocated by British logistics experts in London for soldiers to feed a starving civilian populace. Rations for twelve thousand men for an entire year had been allotted, it was true, but no provision had been made for nearly six thousand hungry Quebecois. Soon, too, as Lieutenant Enys noted in his diary, thousands of Indians eager for the customary presents from the king descended on the city expecting food and drink.

As British warships discharged their cargoes of soldiers along a one-hundred-mile stretch of the St. Lawrence River from Quebec to Sorel, they had also carelessly dumped food supplies for them on the riverbanks. Some of the supplies of bread and flour were bad, some were in flimsy barrels that split open from rough handling, others were in bales that were pried open by hungry Canadians or stolen for sale on the black market. Moreover, the British planners had neglected to send along supply tents or tarpaulins. Large quantities of unprotected supplies were ruined during heavy spring rains.

When British commissaries discovered that much of the first three-month delivery of food had been eaten by the famished garrison, stolen, or ruined, they tried to solve the problem with money. There was £70,000 in the British warchest to buy fodder for livestock and fresh produce from the farmers. But the farmers had nothing to sell. Arnold had stripped the farms, taking with him all the horses and oxen needed to gather the summer's harvest. As he retreated across the Canadian border, he had shot his own horse to prevent its helping even one British officer. He left the British on foot in heavy rains and mud, their food supplies all but exhausted with two months remaining before the next supply convoy was expected from England. In addition, the troops, cooped up and sick from a two-month winter crossing of the North Atlantic, were unfit to fight. To make matters worse, thousands of British troops who had lived on little but salt beef and dry biscuits aboard ships for nearly three months strayed frequently from the line of march as they pursued Arnold and his Americans south, tempted by the unripe fruit on the trees. Soon the army had another problem, what the soldiers called "the quick step," to slow them down.

By the time the men recovered and fresh supplies arrived and were gathered into depots by inexperienced commissaries and quartermasters, it was August and Carleton had had to impress a thousand habitants into British service to transport supplies, clear and build roads, dig trenches, and build fortifications. By this time, there were more than twenty thousand dependent on British rations. The

August resupply, meant to last ninety days, lasted only forty. Obviously, the supplies sent over from England to last one year would not last the winter. Not even a good harvest had much effect, except to slow down the attack further while hungry Canadians took the time to build new barns, wagons, and mills to replace those so calculatingly put to the torch by Arnold. So critical were the shortages of fresh provisions that Governor Carleton ordered that pains be taken to conceal the shortage for his own troops: he ordered newly built storage depots to be stocked with ships' stores of salted meat to give the illusion of plenitude.

In all the weeks that Arnold had been pushing his ship's carpenters to build a fleet at Skenesboro, Carleton had been driving his officers to construct an even larger fleet to carry his army over the lake. He set up three shipyards—at Montreal, Chambly (at the head of the falls), and St. Jean. Every soldier in the British army who had been a carpenter in peacetime was now allowed a shilling extra pay per diem (about $1.50 U.S. a day in 1990) to work in the yards. On July 7, the day of the American council of war at Crown Point, the English frigate *Jailer* had arrived at Quebec from England with ten gunboats that were to be taken apart so they could be hauled overland to Lake Champlain. This first shipment was followed by more transports with more prefabricated craft: thirty long boats, a thirty-ton gondola, more than four hundred bateaux, and a large number of flatboats. All these vessels had to be mounted on carriages and hauled by oxen overland a distance of roughly sixty-five miles from Sorel on the St. Lawrence to Chambly, then on to St. Jean and Isle aux Noix.

At first, Carleton appears to have expected to be able to cross Lake Champlain without building any ships larger than the gunboats sent out from England to escort his troops down the lake. But Arnold's well-publicized shipbuilding efforts—deliberately "leaked" by Arnold to newspapers sure to be carried to British generals—prompted Carleton to build an even larger fleet to protect his troops from attack by Arnold's ships. This decision delayed the British attack by at least a month. It was early September before habitants could clear a road through the forest around the Falls of Chambly and south along the Richelieu River to St. Jean. In a vain attempt to move three large ships from the St. Lawrence to Lake Champlain, a thousand men strained at the hawsers once the first ship was skidded onto wooden rollers, but the weight of the ships was too great; the rollers shattered like matchsticks. Despite repeated efforts, the ships could be moved only one hundred yards before the attempt was abandoned. Rumors of this embarrassing failure reached as far south as Ticonderoga, no doubt helped along by Arnold. But the British engineers, led by Lieutenant John Schanck, persisted: next, they dismantled the three ships and hauled them in sections on ox-drawn sledges around the falls to St. Jean, where other crews worked prodigiously around the clock to reassemble them within twenty-eight days. It was one of these ships, the four-hundred-ton *Inflexible,* that Sergeant Stiles had described to Arnold on September 10. By October 1, it was ready to sail.

If the purpose of Benedict Arnold's comprehensive intelligence report of October 1, 1776, was to sober Horatio Gates and his staff officers at the last possible moment, then it succeeded. For weeks, Gates and his headquarters had been downplaying Arnold's predictions and sandbagging his incessant (although altogether necessary) requests for supplies and men. The combination of such a grim assessment of British strength and intentions and his chilling reminder that he still lacked so much of what it would take to resist the British onslaught finally snapped Gates's complacency. Gates had been predisposed to panic for some weeks, probably because he himself was woefully unprepared for an attack on Ticonderoga. On September 21, when the sloop *Liberty* had fought with British and Indians near the Canadian border, the sounds of Arnold's broadsides from *Royal Savage* had reverberated ninety miles down the Champlain Valley, bouncing between the Adirondacks and the Green Mountains and booming along the lake. At Crown Point, Colonel Hartley had heard the firing. He rushed word to Ticonderoga. Gates nearly panicked, speeding off word to Schuyler at Fort George to put all militia on the alert and have them ready to march to him at a minute's notice.

When Arnold officially reported this brief skirmish, Gates again blew it out of proportion, sending word of it south to Congress and placing a short report in the Philadelphia newspapers. This time when Arnold sent his request for "more seamen and gunners," he got results. As Arnold pointed out to Gates, the men he needed were right under his nose: "There is plenty of seamen in the army." All Gates had to do was offer them more money and rations. Arnold knew this could be a dangerous precedent and he knew Gates did not want to trample on the prerogative of Congress to regulate pay, but he argued that Gates should not worry about Congress: "This emergency will justify the measure." While Arnold had been promised eight row galleys, only two had been delivered: "I am greatly at a loss what could have retarded the gallies so long."[21] Arnold was all the more frustrated because when he left Skenesboro in August, he had left the wood all cut and stacked and four galleys on the stocks, four at the dock. Arnold clearly thought that Gates's indifference to his fleet bordered on incompetence, or he would have ordered the plodding General Waterbury, left in charge at Skenesboro, to do something to speed up production.

To be fair, Gates was not entirely to blame. Eighty percent of all the shipyard workers were down with fevers in the late summer heat. But there were enough able-bodied men to finish one ship at a time, as Arnold suggested. Gates was also unable to furnish the large quantities of rope needed to outfit a fleet, a difficult task so far from seacoast ropewalks even in normal times. Because of longstanding British restrictions on the American iron industry, there was also a dire want of nails to finish planking the ships. They reported that he had dispatched two more row galleys, each with a full complement of eighty men. In addition, there were 110 officers and men, all experienced hands, drafted according to Arnold's suggestions. Gates knew in advance that *Liberty* would take several days to reach Arnold under its load because one vital item was in short supply: oakum to caulk the ships. *Liberty* had been slower than Arnold liked because "the vessel wanted more caulking."[22]

The question of captains for Arnold's ships had also become a sore point between Gates and Arnold, even as it was between Gates and Schuyler. It was Gates's prerogative to appoint all officers under his command, but Arnold knew a bit more about the requirements of commanding a warship, and Arnold was upset that Gates did not always consult him. Gates's choices were not always logical. When one shipwright who had built a row galley asked to be its skipper, Gates urged him on Arnold, pointing out that despite the fact that he had never sailed, he knew a great deal about ships and was, besides, a big, handsome fellow who supposedly would cut quite the figure in a uniform. Arnold's reaction when he read this letter has not been recorded. But then again Arnold had gone his own way when he had written to Schuyler over Gates's head that he had asked five old Connecticut friends to be his captains without consulting Gates. When both Gates's and Arnold's appointees showed up at the dock to claim their ships, there was understandable consternation. Gates countermanded Arnold's appointments and installed his own captains, as was his right. Arnold quietly carried out Gates's wishes for a time, but apparently put such pressure on the unfortunate neophytes that they were soon sailing back "sick" to Ticonderoga as Arnold's handpicked officers took charge.

Unable to outmaneuver Arnold, Gates turned in angry frustration against Schuyler. He wrote to Albany that Schuyler's delay in sending more rope and iron was "lamentable" or even worse, now that the sounds of gunfire on the lake made Gates at last certain the Americans should "prepare for the worst." There were nineteen thousand men at Ticonderoga, five times the remnant of the Canadian army, yet Gates wanted Schuyler to place all New York troops on the alert. Where was the New York militia? Where were "the powder, lead and flints I wrote for so long ago? Pray hurry it up. The moments are precious and not one of them should be lost." Gates intimated that he would have had more suggestions for Schuyler except that "my hands are too full to write more."[23] Then he wrote to Arnold, informing him of his communication with Schuyler. Gates told Arnold that the blame for the delays, the shortfalls, was Schuyler's, Waterbury's, the blacksmith's, anyone's but his own.

Gates had begun to defer to Arnold's military judgment, while Arnold, for his part, kept up the appearance at least of generally accommodating Gates's wishes. As Arnold's weeks on the lake passed, both men's conceptions of the role of the fleet had shifted. Arnold may have first thought that despite Gates's clearcut orders to act on the defensive, he could stretch his orders if he had enough ships and men. Arnold had asked for one thousand to fifteen hundred troops from Gates, claiming they were needed to repulse British boarding parties. Arnold counted on Gates's absolute ignorance of naval affairs when he asked for the men, claiming that the purpose of the double-sized troop transports being built by the British was to attack and send boarding parties over the sides of American ships. Obviously, in the face of scores of swivel guns, the British would have been committing suicide to undertake such a tactic. It was also evident that Arnold was stretching his authority when he sailed up to the Canadian border and blockaded the Richelieu River all through the month of September, leading the British to believe he *was* about to attack. It is possible that if Gates had sent Arnold the troops he requested, Arnold would indeed have attempted to attack the British bases.

As Arnold learned more of the scope of the British forces facing him, he became more cautious, choosing to withdraw to a more protected position. The move pleased Gates, who always preferred the defensive. As Arnold became more cautious, Gates continually revised his orders, allowing Arnold more latitude. After the first skirmish at Isle La Motte on September 21, Arnold informed Gates that he was preparing to drop back to Valcour Island. He had just sent two boats to take soundings around the kidney-shaped island near the New York shore five miles south of present-day Plattsburgh. "It

is an exceeding fine, secure harbor. I am determined to go there the
first fair wind, as the fleet will be secure. We can discover the enemy
if they attempt to pass us. No doubt you will approve of this measure. If not, I will return to any of my former stations."[24] In asking
Gates's permission, in effect, to move the fleet to a position from
which he could attack the British fleet as it sailed by on its way
south toward Ticonderoga, Arnold was giving his commanding officer the opportunity to overrule his plan. But Arnold's wording was
clever, calling for authorization to shift from defensive to offensive
tactics if the British attempted to get by him, which was clearly their
purpose. Far from opposing Arnold's latest plan, however, Gates
now approved it, in writing on October 3. While he had appointed
two wing commanders to the fleet to assist Arnold, and he took it
for granted Arnold would consult them, he gave Arnold clear authority to decide when and where to fight the enemy.

*I take it for granted you will consult with General Waterbury and
Colonel [Edward] Wigglesworth and with them determine when it is
the proper season to retire up the Lake. I am confident your, and
their zeal, for the public service will not suffer you to return one
moment sooner than in prudence and good conduct you ought to do
it. Perhaps some station nearer Crown Point may, about the time
you mention, be proper to be taken, but this must be submitted to
your better judgment in maritime affairs.[25]*

While Arnold confided more and more in Gates and Gates appeared to defer to Arnold, Gates persisted in his intrigues behind
Arnold's back. Indeed, even when his friend Samuel Chase of Maryland wrote from Congress to warn him, Arnold seems to have misunderstood him and asked *Gates* to clear the matter up, so
credulous was he in his dealings with his duplicitous commander.
Much of Chase's long correspondence with Arnold evidently was
destroyed in battle (at least seven letters are missing), but enough
survives along with letters to and from Gates to piece together a
sordid story of backstabbing that no doubt cost Arnold a promotion
and may even begin to explain his later animosity toward many
American leaders. It was Chase who had first introduced Arnold to
Gates. As Gates had been on the point of heading north to the frontier, in May 1776, Chase was on his way south to see his sick wife,
but before leaving Philadelphia, he wrote to Gates, assessing, among
others, Schuyler—"be assured of his integrity, diligence, abilities"—
and Arnold: "General Arnold is brave, active and well-acquainted
with that country. He is acquainted with men and things. Desire him

to show you my letter . . . of my suspicions of some people now in our service."[26] Arnold had, no doubt, confided Chase's secrets to Gates. From this exchange, Gates could only conclude that Arnold and Chase were close friends, and friends to Schuyler: therefore, his enemies.

On August 7, Samuel Chase wrote to Arnold from Congress, filling him in on American and British movements and troop strengths. Evidently Arnold had asked Chase for information when he could get little from Gates. It is a pity that Arnold's letters to Chase have been lost. Chase, in his August 7 letter, praised Arnold's honesty: "I beg you will from time to time communicate with your usual candor and without any reserve the numbers and condition of our army. . . . No more will be disclosed than you desire." Chase went on to warn Arnold, "I am distressed to hear so many reports injurious to your character about the goods seized at Montreal." As the congressional committee hearings into the Canadian debacle got underway in Philadelphia, Arnold's old enemies, Easton and Brown, were busy blackening his reputation. Chase said he was doing his best to stem the smear campaign until Arnold could defend himself. "I cannot but request all persons to suspend their opinion and to give you an opportunity of being heard." Arnold's New England comrades in arms apparently had become his harshest detractors. Chase told Arnold: "Your best friends are not your countrymen." At the same time, Chase asked Arnold to let Gates know that he had written Arnold and that he, Chase, was aware of Gates's intrigues. "Tell him I saw his letter to Mr. J. Adams, that I cannot understand his message to me. . . . I wish he would explain fully and explicitly what he means. I take his letter unkind and think he ought to have wrote to me."[27]

Two days later, Chase wrote to Gates, telling him that Adams had shown him a July 17 letter in which Gates blamed Chase for deceiving and disappointing him into assuming he had overall command in the Northern Army when he had instead become, as commander at Ticonderoga, only "the wretched spectator of a ruined army." Gates had been scathing in his letter to Adams, criticizing Chase's actions during the fact-finding mission with the other Canadian commissioners. "Mr. Chase passed too speedily through this country, he saw superficially and, like a sanguine man, drew conclusions from the consequence, and not the cause. Tell him, if he and I meet, he must expect to be called to a serious account upon this matter. He has deceived himself and his friend."[28] Could Gates have meant Arnold as Chase's "friend"? If so, it could explain his subsequent treatment of him. Next to write Gates was John Adams. "I wish with all my heart that you were dictator at Ticonderoga," he confided, noting that he had indeed shown Gates's letter to Chase and adding that he, Adams, sided with Gates in the controversy over command. Adams derogated Chase for having "too little penetration into the characters of men."[29]

Gates heeded his political ally, Adams, more than his general on the scene, Arnold. Despite all of Arnold's intelligence-gathering, Gates refused, until he actually heard the firing on the lake, to listen to Arnold. The reason was undoubtedly contained in the concluding lines of Adams's letter of August 13 to Gates from Congress: "We expect some bold stokes from the enemy, but I don't believe that Howe and Burgoyne will unite their forces this year."[30] The round of vicious politicking swirled on, coinciding with Gates's letter to Congress blaming Arnold's "temper" at his Ticonderoga court-martial for much of the Wynkoop fracas. Wynkoop, too, had gone to Philadelphia to join the chorus of Arnold critics. Arnold, assuming that Gates had *defended* him to Congress, wrote guilelessly to Gates when he received Chase's warning, asking Gates to write again to Congress on his behalf. From his exposed position aboard his new flagship, the row galley *Congress,* riding at anchor off Wind Mill Point on the Canadian border, Arnold asked Gates, of all people, to intercede for him. "I enclose you a letter from Samuel Chase Esquire. You will observe he requests an explanation of your letter to Mr. Adams. He observes my character is much injured. . . . I beg you will be kind enough to write your sentiments to him on the matter. I cannot but think it extremely cruel, when I have sacrificed my ease, health and great part of my private property, in the cause of my country to be calumniated as a robber and thief at a time when I have it not in my power to be heard in my own defense."[31]

On the eve of the battle that could decide the fate of the new nation, Benedict Arnold had been passed over for promotion by Congress and his reputation besmirched. He felt he was being ignored and neglected by his commanding officer and was being cut off from the chain of command. His calls for men, food, weapons had been ignored while Gates wasted his time on politics. The most serious slight was the withholding of vital information about the outcome of the British attack on New York City. Six times in six weeks, Arnold had implored Gates to provide him intelligence from the south. As he sailed north, he felt more and more cut off. After that first week of storms battering his small fleet, he had written back to Gates: "I am very anxious to hear from New York."[32] When there was no reply in a week, Arnold wrote again. As he himself assiduously collected intelligence under enemy guns and conscientiously relayed it to Ticonderoga, he grew more alarmed at Gates's silence, then annoyed, finally a little sarcastic. "I am surprised you have received no particular accounts of the battle of Long Island,"[33] which had taken place nearly three weeks earlier. The normal time for a messenger to reach Ticonderoga from New York was less than a week. But silence only made Arnold more apprehensive, his pleadings more frequent, insistent. He had to know as soon as possible in order to be able to anticipate British maneuvers, to know whether the Northern Army at Ticonderoga was now the main line of defense to his south and whether the Champlain navy faced Carleton alone. Were Gates and Arnold about to be caught in the deadly vise he had predicted? In his next letter, only three days later, Arnold told Gates that "their army crossing the lake depends entirely on the advice they may receive from New York."[34] If it appeared that Carleton would *not* attack—and if he did not attack in the next two weeks Arnold doubted he would at all that season— then Arnold would drop back to Buttonmould Bay, where his ships and men would be less battered by the cold northeast winds. By now, there was snow on the flanks of the sleeping lion of Mount Mansfield. Winter was coming early to the north country, and there was snow on the men as they slept on the decks of his open boats.

Two weeks more. Still no word. Gates maintained that "no news is good news."[35] Not only was lack of information a bad policy, but Arnold was embarrassed that he could not inform his own officers and men. What little he could learn was in letters from his sister in Connecticut and from Hartley at Crown Point, Arnold told Gates in his last letter to him on October 7 before going into battle, a fact "very mortifying to me." By now, Arnold had managed to piece together his own picture of the news from the south from officers bringing the new galleys to join his fleet. It was the arrival of General Waterbury with little news that finally triggered Arnold's outburst to Gates on the subject. "I fully expected by him to have all the particulars of the evacuation of Long Island and New York. He seems to know little of the matter." Indeed, General Washington had sent off full accounts of the New York City campaign to the provincial congress at White Plains, which had relayed the word north to Schuyler at Albany, who no doubt informed Gates at Ticonderoga. Gates apparently told Waterbury that he had received a sketchy letter from Washington, but there is no such letter in the Washington papers.

Gates's silence about a situation that could affect Arnold's safety and that of his fleet provoked him to criticize American policy for the first time. He criticized Washington, his staff, and those in Congress who would keep him on a leash, preferring to remain on the defensive even as their enemies grew stronger. Arnold was sharply critical of Washington for providing so little information to his frontline general, yet he was equally hard on Washington's strategy, which he felt could be disastrous. To blockade the enemy into Boston by sealing it off from food and supplies had been a good idea, but to mimic that strategy at New York was ludicrous. "What advantage can we derive by blockading the enemy," Arnold wrote Gates, "when they are in possession of a part of the country sufficient to support them." The British could feed themselves from the farms of Long Island and Staten Island alone; they had their huge fleet to roam at will and resupply them from England, and now they had New York City. To what purpose was a blockade? Why had not Washington attacked while the British were unloading their troops on Long Island, striking them piecemeal instead of cowering behind defensive works at Brooklyn? "It appears to me concise measures should be adopted," Arnold wrote Gates.[36] The thing to do was to *counterattack,* not blockade and back away.

When the news finally did arrive from New York City, it was all bad. Even as Gates wrote to Arnold on October 12 in a letter that reached him too late to be of any use, the British were carrying out their third major attack in an offensive that had begun in late August, as Arnold had sailed north. Poor communications were the bane of military planners. Neither British nor Americans knew whether their plans were being carried out or if they had failed. Carleton may not have known before Arnold what the outcome of the assault on New York City was; all that the joint British commanders in New York, General Sir William Howe and his brother, Admiral Lord Richard Howe, knew was that Carleton had been reinforced, his men were in position, and he intended to attack southward to link up with the Howes' drive north.

On August 22 and 25, General Howe had landed twenty thousand British and Hessian troops on Long Island, outflanking the American entrenchments at Brooklyn and routing Washington's main army the next day. As the Americans fled, hundreds drowned; fifteen hundred Americans were killed or wounded out of a force of five thousand. But the British failed to pursue Washington's battered army. Under cover of the same three-day storm that battered Arnold's navy its first week out, Washington was able to evacuate his surviving troops in rowboats at night under cover of a heavy fog to Manhattan.

The British attacked again on September 15, this time at Kip's

Bay, between present-day 30th and 31st Streets, almost managing to cut off the American army in lower Manhattan. But this time General Howe paused for tea with his staff. The American army slipped away, retreating northward to present-day Morningside Heights. There, on September 16, Washington had repulsed a third British attack. For three more weeks Howe hesitated before attacking. During this lull, a mysterious fire broke out in New York City, destroying four hundred buildings, much of the center of the town. All that Benedict Arnold could learn from Gates was that the city had burned and the British had been repulsed.

Warfare had a way of intruding on the savage political infighting of the Revolution, violent outbursts of battle interrupting and altering the incessant round of backroom plotting and public posturing. As the weeks and months passed, the idealism of the writers of the Declaration of Independence seemed to slip away even as its signers did, leaving Philadelphia to go back home to conduct the business of revolution. Arnold, far from the center of power, could concern himself little with politics in the chilly days of October on Lake Champlain. War and a northern winter were bearing down inexorably on him.

For weeks, his ships had kept up a blockade of the British outposts from his base on Isle La Motte, two miles below the northern tip of the island. In a letter to Gates dated September 15, he had described the drill: "I keep the two small schooners continually cruising above and below us. The countersign is never given until four o'clock. Two guard boats are posted every night two miles below us at a proper distance to discover the approach of the enemy. Another boat goes the rounds every two hours all night. Every ship keeps half their men constantly on deck, under arms and matches lighted. It will be impossible for the enemy to surprise us."

As September drew to a close, the storms on the lake grew more severe. Arnold still did not have one spare anchor. He needed to withdraw to a more protected position. "I have sent two boats to sound round the island Valcour who report that is an exceeding fine, secure harbor. I am determined to go there the first fair wind."[37] What Benedict Arnold did not know, could not know for all his intelligence-gathering, was that the British fleet had already sailed. Carleton was coming, looking for him.

11

"SUCH COOL

DETERMINED VALOR"

Should the enemy come up the lake
and attempt to force their way
through, you will . . . give them
reason to repent of their temerity.

Horatio Gates to Benedict Arnold, August 1776

On the blustery cold afternoon of October 10, 1776, General Benedict Arnold, his fleet of sixteen ships riding at anchor between Valcour Island and the New York shore, sat in the cramped stern cabin of the new row galley *Congress*. A cannon protruding behind him, barrels of gunpowder and cannon-balls stacked around him, Arnold needed the relative calm of the small compartment to write what might be his last letter to Horatio Gates before going into battle. The ten-gun *Congress* and its sister, *Washington*, had glided into Valcour Bay under splashing oars only a few days earlier. Arnold fired a five-gun salute as each of the two new galleys approached the fleet. Arnold was eager to transfer the cumbersome *Royal Savage*, his largest vessel, to his Connecticut friend Captain David Hawley and make the smaller, faster *Congress* his flagship. Arnold did not have time to transfer his personal papers or clothing from *Savage*. A courier boat had to clear the anchorage for Ticonderoga before sundown. Arnold had ordered the new galleys into the arc of ships, arranged his field desk in his lap, and begun to write Gates.

Arnold had learned nothing new of the fighting to the south, and was disappointed that New York had sent not one sailor to join his forces in its own defense. Arnold did not immediately mention his greatest disappointment: only three of eight row galleys had been completed. Half his fleet was still unfinished. For want of skilled seamen, he had been forced to adapt his strategy to the defensive, unable to attack exposed British forward positions on the Richelieu River or attempt to destroy the British fleet under construction at St. Jean. When Arnold's intelligence-gathering made it clear by mid-September that the British would have more and larger ships than he could muster and were actually trying to trap his fleet in the northern narrows of the lake between gun emplacements, Arnold had sent scouting parties south to sound a new anchorage. On September 18, he had written Gates from Isle La Motte that he would soon be cut off by a "considerable" British attack unless he moved to Valcour Bay, twenty miles to the south. "'Tis a good harbor. We shall have the advantage over the enemy. If they are too many for us, we can retire." Now, nearly four weeks later, Arnold still had not received official acknowledgment of this plan from Gates, who finally sent Arnold his approval the day *after* the battle began.

In an attempt to offset the British advantage, Arnold wanted the element of surprise on the American side. Carleton would most likely expect to find him farther north, in wide-open Cumberland Bay, where a British fleet had destroyed a French fleet nearly twenty years earlier. Arnold had to eschew an open-water engagement in which the British could sail faster, surround his frail ships, pound them with lethal broadsides, then swarm over them with cutlass-wielding boarding parties, quickly destroying a summer's work, then sailing unopposed up the lake within artillery range of Fort Ticonderoga. If Gates and his raw militia panicked and fled, New York would be split asunder this autumn, the two British armies able to link up and cut the new nation in two. As late as October 9, this was still Carleton's plan. If, on the other hand, Arnold could outwit Carleton and force the British navy to fight on his terms, Arnold could turn their might against them. An oceangoing man-of-war cannot easily maneuver close to shore in shallow channels; the very wind that drives a tall ship can make it tricky to turn it and bring it to bear.

Benedict Arnold had found Valcour Bay on his first exploration of the lake in May 1775, and had sailed past it twice more that summer of 1776, past its three-quarter-mile-wide channel between Valcour Island and the New York shore. At the northern end of the channel, the water was shoaled, blocked by sunken rocks and nowhere more than five feet deep; at the southern end, there was a hidden underwater ledge three hundred yards long. The British, sailing south, must rely on a strong north wind behind them. Too many of their ships, Arnold knew from his scouts, were equipped only with square sails that were useless for beating upwind, and could proceed up the lake only with a north wind at their sterns. The four largest British men-of-war, moreover, would not be able to work in close formation down such a shallow, narrow channel, in places only six feet deep. They would have their wind stolen by the high, spruce-crowned hummock of Valcour Island. Most important, ships anchored behind the island would be invisible from the main channel of the lake. It was near the southern end of Valcour Bay, therefore, that Arnold prepared his trap. Half a mile north of the southern tip of the island, he deployed his sixteen ships in a crescent-shaped line of battle, anchored stem to stern across the channel, their blackened guns bristling, their barn-red sides blending into the red maple leaves of the New York shore. To make their camouflage complete, he had ordered every ship screened with spruce trees sharpened to points and strung upside down around the bulwarks. These evergreen stockades would make it difficult for snipers to pick off his gunners from the nearby shores and, furthermore, discourage boarding parties.

In making his trap work, Arnold was counting on British arrogance to outweigh navigational skill. When "Carleton the Haughty," as Arnold called him, failed to find the Americans in Cumberland Bay, he would no doubt deduce that Arnold had retired up the lake to meet him in the next wide-open stretch of water indicated on the only British map of the lake, which did not even show Valcour Island, twenty-five miles to the south. From his hidden sanctuary, Arnold planned to wait until the British had sailed along the main channel well past Valcour Island. Then he would lure them back against the wind, into his trap, where he could punish the British fleet piecemeal: only one large British ship at a time could tack up narrow Valcour Bay into the curve of Arnold's scimitar formation. There his sixteen ships could hurl nearly six hundred pounds of heavy metal shells at close range with each broadside, not counting grapeshot from a hundred swivel guns.

But Arnold confided few details of his plan to Gates. Instead, he exuded confidence and offered his gratitude for a last-minute infusion of men, ships, and supplies. Arnold was cheered that "we are victualled for about ten days." After two months without fresh meat or vegetables, his men at last could cook a hot meal of beef, biscuits, and fresh potatoes and wash it all down with generous allowances of rum. Aboard *Liberty* as she slipped into Valcour Bay was a barrel of rum for each vessel. In this long, chatty letter, Arnold informed Gates that he had turned the schooner *Liberty* into a hospital ship, stripping her of heavy guns to enable her to sail faster back and forth to Crown Point with the wounded and with dispatches and supplies. Arnold needed *Liberty*'s cannon for *Trumbull*, which had arrived undergunned. Arnold wrote Gates that he was extremely pleased that Gates was finally writing to Congress for more money to build more ships over the winter. More row galleys, not gondolas, were "of the best construction and cheapest for this lake." Arnold again insisted that to control Lake Champlain "perhaps it may be well to have one frigate of thirty-six guns." Was he, in the light of intelligence reports, being sarcastic, or only uncharacteristically delicate? Arnold knew from his soundings of the Richelieu River that no ship larger than a frigate could be floated south from St. Jean. Arnold resumed his usual impatient, impertinent prodding of his commander—they should not wait for Congress: "Carpenters ought to be immediately employed to cut timber and planks" *before* the oncoming winter was over. As soon as the lakes and the rivers were frozen over and there was deep snow in the woods, timber-hauling by sledges and teams of horses or oxen would be easier than in summer. Three hundred winter-hardened axmen should be "set to work at Skenesboro the first of February." Around Arnold, crews rowed loads of shot and shell to stock the fifteen vessels of the first American fleet with provisions and cleared their decks for action. Tonight, there would be laughter and singing over tankards of rum as men proudly sat in new blue uniforms issued to them after months in the tattered, grimy clothes they had worn from home and worked and slept in all summer. Some of the men had been sailing the storm-tossed lake for six weeks now; they had tales to tell the neophytes newly arrived on *Washington* and *Trumbull*. To Gates, Arnold wrote with obvious pride in men he had deprecated at midsummer. Now they were sailors. "We are as well-prepared for the enemy as our circumstances will allow. They will never have it in their power to surprise us. The men are daily trained in the exercise of their guns. If powder was plenty, I would wish to have them fire at a mark with their great guns often. At present, we cannot afford it."[1] Yet every man by now knew the drill of swathing barrel and ramming home cartridge and ball, of hauling out the gun carriages on Casdrop's skids. They had learned a mainsheet from a stay, larboard from starboard; they knew, too, the loneliness, the boredom, the danger of night patrols.

At four o'clock a solitary picket boat, the stripped-down *Liberty*, tacked away from the anchorage and beat upwind to carry the new countersign to the two guard boats Arnold had stationed to the north and east of Valcour Island. On these boats, there could be no cookfires, no talking. Only watching, listening. *Liberty* was back before eight the next morning, October 11, 1776. She came racing south, her square sail filled, her bow plowing into the swells made by the stiff northwest wind. As Captain Premier brought *Liberty* about at the southern tip of Valcour Island, he fired a signal cannon. Minutes before he could tell Arnold personally, the shot announced all. Shortly after dawn, Premier had focused his spyglass on white flecks on the horizon off Grand Isle, seven miles north of Valcour Island. One, two, three, four large ships, one very tall, much larger than the others, then a flotilla of gunboats—there must have been two dozen of them—then an immense ketch with high sloping sides, and finally a hundred canoes, carrying a thousand Indians. Even without the canoes, there must have been three dozen British ships, more than double Arnold's squadron. Premier aimed *Liberty* straight up the narrow channel into Valcour Bay, then dumped her sails to bring her about into the crescent line. In seconds, Premier and the skippers of the other ships were in their longboats rowing toward *Congress* and a last-minute council of war with Arnold.

Unlike most of the American leaders, British Governor Sir Guy Carleton had never doubted the importance of controlling Lake Champlain, but he had moved slowly, methodically, cautiously, maddening such subordinates as his second-in-command, General John Burgoyne. A better politician than soldier, Carleton had taken time to punish pro-American Frenchmen, to stem the flow of American propaganda, to bring the Indians over to his side, to mobilize thousands of habitants. He ordered that French Canadians who had helped the American army were to be disenfranchised and their property seized, and, more humiliatingly, he required the Catholic Church, official state church of Quebec Province, to make them do public penance. And at a series of Indian conferences in Montreal, where he had moved his headquarters to be closer to the front, he had insisted that the Indians publicly burn their treaties with Arnold and denounce their oath to remain neutral before he would allow them to help themselves to the piles of presents from the king that had drawn many of them fifteen hundred miles: guns, blankets, silver jewelry for their necks and noses, knives, tomahawks, war paint. Carleton had also ordered that all American letters, pamphlets, even copies of the Declaration of Independence were to be treated as seditious and burned by the public hangman.

Despite shortages of food and transportation, Carleton's forces were growing stronger by the month as they were reinforced by thousands of Hessian mercenaries. These highly trained and disciplined European professional troops were to be Carleton's reserve, freeing his regulars and Indians for the assault south. Carleton deployed the Hessians in a chain of fortified camps running all along the Richelieu River from the St. Lawrence south to Isle aux Noix. It was, from the start, a strained collaboration between British officers and Hessians, and Carleton let it be known that he was not pleased by what he first saw as he inspected the Hessian camps. Even as his Royal Navy engineers and crewmen assembled his fleet at St. Jean, Carleton and his generals, Burgoyne and Phillips, conducted a surprise inspection of the Hessian base at La Prairie, on the Richelieu.

The German drill began at half past ten in the morning. A brigade of grenadiers, the enlisted men wearing white breeches and blue gaiters, dark blue uniforms with yellow facings, and black hats, the officers with gold trimming their tricorns and highly polished patent-leather boots up halfway on their thighs, braced under the scrutiny of their commander, Baron von Riedesel, and Brigadier General Breymann and his British visitors. After a long lunch, the generals inspected three hundred more men from Riedesel's regiment. Riedesel said that he had a surprise for the British. He displayed his men strung out in a long line to simulate a sharpshooting attack through the woods. In his diary, Riedesel recorded the scene:

As soon as the first line has jumped into the supposed ditch, the command "fire" is given. Then the first line fires, reloads its guns, gets up out of the ditch and hides behind a tree, rock or shrub or whatever is at hand. At the same time firing off four cartridges in such a manner that the line is kept as straight as possible. As soon as the first line has fired, the second line advances and fires off the same number in the same manner. While this is taking place, the woods have been thoroughly ransacked by the sharpshooters.[2]

These tactics were new to the British generals, still accustomed, in eighteenth-century fashion, to having their regular troops fight in open fields in massed formations with no protective cover. What Baron von Riedesel was advocating was to fight Indian-style. Many of his troops were jaegers, professional German hunters and woodsmen who were equipped with short, lightweight rifles similar to those used by Indians and capable of being fired with far greater accuracy than the standard smoothbore .69-caliber Brown Bess muskets that were issued to British soldiers. At the moment, the British officers inspecting the Hessian troops made no official comment, but they left Baron von Riedesel with the impression that they were perfectly satisfied with the performance. One month later, however, when word came down from Carleton's headquarters that the expedition was about to begin, the three thousand crack Hessian troops, with the exception of two hundred Hesse-Hanau artillerists, were left behind on construction details and garrison duty with Allen McLean's Highlanders, who had so capably defended Quebec against the Americans. Only the elite corps of seven hundred British Grenadier Guards and light infantry were to board British ships and move south in the first assault wave.

On October 3, the Grenadier Guards packed their eighty-pound packs, powdered their wigs, and donned their newly issued winter uniforms: warm woolen undervests, white leggings, knee-length white Canadian blanket-coats, and black bearskin caps. One British officer affected a jaunty tone: "We propose, in two or three days, setting out on our visit to Ticonderoga and Crown Point." Beneath their surface bravado the British officers were skittish. One day they thought they heard Arnold firing all his cannon and imagined he must be scaling his gun barrels of rust in anticipation of battle: probably they heard the salute welcoming the row galleys. Then an alarm reached Burgoyne's ears that a force of "five or six thousand rebels was being sent up through the woods in order to burn our base camps." The result, according to this British officer, was a night without sleep for the entire British army: "We lay on our arms for four and twenty hours, but the enemy did not appear." By the morning of October 5, the entire British fleet, except for the largest man-of-war, *Inflexible,* was ready to begin the slow, careful journey from St. Jean to the open lake. It took two days for the forty-mile voyage. It had been discovered at the last moment that the Richelieu was only eight feet deep in places, less than the depth of the loaded men-of-war. To lighten ships, the men, their gear, their food, and ammunition were loaded into scores of bateaux that trailed in each ship's wake as it was guided under shortened sail to Isle aux Noix. Then, the morning of October 7, the schooners *Lady Maria* and *Carleton* and the bomb ketches *Thunderer* and *Loyal Convert* were eased through the east channel past the fortified island of Isle aux Noix, past a thousand white tents, and up the last fifteen miles of straight river toward the open lake. For many in the British fleet, the voyage was, after so many months of waiting, in the words of one British officer, "an unspeakable joy."[3] On the forecastle of Carleton's flagship the royal governor wore the red uniform of a British general as he joined Captain Thomas Pringle, commodore of the Blue Squadron, England's first inland naval squadron, flying its blue pennant for the first time. Carleton had decided to supersede General Sir John Burgoyne and take personal command of the expedition.

The largest ship to navigate the Richelieu that day was the strange-looking ketch-rigged *Thunderer*. A floating artillery battery built to bombard fortifications or anchored ships at long range, she was, at four hundred tons, by far the largest vessel in the fleet. One hundred five feet long at her waterline, she was uncommonly tall and ungainly, her hundred-foot mainmast seeming to tilt forward as if it were moving faster than her hull. Her sides were double-shielded with high bulwarks that sloped inward to protect her gun crews. Designed with a rounded bow and stern and no keel so that she could maneuver close inshore, she consequently sideslipped on a windy day or heeled over radically in a strong crosswind. Her skipper, Royal Engineers Lieutenant Schank, had just invented the keel centerboard, which could be lowered in deep water and raised in shallow, but Commodore Douglas had vetoed it for use on *Thunderer* and the other large vessels. But, under perfect conditions, she was the deadliest of British killing machines. She was fitted out with six heavy twenty-four-pounders (Arnold had not one gun so powerful in his entire navy), six twelve-pounders (alone making her the equal of any American ship on Lake Champlain), and two great eight-inch siege howitzers capable of lobbing heavy shells in high arcs with considerable accuracy. To fire these guns, *Thunderer* carried a complement of German gunners commanded by the Hesse-Hanau chief of artillery, Captain Georg Pausch. By late afternoon October 6, the British navy had arrived on Lake Champlain, dropping anchors off Windmill Point. There had been only one mishap when *Lady Maria* scraped her bottom on a shoal at the mouth of the river and jammed aground until she could be pulled off by bateaux. By nightfall, noted Lieutenant William Digby, "the vessels were all cleared and ready for action, waiting only for *Inflexible*."[4]

Lake Champlain weather shifts rapidly. As the British squadron spread over the anchorage, the wind picked up, and a vast flock of gray-and-pink passenger pigeons flushed in a low, wheeling, cawing cloud. Then the wind backed to the south and blew up into a squall that left the great ships bobbing and heaving at their moorings. Cold autumn rain slashed down hour after hour, turning the decks treacherously slippery. The growing British tent city on the west shore turned into a bog, and the thoroughly drenched soldiers emerged from their wildly flapping tents only to dash to mess tent or privy. Their heavy wool uniforms turned sodden and dank and the soldiers huddled, miserable, for three days until the storm finally subsided.

During the lull provided by the storm, as his subordinates began to despair of ever reaching Crown Point, on October 9 Carleton wrote back to Quebec to Lieutenant Governor Cramahé, "I have got thus far with the armed vessels except the *Inflexible,* which I expect up tomorrow or next day at farthest. . . . We shall take the first favorable wind to proceed upon our expedition."[5] Then he wrote out marching orders for his troops and sailing orders for his fleet. Burgoyne was to have his redcoats ready to row south when Carleton was sure that Arnold could not attack the open troop transports. The fleet was to be led down the lake by "three small boats in front" as a "party of observation."[6] They were to scout the scores of coves and back channels for Arnold's fleet. Next, to sail in single file, were *Maria, Inflexible, Carleton, Loyal Convert,* and *Thunderer.* Half the German artillerists were to be shifted to twenty-seven gunboats. These snub-nosed thirty-footers, each carrying a heavy twenty-four-pound gun in its bow, were to have seven-man gun crews and a dozen British sailors at the sweep oars and the sails. Each crew was under its own officers, one British, one German. A drummer boy, a German, was to bridge the language barrier by banging out orders. Next to come were twenty armed longboats under oars and sails, fast, sleek boats with eager British midshipmen calling the stroke through coxswain's trumpets from their sterns. Four hundred Indians in thirty-foot war canoes would flank the gunboats. In all, when the full fleet glided to the lake's southern tip, the British host would number nine thousand men in 624 vessels, the largest lakeborne invasion England had ever mounted. Now all they lacked was their decisive vessel, *Inflexible.*

The next morning, the 10th, dawned gray. The wind direction was favorable, from the north. But it was stiff, cold, for the first time. In the distant west, there was snow on the Adirondacks. But three cheers went up on the ships as *Inflexible* appeared, gliding majestically under three tiers of sail out onto the open water. Instantly, Carleton gave the order to break out the flag for "Form line of battle." By ten o'clock, the ships were sailing south in search of Arnold.

As the men-of-war took their positions, the fleet seemed to jam the narrow channel between the clusters of islands. Arnold could be anywhere, behind any island or around any headland. Carleton had sent Burgoyne's light infantry and Indian scouts on a sweep down the New York shore to find him. All day, the British fleet ran downwind under full sail, by late afternoon tacking within sight of Cumberland Point. But Arnold was not there. The day that had begun so full of promise ended with a return to the despair that they would *never* come to a decisive battle.

*   *   *

Benedict Arnold did not have much time to brief his captains. As they crowded into the small stern cabin of the *Congress* shortly after eight the morning of October 11, 1776, the British fleet could have been no more than five miles away running downwind on a perfect point of sail. British longboats would even now be probing between Crab Island and the northern tip of Valcour. All evidence points to the fact that until this meeting, Arnold had remained secretive to his officers about his battle plans. He had made last-minute refinements which took into account his new position and intelligence reports of the clear British advantage in ships and guns. Moreover, he seemed to agree with Gates on one fundamental point: he should, by his every written and spoken word, give the appearance of being able to win, even if to win was impossible. At least he must avert panic in order to buy more time for the American armies to be built up. The council of war aboard *Congress* may have been the very first time Arnold took his commanders into his confidence.

In a few minutes, Benedict Arnold could whip up enthusiasm in his officers in a way that few other American leaders in the Revolution ever equaled. His determination and his reckless courage were infectious. Men who dragged themselves into a meeting came out fired with a vigor that carried them into the frenzy of battle. This morning there certainly was enough to dread about the American position. If the attacker does not prevail, an ambush can become a trap, and this shortcoming in Arnold's plan was quickly pointed out by General Waterbury, Arnold's second-in-command. As Arnold unfolded his plan to let the British fleet pass by before luring it into a deadly arc of ships anchored in Valcour Bay, Waterbury argued that they should try to escape while they still could. As a soldier, he saw the chief responsibility of the fleet as protecting the army. They should sail south as fast as they could to defend Crown Point and Ticonderoga, fighting the British if needs be as they retreated.

But Benedict Arnold was respected by his captains as a good sailor. He had pulled together a handful of skilled mariners. Seth Warner of Connecticut had arrived in an oxcart at Skenesboro to supervise construction of the eighty-foot, ten-gun *Trumbull*, smallest of the row galleys. Trusted Connecticut sea captain David Hawley was now in command of the largest American ship, the *Royal Savage*. Arnold himself was resplendent in his new navy-blue general's uniform with its buff sword sash, single gold epaulet, and gold-trimmed tricorn hat. He countered that the Americans *could not* fight the British in the open lake. There were far too many British ships with too much sail, too many guns. On the same point of wind—and the British now had the strong northwest wind that their

big ships needed to crowd on the sail—they could quickly overtake
the Americans in the widest part of the lake, which was sixteen miles
wide just below Valcour Island. With plenty of open water in which
they could maneuver, and with skilled officers and seamen, they
could move in close enough to steal the wind from the American
sails and rake the slender American line of ships with their broadsides. Arnold's intelligence indicated that the British could hurl volleys of more than twelve hundred pounds of iron to his less than six
hundred.

The only American hope was Arnold's plan to force the British
to fight in the narrows behind Valcour Island. Here Arnold had carefully deployed his ships so that any British vessel coming close
enough to fire effectively would be subjected to a murderous
crossfire. Arnold had to fear British boarding parties most of all: his
raw recruits would be no match for veteran British sailors with cutlasses and knives, Grenadier Guardsmen with grenades and bayonets. By lining up his ships in a line across the bay, he could
concentrate fire from all of his ships. The gondolas, built low to the
water, could discourage any attempts at boarding either themselves
or the larger vessels by rapid-firing grape-sized lead shot from their
swivel guns just above the waterline. From as far away as seven
hundred yards, grapeshot would rip apart boatloads of men as they
approached. Against the larger British men-of-war, the galleys could
be rowed out to discharge their cannonades and glide back into their
places in the crescent formation to reload while the sloops and gondolas continued to fire their cannon. Their fire could prove galling to
the most battle-seasoned British tar.

Every detail of the long summer's planning was brought to bear
that morning, charging the air around Arnold. As he went over his
strategy, he showed the captains a master plan that now became
obvious in its simplicity. The arc of American ships would virtually
extend from the New York shore to the island, with ships anchored
on long lines called spring cables that kept them turned broadside to
the British. Naturally, the fast south-to-north current in the bay
would have swung them around nose-in to the northwest wind,
where their broadsides could not be brought to bear. On spring cables, they could be cranked around by their crews turning capstans
aboard each ship and could fire a volley, then the line could be
payed out until they presented only a narrow bows-on silhouette to
British answering fire. The row galleys, moreover, would reef their
sails and use their oars, thus sparing their rigging from the British
canister shot that could rip and tear a ship's sails, leaving it disabled,
ripe for a boarding party. Gondolas, too, should keep their poles

bare and rely on sweep oars, and would be protected by the larger ships. Arnold assigned the galley *Trumbull* to a station at the east end of the crescent, closest to the island, just out of musket range from the tall trees. Next in line, slightly staggered to the north so that *Trumbull* could fire past her into the curving center of the scimitar, were the gondolas—*Boston, Providence, Connecticut, New Jersey, New York.* Then, as the line curved back toward the New York shore, the schooner *Revenge,* with her eight four-pounders; Arnold's flagship, *Congress;* the gondola *Philadelphia;* and the row galley *Washington.* The two biggest ships, *Congress* and *Washington,* Arnold carefully stationed closest to the New York shore to fire across the arc, out of the channel and down the lake at any approaching man-of-war. Nearest to shore, he had placed *Liberty,* his hospital ship and courier to Ticonderoga. It was a carefully considered, brilliant plan. Waterbury, overruled, acquiesced. With little time left now before he expected the British to appear, Arnold quickly outlined just how he intended to lure them into his trap.

It was still dark the morning of October 11, 1776, when boatswains aboard the British warships anchored off the southern tip of Isle La Motte clattered through the holds, spinning their raucous, ratcheting battle rattles to rouse the men. "At five o'clock in the morning," noted Captain Georg Pausch of the Hessian artillery, "we received orders to get in readiness for an engagement." All over Fleury Bay, sailors and soldiers who had spent the night crammed on decks and below them in hammocks and bunks five high unknotted themselves and in the half-light stumbled up ladders. Lining up for a breakfast of bread, pork, and beans, they were issued rum: burning throats and bellies braced the men against the hard hours ahead. The men had barely finished their breakfast when, aboard the flagship *Maria,* Captain John Starke ordered down the mess flag and sent up two more signal flags: "Put out cookfires. Make ready for battle." Aboard *Thunderer,* Lieutenant William Houghton, Fore Master, Royal Artillery, ordered the massive bellows of his brick furnace kept pumping without interruption. He was getting ready to serve up red-hot cannonballs to set American ships afire. By dawn, hundreds of sailors were clambering up into the rigging, hanging, waists doubled, legs dangling, as they unfurled and set the sails. Below them, deep in dark holds away from the wet wind, soldiers put on their blanket coats and stuffed their field packs, which had been ready for days but now were in need of nervous last-minute adjustments. Then they cleaned their weapons once more and dry-fired them. "We raised our anchor and, with a favorable wind, got very early under sail,"[7] recorded Captain Pausch.

The wind, from the north-northwest, was just right for full-rigged ships like *Inflexible* with massed canvas, experienced crews, masts as high as a hundred feet hanging out acres of sailcoth to trap and turn the wind into a hard-driving force. Aboard *Maria,* Governor Carleton pushed pack from the wardroom table. With his younger brother, Colonel Thomas Carleton and Commodore Pringle, he climbed to the quarterdeck, where Captain Starke was now giving the order to get under way. Pringle's new Blue Squadron ensign coursed up the foretop and snapped out the command "Form line of battle."

The men-of-war fell behind Carleton's flagship as she nosed out into the main channel, their fresh orange-painted hulls glistening in the early-morning light. Four low longboats bearing on their transoms the names of mother ships left behind at Quebec—*Blonde, Isis, Canceaux, Lord Howe*—skimmed past the billowing men-of-war, cutting whitecaps and showering their avid young crews with cold spray as they dashed ahead to reconnoiter bays and coves in search of Arnold's navy. The wind picked up and the men-of-war heeled over slightly and soon came abreast of North Hero Island; by eight o'clock, *Maria* had Grand Isle off her port side and Commodore Pringle could make out Cumberland Head off the starboard bow through his glasses. Carleton had been so certain that they would find Arnold there that he had overruled his subordinates at a tense last council of war early that morning.

Nearly a year after the battle of Valcour Bay, an "Open Letter to Captain Pringle" appeared in the *London Gazette* over the signatures of three senior British officers on hand that day, Captains Schank, Starke, and Longcroft, skippers of *Inflexible, Lady Maria,* and *Loyal Convert.* These three officers took the extraordinary step of publicly contradicting their commanding officer's official report of the battle. The letter also underscored the difficulty of reconstructing the battle on Lake Champlain in October 1776, because the three career officers not only virtually accused Governor Carleton and Commodore Pringle of cowardice under fire, but contradicted every significant detail of the official British report of the battle. The letter was apparently written by Starke at St. Jean in June 1777, after the three officers read Commodore Pringle's official report mailed to the secretary of the British Admiralty and then leaked to the *Gazette.* A fourteen-year veteran, Starke had been second lieutenant of *Lizard* and had been in charge of training marines and seamen for the defense of Quebec before he became captain of Carleton's flagship, *Maria,* during the Valcour engagement. After an Admiralty hearing two years later, Starke was rewarded with a promotion to captain of a man-of-war in the Caribbean.

The first major discrepancy in Commodore Pringle's official report, according to the Starke letter, was Carleton and Pringle's denial of the fact that they were told in advance that Benedict Arnold and his fleet were hiding behind Valcour Island. Independent documentation corroborates this charge. Evidently, General John Burgoyne, sent from London as the new commander of the British invasion, was left behind at Windmill Point with his troops when Carleton insisted on personally taking command of the expedition on October 9. Two of the three dissident naval officers had been captains of Burgoyne's troop ships and had sailed with him from England. They were clearly surprised that Carleton, who as royal governor of Quebec Province had no jurisdiction over Lake Champlain, and no right to lead the invasion of New York, had not only superseded Burgoyne but insisted on putting Pringle in charge of the British fleet, promoting him over the heads of Starke, Schanck, and Longcroft. Burgoyne would eventually take his case to England, but for the moment, he could, according to his orders, dispatch scouts south along the Lake Champlain shore without Carleton's approval. The "scouts" he sent were four hundred crack British light infantry with Indian guides dispatched south along both shores all the way to Crown Point, hunting for Arnold. It appears from the scanty surviving records that Burgoyne's scouts discovered Arnold's hiding place on October 10 and rushed word back to Carleton aboard *Lady Maria.* The warning, according to Lieutenant Starke, was indeed given to Carleton and Pringle early the morning of the 11th. Despite this warning, Carleton "formed no plan nor made any disposition of the fleet under [his] command to attack them, which [he] was advised to do the next day, *before* you had seen them."[8]

According to Baron von Riedesel, left behind at Windmill Point with Burgoyne, Carleton's plan of battle was drawn up on the 9th based on reports he received that day. When Burgoyne's reconnaissance reports contradicted Carleton's on the 10th, Carleton refused to alter his plans. Captain Lanodière, skipper of one of the four longboats sent ahead by Carleton to search for Arnold, had reported back on the 9th that he had sailed around Grand Isle and the two Hero Islands "without discovering any traces of the enemy." In consequence of this report, wrote von Riedesel, "General Carleton advanced with all his war vessels with the object of finding and attacking any of the enemy that could be found." But the longboats had forayed south again the next day, Thursday, the 10th. When they returned, von Riedesel said, "It was reported to General Carleton that the American fleet had been seen near Grand Island."[9] (Valcour Island is plainly visible from the southwest shore of Grand Isle.) Surely, such intelligence called for a revision of the plan of battle, argued several of Carleton's senior officers at a hastily convened council of war over breakfast the morning of the 11th. Did the general mean to simply sail down the lake without a coordinated plan of attack? This would mean each captain would be entitled to act at his own discretion, go his own way. It was highly irregular and it assumed that the Americans had no plans of their own. Especially if Carleton knew of Arnold's whereabouts, it seemed reckless to risk spreading out the British sailing vessels with their uneven sailing capabilities so that they could not concentrate their fire. Starke and the others, however, were overruled. When their opportunity for protest came, nearly a year later, they wrote scathingly that Carleton had blundered south: "You formed no plan nor made any disposition of the fleet under your command to attack them, which you was advised to do the next day before you had seen them. This neglect, whether proceeding from want of capacity or want of inclination," the officers wrote, "was the true reason of their not being brought to action."[10]

Carleton presumably was certain that Arnold would either meet him in Cumberland Bay or try to make a run for the protection of Fort Ticonderoga's guns. In either scenario, the superior British fleet could surround the frail Americans. When Arnold was not found waiting for Carleton off Cumberland Head, Carleton dismissed his officers' advice and ordered Commodore Pringle to set a course down the main channel of the open lake, making all possible speed south. Soon *Maria* turned her sternpost to the low islands to starboard—Crab Island, Valcour. With his big ships under full sail, Carleton clearly expected to overtake the Americans and attack them in deep water. By ten o'clock that morning, the British fleet was spread out over nearly ten miles of water, *Maria* coursing past Valcour and running rapidly south, *Inflexible* surging along behind, then the gunboats back two miles or more, not yet abreast of Valcour, wallowing under two-ton bow cannons. Far behind, laboring under oars, her sails all but useless as her flat bottom sideslipped across the current, the leviathan *Thunderer* lumbered, and *Loyal Convert* trailed ignominiously, her lug sail useless, her round bottom sliding off course. Four hundred canoe loads of warriors, whose heads were barely visible above the swells, leaned urgently toward the battle, thrusting and digging their paddles in quick driving rhythms.

*   *   *

Shortly after ten o'clock, as Carleton's ships left Valcour Island five miles astern, a young midshipman at the tiller of one of the long-boats spotted two of Arnold's warships. Under full sail, *Royal Savage* and *Enterprise* were running south on a course parallel to *Maria*. A closer look through a spyglass revealed three row galleys— *Trumbull, Congress, Washington*—knifing through the water nearby, oars dipping, sails lashed to bare poles, above them the new American rattlesnake flag proclaiming "Don't Tread on Me." The Americans were a good three miles north of the three British men-of-war and two miles south of Valcour Island on a course that could cut between the British warships, sail north, and attack the un-protected British troops at Windmill Point. At least this was the im-pression Benedict Arnold wished to create. Instantly, the British longboat's cannon signaled to Carleton and his staff officers aboard *Maria*. Commodore Pringle sent a midshipman to *Maria*'s starboard rail with a glass: in his lens, a three-masted schooner, *Royal Savage,* showed clearly. Close behind came the tall-masted *Enterprise*. At a command from Pringle, *Maria* swung hard to starboard, preparing to come about onto a course calculated to intercept the Americans. At the same time, Pringle ordered up the signal "Engage," even though in the absence of a formal battle plan, every captain, with or without the flag, was free to attack the Americans at will. Already, every British hull strained toward the Americans.

The British ship closest to the Americans was *Carleton,* com-manded by young Lieutenant James R. Dacres, in his first command. *Carleton*'s gun crews poised at her twelve twelve-pounders, waiting for the distance to close between them and the larger American ship. Suddenly, the two American ships changed course, coming about in unison. Arnold's decoys were dashing straight into Valcour Bay, rac-ing *Carleton* up the narrow channel. Then *Royal Savage* came about and, as *Enterprise* continued toward the crescent line, the big Amer-ican schooner veered toward the island's southern tip. Captain David Hawley knew from Arnold's soundings that there was a sub-merged ledge only three feet below the surface. He was trying to lure the bigger British warship aground before he turned sharply once more into the bay. Dacres, aboard *Carleton,* continued to pursue *Enterprise* west across the mouth of Valcour Bay, narrowly missing the American row galleys as they, too, dashed back toward their anchorage. As they streaked up the channel, Dacres could make out more than a dozen American ships seven hundred or more yards from the mouth of the bay. They opened fire and were engulfed by a white cloud of smoke, making them difficult targets. The sound of

American cannon confirmed that this was no accident: Benedict Arnold's navy now beat out a deadly tattoo of welcome.

It was *Inflexible* that won the other race—to overtake *Royal Savage*. At the first signal gun, the British man-of-war had been sailing slightly south of *Carleton*. At Captain John Schank's command she had come about slowly in a great arc, presenting her profile to the American mariners. Her sheer size must have stunned the sailors working feverishly to bring *Royal Savage* safely into the Valcour anchorage. Few Americans on the lake that day had ever seen so vast, so menacing a ship of war. *Inflexible* now bore down on *Royal Savage*. Heavy bow guns roared; shot hissed overhead. In a series of tacks, *Inflexible* steadily closed on the American schooner. As the British man-of-war drew closer, she began firing broadsides at each pass, six eighteen-pounders rapid-firing fore-to-aft with deadly effect. In the first barrage, chain shot tore through *Royal Savage*'s rigging, cutting ropes and ruining tackle. The second volley was aimed lower. Heavy balls smashed through railings, showering her decks with lethal splinters that fell on Americans scurrying for their lives. One shot slammed into the mainmast, shattering it. But Captain Hawley still seemed bent on drawing the British after him. Heeled over now, *Royal Savage* made a tack to starboard and almost came about in time to clear the island's tip and head safely into the bay, but a strong crosswind deflected by the island caught the schooner and fairly lifted her. Her heavy boom swung over, her sails flapped uselessly. At this moment, *Inflexible* fired another broadside through *Royal Savage*'s stern railing. Shot and shell slashed along her deck, shearing off arms and legs, killing at least three men outright. *Royal Savage* sailed straight up onto the underwater ledge at Valcour's tip, screeching. Her tall masts trembled a moment, then pitched forward. *Royal Savage* had jammed hard aground and settled over onto one side, her guns pointed skyward, downward, useless. Hawley lowered a longboat into the water and his men crowded in. Others dived into the chilly water. The largest American ship was out of the battle.

There was little time for British cheering. Around the stranded schooner, the wolfpack of British gunboats that had been swarming in for the kill now scattered and reformed, making its way around the island and rushing up into the channel toward the American line. As it became apparent that Hawley, in his longboat, was trying to use an anchor line to tow off *Royal Savage*, Hessian gunners took deadly aim at him and soon his small boat was hulled by a twenty-four-pound shot. More shots hit it and it quickly sank, and the crews began swimming for the island. As the gunboats turned once again toward Arnold's line, he led his men in aiming a withering fire from their small swivel guns as well as heavy cannon. Running up and down the line of guns aboard *Congress,* he personally aimed them, urging on his men. The accuracy of the American fire surprised the British. Hessian Captain Pausch was in the lead gunboat: the American "gondolas, one after another, emerged from a small bay of the island firing rapidly and effectively. Every once in a while they would vanish to get breath and again suddenly reappear." The gunboat battle, Pausch reported, "became very fierce."[11]

But Pausch could not see what happened next aboard *Inflexible.* Captain Starke, *Maria's* skipper, could clearly see the American row galleys dart out of the crescent formation and open fire as *Inflexible* zigzagged up the channel to get within range. Starke, through his spyglass, was able to make out Arnold aboard *Congress* as he personally sighted the big eighteen-pound bow gun and shouted the order to fire a heavy lead ball straight at *Maria.* It arced over the water and passed directly between the heads of two British officers standing near Starke on *Maria's* quarterdeck—Carleton and his brother. The concussion from the shot knocked Thomas Carleton senseless. Blood rushed from his ears as he fell. The shot had an even more dramatic effect on Governor Carleton. As his personal physician, Dr. Robert Knox, worked over the stricken colonel, the governor stood stunned while Commodore Pringle, in an obvious effort to safeguard the royal governor, gave orders for the most powerful British warship to turn around and sail *away* from the Americans. Nearly two miles from the line of battle, Pringle commanded the infuriated Starke to drop anchor. The British flagship was out of action.

On the surface, Guy Carleton tried to appear nonchalant about the near miss from Arnold's cannonball. Dr. Knox later wrote that Carleton had turned to him a little later and said, "Well, Doctor, how do you like a sea fight?"[12] But by allowing Pringle to take one of four men-of-war out of the battle almost at the start, Carleton mightily encouraged the Americans, dispirited many of the British, and opened himself to criticism even from those inclined to admire him. Aboard *Thunderer,* Lieutenant Digby, who considered Carleton "one of the most distant, reserved men in the world," and had once written, after Carleton's defense of Quebec, that "he possesses a coolness and steadiness which few can attain," now found Carleton's behavior "very unpleasing."[13] And Captain Starke, humiliated by having to give the commands that consigned *Maria* to the rear, made mental notes. A year later, he poured his anger out to Pringle in his open letter. "Yourself in the *Maria*," Starke wrote to Pringle, "lay to with the topsails, and was the only person in the fleet [who] showed no inclination to fight."[14] But had Starke seen Carleton's first official report, spirited off secretly at two in the morning, he might have been even more infuriated.

Indeed, according to Carleton's first official report, it appears that he was completely taken in by Arnold's ruse and was shocked by what appeared to be sudden and unexpected resistance. Writing to General Burgoyne in the rear the next morning, he actually argued to Burgoyne that the Americans, according to prisoners he had taken,

were unapprised either of our force or motions. . . . One of their vessels perceived us only a little before we came abreast of the island, and our vanguard got to the southward of it time enough to stop them just as they were making off. They then worked back into the narrow part of the passage between the island and the main, where they anchored in a line. . . . After we had got beyond the enemy and cut them off, the wind, which had been favorable to bring us there, however entirely prevented our being able to bring our whole force to engage them, as we had a narrow passage to work up, ship by ship, exposed to the fire of their whole line.[15]

That Arnold had successfully snared the British was beyond dispute; that Carleton had fudged about the wind to cover up his own timidity is beyond doubt. Many of his officers never forgave him.

With *Maria* out of action and *Thunderer* and *Loyal Convert* still nowhere in sight, the battle centered, by shortly after noon, on the attempts of the Hessian artillery gunboats to maneuver up the narrow channel in the tricky winds so that they could confront Arnold's fleet formation. "Close to one o'clock," noted the Hessian Captain Pausch, "this naval battle began to get very serious." Pausch and his gunboats had been trying to work their way around Arnold's line to bring it under a crossfire. As one British gunboat under Lieutenant Dufais approached the Americans "a cannon ball from the enemy's guns," wrote Pausch, "went through his powder magazine." The direct hit by American gunners killed half of the men on board. "Dufais's bateau came back burning." The stricken gunboat was full of cold water. "All who could jumped on board my bateau which, being thus overloaded, came near sinking." Even after another British gunboat took off some of the survivors, there were forty-eight men crowded aboard Pausch's boat, twice too many. One, a thirteen-year-old Hessian drummer boy, huddled in shock in the stern. "In what a predicament was I!" Pausch wrote. "Every moment I was in danger of drowning with all on board."[16] American cannonballs then sank two more British gunboats. As the other gunboats dropped back out of American range, a cheer went up from the American fleet, now able to concentrate its fire on a single British warship, *Carleton.*

The grand British invasion had come down to a single ship forced to face the entire American fleet in the spot so carefully selected by Benedict Arnold. And that ship, *Carleton,* no bigger than any of Arnold's row galleys, was in trouble. Lured into Arnold's trap, the twelve-gun, sixty-six-foot British schooner was subjected to murderous fire from the American half-moon as soon as Lieutenant Dacres made the mistake of sailing *Carleton* within one hundred yards of the rebel line. Aboard *Congress,* Arnold was gleeful. As he had hoped, the British were able to send only one man-of-war at a time against his protected position. Up until this point, it had been difficult for Arnold to open up with his heavy guns in any systematic way on a major British target. But Dacres had brought *Carleton* perilously close to the American position, and the British schooner could not have been more vulnerable. Sailing head on into Arnold's broadsides, Dacres was unable to fire his own. Arnold grabbed the opportunity. When Dacres tried to anchor *Carleton* parallel to the Americans so he could fire broadsides, a well-aimed American shot severed *Carleton*'s anchor line. Arnold's crescent crossfire spewed clouds of white smoke as the American guns raked the schooner, which now began to list as it took on water, unable to sail away. American cannonballs punctured jagged holes in *Carleton*'s hull; grapeshot slashed across her decks. Half a dozen officers and men were cut down as they tried to answer the American fire: Captain Dacres was immediately knocked unconscious, hit a glancing blow in the head by a cannonball. Another tore off First Mate Robert Brown's right arm. A nineteen-year-old midshipman, Edward Pellew, assumed command.

Aboard *Congress,* over a two-and-a-half-hour period, Arnold repeatedly gave the order to up anchor and row in closer to *Carleton.* Behind the bulwark of spruce screening, the American gunners were learning to load and fire smoothly, load and fire, slamming hundreds of pounds of shot and shell into the stubborn *Carleton* until virtually all of her officers and crew were dead or wounded. From his vantage point, Sir Guy Carleton could see Arnold darting from gun to gun, rowing to nearby ships to direct their fire. In an attempt to alleviate the pressure on *Carleton,* Sir Guy ordered boatloads of marines and most of his escorting Indians to land on Valcour Island and on the New York shore to harry the American ships with sniper fire. But their fire could only reach the outermost ships of Arnold's formation. *Liberty, Lee, Washington,* along the New York shore, took the heaviest casualties. Aboard *Lee,* Lieutenant Bayze Wells had to take command after the captain and first mate were shot. But the Indians accomplished little more than to round up survivors of *Royal Savage.* Attempts to send boarding parties by bateau and canoe were bloodily repulsed by Arnold, who had blast after blast fired from the small swivel guns. When *Thunderer* and *Loyal Convert* reached the battle scene, they made no attempt to attack, lobbing shells from out of effective firing range. The Indians took to the treetops and engaged in an aerial war with marine marksmen Arnold had ordered lashed to the high rigging and maintops of his vessels. An accurate shot by an Indian sent an American sharpshooter catapulting downward, only to be snapped short of the deck by his lifeline. There, beyond help, he hung bleeding until he could be cut down. Burial was a hasty affair, bodies dumped overboard to avoid further unnerving the men. The wounded suffered lingering deaths, either relegated to the *Liberty* or belowdeck in *Congress* for surgery. More than thirty men were crammed into Arnold's cabin by the time the afternoon was over. But Arnold's forethought had spared many American lives as his men kept cover behind the spruce shields that made Indian sniping largely ineffectual. Much of the damage, as the fighting wore on, came now from Hessian artillery. The German gunners now had the range, and twenty-four-pound projectiles arched toward the sky and crashed through American ships nearly half a mile away. *New Jersey* and *Philadelphia* especially took poundings; *Congress* had more than twenty holes in her hull, mostly above the waterline.

When all his feeble attempts to alleviate the attack on *Carleton* failed, Sir Guy ordered by signal flag that the shattered vessel should retreat. But Midshipman Edward Pellew, one day to distinguish himself as Admiral Lord Exmouth in the Napoleonic Wars, ignored Carleton's command. As a ship's commander, he had that right, since Carleton had not formulated a coordinated plan of battle. As *Congress* kept up the punishing point-blank cannonade, Arnold grew certain he could either sink the schooner or soon board and capture her. But Pellew was determined to sail away. The young midshipman ordered an extra jibsail run up in the bow. Normally, this was the fastest way to catch the wind, get underway. But *Carleton* was held head on to the wind by her main anchor. The canvas merely flapped until the young officer ran out onto the bowsprit, inched along, pulling himself on his knees. Completely exposed to a hail of metal, he stood and kicked at the jib until it began to fill with air; then he ran safely off, bellowing orders. Still, the jib would not draw. By this time, other British captains had come to his rescue. Two longboats, screened by *Carleton*'s hull from American fire, worked close enough for Pellew to throw them lines. Under heavy fire from Arnold's entire fleet, British oarsmen towed the shattered schooner down the channel.

With the way now clear to attack Arnold's line, the largest British warship, *Inflexible,* sailed up into the lengthening shadows of Valcour Bay at five o'clock. *Inflexible* had been forced to hang back all afternoon, and her gunners itched for revenge. The four-hundred-ton man-of-war dropped anchor at close range, her battery of twenty-four-pound guns raking the Americans for nearly an hour. Only the approach of darkness intervened to save several American ships already badly damaged by the Hessians' long-range fusillade. *Washington* especially was hard hit, with heavy casualties. Finally, at dark, the British fired a last salvo and ran downwind out of the bay. A seven-hour battle was over. The day's fighting ended with British boarding parties scaling the sides of *Royal Savage,* capturing Americans attempting once again to tow her off, and setting fire to her. In Arnold's cabin they found his letters and papers. For a long time these were missing: they include his accounts with French Canadians from whom he had bought supplies all the preceding winter, his correspondence with Gates and with his own officers, and numerous letters and documents that could have saved him infinite trouble with courts-martial and congressmen. When the British set fire to *Royal Savage,* the moans of the wounded and the din of cannon fire were momentarily stifled by a tremendous roar of exploding gunpowder. All through the evening, there were lesser blasts.

Exactly what damage had been done was the question Arnold posed to his captains as they crowded into his cabin, which had been doubling as an operating room. Red-eyed with smoke and fatigue, they tallied casualties, the condition of vessels, and remaining supplies of ammunition. About sixty men had died. Three-fourths of their gunpowder was gone, making another sustained battle impossible. Every ship had been badly damaged and was leaking. The gondola *Philadelphia* had been holed so many times that she was sinking and settled to the lake bottom even as they talked.* Every officer on the *Lee* had been killed. *Providence*'s mainmast had been weakened when a heavy shell from *Inflexible* gouged out a large splinter. The row galley *Washington* was badly damaged, her foremast shot through, her hull leaking steadily, all her officers dead or wounded. There were heavy casualties on *Washington* and *Congress*. As they tolled their losses, light from the burning hull of *Royal Savage* played around the cabin. Arnold, instead of reprimanding Hawley, magnanimously gave him command of the *Washington* to replace its wounded captain.

What most of the men in the cabin that night would never forget was Arnold's encouragement and generous praise of his officers and men. There were some, chiefly Waterbury, who did not think they could go on, but Arnold brushed aside their objections. Arnold had a plan for escaping Carleton's navy. Before the night was over, he assured them, they would be miles away, preparing to strike again. Each captain had been provided with chalk and a horned tin lantern, shaped like an inverted cone, with only a small opening in one side to emit light. They were to chalk their stern rails and hang lanterns over them so that light played only on a white band in the night fog, and this only visible for fifty feet or so to a vessel directly behind. They were to give strict orders to their men to lie absolutely still in their ships when, at his signal, they quietly cast off the lines between them and weighed anchor. They would sail through the British fleet undetected, under cover of the thick fog that was settling in. Even Carleton was inadvertently cooperating, by ordering his gunboats back seven hundred yards, his men-of-war even farther.

By the time Arnold's captains clambered onto their ships shortly before seven, he had so infused them with his own enthusiasm that it quickly spread among the crews. By now it was difficult to see from one end of a ship to another and the moans of the wounded had died down. Only the hissing of the smoldering *Royal Savage* and the dull hammering of shipwrights repairing British vessels could be heard as each captain whispered urgent instructions. Every sail but one was to be tied off, except the spanker that would be used to steer. Each oar was to be wrapped in a shirt to muffle its entry into the water. At seven o'clock, Seth Warner aboard *Trumbull* on the New York end of the line lit his lantern, tied it to the fantail, and steered even closer to shore. The other ships fell into line noiselessly, muffled oars dipping slowly, each ship gliding close behind the other. *Enterprise,* then all the remaining gondolas, then *Revenge* and

---

* Raised in 1935, the *Philadelphia,* the oldest extant American warship, is on permanent display at the Smithsonian Institution in Washington, D.C.

Washington slid alongshore between Indian campfires, British gun-boats. They came so close to Carleton's flagship that they could hear carpenters talking, officers laughing in the captain's cabin.

By the time the British woke up the morning of the 12th, Arnold's fleet was seven miles away making its repairs in the lee of long, low Schuyler Island. Three gondolas, *Providence, New York,* and *Jersey*, were too badly damaged and would have to be stripped and scuttled. Arnold was busy writing a long report of the previous day's battle to Gates. *Liberty* would take his dispatch and the wounded and sail quickly to Crown Point, while Arnold led the other vessels under oars and sails toward Crown Point as fast as their leaky hulls would allow. Arnold's report to Gates was matter-of-fact. *Royal Savage* had been lost by "bad management," but all her men had been saved. *Congress* had been hulled more than a dozen times and "received seven shots between wind and water." The battle had been "very warm." One thousand British soldiers had been waiting in bateaux to board his ships, not counting the Indians on shore. "We suffered much from want of seamen and gun-ners"—this was the closest Arnold came to complaining about his fleet's shortcomings. "The enemy [were] very superior to us in ships and men." He would make a run for Crown Point "with utmost dispatch."[17] He badly needed ammunition as well as a dozen bateaux to tow his ships south if the wind shifted.

When Carleton woke up the morning of the 12th and learned that Arnold had, as he later reported to London, "given us the slip,"[18] there was pandemonium aboard *Maria.* He immediately gave orders for the entire fleet to up anchor and sail north after Arnold. He was sure Arnold would try to get between his navy and his army, now exposed to naval attack at Windmill Point. Con-vinced that Arnold could not have sailed right through his fleet, he assumed Arnold must have sailed out the north end of Valcour Bay. Carleton was so flustered and left so precipitately that he forgot to send orders to General Burgoyne to tell him what to do with the redcoats and the Indians he left stranded on Valcour Island. Many of his officers were astonished by the sudden turn—astonished at Ar-nold's daring escape, at Carleton's failure to post proper sentries the night before, at his panicky reaction. Captain Starke in his open let-ter blamed Carleton for moving the three men-of-war at dusk "by which means the rear of the British line was at least one mile from the western shore." It was because of "this disposition," not "the extreme obscurity of the night as you are pleased to say, the rebels escaped."[19] If Carleton had not moved back the gunboats and his men-of-war, Arnold could not have escaped. British navy officers

were humiliated by Carleton's behavior and grudgingly admiring of
Arnold's.

It was nearly noon before Carleton's latest blunder was discovered. Lookouts spotted the sails of Arnold's fleet far down the
lake, heading south, not north. By the time the British could come
about, a hard south wind was blowing, as Arnold had expected.
Fighting against the wind all day, the British returned to Valcour,
where Carleton ordered them to spend the night while Burgoyne and
the Indians searched for Arnold from the shore and by canoe.

But Arnold's luck changed with the wind the next morning, October 13. Although his exhausted, hungry crews had rowed against
the strong south wind and the current all night long in the cold sleet
and rain, at dawn Arnold could see that they had only reached
Willsboro, having covered a mere twelve miles overnight. By eight
o'clock, the fog had dissolved enough for British lookouts to spot
them. Arnold had hoped to make it to Split Rock to form a line of
battle across the narrows, where the British could not get around
behind him, and make another stand, but the wind coming from the
south impeded his progress while, farther to his north, he could see
that it had shifted and was now blowing from the northwest, perfect
for the British men-of-war now beginning to overtake him. The British had passed the Four Brothers Islands and were within five miles
of *Washington* by the time the north wind reached *Congress.* But
Arnold did not dare to dart too far ahead of his slower, leakier vessels. *Washington* was shipping so much water that she was falling
far behind. Arnold had already ordered the other row galley,
Trumbull, and four other less damaged vessels to go ahead to
Crown Point as fast as possible.

Aboard *Washington,* General Waterbury watched helplessly, he
later wrote to Congress, as the towering British ship *Inflexible* overtook him: "My vessel was so torn to pieces that it was almost impossible to keep her above water." To Gates he later explained, "It
began to grow calm and I knew the next wind would be north and
the enemy could spread so much sail and our vessel was so much
torn and dull I thought it best to put my wounded men into the
boats and send them to Ticonderoga and row my galley ashore and
blow her up."[20] As *Inflexible* gained on him, Waterbury sent an
officer to Arnold's flagship to get permission. Arnold refused, ordering him to fight on. Arnold had put Captain Hawley, former skipper
of the *Royal Savage,* in charge of *Washington.* As *Inflexible*'s twelve-
pounders opened fire, Waterbury ordered Hawley to strike his
colors, surrender. A thirteen-year-old seaman aboard *Washington,*
Pascal De Angelis, testified later that "after four or five shots from

the *Inflexible,* the *Washington* galley struck without firing one gun, General Waterbury being on board."21 Waterbury later contended that he didn't fire at the British because they were out of cannon range, but this is difficult to believe if *Inflexible* could hit him. Hawley thus had the distinction of surrendering two ships without a fight in a single battle. Only sixteen of *Washington*'s crew of 122 escaped in a small boat. Arnold sent them with an urgent message to Ticonderoga to hurry up the bateaux he had requested to tow his stricken craft.

With *Washington* out of the fight, the brunt of the British firepower was directed at Arnold's *Congress. Inflexible, Maria,* and *Carleton* all caught up with Arnold and his four gondolas in the narrows and unleashed terrific volleys of round and grapeshot at close range. All afternoon, Arnold's row galley and gondolas dueled with them, Arnold blasting away at them with the two eighteen-pound sternchasers he had mounted to fire out the transom windows of his cabin. Twice he scored direct hits. Arnold's reconnoitering paid off. He knew these waters well. His accurate fire and tricky gusts of wind off the headland at Split Rock made it difficult for the British to get a clean shot at him, but he pounded away at them in a running fight that lasted for five hours, the British twelve times hitting *Congress* below the waterline. Two shots lodged in *Congress*'s mainmast, another shattered her yardarm. Arnold's first mate, John Frost, was killed and tossed overboard with the bodies of three other sailors; wounded men were carried into *Congress*'s bloody cockpit, where uniforms were cut up and applied as tourniquets and bandages. Arnold was everywhere, kneeling to console the wounded, hauling on lines, firing the cannon. Clear of the narrows, the British closed in and began to rake *Congress* with broadsides. Five crashed the length of Arnold's ship, shattering guns, rigging.

"We were then attacked," Arnold later told Schuyler, "broadside within musket shot," by *Inflexible* even as *Maria* and *Carleton* pounded *Congress* from her stern. "They kept up an incessant fire on us for about five hours with round and grapeshot, which we returned as briskly, the sails, rigging and hull . . . shattered and in pieces."22 By now seven British ships surrounded Arnold. Twenty-seven of his seventy officers and crewmen were dead or seriously wounded, his ammunition was gone, and Crown Point was still ten miles away.

Arnold had one more surprise. He refused to let his ships fall into British hands. Slowly, he maneuvered his squadron into shallow Buttonmould Bay, where the deep-draft British vessels dared not follow. Four months earlier, as he had worked his way north to attack the British, Arnold had made careful soundings: now they saved him. He ordered his gondolas to run ashore and jettison their guns. There was one final instruction: they were to burn their rattlesnake flags still flying. *Congress* was the last to sail ashore. Arnold ordered his marines to take positions behind trees on a high bluff and to fire at British longboats now attempting to put boarding parties on *Congress* to salvage her. Peter Ferris, a fourteen-year-old whose family lived near Buttonmould Bay and whose father was a friend of Arnold's, later reported that Arnold ordered his aide, Lieutenant Goldsmith, crippled by a thigh wound, to be carried ashore from a gondola. In the confusion, the gunner forgot to carry off the wounded mate as he set fire to the ship. Lieutenant Goldsmith "then begged to be thrown overboard and the gunner, on returning from the galley, told him he would be dead before she blew up." When the gondola's powder magazine blew up, the lieutenant's body "was seen blown up into the air."[23] When Arnold learned what had happened, he was so angry he threatened to run the gunner through on the spot, but at this moment the British fleet opened fire on the Ferris house and Arnold's men on shore.

That night, as Burgoyne's Indians ran down the narrow road along the Vermont shore searching for Arnold and the 150 bloodstained men he had rescued, young Ferris showed Arnold another less known path. After fighting two battles and rowing for two days and nights, Arnold and his men walked the last twenty miles, carrying their wounded in slings made out of sails, arriving October 14 at Crown Point only hours before the first British landing parties. Before going on to Ticonderoga to confront Gates, Arnold ordered Crown Point, its barracks, warehouses, docks, and blockhouse, burned. "At four o'clock yesterday morning, I reached this place,"[24] he wrote Schuyler from Fort Ticonderoga on October 15, "extremely fatigued and unwell, having been without sleep or refreshment for near three days."

It was October 20 and snow was falling heavily on the tents of Carleton's soldiers by the time Carleton arrived at Crown Point and decided whether to press on and attack Ticonderoga or pause at Crown Point to build winter quarters, an advance base that would solidify his control of Lake Champlain, now firmly in the grip of the Royal Navy. Arnold had stunned him. After the American flight from Canada, Carleton apparently had not been prepared for fierce resistance at the hands of Arnold, who now awaited him at Ticonderoga. Carleton was dazed and confused by the time, a full two weeks after the Battle of Valcour Bay, he finally decided that the "severe season" and the "want of time" to build comfortable winter quarters for his troops before continuing the invasion would, after all, "force us back to Canada."[25]

On November 1, 1776, Carleton ordered his troops back aboard their ships for the return voyage to Windmill Point. The next day, as *Thunderer* sailed past Arnold's Bay,* Lieutenant Digby overheard soldiers calling the place Destruction Bay. "Some of their dead were then floating on the brink of the water, just where the surf threw them," he noted.[26] The British stopped long enough to bury the Americans, then sailed on. As they headed north again, it was snowing. The British invasion of 1776 had been halted by the approach of winter, and the tenacity of Benedict Arnold. Eighty men were dead, 120 more were prisoners. Two-thirds of the first American fleet had been destroyed. The British now controlled Lake Champlain, but they had lost another year, and time was on the American side. Carleton's withdrawal temporarily relieved pressure on Ticonderoga, and Gates was able to send reinforcements to Washington, which arrived in time to take part in his successful attack on Trenton on Christmas night. Arnold had lost a battle and a fleet, but by building a fleet and forcing the British to do likewise, he had imposed a year's delay on Carleton and made impossible the British strategy to divide the colonies and conquer them. "Save for Arnold's flotilla, the British would have settled the business," wrote naval historian Alfred Thayer Mahan. "The little American navy was wiped out, but never had any force, big or small, lived to better purpose."[27]

---

* Near present-day Panton, Vermont.

12

"BY HEAVEN,

I WILL HAVE JUSTICE"

*I spent the last night at the War
Office with General Arnold. He has
been basely slandered and libelled.*

John Adams to Abigail Adams, May 22, 1777

The news that Benedict Arnold had survived the first full-scale American naval battle but that two thirds of his fleet had been destroyed set off a year of infighting in the Continental Army and in the Continental Congress that was only occasionally interrupted by the war. That Arnold had saved the nation and blunted the British divide-and-conquer strategy while teaching both sides that Americans could turn and fight even when outnumbered and outgunned was apparent to the highest rank of generals and to the common people. But to the middle rung of politicians and officers, the fact that he had lost first an army and now a navy made him vulnerable to the attacks of a growing number of jealous personal enemies. Mixed reactions to his stand at Valcour Island surprised Arnold, who was too busy worrying that the British would attack Ticonderoga next and drive on to Albany even to think about the effect on his career. The day after he reached Ticonderoga, Arnold wrote to Philip Schuyler that the British invasion force was "very formidable," yet he still believed that the nine-thousand-man American army at Ticonderoga "if properly supported"[1] could stop the enemy.

318

Most of the letters Gates wrote in the week after Valcour included favorable comments about Arnold. Gates, who preferred the fort to the battlefield, wrote to the Puritan governor of Connecticut, Jonathan Trumbull, "It has pleased Providence to preserve General Arnold. Few men ever met with so many hair-breadth escapes in so short a space of time."[2] A week later, writing again to Trumbull, Gates blamed the loss of the fleet on its very inadequacy: "It would have been happy for the United States had the gallant behavior and steady good conduct of that excellent officer been supported by a fleet in any degree equal to the enemy."[3] He did not mention that he had blocked Arnold's request for a frigate greater in size than *Inflexible* or his own failure to rush the completion of five of the eight row galleys Arnold had counted on when he faced the British. In general orders, Gates was generous in thanking Arnold and his men for the gallant defense they made "against the great superiority of the enemy's force. . . . Such magnanimous behavior will establish the fame of the American army through the globe."[4]

If Gates for the moment went along with public adulation for Arnold, his subordinates did not. While Captain Dacres, the British officer sent to carry word of the battle to England, praised Arnold to the Admiralty—"the disposition of his force and the defense he made against a superior enemy and the management of his retreat did him great honor"[5]—some of the American officers Arnold now had to deal with every day inside Fort Ticonderoga were less generous. General William "Scotch Willie" Maxwell wrote sarcastically to Governor William Livingston of New Jersey, "Arnold, our evil genius to the north, has, with a good deal of industry, got us clear of all our fine fleet. . . . He has managed his point so well with the old man, the General, that he has got his thanks. Our fleet"—and here he relied on the misinformation that was compounding the vindictiveness of attacks on Arnold—"was much the strongest, but he suffered himself to be surrounded between an island and the main land. In the night he gave orders to every vessel to make the best of their way, by which they became an easy prey. This was a pretty piece of admiralship after going to their doors almost and bantering them for two months or more, contrary to the opinion of all the army."[6]

When the news of the battle reached the Continental Congress in Philadelphia, Richard Henry Lee of Virginia denounced Arnold in a letter to Thomas Jefferson. Lee, a member of the Marine Committee in Congress, believed "we had reason to think ourselves in no danger on that water for this campaign," implying that Arnold had turned the expedition into a disaster. Lee and Jefferson were advocating a federation of strong states with their own navies and armies and a weak national government, and Lee seems to have taken this opportunity to cut Arnold down from any heroic size. Lee claimed to have been told by an informant that Arnold had been caught off guard by the British naval attack. "This officer, fiery, hot and impetuous, but without discretion, never thought of informing himself how the enemy went on, and he had no idea of retiring when he saw them coming, though so much superior to his force."[7] The two seemingly contradictory criticisms of Arnold put him at odds with the anti-federalist party, led by the Adamses of Massachusetts, that opposed a strong general staff being built up by Washington and Schuyler.

If Arnold at first chose to ignore party politics in Congress and the army, criticisms of his admiralship and generalship increasingly disturbed him. The Continental Congress's policy of repeatedly promoting over his head officers junior to him in rank and seniority was a bitter affront to him. Indeed, a gentleman in the eighteenth century was expected to resign if he was passed over for promotion: this was an accepted way of forcing resignations and retirements. While out on the lake in September, Arnold had written to Gates that he had "some thoughts of going to Congress" in Philadelphia after the battle and clearing his name, the only impediment he could imagine, to gaining promotion—"Do you think they will make me a major general?" That failing, he was thinking of "begging leave to resign."[8] At Ticonderoga, he grumbled some more about leaving the army "when this disagreeable service is at an end"[9] unless the cloud of calumny swirling about his head could be cleared away.

Festering old feuds burst open again almost as soon as Arnold got his men safely inside Ticonderoga's walls. Colonel Moses Hazen, who had accused Arnold of looting Montreal, now accused him of slander in a military court after Arnold accused Hazen of selling liquor from the public stores at Chambly for his private profit. In addition, Major John Brown now demanded that Gates arrest Arnold for thirteen "crimes," including slandering Brown, depriving him of promotion and calling him a liar, promoting smallpox inoculation, starving his men at Quebec, plundering Montreal, cruelly destroying whole villages, exchanging prisoners illegally, and, as if that didn't cover everything, "great misconduct"[10] from the time Arnold left Cambridge until he returned to Ticonderoga a year later. Leaving no brick of Arnold's reputation standing, Brown demanded a full-scale court of inquiry.

Arnold had continued to underrate the damage his enemies could do among politicians who were willing to believe the worst about him at a time when he had every reason to expect their thanks

Ethan Allen gave Arnold this blunderbuss to use in their joint attack on Fort Ticonderoga. Arnold later gave it to Jonathan Trumbull, muster-master at the fort in the summer of 1776. COURTESY FORT TICONDEROGA MUSEUM

1776 English depiction of Major General Arnold

Fort Ticonderoga, at the southern tip of Lake Champlain. Arnold and Ethan Allen led the attack from Hand's Cove, Shoreham, Vermont, across the lake. COURTESY FORT TICONDEROGA MUSEUM

In this traditional view by R. Dowling, Ethan Allen demands the surrender of Fort Ticonderoga from British commander Captain William Delaplace. Arnold, in actuality, was at Allen's side. COURTESY FORT TICONDEROGA MUSEUM

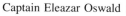

Captain Eleazar Oswald

Captain Daniel Morgan of Arnold's riflemen. By Charles Willson Peale.
COURTESY INDEPENDENCE NATIONAL HISTORICAL PARK COLLECTION

Captain Aaron Burr. By Gilbert Stuart.
COURTESY NEW JERSEY HISTORICAL SOCIETY

Governor Sir Guy Carleton

Captain John Lamb of the New York Artillery. COURTESY ANNE S. K. BROWN MILITARY COLLECTION, BROWN UNIVERSITY

One of Morgan's riflemen in a caped linen shirt and fringed buckskin leggings

A British Grenadier

A French view of Arnold as hero of Saratoga
COURTESY FORT TICONDEROGA MUSEUM

Lower Town of Quebec, where Arnold's main attack came early on January 1, 1776. Watercolor by James Hunter. COURTESY PUBLIC ARCHIVES OF CANADA

Major General John Thomas

Brigadier General Richard Montgomery. COURTESY NEW YORK PUBLIC LIBRARY PRINT COLLECTION

The death of General Montgomery. By John Trumbull. COURTESY YALE UNIVERSITY ART GALLERY

Benjamin Franklin

Major General David
Wooster. Mezzotint pub-
lished by Thomas Hart,
London, 1776. COUR-
TESY THE BRITISH
MUSEUM, LONDON.
BRITISH CROWN
COPYRIGHT

British relief fleet
brings reinforcements
to Quebec in May 1776.

The Reverend John Carroll, S. J. Oil by Gilbert Stuart. COURTESY GEORGETOWN UNIVER-
SITY, WASHINGTON, D.C.

Samuel Chase. By John Wesley Jarvis.

Sawmills and stockade at Skenesboro produced planks to build Arnold's fleet. COURTESY PUBLIC ARCHIVES OF CANADA

Watercolor cartoon by P. Randle in 1777 shows Commodore Benedict Arnold and his fleet on Valcour Bay. COURTESY FORT TICONDEROGA MUSEUM

American schooner *Royal Savage* ran aground at outset of the Battle of Valcour Bay. COURTESY NEW YORK PUBLIC LIBRARY

Continental gunboat *Philadelphia,* which sank in Valcour channel on October 11, 1776, and was raised in 1935. It is the oldest surviving American naval vessel. COURTESY SMITHSONIAN INSTITUTION

Lieutenant James Richard Dacres, skipper of HMS *Carleton,* was seriously wounded at Valcour Bay. COURTESY NAVY DEPARTMENT LIBRARY

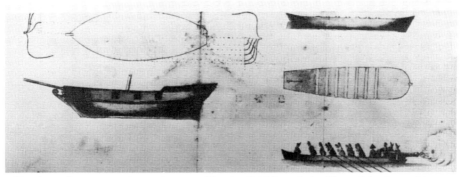

Sketches of a cutter and a gunboat used by the British on Lake Champlain. From Simon Metcalf's sailor's diary. COURTESY FORT TICONDEROGA MUSEUM

British fleet at Valcour Bay. *Left to right: Carleton, Inflexible, Maria, Loyal Convert, Thunderer.* By P. Randle. COURTESY PUBLIC ARCHIVES OF CANADA

General George Washington appointed Arnold to the Northern Department in August 1777. Oil portrait by Charles Willson Peale, 1776. COURTESY BROOKLYN MUSEUM

Major General Philip Schuyler, head of the Northern Department, favored Arnold. COURTESY YALE UNIVERSITY ART GALLERY

Major General Horatio Gates replaced Schuyler and confined Arnold to his tent. By Gilbert Stuart. COURTESY METROPOLITAN MUSEUM OF ART

John Adams backed Gates in the struggle for control of the Northern Army. By Charles Willson Peale. COURTESY INDEPENDENCE NATIONAL HISTORIC PARK COLLECTION

The scalping of Jane McCrea, fiancée of a Loyalist officer, aroused the New York militia to oppose Burgoyne's invasion. Oil by Asher B. Durand, circa 1839. COURTESY FORT TICONDEROGA MUSEUM

Contemporary view of the British encampment on the west bank of the Hudson River at Saratoga

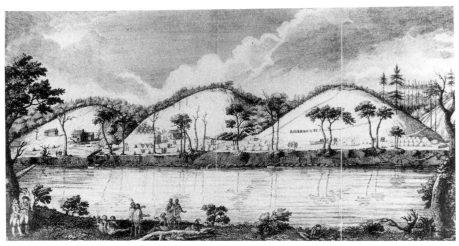

Benedict Arnold was shot from his horse, Warren (actually a chestnut), as he charged the Hessian stronghold at Breymann's Redoubt. Attributed to John Trumbull. COURTESY FORT TICONDEROGA MUSEUM

The Bristish commander at Saratoga was General John Burgoyne.

A French view of Arnold, the hero of Quebec. EMMET COLLECTION, NEW YORK PUBLIC LIBRARY

Benedict Arnold in the uniform of an American major general. Drawn by Swiss artist Pierre Du Simitiere in Philadelphia. COURTESY NEW-YORK HISTORICAL SOCIETY

When Arnold died, his widow gave this mezzotint watercolor of him in an American major general's uniform to his son, Richard. COURTESY FORT TICONDEROGA MUSEUM

A German view of Arnold as the hero of Saratoga. COURTESY FORT TICONDEROGA MUSEUM

Waspish-tongued Rebecca Franks was Peggy Shippen's closest friend and the daughter of a Loyalist merchant banished by Pennsylvania. COURTESY AMERICAN JEWISH HISTORICAL SOCIETY

André sketched Peggy Shippen in the headdress he designed for her to wear in the Meschianza ball. COURTESY HISTORICAL SOCIETY OF PENNSYLVANIA

Arnold purchased this elegant Philadelphia country seat, Mount Pleasant, as Peggy's wedding present.

Silas Deane. By Pierre Eugene Du Simitiere.

John Jay. By Charles Willson Peale. COUR-
TESY MARYLAND HISTORICAL SOCIETY

James Duane

James Wilson. COURTESY FREE
LIBRARY OF PHILADELPHIA

Robert Morris. By Charles Willson Peale.
COURTESY INDEPENDENCE NATIONAL HISTORI-
CAL PARK

Joseph Reed, president of the Supreme Executive Council of Pennsylvania. By Charles Willson Peale. COURTESY INDEPENDENCE NATIONAL HISTORICAL PARK

John André by Sir Joshua Reynolds
COURTESY WILLIAM L. CLEMENTS LIBRARY

Gouverneur Morris. By Thomas Sully. COURTESY NEW YORK PUBLIC LIBRARY

Esther DeBerdt Reed. By Charles Willson Peale. COURTESY HENRY HOPE REED III

André by Sir Thomas Gainsborough

Self-portrait of John André. Engraving by J. K. Sherwin, 1784.

Unpublished silhouette self-portrait cut by André for Peggy Chew in 1777. COURTESY PRINCETON UNIVERSITY LIBRARY

Joshua Hett Smith provided the safe house, Belmont, where Arnold conferred with André, then insisted he change into civilian clothes. Attributed to John Trumbull.

Self-portrait pencil drawing, signed and dated 1775 and addressed to John Cope, while André was under house arrest in Lancaster, Pennsylvania. COURTESY HISTORICAL SOCIETIES OF TARRYTOWN

Colonel Beverley Robinson, a Loyalist leader and boyhood friend of George Washington, accompanied André aboard HMS *Vulture*. COURTESY MUSEUM OF THE CITY OF NEY YORK

Royal Governor William Franklin, son of the revolutionary leader, presided over a Loyalist intelligence gathering in New York City. COURTESY ESTATE OF MRS. G. MANDERSON CASTLE

Sir Henry Clinton, the British commander-in-chief, was André's intimate friend and protector.

The Reverend Jonathan Odell, chaplain of a Loyalist regiment, enciphered many coded messages or decoded them for Major André.

View of West Point from Fort Putnam, the key to the American control of the Hudson River. By W. H. Bartlett.

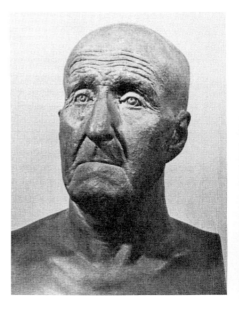

Casts taken from the living heads of Arnold's captors as old men. *From left,* David Williams, John Paulding, and Isaac Van Wart. COURTESY NEW YORK STATE HISTORICAL ASSOCIATION

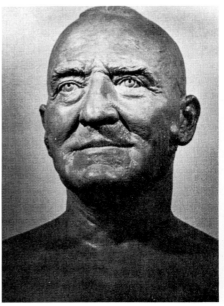

Three American militiamen search André and find compromising documents from Arnold in his boots.

Benedict Arnold escapes from West Point minutes before Washington arrived by commandeering a barge that took him down the Hudson to HMS *Vulture*.

Lieutenant Colonel Richard Varick, court-martialed in the treason plot, was duped by Mrs. Arnold. COURTESY ALBANY INSTITUTE OF HISTORY AND ART

Major David Solebury Franks, Arnold's aide, was devoted to Peggy Arnold and completely taken in by her hysterics. COURTESY HANNAH R. LONDON COLLECTION. AMERICAN JEWISH HISTORICAL SOCIETY

Colonel Alexander Hamilton also refused to believe that the beautiful Peggy Arnold was capable of complicity in treason. COURTESY NEW-YORK HISTORICAL SOCIETY

As the Devil prods a two-faced Arnold, his effigy sits behind a gallows in a wagon drawn through the streets of Philadelphia on September 30, 1780. WOODCUT COURTESY HISTORICAL SOCIETY OF PENNSYLVANIA

Peggy Shippen Arnold in exile in England holds her son, Edward Shippen Arnold, for this 1783 portrait by David Gardner. COURTESY HISTORICAL SOCIETY OF PENNSYLVANIA

The only authentic portrait from life is by the Swiss artist Pierre Eugene Du Simitiere, drawn in Philadelphia when Arnold was the military governor, probably in 1779, and later engraved in Paris. COURTESY NEW-YORK HISTORICAL SOCIETY

Caricature of Arnold, *right,* in a British general's uniform, was printed in London in 1785. COURTESY NEW BRUNSWICK MUSEUM

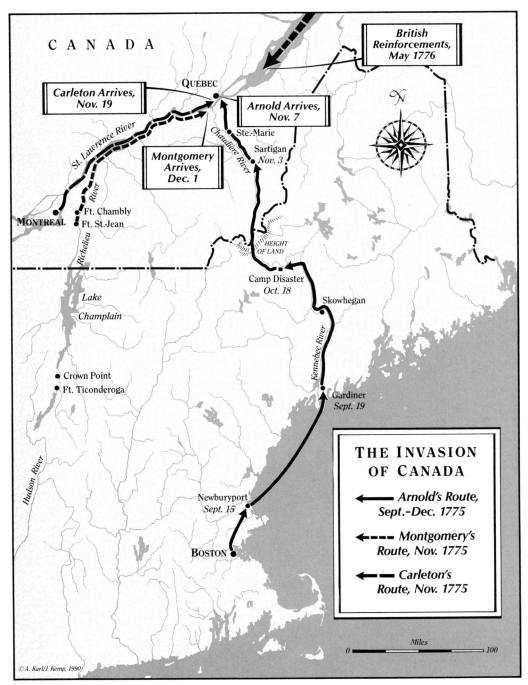

CANADA

British
Reinforcements,
May 1776

QUEBEC

Carleton Arrives,
Nov. 19

Arnold Arrives,
Nov. 7

Ste.-Marie

St. Lawrence River

Chaudiere River

Montgomery
Arrives,
Dec. 1

Sartigan
Nov. 3

Ft. Chambly
Ft. St.-Jean

MONTREAL

River

Richelieu River

HEIGHT
OF LAND

Camp Disaster
Oct. 18

Lake
Champlain

Skowhegan

Kennebec River

Crown Point
Ft. Ticonderoga

Gardiner
Sept. 19

Hudson River

THE INVASION
OF CANADA

Newburyport
Sept. 15

⟵ Arnold's Route,
Sept.-Dec. 1775

◀---- Montgomery's
Route, Nov. 1775

BOSTON

◀— Carleton's
Route, Nov. 1775

Miles

0 ⟶ 100

© A. Karl/J. Kemp, 1990

Invasion of Canada. By Anita Karl and James Kemp. COURTESY *MILITARY HISTORY QUARTERLY*

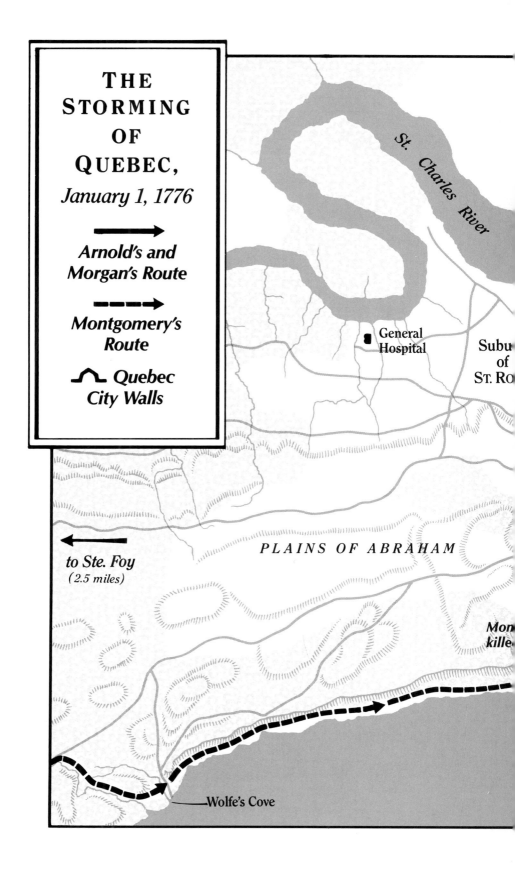

THE STORMING OF QUEBEC,

January 1, 1776

→ **Arnold's and Morgan's Route**

--→ **Montgomery's Route**

⌒ *Quebec City Walls*

to Ste. Foy
(2.5 miles)

General Hospital

Subu
of
ST. RO

PLAINS OF ABRAHAM

Mon
kille

Wolfe's Cove

St. Charles River

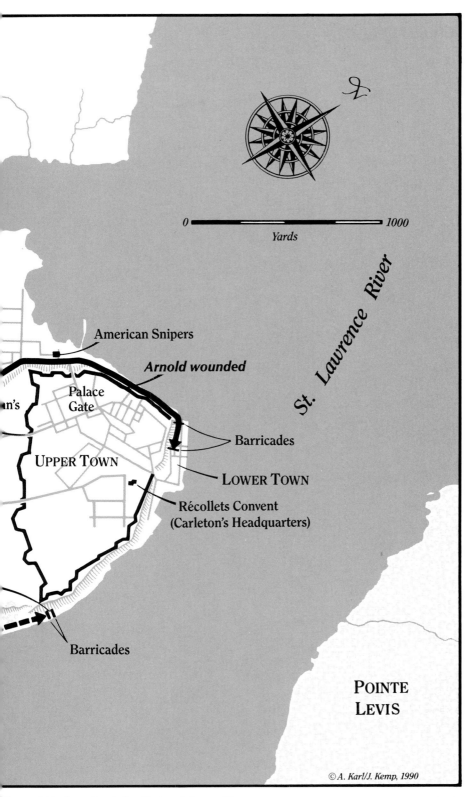

American Snipers

Arnold wounded

Palace
Gate

n's

UPPER TOWN

Barricades

LOWER TOWN

Récollets Convent
(Carleton's Headquarters)

Barricades

St. Lawrence River

POINTE
LEVIS

0   1000
Yards

© *A. Karl/J. Kemp, 1990*

Siege of Quebec. By Anita Karl and James Kemp. COURTESY *MILITARY HISTORY QUARTERLY*

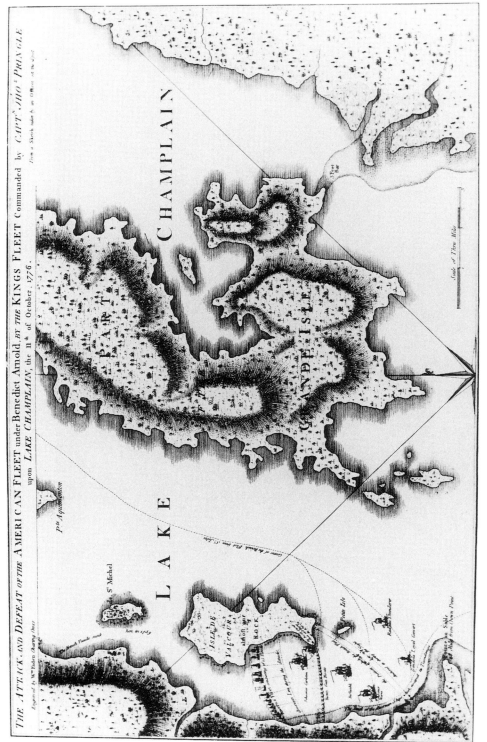

Lake Champlain in the vicinity of Valcour Island. By William Faden, London, 1777.

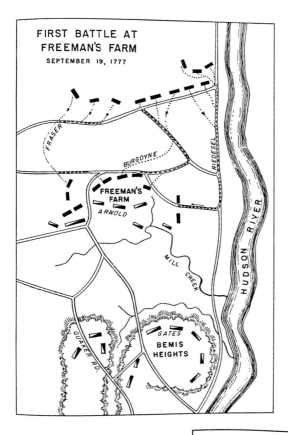

First Battle of Saratoga at Freeman's Farm. COURTESY THE MACMILLAN COMPANY

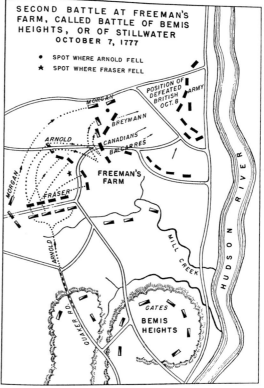

Second Battle of Saratoga at Bemis Heights. COURTESY THE MACMILLAN COMPANY

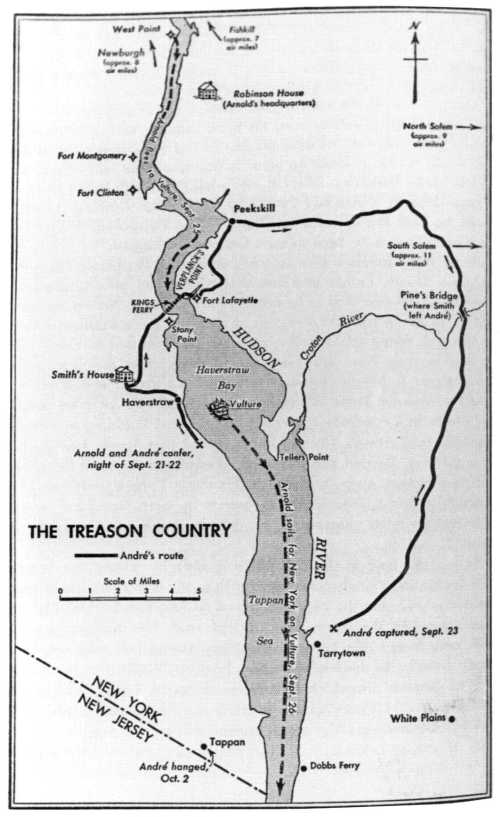

The Treason Country. COURTESY HARPER & ROW

and praise. He left Ticonderoga late in November shortly after it became clear, on the 19th, that the British had actually chosen to head back into Canada for the winter. He was worried more about seeing his family for the first time in eighteen months and straightening out his personal finances than about any detractors. He stopped briefly at Albany to meet with Schuyler and to pick up his strongbox of cash and personal papers he had sent ahead from Ticonderoga when he expected a British attack there. He had grabbed only a cash box when he changed ships at Valcour, and he knew that he had lost many vital personal and public papers on *Royal Savage*. While at Albany, he walked into an unexpected attack, this time from John Brown, his unrelenting foe, who had been busy, with Easton, blackening Arnold's reputation in the Continental Congress just as they had done a year and a half earlier in Massachusetts. Brown, accused with Colonel Easton by Montgomery and Arnold of plundering the personal belongings of British prisoners in Canada, had spent the summer of 1776 in Philadelphia conducting a one-man war against Arnold. Easton had joined Brown in the capital city in April, after his Massachusetts regiment had been disbanded. Ostensibly seeking permission to raise another regiment to go to Canada, Easton and Brown had also submitted a petition to Congress for a court of inquiry to consider the charges of plundering still being pressed by Arnold. Congress had instructed its commissioners in Canada to hold such a court. Easton was not free to go to Montreal: he was in jail in Philadelphia at the moment, clapped into prison for debts totalling £1,500. In yet another petition to Congress, Easton claimed he had money due him in Massachusetts that would pay his debts and that he needed to go to Canada to settle his old regiment's accounts and answer the plundering charges preferred by Arnold. Easton's powerful friends from Massachusetts in Congress ordered his release, and by the time he reached Canada, the retreating army had little interest in his court-martial.

John Brown arrived at Ticonderoga at the same time as the American army, to besiege General Gates for a trial of Arnold. An implacable adversary, Brown brought with him the petition which he had submitted to Congress in the spring and which Congress had approved on June 27, 1776, and referred to Gates for a hearing on the charges. In addition, a committee of Congress was investigating the looting charges and had found evidence that the baggage of captured British General William Prescott had been "plundered by some licentious persons in violation of the faith of the capitulation."[11] Congress ordered Schuyler at Albany to summon a court of inquiry. At the same time, Congress further confounded the matter by appearing to support Brown's claims by granting him the rank and pay of a colonel retroactive to November 20th, 1775, the day Montgomery had promised it to him before learning of the plundering of British prisoners in Canada. Brown swiftly petitioned Schuyler for an immediate hearing in late August, just after Arnold's clash with the Hazen court-martial board. Schuyler's inclination was to ignore Congress and to prosecute Brown for "violent and ill-founded complaints,"[12] but instead he turned the matter over to his subordinate, Gates, instructing him to impanel a court of inquiry on the slander charge alone. On September 3, while Arnold was at the Canadian border proposing to fight the British navy, Brown presented a formal complaint to Gates, asking that Arnold be arrested on his return for defamation of character. Gates, at the time, considered Arnold's other duties too pressing; he ignored Brown's demands, and after Brown pestered him three times in two days, he referred Brown back to Philadelphia to the Board of War, at the same time shunting the Hazen court-martial's findings to the same body in Philadelphia. Realizing that for the moment he had been completely rebuffed, Brown complained, "I have been led an expensive dance from generals to Congress and from Congress to generals."[13]

That left only Colonel Hazen to stand in Arnold's path as he rode south into Albany late in November on his way home. Hazen was also a formidable foe, a rich Canadian merchant and a onetime Tory. On December 2, 1776, as Arnold entered Albany at the side of Gates on his way south, there was a legal roadblock. Arnold had to face a court of inquiry into charges that he had slandered Hazen in June while he had commanded at Chambly. Hazen alleged that Arnold, his commander, had traduced his character by scribbling a remark on the back of a receipt given him at Chambly by Hazen and then passed on by Arnold to the Congressional commissioners for Canada. Arnold had thus tersely accused Hazen in writing of keeping brandy and tobacco belonging to the American garrison for his own use and of selling the garrison's rum to a French Canadian innkeeper. Arnold had written, "Colonel Hazen can best tell how much he sold." After hearing the case, the military court, which included Colonel Wigglesworth, one of Arnold's reluctant galley commanders at Valcour Bay, decided that Arnold's note was indeed "an aspersion of Colonel Hazen's character."[14]

Apparently there were no other consequences except that Arnold was further embittered at his continuing harassment by jealous American officers. Yet, Arnold was becoming alarmed. No doubt he remembered the warning of his friend in Congress Samuel Chase about "so many injurious reports to your character about the goods seized at Montreal."[15] Arnold decided to put off going home and instead go with Gates as he led reinforcements for Washington's retreating army; he would talk to Washington, then to Congress. Driven back from New York across New Jersey, Washington's army had dwindled as the result of massive defections, and large numbers of citizens not only refused to help him but were signing loyalty oaths to support the advancing British army. Schuyler and Gates now agreed with Arnold that the matter was serious enough to warrant sending Arnold to Congress to demand an immediate inquiry to clear the air. On November 27, Gates wrote to John Hancock, president of Congress:

General Arnold, who is now here, is anxious after his long absence to see his family and settle his public accounts. Should the enemy make his presence necessary, I know his zeal for the service will outweigh all other considerations, and induce him to take the route that leads to them.[16]

The route that led to Philadelphia was to be more circuitous, however. Ill-equipped for a winter march, Gates and Arnold led their troops over the New Jersey hills until they finally overtook Washington on the Pennsylvania shore of the Delaware River in Bucks County. Washington was elated at the last-minute arrival of veterans from the northern campaign. This was the first time Washington and Arnold had met since the Kennebec march, and the visit of the general who had held together the tattered American siege in the snows of Quebec provided a heartening analogy for Washington and his troops. At least one of their meetings was to decide how to speed up the exchange of Quebec prisoners still in British hands or on parole at home so they could return to active service. Arnold briefed Washington on officers worthy of promotion. In the course of their secret discussions, Arnold urged Washington to strike quickly against the exposed Hessian outposts in New Jersey now that he had enough disciplined troops and field artillery. Arnold also supported Washington's plans for a three-pronged attack over the Delaware to recapture the New Jersey capital of Trenton. For his part, Arnold was so sure he had Washington's support that he decided to forget his own plans to petition Congress and instead take a temporary new command in New England, when Washington told him another British invasion was expected at Rhode Island.

It had been more than a year and a half since Benedict Arnold had left New Haven. Now he returned a hero. He was still the only living hero of the Revolution. His reputation for reckless bravery in the face of overwhelming odds had been enhanced by the news of the loss of New York City and New Jersey and the pell-mell retreat of Pennsylvanians into the hills and Congress into Maryland. Everywhere Arnold went, crowds came out to meet him—at Hartford, at Middletown, at New Haven. As he approached each town, the Connecticut hills reverberated with cannon salutes, and he was welcomed on the road by veterans of the march to Quebec whose exchange he had helped arrange with Carleton. Men he had last seen scaling the barricades of the Lower Town came out with tears in their eyes to shake his hand, tough men like John Lamb with only one eye now, and Eleazar Oswald, who had lost his youth in British prison, wept with Arnold and embraced him. It was a hero's homecoming, especially on the green at New Haven, as Arnold's own Foot Guards turned out to salute him. Hannah was there, and his three boys, now eight, seven, and four, admiring their famous father.

For the entire week of his visit, there was a steady flow of neighbors, relatives, and former comrades visiting the big house on Water Street. Arnold spent many happy hours talking with the men who had paddled the Kennebec with him, especially John Lamb and Eleazar Oswald, who had been prodding Washington and Henry Knox to form a new artillery battalion. Arnold had interceded with Washington at their Bucks County meeting to hurry up the exchange of Lamb and Oswald, paroled to their homes in Connecticut until they could be swapped for British prisoners of equal rank. Lamb's biographer says it was Arnold who "sustained to the uttermost" Lamb's application for exchange and reappointment to a new regiment: "No man was a better judge of military merit," wrote New York historian Isaac Leake of Arnold, "and the evidence of the necessary qualifications for command."[17] Washington had agreed with Arnold that Lamb was just the man to head a new regiment, and he had arm-twisted Congress into promising the money. When Arnold learned that Lamb had not received from Congress the funds to buy cannon, horses, uniforms, and supplies, he wrote out a note for £1,000, the major share of the enterprise, and sent it to Lamb to draw from Hannah Arnold. The new Colonel Lamb cheerfully accepted Arnold's nominations for his, Lamb's, staff: Oswald, lieutenant colonel; Arnold's late wife's brother, Samuel Mansfield, captain; and Arnold's in-law, John Throop, subaltern.

As Arnold wrote Washington on January 13, he had also raised six thousand militia to hurry on to the commander in chief's winter base at Morristown, New Jersey: he had done "all in my power" to help Washington's decimated army. He sent word that according to his intelligence from inside Newport, the British "have no intention of penetrating the country at present." Arnold congratulated Washington on his successes at Trenton and Princeton, which had driven the British outposts into New York. The news had encouraged New Englanders, "greatly raising the sinking spirits of the country."[18] Then Arnold headed north to Boston, offering his young friend Oswald a ride in his sleigh.

Benedict Arnold's appearance in New England shortly after the British attack on poorly defended Rhode Island had the effect Washington had desired. "His presence will be of infinite service,"[19] Washington had written to John Hancock. British General Henry Clinton, detached from the main British army at New York, had seized Newport on December 7 to counteract the heavy damage being inflicted on British shipping by New England privateers. His appearance off Newport with fifty-three ships and ten thousand men made it appear as if a major invasion of New England had begun even while Howe was driving Washington back across the Middle Atlantic states. But after all the American privateers escaped them, the British seemed content, for the winter at least, to settle into Newport and concentrate on tightening up the blockade of New England's shipping industry.

By the time Arnold reached Providence on January 12, 1777, news of his arrival had excited Major General Joseph "Granny" Spencer and the four-thousand-man Rhode Island militia to expect a swift counterattack to drive out the British, but Arnold found that the Rhode Islanders were too poorly equipped to take on the large British force at Newport. Governor Cooke of Rhode Island had already helped Arnold in his preparations for battle on Lake Champlain and was willing to support Arnold's call for an attack as soon as he had enough men. But Governor Cooke evidently did not know that Washington had ordered Arnold not to attack unless he had enough reliable soldiers to make victory a "moral certainty."[20] Arnold found that he had time on his hands, since further British action in winter was also unlikely. Arnold took the opportunity to ask Washington to permit his young brother-in-law, Sam Mansfield, to be detailed from Lamb's artillery to form a new unit under his command in Rhode Island. Then the two, ostensibly seeking Massachusetts recruits, headed for Boston, where Benedict Arnold found he was now acceptable in the finest society. To dress the part, he stopped off at Paul Revere's shop. General Arnold had an important mission for shopkeeper Revere. Could he do some shopping for him, find a sword knot and sash for his new navy-blue general's uniform, "two best epaulets," and "one dozen silk hose"?[21] Arnold's visit nevertheless proved a high point of Revere's winter, and he sent a long letter by Captain Mansfield to his old friend Colonel Lamb about it.

At the center of Boston society were a handful of *grandes dames* with social connections in both camps. The very idea of Loyalists and Patriots dancing together sent a shiver of revulsion down the backs of firebrands on both sides. Sam Adams wrote back to James Warren, president of the Massachusetts assembly, railing at the great influence the Loyalists strangely enjoyed in Boston when they had all supposedly been driven out with the British. Nowhere would a Patriot like Sam Adams have been more apoplectic than in the Boston drawing room of Mrs. Henry Knox, wife of the three-hundred-pound head of the Continental artillery, the man who had brought the cannon captured on Lake Champlain by Arnold and Allen all the way to Boston on sledges pulled by oxen, even as he was towed in an oxcart himself. The twenty-five-year-old former proprietor of the London Book Store who had gained most of his knowledge of artillery from books was at home for the winter establishing the Springfield Arsenal, and he apparently introduced his friend Arnold to his wife's society. Knox's wife was the former Lucy Flucker, the charming and witty daughter of one of Boston's leading Tories, Thomas Flucker, last royal secretary of the Province of Massachusetts Bay. Flucker had managed to redeem himself in Patriot eyes by revealing that Dr. Benjamin Church had been betraying high-level American secrets to the British; nevertheless, Flucker had fled Boston into exile in London, where he died in 1783. The Fluckers owned much of the land in Maine which Arnold had marched through, and Lucy Flucker Knox had gathered into her drawing room many other ladies of divided loyalties who had come back to Boston to protect family property.

It was in Mrs. Knox's Cambridge drawing room that the elegantly dressed General Arnold was formally introduced into Boston society and, more important to him, introduced to a talkative young lady, apparently as loquacious as his late wife had been incommunicative, the beautiful sixteen-year-old debutante Elizabeth De-Blois. If she was young (and sixteen was not considered too young to seek an eligible suitor at colonial dancing assemblies in those days), she had a polished society matron of a mother to guide her every step. Betsy's father, Gilbert, a rich Tory merchant, had fled to Halifax with eleven hundred other Loyalists and his wife and daughter in the spring of 1776. He, too, eventually sailed to London, where he died, but his wife and Betsy had returned to the family home in Boston, where the despotic Mrs. DeBlois was aghast at the attentions paid her daughter by the lame rebel general Arnold. As Betsy flirted with Benedict Arnold, her mother's choice for her was a young apothecary's apprentice. Arnold's captivation with Betsy made him overlook much: that she was a Tory, first of all, that her mother was a notorious snob who hoped the rebels would leave Boston at the point of British bayonets. The basis for the character Mrs. Flourish in a play then popular in Boston, Mrs. DeBlois tries to be tactful to a rebel officer: "I believe Mr. W[ashington], or General W. if you please, is a very honest, good kind of man." Mrs. Flourish had a low opinion of men generally: "I have found some capable of pleasing, but few, very few indeed, capable of informing me." In the play, Mrs. Flourish refused to let her daughter, Miss Volubility, attend a rebel dance. Betsy rages the night of the party, the next morning inquiring, "How did the he-bears behave? How did they handle their paws?"22

Beyond a certain point, the persistent thirty-six-year-old widower could not besiege the sixteen-year-old Tory belle. He could only resort to the intercession of several ladies he knew, a generous gift to show his financial solidity, and a note to Betsy herself, smuggled through the approving Mrs. Knox. On March 4, he delivered a note to Mrs. Knox, imploring her help in winning the hand of the "heavenly" Miss DeBlois:

> I have taken the liberty of enclosing a letter to the heavenly Miss DeBlois, which I beg the favour of your delivering with the trunk of gowns, etc., which Mrs. —— promised me to send to you. I hope she will soon have the pleasure of receiving them. I make no doubt you will soon have the pleasure to see the charming Mrs. Emery and have it in your power to give the favorable intelligence [that Betsy would marry him]. I shall remain under the most anxious suspense for the favor of a line from you who, if I may judge, will, from your own experience, consider the fond anxiety, the glowing hopes and the chilling fears that alternately possess the heart of, dear Madam,
> Your obedient and humble servant,
> Benedict Arnold23

When Arnold wrote to men, his martial prose was as clear and strong; when attempted to write to women, he could only fall back on the forced phrases of the contemporary form books for gentlemen. Whether his one attempt at a love letter to Betsy DeBlois ever reached her is not known, but while Arnold waited for a response, his pride was shattered by a severe blow to his pride from which he never completely recovered. On February 19, 1777, the

Continental Congress, in the first round of a power struggle between civilian politics and professional soldiers, promoted five brigadier generals to major general over the head of Arnold, number one in line for promotion. All of the officers promoted were inferior to Arnold not only in seniority, but in experience and ability. In February 1777, Washington's rivals in Congress feared that the commander in chief was accruing too much popularity and power. The news that Arnold had been ignored and humiliated by Congress was too much for him. He refused to accept the fact that the promotions were at least in part the result of a new political system. On February 19, the day the generals were promoted, the Congress-in-exile had passed the "Baltimore Resolution," which provided that in voting for general officers, the national legislature had to pay attention not only to "the line of succession" and the "merit of the persons proposed," but "the quota of troops raised, and to be raised, by each state."24 Arnold suspected that the resolution was intended to paper over the fact that Congress could use any criteria to act at its own discretion and was using the argument that Connecticut already had two major generals as a pretext. He believed, probably correctly, that some Massachusetts politicians still resented Arnold's role in the Ticonderoga controversy of 1775.

Washington was also infuriated by Congress's action, since Congress had not deigned to consult him on the promotions. He had first learned of them from the newspapers. Washington was concerned about how Arnold might react to the promotions: any gentlemen would take such an insult as a broad hint to resign. On March 3, Washington wrote to Arnold not to "take any hasty steps" until he could conduct his own inquiry and use his "endeavors" to correct the oversight.25 Could the newspapers have omitted Arnold's name from the list of promotions? There must be some mistake. Secretly, Washington wrote to his old Virginia friend Richard Henry Lee, telling him he was "anxious to know whether General Arnold's non-promotion was owing to accident and design; and the cause of it. Surely a more active, a more spirited, and sensible officer, fills no department in your army. Not seeing him then in the list of major generals, and no mention made of him, has given me uneasiness, as it is not to be presumed (being the oldest brigadier) that he will continue in service under such a slight."26

Arnold, seething in Providence, first wrote back to Washington on March 12. He had been stunned only a few weeks before when Washington had taken the troops Arnold needed to attack the British in Rhode Island and sent them to Ticonderoga under another commander. This double blow had led him to write to Schuyler, worried that he would not be able to return to Ticonderoga, where he thought his knowledge of the northern campaign would soon be badly needed. When he learned from Washington he had been passed over, Arnold's mind leaped to other possible uses of his talents while he waited for Washington to resolve the matter for him. To Schuyler, Arnold suggested he might be more useful, especially considering his experience on Lake Champlain and his years as a mariner, as a naval commander. He had been shocked at Boston's dilapidated defenses and observed that one British man-of-war could "take, plunder and burn" the city. If "a command offers worth my acceptance," he told Schuyler, "I should be fond of being in the navy which, to our disgrace, is now rotting in port when, if properly stationed, might greatly distress if not entirely ruin the enemy's army by taking their provisions ships."[27] At first he was bewildered, then deeply hurt by Congress's action. On March 12, 1777, he wrote the first of two letters to Washington on Congress's

very civil way of requesting my resignation, as unqualified for the office I hold. My commission was conferred unsolicited, and received with pleasure only as a means of serving my country. With equal pleasure I resign it when I can no longer serve my country with honor. The person who, void of nice feelings of honor, will tamely condescend to give up his right, and retain a commission at the expense of his reputation, I hold as a disgrace to the army, and unworthy of the glorious cause in which we are engaged. When I entered the service of my country my character was unimpeached. I have sacrificed my interest, ease and happiness in her cause. It is rather a misfortune than a fault, that my exertions have not been crowned with success. I am conscious of the rectitude of my intentions. In justice, therefore, to my own character, and for the satisfaction of my friends, I must request a court of inquiry into my conduct; yet every personal injury shall be buried in my zeal for the safety and happiness of my country, in whose cause I have repeatedly fought and bled, and am ready at all times to risk my life.[28]

Assuring Washington that he would "certainly avoid any hasty step that would tend to the injury of my country," Arnold brooded about Congress's treatment of him while he went about his job trying to dissuade his titular commanding officer, General Spencer, from a suicidal attack on Newport with untrained militia. After two weeks, believing he had been publicly disgraced, he again wrote to Washington. Since he was not being put to use and there was no need for him either in New England or at Ticonderoga, he could only view Congress's superseding him as "an implied impeachment of my character."[29] Arnold had trouble understanding why the ground rules for promotion were changed just before his turn for advancement came. Washington, besieged by threats of resignation by numerous less qualified officers, considered Arnold's treatment unique and unjust. Washington had to obey the will of Congress, but he also was moved by the unfair treatment of a valued officer whose services he wanted to retain. On April 3, Washington wrote a remarkable letter to Arnold:

It is needless for me to say much upon a subject, which must undoubtedly give you a good deal of uneasiness. I confess I was surprised, when I did not see your name in the list of major generals, and was so fully of the opinion that there was some mistake in the matter, that I (as you may recollect) desired you not take any hasty step, before the intention of Congress was fully known. The point does not now admit of a doubt, and is of so delicate a nature, that I will not even undertake to advise; your own feelings must be your guide. As no particular charge is alleged against you, I do not see upon what ground you can demand a court of inquiry. Besides, public bodies are not answerable for their actions; they place and displace at pleasure, and all the satisfaction that an individual can obtain, when he is overlooked, is, if innocent, a consciousness that he has not deserved such treatment for his honest exertions. Your determination, not to quit your present command, while any danger to the public might ensue from your leaving it, deserves my thanks, and justly entitles you to the thanks of your country.

General Greene, who has lately been at Philadelphia, took occasion to inquire upon what principle the Congress proceeded in their late promotion of general officers. He was informed, that the members from each state seemed to insist upon having a proportion of general officers, adequate to the number of men which they furnish, and that as Connecticut had already two major generals, it was their full share. I confess this is a strange mode of reasoning, but it may serve to show you, that the promotion which was due to your seniority, was not overlooked for want of merit in you.[30]

Casting about for support for a court of inquiry, Arnold brushed aside Washington's advice for a moment and wrote to Horatio Gates, revealing his deepest fears: "I know some villain has been busy with my fame, and busily slandering me." To Gates, Arnold quoted Otway's verse play *The Orphan:* while soldiers were bleeding and dying, there were "selfish slaves" who pretended to serve them while, instead, "like deadly locusts, eat the honey up, which these industrious bees so hardly toiled for." In this contemporary verse, Arnold found inspiration:

> But who will rest in safety that has done me wrong?
> By heaven, I will have justice.
> And I'm a villain if I see not
> A brave revenge for injured honor.

Arnold told Gates he thought the problem was bigger than one man, however: "I think it betrays want of judgment and weakness to appoint officers and break or displace them on trifling occasions," for their "sport or pastime," displace or disgrace him without "giving me an opportunity of being heard in my defense." If Congress continued to treat officers so cavalierly, "no gentleman who has any regard for his reputation will risk it with a body of men who seem to be governed by *whim and caprice*." He felt deeply hurt, he told Gates: "I sensibly feel the unmerited injury my countrymen have done me." Until he received satisfaction from Congress, at Washington's request, he would not resign, but "I cannot draw my sword until my reputation, which is dearer than my life, is cleared up."[31]

Arnold received yet another setback when he was told that Betsy DeBlois would not see him anymore. Lucy Knox wrote Henry, "Miss DeBlois has positively refused to listen to the general, which, with his other mortifications, will come very hard upon him."[32] Rejecting not only Arnold but his trunk of gowns as well, the charming Betsy had her heart set on the apothecary's apprentice. Arnold had been forced to set aside his courtship temporarily when the issue of promotion arose, but he may well have wondered if his public embarrassment was not somehow linked to his private humiliation. His first flirtation with Tory society over, Arnold headed home, wounded and shamed, realizing that there were many people who fully expected him to resign from the army once and for all. Washington himself had said that he expected Arnold to remain on duty only until there was no doubt that Congress really had passed him over. "The point does not now admit of a doubt," Washington's words resounded. "Your own feelings must be your guide."[33]

Rejected by Congress, spurned by Boston's high Tory society, Arnold went home to New Haven, where he consoled himself by joining Oswald's regiment in a furious witch-hunt for Tories in Connecticut that included the roundup of several Loyalists and the hanging of one. Colonel Oswald had apparently alerted Arnold that Loyalists from Connecticut who had fled behind British lines onto

Long Island had formed a regiment, the Prince of Wales Regiment, and were actively recruiting on Connecticut's South Shore. In fact, some 470 Loyalists were on the regiment's muster rolls in 1777 and other Loyalist units were also recruiting in Connecticut. Moses Dunbar, a commissioned officer in the Loyalist King's American Regiment, had been mobbed when the Sons of Liberty persecuted Anglicans in his hometown of Bristol. He was jailed but escaped to the British lines. When he was about to remarry, he had slipped home across Long Island Sound to visit his children and had been betrayed. Arnold, Oswald, and their men decided to make an example of Dunbar, who became the first Loyalist publicly executed in Connecticut. On March 19, after a brief trial, he was hanged before a large crowd on a hill outside Hartford (on the site of the present-day Trinity College).

After the execution, Arnold returned home. He was suffering from an acute attack of gout, and in a deep depression. About three o'clock the morning of April 26, there was a loud pounding on his door and the breathless announcement that the fifteen hundred British regulars and Prince of Wales Loyalists had landed at Cedar Point, some three miles east of Norwalk on the Saugatuck River, and had marched to Weston, where they had bivouacked for the night. Apparently, the courier told Arnold, their target was the main American supply base in Connecticut, located twenty-three miles inland at Danbury. Arnold was soon whipping his horse over muddy roads in a cold downpour, the aged General David Wooster, now commander of the Connecticut militia, and his young friend Oswald at his side. Behind them rode one hundred New Hampshire militia. At Fairfield, they learned that five hundred militiamen under General Gold S. Silliman were also pursuing the British toward Danbury. At five that afternoon, the British reached Danbury and set fire to the ammunition and supply depots. Then they marched to nearby Ridgefield and set fire to the Presbyterian church, which was being used as a military warehouse. They also burned houses belonging to Patriots. A surviving local legend tells how Loyalists painted black and white stripes on their chimneys so they would be spared.

With six hundred men and Oswald's three field pieces, Arnold and Wooster marched through heavy rain all afternoon, coming to Bethel, within two miles of the British, by eleven that night. In the distance they could see the flames of burning buildings. Their guns drenched, their numbers too scanty, they awaited dawn and the arrival of reinforcements. At eight the morning of the 27th, according to a British officer's account, "the militia began to harass us." The number of militia "increased every mile, galling us from their houses and fences—several instances of astonishing temerity marked the rebels. . . . Seven men from one house fired on the army and persisted in defending [the house] till they perished in its flames." The British had marched to within five miles of their ships when they encountered Benedict Arnold at noon: "Arnold had taken post very advantageously with a body of 5,000 men, which obliged us to form [ranks] and lose no time in charging the rebels."[34]

In fact, Arnold's company included only four hundred men detached from Wooster's force. Wooster and his few hundred militia had fallen on the British rear two miles outside Ridgefield, but six British artillery field pieces had raked them with grapeshot and they had broken and run. Wooster had fallen off his horse, mortally wounded, with a bullet in his stomach. His son fought off British attackers on foot, refusing to surrender until he was run through with a bayonet. All night Arnold's men had been digging trenches and building breastworks across a narrow spot in the road between two high ridges, as a second line of defense. At noon, three columns of British approached, the center column charging Arnold and his three cannon. Three British charges were repulsed with heavy losses. The fighting only lasted fifteen minutes, but it was fierce. Arnold's men, outnumbered five to one, took a heavy toll, killing seventy British with a withering fire before the British managed to flank them and charge with bayonets. Arnold was the last to retreat. As he wheeled his horse, he looked up to see a British platoon charging down a ledge of rocks at him. As he turned to fire at them, the platoon fired a volley at him. Nine bullets hit his horse. Seeing their commander fall, the Americans ran, leaving Arnold pinned under his horse, all alone to face the British bayonet charge. As Arnold fell, his pistols flew out of his hands. He struggled to get his boots free of the stirrups and get his leg out from under the dead horse. For a moment, he was helpless. A redcoat soldier ran toward him with a bayonet and shouted, "Surrender! You are my prisoner." At that instant, Arnold yanked free and lunged for a pistol. "Not yet,"[35] he shouted, shooting the redcoat dead. Then, vaulting a fence, he scrambled into a swamp in a shower of musket balls and escaped.

That night, Arnold gathered the militia on Chestnut Hill a mile from the British camp and within sight of the British fleet, in front of a bridge they had to cross. As the British pushed on toward their ships and forded the stream, Arnold attacked, aided by Lamb and Oswald's artillery. Only a reinforcement of Royal Marines from the British fleet rescued the British as the Connecticut militia, heartened by Arnold's stand, turned out by thousands until they outnumbered the British. But despite Arnold's pleas and threats, the militia refused to charge behind him and finally fled before a Royal Marine charge. Arnold was all over the battlefield, urging them to fire from stone walls flanking the British line of march, until a second horse was shot out from under him and a bullet tore through the collar of his coat during a final British bayonet charge that scattered the militia. When the fighting was over and the British rowed away to their ships, 10 percent of their force had been wounded, five times the rate of American casualties. On May 2, receiving the news of Arnold's bravery in Connecticut, an embarrassed Congress finally promoted Arnold to major general.

At the moment of Benedict Arnold's latest military success, he was attacked in print by his nemesis, Colonel John Brown. Disgusted because he could not persuade either Congress or Gates to convene a court of inquiry to prosecute his charges against Arnold, Brown had resigned from the army during the winter and published a pamphlet in his hometown of Pittsfield, Massachusetts, maligning Arnold's character—"Money is this man's god and to get enough of it he would sacrifice his country"[36]—as well as his military ability. Arnold could not leave the charges unchallenged: that would be tacit admission that they were not groundless. He decided to go to Washington, first, to seek his backing, and then to Congress to demand a hearing. After a May 12 meeting with Arnold in his headquarters in Morristown, New Jersey, and a perusal of Brown's handbill, Washington wrote Congress that Arnold was anxious to settle his accounts and clear up the slurs which he thought were so injurious to his reputation. Arnold also wanted to talk to congressional leaders about the terms of his promotion: while Congress had finally appointed him a major general, it had refused to restore his seniority. While Washington's letter of endorsement sidestepped the dispute over Arnold's accounts, he gave hearty recommendation for Arnold as a soldier. "It is needless to say anything of this gentleman's military character. It is universally known that he has always distinguished himself as a judicious, brave officer of great activity, enterprise and perseverance."[37]

Once in Philadelphia, Arnold mounted a campaign to win complete vindication. Dr. Benjamin Rush, one of Philadelphia's doctors and revolutionaries, was little impressed by Arnold but reported that among many Philadelphians, there was "a veneration bordering on idolatry"[38] for Arnold. Writing to Congress on May 20, Arnold enclosed a copy of Brown's handbill with the complaint that he was "exceedingly unhappy to find that, having made every sacrifice of fortune, ease and domestic happiness to serve my country, I am publicly impeached [in particular by Lieutenant Colonel Brown] of a catalogue of crimes which, if true, ought to subject me to disgrace, infamy and the just resentment of my countrymen. Conscious of the rectitude of my intentions, however I have erred in judgment, I must request the favor of Congress to point out some mode by which my conduct, and that of my accusers, may be inquired into, and justice done to the innocent and injured."[39] Arnold certainly took risks by exposing himself to the political crossfire of congressional factions. His boldness was immediately rewarded as he confronted John Adams, who was the most outspoken opponent of giving increased power to Washington and his generals. Adams and other radical leaders were worried about giving the generals political dominance over elected representatives of the people. At this early stage in the nation's creation, congressmen were struggling with fundamental questions of apportioning power between civil and military branches of government, between propertied classes and common people. Benedict Arnold had so far managed to ignore the political split between conservative money interests and radical revolutionaries, who wanted power kept as close to its local roots as possible. But Arnold was a rich merchant as well as a general, and his interest put him on the side of the conservatives in Congress, who supported him and the generals in the struggle over rank and seniority.

Because of his support for the conservatives, Arnold's petition was being opposed by radical congressmen who were worried that the Revolution might end up in a Cromwellian dictatorship. Radicals like John Adams feared that automatic promotion without civilian review would make the army independent of legislatures and the people. Adams was especially disturbed by Washington's growing power, even if Washington was generally scrupulous in his deference to the wishes of Congress. "I have been distressed," Adams had told Congress, "to see some members of this House disposed to idolize an image which their own hands have molded." There were already too many armchair generals who were more antique relics of bygone wars than serviceable field officers. "Schuyler, Putnam, Spencer, Heath are thought by very few to be capable of the great commands they hold. I wish they would all resign. For my part, I will vote, upon the general principles of a republic, for a new election of general officers annually."[40] Washington's open support of his officers on the seniority issue had provoked Adams, Lee, and other radicals at the very moment Benedict Arnold chose to petition Congress for a review of his career. Moreover, European officers with unknowable credentials were flocking to Philadelphia to offer their services to Congress in exchange for pay—and high rank, stirring up resentment among native-born American officers. Congress was considering promoting a French officer, Philippe du Coudray, to major general, despite all its insistence on state quotas, and *three* of Washington's best generals, John Stark, Henry Knox, and Nathanael Greene, all up for promotion to major general, were threatening to resign. When the three wrote almost identical letters to Congress, Congress passed a censuring resolution and sent their letters angrily to Washington, characterizing the generals' behavior as "an invasion of the liberties of the people." The generals were either to apologize "for an interference of so dangerous a tendency"[41]—or resign. The author of the resolution was John Adams.

Benedict Arnold's timing was bold and his frontal attack on Congress could have hurt his case badly, but he wisely admitted he could make errors in judgment. Men like Adams and Lee were open-minded and appreciated his candor. They plainly did not like the kind of backbiting John Brown had engaged in. On the same day that Arnold petitioned Congress and sent along Brown's diatribe against him, Lee, in a remarkable about-face, wrote to his friend Jefferson: "One plan now in frequent use is to assassinate the characters of the friends of America in every place and by every means. At this moment, they are reading in Congress an audacious attempt of this kind against the brave General Arnold."[42] That very day, Congress, incensed by Brown and moved by Arnold's confrontation, voted to make a public statement of its faith in General Arnold, passing a resolution "that the quartermaster general be directed to procure a horse and present the same, properly caparisoned, to Major General Arnold, in the name of this Congress, as a token of their approbation of his gallant conduct in the action against the enemy in their late enterprise to Danbury, in which General Arnold had one horse killed under him and another wounded."[43] Then Congress referred Arnold's complaint immediately to its Board of War.

The next evening, May 21, 1777, the Board of War heard Arnold's testimony until well past midnight. At four o'clock on the 22nd, John Adams sat down to write his wife, Abigail, a letter:

I spent last evening at the war office with General Arnold. . . . He has been basely slandered and libelled. The Regulars say, "He fought like Julius Caesar." I am wearied to death with the wrangles between military officers, high and low. They quarrel like cats and dogs. They worry one another like mastiffs. Scrambling for rank and pay like apes for nuts.[44]

At the late-night hearing, Arnold laid before the congressmen and several generals his private and public letters, orders, and what papers he had salvaged from the Canadian campaign. Fortunately for him, one of the board members was Charles Carroll of Carrollton, who corroborated Arnold's rendition of the chaos at Montreal, as Arnold attempted to stem a smallpox epidemic, defend a city, and feed a starving army, every step taken with the active participation of Carroll and Chase. Still, Arnold had to testify as to every step of his financial dealings from the time he had left to march on Quebec until the end of the battle at Valcour Bay. He reminded the board that in February 1776, besieging Quebec, he had begged Congress for a paymaster to keep track of the "multiplicity of accounts."[45] But Congress had failed to appoint one. Again, at Montreal in May, he had complained bitterly that he had no commissary, quartermaster, paymaster: he had to keep track of everything on the run. He had, he argued, kept the best records he could. But of $66,671 Congress had appropriated to him, he could not produce receipts for $55,000. On the face of it, this was damaging, but, as Arnold explained, he had been forced to divide his cash among divisional commanders on the march to Quebec, and they, with all their records, had been captured. He had also kept records of his purchases from the French Canadians, but many of these records had been aboard *Royal Savage* when it was burned, and others had been left behind in the flight from Quebec.

Indeed, Arnold may have presumed that all the records on the *Royal Savage* had been destroyed, but actually, as recent research shows, they were captured by a British boarding party and were placed in what was apparently the only public archive in Canada at the time, the Jesuit library at present-day Laval University in Quebec. These records show a serious attempt by Arnold not only to keep track of his expenses but, equally important, to document that he had scrupulously carried out Congress's and Washington's instructions to pay the Canadians, not pilfer from them. In addition to spending Congress's money, Arnold declared, he had advanced large sums of his own cash and lent the army money drawn against his own credit, at the same time borrowing "several sums of hard money"[46] from his officers and from such public-spirited men of wealth as Commissioner Benjamin Franklin and Montreal merchants, after Congress's paper money was refused as worthless by the Canadians. Arnold was not a good bookkeeper in the midst of a military disaster, but he emerged from the hearing with his reputation cleared. No proof of his pocketing money during the Canadian campaign has ever emerged.

On May 23, 1777, the Board of War reported to the full Congress that Arnold, with the corroboration of Carroll, had given "entire satisfaction to this Board concerning the general's character and conduct, so cruelly and groundlessly aspersed in Brown's publication."[47] Congress approved the report, officially clearing Arnold of all Brown's charges. However, the radicals prevented the restoration of his seniority as a general. He was temporarily distracted by a British feint across New Jersey as General Howe began the 1777 offensive and Congress again prepared to pack its bags and head for the hinterlands and safety. At Congress's request that he take command of the militia along the Delaware River and defend the capital city against what appeared to be a massive British attack, Arnold set aside his pride for the moment.

When the British temporarily withdrew, Arnold once again bombarded Congress and the Board of War with petitions. At the Board of War, he presented to Secretary Richard Peters a detailed plan for a campaign that was a facsimile of his march on Quebec but, if possible, on an even grander scale. He had been secretly conferring with board members about a surprise attack on present-day Mobile, Alabama, a Loyalist stronghold with a sizable British munitions dump. The expedition would be perfect revenge for the Danbury raid, and it would also deprive the British of an important trading center with neighboring Spaniards and Indians and impinge on British communications in the West Indies. Arnold planned a vast overnight acquisition of real estate for the new nation, making present-day Florida, Alabama, and Mississippi into one enormous fourteenth state. Arnold's intelligence told him that Mobile peninsula was defended by only "two to three hundred" British soldiers. "I should imagine ten or twelve hundred men sufficient for the expedition," he said. Arnold's plan was to do nothing less than travel to Fort Pitt in western Pennsylvania, recruit a regiment of Virginia and Pennsylvania riflemen, and "proceed down the Ohio and Mississippi to New Orleans which might be done in five or six weeks by bateaux." He would leave a captain and fifty men at Kaskaskia "to secure that pass." From the mouth of the Mississippi, he intended to portage to Lake Pontchartrain and "coast it" to the Gulf of Mexico—there would be only one portage of a mile. He asked the Board of War to send two or three frigates via Havana to help him knock out a British navy squadron based at Pensacola before attacking Mobile. Arnold seems to have formulated the plan with his friend Colonial Daniel Morgan, who was "well acquainted with the route and its difficulties"[48] and who would help him. Morgan was familiar with the Ohio and Mississippi, while Arnold knew well the Gulf of Mexico and its exposed British ports and outposts. If the Board of War would not consider him for the expedition, then he recommended Morgan.

Before the Board of War could act on his proposal, Arnold once again requested that Congress restore his seniority, but no longer frightened of an imminent British attack on Philadelphia, the politicians ignored him. This time, Arnold did not hesitate. He would no longer submit to what he considered a calculated insult. John Stark of New Hampshire had just resigned over the commissioning of du Coudray; on July 11, Benedict Arnold submitted his resignation to Congress. "Honor is a sacrifice no man ought to make," he said. "As I received, so I wish to transmit it inviolate to posterity."[49]

Celebration of the first anniversary of the Declaration of Independence at first distracted Congress from Arnold's resignation. Congressmen reveled, danced, and dined in sumptuary style. On the Delaware River, the officers and men of the Pennsylvania navy were joined by scores of flags, pennants, and bunting. At Daniel Smith's City Tavern on Second Street, Congress crowded in with their wives and friends as a Hessian prisoner-of-war band played music for dancing and merrymaking. Outside, an honor guard made up of British deserters serving in a Georgia regiment fired a thirteen-round musket salute. That night, the bells of ten churches and Independence Hall rang. The thick darkness of a humid summer night was broken by thousands of candles illuminating the houses of Patriots, but just as many houses were dark and shuttered: the houses of pacifist Quakers and Tory sympathizers. Before eleven o'clock, when the lights were ordered extinguished, a Patriot mob went on a rampage, shattering the windows of Quakers on Society Hill.

On July 10, one day before Arnold resigned and before Congress had a chance to accept his resignation, George Washington wrote a letter to Congress. Even as Arnold delivered his resignation letter to Independence Hall, a courier rode into Philadelphia with word that an all-out British invasion from the north had begun. Under their new commander, General Burgoyne, nearly eight thousand redcoats, Hessians, Canadian Loyalists, and Indians had swept down the west shores of Lake Champlain on a newly built corduroy road of logs. Trailing some 138 pieces of field artillery, by June 30 they had reached Fort Ticonderoga, now under the command of General Arthur St. Clair. The British attack down Lake Champlain renewed the divide-and-conquer strategy entrusted to Carleton and Howe in 1776. But Carleton had been brushed aside in favor of Burgoyne, a flamboyant member of Parliament, celebrated playwright, and career officer in the Coldstream Guards. Known for fast-moving, bloody, cut-and-thrust attacks with light infantry, he had fought in France, Spain, and Portugal during the Seven Years War, at the same time earning the nickname "Gentleman Johnny" for his humane treatment of his own troops. He had even written a treatise advocating treating soldiers as human beings and opposing frequent and brutal corporal punishment. He was also a reckless gambler in London clubrooms and an amateur actor, and was well enough regarded as a playwright to command the appearance of the leading actor of the age, David Garrick, in his plays. But as a fighter, he had proved a troublemaking correspondent, first causing Gage's removal, then Carleton's replacement—by himself. After Carleton's withdrawal to Quebec following Valcour Island, Burgoyne had sailed for London for the winter and apparently buried his quill in Sir Guy's back. His own plan, which had been approved by King George III, called for Carleton to remain in Canada while Burgoyne commanded a two-pronged offensive southward. Burgoyne was to lead the main attack up Lake Champlain, capture Fort Ticonderoga, and advance to Albany while a second army led a diversion down the Mohawk Valley to link up with Burgoyne at Albany. At the same time, Howe was to attack up the Hudson from his base at New York City.

By the time Washington wrote to Congress about the latest northern invasion, the British had already taken Fort Ticonderoga, the strongest of all American forts, without even firing a shot. Its garrison of 3,500 fled on July 5 after British heavy artillery appeared atop Mount Independence. The incompetent American engineer at Ticonderoga was Jeduthan Baldwin of Massachusetts, who had poured much of the American defensive effort into building a boom across the channel at the head of the lake that was supposed to halt British men-of-war. A small fort intended to protect the boom had been built along the shore, and another fort halfway up Mount Independence was supposed to protect this new redoubt. But Baldwin left the highest hill in the area, Mount Defiance, twelve hundred yards away, unguarded and within easy cannon range of the entire fortress. When Polish-born military engineer Tadeusz Kosciuszko, appointed by Gates, had arrived in June, Baldwin had refused to step aside, and ridiculed Kosciuszko's observation that a few siege guns atop Mount Defiance could pulverize all the forts in short order. When Gates had endorsed Kosciuszko's suggestion to fortify the high hill, the fort's commandant, St. Clair, had ignored Gates's order.

On July 2, as the British army had rattled down the Champlain road, a young Royal Engineer, Lieutenant Twiss, told Burgoyne that he had scouted the hill and thought a cannon could be taken up its steep slope. For two days and nights, artillerists heaved and hauled the siege guns with pulleys, ropes, and blocks and tackles from tree to tree up the steep Mount Defiance while British artificers quietly cleared and leveled and fortified the summit. By dawn on July 5, the Americans could see improvement high above them. By nightfall, St. Clair had ordered a full retreat, abandoning the fort without any attempt to attack and dislodge the British gun crews. That night, two hundred American bateaux slipped south to Skenesboro. St. Clair managed an orderly retreat, taking off the men from the new fort on Mount Independence and ordering the works there blown up. Then he led his forlorn force down Wood Creek and along the west shore of Lake George, following an old cart track.

The powder charges meant to ruin the guns on Mount Independence misfired, the bridge was left intact, defended only by a handful of drunken guards, the boom was shattered by the first British warship, and, in the light of the fires set by St. Clair, British grenadiers without field packs and after only four hours' sleep in three days chased the Americans with fixed bayonets, overtaking the American rear guard at Hubbardton, Vermont, where a bloody but inconclusive skirmish on July 7 left forty Americans dead and at least two-thirds of their numbers captured by the British. Vermont militia led by Seth Warner fought well, using forest terrain, deadly-accurate fire, and skilled tactics to keep the British at bay for two hours until they were unnerved by a fast-moving attack by Hessian jaeger marksmen singing to the music of their band as they charged through the woods at the Americans. Strangely, the British marched slowly south when they could have sailed, taking time to build a road for their enormous wagon train of personal baggage and military equipment. Meanwhile, most of the Americans made it south safely, stumbling and sweating through swamps, woods, and ravines for twenty miles on that first awful day of retreat.

Recognizing the old British strategy to cut off New England from more moderate New York, and thus blocking reinforcements of men and supplies and sever communications from the middle and southern colonies, Washington moved quickly. He turned to Benedict Arnold as the one man who could give the Northern Army the spirited leadership in the field that was needed immediately to stop the British onslaught. On July 10, as Arnold was writing out his resignation in Philadelphia, Washington wrote to Congress to send Arnold to recruit large numbers of militia:

There is now an absolute necessity for their turning out to check Burgoyne's progress or the most disagreeable consequences may be apprehended. Upon this occasion, I would take the liberty to suggest to Congress the propriety of sending an active, spirited officer to conduct and lead them on. If General Arnold has settled his affairs and can be spared from Philadelphia, I would recommend him for the business and that he should immediately set out for the Northern department. He is active, judicious and brave, and an officer in whom the militia will repose the greatest confidence. Besides this, he is well acquainted with that country and with the routes and most important passes and defiles in it. I do not think he can render more signal services, or be more usefully employed at this time, than in this way. I am persuaded his presence and activity will animate the militia greatly, and spur them on to a becoming conduct. I could wish him to be engaged in a more agreeable service, to be with better troops, but circumstances call for his exertions in this way, and I have no doubt of his adding much to the honors he has already acquired.[50]

The next day, July 11, Congress heard Washington's letter—one day before reading Arnold's resignation. Deciding that Congress had been officially ignorant of Arnold's letter at the time Washington's dispatch had arrived, Congress ordered an extract of the parts of Washington's letter pertaining to Arnold sent to him. Congress then directed that Arnold report to Washington's headquarters and follow the commander in chief's orders. Leaving as little as possible to congressional whim, Washington again wrote on July 12: "Being more and more convinced of the important advantages that will result from his presence and conduct, I have thought it my duty to repeat my wishes on the subject."[51] The question of Arnold's seniority would have to wait: his resignation had not been accepted.

Washington's confidence inspirited Arnold. He wrote to Congress, asking that his request to resign be shelved while he carried out his duty. He said he didn't doubt that when he had done what his country required of him, Congress would be more willing to listen to him. And he assured Washington that he would, for the present, be willing to serve under men promoted over him. Moreover, the prospect of being back in action reinvigorated him. He was far to the north on August 8, when Congress entertained a motion for his new commission to restore his seniority backdated to February 19, the day it had passed him over. After a long debate, another motion was made to amend the original motion to add "on account of his extraordinary merit and former rank in the army."[52] It was a rare moment in Congress, so tense that Congressman Henry Merchant of Rhode Island asked that the votes, usually made unanimous after the fact and entered as such, be recorded. Both the original motion and the amended were defeated, six in favor of Arnold's restoration to seniority, sixteen against. Only four states, Connecticut, Georgia, New Hampshire, and Rhode Island, each represented by one member, voted in favor, seven states against. Arnold was supported by one member from the New York delegation and one from Pennsylvania. All of Virginia's and South Carolina's delegates were absent. Only Eliphalet Dyer was present from Arnold's home state of Connecticut, and he voted for Arnold. The entire Massachusetts delegation, including John Adams, who had been so friendly to Arnold at the Board of War, now voted against restoring his seniority. To homely Puritan politicians, Arnold was vainglorious. Another Massachusetts delegate, former Boston schoolteacher James Lovell, may have represented the majority view when he sneered at the significance of "this mighty occasion." Arnold, he wrote, had "conducted himself almost without blemish in resigning, if a man may be said to do so who leaves a patriotic exertion because self-love was injured in a fanciful right which is incompatible with the general interest of the union."[53]

The issue was bigger than Arnold or the generals, Lovell reminded Congress, "really a question between monarchial and republican principles put at a most critical time."[54] A new delegate from South Carolina, Henry Laurens, found the reasoning upon this occasion was "disgusting": Arnold had been turned down "not because he was deficient in merit, or that his demand was not well founded, but because he asked for it, and that granting at such an instance, would be derogatory to the honor of Congress." Congress's behavior toward "good old servant, General Arnold, will probably deprive us of that officer and may be attended by further ill effects in the army."[55] One day later, abandoning its state quotas for the moment, Congress appointed a nineteen-year-old French aristocrat, the Marquis de Lafayette, as a major general with the same rank as Arnold. The Continental Congress made few worse judgments than it did in the matter of Benedict Arnold's rank and seniority, and few with more tragic and far-reaching consequences.

Fortunately for the Americans, it would be many weeks before Arnold knew of his rebuff by Congress; he had rushed to join the dispirited Northern Army, reaching it at dilapidated Fort Edward on the Hudson south of Lake George. The Americans there had retreated after the fall of Fort Ticonderoga on July 5, Skenesborough on July 6, and Fort Anne on Wood Creek which they fled on July 7. It now appeared that all Burgoyne had to do to reach Albany, his target, was to float his troops, cannon, and equipment down Lake George, push through some woods, and cruise down the Hudson to

Albany. American resistance was melting away. Arnold wrote Gates, who had gone to Philadelphia to seek Schuyler's ouster and his own promotion to northern commander, that the Americans would probably have to continue to retreat down the Hudson before they were able to make a stand: "I expect we shall be obligated to retreat to the other side of the Mohawk River, fifteen miles above Albany, whose passage we shall dispute at all events." While Arnold was pessimistic about receiving enough American reinforcements, he was in high spirits and ready to fight: "We have one advantage over the enemy: it is in our power to be free, or nobly die in defense of liberty."[56]

As if American prospects were not bad enough, the British pincers were beginning to close from the other side. Colonel Barry St. Leger and a force of eighteen hundred redcoats, Loyalists, and Indians had sailed up the St. Lawrence and across Lake Ontario, landing at Fort Oswego on the New York shore. Marching southeast along the Oswego River, they had laid siege to Fort Stanwix, which was defended by only 750 New York militia. Eight hundred militia led by rugged old frontier fighter General Nicholas Herkimer had been ambushed by Mohawk Indians and Loyalists led by Chief Joseph Brant and Sir John Johnson, whose father had presided over Indian affairs for the British at Fort Stanwix: a bloody battle, one of the worst of the war proportionate to numbers, began in the deep forest around Oriskany. General Herkimer was badly wounded almost at once, but he managed to draw his men around him on high ground and fight back fiercely. The Indians had retreated when Americans from the fort made a sortie, but Herkimer had lost nearly four hundred men, and he too retreated, leaving Fort Stanwix once again surrounded by the British.

When Benedict Arnold reached Fort Edward on July 24, Philip Schuyler decided to divide the Northern Army into two wings, giving Arnold one, retaining command of the other. Arnold promptly came up with an ingenious expedient to slow down Burgoyne's juggernaut, which depended on hundreds of teams of horses, wagons, caissons, and carts. He sent hundreds of axmen into the virgin forests to chop down trees in the path of the British advance, forcing thousands of British soldiers to sweat all day in the summer sun to clear the road. The British advance was slowed to one mile a day. Once again, Arnold was imposing delay, allowing time to gather American reinforcements. Schuyler's approval of Arnold's strategy, however, only provoked a hot reaction from his critics in New England, who wanted him to stand and fight the British. But Schuyler and Arnold thought that to do so prematurely would only sacrifice the army and open the road for a complete British victory. Schuyler was slow, perhaps plodding, but he was a patient man who hoped that once the American farmers had brought in their harvests and assured their families' survival, they would flock to fight the British.

The turnout of militia was increasing steadily, especially after the scalping of the Loyalist Jane McCrea by Burgoyne's Canadian Indians. She lived on a farm near Fort Edwards and was betrothed to a Loyalist officer in Burgoyne's army. Her fiancé had sent a party of Indians with a horse to bring her and her belongings to Burgoyne's camp. She was accidentally shot three times by pursuing Americans before she was scalped by the Wyandot Panther, who wanted the bounty Burgoyne was offering, equivalent to a barrel of rum, for any American scalp. Many New Yorkers had hoped to remain neutral and let the armies fight it out, but a carefully distorted and propagated story of the murder of a beautiful Tory engaged to a British officer meant that no one, Patriot or Loyalist, was safe from Burgoyne's murderous Indians. Hundreds of farmers took their muskets down and joined the American army; the Jane McCrea myth was quickly circulated throughout New England, and thousands more volunteers began to march. Benedict Arnold had once urged Washington to allow him to employ a large force of Indians on his attack on Quebec. Now he deliberately made the Indians into a vicious enemy to help play on fear to drum up militia recruitment. In his propaganda, he lumped Indians with Tories who would fight fellow Americans. "Infernal savages," he raged, "painted like furies . . . continually harassing and scalping our . . . miserable defenseless inhabitants . . . inhumanely butchered without distinction of age or sex." Arnold was working his men up into a white heat of resentment at Burgoyne for turning the Indians loose. Some farmers and their families "I am credibly informed have been roasted alive in the presence of the *polite and humane British army*."[57] Not only was Jane McCrea's scalping increasing American resistance, but the incident proved doubly damaging to Burgoyne, who wanted to try to execute the Wyandot Panther, but was warned by his staff that if he did so, all the Indians would desert him. But his show of displeasure at Indian depredations cooled the interest of many Indians. Burgoyne had counted on the support of thousands of Canadian Indians who usually turned out on the British side, but only five hundred had come south with him. Most of them defected from the British by early September.

Yet a well-disciplined force of Indians was making a critical difference to St. Leger's army at Oriskany. As Burgoyne inched south, New York troops were desperately holding out inside the run-down old star-shaped redoubt at Fort Stanwix while the British and the Loyalists slowly gathered strength. The rout of Herkimer's reinforcements left only the old wood fort between St. Leger and a complete sweep of the Mohawk Valley to the outskirts of Albany. Schuyler could hardly spare any troops, but in a council of war he argued that unless St. Leger was prevented from taking the valley, the American army would find the British attacking them from the rear. As some of the New England troops whispered that Schuyler was really a Tory who wanted to weaken his army so that Burgoyne could win, Schuyler decided to detach nine hundred Continental volunteers to march to the relief of Fort Stanwix. Actually, Washington had already suggested just such as assignment for Arnold "if anything formidable should appear in that quarter."[58] When Schuyler asked for a brigadier general to lead the dangerous mission, no one stepped forward. Arnold, though a major general who was now second-in-command, was angry at the accusations of cowardice and treason he had been hearing about Schuyler: he volunteered to lead the mission. Schuyler was grateful, and other generals voted unanimously to let Arnold go.

Setting out on August 13, Arnold made his primary destination the settlement of German Flats, some seventy houses clustered around a pair of stockades which were teeming with settlers who had fled to them with their horses and cattle at the first rumor of St. Leger's attack. Arnold realized he needed more than the help of terrified militia: "Notwithstanding my most earnest entreaties, I was not able to collect one hundred."[59] The militiamen, to be sure, remembered the terrible losses of one abortive relief expedition a month earlier. Outnumbered two to one, Arnold decided to turn to two tribes of Indians he knew were friendly to the American cause, the Tuscaroras and the Oneidas, but they too declined to help him. His force was still too weak to attack, but as he waited impatiently for more militia to arrive, he received the encouraging news from Schuyler that Burgoyne had received another setback. He had sent a large British detachment to obtain supplies and forage for his cavalry as well as to link up with New Hampshire Tories, and the detachment had been intercepted and cut to pieces at Bennington, Vermont, on August 16 by raw militiamen from the hills of the Hampshire Grants led by John Stark, the man who had also resigned after being passed over for promotion. The British force, made up of Hessians, Indians, and Loyalists, had been encircled and decimated by Vermont and New Hampshire frontiersmen. Virtually the entire British force had been killed or captured as its Indian auxiliaries fled. Hessian reinforcements had in turn been attacked by Stark, now aided by Seth Warner and four hundred crack Massachusetts veterans, and Burgoyne, in addition to losing one thousand men, now faced critical food shortages.

In an attempt to hearten the settlers and win more recruits, Arnold, still at German Flats, issued a scorching proclamation on August 20, threatening that if St. Leger's troops continued "in their wicked courses" and did not surrender within ten days, he would give them "no mercy."[60] But St. Leger was clearly moving in to finish his siege, his zigzag and parallel trenches bringing him close to the fort's rickety walls. When Arnold wanted to march the next day, however, he was outvoted in a council of war attended by Brigadier General Ebenezer Larned and all six of Arnold's brigade colonels. Reluctantly, Arnold deferred to them, requested more troops from Gates, redoubled his recruiting efforts—and thought of a stratagem. Arnold had spent enough time around Indians in Norwich and in the forests of Maine and Canada to know they could be credulous and superstitious. He also knew that the siege of Fort Stanwix depended on Chief Brant's Mohawk Indians.

Among the Loyalist prisoners he had recently captured and condemned to death for planning an uprising in Tryon County in support of St. Leger's invasion was a half-witted Dutchman named Hon-Yost Schuyler, a man well known to the Mohawks, who revered him as someone protected by the Great Spirit. If Hon-Yost was slow-witted, his mother and brother were not. When they went to Arnold to plead for Hon-Yost's life, it occurred to Arnold that the Mohawks might believe a rumor if Hon-Yost carried it. Arnold told Hon-Yost's mother that he would be spared if he would agree to go to St. Leger's Indians and spread the word that Arnold was approaching with an overwhelming force of thousands of troops. Hon-Yost agreed to the plan. To ensure that Hon-Yost would keep his word, Arnold kept his brother, Nicholas, as a hostage. Arnold had Hon-Yost's coat taken out and riddled with bullet holes, then sent him on his way. Behind Hon-Yost, he sent a trusted Oneida Indian scout, both to keep track of him and, once Hon-Yost was inside the enemy camp, to confirm his story. When the wild-eyed, bullet-tattered half-wit suddenly materialized in the Mohawk camp and was quickly surrounded at gunpoint, he blurted out his story. When the Indians asked him exactly how many men Arnold had, Hon-Yost gestured to the leaves of the trees overhead. The Indians were stunned. Soon, Hon-Yost was standing before Colonel St. Leger, repeating his story. This time he was more specific: Arnold was only twenty-four hours away with more than two thousand troops. The Mohawks, already unhappy at the slow pace of the siege and the paucity of scalps and plunder, had heard before of this fierce American general whom the Abenakis had named Dark Eagle. They were deeply agitated by Hon-Yost's report, and further shaken by rumors spread throughout their camp by Arnold's Oneida scout, who had told Indians whom he knew personally that Dark Eagle was coming to punish only the British and the Loyalists, not Indians who did not oppose him.

When the Oneida was finally brought before Colonel St. Leger, he not only corroborated Hon-Yost's story but further exaggerated the number of Arnold's soldiers. On August 22, Colonel St. Leger tried to persuade the Indian chiefs to stay another day to attack the fort, but it was no use. They insisted on leaving immediately, only pausing long enough to loot British supplies and steal officers' clothing and liquor. St. Leger abruptly decided he had to lift the siege: his men had panicked and were running wildly through the woods, leaving behind all their cannon, tents, equipment. Running behind them came the whooping and laughing Mohawks, shouting "Dark Eagle, Dark Eagle." The British and Loyalists fled all the way back to Fort Oswego on the shores of Lake Ontario; those who straggled behind were killed by drunken Mohawks, who later appeared in Oswego with dripping British scalps hanging from their belts. After a forced march of twenty-two miles on August 24, Arnold arrived at Fort Stanwix and learned just how successful his ruse had been. He wanted to pursue St. Leger and wipe out his force, but heavy rains made it impossible. Not only had Benedict Arnold saved the Mohawk Valley for the Americans, but he had smashed Burgoyne's pincers. Without reinforcements, without Indians, without enough food for his horses or men, Burgoyne now faced the swarming Americans with scarcely five thousand men. With considerable understatement, Arnold wrote Horatio Gates, the new commander of the Northern Department, that "there is nothing to be feared from the enemy in this quarter at present."[61] Then Arnold returned triumphantly to the American headquarters near Albany, ready to take part in smashing the British Northern Army.

Arriving at the latest American encampment at Stillwater on the Hudson River, about fifteen miles above Albany, Arnold found that Gates had reassigned him as divisional commander, in charge of his left wing. Shortly after Arnold arrived, Daniel Morgan rode into camp at the head of his division of riflemen, a timely and well-chosen reinforcement by Washington. There was no more talk between Arnold and Morgan of an expedition down the Mississippi. Now they were ready to finish the work they had broken off that snowy night in Quebec nearly two years earlier. For the first time, the Americans now outnumbered the British, and both sides realized there would be a climactic clash of arms in the forests before the northern winter once again invaded.

At American headquarters, Arnold found the climate completely changed. Gates, so long Arnold's friend, no longer confided in him: he seemed to trust only his twenty-year-old aide, Major James Wilkinson, who made it difficult for Arnold even to see Gates. "Wilky," who had been Arnold's aide for six weeks during the retreat from Canada, had begged Arnold to take him back as his aide before the Battle of Valcour Bay. Luckily for Wilkinson, who had accompanied Arnold on the Quebec march as a volunteer with a Pennsylvania rifle company, his importunate letters to Arnold had been captured aboard *Royal Savage*. They show a pompous, obsequious young man, excessively courtly even for those times, with little or no loyalty. Despite a career absolutely devoid of combat experience, he eventually rose to become commander in chief of the U.S. army before he was finally court-martialed for conspiring to commit treason with Aaron Burr. For the moment, he knew the wind was blowing in Gates's direction and that officers such as Arnold who had been close to Schuyler were now deeply in Gates's disfavor.

The power struggle that had raised Horatio Gates to the number-two generalship in the American army had been fought in the back committee rooms of Independence Hall within days of the fall of Fort Ticonderoga. Gates, after refusing Schuyler's request to stay in command at Ticonderoga and turning the post over to the inept St. Clair, had traveled to Philadelphia just before the long-awaited British invasion had finally come in early July. On August 1, after Gates and the New England delegates met, Congress appointed a committee to find a way to investigate the evacuation of Ticonderoga, as an alternative to the conventional court-martial, which would require the army's participation. After considering this committee's report on August 27, Congress decided to appoint another committee to collect the facts and transmit them to Washington with instructions to "appoint a court-martial for the total of the general officers who were in the northern department when Ticonderoga and Mount Independence were evacuated."[62] Since Gates and Arnold had been in Philadelphia at the time of the fall of Ticonderoga, the "general officers" could only have meant Schuyler and St. Clair. On August 28, John Adams, Richard Henry Lee, and Henry Laurens were chosen by Congress to make up this committee. Once the political machinery for a congressional investigation began to turn,

Adams and the New Englanders who blamed Schuyler for the debacle at Ticonderoga unleashed a smear campaign against him at the
same time they plumped for Gates's promotion.

Regional animosities stirred anew, with New Yorkers livid at the
ferocious attack on their countryman, Schuyler, and New Englanders openly accusing Schuyler and St. Clair of treason. Without
further investigation, Sam Adams wrote that the fall of Ticonderoga
had all the "evident marks of design."[63] And Gates was "always
beloved by his soldiers because he always shares with them in fatigue and danger."[64] In Sam Adams's opinion, there could never be
any question about Gates: "He is an able and honest officer."[65] The
congressmen from New England were proud to have dislodged
Schuyler. "I hope the conduct of Congress will give spirit and vigor
to our arms in the Northern Department," Henry Marchant wrote
home to the governor of Rhode Island. "Our noble exertions may
restore our honor and secure our country."[66] Arnold's request for
seniority had come up only a few days after the call for his mentor
Schuyler's court-martial. Four days after that, Congress made it a
clean sweep, demolishing the Arnold-Morgan plan for an expedition
to west Florida. "The vast expense of money and men and further
disgrace on our arms would be the result of so mad an enterprise,"[67] as Henry Laurens summarized the debate.

When Gates finally faced Schuyler at the Stillwater camp on August
19 after a leisurely march north to relieve him of command, he
rudely rejected Schuyler's offers of conciliation and advice. His
harsh treatment of the long-suffering Schuyler caused more bad feeling at the very moment when New York faced the worst crisis in its
history, invaded in three directions, and every New Yorker was
needed to fight side by side with New Englanders and men from all
over America. The day after Gates's arrival, Schuyler resigned. He
was eventually charged with "neglect of duty in not being present at
Ticonderoga to discharge the functions of his command" but was
acquitted with "the highest honor"[68] in December 1778. While New
Englanders called for his ouster for the loss of the forts that had
traditionally protected their back settlements, in the long run
Schuyler's unglamorous delaying tactics had been useful in slowing
the British, forcing them to use up their supplies and take the desperate risk of resupply that had led to their defeat at Bennington. Further, Schuyler had been bold enough when he needed to be.
Exploiting Burgoyne's sluggish advance, he had turned loose Arnold
and his troops, making possible the relief of Fort Stanwix and the
frustration of Burgoyne's pincer movement. Schuyler had cut off

Burgoyne's left arm and legs, buying a precious month of time for the American army to reorganize, recruit, and regroup. It was up to Gates now to finish the job that Schuyler had started, to finish off Burgoyne's wounded but still extremely dangerous army. Schuyler was philosophical about his removal: he wrote to Gouverneur Morris, "My crime consists in not being a New England man in principle, and unless they alter theirs, I hope I never shall be. Gates is their idol because he is at their direction."[69] To Gates, he wrote, "I have done all that could be done . . . but the palm of victory is denied me, and it is left to you, General, to reap the fruits of my labors."[70]

In their hundred-mile retreat from Ticonderoga in July and August, the Americans under Schuyler had withdrawn south of the Mohawk River, farther than Arnold had wanted, and were camped at Stillwater when he rejoined the army in late August. As soon as Arnold arrived, he saw the danger: the Americans were hopelessly exposed in open country and could easily be surrounded. The army's chief engineer, Colonel Kosciuszko, who was on Gates's staff and had voiced the same fear, now joined forces with Arnold. Kos, as the officers called him (Washington misspelled his name eleven different ways), had a genius for river fortifications and a flair for quick sketches, including caricatures. He was the impoverished son of Polish gentry and had fled his homeland after his attempt at elopement with a rich nobleman's daughter had ended unceremoniously in gunfire. He held a French captain's commission and had been educated at the Ecole Militaire in Paris and at the French artillery and military engineering school at Mézières. Not only was he an expert at river defenses and waterfront fortifications, but he was thoroughly grounded in European warfare: he knew from textbooks what Arnold knew from experience. Later, he would design many of the fortifications and defenses at West Point. He had friends in common with Arnold, who instantly recognized his abilities. He had been recommended to Congress by Arnold's friend Silas Deane and had helped Benjamin Franklin lay out the river defenses at Philadelphia before joining Gates's staff. With Kosciuszko, Arnold set out on horseback in early September to determine the best place to lure the British into battle on American terms. It was Arnold's idea to advance toward the enemy to provoke a British attack. By September 9, he believed he had found just the spot upriver at present-day Saratoga.

Gates and his staff officers joined Arnold and Kosciuszko at Bemis Heights, three miles north of the Hudson's confluence with the Mohawk River. From a bluff overlooking the Hudson, Arnold outlined his plan for the battlefield. Stretching to the west were high bluffs and steep hillsides dropping off into deep ravines to the north. The British could not get around the Americans to the west or past them down the Hudson if there were proper fortifications: the narrow pass would be a perfect place to build strong works and make an all-out stand. The British would have to try to outflank the Americans by attempting to circle to the west of the American line, but in the thick, hilly forests and stump-littered clearings, their artillery and dragoons, indeed all their European battle tactics, would be useless. They would be forced to fight American-style and could be beaten piecemeal.

As the generals looked on, Kosciuszko took paper from his portfolio and quickly penciled in redoubts, earthworks, bivouacs, company streets. Arnold placed Dearborn's light infantry and Morgan's rifles on the far left of the American line to interdict any British flanking attempt. In the center, under Gates's personal command, he put the best battle-hardened New England brigades—Larned's, Poor's, Glover's—and in the heavily fortified right wing, overlooking the river and protected by the bulk of the artillery, a scattering of Continental units to stiffen the spines of two thousand New York and New England militia. Gates gave his approval to Arnold's plan.

For seven days and nights the Americans dug in, their earthworks and redoubts spreading west from the river more than a mile across a narrow flat area and then a ridge of low hills, then turning and running north more than a mile to the farmhouse of John Nielson, a Loyalist who was guiding Burgoyne and would scarcely urge him to attack here. Along the north, the works followed the high natural barrier of a three-hundred-foot ravine, with Mill Creek at its bottom and thick, tangled woods on either side. Making free use of artillery, Kosciuszko ordered high earth-and-log redoubts built to guard a pontoon bridge across the Hudson at Bemis's Tavern, strong redoubts surrounded by abatis—deep, side ditches filled with fallen trees with their branches sharpened—all along the bluffs overlooking the riverbank, all along Mill Creek, and overlooking the Nielson farm to lay down a crossfire at all approaches to the stronghold. For a week, seven thousand men labored in the late-summer humidity, digging in, building breastworks, laying abatis, placing cannon to rake the river and its far bank, the hills across Mill Creek ravine, the hills to the west. By the time the British arrived, the American defensive position was virtually impregnable. No longer relying solely on ambush and wooden stockades, Americans were ready to fight the best troops in the world at the time in a battle that would, everyone understood, influence the outcome of the Revolutionary War.

*   *   *

Gates's acceptance of Arnold's plan for the American defensive network at Bemis Heights was the last time he took advice kindly from his second-in-command. By the end of that very day, September 9, a bitter feud had broken out between the two generals. It seems to have sprung from Arnold's belief that he could pick his own friends and his own staff without insulting, or being answerable to, Gates. Arnold could easily have played the game that Gates expected of him and that was typical of the military politics of the time. All he had to do was renounce his friendship of Schuyler or anyone who had been close to him and become Gates's sycophant. But Arnold refused to purge Schuyler's staff members and went on inviting them into his tent and to his dinner table. Arnold's arrival in camp shortly after Schuyler's dismissal with Matthew Clarkson, a young kinsman of the Livingston-Schuyler clan, as his aide was his first public refusal to remain neutral in the vendetta between Gates and Schuyler. But then Clarkson had invited other friends and members of his family to join the circle around Arnold, who either seemed too distracted preparing for Burgoyne's attack to object or thought the gathering clique was harmless. Next to find a seat at Arnold's table was Clarkson's first cousin, Lieutenant Colonel Henry Brockhulst Livingston, twenty-year-old son of Governor Livingston of New Jersey, who had been Schuyler's aide-de-camp. Another frequent guest was twenty-four-year-old Lieutenant Colonel Richard Varick, Schuyler's former secretary, who still wrote Schuyler twice a day. The young aristocrats around Arnold gave him a link to the New Yorkers turning out to fight for him. Varick, for example, had proved indefatigable in rounding up supplies and men for Arnold's fleet in 1776.

Gates took Arnold's friendliness to Schuyler's relatives as a calculated slap. He had spent two years struggling to overthrow Schuyler, and he was still jealous of his newfound authority. Moreover, Gates had the clever and insinuating young Wilkinson whispering in *his* ear. Wilkinson made no secret of his loathing for the Schuyler-Livingston clan. When Philip Schuyler was temporarily reinstated by Congress back before Ticonderoga fell, Wilkinson had raged that he could no longer "breathe the common air with ingrates, assassins, and double-faced villains,"[71] yet he had stayed on at Schuyler's headquarters corresponding secretly with Gates until his recent promotion. While Gates knew that Arnold had been sent north with the strong personal support of Washington, Gates had a powerful new weapon: virtual dictatorial powers for four months from the Continental Congress, which had passed a resolution empowering Gates "to suspend any officers for misconduct."[72] Gates, with Wilkinson's aid, evidently set out to push Arnold into defying his orders. One way to irritate Arnold was to remind him of John Brown: Gates did it by making Brown a lieutenant colonel under Benjamin Lincoln, who had passed Arnold in the line of seniority, and then inviting Brown into his staff meetings.

The Gates-Arnold feud came into the open when Arnold, who had been given the routine task of assigning newly arrived militia units to such brigades as he saw fit, assigned reinforcements from New York to Poor's New Hampshire brigade and Connecticut troops to Larned's Massachusetts unit. Both regiments were under Gates's direct control. It was a conciliatory gesture on Arnold's part, but also a natural assignment, as the new men would be inside the most heavily defended part of the line.

But the next day, September 10, Arnold was surprised to read in general orders that his assignment had been countermanded and hat the New York militia was being reassigned to John Glover's Massachusetts regiment. Arnold learned that the countermarch had been issued by Gates's adjutant, Wilkinson. Neither man had had the courtesy to inform Arnold of it before he read it in the orders of the day. Arnold, who was already touchy about rank after receiving the news from Philadelphia that Congress had turned down his petition for seniority, complained to Gates about a mere deputy adjutant general countermanding the order of a major general. Wilkinson's action placed Arnold, he argued, "in the ridiculous light of presuming to give orders I had no right to do and having them publicly contradicted."[73] Arnold said it was undoubtedly Wilkinson's mistake and not Gates's; Gates protected his young aide, said he would take full responsibility for the mistake, and promised he would rectify it in future orders, but he never did. Writing to Philip Schuyler, Richard Varick was no doubt happy to report that "a little spirit"[74] had broken out between the two generals.

A much more serious question was whether to go on the offensive when the British advanced south or to remain inside the new American fortifications and force a British assault. Arnold had told Gates that he wanted to "march out and attack"[75] the British, leaving some of the troops behind the fixed positions but turning loose Morgan's regiment and other seasoned units to fight American-style, taking advantage of the terrain, especially the trees. To wait behind earthworks was to invite the British to drag up their heavier artillery and begin a siege, a game at which the British were more experienced. Furthermore, argued Arnold, an American attack, if it failed, could be followed by withdrawal into the fortifications. If the British assaulted the works and drove the Americans out of them, they would have nowhere to go and could be cut up by the British. Gates overruled Arnold on launching an attack, but permitted him to plan a reconnaissance in force with Morgan's riflemen. But, increasingly, Arnold was barred from making any further suggestions and was no longer invited to Gates's staff meetings.

The deadly-serious infighting in the Northern Army was temporarily interrupted by the British attack on Bemis Heights on September 19. While the Americans now outnumbered him by roughly seven to six, Burgoyne still had more than six thousand crack redcoats. He had no desire to retreat to Canada, as his predecessor, Carleton, had done, despite the setbacks at Fort Stanwix and Bennington and the failure of large numbers of Loyalists and Indians to come to his support. He still fully expected General Howe to attack up the Hudson as he pushed on to Albany: he had not yet learned that Howe had interpreted his orders from London to mean that Burgoyne was to support Howe and that Howe had sailed not north to link up with Burgoyne but south, around New Jersey, and up the Chesapeake to attack Philadelphia. There were more immediate problems plaguing Burgoyne. Arnold's scorched-earth policy in Canada was still hurting him: he had too few horses to pull his mammoth artillery and supply train and not enough grain to feed those he had. He had only enough food left for his army for thirty days. He must press on to Albany or return to Quebec: no supplies seemed to be forthcoming from Carleton, no help from Howe. Yet he seemed to move as if he were in no hurry, as if victory were inevitable, perhaps deceived by the precipitate American retreat at Ticonderoga. His intelligence apparently was scanty: he did not know that Gates had more Continentals, more regulars facing him now than untried militia as a result of Washington's sending in some of his best troops. While Burgoyne played cards with his staff and carried on a love affair with Madame Rousseau, wife of his commissary, his troops laboriously built a highway from Canada north toward Albany on the east bank of the Hudson, apparently at the suggestion of Loyalist Philip Skene, whose vast wilderness acreage was thus improved in value by British engineering and labor. By September 19, as the British army crossed the Hudson by pontoon bridge twelve miles north of the American entrenchments, it was already growing cold in British tents at night. Winter was coming early this year, and red maple leaves were already appearing beyond the tall pine fringe along the river road.

Late in the afternoon of September 18, Benedict Arnold and his staff had ridden north to reconnoiter the British advance. Arnold knew roughly the British position: he had continually sent guerrilla parties of Morgan's riflemen out to harass British work crews and snipe at British officers. Varick galloped up to him and said he had spotted some redcoats on a distant hill. Arnold could see that the British would probably reach the Americans by late on the 19th, but for now he wheeled his big sorrel horse and returned to camp, disappointing Varick, who had been "in hopes of the General's ordering a party to attack them."[76] That night, the British camped on high ground less than two miles from the American army.

Just as Arnold had expected, the next day, September 19, 1777, the British tried to outflank the Americans. Burgoyne divided his army into three columns. General Simon Fraser was to be on the British right with 2,200 Loyalists, Indians, and British and German light infantry, trying to skirt the American left and get around behind the long American lines: Fraser's column faced Morgan's riflemen and Poor's and Larned's veterans. Burgoyne personally commanded the British center, leaving the bulk of the Hessians on his left to protect the artillery train and baggage wagons on the river road. It had been cold and foggy that morning, and Burgoyne and his staff had been unable to get a clear look at the American entrenchments as they advanced through the forest. By eleven o'clock, it cleared, and Burgoyne ordered three signal guns fired. The attack was on, as an American patrol quickly reported to Gates's headquarters in the row of tents inside the fortifications atop Bemis Heights. Shortly after noon, the British vanguard reached a 350-yard clearing while Burgoyne awaited word of Fraser's whereabouts on his right. In his command post, Gates was stubbornly refusing Arnold's latest exhortation to march out and attack the British quickly before they dug in. But Arnold already had permission for a reconnaissance force, and he interpreted this to mean he could send out Morgan's riflemen and Dearborn's light infantry from his left to make contact with the British. He also sent orders by his aides to get the rest of his division ready to march out to Morgan's support.

When Morgan's men reached the southern edge of Freeman's meadow, they saw British pickets sitting nonchalantly in the high weeds around the firehouse. One volley from Morgan's rifles scattered the British guard and drove all but its officers back to the woods on the far side: the officers had all been shot dead. When Morgan and his riflemen pursued the fleeing soldiers, they ran headlong into the unyielding center of Burgoyne's army, which now opened up with volley after volley. The riflemen broke and ran back across the clearing into the American side of the woods. For a moment, Daniel Morgan thought his regiment had been destroyed, and the six-foot-two, two-hundred-pound former teamster openly wept. But he continued to make the signal turkey call, and soon his men regrouped around him. When Morgan's men retreated, Burgoyne ordered his redcoats to march into the clearing and line up by regiments: three thousand redcoats with their field artillery took their places for battle. On the American rim of the forest, Morgan and Dearborn drew up their men and ordered them to open fire on the red line in front of them.

As an aide brought word that Morgan's prized regiment was in trouble, Arnold had all the justification he needed to order in Larned's and Poor's New Hampshire brigades. The reinforcements, finding that the riflemen had regrouped and were fighting back, took positions to their left. The American line now erupted in a volley at the silent British line. As scores of redcoats dropped in the tall grass, the British, leaving their cannons, turned and ran to their side of the forest, the Americans pursuing them, trying to capture the cannon and turn them on the redcoats. Before they could open up with the artillery, British grenadiers charged them with bayonets, driving them across the field. Back and forth the charges surged, and the volleys ran all afternoon, for nearly four hours, until there were nearly a thousand dead and wounded bodies in the field between the armies. As Arnold ordered out each fresh American unit, seven regiments in all, he extended the American line farther into the woods, away from the river and curling uphill and around the British right flank. On either end of the British line, for most of the afternoon, men stood and leaned on their weapons, unaware of what was happening until their brigade was sent into the fray, which was confined mostly to Freeman's Meadow. Most of the Americans, like Gates and his staff officers, never left the protection of their breastworks nearly two miles away.

All afternoon, Arnold spurred his men on, personally leading their charges and maneuvers, constantly exposed to enemy fire, preferring to lead by example more than by orders. When Fraser's light infantry suddenly turned and skillfully fell on Arnold's right, Arnold galloped up and down the line, rallying his men, shouting, "Come on, boys. Hurry up, my brave boys!" At the head of five regiments of troops, he charged the British center, attempting to break through. Then he led a rapid countermarch through the woods on the left, trying to break Fraser away from Burgoyne. His attack was bold, brilliant, well disciplined. When he led the charge down from a wooded hill, he very nearly overran the British: only heavy reinforcements of Hessians stopped him. Commuting back and forth between Gates's headquarters and the battlefield a mile and a half away on a big black horse he had named Warren after his old mentor, Arnold "urged, begged and entreated"[77] for more troops from Gates. According to veterans, Gates gave no orders and only once protested. When Arnold led seven regiments into battle, Gates protested that he wanted Scammel's brigade brought back to protect headquarters.

To break the stalemate, Burgoyne, who could see from his horse in the thick of the fighting that the troops in the center of the line were played out and in danger of being outnumbered and outflanked, ordered the Hessians to leave the wagons on the riverbank lightly guarded and relieve the pressure on his troops by charging across Mill Creek ravine to attack the American right. The Hessian reinforcements were led by Major General Baron von Riedesel, whose innovative tactics had routed the Vermonters at Hubbardton. He now was risking annihilation of his vital supply train and bateaux along the river, but Burgoyne was in desperate shape, every bayonet charge being repulsed by heavy American fire. With five hundred infantry and two six-pounders, Riedesel puffed to the top of a hill and ordered his Hessians to advance down into the supposedly impassable Mill Creek ravine, into the weak spot of the American right flank. Surprised, the Americans began to fall back in confusion. At this point, dashing back to Gates, Arnold finally persuaded him to order out Larned's entire brigade from camp to hurry around behind the Hessians from the woods, but Gates refused to let Arnold personally lead the counterattack. He made a point of sending Larned himself.

As Larned's troops went astray, becoming lost in the woods and plundering into Simon Fraser's British light infantry, Arnold paced and fumed. Now the sound of musketry came from the American left and right and grew heavier. Effective leadership at the front at this instant could have given the Americans a smashing victory, making Burgoyne give up the attack and retreat toward Ticonderoga and Canada. Gates and Arnold were outside the headquarters tent when Gates's aide, Colonel Morgan Lewis, rode up. Gates was sure he had made a master stroke by dispatching Larned: he asked Lewis how the battle was going now with Larned on the field. Not well, Lewis reported, the fighting was still indecisive. All afternoon, Benedict Arnold had been impatiently sending off couriers, dispatching regiments, pressuring Gates to attack: now he could not stand to remain on the defensive another instant.

"By God, I will soon put an end to it," he shouted, spurring his horse toward the firing. As he galloped off, Lewis remarked to

Gates, "You had better order him back. The action is going well. He may, by some rash act, do mischief."[78] Gates turned to Wilkinson and ordered him to bring back Arnold. Furious, Arnold had no choice but to obey Gates's direct order and return to headquarters. It was getting dark as the Americans retreated through the woods behind their earthworks, leaving Burgoyne in possession of the bloody clearing. The last army to leave a battlefield is technically the victor, but as he ordered his troops back to their camp two miles away and left behind 620 dead or dying men mingled with three hundred killed or wounded Americans, he was stunned at the American resistance. That night, as camp-following women from both armies stripped the dead, the moans of the wounded carried through the chill night air, haunting men on both sides forbidden to go and help for fear of touching off another round of fighting. That night, as Arnold fumed in his tent, Gates wrote off a long report to Congress, not mentioning that it was Arnold and his division who had stopped and mauled the British invasion, merely alluding to "a detachment from the army."[79] James Wilkinson perpetuated the myth, as late as 1816, after he was forced to resign as commander in chief in the Second War of Independence, insisting that Arnold, by then dead and unable to dispute him, had never even been on the battlefield the day that he stopped the British invasion from the north.

The tether Benedict Arnold usually kept his temper on had already been badly frayed by Wilkinson's reassignment of New York militia just before the British attack. He had only barely restrained himself when Gates, in front of their combined staffs, rejected his plan of attack and then, at the height of the battle, ordered Arnold to return from the front and, instead of delivering the *coup de grâce* to the British, lead the retreat. Gates's slighting of Arnold and his division by not mentioning them by name in the official dispatch to Congress only added to his outrage. Then, after the battle, Arnold learned that, with Gates's approval, General Lincoln, who had taken command of New England militia east of the Hudson, had detached Lieutenant Colonel John Brown to lead a raid on British supply lines between Lake Champlain and Lake George. Brown had succeeded in destroying nearly two hundred British bateaux and large amounts of supplies, and the singing of his praises in camp at Bemis Heights could not have helped Arnold's mood. The last strand of Arnold's self-control snapped on September 22 when, at Wilkinson's suggestion, and without consulting Arnold, Gates published orders that took Morgan's regiment of riflemen away from Arnold's division and reassigned them to his own: Morgan was only to take orders from him. Gates ordered Morgan henceforth to make all returns and reports directly to him at headquarters. Not only did the change make no sense—riflemen were best used on the flanks as snipers, raiders, fast-moving light infantry—but by stripping him of his best troops, especially those of his old comrade Morgan, Gates was publicly humiliating Arnold. Since Gates had not had the courtesy to notify him in advance, Arnold was sure it was a deliberate insult.

Charging into headquarters and brushing aside Wilkinson, Arnold barged into Gates's office and demanded an explanation for Morgan's reassignment. Gates, resenting Arnold's arrogant tone, began shouting at Arnold. The hatred between the two, so long ill-concealed, erupted in harsh tones and loud voices audible throughout headquarters. Arnold's aide, Brockhulst Livingston, said Gates was "rather passionate and very assuming."[80] Gates's aide, Wilkinson, who had done so much to bring on the confrontation and also witnessed the argument, said Arnold was "in great warmth" and "was ridiculed by General Gates: high words and gross language ensued."[81] Gates revealed his secret dealings with Congress, telling Arnold that he was unaware that Arnold was still a major general, since he had submitted his resignation to Congress before coming to join the Northern Army and had suspended it but not withdrawn it. Gates also questioned whether Arnold had a right to command at all. He further told Arnold that when General Lincoln arrived with reinforcements in a day or two, Arnold would be relieved of his divisional command. Adding insult to insult, Gates told Arnold that his services were inconsequential to the army and that he would be happy to give Arnold a pass to leave it whenever he wanted one.

Redfaced and outraged, Arnold broke off the argument and stalked out. He wrote a long and angry letter to Gates, which he evidently intended as a memorandum of record detailing the argument for future use. He itemized Gates's insults to him since he had returned from the Mohawk Valley. "For what reason, I know not," Arnold wrote, "(as I am conscious of no offense or neglect of duty) but I have lately observed little or no notice paid to any proposals I have thought it my duty to make for the public service, and when a measure I have proposed has been agreed to, it has been immediately contradicted. I have been received with the greatest coolness at headquarters, and often huffed in such a manner as must mortify a person with less pride than I have and in my station in the army." In addition to the lack of respect shown him, Arnold concentrated on the wording in Gates's report to Congress and on the general order affecting Morgan's place in the chain of command. In closing, Arnold asked that he and his aides be given a pass to leave camp and travel to Philadelphia, where he proposed "to join General Washington."[82] Later that night, Arnold had an aide deliver the letter to Gates. Gates was preparing for bed, and he did not answer that night. The next morning, without directly answering his note, Gates sent Arnold a brief unsealed letter for him to carry to John Hancock, president of Congress:

Sir,

Major General Arnold desired permission for himself and aide-de-camp to go to Philadelphia. I have granted his request. His reasons for asking to leave the Army at this time shall, with my answers, be transmitted to your excellency. I am sir.
HG
23d Sepr 1777[83]

Arnold returned the note to Gates with another letter the same day, demanding to know why he was not "entitled to an answer" and why Gates did not at least "condescend to acquaint me with the reasons which had induced you to treat me with affront and indignity." Even Gates's note to Hancock, Arnold said, was an insult. "If you have any letters for that gentleman which you think proper to send sealed, I will take charge of them."[84] Several hours passed before another aide darted from headquarters to Arnold's tent with Gates's reply. Denying "insult or indignity," he now sent Arnold "a common pass."[85] He would discuss the matter no further with Arnold, in person or in writing.

The fighting between the generals had thoroughly shaken many officers. Certainly a partisan but no more so than any other in the camp, Henry Brockhulst Livingston fired off a letter to Schuyler on September 23: "The reason of the present disagreement between two cronies is simply this: *Arnold is your friend.*"[86] The following day, Varick wrote Schuyler, "General Arnold is so much offended at the treatment Gates has given him that I make not the least doubt the latter will be called on [for a duel]."[87] Schuyler promptly replied that it was obvious to him that Gates had precipitated the falling-out because he would be indebted to Arnold "for the glory he may acquire by a victory. . . . Perhaps he is so very sure of success that he does not wish [Arnold] to come in for a share of it."[88]

The thought of facing Burgoyne's regulars without their most experienced and bravest general thoroughly disheartened the majority of Gates's officers and men. "The enemy are hourly expected," Livingston wrote to Schuyler. "General Arnold cannot think of leaving camp." The quarrel became public on the 24th, Livingston reported to Schuyler: "General Arnold's intention to quit . . . has caused great uneasiness among the soldiers."[89] To induce him to stay, General Poor (the man who had presided over Arnold's court-martial only a year before) proposed an address from the general officers and colonels of his division returning him thanks for his services and particularly for his conduct during the recent action, requesting him to stay. Two days later, on September 26, Livingston wrote that every line officer in the camp, except Benjamin Lincoln, had signed the petition to Arnold, "requesting him not to quit the service at this critical moment. . . . It gives me pleasure to inform you that General Arnold intends to stay . . . though no accommodation has taken place." While peace among generals had been publicly restored, not so in private. Faced with the opposition of all but one senior officer on the eve of battle, Gates had been working behind the scenes, making his idea of a peace overture. "It has been several times insinuated by Gates," wrote Henry Livingston, "to General Arnold that his mind has been poisoned and prejudiced by some of his [official] family, and I have been pointed out as the person who had undue influence over him."[90] Arnold, in other words, could return to Gates's good graces if he dismissed Livingston. Through an aide, Gates had suggested Arnold make "some overtures," the first of which would be Livingston's dismissal. "When this was told to Arnold he could scarcely contain himself," Varick reported to Schuyler. Arnold's answer was that his judgment had never been influenced by any man. Livingston also reported to Schuyler that Arnold would not sacrifice a friend to please the 'Face of Clay.'"[91] But while Arnold insisted that Livingston stay at his side, Livingston left of his own accord, in the belief that this would benefit Arnold. Varick left, too.

When Arnold still refused to sue for peace, Gates found another pretext for a thundering rebuke. Arnold, as he often did, had given a $50 cash reward to a soldier who had distinguished himself during the retreat from Fort Edward in July. Gates insisted that only he had the right to confer honors. Arnold replied he did not need Gates to lecture him on army procedure: Schuyler had been away and Arnold in command of the army on the day in question and he thus had the right to make the award. Although Gates conceded Arnold's point, from that moment he ignored Arnold altogether, excluding him from staff meetings. Arnold nursed his wounded pride, brooded about the way that the two armies were digging in. The Americans, if they could not fight, would desert rather than submit to camp discipline and boredom. The British could only benefit by waiting for reinforcement, resupply. To Gates, he kept firing off unsolicited letters of advice, unfortunately couched in terms that could only irritate the commander.

. . . Notwithstanding I have reason to think your treatment proceeds from a spirit of jealousy and that I have everything to fear from the malice of my enemies and conscious of my own innocence and integrity, I am determined to sacrifice my feelings, present peace, and quiet to the public good and continue in the army at this critical juncture, when my country needs my support.

Arnold's impolitic letters goaded Gates to action: "The army are clamoring for action. The militia, who compose a great part of the army, are already threatening to go home."[92] Unless Gates attacked, four thousand men, Arnold predicted, would desert. Burgoyne would be able to escape. In fact, cut off from official reports, Arnold was only half right: American reinforcements were swarming to Gates's camp from New York and the south, to Lincoln's growing New England army across the Hudson, until now, as the smug Gates knew, they outnumbered the British nearly four to one. At the same time, however, Arnold may have learned from his own sources that a British messenger had been intercepted with word that a British relief force was moving slowly up the Hudson. The dispatch had been hidden in a specially-made, hollowed-out silver musketball and swallowed by the captured courier, who was given a powerful dose of tartar emetic by his American captors, which produced the message before the man was hanged. In fact, Sir Henry Clinton had belatedly been instructed to make a diversion up the Hudson to draw off American troops from Burgoyne's army and, if necessary, to relieve him. On October 6, the British would land at Peekskill and capture Forts Clinton and Montgomery at the Hudson narrows, then move upriver to Esopus, near present-day Kingston, and burn the town with its important supply depots and shipyards. A fleet of sixty British ships was heading upriver from New York City as Arnold fretted in his tent and fired off one more taunting missive to Gates. He had no desire to command the army, Arnold assured Gates, he only cared "for the cause of my country, by which I expect to rise or fall." But he could not abide what he perceived as Gates's idleness in the face of the enemy. Gates had missed the opportunity to annihilate the British at the Battle of Freeman's Farm by not letting him press the attack, but "that is past." Then Arnold reached back into his childhood for a Puritan proverb that his mother had used to lecture him in letters when he was a schoolboy. To the commander of the Northern Army, he wrote, "Let me entreat you to improve the present time."[93] On October 1, Gates ordered Arnold stripped of his command. Gates himself took over as divisional commander of the left wing and turned over the right wing to General Lincoln. Arnold could either leave Bemis Heights or stay in his tent, but, stripped of command, he no longer had any official place in the Northern Army.

For three weeks, as the American commanders fought among themselves, the British continued to buttress their camp two miles upriver with more earthworks, trenches, and abatis, more redoubts and more artillery. All day and night now, there was the sound of gunfire. Morgan's riflemen, climbing trees hundreds of yards from the British lines, continued to pick off soldiers. At night, wolves howled in the forests. British communications to the north were cut off. Two thousand Canadian habitants had been pressed into service to drive wagons and build roads, and they began to desert in large numbers. Burgoyne ordered one flogged a thousand lashes as an example and warned that renegade Indians had already scalped seven Canadians trying to make it home. Inside the two-mile-oblong hilltop encampment, there was the stench of rotting horseflesh as animals starved and died after grazing the campsite bare. As Burgoyne sent off messengers every day by different routes with appeals to Clinton to hurry to his rescue—"Do it, my dear friend, directly"[94]—he had to cut rations in half. A blind giant in the wilderness, the British army had only nine days' short rations left by the time Burgoyne summoned a council of war in his marquee tent on October 4. He wanted to make a lunge for Albany by attempting to circle the American left wing, to "turn his rear."[95] Von Riedesel led the objections to the plan. Leave the artillery and the wagons, he urged, divide up the food and make a series of forced marches at night to Ticonderoga. Then Burgoyne did what he always did: he postponed his decision. On October 5, they met again in his tent. Von Riedesel was adamant: retreat or wait for Clinton. Simon Fraser supported the Hessian. But Burgoyne wanted to see if there was some way around the Americans, even if his plan was vague and open-ended. He ordered a reconnaissance in force for the 7th: he himself would lead it. He simply had to get close enough to the Americans to see how powerful their defenses were, as if there were some doubt in his mind that he was hopelessly outnumbered. As his troops reconnoitered, they could also forage. If still no help came from Clinton by October 11, then they would retreat to Canada.

At ten o'clock the crisp autumn morning of October 7, 1777, Burgoyne rode out at the head of fifteen hundred slow-marching regulars and six hundred Canadian Loyalists. Behind them came artillery and empty wagons. The men had been fortified the night before by a double ration of beef and rum. They moved some two-thirds of a mile southwest of their entrenchments. Burgoyne ordered a halt on a long rise in a field of sere cornstalks. While his soldiers formed a thousand-yard red line, servants and women camp followers went to work harvesting corn for the horses, heaving it into wagons. From his tent two miles away, Arnold soon heard the ragged gunfire of Morgan's men deployed behind trees, then there was steadier firing, British muskets in volleys, and deep-throated cannon fire, the unmistakable sounds of the British lining up for a pitched battle and American-style resistance. Arnold paced, fumed, finally jumped on his horse, watched what units went out, how many men.

Shortly after noon, Wilkinson rode up to headquarters from the direction of the American outposts along Mill Creek ravine. Morgan had suggested to Gates, his divisional commander, that the riflemen be permitted to attack the British west flank. Gates was not on the battlefield; he remained two miles behind the lines throughout the fighting. Customarily, a commander in chief could choose to remain at his headquarters, but it was expected that a divisional commander be out front with his troops. Instead, Gates sent back Wilkinson with a theatrical order for Morgan: "Order on Morgan to begin the game."[96] Morgan's three hundred riflemen were to work around the hillside to circle the British west flank. Poor, with eight hundred crack New Hampshire veterans, was to lead a simultaneous attack against the opposite end of the British line.

By two-thirty, they were in position, shrugging off losses from British howitzers lobbing exploding shells among them. Coolly lining up at the bottom of a hill occupied by British Grenadiers were New England, New York, and Connecticut militia. The grenadiers opened up with musket and artillery, firing too high, then raced downhill in a bayonet charge. The Americans stood still, fired a volley that shattered the British charge, then surged uphill overrunning the British position. The Grenadiers' commander was captured as he lay helpless with bullet holes in both legs. On the west flank, Morgan had attacked Fraser's Loyalist rangers, which had lost touch with Burgoyne's main party, hurrying through and around them until Morgan's men hit young Lord Balcarres's light infantry on the flank, from the rear. As the British turned to face Morgan, Dearborn's light infantry appeared to the British left, crossfiring them, forcing them to break and run. Balcarres bravely rode up and down the hillside, trying to hold his men, to no avail. His reconnaissance mission obviously turning into a rout, Burgoyne sent Sir Francis

Clarke forward to order a general withdrawal from the cornfield into the fortifications, but one of Morgan's marksmen shot Clarke off his horse. With both flanks exposed, the Hessians fought on, unaware that they had been ordered to retreat. Behind them, the redcoats and the women fled, leaving their artillery and their wagonloads of corn.

The fighting had gone on for a little less than an hour, but it had been a protracted agony for Benedict Arnold. When he could no longer endure the battle going on in the distance, he leaped onto his black stallion, Warren, and rode around the encampment, "betraying great agitation and wrath," as Wilkinson described it. He swore as he saw Gates lounging at his headquarters, at ease with his aides, hardly seeming to listen as messengers brought him news of the battle. At one point, Gates seemed to look toward Arnold; then he looked through him. Disgusted, Arnold spurred his horse toward the lines, where the men cheered him, sure he was about to lead them across the open fields against the British encampment. But Arnold could only wave at them with his sword and ride on. He rode to the ramparts and stared out at the puffs of smoke from cannon, the limp bodies of men being dragged back, the couriers dashing past him toward Gates. Finally, he could take it no more. Insubordination or no he must take part in the kill he had worked for so long on Lake Champlain, on the Kennebec, at Quebec, and in Valcour Bay. Shouting "Victory or death," he plunged his spurs into his horse and hauled in the reins until the big charger cleared a sally port. Then he rode into the woods toward Morgan, Dearborn, his men. Gates came out of his tent to see Arnold disappear toward the battlefield. Gates shouted for an aide, Major John Armstrong, to go order Arnold back. Mysteriously, Armstrong's fast horse never did overtake Arnold, who was by this time far ahead, following a wagon trail between tall trees. Rounding up stragglers, he turned around and led them, cheering, toward the enemy. At the edge of the forest, Larned's smoke-streaked men had paused at a stream to drink. They were familiar faces, cheering men who hurried off after Arnold: "Come on, brave boys, come on!" His horse leaping the stream, Arnold urged it up the exposed hillside toward the Hessians. Suddenly, as the Hessians fired, he realized he was alone: Larned's men had broken and run back toward the woods. Wheeling his horse, Arnold returned to the stream, rallied the men for another charge. This time it was the Hessians who broke and ran, fleeing this madman, leaving him in possession of a cornfield littered with bodies. Wilkinson later arrived and described the scene: "In a square space of ten or fifteen yards, lay eighteen grenadiers in the agonies of death and three officers propped up against the stumps of trees, mortally wounded, bleeding and almost speechless."[97]

As the British fled Arnold's charge, Brigadier Simon Fraser tried to form a new line, his Loyalists turning and unleashing a murderous fire while Fraser rode up and down on a big steel-gray mare, urging on his men. The Americans began to panic as Arnold raged at them to keep up the charge. Turning to Morgan, Arnold shouted, "That man on the gray horse is a host in himself and must be disposed of."[98] Morgan summoned his best sharpshooters. A shot first hit Fraser's saddle as he charged up and down the line, keeping the 24th Regiment firing in volley. A second shot cut through the mare's mane. Fraser's aides urged him to get off to one side, out of the line of fire, but Fraser refused, spurring his horse on up the hill. A third shot tore into Fraser's stomach. He slumped forward. An aide took the reins and led him off the battlefield.

As Burgoyne, who had bullet holes in his collar and coat, led the retreat through a sally port into his encampment, he told Lieutenant Anburey, "Sir, you must defend this post to the very last man."[99] As he spoke, British heavy guns blasted away at the approaching American column on the British right. It was obvious that the Americans intended to attack the camp. The cannon fire became deafening, the clouds of white smoke all but obliterating the view of the attacking troops. The remnants of Fraser's light infantry now took posts on the walls of Breymann's Redoubt with Hessians assigned to hold this fortified strongpoint in front of the main British earth-and-log fort.

Arnold appeared at once deranged and exhilarated, barreling downhill on his big horse, his sword flailing: Morgan's men were reloading and preparing to follow him when Arnold distractedly galloped after one of them, raised his sword, and struck his own rifleman on the head. The man was only stunned: Arnold was not aware that he had ever done it, he later said. As he came up to one group of troops, he shouted, "What regiment is this?"

"Colonel Latimer's, sir."

"Ah, my old Norwich and New London friends. God bless you! I am glad to see you. Now come on, boys. If the day is long enough, we'll have them all in hell before night!"[100]

As Major Armstrong still tried to overtake him, Arnold galloped out of the forest and out onto Freeman's meadow. At the far end of the field was a hollow square of logs: the British were firing cannon and musket as Arnold led his men in a charge across the open space, driving off the Canadian Loyalists. Now he decided to shift the attack. Shouting to his men to follow, he found a narrow path through the long line of pointed abatis that lined the trenches in

front of the British forts. Both armies held their breath as he lashed
his foam-flecked horse the entire length of the British line amid
sheets of grapeshot, musketballs, cannon shells. The path had been
left for British patrols: Arnold now raced its length, leaning over his
horse's mane as he charged right across the British line of fire. Miraculously, neither man nor mount was hit. At the end of the main
British line were log cabins and beyond them a redoubt, a small fort
positioned on high ground to protect the British camp from the right
flank; it was defended by Colonel Breymann and two hundred Hessians. Now Arnold yelled for his men to follow him. Galloping
around behind the redoubt, in a torrent of gunfire, he rode through
a sally port into its rear, his men right behind him. From the walls
inside, Hessians poured a volley of fire down at Arnold's rushing
soldiers: his horse, hit several times, collapsed at the rear of the redoubt, throwing him clear. As he got up and brandished his sword,
a wounded Hessian rolled over and fired. Arnold went down.
"Don't hurt him," he yelled as his men lunged to bayonet the Hessian. "He's a fine fellow. He only did his duty."[101]

Morgan and other officers rushed over: Arnold waved them
away. More Americans crowded into the redoubt, firing British cannon and American rifles at a British counterattack, beating it back in
the last round of fighting in the decisive Battle of Saratoga. Then
they made a sling of a torn tent and ridgepoles for a litter and prepared to carry Arnold, writhing in pain, back inside the American
camp. As officers asked how bad it was, Gates's aide bent over him,
delivering the order to return to his quarters. Arnold was in too
much pain to laugh. Then Dearborn came closer. "Where are you
hit?" he asked.

"In the same leg," Arnold whispered. "I wish it had been my
heart."[102]

13

"AMERICA HAS SEEN ITS BEST DAYS"

See General Gates and Dicky Peters.
With Jimmy Mease of noted worth.
Richard and Tom—the prince of eaters—
Like ancient heroes sally forth!

Anonymous Loyalist ballad, Philadelphia, 1777

For nearly a month, the dull pounding of distant cannon fire had rattled the windowpanes in Judge Edward Shippen's mansion on South Fourth Street in the Society Hill section of Philadelphia. Lawyer and merchant Shippen, a gray-haired, heavy-jowled man with sad eyes and a large nose, had been trying to remain neutral in the Revolution, doing all he could to keep his three beautiful daughters clear of the fighting and the infighting. He had taken them to a farm in New Jersey, but there the neighbors had smashed his windows and called them Tories and accused him of treason. Then they had gone to a country house at the Falls of Schuylkill, just west of Philadelphia, while he shuttled back and forth to be seen in his Philadelphia house. As civil war ebbed and rushed around them, the Shippens had learned a sort of calm that came with prolonged terror. They had watched as hundreds of friends fled the city in panic in the winter of 1776. Then, in early July 1777, at the alarm that the British were marching toward Philadelphia to seize the American capital, the Shippens had fled as congressmen sent their wives home and General Arnold rode out with the Pennsylvania militia to ward off the invaders. But it had been just another British feint to prevent Washington from reinforcing Gates's Northern Army, and as Arnold rode north toward Saratoga and Congress unpacked again, Judge Shippen brought back his wife and daughters and uncrated the family silver.

But there was little respite for Shippen and his Quaker neighbors. Society Hill was deeply divided by the civil war. The Quakers were trying to police themselves to preserve their neutrality and protect their property. In fact, some 418 Quakers were disowned by the Religious Society of Friends for defecting to form the Free Quakers, better known as the Fighting Quakers, who had joined the revolutionary army. The Shippen family itself was sharply divided, with the preponderance on the revolutionary side. Few Philadelphians had better revolutionary connections, but because Judge Shippen had been an official in the old Penn proprietary government, which had tried to block the revolutionaries in the province, he was considered by Philadelphia's radicals to be a *de facto* Tory.

In late August 1777, the Shippens had watched from an attic window as a long stream of rebel soldiers shambled twelve abreast with hemlock sprigs in their tricorn hats down cobbled Second Street for two solid hours on their way south to Wilmington, Delaware, to fend off the long-dreaded British attack on Philadelphia. In early September, as members of Congress and thousands of their adherents crowded their belongings into every available cart and wagon and headed west into the Pennsylvania hinterlands, Quaker refugees streamed into Philadelphia. They were fleeing from the advancing redcoats and Loyalists eager to join the British from Maryland and Delaware and from the Brandywine country of southern Pennsylvania, where a great battle was fought at Chadd's Ford on September 11. For three days, wagonloads of American wounded headed up Second Street on their way to the hospitals of Philadelphia. By late September, the British army under Howe had badly outmaneuvered Washington, cutting him off from the city. On September 19, the news hit home that Philadelphia was actually about to fall to the British.

One week later, on September 26, the great red column of the British army led by Major General Charles Lord Cornwallis marched along the Schuylkill River toward Philadelphia. Radical Pennsylvania leaders, following the orders of the Continental Congress to arrest all "notoriously disaffected"[1] citizens, rounded up forty leading Quakers, all of them friends, relatives, or neighbors of the Shippens. Breaking into suspected Tories' homes, the revolutionary committeemen ransacked the houses for incriminating papers, then herded the Quakers at gunpoint into Masonic Hall, little more than a block away from the Shippens' home. The radicals refused to honor writs of habeas corpus, and twenty-one Quaker prisoners were crammed into carts and escorted toward imprisonment in the hills of Virginia by the elite First Troop Philadelphia City Cavalry. Many of the Quakers were stoned by rebel mobs along the way.

Judge Shippen was spared and induced to sign a revolutionary committee's parole agreement, promising he would not try to leave Pennsylvania or engage in politics in any way. Once again, he trundled his family back to Society Hill, just ahead of the British invaders. On September 26, Elizabeth Drinker recorded in her diary, "Well, here are the English in earnest!" The main British force, led by two Tory guides (both sons of leading Quakers) and a marching band, swung down Market Street behind Lord Cornwallis. Huge crowds lined the streets, waving and shouting with joy as thousands of redcoated British and blue-coated Hessians, a long train of horse-drawn artillery, and another marching band passed by. "Baggage wagons, Hessian women, and horses, cows, goats and asses brought up the rear," noted Mrs. Fisher. Three days later, British quarter-masters were "going about this day, numbering the houses with chalk on the doors."[2] The British occupation of Philadelphia was beginning with a roundup of American sympathizers on Society Hill: their houses would soon be commandeered, looted, turned into British barracks. Edward Shippen hastened to introduce himself and make the point that he had been a *British* official.

As the British army arrived in Philadelphia, the British navy, hampered by adverse winds, was fighting its way up the Delaware River. For nearly a month, British naval gunners dueled with the Pennsylvania navy and British landing parties maneuvered to capture the American river forts before Washington finally withdrew his forces, battered but undefeated, into winter quarters at Valley Forge, twenty-two miles to the west. The American capital became a British fortress.

The Hessian's bullet had shattered Benedict Arnold's left femur. Ordinarily, the leg would have been amputated without question, but Arnold vehemently resisted the efforts of army doctors trying to help him. Carried first to Gates's headquarters in a makeshift litter, he was then taken for an excruciating wagon ride, part of a long cavalcade of the wounded to a three-story military hospital in Albany, thirty miles away. When the doctors insisted his leg had to come off, Arnold argued back that he would rather be dead than crippled. For two days and nights, in great pain, he fought to keep his leg. At the same time, he was extremely anxious that without him, Gates would let the British slip away. Out of danger by the night of October 12, he demanded to be kept posted as the British retreated north, attempting to escape to Ticonderoga. Officers who brought him news found him "much weakened," "in great pain," "very ill." Young Dr. James Thacher, who had first seen Arnold recruiting his Quebec army on Cambridge Common more than two years earlier, sat up with him all night: "I watched with the celebrated General Arnold, whose leg was badly fractured by a musket ball. He is very peevish and impatient under his misfortunes, and required all my attention during the night." Thacher noted that Arnold was strong and seemed to recover "very fast"; by the 15th, there was no more talk of amputation. When Burgoyne surrendered on October 17, Arnold recovered even faster: Thacher reported he was "in great spirits, although he has a touch of gout."3 If Arnold had heard Burgoyne give him credit for the victory to Gates and to the secretary of state, Lord Germain, in London, he might not have lingered in the hospital so long. Gates, on the other hand, gave Arnold no credit for the victory, mentioning to Congress only that Arnold had been wounded. Praising Wilkinson in his official report as a "military genius,"4 Gates had recommended that Congress brevet him as a brigadier general. Wilkinson had, however, annoyed Congress by taking more than three weeks to ride to the provisional capital at York, Pennsylvania, stopping off at Reading to visit his fiancée for a week and to plot and gossip with generals along the way. Samuel Adams at first resisted making the twenty-year-old a general—instead, he wanted Congress to award him a pair of spurs. In the end, Congress gave the boyish messenger who brought the good news a generalship— and made him secretary of its Board of War.

As the wives of generals and congressmen at York began to dance a new step—"The Burgoyne Surrender"—Arnold basked in news sent to him by Washington. Finally yielding to popular pressure, Congress authorized Washington on November 29 to restore Arnold to his old seniority. His victory was complete, even if his wound made further military service doubtful. It was two more months, however, before the busy Washington got around to notifying Arnold of his victory over Congress. In the meantime, Arnold, out of action, brooded daily about a letter that did not come from Washington: he knew of Congress's action weeks before the commander in chief found time to write. Finally, Washington wrote him a congratulatory note signed "affectionately,"5 and sent him a decorative sword knot as a mark of honor, but he also sent one to Lincoln at the same time. It was two more months before Arnold answered Washington with the news that he was still too weak to fight in the coming campaign. By the time he wrote his thanks to Congress on January 11, 1778, for restoring his army seniority, Arnold was finally able to sit up in bed. He still could not walk, but he was about to try his weight on a crutch. In another month, as spring came on, after three and a half months in the hospital, Arnold could finally be carried on a litter to his carriage for the painfully long ride home. He had to make the trip in slow, easy stages. At Kinderhook, New York, a doorjamb had to be ripped out of Dr. John Quilhot's house to allow Arnold's entry on his litter. One day's ride from New Haven, he could go no farther and had to stop at Middletown on the Connecticut River, where he received a hero's welcome and stayed for several weeks with his old merchant-soldier friend General Comfort Sage. Learning to hobble around on crutches, Arnold visited waterfront taverns with Sage and with his new military secretary, Major David Franks. Over a pipe of tobacco and a glass of wine, Arnold talked with successful lawyers, merchants, and militia officers about Congress and the terrible condition of Washington's army at Valley Forge, outside Philadelphia, and of the inexplicable failure of the British to attack it. He heard reports of riches made on privateering voyages. His own ships captured or sold off, his Caribbean and Canadian trade ruined by the war, Arnold had advanced so much money on the public account that he was beginning to feel the pinch. He wrote Hannah for funds to hedge his losses, but she was forced to answer that Congress still had not paid his military salary, now two and a half years in arrears. His friend Sage helped him arrange to buy a one-fourth share in a large privateer, the ten-gun *General McDougall,* a captured British troop transport. He celebrated by going shopping for gold buttons for his uniform, for a new mounting for his officer's sword, for a rose-gold ring studded with four diamonds which he intended to give to Betsy DeBlois: his confidence returning, the lonely Arnold again took up his pursuit of Betsy, now seventeen. On April 8, 1778, he wrote her the first of two letters extant:

Twenty times have I taken my pen to write to you and, as often has my trembling hand refused to obey the dictates of my heart. A heart which has often been calm and serene amidst the clashing of arms and all the din and horrors of war trembles with diffidence and the fear of giving offence when it attempts to address you on a subject so important to its happiness. Long have I struggled to efface your heavenly image from it. Neither time, absence, misfortunes, nor

*your cruel indifference have been able to efface the deep impression
your charms have made. And will you doom a heart so true, so
faithful, to languish in despair? Shall I expect no returns to the most
sincere, ardent and disinterested passion? Dear Betsy, suffer that
heavenly bosom (which surely cannot know itself the cause of misfortune without a sympathetic pang) to expand with friendship at
last and let me know my fate. If a happy one, no man will strive
more to deserve it; if on the contrary I am doomed to despair, my
latest breath will be to implore the blessing of heaven on the idol
and only wish of my soul.*[6]

From Arnold's second letter, two weeks later, it is obvious that
Betsy, or more likely her mother, did not want him to pursue his
siege, but she did not positively forbid it, either:

Dear Betsy—
*Had I imagined my letter would have occasioned you a mo-
ment's uneasiness, I never should forgive myself for writing it. You
entreat me to solicit no further for your affections. Consider, Dear
Madam, when you urge impossibilities I cannot obey; as well might
you wish me to exist without breathing as cease to love you, and
wish for a return of affection. . . . How can I decline soliciting your
particular affections, on which the whole happiness of my life depends.*

That Arnold's infatuation was one-sided, he did not deny: "A union
of hearts I acknowledge is necessary to happiness, but give me leave
to observe that true and permanent happiness is seldom the effect of
an alliance formed on a romantic passion, when fancy governs more
than judgment." His friendship and esteem were the basis for building "lasting happiness." When there is "tender and ardent passion
on one side and friendship and esteem on the other," the result
would be "every tender sentiment." He also apologized for his initial
reaction to her rejection: "Pardon me, dear Betsy, if I called you
cruel. . . . Consult your own happiness, and it incompatible with
mine, forget there is so unhappy a wretch, for let me perish if I
would give you one moment's pain."[7] Since his first assault had
been repulsed by the redoubtable Mrs. DeBlois, Arnold made one
more flanking attack: he sent a letter asking Betsy's Tory father for
her hand. Betsy's mother evidently intercepted the letter. Sending off
his proposal, he left for New Haven, arriving to another hero's welcome on May 4. It was the finest reception Benedict Arnold ever
received in his adoptive hometown. Applauded by people who had

once shunned him, adored by his sister and his sons, he had reached
the zenith of his military career. The American victory at Saratoga
had reversed the tide of the Revolutionary War. After Arnold's
rearguard victory at Valcour Bay and his shocking attacks at
Saratoga, the British would never again mount a major offensive
against the Americans from the north. The defeat of Burgoyne's
army was all Benjamin Franklin in Paris needed to convince the
French that the Americans not only would stand and fight but, with
military and financial help of European allies, could ultimately defeat the British. Before another winter was over, Franklin and King
Louis XVI signed a treaty of alliance. Arnold's bold tactics had
bought a new nation time to build an army, even if they had left
him, at age thirty-six, partially crippled with one leg shorter than the
other and a pain that never completely went away.

Hemmed in on all sides by American forces for nearly three months,
British-occupied Philadelphia was badly overcrowded and hungry.
British soldiers lived on a half-pound salted meat ration a day, while
thousands of their American prisoners had less than an ounce of
meat a day. Two-thirds of the merchants had cleaned out or hidden
their goods and fled: only 120 shops remained open in the entire
city, and they had nothing to sell as long as British transports were
blockaded on the Delaware. The great covered sheds on Market and
Second streets were all but empty as farmer's normal twice-weekly
deliveries were intercepted by Washington's patrols on roads leading
into the city. According to a census made immediately by the British,
only one-fourth of the inhabitants had fled, most of them men of
fighting age. Only 11 percent of the houses had been abandoned:
this meant that the supply of housing for officers and men was severely limited. British quartermasters assigned generals and their
staffs to houses according to a strict hierarchy that ranked the
houses of the city. General Howe was given the Richard Penn mansion at Sixth and Market streets; Major General Grey and his staff,
including Major André, were allotted the square red brick mansion
of Benjamin Franklin on Market Street. The city's mayor, Samuel
Powel, was ordered to move his family into a back wing and make
way for officers in the main house. The old single-story shed-type
barracks on Arch Street quickly overflowed. Redcoats moved into
Independence Hall and the city's almshouse, hospitals, and jails.
Churches were used as stables for cavalry. The Hessians built log
barracks on the northern fringe of the city behind a formidable line
of ten redoubts linking the Delaware and Schuylkill rivers.
    To connect the forts, which were strung all along present-day

Callowhill Street, Howe's engineers ordered deep trenches filled with abatis. Loyalist Joseph Galloway, appointed as city superintendent and police commissioner, could find only eighty Loyalists dedicated or poor enough to take up picks and shovels and help with the fortifications (he had promised five hundred). North of the fortified line, scarcely a mile north of Market Street, all houses were ordered burned to deprive the Americans of cover for their snipers: one night in December, horrified Philadelphians on rooftops watched as seventeen country estates went up in flames. Every farmhouse along Rising Sun Avenue for the eight miles to Germantown was also burned. South of the city, a three-mile line of artillery and cavalry posts was built, extending to Province Island behind Fort Mifflin. More than thirty-seven thousand people were packed into eight square miles of the armed camp that had a few months before been America's most elegant city and its capital.

At Benjamin Franklin's capacious three-story brick mansion, John André was enjoying unaccustomed luxury. Franklin, in Paris for nearly a year now, had lived in the house only eighteen months while a delegate to Congress; his wife had died there three years earlier and his daughter and son-in-law had fled at the approach of the British to the family farm in Lebanon County. André was in many ways at home in the Franklin house that winter, often reading from the richly illustrated volumes of Diderot's *Encyclopédie*. André also liked to tinker in Franklin's workshop, where the rebel philosopher had stored his scientific apparatus, his bell jars, his kites, the vials from his celebrated long-ago electrical experiments. But more than ever, André was putting his talents as a promising artist, poet, and musician to work to assist his rapid climb in the British army.

André's father, a wealthy Huguenot importer, divided his estate among too many sons to leave them any choice but to work. As a result, André seemed consigned to life in a London countinghouse, despite his aristocratic pretensions. The André family had relatives in Switzerland and France and trading connections in the Levant, and he had traveled and studied on the Continent as a boy. Enrolled at the Academy of Geneva, he had majored in military drawing and mathematics and also studied art, taken flute lessons, and become an excellent dancer. He was fluent in German, French, and Dutch. But his principal interest was painting. A brooding young man with the dark skin, hair, and eyes of his ancestral home in the south of France, André was hailed home to London a year before his father's death: at seventeen, he was expected to put aside his sketch pad to study bookkeeping and accustom himself to backbreaking days on a high stool among the clerks. But after hours, he haunted the theaters and taverns of Covent Garden and Drury Lane. He was entranced by the world of acting, of masks and disguises and dramatic writing, but the theater was considered beneath his social status, out of the question for a career.

Shortly after his father's death, André accompanied his mother and two older sisters on vacation to Buxton Spa in Derbyshire, where he met Anna Seward, a bluestocking poetess, and her companion, the beautiful but consumptive Honora Sneyd. Anna was the daughter of another would-be poet, the canon of Lichfield Cathedral, and with her friend Honora had gathered a literary salon around her in the bishop's palace in Lichfield Close. Anna Seward welcomed the poutish André, who was immediately lovestruck by the beautiful Honora. Holding hands with Honora as Anna read her interminable verses, André tried his hand at versifying and occasionally played his flute. André quickly became determined to marry the aloof Honora and proposed to her. She managed a wan acceptance, which was considerably warmer than her father's reaction. Would André be willing to put aside his interest in a military career and apply himself diligently to his mercantile business, becoming rich enough to afford Honora? Would he limit his absences from the countinghouse, in the meantime carrying on his love affair by long-distance letter to Anna, who would write letters for Honora, who herself was too debilitated by the pain in her side to write more than the occasional postscript? Accepting all terms, André returned to London and the prospect of years of gushing out his affection to Honora via Anna. His letters show ambivalence to the military: a friend was still "honest, warm, intelligent" despite enlistment but he "sacrifices the town's diversions." André doubted his own prospects. In his dreams, "I cast my eyes around and find John André by a small coal fire in a gloomy counting-house in Warnford Court . . . in all probability never to be much more than he is at present." He was "cher Jean" writing to his "fair Julia," the name they had coined to mask Honora's identity from a world that was, in fact not interested. He hated his orbit of "books, papers, bills and other implements of gain," and yearned for a life of letters; "it is for thy sake only I wish for wealth."[8] In the end, Honora's father broke off the engagement, certain that André would never amount to enough. Honora apparently made little objection, since she was being pursued by other men of literary aspiration. A few months later, John André sailed for America to begin a soldier's life. He left behind his family's countinghouse and purchased a second lieutenant's commission in the Royal Welsh Fusiliers.

*   *   *

When the British had surrendered St. Jean in November 1775, after
a long siege, one of the officers captured was twenty-four-year-old
John André. As a paroled officer, he agreed that he would remain
within six miles of the town to which he was assigned, in his case
Lancaster, Pennsylvania, sixty miles west of Philadelphia. Already
singled out for special duties by his superiors, it was he who was
sent blindfolded aboard *Enterprise,* Arnold's old flagship, to negotiate the surrender. Then he was sent to Montreal to collect the sixty
wagonloads of baggage of his fellow officers for the journey south
into captivity in Pennsylvania. On the day of the British capitulation,
André had gazed with scorn on the slovenly Americans. He considered them amateurs, a disgrace as an army, their officers a slouch-
ing lot in civilian clothes, their trousers a motley assortment of every
kind and color. Writing later to his mother, he described the Americans as "greasy, worsted-stocking knaves."[9] As André marched out
in his fusilier's red coat with pale yellow facings, he held his grenadier's cap high. He wore clean white lace at his throat and he composed his face as he moved precisely to the tune of the British band.
At a command, he laid his sword before him on the ground. He was
surprised when Montgomery, the English deserter, told him to pick
it up again.

Meandering south, he had stayed a month at Philip Schuyler's
manor house at Albany. The urbane Schuyler hoped that the break
with England would prove only temporary. After a month at
Schuyler's dinner table, André went down the Hudson and stopped
at Haverstraw Bay, where he dined with Joshua Hett Smith, a local
attorney and the brother of New York's Loyalist attorney general.

Once in Philadelphia, André went to seek the help of David
Franks, partner in one of the biggest trading companies in North
America. Franks was the American merchant paid by the British to
supply British prisoners. While the elder Franks attended to the
problems of providing for his fellow prisoner, André had time to
explore "the little society of Third and Fourth Streets,"[10] the opulent townhouses of Society Hill. David Franks's daughter Rebecca
had friends whose fathers were in high places in the old British colonial society of Philadelphia, and this romantic young officer was
ushered into the drawing rooms of elegant houses that strongly resembled London's West End. At the Fourth Street home of Judge
Shippen, he was introduced to Becky Franks's sixteen-year-old
friend Peggy Shippen. Before he left for his indefinite term in captivity, André asked to sketch her.

In the raw frontier county seat of Lancaster, André had looked up Peggy's grandfather, a member of the town's revolutionary Committee of Safety. But even Shippen had trouble finding a British officer a decent place to live. André wound up living in a tavern until the courageous Quaker burgess of the town, Thomas Cope, invited him and two fellow officers to live with him. Three-quarters of a century later, one of the Cope children still remembered that winter and André's "bland manners" (he meant it as a compliment) and the young officer "sporting with us children as if he were one of us."[11] André decided that Cope's thirteen-year-old son John had talent and spent many hours teaching him to draw. André was free, by the terms of his parole, to ride out of town and go hunting. He bought a fine fowling piece from one of Lancaster's renowned gunsmiths and with his prisoner-roommate combed the ridges for pheasant and grouse. At night he began to draw maps of all the terrain in America he had passed through.

As the fighting in Canada worsened and more Pennsylvania troops were called up for service, there were few militiamen to guard the English prisoners. André was transferred to Carlisle, fifty miles farther west. There he was not allowed to ride around, to hunt, to live with a family. Crowded into a tavern, André and his comrades were shouted and spat at. He destroyed his hunting gun so no American could ever use it and stopped writing to Americans—except to offer John Cope advice on his drawings: "My young friend's drawings persuade me he is much improved." He should take "particular care in forming the features in the face and in copying hands exactly." He hoped young Cope would remember the rules he had taught him about "shading with Indian ink"; an anatomical figure was "tolerably well done"—André explained how to improve such figures further by "not blackening the darkest at once but by washing them over repeatedly."[12] When the British were exchanged for American prisoners after a year in confinement, André had time for only one more letter to an American: to John Cope, whom he had once talked of taking to England to civilize and to train as an artist, he now asked only to be remembered.

Despite his capture and house arrest, André was rising rapidly in the favor of British generals, using his artistic talents and his skill with languages to advantage in a society where only an assortment of accomplishments could overcome his real handicap—that he had no relatives among the British nobility. But his knowledge of languages, especially German once the Hessians joined the British forces, and his ability to write clearly and gracefully and spin out flattering literary-sounding toasts at a general's dinner table quickly distinguished him as a staff officer. Shortly after André was exchanged, he found a general who would teach him the art of war, a pig-eyed professional killer, Major General Charles Grey. To his mother, André wrote: "I am now putting my irons in the fire. My wishes are to be attached as an aide-de-camp to some one of your commanders, for which my understanding German qualifies me (if I were equal in other respect) in preference to most others."[13] He also submitted maps he had been drawing to Howe. In the spring of 1777, when Howe went on the offensive, setting aside his attempts to negotiate with the rebels, he assigned André to Grey, a twenty-year veteran who had fought at Minden and in the West Indies, had been twice wounded in the king's service, and had nothing but scorn for rebels, as his bayonet charges at Culloden had bloodily demonstrated. André was billeted with another rebel hater, Major John Graves Simcoe, head of an aristocratic Loyalist light infantry regiment, the Queen's Rangers. Day and night, André imbibed a low opinion of the American revolutionaries.

As Howe's army tried to outmaneuver the Americans outside Philadelphia in late September 1777, Washington detached General "Mad Anthony" Wayne with fifteen hundred men to harass the British flanks. André, keeping General Grey's journal, said Wayne was "watching our motions" and "infesting our rear on the march." How ordered Grey to stop Wayne. At Paoli at one o'clock on the morning of September 20, Grey, with André at his side, ordered his troops to fix bayonets and remove the flints from their muskets. André carried Grey's orders from company commander to company commander, telling the men to be absolutely silent and not fire a shot, that "firing discovered us to the enemy. . . . By not firing, we knew the foe to be wherever fire happened." They were to attack only with bayonet and sword. The increasingly callous André tersely described the killing. The Americans were just waking up and falling out of their tents to begin a raid of their own on the British when Grey's cavalry swept through the camp in a saber charge:

The picket was surprised and most of them killed in endeavoring to retreat. On approaching the right of the camp, we perceived the line of fires, and the cavalry being ordered to form in the front, we rushed along the line, putting to the bayonet all they came up with, and, overtaking the main herd of the fugitives, stabbed great numbers and pressed on their rear till it was thought prudent to order them to desist. Near 200 must have been killed and a great number wounded.[14]

Actually more than three hundred died, half the American force. After the Paoli Massacre, André joined the other British officers in drinking some "good gin"[15] they found as they looted Wayne's camp. So self-satisfied was André with the account he had written that he sent it off to be published in the *New York Gazette*. The destruction of Washington's rear guard at Paoli stunned Washington, who did not resist as Howe slipped across the Schuylkill on a pontoon bridge and marched into the city. For the bloody night's work, André's chief won the nickname "No Flint" Grey. His savage fighting style did not seem to bother André, who wrote to his mother:

I am extremely well and in the most happy situation with my General, who improves upon acquaintance and whom I esteem and am attached to more and more every day. I believe I am fortunate enough to meet with his good will in return. He is much respected in the army, and this last coup has gained him much credit. . . . He seemed satisfied with my assistance and he thanked me in the warmest terms.[16]

And, using his newfound influence, he bought a commission for his younger brother, William, to join his old regiment in Philadelphia.

In late November, Washington prepared to withdraw his battered army to the low hills of Valley Forge, twenty-two miles west of Philadelphia, in time to build his winter quarters of greenwood cabins. It had taken Howe exactly four months, thousands of casualties, and the loss of two men-of-war to move his army and navy ninety miles only to find that the Americans, far from capitulating when their capital fell, were only fighting more fiercely since they had learned of Arnold's victory at Saratoga.

Not until the end of November did the guns stop booming and the men-of-war begin to bring supplies to the British inside Philadelphia. By this time, the British garrison had settled into hundreds of houses and public buildings, but the surrender of Burgoyne and Howe's failure to defeat Washington left the British dispirited. Some officers, including Howe's private secretary, Ambrose Serle, grumbled that there had been little point to taking Philadelphia without gaining a significant victory over the rebels.

At General Howe's headquarters on Market Street, John André was one of many British officers who now decided to follow the example of their commanders in chief and seek some diversions from the toils of war. Howe kept to himself, preferring the company of his blond and beautiful mistress, Mrs. Joshua Loring, wife of the British commissary-general of prisoners, and a handful of cardplaying Loyalist friends, especially poet and bookseller Joseph Stansbury. All but excluded from Howe's company, André and other staff officers fell back on their own resourcefulness. There seemed to be only one general rule binding them: if an officer got a Loyalist woman pregnant, he had to marry her. This dictum led to the establishment of numerous brothels and encouraged a safely platonic social life for the proper young ladies of Philadelphia, who were only interested in having an innocent good time unless it could lead to a suitable marriage. André knew from his earlier visits in 1774 and 1775 that Philadelphia offered a glittering array of attractions. At the city's taverns, the officers formed themselves into eating clubs: for instance, the Friendly Brothers took the motto "Who Will Separate Us?" High-stakes gambling flourished at a number of taverns, as officers followed the example of General Howe. In Moore's Alley off Front Street near the waterfront, Thomas Wildman of the 17th Dragoons established a cockpit, took care of the cocks, and offered £100 purses for mains with no limit on side betting and varying purses for by-battles. Horse racing and cricket matches were more to some officers' tastes, and from January 29 to April 30, 1778, there were weekly subscription balls at Daniel Smith's City Tavern on Second Street in Society Hill, where, under the watchful eyes of proper Philadelphia chaperons, American girls, quite a few of them from leading revolutionary families, could flirt with the redcoats and dance until midnight.

As more and more transports unloaded their cargoes of fine wines, silks, brocades, and fancy foods, many of the city's abandoned shops opened up under the new management of 120 Scottish Loyalist storekeepers from Virginia, who accepted only gold and silver but kept prices as high as they had been when Continental paper money had been accepted. Indeed, nearly five hundred leading Quakers and Tories petitioned Howe to force acceptance of the old provincial currency at two for one (Continental money was still excluded). Soon, Philadelphia hostesses were paying $100 a yard for silk to be made up in the latest fashions for their daughters and were sending out invitations to British officers to come to dinner. Tea was once again politically fashionable, and Philadelphia hostesses poured great quantities of it in their drawing rooms as officers such as John André got to know their daughters. The $60-a-pound price was not a deterrent.

On his way into Philadelphia beside General Grey, André had spent several days in early October at Cliveden, the classically ornamented country summer home of Pennsylvania Chief Justice Benjamin Chew, at the moment under arrest in an American stronghold in New Jersey. André took long walks around Justice Chew's formal gardens with his seventeen-year-old daughter, Peggy, a slim, almost too delicate brunette whose sad eyes brightened whenever André recited verse by poets he said he had actually met. In the evenings, as was his habit, he played his flute for her after dinner, and he talked about paintings by Raphael which he had seen in his tours on the Continent. André and his fellow officers of Grey's command had gone on into Philadelphia, but on the foggy morning of October 4, Washington attacked Germantown. Chew's garden became littered with American corpses after three hundred redcoats turned the thick-walled house into a fortress in the American rear that withstood hours of punishment from Henry Knox's field artillery and repeated American assaults. By the time the firing ceased, eighteen American bodies lay in the front driveway.

As the season of fighting was replaced by a season of feasting, André and his elegant friends began to reconnoiter the best society they could find in Philadelphia to indulge their formalized tastes. By December they were beginning to call on "the little society of Third and Fourth Streets," as André later described the parlors of Peggy Shippen and her young friends. By Christmastime 1777, he had formed the habit of going to call at Judge Shippen's mansion on Fourth Street, accompanied by his friend Captain Hammond of the *Roebuck* and by Lord Howe's dashing young chief of staff, Lord Rawdon, who considered Peggy Shippen the most beautiful woman he had ever seen in England or America.

When Margaret Shippen was born on June 11, 1760, her father, who already had a son and three daughters, wrote to *his* father that his wife "this morning made me a present of a fine baby which, though the worst sex, is yet entirely welcome." Judge Shippen had wanted another son, but after his wife, Peggy, gave birth to two more daughters, who died, he stopped trying. He was usually cheerful about having a big family: he was confident that "by the blessing of God I shall be able to do them all tolerable justice."[17]

The Shippens were one of colonial America's richest and most illustrious families, which assured Peggy Shippen a great deal of attention from the moment she was born. Edward Shippen, the first of his family to emigrate to America, came first to Boston in 1668 with a fortune of £10,000 from trading with the Levant. He married one of the Quakers being persecuted by the Puritans, and they were both granted sanctuary in Rhode Island by Governor Benedict Arnold,

General Arnold's great-grandfather. They resettled in Philadelphia, where he kept herds of deer on his two-mile-deep riverfront estate, invested in land, and expanded his import trade. When William Penn came to Philadelphia to visit, Shippen lent him his mansion. A man of his money and connections was indispensable to Penn's proprietary government. Within a year of his arrival, Edward Shippen was made speaker of the assembly. He was specifically named first mayor of Philadelphia in Penn's charter and became president of the provincial council and acting governor. After Penn went home to die in England, Shippen was the biggest man in Pennsylvania: according to one Philadelphian "he had the biggest person, the biggest house and the biggest coach in the province."[18]

The Shippen name in the first half of the eighteenth century was synonymous with stubborn integrity. Edward Shippen's nephew William was a high Tory member of Parliament who outspokenly opposed the Whigs and the Hanoverian German kings they installed on the throne of England. Once when King George I was making the annual Speech from the Throne at the opening of Parliament, William Shippen "in the course of the debate said the second paragraph of the King's speech seemed rather calculated for the meridian of Germany than for Great Britain and that it was a great misfortune that the King was a stranger to our language and our constitution." The Whigs considered Shippen's comment a "scandalous invective"[19] against the king's person and government, and when Shippen refused to retract, a great majority voted to send him to the Tower of London. Old Shippen was also incorruptible: he returned a £1,000 "gift" brought him by Lord Churchill from the Prince of Wales after one particularly outrageous speech. He often upbraided the Whig prime minister Sir Robert Walpole, who nevertheless had great respect for him. "Some are corrupt," Walpole said of one of England's more corrupt Parliaments, "but I will tell you of one who is not: Shippen is not."[20] Alexander Pope went further: "I love to pour out all myself, as plain as downright Shippen."[21]

It was this reputation for candor which distinguished Peggy Shippen's grandfather, a man who influenced her strongly and who helped her father to remain generally unmolested throughout the Revolution, entering it as a crown official and coming out as chief justice of the New State of Pennsylvania. The second Edward Shippen, Peggy's beloved "Grandpapa," had moved away from Philadelphia to the new town of Lancaster on the western frontier to coordinate the family's import business with the flourishing fur trade: his trade goods from Europe—guns, fishing lines, mirrors, beads, tomahawks, knives—were the mainstay of barter with Indians on the Ohio River. He was a founder of the University of Pennsylvania and Princeton University, serving on Princeton's board of trustees for twenty years. He was a common pleas judge under both the provincial and state governments and took his turn as mayor of Philadelphia. Peggy seems to have lived for her grandfather's visits to town, especially his birthday dinners and Christmases, when they had plump turkeys and preserved fruits from his orchards. It is a pity that her family destroyed all her correspondence they could get their hands on, but an in-law who was the elder Shippen's law clerk wrote a description of her grandfather which helps to explain why she was so fond of him:

I know none happier in their temper and disposition, or any who have greater fund of pleasantry and good humour than the old gentleman. In a minute, he relates to me ten different stories, interlarding each narrative with choice scraps of Latin, Greek and French. . . . Scarce a moment of the day passes over, but I receive some new piece of instruction, either for regulating my judgment or conduct, and even when I take a walk with the old don, seldom fail getting a lesson from him, tho' it be only to teach me to mount a rail fence with safety and dexterity.[22]

Grandpapa Shippen lived to be seventy-five, all through Peggy's childhood acting as *paterfamilias* of the Shippens.

Peggy Shippen's father had little of the family wit or grit. A thoroughly conservative man who seemed to worry constantly about one thing or another, usually about his money and his property, he did not believe in taking risks or in speculation of any kind. Bookish, timorous, even though he lived in London as a law student, he rarely strayed far from Philadelphia's Society Hill. He seemed more inclined to prune the family estates than plant anything new. Rich by inheritance, he followed tradition and his father's dictates as he practiced law—narrowly, upholding the letter if not the spirit. It was the custom for a proper Philadelphia lawyer to marry the daughter of his law praeceptor, so he did: Peggy Francis Shippen was rich, amiable, compliant, and unexciting. Judge Shippen accrued even more wealth. As a hereditary member of the Penn proprietary group that controlled the province until the Revolution, he held what may have been a record number of remunerative offices simultaneously—admiralty judge, prothonotary, recorder—that brought him hard cash. His acceptance of a vice admiralty court judgeship, in 1758, aligned him firmly on the side of the British government in the long colonial struggle that evolved into the Revolution. His tortured reactions to the almost constant tensions that resulted from years of riots, boycotts, and congresses were the backdrop for his daughter Peggy's childhood.

Peggy Shippen was born with the British Empire, only weeks before the French surrendered Canada. Before her third birthday, British America had grown from a strip of small coastal colonies to nearly half of North America: everything east of the Mississippi and much of the Caribbean was added to what had been a small mercantile empire. Philadelphia, the largest town in America by 1763, became a center for trade and its regulation, making it a natural target for protests when resistance to British revenue measures developed in the 1760s. When Parliament passed the Stamp Act shortly before Peggy's fifth birthday, her father was terrified, and he read about "great riots and disturbances" in Boston. He considered the Act oppressive, but he was against the illegal step of destroying the stamped paper. "What will be the consequences of such a step, I tremble to think. . . . Poor America! It has seen its best days."[23] Rather than offend either the local opponents of the Stamp Act or break the law by not using the stamps, he decided to forgo practicing law or carrying out the duties of office requiring stamped paper. Giving up most of his income was better than persecution or prison. When the hated Act was repealed, the gloom lifted in his house briefly and he wrote Peggy's grandfather, "I wish you and all America joy!"[24]

By the time Peggy was eight and learning to read the books in her father's handsome library, the admiralty court, meeting over the market sheds a block away on South Third Street, became the center of the storm over British colonial customs regulations: the young girl saw her father's apprehension grow until, when she was ten, admiralty court judgeship was abolished. As one source of influence and income dried up, Governor Penn provided another: he appointed Shippen to the upper house of the legislature, the provincial council, Pennsylvania's highest governing body. Now more than ever he was a member of the British colonial ruling elite. As the colonial crisis dragged on, Shippen lectured his youngest and favorite daughter on disobedience: bad laws had to be repealed, they could not be ignored or resisted. To do otherwise would open the door to anarchy. Despite his drawing-room bravery, however, Shippen refused to take any public stand, careful to avoid offending radicals and street mobs that might attack his property or harm his daughters. Judge Shippen had come to consider the world, even his privileged and pampered corner of it, a dangerous place where it was wise to keep one's opinions private.

As fighting actually broke out at Lexington, Judge Shippen tried to stay neutral. For a while, he even turned his business affairs over to his eighteen-year-old son, Edward, who made a complete bungle of them. First, Edward recommended moving the family to a newly purchased farm in the hills of Amwell, New Jersey, where he ran a country store. But being far from Philadelphia dried up the well-springs of Shippen political influence, and the family earned no money at all. Instead of customers, the Shippens, obviously rich and therefore suspected of Toryism, earned only hatred in New Jersey. Peggy, at fifteen, heard the word "traitor" applied to her father for the first time in 1776, when the New Jersey legislature passed "an act to punish traitors and other disaffected persons." Unless Shippen renounced his oath of allegiance to the king, he would be charged with treason. Back in Philadelphia, most of the judge's public offices had been abolished with the end of provincial government and the formation of a revolutionary state. As the winter of 1776 approached and there were fresh rumors of British attack, Peggy saw her father burst into a rare fit of rage at Thomas Paine's "book called *Common Sense,* in favor of total separation from England." For years, Shippen had been handing Peggy newspapers and pamphlets debating the great imperial crisis. This one, he rasped, "is artfully wrote, yet might be easily refuted. . . . This idea of independence, though sometime ago abhorred, may possibly, by degrees, become so familiar as to be cherished."[25] No doubt Peggy had learned them by heart. Still, Shippen, a cofounder with Franklin of the Junto discussion group and expert debater, would not speak out, although he firmly opposed the Revolution. He contented himself with writing to his brother-in-law, a prorevolutionary politician in Lancaster, to promote legislation "that would strengthen the hands of the advocates of reconciliation in the Congress." As far into the new politics as Judge Shippen would delve was to invite partisans on all sides, just so they were of sufficient social standing, to air their views at his dinner table. At sixteen, Peggy listened to Washington, Adams, and Silas Deane as well as many high-ranking British officials as they passed through.

Peggy heard Arnold's name frequently in 1776. News of his heroic march to Quebec, his daring attack on the walled city, his naval campaign on Lake Champlain, his wounding, and his promotion often put his name in the Philadelphia newspapers. A few blocks away, a new ship in the Pennsylvania navy, a floating artillery battery, was given Arnold's name. But there was more immediate and personal war news: Peggy's oldest sister Elizabeth's fiancé, Neddy Burd, was missing and presumed killed in the American rout on

Long Island. With her family, Peggy wept. When word came a week later that he was alive but a prisoner of war on a British prisoner ship in New York City, there was a fresh cause for anxiety. Then, in December 1776, even worse news arrived at Judge Shippen's door: Peggy's only brother, Edward, eighteen, had gone for a ride with their cousins, and on the spur of the moment had decided to volunteer in the British army. Riding into Trenton, he lingered there with other Loyalists and the Hessian garrison for the Christmas festivities. When Washington attacked, Edward was captured. More long days of dread followed until the ashen young Edward arrived on Fourth Street, freed personally by General Washington. Peggy cried with relief; Judge Shippen was furious. All his careful neutrality had been jeopardized. The Judge severely punished his only son, vowing never "to put it again in his power to trade or make any improper use of money."[26] Stripping him of any further part in the family business affairs, he turned his son's duties over to Peggy. From that day, too, he was probably a closet Patriot; deeply grateful to Washington. Judge Shippen sometimes slipped and referred to Washington's troops as "our army."[27]

When Judge Shippen had, as a young man, bargained with his future father-in-law over a dowry, he had accepted £500 and spent it all on books. In addition to the predictable lawbooks, he lined his library with Greek and Latin classics and actually read them. When his friend Benjamin Franklin proposed a subscription library, Shippen put his money and his suggestions in the box: Addison, Steele, Pope, Defoe, Berkeley, all the latest French and British writers. Peggy Shippen curled up in a wingback across from her father to read them in her turn.

Peggy's education went beyond that of most young ladies and was as extensive as that of most gentlemen of the times. To be sure, according to her family history, she was instructed in needlework, drawing, dancing, and music. But in all her surviving letters, there is none of the household trivia of women's letters of her time: she had a distinctive literary style and wit and wrote with unusual clarity. She was much too practical, too interested in business and making the most of time and money, to waste her writing on such frivolity. She was devoted to her father and to her older sister, Elizabeth; she was a quiet, serious girl, receiving, in her own words years later, "the most useful and best education that America at that time afforded."[28]

According to one friend, "Peggy Shippen was particularly devoted to her father, making his comfort her leading thought, often preferring to remain with him when evening parties and amusements would attract her sisters from home. She was the darling of the family circle, and never fond of gadding. There was nothing of frivolity either in her dress, demeanor or conduct, and though deservedly admired, she had too much good sense to be vain."[29] Growing up at the elbow of a man agonized by a civil war, Peggy constantly imbibed Judge Shippen's principles of politics as well as business. She read the tracts and newspapers arguing for and against British regulation of trade, the prime grievance of the Revolution. She was exposed as well to the rudiments and, later, the finer points of bookkeeping, accounting, real estate investment, importing and trade, banking and monetary transactions—and she basked in her father's approval.

By the time Peggy was fifteen, she had been studying her sister's manners and social behavior for years. Philadelphia girls with the money and family connections to be invited to join the city's social centerpiece, the Dancing Assembly, began these rituals at an early age, often as young as fifteen. It was at the fortnightly dances of the Assembly season at Freemasons Hall that a young girl was supposed to learn all that she would need to become an eligible debutante and a successful hostess. For days, the young girls and their mothers filled Society Hill households with their own excitement as they tried on new gowns, hurried along servants' preparations of silverware polishing and the cooking of traditional dishes—pepper-pot soup, gammon, roast suckling pigs, duck, rich desserts including syllabub and heavy cream-covered trifle—then, at the last possible moment, they lined up at wigmakers' shops for hours of combing, powdering with white flour, beribboning. The Assembly Balls were a meeting ground of new and old money: members of the Penns' extended political family, including the Shippens, rubbed elbows with the sons and daughters of men with new wealth, such as the children of Benjamin Franklin. Even when Peggy was little, young men who came to visit her older sister began to notice her. She was tiny, blond, dainty of face and figure, with steady, wide-set blue-gray eyes and a determined pursing to her full mouth as she listened intently. Appearing to be shy, she was bright and quick and capable of conversing at length about politics and business to anyone who was not blinded by her sex.

Peggy Shippen's closest friend was witty and sharp-tongued Rebecca Franks, whose father's enormous imports to America had included the Liberty Bell itself but who was now denounced as the "Jew merchant" for acting as commissary of both British and American prisoners. There was also excitable Becky Redman, daughter of a rich Loyalist merchant, and Peggy Chew, who had come back to Philadelphia from Germantown with the British. Becky Franks wrote to a friend in the country to describe the gay whirl of Peggy Shippen's circle after the British joined Philadelphia society that winter:

You can have no idea of the life of continued amusement. . . . Most elegantly am I dressed for a ball this evening at [City Tavern], where we have one every Thursday. You would not know the room, 'tis so much improved. The dress is more ridiculous and pretty than anything that I ever saw, a great quantity of different colored feathers on the head . . . the hair dressed very high. . . . There's no being dressed without a hoop. . . . I spent Tuesday evening at Sir William Howe's, where we had a concert and dance.[30]

To ask for a dance or two at an Assembly Ball required, first, a formal round of introductions, even for a conquering British aristocrat, and the first step was a morning visit to the drawing room of the intended partner. As John André, his sketch pad under his arm, and his officer friends approached the Shippen mansion on the northwest corner of Fourth and Prune streets, they saw, set back between tall pine trees, a grand house for the times, four stories tall and forty-two feet wide and nearly as deep, its handsome red-and-black Flemish-bond brick facade divided symmetrically by a heavy door framed by fluted Bath soapstone doorjambs resembling Greek columns supporting a pyramid-shaped stone pediment. Once inside, there were the obligatory cups of tea, sometimes as many as fifteen, to accompany the talk about the latest books, balls, and plays. Major André and his assistant, New York Loyalist Captain DeLancey, were hard at work at the Southwark Playhouse, turning a former warehouse on South Street into a splendid theater. André and DeLancey were the set designers.

Calling themselves Howe's Thespians, they swept away the cobwebs, installed lamps to illuminate the stage, and painted a waterfall and wooded scenes on the stage curtain. They designed ambitious and romantic sets, one showing a brook meandering through a darkly shaded forest toward a "distant champagne country."[31] Later, a doorkeeper testified that the officers spent days and nights hanging about the playhouse, often with prostitutes, who were offered the female parts. "When any piece was to be rehearsed, they would all flock around the back door."[32] Tickets could not be bought at the door, and there would have been none to buy anyway: they were all sold out at taverns and coffeehouses far in advance, the dollar for a box or the pit or fifty cents for the balcony to go to soldiers' widows and orphans. For five full months the theater was packed as thirteen different plays by David Garrick, Colley Cibber, and Fielding were produced for resplendent audiences, including, among the regulars, an entranced Peggy Shippen. Her friend André often played minor roles, but he was considered by local critics "a poor actor."[33] It did not matter to Peggy, whose head spun with excitement and who talked about the theater for hours with André and company in her drawing room.

After hours of sipping tea and gossiping at the Shippens', André liked to provide his own entertainment, reciting his latest poems and interspersing his readings with passages on the flute, sometimes with Captain Ridsdale playing his violin. The scenes and the rhymes evoked faraway Lichfield Close and Honora Sneyd, especially one poem, entitled "A German Air," which André wrote in January 1778 for Peggy Chew, and which was recently discovered in the archives of Princeton University:

> Return enraptur'd Hours,
> When Delia's heart was mine;
> When she, with wreaths of flowers,
> My Temples wou'd entwine.
> When Jealousy nor care
> Corroded in my Breast,
> But Visions, light as Air,
> Presided o'er my Rest—
> Now Nightly round my Bed
> No airy Visions play;
> No Flowers crown my Head
> Each Vernal Holyday—
> For far from those sad Plains
> My Lovely Delia flies,
> And rack'd with Jealous Pains,
> Her wretched Lover dies.[34]

André flitted from one drawing-room beauty to another, serious about none of them. He liked to draw Peggy Shippen, showing her as elusively elegant and poutish, sometimes turning away, sometimes fixing him with an enigmatic smile. He enjoyed breakneck sleigh rides; with Peggy Shippen wrapped in furs at his side and her friends crowding in with them under heavy bearskin rugs, he would crack a long whip over matched cavalry horses and dash off to the northern line of forts or down to the frozen Delaware. But when Peggy stepped out for the evening, it was more often on the arm of Royal Navy Captain Hammond, who later said, "We were all in love with her."[35] One of the season's highlights was a dinner dance aboard HMS *Roebuck*. Peggy was piped on board the ship, illuminated with lanterns for the occasion. Peggy sat down at Captain Hammond's right for a dinner served to two hundred invited guests, then danced until dawn.

All the frivolity was costing Judge Shippen too much: he had one daughter preparing to marry as soon as her fiancé returned from a British prison ship, and now his sensible practical Peggy was costing him a fortune in clothes, upward of £5,000 in a single year. To his own father on the other side of the American lines, he wrote that "every kind of provision" had trebled in price and that his store of gold and silver was dwindling fast. No money was coming in from rents of lands behind enemy lines or government fees now that the British government had imposed martial law; "There is no remedy for any of us but abridging every article of expense that does not actually supply us with some real comfort in life."[36] In the late spring of 1778, Peggy was becoming jaded by the endless swirl of festivities and more than a little perturbed by some of the immorality she was witnessing. Scandal brewed over Howe's affair with Elizabeth Loring, whose husband was starving American prisoners and pocketing the profits while Howe turned a blind eye toward the commissary's greed. It was also an open secret that British officers were fathering numerous bastards. Oliver DeLancey left at least two without his name, and British officers smirked that rather than leave America depopulated by the war, they saw it as their duty to father at least one illegitimate child. Just so long as the society drawing room was spared the knowledge of such behavior, there were no complaints from proper Philadelphians. But as the winter of occupation came to an end, the British grew bolder. An outraged Becky Redman wrote to a friend that several of her Society Hill beaux had looked right at her and bowed as they waited their turns in line at a notorious brothel only a few doors down the street.

Preferring his various entertainments to attacking Washington in the mild winter of 1777–78, General Howe only occasionally sent out detachments to scour the surrounding countryside for cattle, horses, grain, and firewood, all in short supply in the city. While some of his generals fumed that they could end the war in ten days, in February Howe had learned that France had signed two treaties with the United States, one granting reciprocal most-favored-nation trading status, the other a treaty of military alliance. In August 1777, when he landed in Maryland, he had written to London that he would be unable to subdue Pennsylvania in time to cooperate with Burgoyne on the Hudson. His dispatches had reached London just two days before word that Burgoyne was bogged down at Saratoga, convincing the British secretary of state, Lord George Germain, the plan to divide and conquer America in a single campaign was "totally ruined."[37] Howe estimated he would need 35,000 more troops to end the war in 1778: unless he got them, he would resign. This demand arrived in London one day before news that Burgoyne's army had surrendered. One day later after the news hit, on December 3, the prime minister, Lord North, anticipating French entry into the war, advocated abandonment of British efforts to destroy the Continental Army and occupy the colonies, shifting instead to a series of expeditions from strong coastal bases, a tight naval blockade, and direct negotiations with the rebels. In an intense and protracted power struggle in London, the king, after first refusing Howe's resignation, had finally allowed him to be ordered home. On March 8, Germain sent instructions that the new British commander was to be General Sir Henry Clinton, who was authorized to abandon all offensive operations, withdraw from Philadelphia, and retire to New York. The French alliance had made the American Revolution "a secondary consideration"[38] to war with France.

By late April, Howe was secretly preparing to go home—and John André was preparing a lavish farewell, a Meschianza, a mixed entertainment that would include a waterborne parade, a tournament, a dress ball, and an enormous dinner party. No other effort John André ever made came close to the month-long preparations for the most lavish festival of the American Revolution. Masking his "dejection, regret and disappointment"[39] at Howe's recall, André raised £3,312 in subscriptions among twenty-one staff officers—roughly $9,480 apiece in 1990 dollars—then set to work on the biggest party America had ever seen. It was not an original idea: like many of André's, it was borrowed and embellished, similar to a fête staged by Burgoyne for the marriage of the Earl of Derby, whose younger brother, Major Thomas Stanley, was on Howe's staff and was one of André's subscribers. André's prologues to plays at the Southwark Playhouse and his toasts and introductions of General Howe at dinner parties had made him a Howe favorite: in gratitude for Howe's recognition, he designed his Meschianza, a "tilt and tournament according to the customs and ordinances of ancient chivalry," selecting as escorts for the knights Peggy Shippen and her friends, "ladies selected from the foremost in youth, beauty and fashion."[40] To get around the difficulty of dancing in armor, André adapted court costumes for the knights from the reign of King Henry IV. For the ladies, he designed Turkish harem costumes evoking the Crusades. The metaphor: crusading British seeking the favor of beautiful heathens in a holy quest far from home.

Fourteen knights were divided into two teams: the Knights of the Blended Rose, whose motto was "We droop when separated," and the Knights of the Burning Mountain, their motto "I burn forever." André also designed shields and spears for every knight, every crest combining love and war. André's showed two gamecocks fighting and the claim "No rival." He designed the ladies' elaborate headdresses—"the Meschianza made me a complete milliner"—and his own glittering costume: a white satin vest with full pink sleeves, wide baggy pants, a pink scarf with a white bow draped front and back to his hips, a pink-and-white sword sash girding his waist, and pink bows fastened to his knees. On his head he wore a high-crowned white satin hat "turned up in front and enlivened by red, white and black plumes." His hair he tied with the same contrasting colors, hanging in flowing curls down his back. As his escort, André selected Peggy Chew. To Peggy Shippen, he assigned the youngest of the knights, a boy of eighteen.

If Peggy Shippen was elated that she and her two sisters had been selected out of the fourteen girls from all of Philadelphia, her father was less thrilled. The cost of outfitting three Turkish houris cut deeply into his remaining cash, yet he yielded under intense pressure and sent his daughters off to shop. André designed Peggy's outfit: she

wore [a] gauze turban spangled and edged with gold or silver, on the right side a veil of the same kind hung as low as the waist, and the left side of the turban was enriched with pearl and tassels of gold or silver and crested with a feather. The dress was of the Polonaise kind and of white silk with long sleeves. The sashes which were worn around the waist and were tied with a large bow on the left side hung very low and were trimmed, spangled and fringed according to the colors of the knight.[41]

Judge Shippen shelled out an undisclosed sum of gold that further enriched the London couturiers Coffin and Anderson, whose shop netted £12,000 from the ball. Carrying his penchant for set design to its zenith, André took over Walnut Grove, the deserted riverfront mansion of wealthy merchant Joseph Wharton, a Quaker dying in exile in Virginia. André built a pavilion 180 feet long of wood and canvas and arches supported by Doric columns and with emblems

and devices all over it. He selected Grenadier Guards, the tallest soldiers he could find, to stand in its niches like statues.

On May 18, the day of the Meschianza, the Shippen house
buzzed with the excitement of hairdressing and Peggy and her sisters
modeling their Turkish costumes before mirrors. There are two versions of what happened next. The family version is that after a depu-
tation of somber Quakers urged Judge Shippen that it would be
unseemly for his daughters to appear in Turkish costumes at such a
ball, they stayed home "in a dancing fury."[42] The other version is
that the Shippen girls participated over their father's protests. The
evidence for their participation is stronger than the family's stay-at-
home tradition written after the Revolution. First of all, Judge Shippen and his family were not Quakers anymore: they were Anglicans,
members of Christ Church. Secondly, there are André's sketches, his
detailed accounts in the London *Gentleman's Magazine*, his own letters written home and to Peggy Chew describing their costumes.
And then there is the testimony of leading revolutionaries: among
others, Charles Thomson, secretary of Congress and a member by
marriage of the prominent Dickinson family, states flatly that they
were there. From all available evidence, Peggy Shippen joined the
festive throng described by André in an account he prepared for
Peggy Chew and later submitted to London journals: "The gaudy
fleet, freighted with all that was distinguished by rank, beauty and
gallantry, was conveyed down the river along the whole length of
the city, whilst every ship at the wharves or in the stream was
decked in all her maritime ornaments," André proudly wrote. For
two hours, some thirty decorated barges and galleys floated slowly
downriver against the tide, each boat gaily decked out in bunting,
streamers, and flags and crowded with officers and their ladies. A
mile of waterfront houses and wharves were also decorated. Cannons placed at intervals fired salutes; crowds lining the river cheered
the boats on. As Howe's galley, *Hussar,* neared Market Street wharf,
boatloads of musicians struck up "God Save the King." Hundreds of
small boats filled with merrymakers jammed the river as *Roebuck*
fired a nineteen-gun salute. "The music, the number of spectators
and the brilliancy of the gay tribe which peopled the river made the
whole uncommonly solemn and striking," André reported. Stepping
ashore at Walnut Grove, André's gay tribe paraded behind "all the
bands of the army" under the triumphant Doric arches to an amphitheater where each Turkish maid was escorted to a sofa. André and
six fellow knights in glittering armor rode in on horses "caparisoned
with pink, black and silver, trimmings and bows hanging very low
from either ham and tied round their chest." Then a herald, accom-

panied by three blaring trumpeters, intoned the challenge of the Knights of the Blended Rose: "The ladies of the Blended Rose excel in wit, beauty and every accomplishment. . . . Should any knight or knights be so hardy as to dispute or deny it, they are ready to enlist with them . . . according to the laws of ancient chivalry." Then seven Knights of the Burning Mountain appeared in black satin faced with orange and laced with gold: the two contingents made "a general salute to each other with a very graceful movement of their lances" and then charged each other at full tilt, each tapping his opponent's shield with a spear. Wheeling their horses, they made two more passes, circled, and brandished their lances until the judges ended the combat, deciding that "all the ladies were so fair and the knights so brave it would be impious to decide in favor of either." Riding to decorated booths, the knights knelt to receive the favors their ladies pinned to their turbans.

By now it was growing dark, and the celebrants marched in procession into the gaily lighted Wharton house, where eighty-five mirrors "multiplied every object." After tea and cakes served on fine china, great mounds of delicacies were set out on green-baize-covered tables. Coffee and tea were poured from heavy silver servers, and after an hour of dancing, supper was announced. Cold supper for 430 was served by the twenty-four black slaves: tureens of soup, courses of chicken, lamb, ham, Yorkshire pies, veal, puddings, a choice of rare fruits imported from the West Indies by the Royal Navy. Around the walls were more tables, heaped with fifty pyramids of Philadelphia delicacies: jellies, syllabub, cakes, and sweetmeats, all served from long rows of tables "loaded with 1,040 plates," according to a careful Hessian observer, and illuminated by three hundred white tapers. After dinner, the company toasted the king's health and a band played "God Save the King" as everyone sang along. As the music subsided, the long row of windows facing south from the ballroom was thrown open, showing a brilliant fireworks display on the lawn. Then the north windows were thrown open: this was *not* in the startled André's plan. In the distance, American cavalry, with the help of spies inside Philadelphia, had slipped up to the line of abatis at dusk and dumped kettles of whale oil over the dried and pointed branches, setting them afire. Instantly, the north sky was full of fire. As General Howe tried to assure the ladies that it was all part of the evening's festivities, many of their escorts slipped away, jumping on their horses and lashing them north to a brisk reception from Morgan's riflemen. André omitted this episode from his account, only telling of trumpets blaring and toasts to the king and queen, to General Howe and his brother the admiral, "to the founders of the feast." After dinner, "freighted now with new strength and spirits, the whole repaired to the ball-room."[43] And they danced—or played faro—until dawn. As Peggy Shippen and her friends rode home the next morning, they faced a city more deeply divided than ever by the night's festivities: "We never had, and perhaps never shall have, so elegant an entertainment in America again,"[44] wrote Becky Franks. "Scenes of folly and vanity," wrote Quaker diarist Elizabeth Drinker. "How insensible do these people appear while our land is so greatly desolated."[45] Even some uninvited British officers were disgusted. "The Knights of the Burning Mountain are tom fools," said one, "and the Knights of the Blended Rose are damned fools. I know of no difference between them."[46]

On the searing Philadelphia morning of June 18, 1778, Pierre Eugène du Simitière, a Swiss-born artist who had studied drawing in Geneva with the same teacher as John André, walked down to Benjamin Franklin's house on Market Street to bid adieu to André. He found the major cramming rare books from Franklin's library into packing crates. He also saw Franklin's portrait leaning against the front doorjamb and watched as soldiers crated much of Franklin's scientific apparatus, music and musical instruments he had invented, and personal account books. Objecting vehemently to André's looting, du Simitière was told that André had no qualms about plundering the house of the very rebel who had negotiated the French alliance that had caused André's mentor, General Howe, to be recalled to England. André's pilfering was out of spite more than need, since he was himself wealthy. His will showed an estate of upward of $1 million in modern terms, much of it property in the West Indies that was now threatened by the French fleet. He also told Du Simitière that he was not taking all the loot for himself: the philosopher's portrait was a gift for André's boss, General Grey.*

In the month since the Meschianza, the British had been stripping and packing Philadelphia, at first secretly. Three days after the ball, Howe had actually advised the Loyalist magistrates, according to his secretary, Serle, "to make peace with the rebels who, he supposed, would not treat them harshly." As Tory refugees who had crowded into Philadelphia to join the British now faced "being speedily deserted," they were "chilled with horror," feeling they had been "left to wander like Cain upon the earth without home and without property" as repayment for their loyalty to their king. Serle

---

* Passed down through Grey's family in England, it was given to the United States in 1906 on the two hundredth anniversary of Franklin's birth and hangs in the White House.

called Howe's abandonment of six thousand Loyalists "villainy,"[47] but Howe's successor, Clinton, maintained that he had orders signed by the king to remove his base of operations from Philadelphia. Clinton offered to take with him any Loyalists who wished to leave, as the British had done at Boston. In a panic, thousands of Loyalists tried to sell or transport all that they owned to New York, Maryland, Canada, anywhere beyond the reach of American reprisals. The task was made almost impossible by the British, who had rounded up virtually every horse and wagon to haul their baggage and booty to New York City; the best horses were crammed into ships for the cavalry. Many Loyalists had to pull their wagons and carts by hand through the streets to British ships and then watch helplessly from their decks as sailors pitched overboard any furniture deemed excess in order to lighten the seriously overloaded vessels. Nearly every scrap of food in the city went at high prices to those who could afford it: no one knew how long it would take for the three-hundred-vessel British fleet to sail from Philadelphia to New York. Tory families had to choose between leaving their homes, friends, businesses, and property and risking the wrath of rebels incensed by their open friendship with the British. As the temperature soared in a severe heat wave, five thousand Loyalists crowded their families and belongings onto the three hundred already crammed British transports that had ferried the army to the Jersey shore. There each soldier had been left to carry about one hundred pounds on his back the nearly one hundred miles to the British lines outside New York City, guarding a ten-mile wagon train full of loot. The British retreat from the American capital stunned the city's residents with its speed. At three that afternoon, Benedict Arnold, the new military governor of Philadelphia, led the Continental Army reoccupying the American capital down Second Street, his carriage finally stopping at the Penn mansion on High Street, until a few hours earlier the headquarters of the British army in North America.

BOOK THREE

"TREASON OF THE BLACKEST DYE"

14

"ON YOU ALONE

MY HAPPINESS DEPENDS"

No public or private injury or insult
shall prevail on me to forsake the
cause of my injured and oppressed
country until I see peace and liberty
restored or nobly die in the attempt.

Benedict Arnold to Horatio Gates, August 1777

On May 11, 1778, one week be-
fore the Meschianza, Benedict Arnold, ignoring George Washington's advice, had returned to active duty, reporting to Washington's
headquarters at Valley Forge, where the survivors of a winter of terrible suffering were preparing to pursue the retreating British.
Within a day's march of the indolent British, Washington and his
dwindling army had undergone five months in sharp contrast to the
relatively luxurious conditions enjoyed by Howe's army. The sufferings at Valley Forge had tempered Washington's winter soldiers into
even tougher fighters but had deepened the rift at headquarters, leaving a legacy of bitterness that would finally engulf Benedict Arnold
during the next year.

When the army arrived on the wind-whipped hillsides of Valley
Forge in mid-December, Lieutenant Colonel Henry Dearborn, who
had been with Arnold at Quebec and Saratoga, noted that his men

had for three days been "without flour or bread and are living on a high uncultivated hill in huts and tents, lying on the cold ground."[1] Washington had ordered his army to build log cabins and fireplaces from the thick woods surrounding them. It took a month to get the soldiers under a city of roofs and walls made without nails. Arnold's former aide, Henry Livingston, wrote, "All my men except eighteen are unfit for duty for want of shoes, stockings and shirts, breeches and coats."[2] Washington's own manservant was half-naked. Soldiers dashed through wet snow from hut to hut clad only in blankets: officers had dinners to which they invited only others who did not have "a whole pair of breeches. . . . We clubbed our rations and feasted sumptuously on tough beefsteak and potatoes with hickory nuts for our dessert."[3] Other officers asked to resign and go home because they were embarrassed to be seen by their men in such ragged clothing. Those who left suffered the final humiliation of having to surrender their blankets. Half the army had neither clothing nor blankets and had to stay in smoke-filled, drafty, crowded cabins day and night. Few men were available for duty, as Washington discovered when he had to abandon his plans for an attack on the lethargic British. The clothing shortage was only a prelude to the slow starvation that took the lives of 2,500 men—one in four in his army—over the next few months. Washington could see that his men were near mutiny—or desertion. From the huts of one unit after another he heard the chant "No meat, no meat."[4]

Three times that winter, Washington's food supplies dried up completely as the states, each required by the new Articles of Confederation to feed and provision their own troops, failed to provide any food whatsoever even as farmers near Valley Forge refused to accept Continental money, preferring to sell their goods for hard cash to the British. New York's quota of grain was being sold at high prices to New England civilians and at higher prices to British troops inside New York City. By the third week of February, the last food at Valley Forge had been consumed: there were no rations at all for the men. Desperate, Washington sent his fittest troops on foraging raids, seizing grain from nearby farms and livestock from as far away as Salem, New Jersey, where they took eight hundred cattle from Loyalist farmers. For the moment, the army was saved. In April, when the shad migrated up the Delaware and Schuylkill rivers, Washington sent his cavalry into the river to stir up the fish while his men caught thousands of them. The celebration over a feast of fish was surpassed only by joy at the news, on May 6, that France had joined the Americans in making war against England.

It was the first good news Washington had received in a winter of contention among his officers and their political allies in Congress that had almost led to Washington's overthrow as commander in chief in a shadowy affair known as the Conway Cabal. Even before Gates's victory over Burgoyne, a growing faction in Congress had become dissatisfied with Washington. While his opponents never formed themselves into an easily identifiable group, their most influential members were the Adamses, who believed that Washington and the Virginians had captured too much influence and power in the army. Gates's victory at Saratoga, even though it had been made possible by Schuyler, Arnold, and Washington as well as by Burgoyne himself, fed a growing contention that Washington was incapable of victory. Among those who did not realize all that Washington had to do as commander in chief, it was easy to make the leap that if only the victorious Gates could displace Washington at the head of the army, America would win quickly. Despite Washington's stubborn stalemate at Germantown, his brave stand on the Delaware, and his successful bottling-up of Howe inside Philadelphia, there were more and more politicians and not a few generals who believed that the Virginian was not up to snuff as commander in chief.

By September 1777, they had begun to organize opposition to Washington. John Adams objected not only to Washington's competence but also to his popularity: "The people of America have been guilty of idolatry in making a man their God,"[5] he said in a letter that was rewritten as part of an anonymous circular, "Thoughts of a Freeman," that was circulated among prospective adherents to the anti-Washington faction. One copy, sent by the influential Philadelphia revolutionary Dr. Benjamin Rush to Patrick Henry in Virginia, so alarmed Henry that he sent it directly to Washington. By this time, Washington was beginning to hear who else was involved: Sam Adams, Richard Henry Lee of Virginia, and Thomas Mifflin. Mifflin, who had been Washington's original aide-de-camp in 1775 and had been promoted to quartermaster general of the army, had fallen out with Washington when the commander in chief had refused to put all of his troops into a do-or-die defense of Mifflin's native Philadelphia, deciding instead to reinforce the Northern Army and try to ward off Howe outside Philadelphia. It was Mifflin who had proved such a disastrous supply officer at Valley Forge, rarely showing himself in camp and spending much of his time plotting against Washington. Resigning from Washington's staff in November, he had become a member of the new Board of War, supporting its president, Gates, and working quietly behind the scenes with other anti-Washington generals, including Wilkinson and another

former Washington aide-de-camp, General Joseph Reed, to make
Gates commander in chief.

The movement against Washington received its most vociferous
support from a French-educated Irishman, Thomas Conway, a major in the French army with enormous self-esteem, who impressed
American officers less well trained in tactics and memo-writing than
himself. After performing well in the Philadelphia campaign, he had
lobbied Congress, winning promotion over the heads of all twenty-
three other brigadier generals to major general. The adulation of
such rough-cut officers as John Sullivan of New Hampshire turned
the heads of the anti-Washington bloc in Congress: "His [Conway's]
regulations in his brigade are much better than any in the Army, and
his knowledge of military matters in general far exceeds any officer
we have."6 No general campaigned harder against Washington nor
more openly: at one point, he told congressmen, "No man is more a
gentleman than General Washington, or appeared to more advantage at his table, or in the usual intercourse of life, but as to his
talents for the command of an army"—and here he shrugged—
"they are miserable indeed."7

Washington might have been able to shrug off Conway, too, had
not Congress decided to inflict him on Washington as his adjutant
general, his personal chief of staff. This was too much for the usually amiable Washington who was horrified at Congress's insensitive
meddling and intruding and began to suspect that Gates was collud-
ing with Conway and others in his removal. The plot began to unravel the evening of October 28. James Wilkinson had apparently
been listening at keyholes and rifling files in Gates's office in Albany
even before he slowly made his way not to Washington, as was customary with Gates's official report of the victory at Saratoga, but to
Congress. Stopping frequently en route, he gossiped with Lord Stirling and his aides at Reading, Pennsylvania. Wilkinson confided that
there were some, including Conway, who would rather see Gates in
command than Washington, and he quoted a private letter to that
effect written to Gates by Conway. On November 3, Lord Stirling
wrote matter-of-factly at the end of a report to Washington: "In a
letter from General Conway to General Gates, he says, 'Heaven has
been determined to save your country, or a weak General and bad
councilors would have ruined it.'"8 Such criticism of the commander in chief by one of his generals was considered little short of
treason. Shocked at the evidence of an attempt to discredit him by
two trusted and high-ranking subordinates, Washington reacted
speedily, repeating the words verbatim in a letter to Gates at Albany.
Sending his letter through normal staff channels in his Valley Forge

headquarters. Washington let it be known just what he thought of Conway. Conway responded immediately to Washington, praising him to the heavens, denying he had ever called him weak, offering to show him the original letter, which he never did. A few days later, Conway submitted his resignation to Congress, which shunted his resignation to its powerful new Board of War. The ambitious and jealous Thomas Mifflin was already the board's most powerful member, and Wilkinson was its secretary. Gates soon became its president. During the board's delay to act on Conway's resignation, some congressmen decided to appoint a new inspector general of the army. The position had been vacant since Major General Philippe du Coudray had ridden his horse off a ferry and drowned. On December 13, Congress voted Conway, of all people, to the post, a move that disgusted Washington. When Conway first visited Valley Forge, Washington saw that he was received with the "flawless, cold courtesy," the "ceremonious civility"[9] which he said was tantamount to incivility. Eventually, Conway resigned this post, too. He returned to France after he was shot in the mouth in a duel by General John Cadwalader, a general loyal to Washington.

But by this time it had become clear to the thoroughly alarmed Washington that Conway had been working to shield the real mastermind of the intended coup, General Gates. Conway had gone to see Wilkinson and had obtained his denial that Gates's young aide had uttered the exact words General Alexander had relayed to Washington in November. Conway's loose-tongued lobbying thoroughly alarmed Mifflin, who was aghast at the breach of secrecy by Wilkinson and wrote Gates to be more careful about his papers. Gates, in turn, accused Washington's dapper and diminutive twenty-year-old aide, Lieutenant Colonel Alexander Hamilton, of taking advantage of being left alone in Gates's room during a recent visit to Albany, where he was courting Philip Schuyler's daughter, to copy the Conway letter. In an apparent attempt to destroy both Hamilton and Washington, Gates reported to Washington and Congress that Hamilton had "stealingly copied"[10] his correspondence. Stung into action, Washington outmaneuvered Gates, informing him through Congress that it was his own aide, Wilkinson, who had first betrayed the Gates-Conway correspondence. Gates promptly dressed down Wilkinson in front of his staff; Wilkinson replied by challenging Gates to a duel. Before any more high-ranking officers could shoot at each other, however, Gates and Conway rushed off to York with the original letter, which was, in the words of John Laurens, president of Congress, "ten times worse in every way"[11] than Washington, who never was allowed to see it, thought it was. But, ex-

posed to the light, the Gates-Conway plot evaporated, leaving
Washington shaken with the knowledge that there were few generals
he could trust.

"To the great joy of the army,"[12] Benedict Arnold arrived at headquarters on May 21, 1778, in his carriage from New Haven. In the
camp, many of the men who had suffered with Arnold during an
even worse winter at Quebec had come out onto the company
streets to cheer for him. It took four men to help him into the Dew-
ees mansion for an emotional reunion with Washington, who had
not seen Arnold since he had been shot at Saratoga. Arnold's leg had
not healed entirely: he still was unable to stand without a crutch. He
propped his leg on a stool as he chatted with Washington, who had
urged him not to risk coming back yet. But Arnold wanted some
role in the new campaign, even if it was obvious that he was not
ready to sit on a horse. After a warm welcome—Henry Knox and
his wife, Lucy, were there with Washington and his wife, the plump
and serene Martha, and Arnold's two young former aides. Matthew
Clarkson and Aaron Burr, who had now attached themselves to
Washington's official family. Arnold and Washington sat down to
talk: both Arnold and Lincoln, also still recuperating, were to be
kept in reserve.

But Washington immediately brought up the need for a new
command, a military governorship of Philadelphia, eastern Pennsylvania, and southern New Jersey. Philadelphia was crammed with
goods, much of which the army needed. The British, according to
Washington's spies, would only be able to transport a small fraction
of what was crowded into stores and warehouses. There was also a
large neutral population of Quakers, and there were many revolutionaries in Pennsylvania, just itching for revenge against anyone
they perceived as a Tory collaborator with the British. Washington
also wanted to soothe thousands of artisans he needed to go on with
war work, not flee the city. Furthermore, at least four times, Washington had had to shift his main army to protect the capital whenever the British wished to feint toward the city: a strong military
command headed by a respected officer who could quickly raise militia, as Arnold had often demonstrated he could, would not only
protect the capital but give Washington's main field army much
greater flexibility, allowing it to press the British without having to
worry about another attack from the rear. With French entry into
the war, the American capital could not be packing up and moving
constantly, and a well-known and respected general was needed to
deal as an equal with high-ranking officers. Would Arnold be willing

to take the governorship until he was ready to fight? Arnold cheerfully accepted the high-level rear-area assignment.

It was probably the worst mistake either man ever made, placing Arnold in the middle of a murderous four-way political crossfire: a struggle for control of the nation's capital involving the radical new revolutionary government of Pennsylvania, the anti-Washington, anti-Schuyler, and anti-army factions in the Continental Congress, and the army, which was to be represented only by Major General Benedict Arnold. On May 30, Arnold took an oath of allegiance. It may have seemed a mere formality at the time, and being forced by Congress to take such an oath must have annoyed Arnold. He waited until the last possible day stipulated by Congress, and then, on May 30, his friend Henry Knox administered the oath at the Valley Forge Artillery Park, where Arnold now had his headquarters as the military governor of the region.

By the end of May, as it became obvious that the British pullout from Philadelphia was imminent, Arnold was busy making plans for a peaceful takeover of the city under martial law. First, he appointed his staff. Throughout his convalescence at Albany and in Connecticut, Major David Solebury Franks had been by his side. Franks was the sort of dashing, quick-witted young man Arnold liked and trusted. Because he was the son of a rich Jewish merchant who was a leading supporter of Quebec Governor Carleton, he was under suspicion by revolutionaries who assumed that many of the wealthy were fence-straddling with a family member on whichever side won the war. Many prominent families, including the Franklins and the Livingstons, were eventually laid open to this charge.

Franks had taken great risks for the Revolution, had lent the Americans in Canada whatever money he had, had broken with his father when he left Montreal as an unpaid volunteer on Arnold's staff. When Arnold was appointed military governor, he was able to reward Franks with a major's commission in the Continental Line as his aide-de-camp. But many of Washington's more plebeian officers considered him a fop and a dandy for keeping his wig powdered and his uniform new and spit-and-polish, and some leading revolutionaries were ambivalent about him. Jefferson considered him "light, indiscreet, active, honest, affectionate";[13] Silas Deane denounced him as "volatile and trifling . . . mere wax, and never either too hot or too cold to receive the impression of the last application."[14] As his other aide, Arnold restored to his mess another young patrician who had a knack for arousing criticism: Matthew Clarkson had been the first Schuyler partisan to be forced out by Gates at Saratoga and he was now rewarded for his loyalty to Arnold by being appointed to his personal staff as major aide-de-camp. Arnold's appointments connected him to Schuyler and the New York "gang" and to David Franks of Philadelphia, one of America's wealthiest and most controversial merchants, who had been acting as commissary to prisoners on both sides and whose daughter, the witty and acerbically outspoken Loyalist Rebecca Franks, was not only her father's greatest political liability but Peggy Shippen's closest friend.

On June 18, 1778, only three weeks after Arnold's appointment as governor, the last British soldiers sailed across the Delaware River toward New York. Fifteen minutes later, Arnold's advance guard of light infantry under Captain Allen McLane rode into the city with Major Franks, who carried Arnold's orders, proclamations to be printed in the newspapers, and authority to find him suitable headquarters. The high-spirited Franks had no trouble choosing as Arnold's headquarters the Penn mansion at Sixth and Market streets, until a few hours before, the headquarters of General Howe. The next day, June 19, at the last possible moment, Washington's orders to occupy the capital reached Arnold, and he rode into the city in his coach-and-four with his liveried servants and aides and orderlies at the rear of a parade of Massachusetts Continentals assigned to his garrison contingent led by Philadelphia light horse. Thousands of pro-American Philadelphians lined his route, cheering their liberators. Arnold could see that they were pinched and hungry-looking after the British occupation. What he also saw was a scene of devastation: the city had been turned into a British armed camp, whole neighborhoods of houses on the north, west, and southern fringes burned or dismantled for firewood, virtually every wood fence in the city consumed, gravestones overturned as Presbyterian cemeteries were used to exercise horses, churches stripped of their pews and galleries and pulpits to warm the hearths of barracks and billets. The miles of abatis had been flooded, ringing the city with an immense moat. Windows in some public buildings had been left broken for eight months since the British men-of-war *Augusta* and *Merlin* had exploded. Building interiors had been ruined by moisture and littered with trash, exteriors stripped of their shutters to provide firewood. All of the furnishings of Independence Hall had been burned to warm five companies of British artillery quartered on the first floor; windows and shutters upstairs had been nailed shut to keep wounded Americans from escaping, and other prisoners had been locked in the basement. The city's neat squares and commons had been churned to mud and littered with the debris of a departing army. Near Independence Hall, at present-day Washington Square, was the city's potter's field: returning revolutionaries found it cut with long, freshly filled trenches, the mass graves of some two thousand American prisoners of war who had died in the city that winter. The streets were jammed with broken-down conveyances and the carcasses of horses worked to death in their traces. Only the square-mile enclave of handsome brick townhouses of the city's wealthy Quakers and Loyalists, their shops, meetinghouses and market sheds, appeared conspicuously unscathed by British depredations. Inside his father's mansion on South Fourth Street, Judge Shippen watched nervously with his daughters as the American cavalrymen went by, going grimly to their assigned duty stations.

For two weeks, Congress, sitting at Lancaster, had been debating what to do about Philadelphia. When Congress learned from spies inside British lines that some Philadelphia Tory merchants were trying to hide their goods, then sell them at far higher prices once Continental paper money replaced British gold and silver, Congress had passed a resolution ordering the army to suspend all business transactions in the city once it was reoccupied. An embargo on all trade was to be enforced by General Arnold. Congress asked Washington to prevent plundering or the "removal, transfer or sale of any goods, wares of merchandise in possession of the inhabitants" until a joint committee of Congress and the supreme executive council of Pennsylvania could "determine whether any or what part thereof may belong to the king of Great Britain or to any of his subjects."[15] Public stores belonging to the enemy would be seized. Washington empowered Arnold to "adopt such measures as shall appear to you most effectual, and at the same time, least offensive, for answering the views of Congress."[16]

At the same time, by a resolution passed on June 4, Congress had forbidden any molestation or pillaging of the inhabitants: it would be Arnold's most difficult duty to see that this order was carried out. There was sharp disagreement over how harsh the treatment of Loyalist Philadelphians should be. Congressman Gouverneur Morris of New York thought all citizens should be confined to their houses and forced to pay a collective tribute of £100,000 to the American cause, individual amounts to be determined by wealth and degree of cooperation with the British; Congressman Joseph Reed of Pennsylvania thought that about five hundred Tories of all ranks and stations should be charged with treason and hanged and their property seized by the state. Congress, primarily concerned with any supplies that might have been left by the British and with any goods that belonged to people who could be regarded as British subjects, took milder action, ordering that all goods of types interesting to

Congress—"European, East or West India goods, iron, leather, shoes, wines and provisions of every kind"—be reported to Arnold overnight after the reoccupation, and that nothing be sold or shipped without Arnold's express permission, so that the "quartermaster, commissary and clothier generals may contract for such goods as are wanted for the use of the army."[17]

As Arnold and his staff of ten settled into the Penn mansion, his officers fanned out over the city with contingents of troops to padlock all stores and warehouses to keep out looters. For one full week, Arnold kept Philadelphia closed, even forbidding Captain Peale and his Pennsylvania radicals to carry out the arrests of a long list of "known enemy sympathizers"[18] drawn up by the supreme executive council of Pennsylvania on June 15. This move was interpreted as an attempt to protect Tories and was quickly overturned by Washington. As the roundup of Loyalists and seizure of their homes and businesses began, Arnold immediately found himself the target of charges by radical Pennsylvanians that he was a New England dandy who lived in a palace like a king and was really a closet Tory. The old sectional prejudices had overtaken Arnold at Philadelphia. In Philadelphia, Arnold encountered Joseph Reed, a Gates supporter who, when he had been a member of Washington's staff at Cambridge, had signed the petition to acquit Enos of deserting from the march to Quebec. The first stirrings of revolution in Philadelphia had attracted men of stature like Benjamin Franklin, John Dickinson and James Wilson, but, as Arnold quickly found out, a new and far more radical breed of revolutionaries had come to power in Pennsylvania, and they were out from the beginning of Arnold's governorship to challenge him and trim his sails.

On June 19, Benedict Arnold issued a proclamation drawn up by a committee of prominent Philadelphia radicals, headed by Joseph Reed, member of Congress and vice president of the supreme executive council of Pennsylvania, establishing martial law and closing all stores throughout the city. They remained closed for one week, creating an uproar. Arnold was beset by merchants who blamed him personally for tampering with their trade, even if he was only the military instrument carrying out the orders of Washington, Congress, and the State of Pennsylvania. Part of the groundswell of criticism against him was the result of his highly visible style of living in the mansion of the Penn family, where so recently General Howe had spent an indolent winter living lavishly. As a military governor, Arnold had many guests—congressmen, officers, merchants—and needed many servants to run a great house. The mansion had been stripped by the British: Arnold refurnished it expensively, buying £160.12 in dining-room furniture from merchant Joseph Stansbury and hiring a steward, a cook, three maids, a coachman, and a washerwoman. Instantly, there were accusations that he must be living beyond his means.

There was considerable truth to the suspicions that he was living beyond an officer's pay, but Arnold had enlisted in the army a wealthy man, even if the British blockade had ended his shipping business. Much of his personal fortune he had advanced to feed his army in Canada: two years after the Canadian invasion had ended, his accounts were still blocked in a logjam of audits and hearings by the congressional Board of Treasury. He had received no salary for three years. Meanwhile, Arnold was expected to maintain a suitable house and feed his staff and official visitors out of his own pocket, even as inflation drove down the value of Continental currency every day. To underwrite this establishment, Arnold apparently pursued a number of highly profitable business schemes that were legal in that neither Washington nor the Congress had ever forbidden them, but that brought him into direct conflict with Pennsylvania authorities determined to keep full control in their state.

On June 4, 1778, two weeks before Arnold assumed command of the city, he was visited at headquarters at Valley Forge, where he was acting as officer of the day, by Robert Shewell, Jr., a young Philadelphia merchant and ship captain suspected of having Tory sentiments. Shewell had heard that Arnold would soon control Philadelphia's mercantile fate. He was in partnership with William Constable, Philadelphia branch manager of the large New York firm of John Porteous and Company, and James Seagrove, also from New York, who had rented a waterfront store to sell on consignment for the New York house of Charles McEvers. Business in Philadelphia was bad for the young merchants; Philadelphians had less hard money than expected, and British officers, who purchased most of the goods, insisted on credit, running up large debts. Attempts to sell goods at bargain prices as the British evacuated failed, and like a few hundred other merchants, the three young entrepreneurs were looking around for any sort of vessel to carry their goods out of the city. But the British had commandeered nearly everything afloat, and shipping rates on privately owned vessels had skyrocketed. As hundreds of ships crowded Philadelphia's waterfront, American privateers gathered in Delaware Bay, waiting to pounce. The only protection against capture was a pass or safe conduct signed by some high-ranking Continental or state officer. It was virtually impossible to secure these passes from Pennsylvania authorities, since they regarded merchants doing business in British-occupied Philadelphia as Tories. It was easy to ride out to Valley Forge: the problem was finding an officer willing to sign. Washington himself refused, but he had never issued orders to prevent his subordinates from receiving applicants at headquarters and in special cases granting safe-conduct documents.

In Shewell's case, he arrived at Valley Forge a few days after the new inspector general, Baron von Steuben, who, on learning that Shewell was considered a Tory sympathizer, became so infuriated that he permitted soldiers to manhandle the young merchant and literally throw him off the parade ground. Shewell returned early in June: this time he sought a pass, he said, to move his ill wife and some personal belongings to a farm he had purchased in Maryland. Once again, he was rebuffed, but this time he learned that an old business acquaintance, David Franks, was in camp and on Arnold's staff. Franks introduced Arnold to Robert Shewell, and Arnold authorized and signed a pass allowing them to enter any American port. With *carte blanche* to choose the "personal belongings" for the *Charming Nancy,* the ship they had purchased, Shewell and his partners filled the ship's holds with linens, woolens, glass, sugar, bohea tea, and nails—and then covered the cargo with a thick carpet of salt, a commodity precious in Newfoundland, Canada, their actual destination, but unlikely to be seized by British officers. On June 18, *Charming Nancy* slipped its moorings in Philadelphia, sailed down the Delaware, and was almost immediately captured by a heavily armed Pennsylvania privateer, the *Santippe,* which forced its prize to sail to the crowded privateering port of Chestnut Neck, New Jersey (near present-day Egg Harbor), already crowded with more than fifty captured ships. The ship was ruled a fair prize by Bowes Reed, the sheriff of Burlington County, and a cousin of Pennsylvania vice president Joseph Reed, who was admiralty clerk for the rebel port. But a hearing to libel the prize cargo had to be postponed during heavy fighting in New Jersey.

By October, intelligence reports reached Philadelphia that a British naval force was about to attack Chestnut Neck and seize the valuable prize ships. Once again, Shewell showed up at headquarters, this time in Philadelphia, seeking Arnold's help. But this time, Shewell did not come as a stranger. Two months earlier, in late August, according to his own records Arnold had purchased from Shewell his schooner, investing £1,974.5.4 and renaming it the privateer *General Arnold*. In mid-October, Arnold, concerned that a British raid on Chestnut Neck would only worsen shortages in Philadelphia, rounded up wagons and sent them to New Jersey. On October 16, twelve government wagons, levied in Pennsylvania for military service in that state only, appeared at Chestnut Neck, with written orders and instructions signed for Arnold by Major Franks. The wagon master presented *Charming Nancy*'s skipper orders to release a portion of his cargo for transport to Philadelphia: six casks of sugar, six chests of tea, seventeen bolts of woolen cloth, several bolts of linen, some fine glassware, kegs of nails, coils of rope, and six swivel guns, all to be delivered to the store of Stephen Collins on Second Street. Half of any proceeds were to be held in cash until General Arnold sent for it. Collins later testified that he had assumed Arnold was an "interested party." Collins sold the goods at high prices and paid off the partners quickly: between November 4 and December 8, 1778, £10,108 was paid out, Benedict Arnold coming to Collins's and signing in person for £7,500 for "a share of the same goods."[19] From the admiralty court records, it appears that Shewell offered Arnold a half share of any goods on the ship that could be rescued. Later the ship was released and the remainder of its cargo sailed away after the court ruled over the vehement objection of Pennsylvania that Arnold's pass was valid without being countersigned by Pennsylvania officials.

Arnold's use of his military office was not technically illegal: he had signed Shewell's original pass on June 4 at Valley Forge, one day before Congress, sitting at Lancaster, had ordered all shops and stores sealed by the military governor himself. It is impossible to ascertain whether Arnold knew in advance Congress would ban such transactions. His use of Pennsylvania wagons to haul goods from New Jersey for his own private profit was arguable, since that part of New Jersey was within his military jurisdiction if not in the same state. Moreover, he later testified that he fully intended to pay for their use and his deputy quartermaster subsequently testified that Arnold's use of the wagons caused no public inconveniences at the time. While Arnold had broken no law, he never denied that he had used his authority and the wagons for private gain. As his self-funding schemes became well known, they stirred anew accusations against him of looting and profiteering in Canada.

A second and potentially far more profitable scheme presented itself to Arnold only four days after his proclamation closing the stores and warehouses of Philadelphia. Arnold's census of the ownership of buildings and inventory of their contents, apparently carried out by Clothier General James Mease and his staff, revealed that there were large quantities of goods not belonging to citizens still residing in the city and not needed by the army. These Loyalist-owned goods were about to be confiscated along with other property belonging to a long list of "disaffected persons"[20] now being rounded up by the Pennsylvania state government. Arnold beat Pennsylvania officials to it. On June 23, 1778, he signed an agreement with Clothier General Mease and his assistant, William West, whereby they would buy up any or all Tory-owned goods not on the list of articles needed by the army. "By purchasing goods and necessaries for the use of the army, sundry articles not wanted for that purpose may be obtained," the partnership document stated. "All such goods and merchandise which are or may be bought by the clothier general or persons appointed by him shall be sold for the joint equal benefit of the subscribers Arnold, Mease and West and bought at their risk."[21] They would buy luxury foods, clothing, and medical supplies out of their own pockets at the depressed prices being asked for the goods at the end of the British occupation.

This secret arrangement to buy goods locked away from the competitive reach of other merchants at a time when closing the stores for a week drove up prices by creating demand was probably Arnold's most flagrant abuse of his position. While he did not use public money, he used his office and, apparently, his staff in what, in modern terms, would be at the very least a gross conflict of interest. Arnold apparently commissioned Mease to buy up all sorts of nonessential military goods which they then arranged to sell through a retail store or stores. Whether Arnold actually sold any of the goods has never been proved: all that is certain is that he stocked the basement of the Penn mansion with foodstuffs to serve at his own table to his family, staff, and large numbers of official dinner guests while Congress dragged its feet about providing an allowance for official meals. There were also stories circulating in Philadelphia that Arnold was actually selling contraband out of his governor's palace, but no proof has ever been found. Indeed, Arnold's aides, Franks and Clarkson, later gave sworn depositions before a Philadelphia justice of the peace "that General Arnold did not purchase goods upon his coming into the City of Philadelphia other than for his own private use."[22]

While his secret inside trading with public credit was considered reprehensible by men already his enemies when it was discovered two years later, according to eighteenth-century military ethics it was common practice among commanding generals. One noted historian, Carl Van Doren, comments, "Other American generals besides Arnold paid in falling currency at a time of falling prices, even engaged in speculations, like many citizens whose love of country did not interfere with their love of profits."[23] Such practices were apparently not unheard-of: Arnold felt free to propose a similar deal to General John Sullivan a few weeks later. In case the British abandoned New York City under pressure from the French navy, Arnold drew up plans for another joint venture with Congressman William Duer and, the brother of New York congressional delegate Robert R. Livingston. John Livingston was to buy up a large quantity of goods and hide them inside New York City when the city changed hands. Arnold smuggled offers of partnership through the lines to four leading New York Tory merchants who, unless protected, would certainly, as he pointed out, "suffer greatly in their property"[24] when the Americans came in. But if they would each hide from £10,000 to £30,000 worth of imported goods, giving Arnold and Congressman Livingston a two-thirds share on credit, Arnold would guarantee the safety of all their property and also give them shares in a large quantity of Virginia tobacco which he and Livingston planned to send to Europe in their own ships as part of a convoy protected by the French navy.

Even to send such a message through the lines was illegal: Arnold and his partner offered "a great reward"[25] to the courier. The offer brought only one reply from New York City, and that merchant wanted hard cash, not promises, to pay for sequestering his goods. Unfazed, Arnold formed an alternative plan, a new partnership with trusted aide and former Philadelphia merchant Matthew Clarkson and his friends Seagrove and Constable, Arnold's partners in the *Charming Nancy* deal. They, in turn, recruited Captain James Duncan, who had legitimate business inside New York City. If it appeared that the city was about to be evacuated by the British, Duncan, on his own credit, was to buy up at rock-bottom prices any amount of valuable goods and hide them or smuggle them out. Duncan was to use his own credit to shield Arnold's involvement in the transactions, but in return, Arnold and the others would cut him in for a lucrative share of any "rice and vessels which we shall purchase in Carolina and Georgia."[26]

If Washington disapproved of such activities, he gave little hint of it when reports began to reach him. The day that the British evacuated Philadelphia and Major Franks rode into the city to select Arnold's house, he carried Arnold's secret authorization to buy European or East Indian goods "to any amount" and Arnold would reimburse him. Franks also had Arnold's permission to buy goods on his own account to help him recoup his own losses in the revolutionary cause. While such speculations were acceptable practice, some officers still did not consider them seemly, so Arnold had added to Franks's agreement a "strict charge" that Franks keep secret even from "his intimate acquaintance that the writer [Benedict

Arnold] was concerned in the proposed purchase."27 The unsigned agreement was in Arnold's familiar handwriting. That night, Franks found crowded lodgings with McLane and other officers in a tavern, and the next morning, Colonel John Fitzgerald, an aide to Washington who was familiar with Arnolds's handwriting, saw two open papers "laying on the window:"28 one was Arnold's secret agreement with Franks. Since Arnold's orders were to prevent the sale of any goods until it should be determined what would be seized as enemy property, Fitzgerald thought the letter odd, but he said nothing to Franks.

Not so Captain McLane, who quickly found himself shooed out of headquarters and the city by Arnold's staff and complained back at headquarters at Valley Forge. But when he told Washington what he had seen, he found himself snubbed at headquarters and decided to keep quiet. No details of the profits of these highly speculative ventures have ever been found.

Early in September 1778, Gideon Olmsted, a rugged Connecticut fisherman, and three friends were captured by the British at sea off the Virginia coast and hauled in irons to Jamaica. There they were impressed into the crew of the British sloop *Active,* bound to New York with a cargo of arms and supplies for the British army. Olmsted resolved to seize the ship. One night, he and his friends rose and captured the fourteen British officers and seamen and set sail for Chestnut Neck, New Jersey, the nearest American prize port. But a two-day struggle ensued as the British crewmen desperately tried to recapture their ship, at first melting pewter spoons into bullets, then forcing the hatches and sweeping the deck with their fire. Severely wounded, Olmsted managed to turn a heavily loaded swivel gun and fire it down the companionway to secure control of the deck. Then the British captain cut a hole through the stern of the vessel and wedged the rudder so that Olmsted couldn't steer. Olmsted starved the British and refused them drinking water until they released it. In sight of land, the *Active* was attacked again, this time by two Pennsylvania privateers, who claimed her as their prize. The case was tried by Judge George Ross in Philadelphia under a nine-day-old Pennsylvania law that declared that a "finding of the facts by the jury shall be without re-examination or appeal."29 The Pennsylvania jurors refused to believe that fourteen British had surrendered to four Connecticut men and awarded most of the proceeds from the sale of the prize ship—sold at auction for £47,981—to the Pennsylvania privateers, granting only one-fourth to Olmsted and his friends.

Outraged and destitute, Olmsted turned to his Connecticut

countryman Governor Arnold, who offered to bankroll an appeal to Congress in return for one-quarter shares of any proceeds for himself and for Stephen Collins, his partner in the *Charming Nancy* affair. Arnold and Collins fed, clothed, and housed the crew and paid lawyers for Olmsted to file an appeal with the standing congressional Committee on Appeals. On September 15, the congressional commissioners reversed Judge Ross's decision and ordered the marshal of the Pennsylvania court to sell the sloop and cargo and pay over the entire fund to Olmsted and his friends. Up to this time, state courts had acceded to such rulings, but this time Pennsylvania refused.

Governor Arnold, waiting for a quick £12,000 profit, instead learned that Pennsylvania, in its first serious states' rights challenge to Congress, was about to defy Congress and seize the money. On January 30, 1779, Arnold warned the commissioners that Judge Ross would attempt to get possession of the money for Pennsylvania that evening and had openly directed the provost marshal of Philadelphia, Arnold's aide, Major Clarkson, to deliver the money to him the following morning, boasting that no order of a congressional committee would take the case out of his hands. Arnold begged the congressional commissioners to meet that evening and adopt preventive measures or else the money would be locked in the Pennsylvania treasury the next day. The congressmen decided to proceed cautiously rather than confront Pennsylvania in a jurisdictional fight. It was not until the next morning that they met, one hour after Clarkson delivered the prize money to Judge Ross. The ship itself still had not been sold, and the commissioners drew up an order commanding Clarkson to maintain his custody of all monies from the sale of both the sloop and its cargo. Instead, Clarkson boldly sent them a copy of Judge Ross's receipt for the money. It took two more months before the full Congress considered the matter, asserting the federal power of appeal over state rulings. But it was only a paper victory, for the Pennsylvania assembly countered by ordering Judge Ross to pay the money to the state treasurer. It took thirty more years before Olmsted, long after Arnold's death, finally won a landmark case before the U.S. Supreme Court. In the meantime Arnold borrowed and lost £12,000, roughly his legal share of the prize, to keep the case alive.

Within a few weeks of Arnold's appointment to Philadelphia, his aide, Major Franks, was reporting that Arnold was suffering from "a violent oppression"[30] in his stomach—probably ulcers. A visitor, commissary of prisoners Elias Boudinot of Elizabethtown, New Jersey, also informed Washington that he found Arnold "much

crowded with business" and "in a state of health which I thought
rendered him unequal to the fatigues of his station."[31]

General Arnold's orders from Washington, a rewritten version of a
congressional resolution, brought him into immediate contention
with radical Pennsylvania revolutionary leaders long before they objected to his inside trading on his new position as military governor
by making Arnold the independent military commander of the nation's capital and its environs. "You will take every prudent step in
your power," Washington had instructed Arnold on June 19, "to
preserve tranquility and order in the city and give security to individuals of every class and description; restraining, as far as possible, till
the restoration of civil government, every species of persecution, insult or abuse, either from the soldiery to the inhabitants or among
each other."[32] Arnold took his orders at face value: to him "every
class and description" included not only neutral Quakers but
staunch Loyalists who had stayed behind when the British left.
There was no looting by the returning American army or by angry
revolutionaries, who had every reason to hate the avowed Loyalists
and neutrals who had helped the British and probably prospered
from their presence while fully half the American army died a day's
ride away. Governor Arnold refused to make any distinctions: all
Philadelphians were entitled to his protection if not his friendship,
even if it meant that Patriots' anger and frustrated demands for vengeance were soon redirected toward him.

   The first public confrontation between the returned revolutionaries and the local Loyalists came at the second annual Fourth of
July celebration in a symbolic battle over fashion at City Tavern.
Congress was there, and Arnold. Soon there was a crowd of young
women gathered around him, the latest ribbons decorating their
gowns: the shops were once again open. But not all the women
crowding into the banquet hall wore great mounds of white hair
stacked high above them. Fashion was becoming a revolutionary issue. One American officer who had spent the winter at Valley Forge
reacted to the opulent scene:

. . . Here it is all gaiety and every lady and gentleman endeavors to
outdo the other in splendor and show. The manners of the ladies are
much changed. They have . . . lost their native innocence which formerly was their characteristic, and supplied its place with what they
call an easy behavior. . . . You cannot conceive anything more elegant than the present taste.[33]

*   *   *

Congressman Josiah Bartlett of New Hampshire wrote to his wife to describe Tory ladies "who tarried with the Regulars wearing the most enormous high headdresses after the manner of the mistresses and whores of the British officers."[34] It was a time of celebrating for the young ladies, as Sarah Franklin Bache wrote to her father, Benjamin, in Paris: "There never was so much dressing and pleasure going on, old friends meeting again, the Whigs in high spirits, and strangers of distinction among us."[35] But radical revolutionaries began to take off their wigs and stop powdering their hair and cropped it short. To them, *haute coiffure* was a revolting corruption of American virtue. A gentleman's hat was equally symbolic. Tall conical hats were too similar to Hessian helmets. Officers adopting them were "imitators of the enemy." They preferred the tricorn "à la Washington." Silver toe buckles on shoes also came under fire: such waste of precious metal took away from some deserving soldier "a tankard or a coffee pot." Fur-trimmed coats and capes, large hats with brims "the size of my tea-table," long-shirted greatcoats "dangling below the middle of the leg" were all denounced as being "à la Hesse."[36] To insist on wearing the latest finery became as much a statement as not to. When a bewigged Benedict Arnold refused to yield to the pressure of short-cropped, simply dressed Pennsylvania revolutionaries and instead chose to surround himself with aides such as foppish David Franks, with liveried servants, and with Loyalist ladies of fashion, he risked the wrath of the most radical elements of Pennsylvania, the most revolutionary of states.

When Governor Arnold ignored them, the Philadelphia radicals, loosely organized into the Constitutional Society and led by Joseph Reed and Charles Willson Peale, decided it was time to make a point that women who dressed like "British generals' whores" were the enemy of honest revolutionaries—and officers who allowed themselves to be seen with them *must* be pro-British. In the midst of the nation's second birthday party, the Constitutional Society paraded down Second Street hauling in a cart of toothless old black women in rags and ruined shoes wearing an enormous decorated and powdered wig, the biggest they could find, as they banged out the "Rogue's March" on their drums and bowed and curtsied profusely toward the slave woman. An American officer, Colonel Jack Stewart of Maryland, drifted toward a window inside City Tavern to watch the scene with Peggy Shippen's quick-tongued friend Rebecca Franks.

"The lady is equipped altogether in the English fashion," Colonel Stewart remarked.

"Not altogether, Colonel," she answered. "Though the style of her head is British, her shoes and stockings are in the genuine Continental fashion."[37]

Benedict basked in his new celebrity as the coddled wounded hero of the Revolution. If there was danger at the center of the stage, he was too distracted to notice anything, anything but one particular young lady, smaller, quieter, more intense, and yet lovelier than the rest. The young girl he had once met over dinner at Judge Shippen's enchanted him now, and she was intrigued by him, too, this handsome, brave, proud man with the ruined leg. On the Fourth of July, Benedict Arnold fell in love with Peggy Shippen, a Loyalist, a woman half his age, perhaps, in the eyes of some, the enemy. But all he could see was her steady, quizzical, enticing gray-eyed gaze.

Arnold's duties as military governor of Philadelphia involved a continual round of army business in the daytime—deploying troops around the city, carrying out arrests on the orders of Congress, supervising the prisons, gathering intelligence of British troop movements in the pine forests and mountains of New Jersey, now caught between the two armies. His evenings were filled with social activities, many of them arranged by his sister, Hannah, who had brought his boys down from New Haven and now managed his household as she had once run his store. The once-poor orphan moved in Philadelphia's elite circles. Working at headquarters in the morning and keeping up an afternoon round of tea drinking with the Shippens, Sally Franklin Bache, the Robert Morrises and Sally Morris, the sister of Congressman Gouverneur Morris of New York, the Henry Harrisons (he had been mayor of Philadelphia, she was the daughter of a Loyalist merchant and related by marriage to America's first Anglican bishop). Arnold's new friends were the wealthiest merchants and lawyers in Philadelphia. He enjoyed their company at teas in Society Hill townhouses and at dinners at his headquarters mansion, where his dinner guests included the leaders of Congress, army generals, the entire Massachusetts and Pennsylvania congressional delegations.

At more and more of these gatherings, he met Peggy Shippen, and as the summer progressed, it became common knowledge that she was the general's lady. The Arnold carriage began to be seen parked in front of the Shippen mansion on South Fourth Street, where British officers had come to call only a few months before. At first, resentment that the hero of Saratoga was courting the belle of the Meschianza was confined to a little jealous sniping by Pennsylvania delegates in Congress. The first shot was a petulant congressional resolution demanding that Arnold order his troops guarding Independence Hall to hold down the noise. President of Congress John Laurens, Arnold's frequent dinner guest, wrote that Congress was being "much interrupted" by the "beating of drums and noise of the soldiery at the Guard House."[38] But Arnold's relations with many congressional leaders at this point were smooth.

Only a few days after the Fourth of July celebration, Congress had received word that a great French fleet of twenty-one warships was tacking into Delaware Bay, carrying the first French diplomatic emissaries to America and Arnold's old Connecticut friend Silas Deane, back from a stint as U.S. agent to the French government. Four days later, a French man-of-war anchored in the Delaware off Chester, fifteen miles south of the capital. There a delegation from Congress stepped into a barge, a dozen sailors in scarlet uniforms pulling on the sweeps as a fifteen-gun salute greeted the revolutionaries. At the head of the gangway, the new French minister plenipotentiary, Conrad Alexandre Gérard, greeted the congressional delegates and led them to an elaborate buffet in the ship's great cabin. Then they all headed for Philadelphia in a cavalcade of carriages that finally stopped at General Arnold's, where the official American welcoming reception took place before dinner.

From their seats flanking Arnold that night, America's leaders appraised the man sent by the king of France to help them. President Laurens wrote to a friend in South Carolina that Ambassador Gérard was a "man of politeness, good breeding and affability without troublesome ceremony . . . good sense . . . well-read in history."[39] Elias Boudinot, delegate from New Jersey and another frequent Arnold guest, saw a man "about fifty years of age, modest, grave, decent, cheerful."[40] Arnold offered to put up Gérard and his entire staff in his house until the French found more suitable quarters. Gérard accepted. Over the next week or so, the two men talked at length about the war, and by the ninth day, Arnold felt he could make a bold proposal to the French minister. He wanted to lead a Continental naval force on a joint Franco-American expedition to the Caribbean.

For weeks, the restless Arnold, stunned at first that Washington would not let him lead troops in battle with his leg still unhealed, had been longing for a more active role in the new season of war. If Washington did not think he could sit a horse, then he certainly could not object to his serving on shipboard. Arnold was never happier than when he was in command of a ship. He could not accept the fact that his wound had become his handicap, even if it had become apparent to friends that his damaged leg was now two inches shorter than his good leg and badly bent. To go to sea, to lead a great American naval expedition, was Arnold's answer. He put the plan to Ambassador Gérard and simultaneously launched a lobbying campaign before Congress.

The plan was formally submitted by Gérard to Count de Vergennes, the French foreign minister in Paris and the man running France's new war against England. Arnold proposed that six American frigates join two French ships of the line in attacks on England's two richest offshore islands, Bermuda and Barbados, to take possession of them in the name of the United States. Gérard neither recommended nor dismissed Arnold's plan, which would have given "the pay and privileges of American seamen" to some five to six hundred black and mulatto slaves who would be freed on Barbados for the attack on British merchantmen, and would have provided an opportunity for seizing badly needed military stores and cannon on Bermuda, which would then become the American base for "a swarm of privateers to cruise upon the enemy's West Indian commerce." Gérard only commented in his dispatch to Paris that Arnold was "as ingenious and as active in councils"[41] as he had been on the battlefield. Washington turned aside Arnold's request for his support for the plan and an admiralship for himself. When Arnold told him on July 19 that he was thinking of retiring "from public business unless an offer which my friends have mentioned should be made to me of a command in the navy,"[42] Washington declined to support Arnold "on a subject so far out of my line."[43] Congress ignored the ingenious proposal, certain that France would do all the naval fighting, at no additional cost to American taxpayers. It is one of the more intriguing "ifs" of history to imagine what would have happened to Benedict Arnold if he had been turned loose with a navy in the Caribbean instead of being left to fight it out in the political wars to which he was so ill-suited. In any case, France was not about to share the prize ships and the rich island territories it planned to wrest from its ancient imperial enemy, and Arnold never received an official response from Paris to his plan.

As Arnold chafed for action, he took seriously his role as official host of the French ministry in Philadelphia. On August 25 he marked the birthday of the French king, Louis XVI, with a ball at the Penn mansion to which he invited Philadelphia's leading citizens, even if they were political opponents. Wigless Whigs and Loyalist ladies with powdered wigs wore special cockades, black for the Americans intertwined with white for their French allies, as they filed past Governor Arnold and, at his right, the official hostess for the evening, Martha Washington. Peggy Shippen spent the evening with Arnold, who of course could not dance but was full of anecdotes that more than held her attention. After the dancing had gone on for a while, there was a stirring at one end of the salon and a small dog began barking and ran the length of the room. There was a startled gasp as the dancers saw that the dog was completely covered with the black-and-white cockades, a four-legged harlequin spoofing the Franco-American alliance. Only a few dared titter. Word spread quickly that this was the comment of Becky Franks, whose parents were about to be banished from Philadelphia for their Loyalist views.

Arnold's insistence on inviting Loyalist women to revolutionary social events brought him ever-increasing criticism, yet he seemed oblivious as he spent more and more time at the Shippens' and at the homes of mutual friends. For their courtship to thrive, Arnold needed an intermediary hostess, who seems to have been Mary White Morris, wife of Robert Morris and friend of the Shippens. There, in September 1778, Arnold declared himself a serious suitor in two letters, one to Peggy, one to her father. According to one family member, "there can be no doubt the imagination of Miss Shippen was excited and her heart captivated by the oft-repeated stories of his gallant deeds, his feats of brilliant courage and traits of generosity and kindness."[44] It had recently come to light that Arnold had taken over the support and education of the three children of his mentor Dr. Joseph Warren. The children had been left destitute when their father was killed at Bunker Hill and Massachusetts politicians dragged their feet on his pension and Congress refused to intervene.

But Peggy Shippen had other reasons for falling in love with Benedict Arnold: he was still young, thirty-six, ruggedly built despite his wounded leg, animated, intelligent and witty, strongly handsome and sometimes charming. It was obvious that a life with him would not be dull or unrewarding. If her family's destruction of her letters leaves her mute in courtship, there are some hints in his letter to her. By late September, she had acknowledged her "friendship and esteem."[45] Arnold's habit of keeping a draft of every letter gives some glimpse of their relationship, which was being opposed by Peggy's parents: "I am sensible your prudence and the affection you bear your amiable and tender parents forbids your giving encouragement to the addresses of any one without their approbation. . . . I have presumed to write to your Papa and have requested him to sanction my addresses." It also shows that Arnold, who was not good at this business, hauled out his copy of an earlier letter of proposal to Betsy DeBlois: "On you alone my happiness depends," he copied, "and will you doom me to languish in despair? . . . A union of hearts is undoubtedly necessary to happiness . . . . true and permanent happiness is seldom the effect of an alliance founded on a romantic passion, where fancy governs more than judgment." But there was nothing unoriginal or formulaic about the rest of his longest love letter:

Dear Madam:—

Twenty times have I taken up my pen to write to you, and as often has my trembling hand refused to obey the dictates of my heart—a heart which, though calm and serene amidst the clashing of arms and all the din and horrors of war, trembles with diffidence and the fear of giving offence when it attempts to address you on a subject so important to its happiness. Dear madam, your charms have lighted up a flame in my bosom which can never be extinguished; your heavenly image is too deeply impressed ever to be effaced.

My passion is not founded on personal charms only: that sweetness of disposition and goodness of heart, that sentiment and sensibility which so strongly mark the character of the lovely Miss P. Shippen, renders her amiable beyond expression, and will ever retain the heart she has once captivated. . . . Shall I expect no return to the most sincere, ardent and disinterested passion? Do you feel no pity in your gentle bosom for the man who would die to make you happy? May I presume to hope it is not impossible I may make a favorable impression on your heart? Friendship and esteem you acknowledge. Dear Peggy, suffer that heavenly bosom (which cannot know itself the cause of pain without a sympathetic pang) to expand with a sensation more soft, more tender than friendship. . . . Friendship and esteem, founded on the merit of the object, is the most certain basis to build a lasting happiness upon; and when there is a tender and ardent passion on one side, and friendship and esteem on the other, the heart (unlike yours) must be callous to every tender sentiment if the taper of love is not lighted up at the flame. . . . Pardon me, Dear Madame, for disclosing a passion I could no longer confine in my tortured bosom. . . . Suffer me to hope for your approbation. Consider before you doom me to misery, which I have not deserved but by loving you too extravagantly. Consult your own happiness, and if incompatible, forget there is so unhappy a wretch; for may I perish if I would give you one moment's inquietude to purchase the greatest possible felicity to myself. Whatever my fate may be, my most ardent wish is for your happiness, and my latest breath will be to implore the blessing of heaven on the idol and only wish of my soul.

Adieu, dear Madame, and believe me unalterably, your sincere admirer and devoted humble servant,

B. ARNOLD.[46]

Arnold's letter to Judge Shippen was far more terse. He expected no dowry. He had enough money, he wanted only Peggy. For now, he wanted only permission to court her while the Shippens thought him over:

My fortune is not large, though sufficient (not to depend upon my expectations) to make us both happy. I neither expect nor wish one [a dowry] with Miss Shippen. . . . My public character is well known; my private one is, I hope, irreproachable. If I am happy in your approbation of my proposal of an alliance. I shall most willingly accede to any you may please to make consistent with the duty I owe to three lovely children. Our difference in political sentiments, will, I hope, be no bar to my happiness. I flatter myself the time is at hand when our unhappy contests will be at an end, and peace and domestic happiness be restored to every one.[47]

Judge Shippen did not say yes, but he did not say no, either. The general would have to wait to pay suit to the Shippens' eighteen-year-old daughter while the judge wrote to *his* father to seek advice. Meanwhile, Arnold made light of his forbearance, as Sally Bache intimated to her father, Benjamin Franklin, writing that her baby daughter gave "such old-fashioned smacks. General Arnold says he would give a good deal to have her for a schoolmistress to teach the young ladies how to kiss."[48]

The combination of the most radical Whig state constitution and the largest proportion of Loyalists, neutral Quakers, and pacifists led to persecution in Pennsylvania in the dying months of 1778. There were many Pennsylvanians who were not warlike and, like Judge Shippen, would have preferred to remain neutral, but the British invasion left them exposed to charges of collaboration with the enemy by radical Whigs who had displaced more moderate revolutionaries. The Loyalists were not all periwigged Society Hill merchants. There were Loyalist settlers in the northeastern Wyoming Valley who had been swamped by settlers from western Connecticut and who saw the Revolution as a land grab by the likes of Ethan Allen. There were white settlers all along a five-hundred-mile frontier who chose not to fight Indians loyal to the British crown. There were devout Anglicans, Methodists, Quakers, Mennonites, Schwenkfelders, Moravians, Dunkards, and a host of other sects who either upheld the English crown because it was the settled and established order or because they abhorred violence.

In every feud-ridden neighborhood in every sizable town and county there were two parties: inevitably, one chose the Whig side, one the Tory. Some were victims of religious persecution, like German Dunkard preacher Christopher Sauer, a pacifist whose every scrap of property was confiscated because he did not support the Whigs and who later became a British spy; and his rival, politically innocent German Lutheran clergyman Henry Muhlenberg, who led his congregation off to war and became a patriot general. There were pacifists like Philadelphia merchant Samuel Shoemaker, who served as a magistrate before and during the British occupation but were put on a list of 498 prominent Pennsylvanians accused of treason and who chose to flee to New York City. There were pacifist Quaker schoolmasters like historian Robert Proud, who was accused of treason but stayed on in the city. There were opportunists like merchant Oswald Eve, who thought the British had the money to win and would make him rich: they failed and he fled.

So widespread was Loyalist resistance to the Revolution in Pennsylvania that the radical Whig revolutionaries had to resort increasingly to force when persuasion failed. The Whig radicals by the summer of 1778 would no longer tolerate neutrality or dissent. Since 1776, the Pennsylvania government and the laws it had passed had grown more radical and more repressively anti-Loyalist. First, the Revolution had shattered the Penn proprietary party which had ruled the province since William Penn had founded it in 1682. Penn's heirs, John and Richard Penn, and their top appointed officials had long tried, by manipulating voting districts and proroguing and dissolving the legislative assembly at will, to thwart growing numbers of frontiersmen and radical Presbyterians clamoring for a voice in government all through the long imperial crisis of the 1760s and 1770s. Until the mid-1760s, Philadelphia Quakers controlled most of the power; then, the Anglicans won many converts from their ranks and accrued power and influence. Benjamin Franklin, the political mastermind of Pennsylvania politics, had long led the Quaker party and opposed the Penns, who were growing fabulously wealthy on the sale and rental of their lands.

When the Revolution came, Franklin was the only leader of the party which had so long opposed the Penns to join the revolutionary leadership. He helped to drive the Penns from power and set up the most radical state government with the aid of propaganda writer Thomas Paine. The new government had no governor and no assembly; it was ruled by a revolutionary committee directly elected by the people. Any powers not specifically granted to this supreme executive council were carried out by ad hoc revolutionary committees or clubs, which became increasingly radical. For its power, the council depended on laws, newspaper propaganda, and the support of the clubs, often in the streets. As the Pennsylvania revolution became more radical, revolutionary leaders had to be imported from outside the state to run its government; no Pennsylvanians of wealth or education would serve with the radicals. The vice president of the council was Joseph Reed, a Trenton, New Jersey, lawyer and bankrupt merchant; the leading radical propagandist was Tom Paine, a former corsetmaker from England. The attorney general was Jonathan Dickinson Sergeant, also a New Jersey lawyer. The chief justice was Thomas McKean, from Delaware. Reed himself could find not one able lawyer in the state whom he considered radical enough to work for the Whig side. He wrote to Connecticut to former admiralty judge Jared Ingersoll, who had gone back home to New Haven to escape the war, that it was the perfect moment for his son, Jared, Jr., to come back to Philadelphia to begin a flourishing career on the radical side. "Our lawyers here of any considerable abilities are all, as I may say, in one interest, and that not the popular one."[49] Reed was offered the state's presidency in the summer of 1778, but did not agree until the council hired him as special counsel to prosecute suspected Loyalists, for a handsome £2,000 a year plus his expenses and a confiscated Loyalist mansion, horses, and carriage.

Among the lawyers in the "interest" opposing Reed and the radicals were two signers of the Declaration of Independence, John Ross of Lancaster and James Wilson of Philadelphia, who successfully defended hundreds of accused Loyalists prosecuted by Reed in the state courts. Two other signers, Dr. Benjamin Rush and John Dickinson, also signed petitions pleading for clemency for Tories condemned to death.

As late as 1777, the radical Whigs had such a tenuous grip on power in Pennsylvania that they had had to decree that there could be no treason against the state before passage of the new state constitution of February 11, 1777. Justice McKean ruled that there had been an interregnum from the end of proprietary government until the formal creation of the new state on that date. For the better part of one year, the choice of sides was legal. Since there had been no laws in force and no protection afforded for property, there could be no allegiance and therefore no treason. But after the British invasion of October 1777, the council cracked down, appointing commissioners to confiscate and sell Loyalist property and dispensing with the right to a fair trial for accused Loyalists. The next tightening of anti-Loyalist laws came in March 1778, while the British still held Philadelphia. Confiscation laws were stiffened and commissioners named thirteen prominent Loyalist exiles who had already fled the state, giving them thirty days to appear and surrender to the charge of treason or be attainted, all their property forfeited to the state and their inheritance rights sacrificed. If they refused to submit to a treason trial and ever were captured, they were to be hanged. The power to attaint of high treason was given not to a court of law but to the council. In each county, attainting agents were appointed by the council: they often profited from the sale of confiscated property to friends or revolutionary leaders. Their reports of loyalty or treason were based on hearsay from informers without even the legal nicety of a sworn statement. Between 1778 and 1781, some 487 Pennsylvanians and their families were attainted, 80 percent of them named during the British occupation. Twenty came to trial, one died within British lines, two died in American jails. Three were convicted and sentenced to death, one went insane. Two were hanged for treason. Of the 386 who did not surrender, only six fell into American hands. Five were pardoned. One, the first American ever legally executed without a trial, was hanged. In an attempt to keep their properties from confiscation, many couples were divided, the husbands fleeing with the British, the wives remaining in their homes in Pennsylvania. In June 1780, the council ordered them all expelled. When Loyalists were banished, their properties often passed into the hands of revolutionary leaders, who usually bought them at low prices at auction with depreciated currency. Joseph Reed moved into the house of former speaker of the assembly Joseph Galloway. Reed forced the eviction of Grace Galloway, an in-law of the Shippens, from the house despite the protection of General Arnold, who posted guards in her parlor. When the Pennsylvania council sent around militia Captain Peale and his soldiers to carry her out in her chair, Arnold made a point of sending around his housekeeper to help her pack and his coach-and-four to move her out with dignity, a gesture which infuriated Reed and his council colleagues. The Galloways' five-thousand-acre Bucks County manor, Trevose, went to young General Wilkinson, now in Philadelphia as secretary of the Board of War. In all, the confiscations netted the state £100,000 over an eighteen-year period.

It was the execution of two Quakers denounced by the council as Loyalists that drove Benedict Arnold into open opposition to the radical Whig purges in Philadelphia and led to the largest antirevolutionary protest during the war. John Roberts was a sixty-year-old miller from Lower Merion who was suspected of Tory leanings and had felt compelled to leave behind his family and flee into Philadelphia when the British took over. There he supported himself by selling provisions to the British and raised a cavalry troop, threatening to lead it on a raid to free the Quakers in captivity in Virginia. He also served as a guide on British foraging raids into the countryside. When the British left, General Howe privately warned Roberts to go with the British to avoid reprisals, but Roberts, who also had helped many American prisoners in British hands, followed Howe's public advice to make peace with the Americans. When the supreme executive council on May 8, 1778, issued a proclamation requiring a long list of accused Loyalists to surrender themselves under pain of being attainted of high treason, Roberts left Philadelphia and surrendered himself, subscribing an affirmation of allegiance to the United States and posting bail to stand trial. He was tried on a charge of "waging cruel war against this Commonwealth."[50] Ten of twelve jurors voted for his acquittal and only agreed to a verdict of guilty if they could petition for a pardon. Their petition asserted that Roberts had acted "under the influence of fear when he took the imprudent step of leaving his family and joining the enemy."[51] Although Chief Justice McKean ruled that Roberts had had thirty-five jury challenges, and had only exercised thirty-three of them, the two he failed to use did him in. Despite Roberts's frequent "acts of humanity, charity and benevolence" that had saved many American lives, despite the spectacle of his wife and ten children appealing on their knees before Congress for mercy and the signatures of more than one thousand civic, military, and religious leaders on a petition for clemency, Roberts and a Loyalist gatekeeper, Abram Carlisle, were ordered hanged, their reprieve denied by Reed, who called them "a crafty and designing set of men" and who demanded in the newspapers "a speedy execution for both animals."[52]

On November 4, Roberts and Carlisle were marched through the streets with nooses around their necks at the head of a parade of some four thousand Quakers, the largest demonstration in Philadelphia since the closing of the port of Boston. At the gallows in Centre Square, Arnold's soldiers played the "Rogue's March" and stood at attention as the condemned men were escorted up the gallows stairs. The editor of the *Pennsylvania Ledger,* who fled Philadelphia after witnessing the scene, wrote to Joseph Galloway in England, "Poor Roberts and Carlisle have been wantonly sacrificed. They were walked to the gallows behind the cart with halters round their necks.

Poor Carlisle, having been very ill during his confinement, was too weak to say anything, but Mr. Roberts, with the greatest coolness imaginable, spoke for some time."[53] Another Loyalist eyewitness wrote Galloway that Roberts told the throng "that his conscience acquitted him of guilt, that he suffered for doing his duty for his Sovereign, that his blood would one day be demanded at their hands." Just before the noose was tightened, Roberts turned to his wife, Jane, and their children and "exhorted them to remember his principles, for which he died."[54] After the two men were cut down, the crowd followed the cart carrying their coffins to the Friends Burial Ground.

The night before the execution, Benedict Arnold had demonstrated his sympathy for the city's Loyalists in Philadelphia by staging a public reception at City Tavern, personally inviting leading Quakers and Loyalists. Two days later, Reed began a long campaign against Arnold by writing to General Nathanael Greene, Washington's number-two general: "The Tories are unhumbled. . . . Will you not think it extraordinary that General Arnold made a public entertainment . . . of which not only common Tory ladies but the wives and daughters of persons proscribed by the State and now with the enemy at New York formed a very considerable number. . . . You have undoubtedly heard into what line General Arnold has thrown himself. If things proceed in the same train much longer, I would advise every Continental officer to leave his uniform at the last stage and procure a scarlet coat as the only mode of ensuring respect."[55]

Not all American generals agreed with Reed's assessment of Arnold's public neutrality. Philadelphia's own General Cadwalader, the man who had shot the caballing Conway in the mouth, wrote of Arnold, "Every man who has a liberal way of thinking highly approves his conduct. He has been civil to every gentleman who has taken the oath, intimate with none."[56] Mrs. Robert Morris noted that "even our military gentlemen here are too liberal to make any distinctions between Whig and Tory ladies. If they make any, it's in favor of the latter. It originates at headquarters." But to Mrs. Morris, Arnold's "strange conduct" was the result of romance, not politics. "I must tell you that Cupid has given our little general a more mortal wound than all the host of Britons could. Miss Peggy Shippen is the fair one."[57]

Benedict Arnold's public support of Philadelphia's conservatives during the Loyalist treason trials in the summer of 1778 excited Peggy Shippen and even made her father waver in his opposition to the general's courtship of his beautiful eighteen-year-old daughter. At first, Judge Shippen refused even to hear of their marriage and rejected Arnold's proposal, but Benedict Arnold was not about to be rebuffed. He continued to call on Peggy's family and to invite her to dinners, receptions, and dances at headquarters on High Street, to meet her at the homes of friends, and to roll down cobbled Fourth Street in his carriage for afternoon visits.

Peggy came to relish these pleasantly tense visits, this tug-of-war for her affection. The general, who had thrown away his crutches, came swinging up the walkway in his buff-and-blue dress uniform with two silver stars on each shoulder, tapping his gold-headed cane. Peggy's dignified father sat in one wingback, her suitor in another, discussing politics, war, trade, literature, horses, and the town's latest gossip, while her mother kept their teacups filled and Peggy listened raptly, sometimes surprising both men when she gave her clear, strong opinions. Arnold quickly came to appreciate her "sweetness of disposition and goodness of heart, her sentiments as well as her sensibilities."[58] He trusted her and believed that he could confide in her the way he had never dared with other officers, his first wife, or his New Haven friends. Never had he felt so safe, so appreciated.

At few times in his life, however, had he faced a more implacable adversary than Judge Shippen. The judge had several objections to Arnold. He was worried about his daughter's marrying a cripple, an invalid, a man who would be unable to provide properly for her. Arnold's leg had become the subject of Philadelphia gossip. Congressman Duane wrote to Philip Schuyler that he had heard two socialites "of our acquaintance in deep debate about this same wounded leg. They were as much perplexed as the Widow Wadman. . . . His leg much resembles Uncle Toby's groin [the source of universal speculation by women for five miles around in the novel *Tristram Shandy*]. . . . In the meantime, it is the only obstacle to the lover's happiness."[59]

Arnold had the backing of Neddy Burd, who was about to marry Peggy's sister. To in-law Jasper Yeates he revealed that Judge Shippen was proving intractable and was trying to discourage the match by threatening to move the family away from Philadelphia. That the judge was making Arnold's leg "the only objection" was wrong, Burd argued, especially when Peggy "is firmly persuaded it will soon be well. We have every reason to hope it will be well again, though I am not so sanguine as he is with respect to the time." Burd told Yeates he favored Arnold's marriage to Peggy because Arnold was "a well-dispositioned man, and one that will use his best endeavors to make P—— happy, and I doubt not will succeed." He also liked the sound of Arnold's money: "he has acquired something handsome [for Peggy] and a settlement will be previously made."[60]

Nevertheless, Judge Shippen also saw Arnold as a *parvenu:* he may not have known Arnold's family background. To the judge, Arnold was one of these newly rich revolutionaries who had usurped power from families like the Shippens. Only months before, the British had occupied Philadelphia, and they might come again. He also worried that if the British returned to Philadelphia, years of careful neutrality would be compromised by Peggy's marriage to a rebel general. Yet he must have been aware that he ran less risk of persecution by revolutionaries if Peggy married Arnold. Indeed, Arnold embodied the Revolution, which had stripped Shippen of his offices and much of his income. In December, the judge wrote to his aged father: "My youngest daughter is much solicited by a certain General. Whether this will take place or not depends upon circumstances."[61] There were already hints, deliberately scattered where guests could not mistake them, that Judge Shippen was worried about money. Although he still had plenty of it, he was obviously trying to discourage Arnold from pursuing any of it. An embarrassed Peggy found that she could relax at Arnold's table, where the food and wine never ran out, rather than run the risk that her father would stint on the portions at his dinner table when she did dare to ask the general to stay. She also must have blushed as the drawing-room furniture became threadbare, when the judge did not allow it to be repaired.

When Peggy's father at first refused Arnold's offer of matrimony, Peggy apparently decided that it was unwise to confront him. Instead, she quietly encouraged the general to continue his visits and his invitations. Meanwhile she convinced her father that she was uncertain about Arnold, while she worked behind the scenes to show the man she loved how to outmaneuver the father to whom she was so devoted.

A patient man at few times in his life—on the march to Quebec, building a navy—Arnold showed determination that winter. More than any number of social visits to Fourth Street, two things seem to have brought Judge Shippen around: Arnold's protection of persecuted Quakers and Loyalists and his purchase of a magnificent estate on a hill overlooking the Schuylkill River. Mount Pleasant, preserved by the Philadelphia Museum of Art and located in Fairmount Park, is a handsome ninety-nine-acre country manor, as fine an example of Georgian estate architecture as any of the roughly 150 country houses surrounding colonial Philadelphia. John Adams called it "the most elegant seat in Pennsylvania."[62] It commanded the north bank of the Schuylkill with long views of Philadelphia, five miles in the distance. Its sloping formal gardens, richly paneled and corniced drawing and dining rooms, and tall casement windows would provide a grand backdrop for a governor and his lady to hold elaborate parties. Arnold had visited the house when it was the temporary rented quarters of the Spanish mission to Philadelphia. He paid £7,000 for it, plunking down a £5,000 down payment and taking only a £2,000 mortgage, putting his New Haven house on the market to help pay for it. In an antenuptial agreement, a sort of reverse dowry, Arnold deeded the house over to Peggy Shippen, putting the estate in trust with Judge Shippen, a cousin, and former Mayor Samuel Powel.

By January 1779, Judge Shippen was showing signs of relenting. On January 2, Judge Shippen's own father wrote to Neddy Burd, "We understand that General Arnold, a fine gentleman, lays close siege to Peggy and, if so, there will soon be another match in the family."[63] Everyone seemed swept off his feet except Judge Shippen, who did not like what he was beginning to hear about Benedict Arnold and acceded to his daughter's engagement only when his continued refusal seemed to make Peggy, now thoroughly in love with Arnold, hysterical to the point of fainting spells.

15

"SELF-PRESERVATION IS THE FIRST PRINCIPLE"

I daily discover so much baseness
and ingratitude among mankind that
I almost blush at being of the same
species, and could quit the stage
without regret, was it not for some
gentle, generous souls like my dear
Peggy.

Benedict Arnold to Peggy Shippen, February 8, 1778

Military Governor Benedict Arnold's conspicuous leniency to Loyalists in Philadelphia infuriated radical Whigs. By the winter of 1778, as Arnold publicly escorted Peggy Shippen to dinners, balls, and the theater, the Radicals began, tentatively at first and then with increasing ferocity, to attack him in print. Opposition to Arnold's public and personal policy of treating all Philadelphians as equals had begun as soon as he took office. The first objections came to his invitation of accused Loyalists to Fourth of July festivities, then to his issuance of passes to Loyalist merchants and the families of Tories who had fled to New York City. By the time Silas Deane returned in July 1778 from a diplomatic mission to Paris, Arnold was already so suspected of Tory leanings that Joseph Reed, the man in charge of hunting down and persecuting Loyalists, warned Deane not to move in with Arnold at headquarters or he, too, would be tainted with suspicion of Toryism. Deane ignored Reed, accepted Arnold's invitation—and soon found himself the target of vehement attacks in Congress, where he was eventually accused of spying for the British.

By August, Arnold too was under attack in Congress. Pennsylvania's delegation insisted that the state's rights were being trampled every time Arnold signed a pass to allow accused Loyalists to leave the state. The charge centered around Hannah Levy, niece of a deported Loyalist partner in the mercantile firm of Franks and Levy and a cousin of Arnold's aide-de-camp. With a pass from Arnold, she had gone to New York City to collect money owed to her family. On August 16, Congress forbade Arnold to issue any more passes without the countersignature of Pennsylvania authorities. To most congressmen, the case was one more example of clarifying the cloudy jurisdictions of state and federal governments; to Arnold, it was an indignity to the federal and military authority and a personal insult to himself. To Reed, the congressional victory was an incentive for fresh attacks on Arnold.

Through much of the autumn, Reed was preoccupied with prosecuting Tories. A fundamentalist New Light Presbyterian and disciple of the Reverend Aaron Burr, a leader of the Great Awakening and founder of Princeton University, Reed was zealous in his pursuit of all men moderate or conservative in Philadelphia, convinced that all but the most radical revolutionaries were really British sympathizers bent on subverting the Revolution. After moderate Revolutionary lawyers such as James Wilson successfully took up the defense of almost every one of the accused, Reed won only two of twenty-three cases brought to trial; Roberts's and Carlisle's. Reed was astounded when Arnold openly sympathized with the Quakers and the Loyalists. He wrote to Nathanael Greene at Washington's headquarters, "It would astonish you to observe the weight of interest exerted to pardon them and virtually every other, for none could be more guilty."[1]

When General Arnold began squiring Peggy Shippen to John André's Southwark Playhouse, Reed, still a member of Pennsylvania's delegation in Congress, pressed state legislation to force Arnold to close down the theater. Arnold, continuing to attend plays with Peggy, ignored the ban. Arnold's insistence on publicly courting a leading Loyalist's daughter seems to have been too much for Reed and his wife, a devout Presbyterian born in England. Together, they

watched the lovers with cold eyes. Esther Reed, austere, wraithlike
mother of six, had her own private reasons for disliking Peggy Shippen. She had long been the butt of Loyalist humor and had written
Reed before their marriage that Peggy's in-law, Alice Lee Shippen,
wife of surgeon general William Shippen, "has behaved extremely
unhandsomely to our family and particularly to me. She had endeav-
oured to make me appear not only ridiculous," Mrs. Reed complained, "but really hinted that I have been very ill, that I was sly,
and that religion is often a cloak to hide bad actions."[2] Even though
Reed and his wife were no longer penurious (he was soon earning
£4,000 a year and lived in the former Galloway mansion in winter
and a lavish confiscated country house in summer) they were still
considered outsiders by such families as the Lees of Virginia and
their Philadelphia in-laws, the Shippens.

So long as Reed was only one of a dozen council members and
his anti-Loyalist position was so well known, he was in no position
to attack Arnold in print. That task at first fell to another Presbyterian lawyer, Timothy Matlack, secretary of the council. Matlack
opened the assault on Arnold in the *Pennsylvania Packet* on November 5, 1778, with his "Anecdote for a Military Man," a public denunciation of Arnold's invitation of the wives of Loyalist exiles to
his parties. The next issue of the *Packet,* on November 12, contained
an anonymous article (reputedly written by Matlack) commenting
on Arnold's involvement in the recent admiralty court decision in
the seizure of the sloop *Active.* Reed and the council were furious
that Arnold had stepped in between Pennsylvania and Congress and
had engineered a congressional appeal to a Pennsylvania court case.
Reed and his fellow councillors feared that Congress was trying to
consolidate power at the expense of the states. That Congress, at the
behest of one of its generals, had claimed the right to review the
decision of a Pennsylvania court awakened fears of a centralized tyranny replacing the British monarchy. Arnold had stepped into a
hornet's nest by putting himself in the middle of a test case of state
versus federal prerogative, and Reed and his allies vowed to expose
his financial interest in it and make an example of him. "It is whispered," Matlack wrote, "that some gentlemen of high rank, now in
this city,"[3] had interested themselves in the case. Up to this point,
Arnold had kept secret his dabblings in the profits of prize ships.
Arnold angrily sent an aide to the offices of the newspaper to find
out who had written the paragraph. Refused, Arnold wrote a signed
letter to the *Packet,* which appeared November 19. His reputation,
he argued, was not the issue. He had pledged money for legal costs
to the captain and crew of the *Active* after Reed and the Pennsyl-

vania authorities had seized their ship. "Some of my countrymen [from Connecticut] and neighbors were here in distress,"[4] Arnold responded, arguing that he had invested in the ship only to keep his Connecticut friends from being cheated by Pennsylvania authorities.

On December 1, 1778, Joseph Reed was inaugurated as president of Pennsylvania, an office now considered so important that the investiture was attended not only by the full Congress but by the ministers of France and Spain. At least one French observer, Brissot de Warville, saw Reed as a dangerous upstart, a rival even to Washington. "He was eager to accept the position in order to prevent the pardon [of the Loyalists] and he succeeded," de Warville wrote. "Reed was an ambitious man; he had the soul of Cromwell. He presented himself as a fervent republican because he hoped to seize power for himself one day."[5]

That Arnold now had a powerful new adversary was made plain by virtually every issue of the *Pennsylvania Packet*. Only two weeks after Matlack's taunting hint of Arnold's involvement in the *Active* case, Matlack published another piece, entitled "A Militia Man," ostensibly written by his son, Sergeant William Matlack, one of Arnold's staff orderlies. The nineteen-year-old Sergeant Matlack, a Pennsylvanian assigned to guard duty at headquarters, had been called in one day by the maidservant of Major Franks, who was distressed that some of the powder on his wig had worn away. As would any young soldier who had enlisted to fight the British, the sergeant found it demeaning when Franks ordered him to go fetch a barber. When the sergeant didn't find the major's barber at home, he left him a note and returned to headquarters. Shortly, Major Franks, the sergeant later testified, hurried up to him and tensely "asked me if I had been for his barber." When the sergeant tried to explain, Major Franks grew angry and said "he did not believe he would come." Later, Major Franks came back to the sergeant's post and insisted "I had better go again." Silently, Matlack instead went to one of Arnold's black servants and asked him if it was customary for orderly sergeants to be used on such errands. Told it was, Matlack exploded, "The militia could not be expected to do such duty." He was overheard by Major Franks, who said, "Sergeant, I thought I had ordered you to go for my barber." "I told him," the sergeant later declared, "I had received no such orders. He then told me to go, and I told him, with his orders, I would go, and did go." The next morning, according to the young sergeant, he complained to General Arnold, who "gave me to understand, not in an abrupt manner, that if I did not like such duty, I should not have come there." Arnold added, however, that if "Major Franks had insulted me at this time he gave me the order, it was wrong, and he did not approve of that." When the sergeant left, he went straight home to his father, who sent Arnold a lecture with the theme: "Freemen will hardly be brought to submit to such indignities."[6]

What Arnold apparently did not realize was that there was a revolution taking place within the Revolution, what we would call fundamentalist today, led by Scottish Presbyterians in Pennsylvania, in New York, and in the backcountry all the way south through the Carolinas, rejecting the Anglicized way of life of wealthy merchants and gentry in the coastal towns and tidewater settlements. In Philadelphia, it seems to have been triggered by the juxtaposition of the British occupation with its attendant opulence and waste within miles of the starving American army. The reform movement accelerated under Reed, Matlack, Tom Paine, and the council, publicized in a newspaper war. In an age where educated men and women bowed to the classics, Matlack signed himself "Tiberius Gracchus" after the Roman reformer who argued for land redistribution and republican virtues such as simplicity of dress and style. As the criticism of high-living Tories and Quakers mounted, it became a religious crusade, and Benedict Arnold became the symbol of an opulent and decadent old order as his carriage rattled grandly through a sea of people less well off, more plainly dressed. In this atmosphere of religious fundamentalism, Arnold's enemies were trying to paint him as the devil. Reed and Matlack found they had powerful allies: in Paris, Benjamin Franklin was furious when his daughter ordered fancy feathers for her hair and he admonished her to keep to her loom. From New Jersey, Governor Livingston warned his daughter to avoid the extravagance introduced by the British, spread by the Tories.

Benedict Arnold was a proud man who tried at first to shrug off what he perceived as the insolence of the lowly secretary of the Pennsylvania council: "No man has a higher sense of the rights of a citizen and freeman than myself," he wrote to Matlack privately, but when war made a citizen a soldier, "the former is entirely lost in the latter, and the respect due to a citizen is by no means to be paid to the soldier any further than his rank entitles him to it." Arnold pointed to his own painful experience as a subordinate to General Benjamin Lincoln "who was not known as a soldier until after I had been some time a brigadier."[7] Matlack wrote back to threaten that Pennsylvania militia would no longer enlist if they could be so demeaned. To this, Arnold shot back that they certainly would enlist: "Self-preservation is the first principle of the human race; theirs will induce them to turn out and defend their property."[8]

Next to the tyranny of a strong Congress, the Pennsylvania rad-

icals feared most that generals such as Arnold really aimed at per-
petuating themselves in power as an American military aristocracy
replacing the old British elite. The Whigs resented any threat of sub-
servience to a military order. Matlack fired back another missive at
Arnold: his subordination under Lincoln had been brought about by
"the essential interests of your country" as well as "a regard to your
own fame" and he, too, would have refused to carry out orders
motivated by "pride and insolence."9 An officer could send a man to
his death but not for his barber. Matlack demanded that Arnold
apologize; unless he did, Matlack would withdraw his son from the
militia and publicize his reasons. Arnold, who hated politicians and
was no match in a war of words with lawyers, refused to recant and
fired off another salvo. If Matlack was trying to intimidate him,
Matlack had "mistaken your object. . . . I am not to be intimidated
by a newspaper." But Arnold said he hoped this would be the last
word on the subject, since "disputes as to the rights of soldiers and
citizens may be fatal to both." If Matlack and his son still required
satisfaction, they should take the matter up with his aide, Major
Franks. Arnold was preaching a hard new doctrine to ruggedly indi-
vidualistic militiamen who resisted the mindless monotony of military discipline, the absolute insistence on discipline that prepared
men for battle. Washington had faced this same problem with democracy in New England and had broken resistance with the whip,
the court-martial. Arnold tried in vain by example and now with
words: to him, it was a doctrine "evident from the necessity of military discipline the basis of which is implicit obedience, and however
the feelings of a citizen may be hurt, he has this consolation, that it
is a sacrifice he pays to the safety of his country."10 Arnold had
hoped that his letters would pacify the radicals, showing them the
mix of patriotism and professionalism required to make their republic safe. Instead, it outraged Matlack, who excoriated Arnold for
defending Franks's highhanded conduct. Arnold tried again, thinking Matlack did not quite understand him: "It is needless to discuss
a subject which will perhaps be determined more by the feelings
than the reason of men." He was not swayed by Matlack's threats of
publicity: "To vindicate the rights of citizens I became a soldier and
bear the marks upon me. I hope your candor will acquit me of the
inconsistency of invading what I have fought and bled to defend."11
He again refused to intervene in the dispute between Matlack and
Franks by ordering Franks to apologize, and he himself certainly
would not apologize.

"Militia Man" attacked Arnold in print on November 14:

To be called upon, out of mere parade, to stand at the door of any man, however great, at the whim and caprice of any of his suite to be ordered on the most menial services, piques my pride and hurts my feelings most sensibly. . . . I cannot think that the commanding officer views himself as exposed to any real danger in this city. . . . From Tories, if such there be amongst us, he has nothing to fear, for they are all remarkably fond of him. The Whigs, to a man, are sensible of his great merit and former services. . . .[12]

To Arnold, the word "former" was especially biting.

Matlack made the attack more biting and personal by the day:

When I meet your carriage in the streets, and think of the splendor in which you live and revel, of the settlement which it is said you have proposed in a certain case, and of the decent frugality necessarily used by other officers of the army, it is impossible to avoid the question, "From whence have these riches flowed if you did not plunder Montreal?"[13]

Out came all the unproved charges against Arnold from the long-ago Canadian campaign, and the little booklet of calumnies and accusations printed by John Brown was pulled down off Reed's shelf. The general remained unusually calm when he first responded in print. On December 3, "Observator," undoubtedly Arnold, replied to recent attacks with a public letter of his own calling Matlack and his fellow critics "dogs in the manger" who could "neither enjoy the innocent pleasures of life themselves nor let others without grumbling and growling. . . . This mode of attacking characters is really admirable and equally as polite as conveying slander and defamation by significant nods, winks and shrugs. Poor beings indeed, who plainly indicate to what species of animals they belong by the baseness of their conduct."[14] But Arnold's public sarcasm did not mollify the radical Whigs, who had decided to make an example of him.

No sooner did Joseph Reed become chief executive of Pennsylvania than the attack on Arnold became general. Reed had come to power after running simultaneously for three offices—delegate to Congress, Pennsylvania assembly, and Pennsylvania council—and by switching parties. Brought to power by moderate men, he deserted them to lead the radical attack on his old comrades, including Robert Morris and Silas Deane, and the army officer most closely aligned with them, Benedict Arnold. Reed's change of sides eliminated the moderate element in Pennsylvania, creating a left-wing party, the Radical Whigs, and a right-wing party, the Republicans, whose leaders all were attacked in print and by mobs in the city's streets in the next year. Reed broadened his campaign against Arnold by writing to Washington's headquarters in December that Arnold had become personally and profitably involved in the *Active* admiralty case.

After Reed resigned from Congress to take over in Pennsylvania, it was more difficult for him to attack his federalist foes in Congress. Instead, he concentrated his fire on the visible symbol of a strong central government, Military Governor Benedict Arnold. Reed and his radicals criticized Arnold for his friendships, for his extravagant style of living, even for attempting to stay out of the infighting between moderates and hard-liners. General Cadwalader wrote General Greene at Washington's headquarters that Arnold was becoming "unpopular among the men in power in Congress, and among those of this state in general." He considered the campaign against Arnold ill-founded and the charges circulating against him in the city "too absurd to deserve a serious answer."[15]

When Reed learned of Arnold's private use of Pennsylvania's publicly hired wagons to haul the cargo of *Charming Nancy* from New Jersey into Philadelphia, and of his attempt to help Hannah Levy get a pass to go to New York City illegally and despite the Pennsylvania council's objections, he began his main assault. The council summoned Arnold and his adjutant, Major Clarkson, to testify before them, but Arnold replied in less than tactful terms that he and his staff were accountable only to Congress and their commander in chief. Reed immediately fired off a protest to Congress that Arnold had insulted Pennsylvania, treating its government with "indignity," demanding that Arnold be removed from command in Pennsylvania "until the charges against him are examined."[16] Although no charges had yet been enumerated, Congress appointed a special committee to investigate. Such a committee, Reed realized, was at cross-purposes with the Pennsylvania's council's attempt to assert its own authority. If Pennsylvania had to present evidence to a federal congress, it would be a tacit admission of a higher federal power. But if Reed backed down and did not offer any evidence, Arnold would be acquitted. While Arnold was delighted at Reed's quandary, the council decided to keep its initiative by offering Congress evidence only on the affair of the rented wagons. Reed, in charge of raising Pennsylvania's troops and levying Pennsylvania's share of tax revenues, now added a new threat: if Congress refused to oust Arnold, allowing him "to affront us without feeling any marks of your displeasure,"[17] Pennsylvania would think long and hard about cooperating with Congress in the future. Reed also goaded Arnold by reopening in Congress the question of his rank and seniority; since Pennsylvania supplied more troops than Connecticut, Reed contended, its major generals, Armstrong and St. Clair, should be promoted over his head.

The lines were drawn, and Arnold was determined to contest Reed's every maneuver. When Reed dispatched wagonmaster Jesse Jordan to collect £553 10s., the pay for the teamsters who had ferried the goods from *Charming Nancy,* Arnold refused to pay, protesting that Reed had padded the amount and pointing out that the teamsters themselves had not asked for their pay yet. Finally, after the wagonmaster called on Arnold twice, Arnold left £500 in the hands of Major Clarkson to pay him.

Early in February 1779, Reed and his councillors got wind of Arnold's plan to take a furlough to visit Washington at his winter headquarters in New Jersey and then to travel to New York State to confer with that state's revolutionary leaders. For months, Arnold had been corresponding secretly with Philip Schuyler and meeting with James Duane, William Duer, and Gouverneur Morris. Arnold's friends in New York's congressional delegation had suggested to Schuyler that "the gentlemen of the State of New York"[18] give Arnold a reward for his services in defense of their state during the Canadian campaigns of 1775, 1776, and 1777. They proposed that Arnold be given one of two large confiscated Loyalist manors, either at Skenesboro or Johnson Hall, to colonize with his former troops as a buffer against attacks from Vermont or Canada. Arnold was agreeable: he preferred Skenesboro's forty thousand acres on Lake Champlain, which were suitable for "iron works, mills, etc."[19] He expected to pay for the land, but hoped the grateful legislature would sell it to him very cheaply. On February 3, he planned to ride north to Kingston to negotiate with the legislature. He had the backing of his powerful friends in the New York delegation to Congress, even if his Philadelphia Loyalist friends, including his beloved Peggy, considered the lands tainted because they had been seized from other Loyalists. On February 3, as Arnold was preparing to go to New York, John Jay sat down to write a strong recommendation to Governor Clinton for Arnold, one which reveals how far Arnold had gone in his plan to leave the army and found a major new settlement on the New York frontier:

Major General Arnold had in contemplation to establish a settlement of officers and soldiers who have served with him . . . and to lay the foundation without loss of time. . . . He gives our state the preference. . . . The necessity of strengthening our frontiers is ob-

vious. . . . To you, Sir, or to our State, General Arnold can require no recommendation. A series of distinguished services entitles him to respect and favor.[20]

Reed and his council were outraged that Arnold should escape them at the very moment they were preparing formal charges against him. On February 2, Reed rushed off eight charges against Arnold to the printer's. A proclamation issued the next day, as Arnold's portmanteau was hoisted onto his carriage and Major Clarkson helped him up, charged that (1) Arnold had granted illegal passes to persons of "disaffected character" to enable *Charming Nancy* to get away from British-occupied Philadelphia to any American-held port; (2) Arnold had closed the shops of Philadelphia so that he could make sizable purchases of foreign goods; (3) Arnold had imposed degrading services on militiamen; (4) Arnold had interfered in a prize case (the sloop *Active*) by illegal purchase at an inadequate price; (5) Arnold had used public wagons to transport private property; (6) Arnold had tried illegally to help an improper person, Hannah Levy, through the lines into New York City; (7) Arnold had made "an indecent and disrespectful refusal" when he had been "requested" by the council to explain about the wagons; (8) Arnold's "discouragement and neglect" of patriotic persons and his "different conduct toward those of another character are too notorious to need proof or illustration." To put teeth in its charges, the council proclaimed that so long as Arnold remained in command in Pennsylvania, they would pay none of the army's costs and would call out the militia only in "the most urgent and pressing necessity."[21] No more militia would do Arnold or his staff's bidding. The charges were made public, Arnold's aide Clarkson testified later, before Arnold saw them or could respond to them and hours *after* Arnold drove across the frozen Delaware: Arnold recrossed the river at Bristol the next day when he learned there was an express for him from Philadelphia. Reed dispatched copies of the charges to every state and its Congressional delegation and to Washington's headquarters in New Jersey, but according to Arnold, the first he knew of them was when Clarkson overtook him on the road with a copy of the *Pennsylvania Packet* carrying the proclamation. That day, the council further resolved that, except in "the most urgent"[22] emergencies, it would no longer call out wagons or militia to serve under General Arnold. The council also ordered that the attorney general of Pennsylvania was to prosecute Arnold in the state's courts. Facing indictment by Pennsylvania, Arnold had only two choices—to return to Philadelphia immediately to submit to the state's authority, or to ignore the risks and press on to the army's headquarters, hoping for Washington's support. He decided to go on. To many Philadelphians, however, it appeared that Arnold had fled north toward the British lines.

Alarmed at Reed's thoroughgoing denunciation, Arnold rushed to Washington's camp deep in the snow-covered northwest highlands of New Jersey. As soon as he arrived, Arnold fired back a statement to the Philadelphia newspapers, protesting that he was being "persecuted":

The President and Council of the State have preferred to Congress eight charges against me for mal-administration while commanding in the State. . . . Not content in endeavouring in a cruel and unprecedented manner to injure me with Congress, they have ordered copies of the charges to be printed and dispersed through the several states for the purpose of prejudicing the minds of the public against me while the matter is in suspense. Their conduct appears the more cruel and malicious in making the charges after I had left the city, as my intention of leaving it was publicly known for four weeks. . . .

Arnold would not, he declared, submit to the authority of Pennsylvania; instead, he said, he would request that Congress order a court-martial to prove the council's allegations "as gross a prostitution of power as ever disgraced a weak and wicked administration."[23]

No official report of Arnold's visit with Washington survives, but whatever happened there made Arnold decide to abandon his plan to press on to New York to negotiate for land. Instead, a few days later, he returned to Philadelphia. As Arnold explained privately to Peggy, Washington was sympathetic to him, expressing outrage at the charges against him and bitterly excoriating Mr. Reed and the council for "their villainous attempt to injure me."[24] Washington, he said, had urged him to request a congressional inquiry to hear the charges after Arnold protested that he did not trust the politicians and would feel safer being tried by his fellow officers in a court-martial. Arnold's letter to the press shows that he acceded to Washington's advice and passed it off as his own idea, despite the underlying fact that he was trying to avoid having the charges tried in Pennsylvania. Washington's account of their meeting, written immediately after Arnold's treason, was somewhat different: when President Reed demanded of Washington whether it was, as rumor had it, true that he had received

Arnold cordially, Washington replied that he could not even remember the conversation, "the conversation made so little impression on me."[25] Washington's cool politeness that day thoroughly rattled Arnold. It was that unmistakable Washington civility that amounted to incivility, and Arnold got the message. He quickly abandoned his plans to go on to New York. He dashed off a letter to Philip Schuyler, blaming the bad roads and the worst winter in anyone's memory for putting off his visit. But to Peggy Shippen, now his fiancée, he revealed the depth of his disenchantment and the sharpness of his pain:

> *My dearest life,*
> *Never did I so long to see or hear from you as at this instant. I am all impatience and anxiety to know how you do. Six days' absence without hearing from my dear Peggy is intolerable. Heavens! what must I have suffered had I continued my journey: the loss of happiness for a few* dirty *acres. I can almost bless the villainous roads and the more* villainous *men who oblige me to return. I am heartily tired with my journey and almost so with human nature. I daily discover so much baseness and ingratitude among mankind that I almost blush at being of the same species, and could quit the stage without regret were it not for some few gentle, generous souls like my dear Peggy who still retain the lively impression of their Maker's image, and who with smiles of benignity and goodness make all happy round them. Let me beg of you not to suffer the rude attacks on me to give one moment's uneasiness; they can do me no injury. I am treated with the greatest politeness by General Washington and the officers of the army, who bitterly execrate Mr. Reed and the Council for their villainous attempt to injure me. They have advised me to proceed on my journey. The badness of the roads will not permit, was it possible to support an absence of four weeks, for in less time I could not accomplish it. The day after tomorrow I leave this, and hope to be made happy by your smiles on Friday evening. 'Til then, all nature smiles in vain; for you alone, heard, felt, and seen, passes my every thought, fill every sense and pant in every vein. . . . Make me happy by one line, to tell me you are so. . . . Please present my best respects to our Mama and the family. . . .*[26]

Arnold returned to Philadelphia to face criminal charges that involved virtually every major political controversy dividing the new republic. The case set off a tumult of "great debates,"[27] one of which tabled a motion that Arnold be tried by a military, not a civilian court, on the grounds that to give in to Arnold's request would give the radicals a chance to accuse Congress of putting the interests of the military over those of the nation. A motion by Reed's adherents in Congress that Arnold be removed from his command was defeated in a roll-call vote. Only Pennsylvania had a majority in favor of suspending Arnold. On February 16, every other state but Pennsylvania voted in Congress to refer the charges against Arnold to the committee presided over by William Paca of Delaware, already investigating Arnold's conduct. It in turn was to confer with the Pennsylvania council and hold a public hearing. Paca, a rich Maryland planter married to one of Peggy Shippen's friends, immediately called for evidence. Meanwhile, the Pennsylvania council kept up its barrage of mudslinging. While the council had little evidence to turn over to Congress, Secretary Matlack dug up all the old dirt he could find, printing all of the unproved accusations made by Brown and Hazen in the February 27 *Packet*. The council offered no real evidence to the public, except on the charge of misuse of public wagons. Reed and Matlack conceded in print that they had nothing more than "an opinion operative only as the world shall give it weight drawing with it no civil or military punishment."28 On March 4, the day set for his hearing before the Paca committee, Arnold replied in print: "Envy and malice are indefatigable. Where they have not invention enough to frame new slanders, or the slanders newly framed are found totally inadequate to their purpose, they will call in the feeble aid of old calumnies."29 When Arnold pointed out the fact that Congress had dismissed Brown's charges as groundless and the Board of War had acquitted him, Matlack contended that Congress's acquittal of Arnold was meaningless, since Congress had never allowed Brown to testify.

For two weeks, Paca's panel was "repeatedly pressed by General Arnold for a hearing, with all the sensibility of a soldier injured in his honor."30 As the Pennsylvania council's lawyer-leaders obfuscated, turning over only its evidence on misuse of wagons, Reed refused to send a representative to confer with the congressional committee, complaining that Paca was meeting secretly with Arnold and, furthermore, if the Paca committee dared to consider any of the charges except the matter of the wagons, Congress's action would be "derogatory to the rights and interests of the state and the honor of this council." Then the council menaced the Paca committee: "If any misstep should be taken, you shall be accountable for it."31 Reed's threats brought back a rebuke from Paca: "As to the honor of the council, you have nothing to fear from our report."32

Arnold was quick to forward his own evidence and explanations to the congressional committee. Arnold hoped Congress would move at once to give him a fair trial. On March 5, Arnold alighted from his carriage at Independence Hall for the Paca committee's hearing; Pennsylvania again refused to send a representative. Arnold's defense was concise and almost straightforward. He defended his authority, as military governor, to grant passes. He presented affidavits from the crew of the *Active* but omitted mention of his financial interest in the case. He presented, without comment, his correspondence with Matlack in the case of Major Franks, the barber, and Matlack's son. He pointed out that he had already turned over to Congress his papers about the wagons. He stated "upon my honor" that he had not made any purchases while the shops were closed (he did not mention that while this was technically true, at his behest the purchasing was actually done by Clothier General Mease). All of his correspondence with the Pennsylvania council, he maintained, was as respectful as that body "had any right to expect or were entitled to." And he insisted that he had always been courteous to all Patriots "who have put it in my power to take notice of them," and also to all Loyalists: "The president and council of the state will excuse me if I cannot divest myself of humanity to my enemies and common civility to all mankind in general, merely out of compliance to them."[33]

Arnold's fate was decided quickly, or so it seemed: the Paca committee cleared Arnold of the six charges they considered it within their power to try and recommended a court-martial for the charges of misuse of militia and wagons. Arnold was elated, certain that Washington or a board of officers would dismiss these two trivial charges. Sure that he was about to be vindicated, Arnold decided to resign as military governor of Pennsylvania.

But the contest had become bigger than one man. It was a confrontation between state and nation. If a state could seize ships, as in the *Active* case, it could provoke wars that dragged in the entire nation: if a state could disband its militia and refuse the authority of Continental generals, then the quotas of Congress and the reserves of the national army would be rendered unpredictable and unreliable. The confrontation between Arnold and the Pennsylvania authorities had the potential not only for forming political parties in one state but dividing Congress into factions that could lead to the dreaded formation of national political parties that would, it was widely feared, injure the war effort. The rupture had grown so serious that there was even talk of moving Congress out of Philadelphia. The fact that Reed and his Radicals faced increasing political opposition in Pennsylvania, where the new Republican Society was working to overturn the state's radical constitution of 1777, only poured fuel on congressional fires. Reed accused many congressmen, especially Arnold's New York friends, of working secretly to overthrow his state's constitution, the basis of his power.

Considering Arnold's reputation to be less important than the danger of an open left-right split in Congress, the full house voted to set aside the Paca report and the findings of the March 5 hearing and voted to create a new committee to attempt to reach a compromise with the powerful Reed and his Pennsylvania council. After a stormy all-night negotiation, Henry Laurens of South Carolina wrote, "I feel this morning as if my life was breaking."[34] The new committee recommended ignoring the Paca report and, even if it meant putting him in double jeopardy, ordering Arnold tried by court-martial. The debate in the full Congress was, according to Thomas Burke of North Carolina, "peevish and childish,"[35] four states supporting Arnold, but the majority resolved that Arnold should be tried by court-martial on four charges: the passes for the *Charming Nancy;* illegal purchases from closed shops; ordering militia to perform menial duties; and misusing public wagons. On April 3, Congress reached an agreement with Reed allowing the charges against Arnold to be turned over to Washington for trial by court-martial.

Benedict Arnold accepted stoically the news that he must once again leave Philadelphia and journey to Washington's headquarters, this time to face a court-martial. He had just won one court battle, which no doubt helped to reassure him: on April 5, 1779, a Pennsylvania jury repudiated the Pennsylvania council's charge that Arnold "by force and arms"[36] had interfered in the case of the sloop *Active,* once again awarding it to its crewmen and their backer, Arnold, who triumphantly praised the Pennsylvania jurors for resisting "all the arts made use of to poison the fountains of justice."[37]

Three days later, Arnold rode down Fourth Street in his carriage with his sister, his sons, and his aide, Major Clarkson, alighting at the Shippen mansion early in the evening of April 8, 1779. There, in a ceremony as spartan and private as their courtship had been lavish and public, Benedict Arnold, thirty-nine, in his major general's blue uniform, married the nineteen-year-old Peggy Shippen in Judge Shippen's drawing room. Months of attacks on Arnold's character had only made Peggy more determined to marry Arnold and had won him more support among her friends and relatives. Judge Shippen had wavered after he heard his own father's worries about "a number of things laid to the charge of G—— A——,"[38] but according to family tradition, the judge finally gave in to the marriage for fear his daughter would become ill if he continued the months of tense indecision in the Shippen household. The Shippens invited only immediate family members of the bride's and groom's families and Arnold's closest aide, Clarkson, on whose arm the general had to lean throughout the brief ceremony. A young relative wrote that Peggy was "lovely," a "beautiful bride."[39] Her sister Betsy told her how delighted she was to see her "Burgoyned" at last by her "adoring general."[40]

After three days of being "at home" with the Shippens in which they received scores of guests, the newlyweds climbed into the general's carriage and drove the short mile to the former Penn mansion. There Peggy began to settle in with Arnold, his sister, and his youngest son. For a year, his two older sons had been in Samuel Goodrich's school in Middletown, Connecticut; then in May 1779, Arnold enrolled them at the Hardwood School near Hagerstown, Maryland, run by an Anglican Loyalist, the Reverend Bartholomew Booth. "This city," Arnold wrote Booth, "is a bad school, and my situation has prevented me paying attention to them." As a man just married and ordered to stand trial, Arnold would have little time to spend with them, so he packed them off with £300 and orders for Booth to treat them as his own, not to spare the rod as he forged them into practical citizens. "I wish their education to be useful rather than learned. Life is too uncertain to throw away in speculation on subjects that perhaps one man in ten thousand has a genius to make a figure in."[41]

Four days after the wedding, Arnold, once again expansive and optimistic, decided to make a fresh effort with Congress, writing to appeal to them in his most conciliatory tone to accept the Paca committee's recommendations and dismiss the four charges against him as improper for trial by a military court:

As an individual, I trust I shall ever have spirit to be the guardian of my own honour; but as the servant of Congress, when attacked by a public body I consider myself bound to make my appeal to that honourable body in whose service I have the honour to be. And whilst my conduct and the charges against me are under their consideration, I think it my duty to wait the issue without noticing the many abusive misrepresentations and calumnies which are daily circulated by a set of wretches beneath the notice of a gentleman and man of honour. Yet permit me to say that there calumniators, employed and supported by persons in power and reputable stations, whilst my cause remains undetermined before Congress, consider themselves secure, and industriously spread their insinuations and

false assertions through these United States to poison the minds of
my virtuous countrymen and fellow-citizens and to prejudice them
against a man whose life has ever been devoted to their service and
who looks on their good opinion and esteem as the greatest reward
and honour he can receive.[42]

But Congress, afraid of arousing the wrath of Pennsylvania, tabled
his request. The rebuff stunned Arnold, who now wrote to his old
friend Washington asking that there be a speedy court-martial to end
his months of agony. He complained that Reed had "kept the affair
in suspense" for two months and was ruining his health and his
reputation by the delays. Reed would "I make no doubt use every
artifice to delay the proceeding of a court-martial, as it is to his
interest that the affair should remain in the dark." Pleading for an
early trial date, he warned that Reed would seek further delays "for
want of their evidence; mine will be ready on the shortest of notice."
The case, he argued to Washington, had become an affront to the
entire army: "Every officer in the army must feel himself injured"[43]
by the way one of them was being persecuted. He received a swift
answer from Washington, who wrote to Reed to set the trial date for
May 1.

Until now, Joseph Reed had considered the court-martial a compromise: he mistrusted a military tribunal as much as Arnold mistrusted him. Moreover, he still lacked proof. He wrote to threaten
Washington on April 24 that unless the army adjudged Arnold's
misuse of Pennsylvania's wagons a serious offense, the state would
never again provide transportation for Washington's army. Reed
knew that Washington was preparing a major new offensive that
depended on Pennsylvania and its Conestoga wagons.

"Such is the dependence of the army upon the transportation of
this state," Reed reminded Washington, "that should the court
[-martial] treat it as a light and trivial matter, we fear it will not be
practicable to draw forth wagons in future, be the emergency what it
may, and it will have very bad consequences."[44]

Then he demanded an indefinite postponement to gather evidence and witnesses. When Arnold first heard of this postponement
in a letter from Washington, he completely misunderstood it. He
thought the delay meant that Reed was backing off because Arnold's
case was so strong. That the news had come in a letter from Washington to Reed, delivered by a Pennsylvania militiaman, was a further affront to Arnold. He dashed off another request to Congress
for dismissal of all charges. Indeed, sympathy for Arnold had been
building in Congress, which now wavered. But when Pennsylvania's

delegates warned Reed that Congress was about to dismiss all charges against its wounded hero for lack of evidence, Reed fired off his own letter to remind Congress of Pennsylvania's "confidence, veneration and respect" and its understanding that Congress had agreed to bury the Paca report and press for a court-martial. If Congress now favored Arnold, the nation faced "a melancholy prospect of perpetual disunion between this and the other United States."[45] Faced with the possible secession of Pennsylvania from Congress, and from the war, Congress backed down and ignored Arnold's appeal.

It was at this very moment that Benedict Arnold tore open the letter from headquarters bearing the seal of the commander in chief:

Dear Sir,
I find myself under a necessity of postponing your trial to a later period than that for which I notified your attendance. I send this information in a hurry, lest you set out before it might arrive, if delayed an hour of more leisure. In a future letter, I shall communicate my reasons, and inform you of the time which shall be finally appointed.[46]

Terse, polite, vague, Washington's note left Arnold shaken. Arnold's old friend, the man on whom he relied when his ungrateful country and its Congress deserted him, had now left him hanging and twisting for an indefinite sentence. Out of his command, out of the war at least for a season, Arnold had sent off his aides to South Carolina to buy a ship and cargo. Any chance he had for a peaceful honeymoon had been dashed. Washington's brief note reached him April 27, three days before the day scheduled for his trial. Nine tormented days later, when no further word came from Washington, Arnold could restrain his hurt no longer. He wrote a drastic letter to Washington:

If your Excellency thinks me criminal, for heaven's sake let me be immediately tried and, if found guilty, executed. I want no favor; I ask only justice. If this be denied me by your Excellency, I have nowhere to seek it but from the candid public, before whom I shall be under the necessity of laying the whole matter. Let me beg of you, Sir, to consider that a set of artful, unprincipled men in office may misrepresent the most innocent actions and, by raising the public clamor against your Excellency, place you in the same situation I am in. Having made every sacrifice of fortune and blood, and become a cripple in the service of my country, I little expected to meet the ungrateful returns I have received from my countrymen; but as Congress have stamped ingratitude as a current coin, I must take it. I wish, your Excellency, for your long and eminent services, may not be paid in the same coin. I have nothing left but the little reputation I have gained in the army. Delay in the present case is worse than death.

This tortured letter to the man Arnold admired as a father, the man who had urged him back into the fight after so many rebuffs, had a ring of farewell about it. Arnold had given up hope of ever being appreciated or repaid by an ungrateful nation. He said he wished only that Washington would not meet a similar fate at the hands of an ungrateful people manipulated by a "set of artful, unprincipled men in office." He considered his actions, far from criminal, "the most innocent."[48] He was probably telling the truth when he said he had now lost everything. He had never been paid his Continental Army salary, in the three years and seven months since he had been commissioned to lead the expedition against Quebec: he now totaled up the arrears, plus the expenses allowed for a colonel's, a general's, a governor's table for his officers and guests. He had been reimbursed in part for his personal loans to keep the army from starving in Canada, but not in full. On April 27, the day Washington notified him his court-martial had been postponed indefinitely, Arnold was also notified that his accounts, bucked from Massachusetts to the Northern Department to Congress to the Board of War, were now to be scrutinized again by a congressional treasury committee. He was trying to sell his New Haven house to help meet his mortgage payments for Mount Pleasant, which was rented out to the Spanish minister. His privateering ventures had foundered; his share of the profits from *Charming Nancy* were probably going fast. He had borrowed £12,000 from a French trading firm to underwrite his legal battle for the prize sloop *Active*. No wonder there were suspicions of his sources of income. He still had money, but he was eating up his capital even as Continental currency had depreciated to one-sixtieth its 1777 value. Only Hannah's shrewd investments seem to have saved him for the time being, giving him the money to send off with Clarkson and Franks to invest in a new ship to be loaded with rice and indigo, to sail through the British blockade and trade in the Caribbean. But Arnold had grown tired of waiting for the politicians to rescue the economy of this new and ungrateful nation. He had decided, almost hysterically it seems from the tone of this desperate letter to Washington, to turn his back on the people who had so rejected and wounded him, and make his peace with the British. Sometime early in May 1779, with the full knowledge and consent of his bride, Peggy, Benedict Arnold secretly offered his services to the British.

16

"MY LIFE AND EVERYTHING IS AT STAKE"

Unless a system very different from
that which has long prevailed be
immediately adopted throughout the
states, our affairs must soon become
desperate, beyond the possibility of
recovery. Indeed, I have almost
ceased to hope.

George Washington to Robert Howe, May 25, 1780

That the hero of Saratoga was being hounded and kept at bay by radical politicians had become a topic of gossip even in the Loyalist press inside British-occupied New York City by February 1779. The *Royal Gazette*, praising Benedict Arnold for being "more distinguished for valor and perseverance" than any other American, including Washington, wondered why the enemy was wasting his "military talents" and had permitted him "thus to fall into the unmerciful fangs of the executive council of Pennsylvania."[1] Such speculation in a Tory newspaper, one that was frequently smuggled through the lines into Philadelphia and read avidly by Arnold's Loyalist friends, may have fed into a growing channel of encouragement for Arnold to leave the American cause. By the spring of 1779, when Arnold put out his first feeler to see if the British would make use of his services, a chorus of Tories had joined in denouncing Arnold's enemies for their ungrateful treatment of Arnold.

The fiercely independent Arnold did not need the encouragement of Loyalists: he may have thought of changing sides as early as the seniority controversy two years earlier when he wrote to his then friend Horatio Gates in August 1777 that "no public or private injury or insult shall prevail on me to forsake the cause of my injured and oppressed country until I see peace and liberty restored or nobly die in the attempt."[2] Yet the years of political infighting, even as the British held out the olive branch of reconciliation, had turned Arnold against many of the original revolutionaries. As the economy deteriorated and the revolutionaries became more radical, Arnold moved ever closer to sympathizing with conservative Americans who were swelling the ranks of Loyalists. Added to his natural affinity for men of industry and thrift who feared they would lose everything if radical revolutionaries were permitted to continue on their ruinous course, Arnold was flattered more and more by Loyalists and disaffected revolutionaries around him. In addition, he was itching for a chance to get even with the likes of Joseph Reed. By early 1779, there were reportedly fifty thousand Loyalists under arms or offering their services to the British—more than double the force Washington had at his disposal. Arnold would have his revenge by leading American Tories in a decisive civil war that would return America to peace with England. By 1778, British peace commissioners were offering to rectify all the American grievances of 1776, ignoring only the demand for independence.

More and more, conservative men that Arnold had come to respect were urging return of the colonies to their *status quo ante bellum*, before the age of tumults had begun in 1763, as the British now said they were willing to do. Persecuted and disenchanted by his old compatriots in revolutionary politics, Arnold opened up a secret correspondence with British military leaders inside New York City. That Arnold made such a fateful step that involved his wife in such grave risks and clandestine activities without consulting her is impossible to believe, especially given the intimate nature of their relationship. Indeed, there are indications that she urged him to give up the cause of the ungrateful Americans and serve with friends who respected him. As Arnold clearly understood by May 5, the time he wrote his letter to Washington, he could be executed if he was caught and convicted, hardly his wish now that he was blissfully married.

Arnold revealed how happily married he was and how close to Peggy in a letter he wrote more than a year after his marriage to a bachelor fellow officer, Major General Robert Howe, commandant at West Point:

Be assured, sir, sensations can have a comparison with those arising from the reciprocity of concern and mutual felicity existing between a lady of sensibility and a fond husband. I myself had enjoyed a tolerable share of the dissipated joys of life, as well as the scenes of sensual gratification incident to a man of nervous constitution, but when set in competition with those I have since felt and still enjoy, I consider the time of celibacy in some measure misspent.[3]

So sensitive a wife and one so intelligent could not have been unaware of Arnold's agony as he thought of execution, talked of revenge, brooded about his ungrateful treatment, even if she had not thought her husband wronged and abused. Moreover, she came from a family with strong Loyalist leanings, and while she may have resolved to endure his revolutionary activities, the shabby treatment of her husband may have helped her change her mind. Peggy Arnold undoubtedly supported Arnold's decision and probably helped him plan and carry out his treason at every step.

While corresponding with the enemy was a dangerous act of treason and could have meant hanging for everyone involved, communication with the British was a routine and almost trivial fact of wartime life in Philadelphia, as Peggy Arnold well knew. Indeed, since the British had retreated to New York City, Peggy Arnold's friends had stayed in touch with their old redcoat beaux behind enemy lines one hundred miles away. One route open for the Arnold treason correspondence was through Peggy's closest friends. In her diary, Grace Galloway, Peggy's in-law, relates the existence of an innocent-appearing birthday pact that her friends, the Chew sisters, Peggy and Nancy, had made with Major André and his friends and, in the spring of 1779, revealed to her over tea:

All their discourse was of the [British] officers. . . . They said André and Campbell and Ridsdale, with many others, sent them cards and messages, and that they kept the birthdays of six of them by meeting together and drinking their healths in a glass of wine and that the gentlemen kept theirs in ye same manner.[4]

Peggy Arnold undoubtedly knew of the birthday club and may have told Benedict about the practice of her circle of sending not only cards and letters but orders for the latest finery through the lines to

British officers in New York City, with the aid of one Philadelphia merchant in particular. Arnold decided to summon that merchant and send him with a secret message to Peggy's old friend John André.

Joseph Stansbury later testified under oath before a British commission investigating Loyalist claims that "about the month of June, 1779, General Arnold sent for me and, after some general conversation, opened his political sentiments respecting the war carrying on between Great Britain and America, declaring his abhorrence of a separation of the latter from the former as a measure that would be ruinous to both."[5] According to documents in the British Headquarters Papers, however, their first treasonous conversation had to be in the first week of May. Arnold himself corroborated Stansbury's testimony in London after the war when Stansbury attested Arnold's narrative of his treason, but in retrospect the date may have seemed only a minor discrepancy. By the time Arnold invited the dapper thirty-year-old Stansbury to come talk to him alone in a secluded room in the Penn mansion, Arnold knew a great deal about the man. Arnold had been in charge of gathering intelligence in the state for Congress and for the army, and he would have come across Stansbury's name in a variety of ways. He also may have met him before, since his personal records indicate he paid Stansbury £160 to furnish his dining room in June 1778, a fact that gave Stansbury easy access to his house.

Born in London in 1740, Stansbury had been a brilliant student at St. Paul's School. Put to trade by his parents, he had emigrated to Philadelphia, where he had lived through most of the colonial crisis. Known as a mild-mannered, compliant little man, a dealer in glass and china with a shop up Fourth Street from the Shippens, he had at first been mildly critical of British legislation that restricted American trade, but he abhorred the thought of independence from England. He had made a name for himself as a writer and singer of songs in Philadelphia society, but in October 1776, a revolutionary informer reported Stansbury for having "sung 'God Save the King' in his house [as] a number of persons present bore him chorus."[6] Confined to his house under arrest by the Whigs, he had stayed in Philadelphia to welcome the British the next year. In turn, General Howe made Stansbury an ornament at his table, his own resident poet, adding cash to the bargain by appointing Stansbury one of the British commissioners for selecting and governing the city police under Superintendent Galloway. Howe also named Stansbury a director of the Library Company and a manager of the British lottery for the relief of the poor, but he was most grateful for Stansbury's Loyalist songs and verses, which he could dash off with amazing ease at dinners and meetings of the Sons of St. George and the Church-and-King Club. A Stansbury poem had saluted Howe's arrival in the city, and one sent him off when the British withdrew.

Bidding goodbye to his British friends, Stansbury was careful to swear a fresh oath of allegiance to the returning Americans, reopening his shop and resuming his rounds of Society Hill circles, one of some seventy to eighty former members of their secret police that the British left behind undetected in Philadelphia. Arnold found out enough about him to know that Stansbury had a lot to lose if he was ever arrested by the Americans and, moreover, that the discreet Stansbury had the connections in both New York and Philadelphia to be his best possible emissary. Peggy reassured Arnold that Stansbury was not only able to contact high-ranking British officers such as Major André, but could be trusted absolutely. In his testimony after the war, mentioned above, Stansbury tersely disclosed the routineness of his errands for Arnold: "In order to facilitate the completion of his wishes, I went secretly to New York with a tender of his services to Sir Henry Clinton." At first, Arnold's identity was to be concealed. Stansbury was merely to deliver a letter offering the services of a high-ranking American general who was willing to aid the British "either by immediately joining the British army or cooperating on some concealed plan with Sir Henry Clinton,"[7] the British commander in chief. Stansbury was to take no one else into his confidence.

Leaving Philadelphia immediately, Stansbury made his way across New Jersey and through the British lines. Disregarding Arnold's instructions, he went immediately to his close friend the Reverend Jonathan Odell. An Anglican priest who had been pastor of St. Mary's Church in Burlington, New Jersey, Odell was an even better known Loyalist poet than Stansbury. Odell was now supporting himself and his family as chaplain of a Pennsylvania Loyalist regiment camped on Staten Island. Princeton-educated, he had served as a surgeon in the British army before he was ordained as an Anglican priest. As a missionary physician in New Jersey, Odell had been the close friend and protégé of the royal governor, William Franklin, illegitimate son of Benjamin Franklin. He had been elected to the American Philosophical Society for "his medical character."[8] While he personally opposed the colonial tax protests, he had publicly abstained from politics for nearly ten years, confining his political views to conversations in the drawing room of his close friend Governor Franklin. But after the Battle of Bunker Hill, he had been arrested by revolutionaries who had opened his mail to England.

Taking an oath to keep his own views private, he had been released. Then, on the night of June 4, 1776, on the birthday of
George III, he had written a birthday ode to the king which he read
to captured British officers on parole on an island in the Delaware
River a few miles from the congressional debates on independence.
John André had been one of the prisoners who heard Odell call for
all loyal subjects to rally behind their young king. Odell was arrested
again by the revolutionaries and ordered to stay on parole in Burlington. When war swept through the town that December, he was
hunted down by a band of rebels ordered to take him dead or alive.
He left behind his wife and three small children and for weeks was
hidden by parishioners in a windowless priest's hole in Governor
Franklin's abandoned riverfront house before he could make his escape to New York City. Many of the British officers were his former
compatriots from the French and Indian War, and they helped him
to subsist on army rations and the small wages of a Loyalist chaplain. He poured out what one critic has called his "deathless hate"[9]
in anti-American verses that lampooned revolutionary leaders, becoming the foremost Loyalist satirist and regularly publishing such
diatribes as this on George Washington in the *Royal Gazette:*

> Was it ambition, vanity or spite
> That prompted thee with Congress to unite?
> Or did all three within thy bosom roll?
> Thou heart of a hero, with a traitor's soul.[10]

He also carried out a number of confidential tasks, including trans-
lating captured French and Spanish documents. When Odell's old
mentor Governor Franklin set up the Board of Associated Loyalists,
Odell became its assistant secretary and the man in charge of its
elaborate Loyalist spy network.

As the go-between in Benedict Arnold's treasonable correspondence with the British, Jonathan Odell reported secretly to Governor
Franklin. Governor Franklin had been urged by his father, Ben
Franklin, to resign as royal governor at the outbreak of the revolution and take a high post with the rebels. Refusing, he had been
arrested and jailed in Litchfield, Connecticut, where he had spent
nearly a year in solitary confinement in a filthy death cell. Near
death when he was exchanged in November 1778, by the time Arnold wrote to the British in May 1779 Franklin was in the process of
organizing thousands of Loyalist refugees in New York City and on
Long Island into the Board of Associated Loyalists. Ultimately, he
would be appointed its president by the king. A master at espionage

who, as royal governor, had long transmitted intelligence from his friend Galloway inside the Continental Congress to officials in London before his detention and imprisonment, he was busy setting up safe houses and coordinating agents who could pass information to British headquarters in Manhattan from Loyalists as far away as the prison camps of Burgoyne's captured army in Virginia. He had met with British peace commissioners sent to America to negotiate with Congress: the Carlisle Commission had arrived in Philadelphia just before the British withdrawal, only to be rebuffed by Congress, and for six months had lingered in New York City. Governor Franklin had received their backing for his plea for "procuring, digesting and communicating intelligence of the motions of the enemy"[11] to the British Secret Service.

Franklin's proposal dovetailed with the recommendations the Carlisle Peace Commission would make to the British secretary of state on its return to London. Unable to talk peace, they urged waging political warfare, using British troops to subdue a district and then to raise Loyalist militia, offer amnesty to rebels, and set up Loyalist civil government in each area returned to British submission. Lord Carlisle, commission chairman, had supported Franklin's plan, especially since it was evident that the British army had failed to defeat the Americans and had only made matters awful for Loyalist Americans. Like Franklin, he saw a great opportunity being squandered as British generals failed to exploit Loyalists fully: "In our present condition, the only friends we have, or are likely to have, are those who are absolutely ruined for us."[12]

Carlisle's commission had persuaded the British commander, Sir Henry Clinton, to provide a house on King Street in Lower Manhattan to serve as headquarters for Franklin's refugee organization. Here Franklin, Odell, and other Loyalists were drawing up plans for a Loyalist army which would need the leadership of a respected American general: "Unless the refugees and other Loyalists are put under the command of a person in whom they confide and to whom they have an attachment, they can answer no valuable purpose."[13] Odell's report that just such a man, the best American battlefield commander, was about to defect must have electrified Franklin. On May 10, 1779, Joseph Stansbury was handed from Odell to Franklin to the new British spy chief, Major John André. Benedict Arnold had been made the first link in a dangerous chain of espionage reaching one hundred miles from the former military governor's bedroom in Philadelphia to British headquarters in the white-painted brick mansion at Number One Broadway in Lower Manhattan.

* * *

John André had only two weeks before been promoted to the position of chief of the British secret service, an office which instantly involved him in Arnold's negotiations with Clinton. André was eager for an espionage coup that would further ingratiate him with his new boss, General Clinton. When the Howe brothers had been recalled to England and Clinton had taken over as commander in chief at the British withdrawal from Philadelphia, John André found he was, like all of the Howe's favorites, in official disfavor. Clinton had his own aides and his own style, and he despised the Howes and all their sycophants. A reserved man by nature and not given to flattery, Clinton liked solitude, his mistress, a good bath, and a fast ride, but none of the arts and artifice so typical of highborn British officers of the time. Because he had ducal relatives, he had never had to toady to other officers to gain promotion, and he did not respect those who did. With the exception of André, all of Howe's old aides broke with Clinton. Before returning home with the Howes, André's mentor General Grey found opportunities to push André at Clinton, especially on shipboard during an abortive British attack on Rhode Island. Clinton had sailed to the rescue of the trapped British garrison at Newport, but adverse winds impeded his expedition even as the same winds drove off the French. During stormy days at sea on the frigate *Carisfort,* André, introduced by Grey, had time to cultivate the aloof Clinton, cautiously chipping away at Clinton's reserve. André was much too careful ever to put into writing how he regarded Clinton, much too determined to avoid a life in business to give up his decorous assault on the new commander, described variously by Loyalist Judge Thomas Jones as "haughty, morose, churlish, stupid and scarcely ever to be spoken with"[14] and by William Franklin as "gallant to a proverb and possessing great military knowledge in the field but . . . weak, irresolute, unsteady, vain, incapable of forming any plan himself, and too weak, or rather too proud and conceited to follow that of another."[15] André had made some inroads by the time Grey finally sailed home to England. Clinton accepted André as one of his aides-de-camp, giving him a provincial major's commission, a desk at headquarters in the Archibald Kennedy mansion at One Broadway, and a succession of ever more confidential assignments.

At his new commander's beck and call all morning, André went briskly about his paperwork with his fellow staff officers, old Philadelphia comrades such as John Graves Simcoe and Lord Rawdon, cavalry Colonel Banastre Tarleton, highborn Scotsman Lord Cathcart. After lunch, they all rode down to the brothel district near the ruins of Trinity Church, where Loyalist girls who would have been housewives in peacetime serviced a redcoat every fifteen minutes. While other officers diverted themselves with the prostitutes or with games of billiards or bowling, Clinton and André worked up a sweat playing handball. Then Clinton and his entire entourage mounted up for a quick gallop up Broadway and out into the countryside. Loyalists complained that Clinton spent very little time fighting. One Loyalist diarist wrote, "I saw him at 3 o'clock pass my window, following a Hessian jaeger who dragged a bone pursued by a dog. All full speed over fences, through fields, etc."[16] There were also golf matches, cricket matches, cockfights, bullbaiting, boxing matches, and horse races. In New York, too, André was the pet of Tory hostesses, but he had no special female partner, preferring to expound in public lectures on "Love and Fashion," regaling Clinton's dinner parties with fanciful accounts of his dreams and rebels who appeared as animals in them. Judge McKean, hanging judge of Roberts and Carlisle infamy, was a bloodhound; John Jay, president of Congress, a serpent, "a mixture of the lowest cunning and the most unfeeling barbarity." Clinton's hated predecessor, General Howe, appeared as a gamecock "who at once began to crow and strut about as if he was meditating combat."[17] Clinton howled at his aide's savagely disloyal lampoons.

There were many high-ranking British who considered Clinton an armchair general who preferred his bottle and his lass and playing favorites to risking a fight against the Americans and their French allies. General James Robertson, military governor of New York City, called Clinton "inconstant as a weathercock."[18] Clinton's deputy adjutant general, Stephen Kemble, a career soldier, was horrified at Clinton's "unheard-of promotion to the first departments of boys not three years in service, his neglect of old officers and his wavering strange, mad behavior."[19] Aides such as André disgusted Chief Justice Smith: they were "without reputation, young and raw," especially André, who wasted half his time "acting upon the stage all winter."[20] Indeed, whenever he could pry himself away from Clinton, André hurried to the Theatre Royal, the playhouse on John Street where, with his fellow officers, he had formed a stock company that staged *Macbeth, Richard III,* and *She Stoops to Conquer,* among others. André once again appeared in several minor roles, wrote long poetic prologues, painted scenery with his closest friend, Loyalist Oliver De Lancey.

There were also some Loyalists in New York City who believed that John André had risen so far so fast because he was having a homosexual affair with the commander in chief. There is no proof and very little in print on the subject, but there have been persistent rumors ever since. There is that suggestive remark by the staunch Chief Justice Smith about young men, men "without reputation, young and raw," rewarded for no apparent military ability or achievement and former staff officer Stephen Kemple's disgusted comment about the "unheard-of promotion" of "boys not three years in service." But if Clinton chose to alternate his dalliances between the sexes, he was much too discreet, as was André, to leave any evidence behind. André, the would-be thespian, was always playing a role, but there seems more than acting or the obsequiousness of the courtier in his notes to Clinton, nor are they a son to his father. His letters to Sir Henry are strikingly intimate, self-deprecating, and ever solicitous to cover up Clinton's faults. And Clinton would one day be even more immobilized than usual when he lost his intimate young friend. Moreover, the evidence of the documents does not fully explain the venom directed toward Clinton by other career officers and Loyalist leaders.

On the morning of May 9, 1779, André, appointed only two weeks before as the officer in charge of Clinton's secret service, had two visitors at One Broadway, fellow poets Joseph Stansbury and Jonathan Odell. To visit British headquarters with the message of a traitorous American general was a nerve-racking business for Stansbury, exhilarating in that he was helping to deliver a vital blow for the British, potentially rewarding (for the British paid well for information), but dangerous. Two of Galloway's spies in Philadelphia had already been caught and hanged. In 1777 alone, a dozen Tory spies had been put to death by the Americans. Stansbury and Odell had to wait nervously to be ushered in to see Major André. Then they asked to talk to him in private. Stansbury told his story. General Arnold, a customer of his, had sent for him. He had sworn Stansbury to secrecy, told him he abhorred the war with England, feared it would ruin both countries if it went on. He had spoken cuttingly of Congress and of the French alliance, and he'd said he had decided to offer his services to Sir Henry Clinton, either at once or as part of a concerted plan that would put an end to the usurpations of the politicians of Congress and restore peace and order to his country. He wished Stansbury to convey his offer and to ascertain whether the British were serious about fighting the war to a successful conclusion. Arnold's choice of the code name "Monk" offers some insight into his motives. George Monk had been one of Cromwell's generals in the English Civil War, and when the English Revolution had devolved into chaos and splintered into radical groups incapable of governing England, George Monk had conspired to restore monarchy to his country. For his change of sides, Monk had become a national hero and had received a dukedom and a large pension from the king. Arnold obviously would have his price, too.

For weeks, now that the French had entered the war and Congress had refused to negotiate peace, British generals and Carlisle commissioners had been speculating which American generals could be counted on to change sides. New Englanders generally were less enthusiastic about making common cause with the old enemy. With a shift in British strategy necessitated by the Franco-American alliance, Clinton had been told he would be getting fewer reinforcements from England. He had been devising a strategy of posts, striking out on raids against key military targets and supply dumps and avoiding bloody campaigns that alienated more Americans from reconciliation with the king. Indeed, he had recently had André prepare a report and proclamation forbidding looting, and he had severely chastised generals who had burned houses and churches during recent coastal attacks on Connecticut and New Jersey. Clinton agreed with William Eden, a Loyalist and a member of the Carlisle Commission, that every attempt should be made to carry on a war of espionage to win by conspiracy, bribery, and reward what could not be gained by his limited number of troops. His network of spies would eventually put him in touch with numerous high-level revolutionaries flirting with the idea of defection, including Ethan Allen, who actually negotiated to annex Vermont to British Canada. But Clinton had probably never dreamed that Benedict Arnold could be induced to change sides.

While Stansbury laid out the details of his meeting with Arnold, André, excited to the edge of disbelief, listened, then disappeared toward Clinton's office. Stansbury was anxious to get back, worried that he would be missed in Philadelphia.

That afternoon, after conferring with Clinton, André sat down to draw up a careful letter of instructions for Stansbury, fleshing out the blanket approval given by Clinton. "On our part," André began, "we meet Monk's overtures with full reliance on his honorable intentions." Stansbury was to assure Arnold, first of all, that "no thought is entertained of abandoning" the war effort. On the contrary, more powerful steps were to be taken, and they could be coordinated with Arnold. André assured Arnold that he would be rewarded with "liberality." If Arnold helped the British seize "an obnoxious band of men," the British nation would reward him with a generosity that would exceed "even his most sanguine hopes."[21]

This cryptic message poses several questions: Had Arnold hinted through Stansbury that he would help to seize the Congress? The Pennsylvania council? Washington and his generals? What "band of men" was obnoxious to the British? André further stipulated that if Arnold failed and was forced to flee, the British would indemnify him for his losses. Then André detailed to Stansbury the services Arnold might provide: interrupting and leaking French dispatches, original American dispatches, the names of American agents, the number and position of troops and reinforcements; influencing other leading Americans to come over to the Tory point of view; and "fomenting any party" that would help the British. Military objectives would be as well rewarded as political. Arnold could pinpoint new American supply magazines for British raiders to destroy as they had at Danbury as the result of Loyalist spying. He could help to arrange an exchange of prisoners of war. This last suggestion was especially important to André, who was negotiating prisoner exchanges of war at the time. Clinton believed that the British would be able to benefit more than the Americans from such prisoner exchanges, augmenting their forces at a time when reinforcements from England were curtailed. The redcoats were trained regulars, in the war for its duration, while the Americans to be released in exchange were mostly American militia, whose enlistments had expired and who would go home.

Just how the treacherous Arnold-André correspondence was to be carried out was something André had taken especial pains to work out. Arnold was not to send messages through the "birthday club": the young ladies of Society Hill "must be kept unacquainted with this," André decided. But one woman in particular, "the Lady," Peggy Shippen Arnold, "might write to me at the same time [as] one of her intimates, she will guess who I mean." That intimate was to be Peggy Chew, André's escort to the Meschianza, who was to be kept ignorant of the plot and led to believe by Mrs. Arnold that her correspondence was innocent. "I will write, myself, to the friend [Peggy Chew] to give occasion for a reply. The letters may talk of the Meschianza and other nonsense." Finally, Arnold was to give Peggy Chew's letters to Peggy Arnold. Either she or Arnold was to write Arnold's secret messages between the lines with invisible ink and in code. Despite the fact that he knew that Peggy Chew's father was a prisoner of the Americans, André was ruthlessly involving her in the plot, without her approval, and making her subject to reprisals. At the time, the British were using three different codes: André chose the simplest. The code was to be made up of three-number groups each signifying a word from "a long book similar to yours."

The first number of each group was to indicate the page number in Blackstone's *Commentary on the Laws of England,* the second number, the line on that page, the third number, the word itself. Letters could be read either by holding them over a candle until the interlineations became legible or by brushing the entire page with acid to make the ink disappear and the invisible ink darken. Ordinarily, the British secret service sent messages in code, but Arnold's correspondence was to be doubly guarded, written with invisible ink and in code. Finally, Stansbury was instructed to take "mysterious notes"[22] of this letter of instructions and then to burn it. Stansbury was to be Arnold's regular courier from Arnold to Odell, who was fast becoming André's code specialist. It was a risky business. Even if a message made its way through the dangerous no-man's-land surrounding New York City, if it ever became damp, the decoding acid could turn a critical cipher into an indecipherable blot. Odell would carefully decipher Arnold's messages at Loyalist headquarters, then personally carry them to André. André would then pass to Odell his answer, which André himself, trusting no one, would have encoded. At his end, Arnold was to use a code name to sign his letters, talk about mercantile matters if he wrote directly (he chose the Swedish name "Gustavus," at first, later switching to "John Moore"; André was to be "John Anderson," a New York City merchant). André sent a copy of his instructions to Clinton with his own covering note. He admitted to "the kind of confusion such sudden proposals create when one must deliberate and determine at once. . . . I hope, sir, you will think that a sufficient foundation is laid." André rode off to Clinton's farm on the Beekman estate in Brooklyn after sending the two papers to Clinton. "Not finding myself very well, I, in consequence of your indulgence on these occasions, came into the country."[23] As he often did, John André had acted boldly, then gotten sick.

That night, May 10, 1779, Stansbury was taken by secret service sloop and whaleboat to Prince's Bay, turned over to the Royal Navy commander of an armed patrol vessel stationed there, then rowed ashore at South Amboy for his clandestine journey across New Jersey to Philadelphia. The man who met him at Perth Amboy was another vital link in the Loyalist espionage network. Merchant John Rattoon, code-named Mercury, a close friend of Governor Franklin's, stayed in the old eastern capital of New Jersey when most other Loyalists had fled, spying for the British all through the war and buying William Franklin's former governor's palace and becoming mayor of Perth Amboy. His espionage activities for the British were never detected in his lifetime and were not made public until

Clinton's headquarters papers were purchased in England and brought to America in the 1930s. Rattoon rowed Stansbury ashore and provided him with a horse and enough goods to make it look as if he had been on a buying trip in New Jersey. Then Stansbury hurried back to Arnold in Philadelphia.

It must have been several days before André was able to write to Peggy Chew. The copy in the British Headquarters Papers is undated: "I hardly dare write to you after having neglected your commissions," he began. "I would with pleasure have sent you drawings of headdresses had I been as much of a milliner here as I was at Philadelphia in Meschianza times." He spoke of "ill health" and said it had obliged him "to abandon the pleasing study of what relates to the ladies." He recalled his pleasure at "frequenting yours and the Shippen family. . . . I trust I am yet in the memory of the little society of Third and Fourth Streets and even of the *other Peggy* [now Mrs. Arnold]." He wanted Peggy Arnold to "peruse not disdainfully this page";[24] the words were tucked away in felicitations and gossip of other officers. He marked the letter "A" for acid, sending it off on May 16. There is no record that it was ever received, ever answered by Peggy Chew. Someone at the Philadelphia end of the treasonous line decided not to involve her, maybe Arnold, who wanted as few people as possible involved.

On May 21, Arnold sat down with Peggy Arnold at their Market Street house and pored over the pages of the twenty-first edition of *Bailey's Dictionary*—he had rejected *Blackstone*'s as too unwieldy. Stansbury used the new cipher for a covering note of his own:

To write with dispatch G[eneral] A[rnold] had made use of Bailey's. . . . This I have paged for him, beginning at A. . . . Each side is numbered and contains 927 pages. He adds 1 to each number of the page, of the column, and of the line, the first word of which is always used, too. Zoroaster will be 928.2.2 and not 927.1.1. Tide is 838.3.2 and not 837.2.1 When he would express a number, so (11,000). He depends on me for conveying, which is dangerous. He goes to Camp next week, from thence he will write to you. . . . His signature will be AG or a name beginning with A.[25]

This time, it took ten days for Stansbury to slip through New Jersey and make his way to Odell's house in Manhattan. Before he handed it on to André, however, Odell wanted to try to read the coded letter. He went to his fireplace and tore open the letter. In a few minutes, he was writing an embarrassed note to André. He was "mortified to death" that he had, "perceiving it contained an invisible page for you, assayed it by the fire." To his "inexpressible vexation," Odell found that the paper had gotten damp and the invisible-ink solution had spread "in such a manner as to make the writing all one indistinguishable blot, out of which not the half of any one line can be made legible." Warning Stansbury to be more careful in the future, Odell offered his future services in decoding and encoding André's messages "if you think proper to confide so far in my discretion."[26] André agreed. Most of the Arnold-André correspondence that survives is Odell's deciphering in Odell's handwriting.

There were other lapses and mishaps as the two correspondents tried to set up their cumbersome linkage. On May 24, food riots broke out in Philadelphia as Reed's Constitution Society protested rising prices on bread caused by the rapidly depreciating Continental currency. A parade by clamorous militia was followed by a mass meeting on the 25th at which Arnold's friend, the merchant Robert Morris, who had warehouses full of precious flour destined to supply the French fleet, was denounced for driving up prices by hoarding. The leader of the mob warned the city magistrates and President Reed "to be out of the way, if possible, on this day."[27]

Joseph Stansbury decided to get out of the way, too: "The confusion of a town meeting," he wrote to Odell, "hath banished me to Moorestown [New Jersey] for preservation." From the safety of Quaker Moorestown, Stansbury sent off his letter to Odell by way of Shrewsbury on the New Jersey coast, a Loyalist enclave from which ships routinely passed to New York City. It was carried by two young Loyalists, Tilton and Hulitt, for whom Odell was seeking commissions in a Loyalist regiment.

On June 4, 1779, Stansbury wrote to Odell again that he was "cut off from my favorite sphere of usefulness." He had tried "in a circuitous manner" to procure a response from Arnold to forward by Rattoon, but for some unknown reason, he had received no reply. The reason was that Arnold had left Philadelphia to go to Washington's headquarters for his court-martial just after he and his wife had put together their May 21 response to André's first letter. By June 9, Stansbury was writing to Odell again. "Mr. A.G. is at present out of town on private business," but had forwarded, through Stansbury and in Stansbury's handwriting, a "plan of trade."[28]

That very day, Odell had written to Stansbury that "Lothario (André) is impatient."[29] Arnold's dictated letter more than repaid André and Odell for their months of waiting. "Our friend S——," Arnold had dictated to Stansbury, "acquaints me that the proposals made by him in my name are agreeable to Sir Henry Clinton and that Sir Henry engages to answer my warmest expectations for any services rendered." His first concern was enough money for his family, he later explained to Clinton, and he began to earn it by sending Clinton vital military and political secrets. To convince Clinton that his confidence was not misplaced, Arnold sent Clinton word that Washington would move north to the Hudson for the summer campaign "as soon as forage can be obtained." This meant in early June, as soon as the first hay was harvested. This vital leak gave Clinton time to strike first up the Hudson before Washington could reinforce his forts there. Next, Arnold disclosed that Congress had decided to all but write off Charleston, South Carolina, the largest and most important town to the South, if the British once again attempted to take it. Arnold brushed aside André's suggestion that he try to filch original French or American dispatches: "Seizing papers is impossible." It was also unnecessary, since it was easier to learn over dinner what was in them: "Their contents can be known from a member of Congress."

Arnold wrote at some length about American currency problems and about congressional refusal to give agents in Paris full powers to negotiate a peace treaty with Britain. Arnold thought the French alliance was shaky, and that if it fell apart the Americans must sue for peace. He believed he could then be valuable, and would be well rewarded by the British for bringing about a reconciliation of responsible Americans with the British:

I will cooperate with others when an opportunity offers, and as life and everything is at stake, I shall expect some certainty, my property here secure and a revenue equivalent to the risk and service done. I cannot promise success: I will deserve it. Inform me what I may expect. Could I know S.H.'s [Sir Henry Clinton's] intentions, he should never be at a loss for intelligence. I shall expect a particular answer through our friend, Stansbury.

Arnold added a postscript: "Madam Arnold presents her particular compliments."[30] Peggy Arnold was acknowledging to André that she was in on the plot, a partner in Arnold's treason, from the moment of its conception. It would be another tense month before the Arnolds heard again from André.

Virtually incapacitated by pain from his wounded left leg and from the worst attack of gout in years in his good right foot, Arnold was agonizing over a last attempt at reconciliation with Washington and his old comrades. In May 1779, Washington had written to him that the Pennsylvania council had requested a further postponement in Arnold's court-martial so that Reed could subpoena witnesses from distant states. The inquiry would be convened by June 1, or, that failing, by July 1 at the latest. On May 14, Arnold wrote back to Washington, asking to rejoin the army and

to render my country every service in my power at this critical time, for though I have been ungratefully treated, I do not consider it as from my countrymen in general but from a set of men who, void of principle, are governed entirely by the private interest. The interest I have in the welfare and happiness of my country, which I have ever evinced when in my power, will, I hope, always overcome my personal resentment for any injury I can possibly receive from individuals.[31]

Washington brushed aside Arnold's letter. "Though the delay in your situation must be irksome, I am persuaded you will be of opinion, with me, it is best on every principle to submit to it rather than that there should be the least appearance of precipitating the affair."[32] Arnold's letter to Washington had a disturbing, sinister quality to it, especially in the light of his response to André. It was manifestly and calculatingly deceitful. He did not want to rejoin the army to serve the Revolution; he only wanted access to more information to convey to the British to prove his usefulness.

The new date for Arnold's court-martial scheduled, Arnold set out for Washington's camp at Middlebrook, New Jersey, in such pain that he had to be lifted into his carriage. He still had heard nothing from the British. Perhaps it was better this way. He would be vindicated by his old friends in the army and his enemies would be discredited. He would not have to throw away all his laurels, leave behind his good friends from the Kennebec, from Champlain and Saratoga. So many Americans really did revere him as the hero of the Revolution. With him, he carried a letter from old friend Silas Deane to Nathanael Greene at Washington's headquarters:

Great God! Is it possible that, after the bold and perilous enterprises which this man has undertaken for the service and defense of his country, the loss of his fortune and the cruel and lingering pains he has suffered from the wound received fighting their battles, there can be found among us men so abandoned to the base and infernal passions of envy and malice as to persecute him with the most unrelenting fury, and wish to destroy what alone he had the prospect of saving out of the dreadful wreck of his health, fortune and life: his character?"[33]

But Deane himself was under a congressional cloud, accused of financial misdeeds as agent in Paris, and Greene had been listening to President Reed's hectoring of Arnold long enough to have made up his mind without awaiting the outcome of the court-martial. Dismissing Deane's "sly letter,"[34] Greene invited Pennsylvania secretary Matlack, who was to prosecute the council's case against Arnold to the court-martial, to stay with him at Washington's camp. Matlack, however, declined, since Greene's quarters were too close to Arnold's.

Happy to be surrounded by the din and bustle of camp life, Benedict Arnold's mood swung mercurially to an optimism that only brought him a fresh rebuke from Washington when Arnold "self-invited some civilities I never meant to show him, or any officer in arrest, and he received a rebuke before I could convince him of the impropriety of his entering upon a justification of his conduct in my presence."[35] Barging in on Washington at headquarters, Arnold had tried to clear his name, only to mortify himself. Caught between old favorites, Washington insisted on a neutrality that was crushing to the tactless Arnold, who backed redfaced out of headquarters. Arnold blundered by discussing his case around camp, especially at headquarters. To the strictly impartial Washington, Arnold's attempt to discuss his case with the commander in chief while under arrest was a serious transgression. Utterly incapable of perceiving Washington's need for judicious neutrality, Arnold did not see that he had embarrassed himself. Instead, he took Washington's rebuff as a personal affront to his honor in front of fellow officers. No longer would he rely on Washington to defend him against his enemies, no longer would he consider Washington his champion.

Benedict Arnold's court-martial convened at eleven o'clock the morning of June 1, 1779. Washington had chosen Major General Robert Howe of North Carolina as president "for particular reasons":[36] Howe had experienced similar controversies as commander of Charleston and Savannah. In making appointments to the board of officers, Washington had assured President Reed that he would "have the affair conducted in its future progress with unexceptable propriety."[37] Arnold strained this atmosphere of studied propriety at the outset by issuing a peremptory challenge to the court's makeup. Confidently conducting his own legal defense, Arnold faced Howe, four brigadiers—his old friend Henry Knox, William Smallwood of Maryland, William Woodford of Virginia, and William Irving of Pennsylvania—plus six colonels and three lieutenant colonels, in all fourteen officers instead of the required thirteen. Arnold objected to the inclusion of so many Pennsylvanians. Under the articles of war, there was no provision for a peremptory challenge, yet President Howe allowed it before adjourning to the next day. That night, at a hurried conference with Washington, the officers learned that the hearing would have to be postponed indefinitely because the British were attacking fifty miles north of New York City. The court voted hastily to postpone the hearing for two or three days. Washington wrote Arnold and Matlack that "the movements of the enemy may possibly admit" resuming in a "few days." Washington also informed Matlack that Arnold "intends to go to Morristown and to wait events."[38]

As Washington and his able-bodied officers rushed north, Arnold, left behind, traveled to Washington's headquarters, where he waited for three weeks. But it was to be six more months before Washington got around to the case of Benedict Arnold again. In those humid weeks of June, Arnold was busy talking to other officers, asking about troop numbers and Washington's plans for the coming season of war. Before he finally left Washington's headquarters, Arnold sat down in his quiet quarters near Washington's mansion and wrote a letter to André, as he had promised, sending it through his old Quebec merchant friend Edward Antill, inside New York City. Arnold disclosed top-secret American troop strengths, dispositions, and destinations. Sullivan was at Easton with "three brigades against Detroit and Niagara to destroy the Indian settlements." Washington's whole remaining force was only eight thousand men.

Arnold's political intelligence was of less value to Clinton but more self-revealing of Arnold: "Congress has done nothing towards obtaining a loan or appointing commissioners to negotiate a peace. Their time and attention are taken up with trifles."[39] He was anxious to learn how generous the British would be when he openly defected. Nearly three weeks passed before he heard again from André, who had gone along on Clinton's attack on the American forts in the Hudson highlands. Although Arnold's information could have helped him with the attack upriver against Stony Point, Clinton had already embarked on this expedition before he received it. Ironically, it was this attack by Clinton that had caused the postponement of Arnold's court-martial. When Arnold finally heard from André again in late June, his reply was disappointingly vague and not a little condescending. André observed that Clinton could not be expected to treat Arnold as an equal, either concerting his plans with Arnold's or telling him in any detail what these plans were.

Indeed, André had just had a small taste of glory as he accompanied Clinton's sudden attack on the Hudson forts at Stony Point and Verplanck's Ferry. Sent by Clinton under flag of truce to Fort Lafayette, André had melodramatically accepted its surrender on the fort's ramparts in full view of both armies. Now there seemed to be a shift in André's attitude, his tone. Indeed, André did not see how foolish his pompous acceptance of the American surrender of a mere blockhouse made him appear. To him, it was one more mark of Clinton's favor. But it further annoyed André's growing circle of enemies. "What excuse," one of them wrote to the newspapers, "will a person of Mr. André's reputed sense make for this parade?"[40] Clinton nevertheless wrote to London to boast of the important contribution of his aide-de-camp: "I refer you to André [who enclosed a report] for foreign intelligence."[41] For the first time, André received official notice in London.

André needed Clinton's approval more than ever: he had just learned that the French fleet under Admiral d'Estaing had seized the West Indian island of Grenada, where sugar plantations provided most of his family's income. A mere captain with only three years seniority, he needed money to buy a major's commission at the going rate of £2,100. If he had the cash, he was sure Clinton would promote him over the heads of officers with twenty years more seniority. "While I was lamenting my disappointment" at d'Estaing's seizure of Grenada, André wrote home to his mother, "the post of adjutant general became vacant by the resignation of Lord Rawdon, and the deputy adjutant general, Colonel Kemble, became desirous for private reasons to withdraw."[42] Actually, both Rawdon and Kemble had come to loathe and fear André, whom Clinton had effectively put over their heads. Old Judge Thomas Jones, who interviewed hundreds of Loyalists for his scathing two-volume history of New York, had a variety of sarcastic epithets for André: he was Clinton's "first friend," his "bosom confidant." André had "the address to insinuate himself so much into the favor for the commander in chief" that he could gain "absolute ascendancy over that officer."[43] André, to be sure, was accruing such personal power that he could dispense offices and drive out of Sir Henry Clinton's official family all Clinton's former friends and favorites.

That André was widely considered a "cringing, insidious sycophant"[44] by senior officers who fumed at orders he wrote and signed without reference to their mutual superior, General Clinton, did not lessen this power, which was becoming more absolute as

Clinton slipped further into sloth and indecision. As the British prepared to invade the South in late 1779, it was André who made nearly all the arrangements and signed the orders as adjutant general (even though he was deputy, Clinton promoted no one over him to the top staff job and allowed André to run his headquarters staff). The tone of Clinton's official correspondence changed when André took over, and Benedict Arnold detected the shift when André wrote back to him in late July 1779. André had learned that Arnold had fallen out of favor in the American officer corps. A British officer who had escaped from Philadelphia informed Clinton that Arnold was "in no repute"[45] and had no command. Arnold was now told he should be satisfied with Clinton's general assurances. Until he had a command again, his value to the British was diminished. "Join the army," the young subaltern André archly lectured General Arnold in Clinton's name. "Accept a command, be surprised, be cut off: these things may happen in the course of maneuver, nor can you be censured or suspected. A complete service of this nature involving a corps of five or six thousand men would be rewarded with twice as many thousand guineas."

As to where or how Arnold was to surrender such an army, Clinton was leaving that to Arnold's ingenuity. In the meantime, Clinton would only tell Arnold that he had shifted the base of his operations fifty miles north up the Hudson. Arnold could choose his own maneuver and rely on Clinton's cooperation. "You must know," André wrote, "where the present power is vulnerable, and the conspicuous commands with which you might be vested may enable us at one shining stroke, from which both riches and honor would be derived, to accelerate the ruin to which the usurped authority is verging and to put a speedy end to the miseries of our fellow creatures." Arnold could see through the lines of André's latest dramatic prologue: Clinton did not trust him. How could Clinton be sure that Arnold was not using Stansbury to extract vital intelligence from the British? Indeed, by urging Arnold to seek a command in the Carolinas, André had gone too far, giving away Clinton's plans for a major attack on Charleston. André had also revealed Clinton's growing anxiety. Was it really Arnold out there? Arnold had written nothing in his own handwriting, done or said nothing that he could not deny.

André's solution was to ask Arnold for a face-to-face meeting, even if it was dangerous and violated the rules of war. Such a master stroke or the intelligence coup that would lead to it was what André was looking for, and "it is such as these [Clinton] pledges himself shall be rewarded beyond your warmest expectations."[46] In the meantime, André wanted Arnold to use his influence to help bring about the exchange of Burgoyne's captured army for American militia. Clinton needed the regulars, and who was in a better position to work for their release than the man who had brought about their defeat? Clinton also wanted Arnold to work on the exchange of his close friend General Phillips, captured at Saratoga. André's letter revealed his own dreams of glory, of a great master stroke to win the war, one in which his part would be conspicuous, more than it provided Arnold with any useful instructions. André's note did little to reassure Arnold. It appeared that their negotiations had bogged down. Could it be that Arnold's letter of June 8 from Washington's camp had gone awry?

In fact, André's impertinent letter, written as he basked in the afterglow of the stagy surrender of the Hudson River forts, had crossed with Arnold's invaluable intelligence, written only a few days before, as couriers picked their way cautiously between the lines. It was July 7, nearly two months after André had first written to Arnold, before Stansbury reached Arnold again, and then Stansbury could not get an audience with Arnold for four days and had to deliver André's letter to Peggy Arnold, code-named "Mrs. Moore." Stansbury wrote back anxiously to André on July 11 that he had finally met with the general and that André's offer was "not equal to his expectations." Whether he succeeded or not, Arnold expected to be indemnified for his losses; whether the war was finished "by sword or treaty," he expected £10,000 for his services. Indeed, the amount was not a great shock to Clinton, and Arnold had not pulled the figure out of the air. The Continental Congress had awarded General Charles Lee exactly this amount when Lee had resigned his British army commission and forgone his British pension at the outset of the Revolution. As evidence of his continued cooperation in the plot, Arnold had given Clinton additional valuable intelligence: the latest troop strengths and expected turnout of militia, the state of the army and the location of its supply depots, the number of men and cannon bound for Detroit by the "usual route"[47] Gates's location and the strength of his force in Rhode Island; Heath's and Lincoln's troop strengths and weaknesses; the state of the navy and location of its ships; news of the movements of the French fleet. Despite the effusion of top-level intelligence which Arnold sent off with Stansbury, the tone of his meetings with Arnold disturbed Stansbury, who conveyed his apprehension to Odell. It had taken Arnold fully ten days to answer André's missive this time, and then it was not in writing. The British, who had taken more than six weeks to answer Arnold, now worried when Arnold kept them waiting. Arnold was too busy even to see Stansbury, Peggy Arnold had explained to Stansbury, asking him to return in several days for an answer. Mrs. Arnold then claimed that "a multiplicity of business" prevented his meeting personally with Stansbury. Three days later, Stansbury reported, he had called again. Arnold had, by now, "made some progress with an answer," Mrs. Arnold informed him. A note would be sent around to Stansbury's china shop that night. A servant in Arnold's livery did appear as scheduled, but the note Stansbury tore open informed him that Arnold "had carefully examined the letter, and found by the laconic style, and little attention paid to his request, that the gentlemen appeared very indifferent respecting the matter." Reporting to Odell, Stansbury added that Arnold had "therefore omitted sending me the memo he intended in the morning, and wished to see me."

The next morning, Stansbury went to the Arnold residence, and in a locked room, heard Arnold's angry demands. First, why was this latest message in an unfamiliar handwriting—hadn't Arnold's note insisted that no one be taken in on the plot? Stansbury assured Arnold that Odell had no idea to whom he was encoding André's messages. As for payment, Arnold insisted that he must be paid for his defection no matter the outcome of his treasonous efforts. "He expects," Stansbury wrote André, "to have your promise that he shall be indemnified for any loss he shall sustain in case of detection, and whether this contest is finished by sword or treaty, that £10,000 shall be engaged him for his services." Arnold had finally sent to Stansbury a note, saying that "he had carefully examined [André's mid-June] letter and found by the laconic style and little attention paid to his request, that the General [Clinton] appeared very indifferent." Stansbury reported that Arnold's reception of him had been so cool that Mrs. Arnold had stepped in ever so gingerly, asking Stansbury to deliver a letter of her own to André as a signal that she would see that the conspiracy remained alive. Her stepping in to keep the negotiations alive indicates that she was becoming the driving force behind Arnold's going over to the British. Far more than just an observer, she had become a go-between, a delicate negotiator, and the diplomat who kept the negotiations alive. "Mrs. Moore requests the enclosed list of articles for her own use may be procured for her and the account of them and the former sent and she will pay for the whole with thanks."[48] The "shopping list" included cloth for napkins, for dresses, a pair of spurs, some pink ribbon. It was in Arnold's hand.

Stansbury was not the only one alarmed, he wrote to André. Odell, too, was worried that the busy André would not spend any more time on what was beginning to look like "a seemingly fruitless correspondence."[49] Odell needed a fast answer. Stansbury was under suspicion by the Americans and had to get to Philadelphia. If André was too busy, Odell would write for him, putting Stansbury off the scent by saying that André was out of town. But by now, André, too, was becoming alarmed. He saw through Peggy Arnold's list. Although the negotiations with her husband had been disappointing so far, she was telling him that they were not hopeless. André put aside Peggy's shopping list and informed Clinton that Arnold had finally stated his price: £10,000. But Clinton was preoccupied. At bayonet point, the American general Anthony Wayne had taken back Stony Point, jeopardizing Clinton's new Hudson River strategy. It was fully two more weeks before André could meet with Clinton again about Arnold. But then it was Clinton who feigned exasperation at Arnold. "We are thankful for the information transmitted," André wrote to Arnold, but "permit me to prescribe a little exertion." Especially after the setback at Stony Point, what Clinton wanted was detailed plans of West Point, the new American stronghold fifty miles up the Hudson, of Washington's Hudson River camp at new Windsor, and of Constitution Island in the Hudson opposite West Point. It was the first time either party had referred to West Point. And then André introduced a new and dangerous note: Clinton wanted Arnold not only to press for a new command, but to meet face to face with a high-ranking British officer under the guise of an exchange of prisoners of war. Clinton insisted on confirming Arnold's participation in the plot by a face-to-face meeting. So far, Arnold had not exposed himself to any great risk. Only Stansbury had seen or talked to him. None of the intelligence that had passed between the lines was ever in his handwriting. Clinton now demanded that Arnold involve himself personally in obtaining the exchange of his close friend General Phillips, captured at Saratoga. Phillips could then stop off in Philadelphia to confer with Arnold en route to New York, even if such a meeting would be a blatant violation of the rules of war. Arnold must make his move. It must be more strenuous than "general intelligence" at a time when "so much greater things may be done."[50] Full of inspiration to deeds of daring, André's letter contained, nonetheless, no guarantee of the indemnification Arnold was demanding. Disgusted, his dalliance with treason apparently at an unprofitable end, Arnold had Peggy write André.

When the nerve-racked Stansbury had carried the Arnolds' list of goods for André to purchase back to New York, André had responded in kind, sending her a coy answer in a note carried by a paroled American officer (André was thus violating the man's parole and risking his life for him). "It would make me happy to become useful to you here," André wrote Peggy, listing the purchases of finery as "trifling services from which I hope you would infer a zeal to be further employed."[51] It was two months later, late October, before André received another note from Peggy Arnold:

Mrs. Arnold presents her best respects to Captain André, is much obliged to him for his very polite and friendly offer of being serviceable to her. Major Giles [the paroled prisoner] was so obliging as to promise to procure what trifles Mrs. Arnold wanted in the millinery way, or she would with pleasure have accepted it.[52]

But not a word of intelligence, of a new command for Arnold. In other words, the Arnolds were breaking off the negotiations. Stansbury transmitted one last oral message from Benedict Arnold himself. "However sincerely he wished to serve his country in accelerating the settlement of this unhappy conflict," Stansbury wrote to André, he considered it unfair for him to "hazard his all" and to "part with a certainty for an uncertainty." He would write nothing more until he received guarantees, and as they did not appear to be forthcoming after five months of preliminaries, he was about to rejoin the American army.

Only two days later, Arnold turned to his former mentor, Washington, and urged him to reconvene the court-martial quickly, to consider "the cruel situation I am in." He could not stand another year on the sidelines. If the British would not meet his terms, then he must make his peace with Washington. He would do anything to get back into the fight: "My wounds are so far recovered that I can walk with ease, and I expect soon to be able to ride on horseback." If Washington could not promise a speedy trial, Arnold wanted to be released from his arrest in Philadelphia for "a few months' absence on my private affairs."[53] But more months were to drag by before Washington, busy planning the recapture of the other Hudson River forts and the destruction of the Six Nations Indian villages in western New York, could spare enough general officers to reconvene the court-martial.

Benedict Arnold's treasonous correspondence might have remained a dark secret if the tension between radical and conservative factions in Philadelphia, where he was awaiting trial, had not flared anew in the autumn of 1779, culminating in food riots and the mobbings of leading revolutionaries, including Arnold himself. The arrival of

French ships off the American coast had only added to food shortages. French sailors and soldiers had to be fed, and the French were
paying in gold. Philadelphia's waterfront warehouses bulged with
grain, but most Americans could not buy it because French commissary officers ranged the countryside paying inflated prices in gold
that further drove down the value of Continental paper money. By
1779, prices were rising at the rate of 17 percent a month while
Continental currency, according to Arnold, had depreciated to one
forty-fourth of its 1776 value. Many city-dwelling Philadelphians
were confounded by unaffordable provisions in a region of agri-
cultural abundance. Organizing into political clubs such as Joseph
Reed's Constitution Society, they spilled over out of the state house
into the streets, blaming inflation on wealthy Loyalists and conservative merchants, such as Morris, who were allegedly manipulating commodity markets and refusing to accept Continental currency,
growing richer by buying up grain and holding it for hard-money
payment by the French. This practice, known as "forestalling,"
made revolutionary tempers boil over.

When Reed and his Radicals had come to power in Pennsylvania in December 1778, Washington had congratulated him and
urged him to bring to trial "those murderers of our cause," the
rich-merchant "monopolizers, forestallers, and engrossers of con-
dign punishment":

*It is much to be lamented that each state, long ere this, has not
hunted them down as the pests of society and the greatest enemies
we have to the happiness of America. I would to God that one of
the most atrocious in each state was hung in gibbets upon a gallows
five times as high as the one prepared by Hamen. No punishment, in
my opinion, is too great for the man who can build his greatness
upon his country's ruin.[54]*

Writing from Valley Forge, Washington had enflamed the passions of Reed's Radicals. Nine months later, they began attacking
Philadelphia merchants accused of forestalling grain sales in the
city's markets. When a cargo ship, the *Victorious,* entered the port
loaded with grain consigned to Robert Morris and destined for the
French army, Morris was publicly accused of forestalling to raise
prices before delivery. In May, after a mass meeting in Independence
Hall Yard, Radicals organized into armed committees with the express mission of forcing merchants to roll back their prices. On July
4, 1779, when General John Cadwalader, leader of the conservative
Republican Society, attempted to speak against price controls at an

Independence Day rally, one hundred Radical militiamen armed with clubs crowded the front rows near the stage, shouting down Cadwalader and breaking up the meeting. By this time, not only Arnold but many conservative Philadelphians, as one merchant wrote to his brother, regarded Pennsylvania as a state whose only law was now the mob: "Every man who takes a club in his hand to town meetings (which, by the way, have been very frequent of late) undertakes to be governor."[55] Soon, Philadelphia and surrounding towns as far as Lancaster were in the grip of Radical committees enforcing lower grain prices.

Late in July, a merchant wrote an attack on the Radicals and published it under an assumed name in the conservative *Evening Post*. The radicals hauled the publisher, Benjamin Towne, before a committee and extracted the identification of the merchant, Whitehead Humphreys. A mob then went to the merchant's house and, finding him absent, roughed up his sister and menaced a boarder, Edward Langworthy, a member of Congress from Georgia. When Humphreys came home, he armed and barricaded himself and some friends inside the house while the mob brought up a party of Continental soldiers. When Humphreys still held his ground, the mob dispersed. Congressman Langworthy told Congress that the Radicals planned to seize him along with several other Republican members of Congress. Congress referred the charge of misuse of Continental troops to the Board of War for an inquiry. The incident blew over, but it encouraged conservative merchants to resist radical pressures. Early in September 1779, eighty merchants protested to the Pennsylvania council that any attempt to compel a trader to accept less for his goods was an invasion of property rights. The Radical leadership, frustrated at its own inability to solve the growing financial crisis, once again stirred up the mob to seek a scapegoat. The mob isolated a target: James Wilson, constitutional lawyer and signer of the Declaration of Independence who was hated by Radicals for defending Loyalists prosecuted by Reed and, more recently, for defending Robert Morris.

On Monday, October 4, 1779, the Radical revolution in Philadelphia reached its peak when two days of rioting broke out in the capital city. Accounts of what happened in the next few days are highly partisan and include biased family papers of the rival participants and accounts placed in the city's newspapers by spokesmen for opposing factions. A family biography of Reed insists that Arnold took no part, a view repeated by the only modern biographer of Reed; Shippen family records indicate that Arnold was a key figure. Unfortunately, no court records survive and events can only be re-

constructed with difficulty from journals, diaries, letters, and newspapers. Yet a picture does emerge and many of the facts are not in
dispute. What is open to interpretation is Arnold's role. Reed's biog-
raphers say that Reed was in command of the events and sent Arnold home under threat of arrest. But all other accounts, including
those of some of Reed's partisans, place Arnold in the thick of the
fighting.

For weeks, Radical committees had been meeting, planning to
seize all the women and children of Loyalists who had already gone
over to the British and deport them in boatloads to New York City
to ease food shortages in Philadelphia. As October began, Radical
handbills appeared, calling a mass meeting of militia. At the meeting, the Radicals broadened their immediate goal to include rounding up and driving out of the city all of the leading Republicans,
some of whom were attracting wide support and were about to
stand in opposition to Reed's Radicals in the assembly elections a
week later. Getting wind of the plan, the Republicans armed themselves and gathered at the stout three-story brick mansion of James
Wilson on the southwest corner of Third and Walnut streets in Society Hill, which they dubbed Fort Wilson. They were soon reinforced
by the socially elite dismounted cavalry of the First City Troop.
Across town, the Radicals were gathering at Paddy Byrne's Tavern
on Tenth Street between Vine and Race, just off the Commons. They
were a mix of militiamen and street loiterers who quickly decided to
capture Fort Wilson, though at first there were too few of them. All
morning, they prowled the streets aimlessly, banging a drum and
shouting.

When no attack came by noontime, the City Troopers went
home for dinner. Meanwhile, Wilson and General Thomas Mifflin
had been drilling about thirty Republicans on Second Street south of
Market in front of the courthouse. Wilson appealed for protection
from the Pennsylvania assembly and the executive council, but he
was not sure that they could preserve order. It was at this point,
according to some sources, that Benedict Arnold arrived and joined
the conservative volunteers, who included three signers of the Declaration of Independence: Wilson, Robert Morris, and George Clymer.
Two of the Republicans, Major Francis Nichols and Daniel Clymer,
ran to the city arsenal at Carpenters' Hall and grabbed armloads of
muskets, stuffing their coat pockets with cartridges.

Shortly after noon, President Reed, who had been ill in bed, received word that when the troopers had gone home to eat, the mob,
now gathered on the Commons, had suddenly grown larger: by
now, there were about two hundred Radicals, including many Penn-

sylvania German militiamen equipped with two field artillery pieces. The message, from the executive council, said that their target was Wilson's house. Reed sent the messenger to the homes of City Troop officers and told him to gather their men and meet him at their stables on Dock Street. Reed jumped on a horse and headed for the rendezvous. But only two troopers were waiting for him. Together, they raced toward the sound of small-arms fire on Walnut Street.

While the troopers had been dining, the mob had been gathering strength and marching down Second Street, the main north-south artery, stopping to seize suspected enemies from their homes. They allowed John Drinker to finish his dinner, then paraded him with two other suspected Loyalists up Walnut Street toward Wilson's, their drums beating the "Rogue's March." Wilson and the Republicans, now numbering between thirty and forty, retreated inside Fort Wilson. The Radicals gave three cheers and rushed the house amid imprecations on both sides. Inside, Captain George Campbell opened a third-story window and fired his pistol. The German militiamen in the street below fired a volley at him. Campbell fell, dead.

Inside Fort Wilson, it seems certain that Benedict Arnold was in command: the stubborn resistance of a small number of men outnumbered by more than seven to one could only have been organized by an experienced officer, and none of the other combatants had been under fire. Arnold evidently divided the command with Mifflin on the ground floor and himself upstairs. Arnold deliberately showed himself at a third-story window and then blazed away with his pistols. Soon there were four dead bodies in the street, a dozen more wounded; inside, three more men had been hit. The deadly firing from inside was at first accurate and drove back the Radicals, but then the German artillerymen dragged up a field piece as one of them, a giant named Huler, battered down the front door with a sledgehammer.

As the Germans rushed inside, they were confronted by Colonel Stephan Chambers on the stairs, who fired at them, wounding one. Huler rushed Chambers before he could reload, dragged him downstairs by the hair, and ran him through with a bayonet. Huler was pulled off by Philip Hagner, a noncombatant, who helped carry away Chambers. Now a heavy fire hit the mob from the staircase, cellar windows, upstairs windows. The crowd retreated and Wilson and his friends barricaded the doorway with his dining table and living-room chairs. The militia rallied and surged in again as Arnold directed the fire from upstairs. It was at this moment, Philip Hagner later remembered, that Reed arrived, "as if he had just risen from bed, his knee-buttons being unfastened and his boots down, a pistol in his hand, but no sword." With Reed was militia Captain Peale, who later insisted that he tried to discourage the mob before going to rouse Reed: Peale, a Reed partisan, wrote that Arnold not only was at the scene but taunted him from the window, "Your President has raised a mob, and now he cannot quell it."[56] The Germans had fought their way to the main staircase by the time two more squads of troopers from Baylor's Virginia Regiment galloped up Chestnut Street, charging around the corner, slashing at the rioters amid shouts of "The horse, the horse!"[57] Inflicting severe saber wounds, the Continental troopers trapped the militia and Reed ordered everyone, inside and outside the house, arrested. Able to post property bail, Wilson, Morris, Arnold, and the other Republicans were immediately released, but the militiamen were ordered held in Walnut Street Prison which was surrounded by cannon and City Troopers.

When German militia north of the city learned that night that several of their countrymen lay dead and more were in jail, they marched down Germantown Pike the next morning to free their comrades. Reed, Matlack, and the City Troop rode out to meet them and, promising to release the prisoners, finally persuaded them to turn back. That same day, Reed went before the Pennsylvania assembly and tried to explain away the bloodshed as one of the "casual overflowings of liberty."[58] He sought and won amnesty for the militia. As the assemblymen voted, another mob was gathering, this time to attack and stone Benedict Arnold as he returned home from a meeting of Republicans at Grays Ferry. As two men moved in menacingly, Arnold drew his pistols and threatened to kill them. The crowd withdrew momentarily as Arnold hurried into his house.

Appealing to the Board of War for a guard, he told Congress that he had been warned, along with all the others who had made up the garrison of Fort Wilson, that they would be driven out of the city. Only James Wilson left, going into hiding in New Jersey. But Arnold would never leave, he announced. Arming his servants, he barricaded his pregnant wife and his family and servants inside the Penn mansion and waited for word from Congress. More furious than frightened, he had reason to smart, for he had become so unpopular with the militia that they had stoned him and jeered as he had ridden up to Wilson's house the day before and now they were besieging their former commander in his house.

Arnold had little time for brooding: a fresh mob was gathering outside his house. Sending off a runner with a second appeal for help, he asked for soldiers and a good officer because "a mob of lawless ruffians" was threatening to attack him inside his own house.

As there is no protection to be expected of the state for an honest man, I am under the necessity of requesting Congress to order me a guard of Continental troops. This request I presume will not be denied to a man who has so often fought and bled in defense of the liberties of his country.[59]

But Congress refused, declining to become involved, it argued, in a jurisdictional dispute with Pennsylvania. Instead of troops, Arnold received a curt note informing him that he should have applied for protection to Reed, to "the Executive authority of the state of Pennsylvania in whose disposition to protect every honest citizen Congress have full confidence, and highly disapprove the insinuations of every individual to the contrary."[60] As the mob swarmed around his house, Arnold fired off yet another message to Congress. He had not meant to insinuate anything more than the feebleness of the state: "Their disposition to protect the honest citizens I did not doubt, their abilities I doubted and still have reason to doubt from the fatal consequences of yesterday's commotions."[61] By nightfall, as the First City Troop returned to the city and began patrolling the streets, President Reed sent out a squad of guards that half-protected, half-watched Arnold. Benedict Arnold realized now that after all his years of fighting for the revolutionary cause, there were few patriots who would lift a finger to protect him, his wife, his children.

17

"CONSCIOUS OF MY OWN

RECTITUDE"

I will furnish you
with opportunities of
regaining the esteem
of your countrymen.

George Washington to Benedict Arnold, April 6, 1780

Benedict Arnold was besieged not only physically but financially and legally in the autumn of 1779 as he pressed Congress to settle his accounts, some of them tied up since early 1776, and prepared to defend himself before the court-martial which Washington had postponed until the year's military campaigning was over. His tangled finances had dragged him through a series of audits and committee hearings that were to last for many months more. By the time of the Fort Wilson riot, Arnold's court-martial was imminent. He was as expert in military law as most of the judges he would face, having served on numerous courts-martial and already defended himself twice. He had lost two preliminary legal rounds. In the first, Arnold had tried to prevent his aides from having to testify in the case. Arnold had sent Clarkson and Franks to Charleston, South Carolina, late in March when he had learned that Congress, ignoring the report of its own investigating committee, was insisting on trying Arnold on four counts of malfeasance in office. To avoid contempt charges and to have the benefit of their friendly testimony before they left for Charleston, he had sent his aides around to Benjamin Paschall, a Philadelphia justice of the peace, to swear depositions before him that Arnold "did not purchase goods upon his coming into Philadelphia other than for his own private use."[1] Arnold's second motive for sending them on furlough to Charleston was to oversee his purchase of a merchant ship to trade in rich cargoes of rice and indigo to France. Since it was Clarkson who had actually issued the pass that had permitted Hannah Levy to cross enemy lines into New York, Reed and Matlack requested Clarkson to attend an inquiry. Probably at Arnold's behest, Clarkson refused, denying the Council's authority to question him. Pennsylvania submitted contempt charges against Clarkson to Congress in a letter signed by Reed. Clarkson, again no doubt acting on Arnold's instructions, then challenged the authority of Congress to summon him to give testimony. On March 24, Congress subpoenaed Clarkson and officially reprimanded him for his disrespect to the president of Congress.

A second legal setback for Arnold had come in May 1779, even as he was initiating his treasonous correspondence with the British. In a letter to Congress, Arnold had requested "copies of all the papers relative to the charges against me."[2] His request was referred to a committee headed by William Paca, which replied that "the whole of the evidence which relates to the charges on which you are to be tried is transmitted to General Washington with the charges. There is nothing kept back which you could avail yourself of in your defense." The letter did not, however, mention the fact that the Paca committee had strengthened Pennsylvania's hand by passing resolutions that Congress held the Pennsylvania authorities in great respect and supported Pennsylvania's right to object to disrespectful and indecent behavior by any officer to the civil authority of a state. Resolutions so prejudicial to Arnold's case were clearly being concealed from him by Paca, who stated that "the resolutions of the committee can have no operation whatever"[3] now that Congress had reached an accord with Pennsylvania and decided on a court-martial.

As harried as he had ever been in battle against an array of enemies, Benedict Arnold nevertheless exuded self-confidence as he alighted from his carriage at Dickerson's Tavern in Morristown, New Jersey, on December 23, 1779, for his reconvened court-martial. On a good day, Arnold's crippled right leg was merely an annoyance and he limped only slightly on a built-up boot. But Arnold under stress or exhausted was a cripple. His leg muscles contracted, pressing nerves against broken ends of bone, causing him intense pain and making him hobble conspicuously. Today, aiming to remind his fellow officers of his services to his country, Arnold dressed in his handsome pale-blue-and-buff major general's uniform with the gold epaulet of honor presented him by Washington after Saratoga and put on a short ceremonial sword hanging from the decorative gold knot that Washington had given him. Arnold swung confidently up the walkway and into the crowded, low-ceilinged great room of the tavern. The thin pale light of late December was warmed by a crackling fire, illuminating a row of field officers who now faced him across a long, low table. At its center, presiding over an all but new panel of officers, sat Major General Robert Howe, an ardent Whig and once-wealthy southern planter who had lost virtually everything to British raiders. Punctilious about honor, an expert on the gentlemen's code of the day, Howe had shot Congressman Christopher Gadsden in the ear after one minor disagreement—then the two had become close friends. After the Americans lost Savannah to a British expedition early that year, Howe had been court-martialed on charges similar to Arnold's and acquitted. Washington's appointment of Howe as president of the Arnold tribunal may have been a reminder to many officers in the room of the struggle between civilian politicians and the military, but Arnold took from it the meaning he wanted. The only other familiar face at the long table was Arnold's old friend from Boston Henry Knox, now a brigadier general. The Pennsylvanians were gone, supplanted by Brigadier Mordecai Gist of Maryland and, to Arnold's horror, Moses Hazen, who had been first to accuse Arnold of looting Montreal. Arnold had scarcely heard Howe read the charges before he was on his feet, peremptorily challenging Hazen's inclusion among the judges. Howe acceded and Hazen was banished from the board, although four members of the Hazen court-martial at Fort Ticonderoga still remained. Had Arnold known what another member of the court had written about him after Valcour Island, he might have attempted one more peremptory challenge: "Scottie Willie" Maxwell of New Jersey was one of those who had served on the earlier court-martial on looting charges and had written to Governor Livingston that Arnold was an "evil genius."[4] But Arnold remained ignorant of Maxwell's barb and considered Maxwell an ally, since he was close to Schuyler. Arnold was no doubt pleased that Pennsylvania Secretary Matlack had been replaced as prosecutor by John Laurence, judge advocate general of the Continental Army, a New York lawyer who was a veteran of the invasion of Canada and a member of the Livingston-Schuyler political clan.

Congress had indicted Arnold on only four of the eight charges preferred by Pennsylvania, but Arnold insisted on a full-dress review of all eight allegations: unless he cleared himself of all charges, he felt that his honor would remain tarnished. After months of plotting treason, Arnold rose and launched into a lengthy defense of his entire service in the American army, at the same time boldly counterattacking his accusers. His speech may be the clearest statement of his views on the Revolution and his role in it. Taken together with his secret writings to André, it reveals his thoughts as he shifted from patriotism to treason and back again:

Mr. President and gentlemen of this honorable court: I appear before you to answer charges brought against me by the supreme executive council of the commonwealth of Pennsylvania. It is disagreeable to be accused, but when an accusation is made, I feel it is a great source of consolation to have an opportunity of being tried by gentlemen whose delicate and refined sensations of honor will lead them to entertain similar sentiments concerning those who accuse unjustly and those who are justly accused. . . .

When the present necessary war against Great Britain commenced, I was in easy circumstances and enjoyed a fair prospect of improving them. I was happy in domestic connections and blessed with a rising family, who claimed my care and attention. The liberties of my country were in danger. The voice of my country called upon all her faithful sons to join in her defense. With cheerfulness, I obeyed the call. I sacrificed domestic ease and happiness to the service of my country, and in her service have I sacrificed a great part of a handsome fortune. I was one of the first who appeared in the field and, from that time to the present hour, have not abandoned her service.[5]

Arnold asked indulgence to read before the court complimentary citations from Washington as well as Washington's letters to Congress recommending him for promotion. He stressed passages calling him an "active, judicious and brave" officer "in whom the militia had great confidence." He didn't blush to take up the court's time with such a recitation:

When one is charged with practices which his soul abhors and which conscious innocence tells him he has never committed, an honest indignation will draw from his expressions in his own favor which, on other occasions, might be ascribed to an ostentatious turn of mind.

After a full-dress review of his military career, he asked if it was probable that he "should all at once sink into a course of conduct

equally unworthy of a patriot and a soldier" and stated, "My conduct from the earliest period of the war to the present time has been
steady and uniform." Complaining bitterly that the long and cruel
delays to obtain a fair trial had been caused by his persecutors in
Pennsylvania, Arnold declared his confidence that he could prove
that all of the charges against him were "false, malicious and scandalous."

The first charge allowed to stand by Congress against Arnold
was that he had issued a pass to the owners of the *Charming Nancy*.
Had he known that they were "disaffected persons"? Arnold tried to
justify granting the pass by pointing out how easy it was to mistake
the loyalties of Philadelphians at the time. Then he boldly unleashed
a scathingly sarcastic attack on Reed and the Pennsylvania council
for insinuating that they had to act for Washington in preventing a
Continental officer from violating the State's prerogative:

*I think it peculiarly unfortunate that the armies of the United States
have a gentleman at their head who knows so little about his own
honor, or regards it so little, as to lay the president and council of
Pennsylvania under the necessity of stepping forth in his defense. . . . The General is invested with power, and he possesses
spirit to check and to punish every instance of disrespect shown to
his authority, but he will not prostitute his power by exerting it
upon a trifling occasion. . . .*

Arnold argued that the attack for issuing passes was just one
example of the slanders he had endured as military governor at the
hands of officials clearly out to get him. He excoriated Reed, who
was not present, for such a petty misuse of office when a war hung
in the balance: "Such a vile prostitution of power and such instances of glaring tyranny and injustices I believe are unprecedented
in the annals of any free people." In fact, Arnold revealed the tyranny of Pennsylvania revolutionaries was making him have serious
second thoughts whether Americans were ready for independence.

Arnold stood accused of inflicting menial duties on Timothy
Matlack's militiaman son. It was a complaint, he said, made merely
to alienate him from the soldiers who had always respected him,
despite the recent riots at Fort Wilson:

*My ambition is to deserve the good opinion of the militia of these
states, not only because I respect their character and their exertions,
but because their confidence in me may . . . prove beneficial to the*

general cause of America. But having no local politics to bias my voice or my conduct, I leave it to others to wriggle themselves into a temporary popularity by assassinating the reputation of innocent persons and endeavoring to render odious a principle . . . essential to the good discipline of the militia and consequently to the safety of these states. . . . The time is not far off when, by the glorious establishment of our independence, I shall again return into the mass of citizens. 'Tis a period I look forward to with anxiety. I shall then cheerfully submit, as a citizen, to be governed by the same principle of subordination which has been tortured [by Pennsylvania's charge] into a wanton exertion of arbitrary power.

In defending himself against Pennsylvania's charge that he had acted illegally in buying a share in the prize claim of the sloop *Active,* Arnold argued that this was a civil, not a military case and that a grand jury had already dismissed the indictment against him for want of evidence. He had helped Olmsted, the captain of the sloop, and the other crewmen out of sympathy for their plight. Arnold stayed silent about his own self-interest in the ship and he did not mention that he had asked witnesses to appear before a grand jury to swear that he had no interest in it at all. But the court-martial never asked him outright if he stood to profit from the case, nor did the prosecution produce any evidence that he did. Under English common law, he was under no compulsion to incriminate himself. Instead, he again attacked Reed and his committeemen, claiming that they had been interested financially in the case, seizing the proceeds of the prize sale for their own use, and they had been motivated by vengeance against him.

On the serious charge of misusing government wagons, Arnold did not deny that he had used them to haul private property in which he had an interest, but he did deny that the public needed the wagons at the time and he insisted that he intended to pay for them. He further accused Reed of persuading the wagonmaster not to accept the £500 Arnold had ready for him but to then sue him for double the amount. Arnold raised the issue of double jeopardy in the case, since he was being tried in a Pennsylvania court for the same charge. Pennsylvania had charged Arnold with "indecent and disrespectful refusal of any satisfaction whatsoever" when he had refused orders to appear before state authorities to answer questions about the wagons.

When public bodies of men find themselves actuated by the passions of anger or envy, and apply their efforts to sap the character of an

individual and to render his situation miserable, they must not think
it extraordinary if they are not treated with the deference which they
think their due.

The key witness in the case of the public wagons was Colonel
John Mitchell, deputy quartermaster general and wagonmaster of the
army. Had he done Arnold a favor and was he therefore himself the
one at fault, or had he been obeying the order of his superior officer
by dispatching the wagons? It was a question Mitchell tried to duck.
When he did not appear by the fourth day of the trial, the court was
adjourned until he could be subpoenaed from Philadelphia. Peggy Arnold, now six months pregnant, tried to persuade the elusive Mitchell
to hurry to Morristown to testify, but Mitchell refused. The parade of
witnesses promised by Reed had dwindled to a mere handful:
Matlack and his son William; Arnold's aide, Major Franks; Washington's aide, Alexander Hamilton; Mitchell's aide and a clerk whose
testimony was stricken from the record. The court-martial had to be
adjourned three times to await witnesses. On December 30, General
Howe ordered the inquiry recessed until Mitchell appeared. Arnold
rushed back to Philadelphia, but it was three more weeks before he
could drag back the reluctant Mitchell, who then testified that it had
been his idea to lend Arnold the wagons.

To the charge that Arnold had privately made purchases from
the stores of Philadelphia while they were closed to the public and
then sold the goods for his own profit, "as is alleged and believed,"
Arnold testified:

If this is true, I stand confessed in the presence of this honorable
court the vilest of men. I stand stigmatized with indelible disgrace,
the disgrace of having abused an appointment of high trust and im-
portance to accomplish the meanest and most unworthy pur-
poses. . . . But if this part of the case is void of truth, if it has not
even the semblance of truth, what shall I say of my accusers? What
epithets will characterize their conduct? Where is the evidence of this
accusation? I call upon my accusers to produce it. If I made consid-
erable purchases, considerable sales must have been made to me by
some person in Philadelphia. Why are not these persons produced?

It was to the charge that he had favored and protected Loyalists
that Arnold gave his most withering rejoinder:

Conscious of my own innocence and the unworthy methods taken to
injure me, I can with boldness say to my persecutors in general, and

to the chief of them in particular, that in the hour of danger, when the affairs of America wore a gloomy prospect, when our illustrious General [Washington] was retreating through New Jersey with a handful of men, I did not propose to my associates basely to quit the General and sacrifice the cause of my country to my personal safety by going over to the enemy and making peace. I can say I never basked in the sunshine of my General's favor and courted him to his face, when I was at the same time treating him with the greatest disrespect and vilifying his character. . . . This is more than a ruling member of the council of the state of Pennsylvania can say.

It was indeed a serious charge, one calculated to discredit Reed before his former comrades, and Reed was not present to rebut it. Arnold had been far to the north when Reed had resigned from Washington's staff in the winter of 1776, but General John Cadwalader later admitted to Reed that it was he who had told Arnold that Reed had quit as Washington's aide-de-camp out of cowardice. Reed at the time said he was resigning because he had lost confidence in Washington. His resignation had come immediately after Washington had refused to appoint him as head of the American cavalry, a post which he had neither training for nor experience in.

Arnold's friendships with Loyalists and his marriage to the daughter of an accused Tory could not be dismissed by such an attack, however. Arnold confronted the charge directly:

I am not sensible, Mr. President, of having neglected any gentlemen, either in the civil or military line, who have adhered to the cause of their country and who have put it into my power to take notice of them. . . . I can appeal to the candor of Congress and to the army, as scarcely a day passed but many of both were entertained by me. They are the best judges of my company and conduct. With respect to attention to [Loyalists], I have paid [no attention] but such, in my situation, as was justifiable on the principles of common humanity and politeness. The president and council of Pennsylvania will pardon me if I cannot divest myself of humanity. It is enough for me, Mr. President, to contend with men in the field. I have not yet learned to carry on warfare against women, or to consider every man disaffected to our glorious cause who, from opposition to those in power in Pennsylvania, may, by the clamor of party, be styled a Tory. This odious appellation has been applied indiscriminately to several of illustrious character.

Benedict Arnold had turned the tables on his accusers, making his defense an attack on Pennsylvania's rulers. By so doing, he made the deliberation far more difficult for the court, reminding his judges over and over of the clash between a Continental officer and state authorities.

Strong, resolute, Arnold strode into the makeshift courtroom for the last time on January 26, 1780, feeling vindicated, expecting exoneration. There was no evidence against him for which he had not been prepared, to his mind no crime worthy of the name of more than bad judgment. He had awaited the judgment of his comrades "with pleasing anxiety," expecting acquittal. His comrades indeed acquitted him of mistreating militia and of buying up goods when stores were sequestered, but they adjudged him guilty on two counts. Arnold was found guilty of violating a catchall provision in the articles of war which forbade all acts "to the prejudice of good order and military discipline." At the same time, the court absolved him of any fraudulent intent in using the wagons, but "considering the delicacy attending the high station in which the government acted and that requests from him might operate as commands, they are of opinion the request was imprudent and improper." The court acquitted Arnold of any intentional wrongdoing and all illicit private speculation, findings which usually resulted in acquittal with honor. Arnold, however, was acquitted yet sentenced to a reprimand from the commander in chief. The four officers who had sat on Hazens's court-martial secretly voted for a much more severe sentence, Arnold's expulsion from the army.

At first, Arnold considered himself vindicated. He expected only a mild rebuke from Washington. So strongly did he believe himself cleared that he arranged to have the entire 179-page court record printed at his own expense and circulated in America and Europe in both English and French! He went cheerfully about his rounds in Philadelphia, expecting a new command in the army, then writing to Washington again to revive his request to be put in charge of an enlarged Continental Navy. On March 22, Arnold wrote to Silas Deane that he proposed to the Board of Admiralty "an expedition which will require three or four hundred land forces to act in conjunction with the ships; the matter rests with General Washington. If the men can be spared, and my plan takes place, you will hear from me soon. If it should not, I propose going to Boston, with the intention to take a command of private ship."[6] But in two letters to Washington two weeks apart, Arnold on March 6 and 20 insisted that the expedition was the Admiralty's idea. "They wish to be informed if the men can be spared from the army . . .";[7] "From the injury I have received in my leg and the great stiffness in my ankle, my surgeons are of opinion it will not be prudent of me to take a command in the army for some time to come."[8] But Washington did not reply. Instead, he informed the Admiralty that the men could not be spared. He could not express his opinion about Arnold's naval abilities, but said he had no objection if the Admiralty gave Arnold the command. But without marines, Arnold's hopes for the naval expedition were dashed. It must have been galling that Washington had detached Benjamin Lincoln and not Arnold with a corps of troops to Charleston, an assignment that now also scotched Arnold's naval plans.

There had been good news in the Arnold household. Peggy Arnold gave birth, on March 19, 1780, to their first child, a boy, named Edward after Judge Shippen, and the proud father had written to Washington of his fourth son's birth. Arnold had already heard from the Admiralty Board that there would be no expedition; now he requested a leave of absence from the army.

The day after Edward Shippen Arnold was born, Benedict Arnold resumed his campaign to clear his name. On March 20, 1780, he wrote a letter, previously unpublished, to Jeremiah Powell, president of Massachusetts:

Sir:
The President of Council of the State of Pennsylvania having published and officially transmitted to the different states sundry resolutions of theirs, dated Philadelphia, Feb'y 3, 1779, containing heavy charges tending to prejudice the minds of my fellow citizens against me previous to a trial, which with much difficulty I have at last obtained—The justice due to my own character (and to the public who have been so greatly deceived) will, I trust, excuse the liberty I take in transmitting to your Excellency the proceedings of the courtmartial. . . . I would wish to take from the minds of those Gentlemen [of the Massachusetts government] every unfavorable impression . . . to convince them that my character has been most cruelly and unjustly aspersed.[9]

On March 28, Washington sent a letter extending his congratulations to the Arnolds on the birth of their son and granting Arnold's request for an unpaid leave. But Washington once again drew the line between the Continental Army's authority and the civil authorities: Arnold would have to apply to Congress for a furlough from Philadelphia if he wished to leave the country to go to sea, "as

I have in no instance whatever ventured to grant a furlough to any place not within the United States."10

This line should have held a worrisome hint for Arnold that Washington was now finally reading the entire court-martial record. It was now entirely up to Washington whether he would issue a formal reprimand or let the matter drop. He had to consider the wishes of Congress, which had ordered the court-martial and confirmed its sentence, and he had repeatedly demonstrated that he was worried about Pennsylvania's threats to withdraw support for his army unless he made an example of Arnold.

Arnold was totally unprepared for the sledgehammer blow that fell from Washington's headquarters a full ten weeks after the court-martial. Congress had protracted the ordeal by not sending the court record to Washington until late March, even though it had secretly voted twenty-three to three to confirm the sentence six weeks earlier. On April 6, less than a week after Arnold received Washington's warm congratulatory note, Washington issued his own verdict on Benedict Arnold, publishing it in his general orders for the day, to be distributed throughout the army and picked up by the newspapers:

The Commander-in-Chief would have been much happier in an occasion of bestowing commendations on an officer who had rendered such distinguished services to his country as Major General Arnold; but in the present case, a sense of duty and a regard to candor oblige him to declare that he considers his conduct in the instance of the permit [to the Charming Nancy] *as peculiarly reprehensible, both in a civil and military view, and in the affair of the wagons as imprudent and improper.11*

Arnold still could see no wrong, no tactlessness, no arrogance, no indelicacy in his public behavior toward the Pennsylvania authorities. To his friend Silas Deane he wrote:

I believe you will be equally surprised with me when you find the court-martial have fully acquitted me of the charge of employing public wagons, of defrauding the public or of injuring or impeding the public service, and in the next sentence say "as requests from him might operate as commands," I ought to receive a reprimand: For what? Not for doing wrong, but because I might have done wrong, or rather, because there was a possibility that evil might have followed the good I did.12

But it was obvious that Washington did, and Washington's favor or ill will were crucial to him. Indeed, Washington wrote Arnold a letter that immediately preceded the reopening of Arnold's negotiations to leave behind his ungrateful former comrades and exchange his blue uniform for a red one. "Our profession," Washington began,

is the chastest of all. Even the shadow of a fault tarnishes the lustre of our finest achievements. The least inadvertence may rob us of the public favor, so hard to be acquired. I reprimand you for having forgotten that, in proportion as you have rendered yourself formidable to our enemies, you should have been guarded and temperate in your deportment towards your fellow citizens. Exhibit anew those noble qualities which have placed you on the list of our most valued commanders. I will myself furnish you, as far as it may be in my power, with opportunities of regaining the esteem of your country.[13]

It was as considerate a letter as Washington ever wrote, yet in Washington's eyes, Arnold had undeniably already lost his country's esteem. He had become the main subject of gossip, "served up as a constant dish of scandal to the breakfast of every table on the continent in this general rage for abuse."[14] Nevertheless, Benedict Arnold had, in fact, gotten off easily in the legal sense. Had his agreement with Mease or his payments by Collins or his interest in the sloop *Active* become known at the court-martial, he would no doubt have received more than a public slap on the wrist from Washington.

During the ten weeks of congressional delay between his court-martial and the official reprimand, Benedict Arnold faced a battle on a second front. Nearly four years had passed since the end of his Canadian campaign and he was still waiting for his accounts to be settled. In February 1780, as Congress mulled his punishment for questionable practices as military governor, it also considered his tangled financial affairs. By his own sworn accounting to a British investigating commission after the war, Arnold in 1780 was still rich on paper, a millionaire in modern terms, but cash-poor. But like many other revolutionary leaders, he had seen his fortune dwindle as he focused all his attention on the affairs of the country. Moreover, British naval blockades, raids on land and sea, currency depreciation, and runaway inflation had all taken their toll. By June 1780, Continental currency had depreciated to one forty-fourth of its original worth. Arnold's money was tied up in real estate and shrewdly purchased low-yield stocks, and he was desperately short of cash. He valued his Mount Pleasant at £7,000, but it was rented out to

the Spanish ambassador to make the mortgage payments, and he
and his bride never got to live in it. He had a handsome house in
New Haven and a small farm in Connecticut, which he had tried to
sell to pay off some of the debt on Mount Pleasant, but he was
unable to find a buyer, even when he asked less than half of their
prewar value. His expenses were high: he still drove around Philadelphia in a fancy carriage worth £100, pulled by a fine pair of
matched horses for which he said he had refused £200, driven by a
twenty-two-year-old black slave he valued at £100.

He was unable to sell goods that sat rotting by the New Haven
waterfront. He needed some of the money owed to him, in all an
astronomical £7,131, by his own accounting. Customers and creditors in Connecticut owed him £2,950, which he hired a lawyer to
collect. He had advanced, according to his records, £2,919 out of his
own pocket while he commanded in Canada. His pay and table
allowance as a general was four years—£1,791—in arrears and
had, by Arnold's calculations, depreciated in purchasing power another £1,125. Seagrove and Constable had still not paid him the
final £1,200 that was his share from *Charming Nancy*'s goods, and
his £1,890 share of the sale of *Active,* the reduced portion allowed
by the Pennsylvania courts, had never been turned over to him. He
had invested in another ship, the sloop *John,* sailing out of
Charleston to the Caribbean, but still had received nothing from its
£1,070 cargo of rum, sugar, and molasses.

Arnold had pressed his claims for back pay and expenses in
Congress, but with little success. Nearly a year before, in April 1779,
his tangled accounts had been referred by the Northern Department
of the Army to the newly formed Board of Treasury of Congress. Six
months later, on October 1, 1779, the board declared that the records were so confusing that Congress had decided to appoint a five-
man committee to unravel them. Another four months passed: that
committee, on February 14, 1780, two days after the full Congress
had overwhelmingly voted to censure Arnold for misconduct in office, threw up its hands. With other matters pressing, they found
such a committee "impracticable" for adjusting accounts "with that
accuracy and attention which the nature of them demand." The
committee persuaded Congress to return the case to the Board of
Treasury where "the business of liquidating accounts is now carried
on in a regular manner."15

That was the last place Arnold wanted his accounts scrutinized.
He insisted that he had an enemy on the board who had deliberately
lost or hidden key expense vouchers. There was his public enemy
Elbridge Gerry of Massachusetts, who had delayed his payments for

two years already before forwarding them from Massachusetts to Gates's headquarters at Albany. Gerry also had worked behind the scenes in Massachusetts to deprive the estate of Joseph Warren of a general's pension, even as Warren's four orphans remained threadbare. Arnold had pointedly undertaken their support and education, sending another £500 payment to Boston for them in February 1780, right at the moment his accounts came before Gerry and the Treasury Board. Arnold chose this moment to protest the board's makeup to Congress, alleging that Gerry and his clerks were motivated by "private resentment." He had been at sword's point with several board members, in fact, who were "by no means disinterested and proper persons to judge"[16] his accounts and claims. There was also an enemy he probably did not recognize: a key clerk at the board was Joseph Reed's brother-in-law, Charles Pettit, who for two years had secretly been providing information on Arnold's private financial affairs to Nathanael Greene at Washington's headquarters. But when Arnold protested to Congress that he was being thwarted by the board for political reasons, Congress ignored his protest.

More than two months later, on April 22, 1780, two weeks after Arnold's official reprimand, the Treasury Board issued its lengthy report. The board found Arnold indebted to the United States in the amount of $70,000,* most of it the $66,667 in gold and silver coins which Washington had given to Arnold to pay his way in Canada. Arnold had been able to account for all but £1,000 of this sum, which the board now declared he owed to Congress. Arnold contended that he had given the missing $3,333 to John Halsted, commissary of provisions in the Canadian campaign, but Halsted denied having ever received the sum. The board refused to place the sum to Arnold's credit unless he could produce a voucher for it. Arnold insisted he had already deposited the receipt with the board and that someone there had deliberately removed it from his files. A long search ensued, but the paper was never found.

Actually, even if there was no mole on the board working against him, neither Halsted nor Arnold could produce complete records because some of them were in British archives in Quebec, where they had been deposited after they were captured during the American retreat from Quebec and aboard *Royal Savage* at Valcour Bay. They remained in Canada among the Arnold papers at Laval University, the only archives in Canada at the time, and at Château de Ramezay, American headquarters during Arnold's siege of

* There were $3.334 Continental to £1 sterling when U.S. currency replaced British in 1776. One dollar in 1776 is equivalent to approximately $30 in 1990.

Quebec. Analysis of the missing papers shows that Arnold did as he said: he paid cash. In the words of one Canadian historian, "Large sums of money were disbursed for the purchase of beef and other supplies. To give the invader his due, he paid his way."[17] Arnold's lost records reveal he kept careful track not only of congressional funds but of money he owed to Canadians once his cash ran out. He used a number of commissaries to buy up provisions, and ordered them to keep careful records of stoves, shoes, blankets, wine, beef, rum, flour, sheep, horses, potatoes, gunpowder, even the paper on which he wrote such records.

Arnold erred when he said he had given the cash to Halsted, however. In fact, a journal left behind at Château de Ramezay shows that Arnold made large cash advances to his French Canadian commissary, Colonel Mercier. The amounts and their distribution were logged by Mercier's assistant, John Halsted, who apparently forgot the ledger book during the hasty American evacuation. If there was understandable confusion, Arnold was impotent to clear up one nagging question: if John Halsted logged the money that Arnold gave Mercier, then why didn't he tell the investigators that the money had been given to Mercier, rather than just deny that it was given to him? That would have solved all the confusion. But without the lost ledger, Halsted had no proof, and neither did Arnold, and Congress would not take his word.

Neither the Treasury Board nor Congress seemed to take into account the chaotic conditions during the Canadian winter campaign of 1776 and the ensuing spring retreat, preferring to disbelieve Arnold. For example, when he had reached Quebec, Arnold had found that his brig *Peggy* had been hidden by friends behind Ile d'Orléans. He had used it as a fireship on May 3, 1776, in a futile attempt to incinerate the British relief convoy. The board allowed him $2,666 in depreciated Continental currency for the ship: his sister, Hannah, had sold a similar vessel for nearly double that amount before depreciation. The Treasury Board also disallowed Arnold the value of the full cargo of oats, hay, fish, provisions, and twenty-five horses, which Arnold had taken ashore and turned over to the army. Arnold's documentation included an affidavit from the late General Wooster that part of the cargo had been used as fuel for the fire on the ship. Commissary John Taylor declared that all of the twenty-five horses were eventually employed by the army and not returned to Arnold. But the Treasury Board declined to pay Arnold anything for the horses, claiming insufficient documentation, and granted him only $369 for the ship's entire cargo.

The board never paid Arnold's four years of back pay as a Continental officer, even with depreciated dollars, and reported to Congress that Arnold was to receive nothing for his $9,720 in claims. Instead, he owed the United States $2,328 in gold or silver. The Treasury Board also disallowed Arnold's request for his table allowance. After advancing him $8,000 in depreciated currency to meet his expenses in his early months as military governor, which included official receptions for Congress and the French, the board refused to repay him for the rations he said he had provided for his guests and staff. In four years as a general, he was entitled to fifteen rations per meal. Arnold calculated that Congress owed him for ten thousand meals. He was never reimbursed for them except for the advance of $8,000 in August 1778, paid in depreciated currency worth only $600 in hard money, not enough to sustain his establishment for more than a few weeks. In effect, Arnold could no longer afford to serve as an American general. The Treasury Board's ruling left Arnold with a $9,164 loss in gold and silver, roughly $275,000 in today's U.S. dollars.

The truth was that the scandal of Arnold's conviction on malfeasance charges had spilled over to taint his valid claims for expenditures. Humiliated by his court-martial, left with only his meager officer's pay, a frustrated, infuriated Arnold made one last request for an appeal to Congress, took his leave of absence from the American army, and with his family moved into a smaller house owned by his father-in-law, Judge Shippen.

For fully two years since he had come to Philadelphia, Benedict Arnold, even as he was attacked by radicals in the state and federal governments, had also been surrounded by critics of these same radical revolutionaries. For weeks, his good friend Silas Deane had sat at Arnold's dinner table at the Penn mansion, along with his friends berating enemies in Congress for their ungrateful treatment of him after his term as American agent to Paris had ended amid charges of fraud and conspiracy. Many of Arnold's other friends had been roughly handled by Congress and committees—Daniel Morgan and Eleazar Oswald had resigned from the army after run-ins with Congress. His friend in Newburyport Nathaniel Tracy had been all but ruined by currency depreciation. Peggy Arnold's private encouragement of his secret negotiations to change sides was constantly being seconded by a Greek chorus of Loyalists and conservative Philadelphia merchants and lawyers.

The most powerful and persuasive arguments for Arnold to abandon the Revolution and take a leading role among Loyalists who wanted to end the war and return to the *status quo ante bellum* may have come from a boyhood friend of George Washington, Colonel Beverley Robinson, whose father and grandfather had both been members of the governor's council. He had married the daughter of a Hudson River patroon and built one of the great New York fortunes on land speculation and managing sixty thousand acres and 146 tenant farms in Dutchess County, where he was the first colonel of militia and judge of common pleas. A political rival of the Livingstons and the Schuylers and a leader of New York's conservative majority, he was nevertheless elected to the first revolutionary provincial congress, largely because he had supported the boycotts of British exports and imports, ordering all his dependents to do likewise. When fighting broke out, he had retired from public life and remained neutral at his riverfront mansion across from West Point until British armies advanced toward his estates from both north and south in mid-1777. Then he had raised a Loyalist regiment, mostly relatives and tenants, and joined the British in New York City, where he had become a friend and trusted adviser of General Clinton. Sometime early in 1779, he wrote an undated letter to Arnold calling on Arnold to take over the leadership of the Loyalist Americans, to end the war, staunch the bloodshed, help to found a new American government with its own two-house Parliament with only native-born American members, a viceroy appointed by the king, the power to make its own laws, set its own taxes, enjoy the same citizenship rights as Englishmen at home. "They will enjoy, in every sense of the phrase, the blessings of good government. They shall be sustained, in time of need, by all the power necessary to uphold them." The American colonies would win redress of all the grievances that had led to the Revolution, but the British would not grant America independence. To refuse to grant independence to colonies which had produced such leaders as Arnold's enemies in Congress and on the Pennsylvania council was a position Arnold undoubtedly found reasonable.

But Britain must be helped to put an end to the bloodshed.

It is necessary that a decisive advantage should put Britain in a condition to dictate the terms of reconciliation. . . . There is no one but General Arnold who can surmount obstacles so great as these. A man of so much courage will never despair of the republic, even when every door to a reconciliation seems sealed. Render, then, brave General, this important service to your country. . . . Let us put an end to so many calamities. You and ourselves have the same origin, the same language, the same laws. . . . Beware, then, of breaking forever the links and ties of a friendship whose benefits are proven. . . . United in equality, we will rule the universe, we will hold it bound, not by arms and violence but by the ties of commerce—the lightest and most gentle bonds that human kind can wear.[18]

Early in April 1780, Arnold met with Philip Schuyler, who had come to Philadelphia as a New York delegate to Congress. On April 13, Schuyler was elected chairman of a congressional committee to confer with Washington at his Morristown headquarters on the reorganization of the army departments and American cooperation with the French. Schuyler agreed to speak to Washington about a new command for Arnold, this time as commandant of the key American stronghold at West Point, an assignment of critical importance to the New York delegate and one which Schuyler's weight could help swing Arnold's way.

Sometime after Schuyler left for Morristown, probably after his appeal to Congress of the Treasury Board's decision was shunted to yet another congressional committee, Arnold apparently decided once and for all that he would desert the cause of the ungrateful American revolutionaries to join the standard of Loyalist Americans and their British king. Like every other American revolutionary he was already a rebel, a traitor to the English citizenship of his birth. But in shifting back again to British allegiance, he would risk losing all of his property and most of his assets—his houses, farm, wharves, warehouses, ships—if the British lost. To prevent this loss and be able to support his large family, he needed to make himself valuable to the British. He decided to use Philip Schuyler's friendship to gain the command at West Point. Arnold would later maintain that at the time, he believed that if he had the courage to renounce the Revolution and resume his allegiance to the king, other men like Philip Schuyler who had lost so much in the deteriorating conditions of civil war would follow his example, desert the radical revolutionaries, bring back peace and prosperity in America.

Schuyler hated to see the revolutionary cause fail to make use of Arnold's services. By May 11, 1780, Schuyler had spoken to Washington about Arnold. When Arnold did not receive an answer right away, he pressed Schuyler again on May 25:

I have not had the pleasure of receiving a line from you since you arrived at Camp, and know not who is to have the command at the North river [the Hudson River forts]. . . . When I requested leave of absence of His Excellency General Washington for the summer, it was under the idea that it would be a very inactive campaign, and that my services would be of little consequence, as my wounds made it very painful for me to walk or ride. The prospect now seems to be altered, and there is a possibility of an active campaign in which, though attended with pain and difficulty, I wish to render my country every service I have in my power and with the advice of my friends, am determined to join the army.[19]

On June 2, Philip Schuyler wrote Arnold claiming that he had written as long ago as May 11 to advise him that

I had conversed with the General on the subject which passed between us before I left Philadelphia, that he appeared undecided on the occasion, I believe because no arrangement was made, for he expressed himself with regard to you in terms such as the friends who love you could wish. When I received yours of the 25th of May, I read it to him. He was much engaged. Next day, he requested to know the contents again. I put it into his hands. He expressed a desire to know whatever was agreeable to you, dwelt on your abilities, your merits, your sufferings, and on the well-earned claims you have on your country, and intimated that as soon as his arrangements for the campaign should take place, he would properly consider you.

I believe you will have an alternative proposed, either to take charge of an important post with an honorable command, or your station in the field. Your reputation, my dear sir, so established, your honorable scars put it decidedly in your power to take either. A state [New York] which has full confidence in you will wish to see its banner entrusted to you. If the command at West Point is offered, it will be honorable; if a division in the field, you must judge whether you can support the fatigues, circumstances as you are.[20]

By the time Arnold received Schuyler's generous letter, Arnold had communicated once again with British headquarters in New York City. André was absent when Joseph Stansbury arrived at headquarters at One Wall Street and was ushered into the office of the Hessian officer in charge, Major General Wilhelm von Knyphausen, commanding in New York City while Clinton was absent in South Carolina. Benedict Arnold had informed Stansbury that he was to tell Clinton or Knyphausen, whoever was in command at New York, "that he will undertake the part in question," provided he obtained "the security as expressed in the enclosed note written by His Friend." Arnold had apparently dictated his terms to Stansbury, who was to take them directly to André. The "certain indemnifications for himself and family required, are as follows: first, the loss of his private fortune £5,000 Sterling; ye debt due to him by the *community* £5,000 Sterling to be made good, or whatever part is lost." Arnold also demanded "to have a new-raised battalion here upon the common footing," a Loyalist battalion with himself at its head, giving him the rank of a provincial brigadier general, and an independent command. "Were it not for his family," Knyphausen wrote down Stansbury's words, "he declares he would join the army without making any terms." He asked for "a small sum of ready money to employ in a particular channel"[21]—to pay for his own couriers; he evidently was growing suspicious of Stansbury. Arnold gave more direct hints of his identity than usual: "He is not at Phil," Knyphausen noted—"goes in a few days to Connecticut on his private affairs, after which he returns to Camp [Washington's headquarters] and remains there in a military capacity." Arnold thus notified Clinton that he had rejoined the American army, and where he could be found. He added a note of urgency. He must have "a conference with an officer of confidence" about his best use: "He will take a decisive part in case of an emergency or [in case] a capital stroke can be struck." Knyphausen added in a note of his own that "the matter in agitation is of so important a nature that G. K. [Knyphausen] does not think himself authorized to give an answer to it." But Knyphausen wisely decided to send Arnold £200, a "trifling expenditure" to help in "cultivating the connection." Knyphausen also responded to Arnold's request for a "token" to prevent any "fraud" by American agents. He procured for Arnold two rings "which are exactly alike for the purposes of communication" and sent him one, retaining the other for the "officer of confidence" who would later meet secretly with him.[22]

As soon as Stansbury could reach Arnold's new residence in Philadelphia, he gave Arnold the ring, the expense money, and Knyphausen's assurances he would take up the matter with Clinton on his return. Arnold responded quickly with proof of his intentions. He had just heard of a secret Franco-American invasion of Canada. An American army headed by Marquis de Lafayette was to sail up the Connecticut River and march across Vermont to attack St. Jean as a diversion while a French fleet with eight thousand French troops aboard, the main invasion force, was to attack Quebec. Washington had sent Arnold several copies of a proclamation to have translated into French. Arnold had taken them around to his former headquarters and pumped the rest of the information out of the French minister, Luzerne. Now Arnold sent a coded copy of Washington's proclamation back to New York with Stansbury with a detailed warning of the invasion plan and its route. He also said he would arrive at Washington's headquarters in Morristown "by the 4th of July." If he met a person "who has the token agreed upon, you may expect every intelligence in my power which will probably be of consequence."[23] Arnold informed Knyphausen that he would also reach Washington's headquarters at Morristown on his way north on June 12.

The day he arrived in camp he sent a message, giving Clinton even more details of the Canadian invasion. If he moved quickly, Arnold wrote, Clinton could intercept the French fleet, six ships of the line and six thousand French troops, at Rhode Island, where they were to rendezvous with Washington and four thousand Americans. If the Americans were not intercepted, Washington would soon have twenty thousand men. Actually, the report of a Franco-American invasion to the north was a ruse deliberately concocted by Washington and promulgated by the French ministry in Philadelphia to draw off the British navy and supporting troops from New York City, the real target. Washington had long felt that Philadelphia was a sieve for intelligence, and he wanted the capital moved out of the city into a small town in the Maryland hinterlands not only because Philadelphia was heavily Loyalist and too close to British headquarters but also because whatever he told Congress seemed to be instantly communicated to the British. Arnold had written Clinton the year before that it was unnecessary to steal French or American documents because he could learn everything from congressmen and French diplomats who lived under his roof. Washington, aware of the leaks if not their exact channel, was perfectly capable of making his own use of Congress's abysmal ability to keep secrets. If Clinton had been able to follow Arnold's suggestions, the British would have started north and Washington could have attacked New York City when it was virtually undefended.

Before continuing his June 1780 trip north, Benedict Arnold added a hasty postscript to the coded message he sent through the lines into New York City on June 15: "Mr. Moore expects to have the command of West Point offered him on his return." Arnold dashed off a preliminary assessment of West Point for the British based on his conversations with Schuyler: "Troops and provisions wanting there. . . . Only fifteen hundred [men]. . . . Mr. M. thinks it would be a good stroke to get between General Washington and West Point."[24]

As he headed north the next day, June 16, he stopped off to inspect West Point. From Fishkill on the Hudson, Arnold sent another coded message, deciphered by Odell. In devastating detail, Arnold told the British commander what he had seen as he had ridden around the hilltop fortifications and riverfront batteries at the side of West Point's present commandant, General Robert Howe, the man who had presided over his court-martial. Howe had allowed the strategic base to fall into disrepair: Arnold was "greatly disappointed both in the works and garrison." Its garrison was not strong enough to "half man the works," which were made up of seven different forts, even though another twelve hundred men were being transferred from Albany. "General Howe tells me there is not ten days provisions": the forts could not hold out against a British siege. "If the English were to cut off the communication with Pennsylvania"—source of West Point's grain supplies—"they would be distressed. . . . It is surprising a post of so much importance should be so totally neglected. . . . The works appear to me to be most wretchedly planned . . . to stop the passage of the river. The Point is on a low piece of ground comparatively to the chain of hills which lie back of it." Arnold spelled out the strong points and weak spots, their garrisons and guns. Of the key fort atop the highest hill, Rocky Point, he noted that while the walls overlooking the river were six feet thick, the fort was "defenseless on the back." An English force could "land three miles below and have a good road to bring up heavy cannon to Rocky Point." The redoubt could be taken by "a handful of men." Scores of American cannon in forts on a bluff overlooking the great bend of the Hudson River and in redoubts opposite the Point on Constitution Island were positioned to fire on any ships which tried to run through an enormous chain blocking the channel. But, Arnold wrote, "I am convinced the boom or chain . . . cannot be depended upon. . . . A single ship, large and heavy-loaded with a strong wind and tide would break the chain."[25] Late the night of the 16th, at Fishkill, Arnold encoded his long blueprint for a British attack on West Point, sending it with a paid and trusted courier off to British headquarters. Then he drove on to New Haven, where he was trying to sell his house and collect his debts.

Just two days later, Clinton and André sailed into New York Harbor from their victorious campaign in South Carolina, where Benjamin Lincoln's 5,400-man army had surrendered, the largest American loss of the Revolution, after a ten-week siege largely planned and executed by André. But André found Clinton much too preoccupied with Arnold's intelligence reports to answer Arnold's messages. Clinton returned just in time to receive Arnold's message that Washington and his army were about to rendezvous with the French in Rhode Island, and he wanted to move quickly. He believed that New York, not Canada, was the intended French target, but he had been unaware that the French planned to link up with the Americans at Rhode Island. He needed to deprive them of a base in New England, and he most of all wanted to keep them from joining forces with Washington. If the redcoats who had returned from South Carolina with Clinton could reembark on Royal Navy ships and sail immediately to Newport, they could reoccupy Rhode Island and prepare a hostile reception for the French. The British ships could then deploy to intercept and destroy the French fleet before the French army could disembark.

But Clinton had long been plagued by British infighting at the highest levels. Admiral Marriott Arbuthnot, the irascible and probably senile head of the Royal Navy on the North American station, declined to provide the necessary ships. Furthermore, he refused to believe the intelligence provided by Arnold, preferring to gather his own naval intelligence and await reinforcements from England before attacking the French fleet. The major stroke that Arnold and Clinton so desperately wanted was, for the moment, lost. On July 7, 1780, Clinton learned that the French had been spotted off the Virginia coast; three days later they arrived off Rhode Island. It was now more important than ever to keep Washington's army from linking up with the French. More and more, Clinton's mind turned toward driving a wedge between them, as Arnold had suggested, at West Point.

After surveying the fortifications at West Point, Benedict Arnold had driven to Hartford, Connecticut, where the assembly was in session. Arnold persuaded the leadership to add his name to a list of officers of the Connecticut line in the Continental Army who would be paid the difference between their salaries and what had been lost by depreciation of the Continental currency. Months later, when the committee in charge of settling his back-pay account still had not met, Arnold hired a Middletown lawyer to collect the money for him and himself hurried to New Haven: he needed cash, and the legislature was only offering promissory notes worth £1,125 in four annual installments, not to begin for another two years. Arnold turned the *Active* case, still pending in the courts in Philadelphia, over to the same lawyer, and offered $1,000 in gold to any lawyer who could settle the case or interest the Connecticut legislature in thinking it "their duty to obtain justice to a subject of the state and defend its rights and dignity so grossly violated."[26] Arnold was steadily collecting old debts. He offered to sell his house in New Haven to Enoch Brown of Boston for £1,000, a little more than half what he had spent to build it. Arnold refused to take Continental money for the house. He was already shifting his assets to London through friends in New York City, and he told Brown he wanted only good sterling bills drawn on an English, French, or Dutch bank.[27]

Back in Philadelphia sooner than he had told Knyphausen to expect him, Arnold learned the disappointing news from Peggy that there was still no word from the British, no guarantee of the indemnity he had demanded. On July 7, Stansbury wrote from Philadelphia to Odell: "My partner is come to town. . . . He thinks it strange that no steps are taken on your part to come to a settlement." Arnold had kept Stansbury waiting all day before seeing him, and Stansbury in turn had kept a courier waiting until midnight before Arnold sent his servant around to Stansbury's shop on Walnut Street to fetch him. Stansbury memorized what Arnold wanted encoded and sent it right off: "Mr. Moore requests a very explicit answer to his letter of June 7th." He also wanted an interview with Major General Phillips, head of British artillery, or "some other proper officer, as nothing further can be done without it." Arnold suggested that Phillips come out of New York City to negotiate a prisoner exchange under a flag of truce.

Then Arnold hastened to correct the misinformation he had sent Clinton from Washington's camp: New York was to be the target of the French, Canada "a secondary object in case the other fails." Arnold gave Clinton more information on Washington's intended movements and added fresh details about the Highland forts, which he had visited again on his way back from New Haven. He also informed Clinton that "two or three persons in whom you confide as spies are in his [Howe's] pay and often give him important intelligence. . . . [Arnold] begs you would write to him only by such channels as may be depended upon. He is to take the command of West Point immediately on the [French] fleet's arrival, or at any rate in the course of a month." Although Arnold's appointment to West Point was far from sure, Arnold no longer said he expected the West Point command, he asserted that he was certain of the appointment to enhance his value in the dealings. Arnold held out even more enticing bait, a "drawing of the works on both sides of the river done by a French engineer," by means of which "you might take [West Point] without loss." In addition, if only Arnold could meet with the right officer, they could "lay down a plan of communication whereby you should be informed of everything projected at [American] headquarters."[28]

While Arnold stewed in Philadelphia, John André had been busy checking out Arnold's activities. Three days after his return from South Carolina, André had already confirmed that Arnold was, as he had said, traveling through New Jersey, en route from Washington's headquarters at Morristown to Connecticut. André was also having Arnold's movements in Connecticut watched by Loyalist operatives there. Joseph Chew, a Tryon County, New York, Loyalist working for British intelligence in Manhattan, wrote to André on the 20th that he had "put two persons out in order to obtain an account of Mr. Arnold's movements."[29] André was being prudent, but Clinton was already convinced of Arnold's veracity as well as his extreme usefulness. He wrote to London to British under secretary of state William Eden, head of the British secret service, that "immediately on my arrival from the southward, I received, from such authority as I should have risked an action upon, intelligence that the French fleet"[30] was expected at Rhode Island. Clinton now believed that Arnold had betrayed one of Washington's most important secrets. Preoccupied with moving his troops up the Hudson to get between Washington and the French, Clinton neglected to communicate with Arnold.

Arnold did not wait for an answer to his July 7 message. Four days later, he wrote in stronger terms to Clinton that unless there was definite progress in their arrangements, he would break off their negotiations. He sent his July 11 message not by Stansbury through Odell but by Samuel Wallis, a Philadelphia Quaker businessman long involved in spying for the British. (Arnold did not know that Wallis already worked for André with Stansbury and Odell.) Arnold's stern letter reiterated all that he had said in the past month about his terms, just in case Stansbury had failed to deliver his messages. There was a strong preamble to this letter, however, that certainly must bring a response from Clinton: either

a mutual confidence between us is wanting, the persons we have employed have deceived us, or we have been unfortunate in our negotiation, in which on both sides, we are deeply interested. If the first, here our correspondence ought to end. If the second, an opportunity offers of redressing any abuse. If the latter, a stricter attention and proper regard to the interests of both parties may remedy the misfortune.

Arnold was anxious to know whether he could count on the British. "I have advanced several sums already," he wrote (had Stansbury pocketed the gold sent by Knyphausen?), "and risked still greater without any profit. It is now become necessary for me to know the risk that I run in case of a loss."[31]

Not satisfied with this ultimatum, written in a disguised handwriting, Arnold made Wallis wait while he wrote another letter the next day, July 12, its cipher keyed to the pocket dictionary that Knyphausen had sent him. He made his offer to betray West Point even more explicit: "If I point out a plan of cooperation by which S.H. shall possess himself of West Point, the garrison, etc., £20,000 I think will be a cheap purchase for an object of so much importance." If Stansbury had not delivered his earlier messages, Clinton would now be able to isolate him as the problem. But he also pressed for a meeting with a high-level officer; "the necessity is evident." He also wanted to assure Clinton that if the British could only frustrate American war efforts through one more year, the revolution would collapse:

The mass of the people are heartily tired of the war, and wish to be on their former footing. They are promised great events from this year's exertion. If disappointed, you have only to persevere and the contest will soon be at an end. The present struggles are like the pangs of a dying man, violent but of a short duration.

Arnold sent off Wallis with "great confidence," but he asked Clinton to "threaten him with [your] resentment in case he abuses the confidence placed in him, which will bring certain ruin on me."[32] And to seal the bargain, he insisted that André give Wallis £1,000 to bring to him as a good-faith down payment on West Point.

It was two more weeks before Arnold received his first answer from André in more than a year, and then, as Arnold had wished, it was guarded, perhaps more cautious than he had wanted: it still contained no firm offer of money or compensation for losses, no timetable, no outright acceptance of Arnold's offer to surrender West Point. It did confirm André's implicit trust in Stansbury and, indeed, was addressed to Stansbury under the code name "Carleton" and then delivered by Stansbury to Arnold. André did not apologize for the delay in answering—"You must not wonder if we take a view of our new-arrived foe [the French]," he wrote—but, in a move to placate Arnold, informed him that his plan for turning over the Hudson River forts was "our main purpose."[33] He also hinted to Arnold that it would be André who would come to meet secretly with him, since Phillips had refused on the grounds that he was in the process of being exchanged for Benjamin Lincoln, and any breach of the rules of war at this time could cost him the revocation of his parole by the Americans.

Arnold sent off his answer to this letter via Stansbury and Andrew Furstner, a veteran British secret service spy who had been carrying secret messages from Pennsylvania to New York for more than three years. On July 24, 1780, one day after Arnold's strong letters of July 12 and 13 finally were placed in André's hands and fully five weeks after Clinton's return to New York, André finally had a long conference with Sir Henry. André sent for Odell, who encoded the long-awaited message. If Stansbury was captured, it was supposed that nothing in the letter pointed to Arnold:

His Excellency authorizes me to repeat in the strongest terms the assurances so often given to your partner that if he is in earnest and will to the extent of his ability cooperate with us, he shall not in any possible event have cause to complain. . . . Essential services shall be even profusely rewarded, far beyond the stipulated indemnification. . . . Indemnification is what S.H. thinks highly unreasonable. However, he has not the smallest doubt but that everything may be settled to mutual satisfaction when the projected interview takes place at W.P., from whence it is expected Mr. Moore will take occasion (upon entering his Cd [command] there) to correspond with S.H. by flag of truce. Mr. Anderson is willing himself to effect the meeting.34

Enclosed with the Odell-Stansbury cipher was a second coded message, keyed to the pocket dictionary, for the first time flatly promising Arnold terms: "Should we, through your means, possess ourselves of 3,000 men and [West Point's] artillery and stores," André himself wrote, "the sum even of £20,000 should be paid you." If Arnold failed, he would not "be left a victim." Clinton flatly rejected Arnold's demands for indemnification for losses. He would only be paid for services rendered. Clinton cut in half Arnold's request for £1,000 as a down payment for his services. He authorized André to give £200 to Wallis to transmit to Arnold, and gave André another £300 to keep at Arnold's "disposal."35 Arnold had apparently instructed Wallis to entrust the money to his friend Daniel Coxe, vice president of the Board of Associated Loyalists in New York City and the husband of Peggy Arnold's friend Becky Redman. There it would remain at Peggy's disposal. Arnold did not wait for Wallis to bring him André's letters assuring him that Clinton would meet his price. He had already left for West Point to meet with Washington and accept his new command. Yet when Wallis returned to New York City on July 29, he brought word to Odell for André that Arnold "will no longer hesitate."36

At midnight, July 30, 1780, a sick and exhausted Captain

George Beckwith, worn out from the summer's heat, transmitted Arnold's missing letters of July 11 and 12 to André along with Odell's note that they could not expect Arnold's full cooperation. Beckwith also told André that he had worked out arrangements, albeit cumbersome, with Arnold at West Point, through Peggy Arnold in Philadelphia. The American army was on the move with Washington, making espionage more difficult. It took John Rattoon two weeks to make it through the American lines to Philadelphia to Stansbury, reaching him on August 15 with Clinton's final offer of £20,000. Another full month passed before André knew that his letters had been delivered. On August 23, three weeks after Arnold actually took command at West Point, André, fifty miles away, knew only that Peggy had received the British offer—and still did not know if Arnold had accepted it. "Mr. Moore commands at West Point," Stansbury wrote André, "but things are so poorly arranged that your last important dispatches are yet in *her* hands."[37] So far, Peggy had found no "unquestionable carrier" to take the British offer to Arnold. Stansbury was completely disgusted with this tedious and dangerous triangular correspondence, and recommended that André deal directly with Arnold from now on.

By August 24, neither side knew whether the other would accept its terms. Peggy had already received letters from her husband at West Point, and now she had Stansbury copy extracts from them to encode and carry to André in New York. Arnold's letters appeared chatty and innocent enough, so that if they were intercepted, they would seem to be just newsy letters from Arnold to his wife back home. In fact, they were crammed with intelligence that could be extremely useful to the British. Washington, Arnold wrote, had gone to Stony Point to take his army across the Hudson at King's Ferry. Ten thousand American troops were on the march, heading toward New York to distract Clinton from Rhode Island. Stansbury transmitted information from Arnold that would be crucial to Clinton's plans, if only Stansbury and Rattoon could move quickly enough. "I wish our force and the provision made for it would enable us to attack New York in his [Clinton's] absence and end the dispute; but I am sorry to say that I believe it will be unequal to the undertaking, and am apprehensive for the French fleet and army, who are in a critical situation."

Arnold also passed along intelligence about French reinforcements that could be invaluable to Clinton's timetable. Another division of 2,500 men and several ships were to sail from Brest as soon as transports could be procured. Arnold's words warned Clinton to move quickly and decisively. "If this division should arrive soon, they will probably make the French fleet nearly equal, perhaps superior, to the British, and there is some expectation of [French] reinforcements from the West Indies."38

In a second letter, Arnold had written Peggy that Washington had marched south to Dobbs Ferry, "to establish a post and build works which will confine the British within narrower bounds and shorten our communication with New England."39 On August 3, Arnold wrote Peggy that American preparations for attacking New York City were being shelved because so few Americans had responded to the latest call for recruits. The entire American army was, however, marching to Dobbs Ferry so the British would believe they were about to attack the city. To appear strong enough to ward off a British attack, Washington had stripped West Point of all its Continentals, having only raw militia and invalids for its garrison.

Privately, George Washington, too, was on the point of despair. Robert L. Livingston and Philip Schuyler were pressuring Washington to remove Robert Howe as commandant in the Highlands and appoint Arnold, on the grounds that Howe had neglected his duties and weakened West Point. Resorting to half-truth, Washington argued that there was no "danger to the post at West Point" and that, indeed, he was "so well persuaded of the safety of West Point" that he had "dismissed all the militia that were called in for the defense of the posts on the [Hudson] river."40 The letter directly contradicted what he wrote to Howe himself. On July 6, he wrote his brother, "It is to be lamented, bitterly lamented, and in the anguish of soul I do lament, that our fatal and accursed policy should bring the 6th of [July] upon us, and not a single recruit to the Army." The army was "reduced almost to nothing [by short enlistments]," went "five or six days together without bread, then as many without meat," "two or three times without either."41 The harvests were plentiful, but army commissaries were driving herds of cattle paid for by Congress and destined for Washington's army to the French in Rhode Island, who were paying in gold, not depreciated paper money. When Benedict Arnold joined Washington's army on the Hudson a few weeks after this, he confirmed Washington's bleak view, but he did so in a letter to Peggy. The army had been "three days without a mouthful of meat, and [West Point] is very little better."42 He sent this latest morsel of treasonous intelligence on August 25, one day after Peggy finally got word through to him that Clinton was willing to meet his price for West Point and its garrison, a price roughly equal to Benedict Arnold's entire net worth, including all the debts, public and private, that were owed to him.

18

"I HAVE
NO CONFIDANTS"

*It is a matter much to be lamented
that our army is permitted to starve
in a land of plenty. There is a fault
somewhere. It ought to be traced up
to its authors [and] capitally
punished.*

Benedict Arnold to Nathanael Greene, September 12, 1780

With the British navy sailing virtually unopposed along the Atlantic seaboard, all revolutionary communication between New England and the Middle Atlantic states moved inland. The main strategic links were the Hudson River and the Post Road along the east shore. British generals since Gage had considered New England the head of the Revolution, and the Americans knew that if they lost New England, they would soon lose the war. As recently as June 15, 1780, as Knyphausen attacked his army in New Jersey, Washington remained convinced that this was only a diversion, that the real British objective was the Hudson Highlands, with its fifteen-mile chain of forts.

In short, Washington had come to think of West Point as "the key to America."[1] As long as he held it, he could maneuver his army and, in effect, neutralize Clinton's powerful base at New York City. Arnold and Washington had agreed on the Hudson's strategic importance from the beginning of the war, when Arnold had marched to Canada and then fought desperately on Lake Champlain to keep the British from sailing down the Hudson to link up with their army and navy attacking northward up the Hudson River from New York City.

The road along the west bank of the Hudson and the ferry crossing over the wide river just below West Point were the vital line of communication between the French army now based in Rhode Island and Washington's main army. Roughly equidistant from Washington's winter encampments in Morristown, New Jersey, and his supply bases at Albany and Hartford and in northwestern Pennsylvania, the forts at West Point were at the heart of Washington's quadrilateral strategy of offensive as well as defensive warfare, and he would commit its command only to a skilled and trusted general.

At West Point the two-hundred-foot-deep channel narrows and bends nearly ninety degrees, then immediately bends another ninety degrees, squeezing between high cliffs on the west bank and the rocky shores of Constitution Island to the east. Once the point was fortified, a British man-of-war that dared to run the gauntlet against the river's strong tidal current would still have to come about twice past the lethal broadsides of scores of well-placed heavy cannon. In 1775 Arnold's friend the military engineer Bernard Romans had laid out redoubts and batteries on the east side of the Hudson and recommended that the west point of land overlooking the island also be fortified. The first fort at West Point, modeled after Ticonderoga, with high earth-and-log walls and four triangular ramparts on a bluff at the river's bend, was named Fort Arnold when it was built after Saratoga, and bristled with the heavy artillery Burgoyne surrendered. The fire of the guns from Fort Arnold and Constitution Island protected a 1,097-foot chain, each twelve-by-eighteen-inch link of two-inch-thick bar iron weighing at least one hundred pounds, which floated on log pontoons just below the river's surface to block passage of the river.

When Tadeusz Kosciuszko arrived to take over as chief engineer in the Hudson Highlands in March 1778, he could see how vulnerable the fortifications would be to British artillery placed above and behind them. From a sheer cliff atop Rocky Hill, half a mile west of Fort Arnold, he looked down and watched masons and carpenters working beneath him inside a new hilltop redoubt called Fort Putnam, and he could clearly make out other men working all over the great plateau below him, inside the works at Fort Arnold, and across the Hudson on Constitution Island, less than a mile away. All were within range of an eighteen-pound gun. When Kosciuszko reminded his superiors of the consequences of ignoring his advice at Ticonderoga, he received approval to build the formidable Redoubt No. 4, with six-foot-thick stone walls open on the back against the sheer hillside. In twenty-eight months of nearly constant construction, Kosciuszko had supervised the erection of four major forts, a blockhouse, and a chain of new hilltop redoubts, as well as repositioning and reinforcing a string of river-level gun emplacements. By the late summer of 1780, there were ten forts in all at West Point. When the Marquis de Chastellux visited the stronghold that autumn, he described West Point as a ring of forts perched on hills and cliffs in the shape of an amphitheater, protecting each other. In addition, there was, on the outer plateau behind Fort Arnold, a small city, including rows of wooden officers' barracks, a hospital and tents, a bakery, a powder magazine, storehouses, a jail.* Fifteen hundred men made up the garrison.

At the end of July, after Clinton called off the British attack on Rhode Island and withdrew his armies from eastern Long Island and New Jersey into his heavily fortified defensive lines, Washington and the American army marched and countermarched, trying to entice Clinton into leaving New York City, leaving it vulnerable to a French naval attack. But Clinton was biding his time, waiting for Arnold to betray the Hudson forts. On the last day of July 1780, Arnold overtook Washington on a high bluff opposite Peekskill, New York, where he was watching the last of the American brigades being rowed across the Hudson at King's Ferry. It was a sweltering midsummer day, and thousands of weary soldiers were taking all of it to march down the twisting dirt road to the landing below Fort Lafayette, cross the river, and tramp up the steep grade at Stony Point for a twenty-five-mile march south to Tappan, the main American base camp.

As Washington sat on his tall bay charger, he could see long columns of tired Continentals, their flintlocks shouldered as they shambled along, saddle-weary dragoons and artillerymen trudging beside their horse-drawn cannons; groaning wagons full of wounded men suffering in the hot sun from dysentery, cholera, fever; more than two hundred creaking Conestoga wagons filled with barrels of wheat and salt pork, rolling along behind a thousand huge dray-horses.

Among George Washington's attributes as a general was his

* The U.S. Military Academy was not established at West Point until 1802.

stubborn unpredictability. Off and on for weeks, people had been prodding him to give Benedict Arnold the command at West Point. But Washington not only was resisting congressional pressure, he was short on good battle-seasoned major generals. Lincoln was a prisoner; Greene had been removed from command in the Hudson Highlands and was going south with a detached command; old William Heath was coming out of semiretirement and Washington hoped to put him, not Arnold, in charge of the rear-area base at West Point. Washington later explained to Joseph Reed what he had told Arnold when he had met with him in June:

As we had a prospect of an active and vigorous campaign, I should be glad of [his] aid and assistance, but saw little prospect of his obtaining such a command as [West Point]. . . . It was my intention to draw my whole force into the field . . . leaving West Point to the care of invalids and a small garrison of militia; but if, after his previous declaration, the command of the post, for the reasons he assigned, would be more convenient and agreeable to him than a command in the field, I should readily indulge him.[2]

When Arnold had written to Clinton that he already had the assignment, he had been overstating his case vastly. By the afternoon of July 30, 1780, Washington had changed his mind.

He decided that he needed Arnold in command of the entire left wing of the army, one half of his best infantry. It was the post of honor, an appointment that would have resuscitated Arnold's reputation in a single stroke by making it apparent that Arnold was back in Washington's favor. Washington no doubt expected Arnold to accept it, gratefully. That hot August afternoon in 1780, Arnold rode up next to Washington at King's Ferry and the commander in chief, turning from watching the loaded barges glide across the Hudson, nodded to him with his usual grave courtesy. Washington later recalled that Arnold "asked me if I had thought of anything for him." Washington was pleased to see the brave Arnold back on a horse, reporting for duty, back in the fight. Yes, yes, he answered Arnold, smiling. Arnold was to have "a post of honor." Arnold smiled, too: the post of West Point was his, in his gift to deliver to the British. But Washington went on: Arnold was to be a divisional commander, in command of the left wing. "Upon this information," Washington remembered, Arnold's "countenance changed and he appeared to be quite fallen, and, instead of thanking me or expressing any pleasure at the appointment, never opened his mouth."[3] Officers closer to Arnold that day said his face had turned dark red, almost purple, as if he were angry. Washington, perplexed, asked Arnold to ride on to his headquarters and wait for him.

Arnold may have been the only high-ranking American officer who did not know that Washington had already restored him to a field command, and that the general orders for August 1 had already been written. As Washington rode back toward headquarters, he was intercepted by Colonel Tench Tilghman, his chief of staff, who said that Arnold was limping back and forth at headquarters, arguing that his leg was bad, that he could not last very long on horseback, that only a stationary command such as West Point would suit him. Arnold did not seem as crippled as he said he was, however. Tilghman's comments disturbed Washington, but not to the point of suspicion. Washington was sad that the years of political wrangling and inactivity seemed to have sapped Arnold's martial spirit so badly that he would now settle for such an inferior command. Washington rode on to his headquarters and patiently argued with Arnold, trying to prod him, embarrass him into fighting at his side. But Arnold was adamant, arguing passionately about his wound, his need for a rear-area assignment. Washington would agree only to think this matter over.

Two days later, Washington issued new general orders. Arnold was to "proceed to West Point and take command of that post and its dependencies." To justify assigning such a senior officer to West Point, Washington expanded Arnold's duties to include not only all the Hudson River forts from West Point south to Dobbs Ferry on both sides of the river but also command of a corps of infantry and cavalry "advanced towards the enemy's lines."[4] Washington himself was marching south to the New York–New Jersey border. Arnold would be in charge of a vast territory extending from Albany to the British lines at North Castle, just outside New York City—the exact region through which Clinton would have to send troops or ships attacking West Point or troops marching to fight the French on Rhode Island.

Peggy Arnold was at a dinner party at the home of Robert Morris when the news reached Philadelphia that Washington had appointed her husband to the command of the left wing of the Continental Army, not to the command of West Point. She fainted.

Benedict Arnold lost little time assuming his new command at West Point, but even before he got to his Hudson River headquarters, he stopped along the road to recruit an accomplice, a man who turned out to be the perfect patsy for Arnold's conspiracy. He was Squire

Joshua Hett Smith, a pompous, garrulous lawyer and country gentleman who lived in a big white house called Belmont overlooking
Haverstraw Bay near Stony Point. A man trusted completely by neither side, Smith was the younger brother of the completely Loyalist
chief justice of New York; he himself had been an active Whig early
in the Revolution, a member of the revolutionary provincial congress, a militia officer. But he was also a man with a loose tongue,
and Arnold was not the first American or British officer to sense that
Smith's pliability could be useful.

It was Smith who supervised the West Point spy network under
the command of Arnold's predecessor, General Robert Howe, a ring
of operatives that was selling information to both sides. Arnold may
have learned all he needed to know about Smith by the time he
stopped off at the squire's house the night of July 31, awaiting orders from Washington. Arnold had met Smith in Philadelphia in
1778 when the squire was riding to South Carolina to fetch his
bride, a friend of General Robert Howe's. When Arnold had traveled to West Point earlier in 1780, he had stopped off again at
Smith's manor house at least once. When Arnold asked Howe for
names of his secret agents, Howe had refused to give him all but
one: Squire Smith. Smith enjoyed the confidentiality of generals and
was eager to ingratiate himself with the new commandant. He solicited Arnold's friendship, he later wrote, because "I felt myself happy
in rendering him every aid in my power and cultivated his acquaintance from motives of security." But while Smith did not know he
was being made an unwilling accomplice in treason, he was no fool:
many families at the time wished secretly for a powerful friend on
each side. Smith not only wanted to protect his property from the
depredations of passing American soldiers, he needed a highly
placed revolutionary job that might someday be more valuable to his
largely Loyalist family: "My family in general were suspected of dis-
affection to the American cause."[5] Before he left, Arnold invited
Smith and his wife to come visit him at West Point. He also asked
Smith to help him find bedding and to prepare a list of all his American operatives. He no doubt made a mental note that Smith's house
would make a perfect rendezvous with British agents, so near was it
to the no-man's-land separating the lines, so accessible to ships passing in either direction.

At West Point, Benedict Arnold selected headquarters that were ideally situated for clandestine activities. With his staff and servants, he
took over Beverley, the confiscated mansion of Colonel Beverley
Robinson, commander of the Loyalist King's American Regiment

and the man who had recently written to Arnold to persuade him to assume a leading role among the Loyalists. The sprawling white clapboard house was set back a mile from the Hudson on a bluff among dense trees at present-day Garrison, two miles south of the ferry crossing to West Point. The house and its approaches could not be seen by officers at forts across the river and was safely out of range of British naval cannon firing on the American fortifications. The choice was also natural enough: Robert Howe had used Beverley as his headquarters.

Benedict Arnold confided in no one at West Point, yet he was careful to surround himself with old friends and trusted aides. Major Franks continued as his aide-de-camp, but Arnold never involved Franks in his defection. Indeed, Arnold did not even use him to write the orders and letters that were his covers for coded messages. To handle all the paperwork of an extensive command, Arnold called on his old aide from the Northern Department, Lieutenant Colonel Richard Varick, who had recently resigned from the army and was studying law at his father's house in Hackensack, New Jersey. Arnold had checked with Philip Schuyler, who wrote Varick "that he believes it would be agreeable to you, as the duty would engross only a part of your time."[6] Varick could hardly refuse the flattering invitation of his two former commanders, especially if it still left him time for his studies. Varick gladly accepted the post as Arnold's writing aide, happy to serve again "under an officer than whom none in the army claims greater respect."[7]

Arriving at Beverley on August 4, Arnold found two other old comrades-in-arms waiting to welcome him: one-eyed Colonel John Lamb, half his face blown away in the assault on Quebec, was the ranking artillery officer on the West Point side of the river; and Colonel Return Jonathan Meigs, who had led a division of Arnold's army on the march to Quebec, was in charge of a regiment fortifying the hills behind Fort Arnold. Arnold kept them waiting, taking several days arranging himself at Beverley before crossing the river. He organized a life-guard force of one hundred picked men, two drafted from each company and nine of them assigned to an eight-oared thirty-foot bateau with lugsail that could speed him up and down the Hudson. Arnold arranged them around his headquarters in tents and barracks. Always under arms, they guarded his house and did errands for him. He sent off one of his life guards, an orderly, to Connecticut to deliver a stream of personal letters, many of them demanding payment of debts. As he made excuses to subordinates, Arnold also wrote harmless-looking letters to Robert Howe and to Lafayette, asking the names of all spies operating in the Highlands.

It was a normal enough request from a new commandant, but both generals refused to divulge the identities of their operatives. Howe suggested that Arnold ask Squire Smith for particulars, and Smith hurried up to Beverley to divulge all the names he knew. But Arnold still lacked a trustworthy courier to New York and Philadelphia, and for most of August, his treasonable correspondence lagged.

There was no respite, however, to his preparations for selling out West Point. When Richard Varick arrived on August 13, he found that Arnold had changed since Saratoga. Now this man who had relied so much on his young staff officers had become "very tenacious of ordering and attending to everything himself."[8] Arnold assigned Varick to a desk at the opposite end of a large ground-floor office and promptly buried him in all but his most confidential paperwork. Then he retreated into an inner office, off-limits even to Varick.

Arnold's first run-in with honest, outspoken John Lamb came after days of neglect and, ironically, was over the treatment of a notorious Loyalist being held prisoner in the West Point underground dungeon at Fort Putnam. A lieutenant in the Loyalist 1st Battalion of New Jersey Volunteers, James Moody was one of the most valuable spies employed by the Board of Associated Loyalists in New York City. Absolutely fearless, Moody had carried out numerous successful raids and intelligence missions in New Jersey. With his raiders, he had captured high-ranking revolutionaries, destroyed rebel supply depots, repeatedly scouted Washington's positions, and broken out captured Loyalists from jail. In May 1780, he had tried and failed to kidnap the rebel governor, William Livingston, and had been captured after a massive manhunt. When Washington moved north, he ordered Moody taken north to West Point with other Loyalist prisoners, out of the reach of British rescue parties. But nine of the Loyalists had broken out of the poorly guarded West Point jail by mid-August when Colonel Lamb ordered Moody locked in leg irons and handcuffs.

Less than a week after Arnold's arrival at West Point, he received a letter from his friend William Duer, one of Schuyler's New York "gang" and a delegate to Congress. Duer had been tipped off that Moody, although on his parole-of-honor as a British officer, "will probably soon make his escape to the enemy and thereby escape the fate he so richly deserves, of being hung as a spy."[9] On August 9, Colonel Lamb wrote to Arnold for orders: "I do not think myself authorized to order him in irons. . . . No dependence can be placed upon [the guards]."[10] Lamb asked Arnold to write to Washington for instructions, but without waiting for an answer, the nervous Lamb ordered Moody locked in manacles and leg irons. Somehow, Moody contrived to write and smuggle a letter across the river to Arnold to complain of ill treatment. A fellow prisoner later swore an affidavit that Moody's handcuffs were "ragged on the inside next to the wrist, [causing] his wrists to be much cut."[11]

At first, Arnold tried to duck Moody's petition. Once himself the man who hunted, flogged, and hanged Loyalists, Arnold was now married to one and involved in a conspiracy with others. Yet he did not dare appear lenient to Lamb or other American officers already alarmed by Squire Smith's friendship with the commandant. Lamb later insisted that Moody "grossly exaggerated the rigors of his confinement,"[12] but Arnold dispatched an aide, probably Franks, who verified that the irons were too rough even for Loyalist prisoners. Still ducking a visit to Lamb, claiming his own leg was "a little inflamed," Arnold sent orders to Lamb on August 11: "I don't think it justifiable to put prisoners-of-war in irons." Arnold believed Moody "a bad man" but reminded Lamb he was a prisoner of war. If Moody had observed his parole, Lamb could not "discriminate" against him. "I know not by whose order he has been put in irons, but suppose by yours," Arnold wrote to Lamb. "I could therefore wish they might be taken off by you, without his knowing that I have interfered in the matter."[13] But Lamb remained adamant. He ignored Arnold's order. He wrote back, "I view him in the light of a spy." Moody had been brought into West Point "in open daylight" and knew the weakened state of the garrison. Moody would escape "in forty-eight hours if he is unshackled." Refusing to uncuff Moody, Lamb insisted Arnold write to Washington for further orders: "Every method ought to be taken to prevent the enemy from knowing the real state of this post, for although they may not at present have it in contemplation to attack it, when they are informed what kind of troops [defend it], it may become an object."[14] Shaken by Lamb's unflinching courage, unwilling to argue any further to spare a Loyalist, Arnold countermanded his own order, and the Loyalist officer remained in irons.

As Benedict Arnold exchanged visits with suspected Loyalist Joshua Smith, Arnold's aide, Major Franks, grew more openly hostile to the squire. As soon as he learned that Clinton had accepted his terms, Arnold, also careful to keep his longtime aide from openly insulting his valuable new henchman, sent off Major Franks to Philadelphia to bring Peggy and baby Neddy, now six months old, to West Point. Writing to his former in-laws, the Mansfields, in New Haven that Peggy was only coming for a visit of several weeks, Arnold wrote out detailed instructions for Peggy, who was to come in a light covered wagon with the baby's nurse and her personal servant while a slave drove the carriage. When he arrived in Philadelphia on August 28, Franks wrote Arnold that he would set out with Peggy's party in a few days, and "soon [would] put safe into your hands the greatest treasure you have."[15]

As soon as Arnold had learned, in late August, that Clinton had approved the £20,000 payment for his defection and the surrender of West Point and three thousand men, he called for returns of troop strengths from all his posts and then added them up: they came to 3,086 men—eighty-six more than the minimum. His problem was that he did not want to obtain more troops, but as inconspicuously as possible to deploy those he had so that West Point could not be defended against the impending British attack. He went about his clever shell game in a way that made it appear that he was carrying out Washington's orders to buttress West Point's incomplete defenses even as he crippled the fortress's garrison. Some of his task was easy: a French engineer had concluded that the pontoons supporting the great chain across the river were rotted and that the large iron staples holding either end needed to be reinforced, and Arnold simply did nothing to repair it. But to shift large numbers of men, he had to overcome the objections of John Lamb and Varick, who, more and more, was meddling in Arnold's affairs, no longer content to sit quietly and copy out his orders.

On August 12, Arnold began systematically to weaken the garrison by ordering two hundred of the fifteen hundred soldiers up the river to cut firewood. Usually, Arnold would have taken care of this routinely, but to keep alive the myth of his own decrepitude, he began to pester Washington about all sorts of minor business. At first he complained that there were no camp kettles at West Point for incoming recruits and not even enough tents: Arnold bombarded the new quartermaster general, Timothy Pickering, with complaints about "this poverty-struck place." On August 16 he wrote, "Everything is wanting." He claimed that he could not carry out badly needed repairs on the redoubts, the barracks, the provost, without harnesses for ten teams of horses. Since the barracks could house only eight hundred men, he needed tents for that number again, but could find none: his men were living in lean-to sheds. And there was only one camp kettle for "80 or 100 men." Without a rapid infusion of supplies, "the garrison will be in a wretched, uncomfortable situation next winter," and by the next spring, West Point would be "defenseless."[16] Arnold may have deliberately been trying to drain supplies from the main army to weaken his new enemies further; at the very least he was papering files in Congress and at Washington's headquarters to explain why he was doing little or nothing to strengthen West Point.

In all, Benedict Arnold was able to weaken West Point's garrison by one-half in less than two months. He did not raise a protest when Washington requisitioned four companies of artillery. He sent another two hundred men down the river to Haverstraw for outpost duty. He detached even more men, some of his precious artillerymen, to escort the Loyalist prisoners all the way to Washington's camp at Tappan. He would have sent even more troops away if vigilant John Lamb had not objected. By August 19, Lamb was really getting worried. "What will become of this garrison? Exclusive of the guards, we have between four and five hundred men. . . . This is murder to a garrison."[17]

While he was dissipating West Point's troop strength, Arnold also set about depleting its provisions, doing all in his power to make a long siege impossible. Arguing with his aide, Franks, that an ungrateful Congress owed him ten thousand rations, he drew his share of provisions—fifteen portions per meal—months in advance. Soon some of those newly acquired horses and wagons were hauling barrels of pork and salt pork, hams, and bags of grain out of West Point's supply basements and down to the riverbank for the barge ride over to Beverly, where Arnold ordered them locked in a huge storeroom to which only he and his housekeeper had the keys. Major Franks, grumbling that he refused to be Arnold's steward, complained to Varick that if the British ever attacked they would have to choose between saving their personal baggage or Arnold's provisions. Varick hotly replied "that the stores should go to the devil before I lose my baggage" and that he flatly refused to have anything to do with the Arnold household or stores "as caterer or steward."[18] Arnold kept some of the supplies for his table, where a dozen officers often dined with his other guests and staff, but when John Lamb came for dinner twice, Arnold each time served salt cod. There were wine and fruit and fresh vegetables, a result of Arnold's sharp trading with neighboring farmers from his well-stocked larder, but Arnold was selling off barrels of pork and rum and hams for hard cash, repaying himself, he told Franks, for all the meals for which Congress had never paid him. Franks and Varick compared notes and swore to each other, they later testified, that they would no longer cover up for Arnold's black-market dealings. One day when a Loyalist ship's captain came to headquarters to buy three barrels of port from Arnold, Varick blurted out that every time Ar-

nold sold provisions for gold or silver, it made it that much harder
to induce farmers to sell provisions to the garrison for Continental
paper money. Arnold ignored Varick. He dropped his voice to a
whisper, apparently agreeing to the sale, and then waved the ship's
captain out of the room.

Arnold's sale of army provisions seems at least to have been
provoked by the news that not only would Congress not speed up
the review of his claims for table allowances, but on August 12, it
had turned down a petition for pay raises for general officers. Arnold could not grasp the fact that Congress had no money. A desperate Congress sent the generals not a raise but a sermonette that
left Arnold livid:

*Patience and self-denial, fortitude and perseverance, and the cheerful
sacrifice of time, health and fortune are necessary virtues which both
the citizen and soldier are called to exercise while struggling for the
liberties of their country; and that moderation, frugality and temperance must be among the chief supports, as well as the brightest
ornaments of that kind of civil government which is wisely instituted
by the several states in this union.*[19]

Congress reiterated its two-year-old promise that Arnold, like other
major generals, would receive a bonus of seven years' half pay and
eleven hundred acres of land after the war. Furious, Arnold sent the
resolution with a sarcastic letter to General Parsons, head of the
Connecticut militia, observing bitterly that it was "founded on principles of genuine Congressional virtue, magnanimity, benevolence,
patriotism and justice. I hope they meet with a proper reception. . . .
The insult added to injury is too pointed to pass unnoticed."[20] Arnold proposed that a committee of a thousand or fifteen hundred
soldiers march on Congress.

Plagued by poor communications through the lines to New York
City as Arnold waited for Peggy's arrival at the end of August, he
finally found a suitable messenger for a long-overdue letter to André.
He was William Heron, a member of the Connecticut assembly and
friend of General Parsons, who thought Heron wanted to go into
New York City to collect a debt and sent him to Arnold for a pass.
"Mr. Heron is a neighbor of mine, for whose integrity and firm attachment to the cause of the country I will hold myself answerable,"[21] Parsons wrote to Arnold. On August 30, Arnold had Heron
wait two hours in the outer office with Varick before Arnold came in
and asked Varick to write Heron a pass that Arnold signed. Arnold

then "retired to his room and immediately sent word to me that he wanted to speak to me." Arnold asked Heron "if I thought the person with whom I expected to transact my business at the enemy's lines could transmit that letter meaning a letter he held out to me to the person to whom it was directed." Heron said he saw immediately that Arnold's letter was written "in a feigned hand." Later, Heron testified he was immediately suspicious in a way "that I never before experienced concerning any person of his rank." Arnold pretended that the letter was from someone else, that he had broken its seal, inspected it, and then resealed it. Heron insisted the seal was "entirely whole." Arnold was obviously sending a secret message to New York that he didn't want Varick to know about. Once inside New York City, Heron went about his own business first—which was to offer his services to the British as a spy. He met for three hours with Loyalist Chief Justice William Smith, told him he knew his brother, Joshua, of Haverstraw, and had met Arnold at Belmont, but he kept Arnold's letter in his pocket until he got back to Connecticut and handed it over to Parsons, who thought it referred "merely to commerce"[22] and put it in a desk drawer. The seemingly mercantile letter brimmed with details André needed:

A speculation might at this time be easily made to some advantage with ready money [British forces], but there is not the quantity of goods [soldiers and supplies] at market [West Point]. . . . The number of spectators [American troops] below [Tappan] I think will be against your making an immediate purchase [attack]. . . . Goods will be in greater plenty and much cheaper in the course of the season. . . . Mr. Moore flatters himself that in the course of ten days he will have the pleasure of seeing you."[23]

What Heron had taken to Parsons was nothing short of Arnold's acceptance of the British terms and a proposed delay in the timetable to arrange the surrender of West Point. Four days later, on September 3, Arnold wrote another letter, a coded one, this time giving it to Mary McCarthy, the wife of a British prisoner of war. Arnold issued her a pass to go through the lines with her two children and had her rowed down the river by a lieutenant and a detail of Continentals. In a letter she carried was a message to "a person in New York whose fictitious name was John Anderson," Colonel Varick later recalled, "to establish a line of intelligence of the enemy's movements."[24] Arnold had decided to tell Varick that he was corresponding with an American secret agent inside New York—and he boldly dictated the letter to Varick, who handed it to the woman to take to Jonathan Odell, code-named James Osborne.

As September began, André and Clinton were still unsure of Arnold's reaction to their offer. When neither side heard back from the other, both contemplated bolder steps. It seems that it was André who decided that the safest subterfuge would be to appear at an American outpost in the guise of a secret American agent working for Arnold. Once he was inside, no American officer would have the nerve to question him. In the letter Mary McCarthy delivered for him, Arnold asked that André or his agent meet him at the quarters of Colonel Elisha Sheldon of the dragoons at the forward outpost at South Salem. Sheldon had his own double agent, Elijah Hunter, who was trusted by the British but loyal to the Americans. Arnold may have learned about Hunter from Squire Smith, and on September 1, he wrote to Sheldon, "I wish to be informed if the person you mentioned is returned from his excursion [to New York City]." Arnold had obviously already begun to prepare Sheldon for a visit from John Anderson: "I am convinced that material intelligence might be procured through the channel I mention."25 Arnold was making André appear to be a spy loyal to the Americans, like Hunter.

Sometime in late August, Arnold received a letter from Peggy that she wanted transmitted to Major Giles, the British officer who had agreed to smuggle finery for her from New York City to Philadelphia the year before. Arnold sent the letter to Sheldon, who wrote back on September 6 that he had forwarded the letter to Colonel Oliver Delancey, André's friend and assistant. Delancey had written back to Sheldon across the lines that "if any articles are sent to him for Mrs. Arnold he will take particular care of them and inform me immediately,"26 Sheldon reported. Arnold, after trying for five fruitless weeks, had found a way to smuggle letters in and out of New York City. But Sheldon quickly dashed Arnold's hopes of helping him any further: he was relieved the next day by General Parsons. Arnold lost no time writing to Parsons. "A lady of my acquaintance," he confided to Parsons, had a friend in New York buy some "trifling articles." He had already arranged for Sheldon's cooperation in their delivery:

I beg the favor of you to take care of them and send them to me. I am told there is a general order prohibiting any goods being purchased and brought out of New York, but as the goods were bought many months before the order was issued, I do not conceive they come under the intentions or spirit of it. However, I would not wish my name to be mentioned in the matter, as it may give occasion for scandal.[27]

Arnold had paved the way for an answer from André. On September 8 he finally heard from him, but in a most unsettling fashion. "Enclosed I send you a letter," Colonel Sheldon of the Dragoons wrote to Arnold, "which I received last evening from New York, signed John Anderson, who mentions his name being made known to me. If this is the person you mentioned in your favor of yesterday, he must have had your information by letter, as I never heard his name mentioned before I received the letter."[28] Was Sheldon suspicious? Quickly scanning the letter, Arnold could see that his letter to André via Mary McCarthy had reached André, who had promptly written to Sheldon. But André was proposing a different meeting place and talking about a British officer instead of a merchant coming. Sheldon had been expecting a civilian. An agent identifying himself as an officer would not do as well as André seemed to think. Sheldon might suspect that an officer came with official British backing.

Arnold could not know that his proposal for a meeting with the "merchant" John Anderson had been considered too risky by Sir Henry Clinton, who told André that a disguised British officer inside the American lines would automatically be considered a spy. Clinton insisted that the meeting should be held on neutral ground between the lines or on the Hudson where British ships would be standing by to rescue him. Writing to Sheldon on the 7th, André, as the merchant, said he would try to get a pass to come out of New York at noon on the 11th under a flag of truce "when I shall be happy to meet Mr. G——." (Arnold had signed his last letter "Gustavus.") "Should I not be allowed to go, the officer who is to command the escort, between whom and myself no distinction need be made, can speak of the affair."[29] André's careful letter left Sheldon no idea that a British officer was involved. Only Arnold knew that both the officer and Anderson were the same person. But Arnold decided he must write Sheldon to ward off any suspicion about his own involvement with an American spy who could be in league with a British officer who might be trying to communicate with his headquarters. "You judge right," he wrote Sheldon. "I wrote to Mr. Anderson on the 3rd, requesting him to meet me at your quarters. I did not mention his name in my letter to you because I thought it unnecessary. I was obliged to write with great caution to him. My letter was signed Gustavus to prevent any discovery in case it fell into the hands of the enemy." Arnold pretended he did not understand why Anderson would be represented by an officer. Perhaps his letter to

Anderson had been intercepted, he told Sheldon, and the letter Sheldon had reviewed was a fake, after all. Yet Arnold would come to Dobbs Ferry by boat on the 11th anyway, he said. If, in the meantime, Anderson appeared at the forward outpost, "send an express to let me know, and send two or three horsemen to conduct him on his way to meet me, as it is difficult for me to ride so far. If your health will permit, I wish you to come with him. I have promised him your protection, and that he shall return in safety."[30] Sheldon could tell Parsons, too, about the meeting.

To André, Arnold wrote another secret letter. He feared that since the letter he had sent by Heron had never been answered, it and his letter via Mary McCarthy had been intercepted: thus his pretense at openness with Sheldon. André must realize that no one, certainly not Sheldon or Parsons, had been drawn into the plot, which *must* be carried out by stealth. Arnold was sure to be watched if a redcoat officer appeared under a flag of truce, as André had proposed, to talk with a high-ranking American general. Arnold insisted that if André came "to our lines by stealth," he could promise that "you shall be perfectly safe here."[31] Nevertheless, disagreeing with André's plan but uncertain whether his latest letter would alter it or even reach British headquarters in time, Arnold stepped into his barge and, rowed by eight Continental oarsmen, glided down the Hudson to Squire Smith's house on Sunday evening, the 10th, where he spent the night before going on south to Dobbs Ferry the morning of the 11th.

Almost a year and a half had passed since Benedict Arnold had first written to Sir Henry Clinton, and all parties to the plot were growing desperate for its consummation, none more so than John André, whose rise to power had been slowed by a series of recent reverses. André needed a brilliant success, a master stroke that would distinguish him from all the other British officers, hundreds of whom were ahead of him in line for promotion and pay raises. To mastermind the capture of the vital Hudson River forts and bring back to the king's standard the most successful American field commander would be a double coup that certainly must bring him high permanent rank in the army, perhaps even knighthood, and would certainly end the financial problems that the war had brought about. Many British officers considered him an opportunist and wanted to see John André fall from Sir Henry's grace, and some worked secretly to thwart him even as they appeared to flatter him. Highborn officers considered André an upstart son of a countinghouse tradesman. When Lord Cathcart received orders signed only by André and not by Clinton, he complained bitterly. André wrote his lordship apologetically, "I imagined, perhaps, improperly, that a signature in an official capacity implied the commander-in-chief's authority. Every future letter will have every formality his Lordship wishes."[32] When Clinton led an invasion of the South in December 1779, André drafted all the orders and made all the logistically arrangements for 8,500 men, acting as the liaison between stubborn Sir Henry and the moody and irascible Admiral Arbuthnot.

It was very much John André's attack on Charleston. Not only did he supervise all the staff work but, drawing on his years of textbook training as a military engineer in Germany before the war, he drafted all the detailed plans for the extensive siege of Charleston, the most important city in the South. The twenty-eight-year-old regular army captain with only three years seniority had an easier time with Benjamin Lincoln's pathetic defenses than with his own officers. One day, redcoats gathered on the parade ground, but refused to march. Someone had given orders countermanding André's, "I know not for what cause; I know not by whom."[33] But the troops, British troops, didn't move when Hessian officers gave them orders. It quickly became clear that André, the linguist, had ordered out special work details with Hessian officers unable to speak English giving orders to British troops unable to understand German. Hessians bellowed at him in German; British officers offered him suggestions in unmistakable Anglo-Saxon terms. Major General Alexander Leslie, in command at the time, turned on André: he was "concerned to see so much displeasure."[34] All the months of suffering the condescension of Sir Henry's current pet boiled over in Leslie's accusation that André "supinely decreed" orders to do work he knew nothing about. Finally, Sir Henry was drawn to the field of battle by the Babel directed at his favorite. In front of the British army's top brass, Clinton icily refused to support André. What had happened had been the result of André's naive ideas that special forces could be organized for special tasks under unfamiliar officers, instead of brigades taking orders from their own brigadiers. Publicly humiliated, André went back to his tent and wrote a defense of his actions to Clinton. "For my own part, I have seldom suffered so much anxiety." But then he put a line through the words and started over. "These are matters which gave me much anxiety."[35]

There was another reason for André's unpopularity with fellow officers: to clinch his promotion as deputy adjutant general, André had written a supposedly confidential memorandum for Clinton on the evils of British looting. André was not interested in the usual forms of graft and plundering sometimes attached to his office, and

he had never led troops who had only joined the army and endured
its hardships, dreadful risks, and brutal discipline for the booty. André's memo on plundering, widely circulated throughout the British
establishment, was filled with strong language about "the stripping
and insulting of inhabitants" for "wanton pleasure." Much of his
purple prose was gleaned from his Loyalist friends, often the victims
of British and Hessian plundering, a "conduct so atrocious [when it]
involves our friends in ruin."[36] Whether his report was accurate or
not was beside the point: while it pleased Clinton and helped bring
about André's promotion, it made André many enemies.

Even his Loyalist friends were growing impatient with André,
who had opposed the establishment of an independent Board of
Associated Loyalists, fearing that its activities, especially in intelligence-gathering, would undermine his own adjutant general's office.
Loyalist leaders were also unhappy about the large amount of time
André spent away from his staff duties, writing and designing sets at
the John Street Theatre in Manhattan, penning odes and poetry for
the newspapers, and composing elaborate toasts for lavish dinners.

Since a French fleet had seized Grenada, André had to live entirely on his captain's pay, and his rank was at "the bottom of the
captains"[37] in the 26th Regiment. André badly needed a promotion
to major that would give him a substantial increase in pay and a
permanent commission after the war; otherwise he would have to
return to only a captain's half-pay pension and to his bench in the
countinghouse. In an attempt to help him, Clinton recommended
him for promotion to the post of adjutant general of all British
forces in America, an unheard-of position for a young captain. With
the post came the temporary rank of major, but a major's rank had
to be confirmed in England. Short on cash, André nevertheless was
exultant at this latest mark of Sir Henry's favor. André was not prepared for the reaction of Lord Jeffrey Amherst in London, commander in chief of all the British forces, who insisted on strict
seniority in the army. Amherst told Lord Germain, to whom Clinton
had written to recommend André for promotion, that he had never
heard of André, could not even find him on the list of the 54th
Regiment, only "a Capt. John André of the 26th Regt. [André's former unit] who has been a captain twenty months." There were some
captains with twenty years seniority.[38]

André and Clinton chafed impatiently as they waited for British
naval reinforcements to arrive to give the British the superiority they
felt they needed before attacking the French on Rhode Island. To
while away the devilishly hot, muggy summer hours in New York
City, the penurious André wrote poems satirizing the Americans and

had them published in Rivington's *Royal Gazette*. In July, the American general Anthony Wayne had attacked a Loyalist blockhouse on the New Jersey shore. Beaten back, Wayne captured instead a herd of cattle. André dipped his quill in venom and wrote "The Cow Chace" which appeared in three installments in the *Royal Gazette* and was read on both sides of the lines. André informed his readers that Wayne had been, before the Revolution, that most despicable tradesman a tanner, a man who gathered manure to cure the skins of dead animals. André warned Wayne, whose night attack had reclaimed Stony Point the year before, that he could soon expect "the tanning of his hide." The bard of One Wall Street went on to pillory other "dung-born" American generals, men who dressed horridly in homespun "blue stockings and brown breeches," including Arnold, whose humble early career as an apothecary earned him the sobriquet "the Vender of the Pill." The unsigned cantos appeared as André wrote them from mid-August to mid-September, the last, going to press on September 23, ending:

> And now I've closed my epic strain,
> I tremble as I show it,
> Lest this same warrior-drover Wayne
> Should ever catch the poet![39]

On September 10, 1780, before he glided down the Hudson to Dobbs Ferry to meet John André, Benedict Arnold, apparently late that night at Squire Smith's country house on Haverstraw Bay, began to write the most daring and important letter of his eighteen-month-long treason. Interrupted, Arnold went to his meeting the next day, failed to connect with André, was almost killed, then returned to West Point, where he finished writing the letter, hastily in disguised handwriting, and smuggled it into New York City. By September 15, he had sealed his bargain to meet with André late at night on the 20th, to make final arrangements to surrender West Point. It appears that both sides were poised and ready to spring the trap that would turn over America's most important stronghold to the British, in all likelihood helping to bring the dragged-out five-year-long revolution to an abrupt close. A man so patient that he appeared perpetually lethargic, the British commander, Sir Henry Clinton, was confident that Benedict Arnold's treasonous plot would succeed, and he had prepared his army and the British navy for simultaneous attacks on Washington on the Hudson and the French on Rhode Island.

While Clinton kept Admiral Arbuthnot completely in the dark about the Arnold affair, he confided his plans to two other British admirals who reinforced New York City late in the summer of 1780. Rear Admiral Thomas Graves had raced the French fleet across the Atlantic, arriving off New York on July 13 with six ships of the line; Admiral Sir George Rodney and ten more ships of the line arrived on September 13. Suddenly, the British navy had considerable superiority in American waters. In Rhode Island, according to one of Sir Henry's Loyalist informants, the French "gave themselves up for lost on the arrival of Rodney,"[40] believing that the war would be lost, along with their army and navy. Clinton, who had given up his earlier plans to attack Rhode Island, now outlined new plans for an attack up the Hudson. Rodney, fresh from a series of naval victories in the Caribbean, and Clinton, excluding Arbuthnot, had "several very unreserved consultations." Clinton had also just received word that his second-in-command in the South, Lord Cornwallis, had smashed the American southern army under Horatio Gates at Camden, South Carolina. Clinton told Rodney about his plot with Arnold, of the "most material intelligence" Arnold had already provided him, "that the obtaining possession of [the river forts] at the present critical period [was] a most desirable circumstance, and that the advantages to be drawn from Mr. Arnold's having command of them struck me with full force the instant I heard of his appointment." But as Clinton told Admiral Rodney, he first had to "reduce to an absolute certainty whether the person I had so long corresponded with was actually Major General Arnold."[41] So sure was Rodney that Clinton's attack on West Point was imminent that he canceled shore liberty for his crews and, instead, ordered them to help Clinton's soldiers pack their gear aboard ships for the assault up the Hudson.

As redcoats boarded Royal Navy ships and Benedict Arnold clambered aboard his bateau at Squire Smith's wharf to be rowed to the American outpost at Dobbs Ferry, Sir Henry dashed off a brief note to André. After weeks of steadfastly refusing André permission to follow Arnold's advice and come "mysteriously" to meet him, Clinton now gave André permission to go and verify that he was the man who had written him so many valuable letters:

> Dear André
> Col. Robinson will probably go with the flag [of truce] himself, [but] as you are with him at the fore-post [Kingsbridge], you may as well be of the party. You will find me on your return at Gen. Knyphausen's.
>
> Faithfully yours,
> H. Clinton[42]

*   *   *

André and Colonel Beverley Robinson had worked out a pretext, approved by Clinton, for a meeting with Arnold on the edge of the American lines under a flag of truce which would have provided the least physical risk for any of them, as Clinton insisted. Three years earlier, while General Israel Putnam had commanded at West Point and was making his headquarters at Beverley, Colonel Robinson had gone upriver, supposedly to make arrangements for the household goods he had left behind in the mansion when he had led his Loyalist neighbors into the British camp. Once again, Robinson would make the disposition of his property his excuse for using a flag of truce and talking to the American general occupying his house and lands. Under Robinson's covering flag, André was to confer with Arnold, right in the tent of the American officer in charge of the advance post at Dobbs Ferry. So crucial was the meeting that Clinton, in the late-summer heat, rode the length of Manhattan Island to wait for André at Jumel, the jonquil-colored Hessian headquarters in Upper Manhattan.

Boarding the sloop-of-war *Vulture,* stationed off Kingsbridge at Spuyten Duyvil, André and Robinson sailed up the Hudson to Dobbs Ferry Monday morning, September 11, alighting on the east bank, where they expected to meet Arnold. As they approached shore, they could see several British gunboats on patrol in the river. André had not thought to tell the officers in charge of the patrol boats that an American general in a bateau was coming to meet British officers under a flag of truce. As Arnold's bateau slid into sight off Dobbs Ferry, at least one British gunboat came about and opened fire on it. Shells raked the water and found the range, and Arnold and his unarmed crew very narrowly escaped to the western shore, where they remained under the cover of fire of an American blockhouse for nearly nine hours until sunset. More than a mile across the Hudson, on the eastern shore, Robinson and André waited, too, until they became convinced that Arnold wasn't coming. They sailed back to a disappointed Sir Henry. When Arnold got back to West Point, he pretended that he had been on an inspection tour and he wrote John Lamb to send some heavier artillery pieces down the river to ward off British patrol boats. "Two nine or twelve pounders are wanted in the redoubts at Dobbs Ferry. . . . The enemy's boats come up almost every day and insult the post."[43] Lamb had the guns ready the same day, but Arnold was careful not to send them downriver too quickly.

It was September 15 and Arnold was back at Squire Smith's before he could get another message off to André. He finished the letter he had begun on the 10th, telling André that he had tried to meet him on the 11th "but was prevented by the armed boats of the enemy, who fired several times upon us." His letter had originally been intended "as a caution to you not to mention your business to Colonel Sheldon or any other person. I have no confidants. I find I have made one too many already, which has prevented several profitable speculations." But if André still wanted to "pursue your former plan," it would be "perfectly safe" to come upriver again, either to the quarters of Sheldon's replacement, General Parsons, or of Major Benjamin Talmadge, both Arnold's subordinates now that two regiments of Connecticut militia had arrived at the southern outposts and been put under Arnold's command.

Before he returned to headquarters at West Point to rendezvous with the "very honest fellow"[44] who would take his latest scheme for a meeting with André to the British lines, Arnold put aside all business for a few hours to spend the night of the 11th at Smith's, where he met Peggy and Neddy, who had just arrived from Philadelphia. With her baby, her luggage, and her servants, Peggy Arnold brought a letter to Benedict from his sister, Hannah. Approaching forty, increasingly spinsterish, Hannah had a hard time getting used to Peggy, half her age, living in the huge Penn mansion, and had even more trouble at closer quarters with her. Arnold's constant controversies had not only strained his relations with fellow officers but had led to an atmosphere of tension between brother and sister. Hannah was a small-town New England girl, simple, devout, forthright. She could never abide his treason, had she known about it in advance, even if she sympathized with him during all the years of slights and political attacks. She didn't like the change in the tone of his letters to her—they had become diatribes—and she told him so: "Ill nature I leave to you," she began, "as you have discovered yourself to be a perfect master of it." She couldn't stand the atmosphere of conspiracy around Peggy and her friends after Benedict left Philadelphia to rejoin the army. On September 4, as Peggy supervised the packing, Hannah wrote a long letter to her brother. Just as she loathed Philadelphia drawing-room society, she was certain she wouldn't like the Hudson's "barren hillsides" and was sure Peggy would hate West Point. "As you have neither purling streams nor sighing swains at West Point, 'tis no place for me, nor do I think Mrs. Arnold will be long pleased with it, though I expect it may be rendered dear to her for a few hours by the presence of a certain chancellor." This was what was really on Hannah's mind—the incessant visits by the Arnolds' closest friend Congressman Robert L. Livingston of New York. Hannah had no time for all the well-mannered flirtatiousness of Peggy and her friends and mistook Livingston's constant attentions for more than friendship. Despite all the accusations cast at Peggy in later years, no one but Hannah ever accused her of infidelity, but Hannah was jealous, even if she knew her brother would not welcome her gossip. "I could say more than prudence will permit, I could tell you of frequent private assignations and of numberless billets doux, if I had an inclination to make mischief. But as I am of a very peaceable temper, I'll not mention a syllable of the matter."[45]

After two months apart, the Arnolds' nights and days at Belmont and at Beverley took on the added excitement of their opportunity to plot the last details of defection to the British. Arnold's weeks without Peggy, the longest he had ever been away from her, had been one of the loneliest periods in his life, filled with desperate anxiety relieved now by her safe arrival at Squire Smith's house. Arnold had been forced to take Smith more and more into his confidence. Before the Arnolds left for the bateau ride up the river to West Point, they invited the Smiths to join them the following weekend at Beverley. If Clinton approved his latest proposal, Arnold would need Smith's house for his midnight meeting with André.

When the Arnolds arrived at West Point on the 16th, they found a letter which cut short the time they could expect to have together. Washington was coming north, he wrote in a letter with a confidential postscript:

I shall be at Peekskill on Sunday evening, on my way to Hartford to meet the French admiral and general. You will be pleased to send down a guard of a captain and 50 at that time, and direct the quartermaster to have a night's forage for about 40 horses. You will keep this to yourself, as I want to make my journey a secret.[46]

Arnold knew how rarely Washington traveled without his army, how vulnerable he would be. Not only Washington but Marquis de Lafayette, chief of artillery Henry Knox, and their combined staffs would be crossing the Hudson en route to Hartford for secret talks with the French command. Arnold put a terse footnote on his interrupted letters of September 10 and 15 and sent off his most trusted courier under an illegal flag of truce to Clinton with word that Washington was coming. If the message arrived in time and the British moved quickly, their warships on the Hudson with the help of a few hundred dragoons could capture Washington as he crossed the river with a few score troops that Sunday night, the eighteenth. If they did not arrive in time to take him during the ferry crossing, Washington would be spending the night at an inn at Peekskill, within an easy ride of the nearest encampment of British dragoons. Washington's former second-in-command, General Charles Lee, had been captured in just such a raid in 1776. Arnold now dispatched an express rider to Washington's camp. He had received a letter a week earlier from Washington, asking for details on West Point's defenses. At a September 6 council of war with his generals at Tappan, Washington had asked a number of questions which no one but Arnold could answer about the fortress's ability to hold out under a major British attack. "My answers to the questions proposed by your Excellency to the council-of-war I will do myself the honor to deliver in person." Now Arnold had the perfect excuse to gather up-to-the-minute intelligence for the British from the post's officers to turn over, not only to Washington, but to André. He wrote down a complete inventory of the 120 cannon at West Point, the brigade major's detailed orders for the garrison "in case of an alarm," and the engineer's report of the minimum number of men needed to man the works, 2,438 (there were fewer than fifteen hundred now on duty).

Then Arnold wrote a second report, one that he never showed Washington, but would give to André his own expert analysis of the defects of the forts and redoubts. Between the two, there was everything the British needed to know to carry out a successful attack on West Point. Arnold's covering letter to Washington was all duplicity: a British attack would not be "very dangerous," with "little probability of succeeding." Washington had asked if Fort Arnold, the main fort, could hold out if the British took the weaker outer redoubts. Arnold responded that Fort Arnold, with a thousand men protected by bombproof casements and twelve hundred yards from Fort Putnam, the nearest outwork, "of course would not" fall to the British. Arnold's tone was brusquely reassuring: it would take a British army of twenty thousand a long and bloody siege to capture West Point. His words were ironic. "Everything could be changed by the fluctuating situation of our affairs." The outcome of the war "may be totally changed in a short time by a variety of circumstances which may happen." Arnold hemmed and hawed at Washington's request for strategic advice: "It appears extremely difficult for me to determine with any degree of precision the line of conduct proper to be observed."[47] Arnold had learned of Gates's disastrous defeat in South Carolina. Arnold resisted the urge to volunteer for the now-vacant southern command, once again his, by right. He had already written to Nathanael Greene, calling Gates "that hero," suggesting his defeat would "blot his escutcheon with indelible infamy." Gates's cowardly retreat before the British at Camden had "in no wise disappointed my expectations or predictions on frequent occasions."[48]

Peggy Arnold's first and only Sunday dinner at Beverley was a tense affair, Arnold's aides bracing as they filed into the wainscoted dining room to take their seats with the Arnolds' Loyalist weekend houseguests, the Smiths. It was an early dinner because Arnold was leaving that afternoon to go downriver with Washington's escort. Dr. William Eustis, head of the military hospital at West Point, took his place near Colonel Varick and Major Franks. They were hardly seated when a messenger arrived, bringing two letters for General Arnold forwarded by Colonel Livingston at Verplanck's Ferry at the upper end of Haverstraw Bay. The courier explained that the day before, the British sloop *Vulture,* had come upriver from Spuyten Duyvil and dropped anchor, sending the letters ashore in a small boat under flag of truce. One letter was addressed to General Israel Putnam, who had recently visited Arnold at West Point; the other was to Arnold himself. The letters, in the hand of André, bore the signature of Beverley Robinson. The pretext was that he wanted to meet with Putnam or his replacement. Arnold broke the seal of the covering letter to Putnam and scanned it hastily. Robinson did not specifically say what he wanted "for prudential reasons" until he had "some assurances that it shall be secret if not granted." Arnold's heart must have raced as he read that Robinson had sent the letters through the commanding officer at Verplanck's Ferry instead of "by my servant, James Osborne,"[49] the code name for the Loyalist intermediary Odell. Robinson obviously was writing to him and waiting to meet him with John André.

Trying not to betray his excitement, Arnold quickly pocketed the letters. He told his guests that they came from the man in whose house they were dining. Turning to John Lamb, Arnold explained that Robinson wanted an interview. Lamb later testified that his immediate response was that Arnold should not grant Robinson's request, that if such a notorious Loyalist had anything to say "of importance to this country, he might do it by letter." If he wanted to communicate about private business, "his business would be with the governor of the state, not with the general commanding in the department."[50] Such a meeting, Lamb warned Arnold, would induce suspicion of an improper correspondence between him and Beverley Robinson. Lamb urged Arnold to take the matter up with Washington that evening at Peekskill and let him decide what Arnold could and could not do. Shrugging off Lamb, Arnold said that whatever Robinson had in mind, he should at least be offered a chance to speak "through some channel,"[51] and with that Arnold changed the subject. Joshua Smith, who still remained in the dark about Arnold's real intentions and thought he was helping the American cause by helping Arnold, interjected that he agreed with Arnold that Robinson was probably bringing secret intelligence that would be useful to him.

Late the afternoon of September 18, 1780, Arnold personally led his handpicked guards to meet Washington at King's Ferry, where he met Washington, the commander in chief, at Belmont before accompanying him across the Hudson to Peekskill. With Washington rode young Marquis de Lafayette and his aide, Captain James McHenry; Henry Knox, Washington's aide; Colonel Alexander Hamilton; and a squad of nineteen of Washington's life guards. As the ferryboat crossed the river, it came within spyglass range of the *Vulture,* but Arnold's message about Washington's crossing evidently had reached New York City too late for a British raid: the three-masted sloop-of-war *Vulture* floated silently in the distance. Washington's twenty-year-old legal aide, Alexander Hamilton, joined the commander in chief and Arnold at Peekskill after supper and went over Robinson's letters. Hamilton later wrote to a friend that Arnold "asked for Washington's opinion of the propriety of [complying] with [Robinson's] request." Washington "with his usual caution" dissuaded Arnold from meeting Robinson and "advised him to reply to Robinson that whatever related to his private affairs must be of a civil nature, and could only properly be addressed to the civil authority."[52] According to Hamilton, Arnold promised Washington he would have Robinson write to Governor George Clinton. Riding along with Washington's party to its next stop, Arnold turned over his long written answer on the state of the defenses at West Point to Washington, who was already worried about the weakened condition of the fortress. It was the last time Arnold ever saw George Washington.

As they rode east, Washington had his own misgivings about West Point, if not about Arnold. He had received a warning from a trusted spy on Long Island that one of the American generals "high up" was in league with the British. But the vulnerability of an undermanned West Point to sudden British attack had worried him for months. In recent weeks, Washington had diverted an entire regiment of Continentals to Haverstraw Bay, their picket posts within shouting distance of Squire Smith's Belmont. He had built up forward bases at Dobbs Ferry to keep pressure on Clinton in New York

City and beefed them up with two regiments of Connecticut militia. Only two weeks before, he had ordered Ethan Allen, now a Vermont militia major general, to be ready to support Benedict Arnold at West Point in case of a British attack up the Hudson.

Leaving Washington and circling back to Beverley with his aide, Major Franks, Benedict Arnold had reason to worry about Washington's direct order not to meet with Beverley Robinson under a flag of truce. That night he was up late discussing his predicament with Peggy: now their cover of an open meeting with Robinson and André had been blasted by Washington's refusal to write an order for the flag of truce. By the next morning, Monday, September 19, Arnold had decided to ignore his agreement with Washington and write directly to Robinson aboard the *Vulture*. Still trying to keep up the pretense of a legal parley under a flag of truce, Arnold dictated the letter to Varick, who insisted that Arnold revise it because it "bore the complexion of [a letter] from a friend rather than one from an enemy."[53] He told Robinson that he had taken the matter up with Washington, who had ruled that Robinson must go to the civil authorities, but Arnold boldly managed to keep his channel to Robinson open even as Varick took down his words: "If you have any other proposals to make, and of a public nature of which I can officially take notice, you may depend on it that the greatest secrecy shall be observed, if required, as no person except his Excellency General Washington shall be made acquainted with them. The bearer, Captain Archibald, will take particular care of your letters and deliver them to me with his own hand."[54] Arnold had no intention of showing any more letters to Washington, but threw in the commander in chief's name to disarm his aide's objections.

Arnold did not show Varick a private letter to Robinson which he slipped in with the letter: it would not be safe now to meet with Robinson in public. The meeting would have to be secret, as he had said all along.

I shall send a person to Dobbs Ferry, or on board the Vulture, *Wednesday night the 20th, and furnish him with a boat and flag of truce. You may depend on his secrecy and honor, and that your business, of whatever nature, shall be kept a profound secret. . . . This matter must be conducted with the greatest secrecy. I think it will be advisable for the* Vulture *to remain where she is until the time mentioned. . . . I have enclosed a letter for a gentleman in New York [André] from one in the country [Arnold] on private business, which I beg the favor of you to forward, and make no doubt he will be permitted to come at the time mentioned.*

*   *   *

Then Arnold added a postscript, a signal meant to be transmitted to
Sir Henry Clinton. The British would have a second chance to capture Washington and his generals on September 24 when they came
to West Point "to lodge here on Saturday night next [September
24]."[55] If Clinton wanted to bag Washington as well as capture
West Point, there would be no better time.

Two attempts to meet André had now slipped behind Arnold. A
meeting with Robinson, who was recognizable by too many of his
former neighbors, was now out of the question. But no one at West
Point was likely to have ever seen John André or would think that
John Anderson was anything more than the young New York countinghouse merchant he said he was. With Peggy's help, he must now
stitch together a flawless final plan. He rehearsed for her all the steps
he had already taken to weaken West Point for Sir Henry's attack. If
Clinton decided to widen the conspiracy to include the capture of
Washington, Lafayette, and their staffs, there would be no better
place than Beverley, where Washington and his party would stop
over at noontime Saturday for dinner: Peggy must prepare a suitable
feast, one that would last as long as possible. Arnold would arrange
for Washington's party to make a leisurely afternoon inspection of
West Point. Once again, delay was Arnold's weapon of choice. But
Arnold's meeting with André must happen swiftly and smoothly.
Washington and the French no doubt were making final plans for a
joint attack on New York City. Clinton must strike first.

When he sat down weeks later to write his version of the West Point
conspiracy, Sir Henry Clinton summarized his strategy for exploiting
Arnold's defection in very few words:

*General Arnold surrendering himself, the forts and garrisons, at this
instant, would have given every advantage which could have been
desired. Mr. Washington must have instantly retired from Kingsbridge [at the outskirts of New York City] and the French troops
upon Rhode Island would have been consequently left unsupported
and probably would have fallen into our hands. The consequent advantage of so great an event I need not explain.*

Washington would be sent reeling, and when the Hudson was
brought under British control and New England was cut off from
the South, the Revolution would, at last, sputter out. Arnold's message that Washington would be crossing the Hudson at Peekskill
with a corporal's guard and could easily be captured the night of the
eighteenth did not reach Clinton in time, but by September 19, Clin-

ton was so sure of the success of his own plan that he requested Rodney's ships be ready to dash up the Hudson as soon as Beverley Robinson and John André returned from a brief meeting with Benedict Arnold. Sir Henry later explained to Lord Germain, in London, that he was "determined not to make the attempt" but under "particular security" that Arnold was not planning a counterplot, that his surrender of the forts and their garrisons was part of "a concerted plan between us [so] that the King's troops sent upon this expedition should be under no risk of surprise."[56] Clinton gave André three oral orders intended to safeguard his impetuous young spymaster. First, André was not to venture behind enemy lines: he was to meet Arnold ashore in the Westchester County no-man's-land or on the Hudson, where a British warship could more easily rescue him. Second, he was not to disguise himself but to stay in his British uniform. Finally, he was to carry no compromising papers. If he violated any or all of these hard-and-fast rules of war, he could be hanged as a spy.

On September 19, his last night in New York City, André, after sending off the last cantos of "The Cow Chace" to the *Royal Gazette,* joined Sir Henry for a ride out to the house of Baroness Frederika von Riedesel. André bantered in German with the Hessian officers and the ladies at the baroness's. André was basking that night in the commander in chief's favor. When he shook hands with Sir Henry the next morning and climbed into a launch that was to take him to the *Vulture* on Haverstraw Bay, he tugged at the long navy-blue cape that all but covered his red British uniform and his white-topped, hand-tooled English riding boots.

A season of drought along the Hudson River had already speckled the forest riverbanks and close-pressing mountains brown with dead oak and chestnut leaves as Major John André, resplendent in his scarlet uniform, pulled himself quickly up a gangplank onto the armed Royal Navy sloop *Vulture,* which was riding at anchor off Tellers Point, roughly fifteen miles downriver from West Point. It was seven o'clock when Captain Andrew Sutherland and Colonel Robinson greeted André warmly and led him astern to the captain's cabinet for a drink and a meal. André turned over two letters from Clinton to Sutherland and Robinson. Clinton had ordered Sutherland to move *Vulture* down to Dobbs Ferry, where André had tried to meet Arnold before, on the eleventh. André was supposed to have waited for *Vulture* to come downriver, closer to the British lines, but he was already disobeying Clinton by acting as his own courier to Sutherland. Sutherland was already nervous enough: earlier that day, some Americans had raised a white flag on the eastern shore and, thinking Arnold was trying to send Robinson a message, Sutherland had sent in a boat. As it approached shore, the Americans had fired on it, driving it back to *Vulture*. Sutherland was in a quandary: while Clinton explicitly ordered *Vulture* back to Dobbs Ferry, Arnold had written him to remain at Tellers Point so that he could send a trusted emissary aboard that night. The three British officers conferred and decided to stay put in Haverstraw Bay.

When no one came from shore all night, André, after hours of pacing the deck with growing anxiety, made another decision that ran counter to Sir Henry's orders: if he left now and returned to New York, he would upset the whole timetable of conspiracy. Before he could communicate again with Arnold and create a fresh pretext for coming back upriver, another vital week or more could slip away. André now feigned a sudden return of a sick stomach, and Sutherland invited him to stay aboard until he felt better. André sent a note to Clinton that he would return to the city the next day, but he surreptitiously included in it another note: "This is the second excursion I have made without an ostensible reason, and Colonel Robinson both times of the party. A third would infallibly fix suspicions. I have therefore thought it best to remain here on the pretense of sickness, as my enclosed letter will feign, and try further expedients."[57] André peremptorily scrapped the carefully worked-out British plan and began to improvise.

Apparently the first step André took on his own was to persuade Sutherland to write Arnold to protest American firing on his flag of truce: Sutherland's letter was in André's handwriting, unmistakable by now to Arnold, and was countersigned "John Anderson, Secretary." Arnold would know beyond question that André was waiting for him. Robinson also wrote Arnold to complain that Arnold's messenger had failed to appear the night before: both letters were carried under flag of truce in a launch from *Vulture* to Arnold, who was nearby at Verplanck's Ferry ostentatiously inspecting the fortifications with the commanding officer, Colonel James Livingston, his old comrade from the Canadian campaign.

Arnold was being plagued by last-minute problems, the largest of which was Squire Smith. Arnold had to rely more than he liked on Smith, whose visits had provoked frequent anti-Loyalist outbursts from Arnold's aides. After Arnold had gone downriver to meet Washington on Sunday, the 17th, Varick had decided to pick a fight with Smith at the supper table. When Smith blithely commented that the American party could have made an honorable peace with Britain in 1778 during the visit of the Carlisle Commission, sent to offer America home rule, Varick fairly exploded. But he could not ruffle the unflappable Smith, who left the next day to take his family to Fishkill. While their departure cleared the way for Arnold to meet André at Smith's house, Smith's absence made it difficult for Arnold to get last-minute instructions to Smith in time for the rendezvous with the mysterious John Anderson, whom Smith evidently still believed was an American agent working for the general. Smith then failed to appear at Beverley in time to carry Arnold's passes out to André on the *Vulture*. On September 20, Arnold had drawn up a pass for Smith and André: "Permission is given to Joshua Smith, Esquire, a gentleman, Mr. John Anderson, who is with him, and his two servants, to pass and repass the guards near King's Ferry at all times."[58] Arnold had also given Smith a requisition for a light boat from the American quartermaster at King's Ferry. Although Arnold's pass and instructions reached Smith in time on the afternoon of the 20th, Smith did not draw the boat or line up his own tenant farmers as boatmen, aborting the long-awaited meeting of Arnold and André that night.

When Arnold learned on his arrival at Belmont before dawn on September 21 that André was not waiting for him there, he went on, disappointed, to Verplanck's Ferry and was visiting Colonel Livingston there when Sutherland's and Robinson's messages were rowed ashore from the *Vulture* under flag of truce. Crossing quickly to Stony Point, Arnold learned that Smith had not drawn the boat because no boat was available. He ordered his bateau up to West Point to tow one back and left orders for it to be brought up Haverstraw Creek as close as possible to Belmont. Arnold explained to Major Edward Kiers, Quartermaster at Stony Point, that Smith "had furnished General Howe with very good intelligence" and now "was going down the river"[59] for Arnold. Then, as the sun disappeared behind the mountains, Arnold rode quickly to Belmont, where Squire Smith was upstairs, having trouble persuading a tenant farmer to row him that night.

Samuel Colquhoun later testified that he had been very tired after a long day of farm work. "Mr. Smith spoke to me as I was going for the cows, and told me the General wished to speak to me." Arnold "asked me to go with him a piece that night. I said I could not go, being up the night before, and told him I was afraid to go. But General Arnold urged me to go and told me if I was a friend to my country, I should." Colquhoun wanted to know where they were going: Arnold told him "on board of the ship in the river, that there was a man there the general wanted to see very much." Colquhoun wanted to know why they couldn't wait until morning. "General

Arnold said it must be done that night." Colquhoun insisted he wouldn't go alone. Smith sent him to fetch his brother, Joseph, but when Samuel came back he was alone. He said his wife now objected. "I went back to General Arnold and told him that I did not want to go, there were guard boats out." All of this was getting on Arnold's nerves. There was no danger, Arnold insisted. He would take care of everything. Besides, if Colquhoun didn't go, "he would look upon me as a disaffected man." He *was* a Patriot, wasn't he? "I then went and fetched my brother. We stood out a great while before we consented to go."[60] The brothers had held out for nearly four hours. Arnold finally offered them a precious fifty pounds of flour each if they would go, and then Smith poured them each a good stiff drink of whiskey.

Then Arnold sent Smith's black slave down to the boat landing. He did not have to worry about a slave, who could not testify in a court of law. The manservant came back quickly with word that the boat was ready. Again, the Colquhouns protested. Arnold threatened to arrest them immediately if they would not go. Smith left with the Colquhouns while Arnold accompanied the slave down the riverbank with a spare horse. The servant was to wait with the horse in the fir trees atop the riverbank, opposite *Vulture*. It was almost midnight as Arnold rode off. Stepping into a heavy oversized rowboat, Smith's reluctant crewmen hauled on the oars, muffled, by Arnold's order, in sheepskins, pulling him out into the darkened channel for the six-mile row down and across the river to *Vulture*. The tide was running out fast, carrying them along swiftly. At last, the three men could make out the outline of *Vulture*. Smith instructed the oarsmen to stay in the boat and say nothing while he went aboard. As the rowboat neared the sloop-of-war, a loud voice ordered them to come to. The British watch officer demanded where they were from and where bound before he unleashed, as Smith later testified, "a volley of oaths" including orders to come alongside or they would be blown out of the water. Unperturbed, Smith climbed a rope ladder to the main deck. A cabin boy darted between Smith and the officer of the deck: "The captain orders the man below." In the spacious stern cabin, Smith was brought before "a venerable looking"[61] Colonel Robinson dressed in his red-and-green Loyalist regimentals. Robinson put Smith at his ease and introduced him to Captain Sutherland, who was lying ill in his berth.

Ordering some refreshments, Robinson studied the papers Smith handed over, then left to bring André. The two army officers carefully studied the letter and the passes provided by Arnold: first, Arnold's covering letter to Robinson, meant to deceive Smith if he opened it or to lull any watchful American officer. It ended with the words "I take it for granted Colonel Robinson will not propose anything that is not for the interest of the United States." Then a small piece of paper marked "Gustavus to John Anderson."[62] There was also Arnold's pass for Smith and three men, naming John Anderson, but not Robinson. Obviously, Arnold wanted to meet only with André, not Robinson, despite Sir Henry Clinton's wishes. André decided to go alone. Wearing a covered-up British uniform, he was still passing himself off as John Anderson, a civilian merchant. Smith did not think to question André why, if he was a merchant acting as an American agent, he did such an odd thing as put on a British uniform to go behind American lines. Smith did think that they were under a valid flag of truce. When Colonel Robinson observed that the oarsmen would be hard pressed to pull four men in a heavy boat six miles upriver, this time against the tide, and that a British boat could tow them faster, lawyer Smith objected that this might be an infringement of the flag of truce. But there *was* no flag of truce. So far, André had broken two of Clinton's dicta: he came at night, disguised and by stealth, using a false name as he went behind enemy lines to make final plans for a treason. Bunching up his high-collared coat around him and pulling down the brim of a wide, flat hat, he sat silently in the stern beside Smith, who was working the tiller.

The open boat thumped ashore at the foot of Long Clove Mountain, two miles below Haverstraw and a considerable distance from the spot where Arnold had told Smith he would be waiting with the horses. But Arnold had been watching, and he rode down quickly from the road. "When we came on shore," Samuel Colquhoun recalled, "I heard the noise of a man at the bank above, and Mr. Smith went up, and returned immediately, and the person we brought on shore [André] went up, and Mr. Smith stayed with us."[63] According to Smith, Arnold did not show himself but "hid among the firs."[64] They were already behind Arnold's timetable. It was nearly two o'clock. In two hours it would begin to get light. It was two hours later before Smith got up the courage to climb back up to the grove of fir trees where Arnold and André had been talking. No one ever found out exactly what they discussed. Was it about the British assault, the rewards for Arnold? André never had the chance to recount the conversation, and Arnold only related, in a letter to Clinton, what he said André had promised him. No doubt Arnold's price was the first thing they had to agree on before the details of attack and surrender. According to Arnold's version,

[Major André] was so fully convinced of the reasonableness of my proposal of being allowed 10,000 pounds sterling for my services, risks, and the loss which I should sustain in case of a discovery of my plan should oblige me to take refuge in New York before it could be fully carried into execution, that he assured me, though he was commissioned to promise me only 6,000 pounds sterling, he would use his influence to recommend it to your Excellency.[65]

There was still plenty of time to go over the documents which Arnold had brought to the meeting: a summary of the American army's strength, a report of the troops at West Point and in the other Hudson defenses, an estimate of the forces needed to garrison the defenses properly, a return of the ordinance on hand, the plan of artillery deployment in event of an alarm, a copy of the minutes Washington had sent Arnold of the council of war of September 6, and Arnold's detailed analysis of the defensive defects of West Point. Arnold did not have to waste any time describing West Point's terrain. André had stopped off at West Point when he had passed south from St. Jean as a prisoner of war in 1776. Moreover, Clinton had been familiar with the Hudson's forts since he had captured and destroyed Forts Montgomery and Clinton in 1777. But Arnold could point out to André, who was to lead the assault on Fort Putnam, that this stronghold was in poor repair. They must have discussed a timetable: Arnold had hinted, in his last smuggled message to Clinton, that the attack should come on Sunday, September 24, while Washington was still there. But it was already Friday, the twenty-second, and André would need time to get back, consult with Sir Henry, and work out all the plans for the army and navy.

It was getting light as Squire Smith dared to interrupt them shortly after four o'clock. Smith later testified he "deemed it expedient to inform them of the approaching dawn of day."[66] According to Smith, Arnold went back down the riverbank with him and tried in vain to persuade the Colquhouns to row André back to *Vulture;* the farmers testified they never saw Arnold. According to Samuel Colquhoun, it was Smith who "asked my brother and myself if we would go on board the vessel again that night. . . . I told him I was fatigued, being up the night before, and could not go."[67] Ignorant of the danger to André, certain that Arnold had everything under control, Smith went off in the boat to return it to Haverstraw Creek by dawn. André had little time to argue when he discovered he would not get away to *Vulture* that day. "I was told," he testified at his own court-martial, "that the approach of day would prevent my return, and that I must be concealed until the next night."[68] Arnold was prepared for hours more of talk with André. He had brought along a horse for André in case their business required a visit to Belmont. Arnold had decided unilaterally that it would be perfectly safe for André to stay ashore all day before returning to *Vulture*. But things began to go wrong as Arnold and André rode toward Belmont in the half-light. On their way down the river road, they were stopped by an American patrol, which promptly allowed General Arnold and his escort to pass. This was apparently André's first inkling that he had come ashore behind American lines.

A second jolt hit him within minutes of their arrival at Belmont. While Smith roused the servants and had them get breakfast, Arnold and André went to an upstairs bedroom. Their talk was interrupted by the repeated booming of cannon fire across the river. As both men ran to the window, they could see that American heavy guns on Teller's Point were firing on *Vulture,* despite Arnold's direct order to Colonel Livingston not to fire on the ship. But Livingston had long been worried that the presence of the British warship was an open invitation for Loyalists to row out and plot mischief. While Arnold and André were parleying in the woods, Livingston had personally dragged a howitzer and a four-pounder out onto the point to harass *Vulture* and drive it off and his gunners hauled a twelve-pounder and a howitzer close enough to *Vulture* to pound the British sloop, which could only fire back ineffectually from her anchorage. Colonel Robinson, aboard *Vulture,* reported to Clinton "a very hot fire on us which continued for two hours. . . . Though every exertion was made to get the ship out of their reach sooner, six shot hulled us, one between wind and water."[69] That shot raked the quarterdeck with splintered oak, one shard slashing Captain Sutherland's nose. *Vulture* finally scored a telling hit, blowing up Livingston's powder magazine, but by this time, *Vulture*'s sails, rigging, and boats were in ruins.

Sutherland was not the only casualty: Arnold's entire plan for getting André back to Clinton had been shattered. As *Vulture* dropped downriver at nine the morning of September 22, with it went the chance for a quick return for André to British headquarters and a speedy attack on West Point. Smith never forgot the look on André's face—"the impassioned language of his countenance and the energy with which he expressed his wish to be on board."[70] Arnold now argued that it was preferable for André to overtake *Vulture* at Dobbs Ferry, but in case that was impossible, he began to improvise another plan, writing out two passes for André, one for a water passage, another if he had to escape by land.

Dazed and frightened, André still believed he would go back to

New York City aboard *Vulture,* but he accepted the passes Arnold
pressed on him. Then Arnold handed him the plans for West Point
and urged him, if he was intercepted, to destroy them. Apparently
thinking Arnold meant intercepted in an open boat on the way back
to *Vulture,* André replied that he would "have them tied about with
a string and a stone." Just why André accepted the six compromising documents, five of them in Arnold's handwriting, is unclear. No
British officer had to follow the orders of an American rebel, no
matter how high-ranking, yet André maintained that Arnold "made
me put the papers I bore between my stockings and feet."[71] Arnold
apparently insisted that Clinton would give more weight to Arnold's
plans if he could see them. But Clinton had plenty of other excellent
intelligence reports about the forts from his own spies, so that Arnold's documents "were not wanted for my information."[72]

By ten o'clock Friday morning, the twenty-second, Arnold was
ready to return to Beverley on the scheduled arrival of his bateau at
Stony Point. Smith rode with him to the bateau. Before he left, Arnold had a brief disagreement with André. André later testified that
"some mention had been made [by Arnold] of my crossing the river
and going by another route, but I objected much against it, and
thought it was settled that in the way I came I was also to return."[73]
Riding to Stony Point with Smith, Arnold apparently left it to the
squire's discretion which was the best way back, according to circumstances. By now, Arnold had realized that the Hudson would be
crawling with American gunboats after the engagement with the
Vulture, making it virtually impossible for André to escape downriver, regardless of Arnold's pass. Evidently certain that André
would be safe in Smith's hands and that the conspiracy had been all
but consummated, Arnold went back upriver to Beverley in his
bateau to await the British attack on West Point.

Benedict Arnold's aides greeted his return to Beverley with more
than their displeasure, thinking he had once again spent the night at
Squire Smith's. The two aides had been talking about Arnold's commercial dealings while he was away, assuming that his latest visit to
Smith and his open correspondence with Robinson involved illicit
trade with New York City. They had concluded, they later testified,
that Arnold was "an avaricious man." But they were more disturbed
by his continued association with "the rascal Smith," and in Arnold's absence had taken the extraordinary step of complaining to
Mrs. Arnold about their fears. They "begged Mrs. Arnold to use her
influence with Arnold" to prevent his continuing friendship with the
suspected Loyalist. Peggy pretended to agree, telling them that she,

too, had an "unfavorable opinion of Smith both as a gentleman and a man of sincerity."[74] She promised to talk to her husband about Smith, but before she could, Squire Smith appeared at Beverley just before dinnertime on Saturday, September 23. Arnold was unusually friendly at Squire Smith's arrival: he disappeared with Smith and quickly learned the details of Smith's journey south as he escorted André toward the British lines.

After Arnold had ridden off toward Stony Point the morning of the twenty-second, André had tried to get some sleep. At some point late in the afternoon he asked Smith when they would be leaving to go down the river to overtake *Vulture*. Smith later lied under oath when he testified at his own court-martial that Arnold had come back toward evening and found Smith suffering from a fever and unable to go by boat, and that Arnold had then ordered him to escort André by the land route. Arnold did not return to Belmont that night, and Smith may also have lied to André, claiming that Arnold had insisted that they go on horseback. André must have objected, but he could not reveal to Smith why it was so much more dangerous. If Smith had known that André was a British officer and not a civilian merchant, and how risky it was for him to put on a disguise, he might have decided to make an effort to get him, undisguised, aboard *Vulture*. But Smith ignored André's protests, and to André's "great mortification, persisted in his determination."

Listening to Smith's plan, André, as he later put it, began to think of himself as a prisoner who must "concert my escape."[75] When Smith insisted that Arnold wanted him to wear a disguise, André, once again ignoring Sir Henry's verbal orders, took off his scarlet coat and put on an old claret-colored coat of Smith's with gold-laced buttons and buttonholes and a yellow cotton nankeen waistcoat and breeches. He kept on his shiny white-topped riding boots. Over Smith's old coat, he put on his own blue cape. Smith also gave him a round beaver hat, which he wore uncocked. They went downstairs and a servant helped André onto a large bay horse with a Continental Army brand. André had lost nearly a full day before setting out with Smith and his servant. Everyone who saw the threesome that evening and the next day remembered Smith as garrulous and jovial, his companion as silent. Smith and André first overtook Major John Burroughs of the New Jersey Line: Smith invited Burroughs to come over soon for tea at Belmont. Three miles farther, on the Verplanck's Ferry side of Stony Point, Smith paid a call on Colonel Livingston, at Fort Lafayette. "I asked him where he was going," Livingston later testified. "He said up towards General Arnold's. . . . I then urged him to stay awhile and take supper of a drink of grog. He then informed me that there was a gentleman waiting for him who had just rode on."[76] André could breathe easier when Smith caught up with him.

It was André's desire to ride quickly without stopping to White Plains, and their big horses cantered eastward toward Crompond along eight miles of uninhabited woodland roadway until a half-dozen New York militiamen stepped out and blocked their path, muskets cocked. Smith shouted, "Friends!" as they closed in. Captain Ebenezer Boyd walked up, asking where they were from and why they were out past nine at night. Smith said they were on an errand for General Arnold. Boyd asked to see their passes and went for a lantern. André squirmed in the saddle. Satisfied by the passes, Boyd offered to find them lodgings for the night. Andreas Miller in Crompond had a room. They would be wise to go no farther that night, since the Cowboys were out. Smith needed no explanation about the gangs of would-be Loyalists who robbed from both sides in the thinly populated no-man's-land, selling stolen livestock to the British. Cowboys had just raided Andreas Miller's farm: he could put up the travelers, but not feed them. Soon, André and Smith were sharing a four-poster bed, the only piece of furniture in the room. Both men went to bed fully dressed, André keeping his boots on. Smith's sleep was "often disturbed with the restless motions and uneasiness of mind exhibited by my bedfellow."[77] Up before dawn, André helped the servant saddle the horses and waited nervously as Smith thanked Miller.

Dense early-morning fog shrouded the riders as André, smiling and talkative now, said he hoped they were past their last sentry post. But at Crompond they were stopped again by youthful Captain Ebenezer Foote of the New York militia. Scanning their passes, he waved them on. Soon they would reach Wright's Mill, where Sheldon's dragoons were stationed and the officer in charge might give them an escort. As they turned south toward Pine's Bridge, the fog was burning off. Suddenly they came upon an American officer whom André instantly recognized and who eyed André closely as he rode past. He was Colonel Samuel Blachley Webb, a recently released prisoner of war who had spent three years on parole in New York City. Webb did not recognize André. As they approached the British outposts, André relaxed. Smith reined in at a farmhouse, where an old woman, Sarah Underhill, apologized that her larder had been stripped by marauding Cowboys. All she could sell them was a little suppon, a cold cornmeal mush that André had recently derided in "The Cow Chace." André took his bowl out onto the back stoop and ate all he could get down, alone. After this hasty breakfast, Smith came out and announced that he and the servant were turning back, that André had only about two and a half miles to go to the nearest British outpost (actually it was more like fifteen miles). If André avoided the Post Road and used the map Smith gave him, taking a slight loop around, staying on this road, he would be safe from the Cowboys. André was too shocked to object. Smith, who knew the roads, turned loose André, who did not, in the dangerous neutral ground between the lines where Smith, if he had been stopped by partisans of either side, would have been safe. Without Smith, André would have to depend on his pass from Arnold and hope to pick the right road to safety. André needed money and asked if Smith would accept his gold watch as security. Smith refused the watch, but gave André a few coins. They wished each other Godspeed and Smith rode off toward West Point to report to Arnold.

Smith's arrival at Beverley just before noon Saturday was more than Varick and Franks could endure silently. Varick had told Franks earlier that he considered Arnold's continued friendship with Smith "very ungenteel." Now the two conspired to provoke Squire Smith when Arnold's official family gathered in the dark-paneled dining room. John Lamb remarked that there was "a scarcity of butter at the table."

On Mrs. Arnold's calling for more butter, she was informed by the servant that there was no more. Arnold immediately said: "Bless me, but I had forgot the olive oil I bought in Philadelphia. It will do very well with salt fish." . . . The oil was produced and, on Arnold's saying it cost eighty dollars, Smith replied, 'Eight pence,' that a dollar was really no more than a penny, upon which [Varick] said with some warmth, 'You are mistaken, Mr. Smith,' in such a tone of voice as convinced me [he] was determined to affront him.

Varick testified that "a very high dispute took place" in which Franks "became a volunteer with me." Arnold soon joined the battle, answering Varick's charge in angry rejoinders directed at Franks. Varick then answered Arnold's objections, "addressing myself to Smith." The argument raged "till Mrs. Arnold, observing her husband in a passion, begged us to drop the matter." Others remembered that she shrieked for them to stop it. Varick left the table and went to his room. After Smith left that afternoon to go to get his family, Arnold came into Varick's room with Franks and "took [Franks] to task in very illiberal language for affronting Smith. . . .

He lashed me over [Franks's] back without addressing himself to me. He declared that, if he asked the Devil to dine with him, the gentlemen of his family should be civil to him." Franks told Arnold that if Smith had not been at Arnold's table, he would have "sent a bottle at his head, and would thereafter treat him as a rascal." Franks accused Arnold of becoming "prejudiced" against him, asked to be discharged from his staff, and left. Varick continued assailing Smith, calling him "a damned rascal, a scoundrel and a spy." Arnold listened quietly until Varick had finished, then icily told him he was "always willing to be advised by the gentlemen of his family, but, by God, would not be dictated to by them."[78] Later that evening when Varick went to Arnold to offer his resignation, Arnold assured him that he would have nothing to do with Smith. Still stinging from Arnold's tongue-lashing, Major Franks did not come down to breakfast on Monday morning, and Varick, running a fever, stayed in his room. Peggy had planned a breakfast reception for the commander in chief's arrival, but Washington had sent ahead his aide, Captain Samuel Shaw, and Lafayette's aide, James McHenry, with word that he would be late and that breakfast should go ahead without him. The commander in chief had taken a longer route back from Hartford for reasons of security and had spent the night at Fishkill, having supper at the same house as Squire Smith. Peggy Arnold stayed with the baby in the master bedroom with its big windows and balustraded porch, a sunny, quiet place. She was exhausted not only from nine days in an open wagon but from anxiety over the safety of her friend André. She planned to go downstairs later, when Washington arrived. Arnold had come to the table with Dr. Eustis, Hamilton, and McHenry. They had just been served when Lieutenant Joshua Allen, muddy and dripping from riding through a downpour, clambered into the foyer with an express message from Colonel Jameson, in command at North Castle.

> *Sir*
> *I have sent Lieutenant Allen with a certain John Anderson taken going into New York. He had a pass signed with your name. He had a parcel of papers taken from under his stockings, which I think of a very dangerous tendency. The papers I have sent to General Washington.*[79]

John André's luck had run out as he approached Pine's Bridge over Clark's Kill, half a mile north of Tarrytown, between nine and ten o'clock on Saturday morning, September 23, 1780. Seven young militiamen who were absent without leave from their unit had banded together into a gang to waylay and rob Loyalist travelers. Their leader was a twenty-two-year-old giant in the torn green-and-red uniform coat of a Hessian jaeger: John Paulding had worn the uniform to help make good his escape four days earlier from a British jail in New York City. Playing cards with Paulding as they waited for word from their four lookouts were twenty-year-old Isaac Van Wert and twenty-five-year-old Daniel Williams. As André neared Pine's Bridge, he was startled by the three men, who darted out, flintlocks ready. Paulding grabbed the bit of André's horse. "Gentlemen," said André, who could see the British lines in the distance and was sure he was among friends, "I hope you belong to our party."

"What party?" Paulding demanded.

"The lower party," André replied, alluding to the Loyalists based in New York City. He quickly added, as Paulding nodded, "Thank God, I am once more among friends, I am glad to see you. I am an officer in the British service, and have now been on particular business in the country, and I hope you will not detain me. And for a token to let you know I am a gentleman"—and here the exuberant André pulled out his gold watch. But Paulding was not impressed, and André realized he had been mistaken, that the three men were not Cowboys but Skinners, the Patriot equivalent.

"Get down," Paulding growled. "We are Americans."

"My God, I must do anything to get along," André rejoined with his best stage laugh. Fishing in his pocket for Arnold's pass, he brandished it before Paulding. Only Paulding could read—barely—and he mouthed the words. But he was already suspicious.

"Damn Arnold's pass! You said you was a British officer. Get down. Where is your money?"

André leaped from the horse, talking fast. "Gentlemen, you had best let me go, or you will bring yourselves in trouble, for, by stopping me, you will detain the general's business."

Paulding and Williams swore at André and moved closer, pointing their weapons. "God damn it! Where is your money?"

"Gentlemen, I have none about me."

"You are a British officer, and no money? Let's search him!"

They forced André into the woods beside the road and through a gate into a thicket, where they ordered him to strip. They searched every piece of clothing, finding his watch and some Continental dollars given him by Squire Smith. By now, André was naked except for his boots and stockings. André's and the Americans' testimony about the strip search is quite different. To a sympathetic American, Dr. Isaac Bronson, who examined André late in the day, André confided what happened next. They had ripped up the housings of his saddle and the collar of his coat and, finding no money there, were upon the point of letting him go when one of the party said, "Damn him! He may have it in his boots!" They threw him down, drew off his boots, and discovered the papers. David Williams, one of the highwaymen, testified:

We told him to pull off his boots, which he seemed indifferent about, but we got one boot off and searched in that boot, but could find nothing. . . . We found there were some papers in the bottom of his stocking, next to his foot, on which we made him pull his stocking off, and found three papers wrapped up.

As the naked André anxiously watched, Paulding struggled to read the documents, finally shouting to the others, "This is a spy!" Ordered to get dressed, André listened as the men argued about what to do with him. Williams turned to André and asked whether he would give up his horse, bridle, watch, and a hundred gold guineas, "upon which he said, 'Yes,' and he told us he would direct it to any place, even if it was to that very spot, so that we could get it. I asked him whether he would not give us more. He said he would give us any quantity of dry goods or any sum of money, and bring it to any place we might pitch upon, so that we might get it." But André's voluble nervousness only reinforced Paulding's dogged conviction that he was a spy who would be worth something to his American enemies, and that they could still have his horse and personal possessions. Besides, he had just come from a British prison and did not want to be tricked back into one. When André suggested that two of them hold him while the third went into New York City, for "five hundred or even a thousand guineas," Paulding argued convincingly that a British "party would be sent out to take them and then they should all be prisoners."

Prodded as he dressed and mounted, André had his arms tied behind him as his horse was led over the roads he had just followed. The three robbers were soon joined by their four partners, who had been watching another road. Van Wert later recalled André's state of mind:

You never saw such an alteration in any man's face. Only a few moments before, he was uncommonly gay in his looks, but after we made him prisoner, you could read in his face that he thought it was all over with him. After travelling one or two miles, he said, "I would to God you had blown my brains out when you stopped me!"[80]

Benedict Arnold did not take time to read Colonel Jameson's list of documents found in André's stocking: he knew them only too well. Excusing himself from the breakfast table, he hurried upstairs to Peggy, locked the bedroom door, whispered to her that André had been captured, the plot discovered, and incriminating papers were on their way to Washington, who was expected any minute. If Arnold had any question what he must do, Peggy must have reassured him that she would be safe: it is unlikely that Peggy tried to talk him out of fleeing for his life. Arnold evidently instructed Peggy to burn all of their papers and stall for time. Embracing her and taking a last look at Neddy, Arnold stiffened as a knock resounded on the bedroom door.

"In about two minutes," testified Franks, "General Washington's servant came to the [front] door and informed me that his Excellency was nigh at hand. I went immediately upstairs and informed Arnold of it. He came down in a great confusion and, ordered a horse to be saddled, mounted him and told me to inform his Excellency that he was gone over to West Point and would return in about an hour."[81] Franks had no idea what was in the letter Arnold had just read, much less that Arnold was lashing his horse down a precipitous short cut to the boat landing where the crew was eating breakfast. Life guard Alpheus Parkhurst, on sentry duty, saw Arnold leaving. Franks "rode up in great haste and the general came to the door and the aide-de-camp ordered the general's horse [a big bay] to be brought as quick as it could be done. The general and his aide started off together for the river, and the aide soon returned and brought back the general's horse." Parkhurst saw Arnold dismount and step into his bateau and draw his sword. Arnold brought along his saddle, two pistols in holsters still attached to it. He told his crewmen he would give them two gallons of rum if they would get him downriver to Stony Point and back in time to meet Washington. The bateau, according to Parkhurst, "started off in great speed"[82] with Arnold sitting in its stern.

19

"THE WORLD

SELDOM JUDGES RIGHT"

Thy public life was but a specious show,
A cloak to secret wickedness and shame
Hence thou has lurked beneath the fair guise
Of freedom's *champion,* mammon's
sordid slave.

"The Fall of Lucifer," anonymous, Hartford, 1781

When André was brought into North Castle, the nearest American outpost, by his captors, white-haired Colonel John Jameson wrote two letters to Arnold, which were sent along with all the captured documents and André himself under guard to West Point. Lieutenant Allen had already set out with the prisoner, who could breathe a little easier now, thinking that Arnold could intercede for him, by the time Major Benjamin Tallmadge, a high-ranking officer in Washington's secret service, arrived at New Castle. Tallmadge instantly suspected that André was a spy and that Arnold was his accomplice. Why else was André heading south, toward British lines, with documents in the handwriting of Benedict Arnold? At a hastily summoned council of war, Tallmadge argued against sending anything to Arnold until Washington saw the papers. But Jameson, who outranked him, overruled him: not to inform their superior, Arnold, was insubordination, and, besides, it was serious business to make such a charge against a commanding general. But Tallmadge did persuade Jameson to make one change of plans, and a messenger rode north to overtake Lieutenant Allen, rescinding his orders: he was now to take André to South Salem, fifteen miles east of the river and away from British ships, leave him under heavy guard, then take Jameson's letter to Arnold. The courier was then to take the intercepted document not to Arnold but to Washington, following the road through Peekskill and Danbury to Hartford, the route Washington had taken the week before on his way to confer with the French.

By the time the messenger reached Danbury and learned that Washington had not returned that way and then rode through a heavy storm back to Jameson at North Castle for further orders, Arnold had been unwittingly tipped off by Lieutenant Allen and had fled. At ten-thirty, Washington, Knox, Lafayette, and their 160-man entourage arrived at Beverley. Washington had not planned to have breakfast until he had inspected West Point, but Marquis de Lafayette was eager to pay his respects to the beautiful Mrs. Arnold, who was noted, he told Washington, for her cooking and her hospitality. "Ah, Marquis," Washington chided him, "you young men are all in love with Mrs. Arnold. I see you are eager to be with her as soon as possible. Go and breakfast with her, and tell her not to wait for me."[1] Lafayette, embarrassed, rode on with Washington and Knox, but Hamilton and Lafayette's aide, McHenry, rode up to Beverley, where Major Franks apologized that breakfast was not ready and that Arnold was not there to greet him—he had gone over to West Point—and Mrs. Arnold and Colonel Varick were sick in their beds.

As Washington crossed the river, he expected Arnold to have arranged a cannon salute, as much for the French officers as for himself, and he expected Arnold to be there to receive them properly. Washington later said, "The impropriety of his conduct when he knew I was to be there struck me very forcibly, and my mind misgave me, but I had not the least idea of the real cause."[2] Much more shocking was the condition of the defenses at West Point, its garrison scattered, its barracks falling down, its earthworks half completed. For two hours, Washington rode and walked over them, stunned by the neglect. Only days before Arnold had assured him that West Point could withstand any British attack. It was the second blow Washington had sustained in a few days, the French informing him at Hartford that the British had them bottled up on Rhode Island and that they could not support his attack on New York City.

Now Washington realized that the American lifeline on the Hudson was vulnerable.

Crossing back to Beverley, Washington went with Lafayette upstairs to the rooms reserved for them to await the noonday meal. They had barely taken off their cloaks and gloves when a messenger arrived, this time from Colonel Jameson for the commander in chief. As Washington broke open the seal and paged through the documents, the terrible, incredible truth struck him: Benedict Arnold had sold out to the British. Remarkably clear-headed under fire, Washington was the only one at West Point that day to act calmly. He immediately ordered Alexander Hamilton and James McHenry to go after Arnold. Lafayette came into the dressing room where Washington was sitting, head down, hand trembling with its load of treasonous papers, murmuring to Henry Knox, "Arnold has betrayed me. Whom can we trust now?"[3]

While Washington had been across the river at West Point, Peggy Arnold had run down the hallway in her dressing gown, her hair disheveled, shrieking. She had gone to Varick's room the day before, he testified at his court-martial, "while I lay in a high fever, made tea for me, and paid me the utmost attention in my illness." Still running a fever from a long bout of dysentery, Varick now rushed up the stairs, where he found Peggy screaming and struggling with two maids, who were trying to get her back into her room. "The miserable lady" was "raving." Peggy grabbed the young aide by one hand, cried, "Colonel Varick, have you ordered my child to be killed?" Varick testified that Peggy then "fell to her knees at my feet with prayers and entreaties to spare her innocent babe." Varick "attempted to raise her up, but in vain." Major Franks and Dr. Eustis, the fort's physician, "soon arrived, and we carried her to her bed, raving mad." Years later, Varick would say that Peggy was acting to protect herself and her baby, to buy time for her husband's escape. But on September 25, 1780, when she was twenty years old and he was twenty-seven and devoted to her, Varick was only the first to be taken in by what at least began as a brilliant piece of acting, but apparently developed into a true dementia fueled by her fear that she might never see her husband or her friend André again. Her world had been exploded by a plot she had encouraged, aided, and abetted, and the sheer nervous tension on the day of discovery completely fooled everyone around her. It would be the twentieth century before the opening of the British Headquarters Papers at the University of Michigan proved what the eighteenth century refused to believe—that a young and beautiful woman was capable of helping Benedict Arnold plot the greatest conspiracy of the American Revolution and then completely fooling the astute warriors around her. Varick, like the others, could see "no cause for all this." He still did not know of Arnold's treason.

When she seemed a little composed, she burst again into pitiable tears and exclaimed to me, alone on her bed with her, that she had not a friend left here. I told her she had Franks and me, and General Arnold would soon be home from West Point with General Washington. She exclaimed: "No, General Arnold will never return. He is gone, he is gone forever. There, there, there, the spirits have carried [him] up there, they have put hot irons in his head"—pointing that he was gone up to the ceiling. . . .

When Peggy learned that Washington had come back from West Point without Arnold, she cried out to Varick again that "there was a hot iron on her head and no one but General Washington could take it off, and [she] wanted to see the general." After Dr. Eustis examined the hysterical woman, he left the room with Varick and Franks and told them that they must send for Arnold "or the woman would die." By now, her repeated insistence that Arnold was gone forever had made the two aides suspect that Arnold had indeed gone forever, over to the enemy. They confided their fear to Dr. Eustis, but added they were afraid to make such an unfounded charge about their commanding officer to Washington, who still had not told them by noontime that he already knew. The threesome decided they must make the first move by letting Washington "see her unhappy situation." Varick went to Washington's room and told him all he knew, then accompanied Washington to Peggy's bedside. Varick told her, "Here is General Washington." Clutching her baby at her breast, Peggy said it was not Washington:

She said no, it was not. The General assured her he was, but she exclaimed: "No, that is not General Washington; that is the man who was going to assist Colonel Varick in killing my child." She repeated the same sad story about General Arnold.[4]

Washington retreated from the room, certain Peggy Arnold was no conspirator.

Peggy Shippen could not have played a more brilliant part to a wider audience. Hamilton, always with an eye to public opinion, sent his letter to his fiancée for publication in the *New York Post* and the *Pennsylvania Gazette*. It was soon reprinted all over North

America. Her performance, part acting, part desperate fear, exonerated her, made her husband all the more hated. The next day, when Peggy summoned Hamilton and Lafayette to her room and appealed to them to intercede with Washington for a pass for her to leave with her baby, Hamilton was able to come back almost immediately and tell her that she could either go to her father's home in Philadelphia or to her husband in New York City. She chose Philadelphia. Her deception was now complete. She could give the appearance of spurning her traitorous husband and fleeing to her father when, in fact, she had another mission: like the wives of many Loyalists who had fled to the British, she was trying to protect the family's valuable property. But Washington saw no reason to stop her. He believed Peggy Arnold.

When Hamilton had come back from his chase after Arnold he brought Washington a letter from Arnold:

On the Vulture, *25 September, 1780*
Sir; The heart which is conscious of its own rectitude cannot attempt to palliate a step which the world may censure as wrong. I have ever acted from a principle of love to my country, since the commencement of the present unhappy contest between Great Britain and the Colonies. The same principle of love to my country actuates my present conduct, however it may appear inconsistent to the world, who very seldom judge right of any man's actions.

I have no favor to ask for myself. I have too often experienced the ingratitude of my country to attempt it. But from the known humanity of your Excellency, I am induced to ask your protection for Mrs. Arnold from every insult and injury that a mistaken vengeance of my country may expose her to. It ought to fall only on me. She is as good and as innocent as an angel, and is incapable of doing wrong. I beg she may be permitted to return to her friends in Philadelphia, or to come to me, as she may choose. From your Excellency I have no fears on her account, but she may suffer from the mistaken fury of the country.

I have to request that the enclosed letter may be delivered to Mrs. Arnold, and she be permitted to write to me.

I have also to ask that my clothes and baggage, which are of little consequence, may be sent to me. If required, their value shall be paid in money. I have the honor to be with great regard and esteem, your Excellency's most obedient humble servant.
Benedict Arnold
N.B. In justice to the gentlemen of my family, Colonel Varick and Major Franks, I think myself in honor bound to declare that they, as

*well as Joshua Smith, Esq. (who I know is suspected) are totally
ignorant of any transactions of mine that they had reason to believe
were injurious to the public.*[5]

There was something still honorable in the way Arnold had taken all
the blame to himself and lost no time trying to protect his wife, his
aides, even the shifty Squire Smith. Washington, informing Franks
during a walk after lunch that Arnold had defected and Franks must
consider himself under arrest until a court-martial could be summoned, then gave Franks permission to accompany Peggy and the
baby to Philadelphia.

Despite his surface calm, Washington knew better than anyone
that this was the most serious crisis of the Revolution. He quickly
shifted regiments, called his best battle-seasoned units in from New
Jersey, Connecticut, and Massachusetts, units headed by men who
had fought under Arnold—Scammell, Meigs, Dearborn, Lamb. He
put West Point under Nathanael Greene's command. He gathered
his army around him like a cloak, evidently expecting the British to
attack, with Arnold as their guide. Years later, honest, angry John
Lamb would describe the consternation at West Point in 1780. Had
André "exhibited a presence of mind worthy of his reputation for
sagacity, the die had been cast which [would have] sealed the fate of
the Highland passes, and of the army." West Point, "weakened as it
was by the contrivances of Arnold, could not have made a successful
resistance." The formidable British forces gathering for the kill were
"sufficiently numerous to assault it on all sides at once."[6]

Washington moved quickly, decisively, ordering André brought
to West Point for interrogation and a speedy court-martial. Ignoring
Arnold's disclaimer, he had Squire Smith immediately arrested: he
was seized in his nightshirt at his in-laws' in Fishkill. Washington
especially did not trust Smith and personally interrogated him as
André was questioned in the next room. It was one of the few times
Washington let go of his temper. According to Smith's own account,
not published for thirty years, he did not learn of Arnold's escape
until he faced Washington and five other interrogators. Washington,
he said, exploded at him:

*Sir, do you know that Arnold had fled and that Mr. Anderson,
whom you piloted through the lines, proves to be Major John André, the adjutant general of the British Army, who is now our prisoner? Unless you confess who were your accomplices, I shall
suspend you both from that tree!*[7]

Washington also vented his anger on Colonel Jameson for his "egregious folly." If it hadn't been for Jameson's "bewildered conception" of his duty to tell Arnold that he had captured André, "I should as certainly have got Arnold," Washington wrote to Lieutenant Colonel John Laurens in Philadelphia. Publicly, Washington refused to concede the possibility that the Arnold-André conspiracy had included their attempt to betray him to the British, a belief that spread quickly throughout the country and persisted, making Arnold's treason more personal, evil, Judas-like. "How far he meant to involve me in the catastrophe," Washington wrote Laurens, "does not appear by an indubitable evidence, and I am rather inclined to think he did not wish to hazard the more important object of his treachery by attempting to combine two events, the lesser of which [Washington's capture] might have marred the greater."8 To Joseph Reed in Pennsylvania, Washington confided there had been reasons for doubt. "I am far from thinking he intended to hazard a defeat of this important object by combining another risk, although there were circumstances which led to a contrary belief."9 One of these was Arnold's knowledge of Washington's movements. To Major General William Heath, Washington acknowledged that Arnold "knew of my approach and that I was visiting [Beverley] with the Marquis [de Lafayette]."10 To John Laurens, Washington's aide-de-camp, Alexander Hamilton wrote a full report which concluded that while Arnold would have been "unwise" to try to capture Washington at the same time he surrendered West Point, he admitted "there was some color for imagining it was a part of the plan to betray the General into the hands of the enemy. . . . Arnold was very anxious to ascertain from [Washington] the precise day of his return, and the enemy's movements seem to have corresponded to this point."11

If Washington chose not to believe that his capture at West Point was Arnold's real objective, there were others who did. Lafayette, with him that week and a member of John André's court-martial, apparently propagated the enduring French view. "The plan was [for the British] to come up suddenly before West Point and to present all the appearance of an attack," Lafayette wrote to the Chevalier de La Luzerne, French minister to the United States. "Arnold intended to say that he had been surprised by a superior force. . . . After retreating to the redoubts at West Point across the river, [he was leaving] Washington, Lafayette, Knox and the rest to be captured while he stood wringing his hands."12 An American officer who was a prisoner of war in New York City added more details. "The plan was that Sir Henry Clinton on a certain day agreed upon between himself and General Arnold, was to lay siege on Fort [Arnold], which is reckoned almost impregnable," wrote Colonel George Matthews of the 9th Virginia Regiment. "General Arnold was immediately to send to General Washington for a reinforcement, and before that could arrive, was to surrender." Clinton was then "to surprise the reinforcement, which probably would have been commanded by General Washington in person. . . . Had this plan succeed, it must have put an end to the war."[13]

That Washington was Arnold's real quarry was beyond doubt to others close to him. From New Jersey, Governor William Livingston joined a chorus of congratulations on "the timely discovery of General Arnold's treasonable plot to captivate your person."[14] And young John Laurens, writing to Washington from Philadelphia on October 4, had no doubt of Arnold's intent. "I congratulate my country, whose safety is so intimately united with yours, and who may regard this miraculous rescue of her champion as an assurance that Heaven approves her choice of a defender."[15] The only other man in a position to know was Sir Henry Clinton, the man in charge of the entire operation. Clinton was already trying to justify his loss of André: "The interview with Arnold was absolutely necessary to ascertain whether he had really been corresponding with Arnold," Chief Justice William Smith recorded. "He regretted this disappointment as the loss of his hope of an instantaneous termination of the war. [He] said he should have had both Washington and Rochambeau prisoners, for they were both there now [at West Point]."[16]

The news that Benedict Arnold had defected to the British after plotting to surrender West Point set off a firestorm of newspaper attacks and angry outcries from old friends and comrades. At West Point, the name of the main fort was immediately changed from Fort Arnold to Fort Clinton after New York's General George Clinton. "Every memento of his name was expunged from the garrison which he had so basely undertaken to betray," wrote John Lamb. "The original appellation of the first fortifications erected at West Point [would be] unknown in history and only to be found in the military correspondence and garrison orders of that day." Lamb, trying to understand what had driven his old friend to such a drastic step, concluded that "there is little doubt that his beautiful and accomplished wife was the prime mover of the grand conspiracy."[17] Lamb corresponded for weeks with his old Quebec comrade Eleazar Oswald, Arnold's former secretary, who told Lamb he wished Arnold had been killed at Saratoga.

But George Washington did not share Oswald's belief that Arnold faced a fate worse than death on the gibbet. "I am mistaken if at this time Arnold is undergoing the torments of a mental Hell. He wants feeling!" Washington wrote John Laurens, saying that he considered Arnold "so hackneyed in villainy and so lost to all sense of honor and shame that while his faculties will enable him to continue his sordid pursuits, there will be no time for remorse."[18] When Benjamin Franklin learned of Arnold's defection, he put it in pecuniary terms. "Judas," he wrote, "sold only one man, Arnold three millions. Judas got for his one Man 30 pieces of silver, Arnold got not a halfpenny a head. A miserable bargain!"[19]

While old friends tried to efface Arnold's memory, some Patriots worried that Arnold would inspire even more defections. Lamb reported desertions at West Point, where Arnold's Life Guards marched home. As a British intelligence report written in early October put it, the reaction of many Americans to Arnold's treason revealed their own "distrust of themselves."[20] A mob rushed into the cemetery in Arnold's native Norwich, Connecticut, and destroyed both his father's and his infant brother's grave markers in an attempt to obliterate the name of Benedict Arnold. Arnold became the scapegoat for all that was evil in the Revolution. In Philadelphia, where his memory was so strong and fresh, within days of his defection radicals paraded a two-faced effigy of Arnold in a horse-drawn cart, its head turning constantly as a black-robed devil jingled a bag of gold coins next to his left ear and prodded him with a pitchfork into the flames of Hell. The figure of Arnold held a mask and sat behind a lantern painted with a gallows. In New Milford, Connecticut, a large crowd paraded figures of Arnold and Satan through the town to the sound of firecrackers as every house window was illuminated with candles. And all over America, men swore that if they caught Arnold, they would cut off the leg wounded in the nation's service at Quebec and Saratoga, bury it with full honors, and then hang the rest of him on a gibbet.

If Washington could not catch Benedict Arnold and hang him for his treason, then there was André. Someone must die for so blatant a conspiracy. Hamilton, legal aide to Washington, wrote to Colonel John Laurens on October 11 to explain why John André was condemned to death by a court-martial within a few days of his capture. "There was, in truth, no way of saving him. Arnold or he must have been the victim, and Arnold was out of our power."[21] Arnold, in fact, had safely boarded the British warship *Vulture* before Washington even knew of his treason. Gripping hard on the tiller of his bateau, his sword and pistols at the ready, Arnold had sailed as fast as he could down the Hudson to Stony Point, then searched for the

Vulture, giving the captain and crew of his bateau the choice of joining him in going over to the British and receiving promotions, or turning back. Two of them stayed aboard; the others rowed back to West Point. Arnold himself received a nervous welcome from Colonel Robinson and Captain Sutherland, gave them the bad news of André's capture, and, retiring to the stern cabin, wrote to Washington and to Peggy. After Sutherland sent Arnold's letters ashore to Verplanck's Ferry, he gave orders for the big sloop-of-war to up anchor and run downriver with the outgoing tide to Spuyten Duyvil.

By late the night of September 26, Sir Henry Clinton knew the worst. Clinton instantly enlisted Arnold in his efforts to save André. As André and Smith were escorted south from West Point under heavy guard to the main American camp at Tappan, Arnold wrote a letter to Clinton which was to be sent on to Washington. It asserted that André had been operating legally under a flag of truce granted by Arnold and thus should be immediately released. Once again, Arnold took full responsibility:

Thinking it much properer he should return by land, I directed him to make use of the feigned name of John Anderson under which he had by my direction come on shore. . . . This officer cannot fail of being immediately sent to New York, as he was invited to a conversation to me, for which I sent him a flag of truce. . . .[22]

But Washington was not swayed by Arnold's attempt to portray André's spying as a protected negotiation. Under the articles of war, Washington could have hanged André outright as a spy without a trial. André had been caught in disguise with hidden papers, behind enemy lines, violating not only Clinton's advice to him but the articles of war: Washington had already executed eight British spies in the war. He wanted to assert the sovereignty of the United States and he wanted a showcase trial, but not a long one. He named fourteen high-ranking generals, presided over by Nathanael Greene, and charged John Lawrence with cross-examining André. The generals were to weigh the evidence and make a recommendation of guilt or innocence to Washington, the final authority. The trial was to proceed immediately, to avoid dragged-out British appeals and the danger of reprisals or attempts to rescue André.

The court-martial took one day. It was convened in the old Dutch church at Orangetown, New Jersey, on September 29. Even before his interrogation, André did not deny the charges, but he did not consider himself a spy, only Clinton's deputy. He had become a spy by accident, he insisted. He had expected to meet Arnold aboard *Vulture.* He had crossed enemy lines by accident, against his wishes. He had traveled south in disguise against his will, urged on to his "great mortification," and he had "objected much against it"[23] (he never did mention Smith's name, a gallantry which saved Smith's life). Arnold had pressed the hidden papers on him. André considered himself a brave officer on a high-level mission for Clinton. The board of generals considered him a spy. The court-martial also studied Arnold's letter and those of Clinton and Robinson, insisting that there had been no valid flag of truce. No witnesses were called, and the same day, the board, its opinion unanimous, reported to Washington that André "ought to be considered as a spy from the enemy and that, agreeable to the law and usage of nations, it is their opinion he ought to suffer death."[24] The next day, on Saturday, September 30, Washington announced that André was to die on October 1, at five in the evening.*

In a letter to Clinton notifying him of his verdict, Washington maintained that it was "impossible for him [André] to suppose he came on shore under the sanction of a flag"[25] of truce, and even if he had, his actions were those of a spy. Washington's courier also carried a letter from Peggy Arnold to Benedict, since lost, a letter from André to Clinton, and an anonymous message in disguised handwriting from Alexander Hamilton to Clinton, proposing the exchange of André for Arnold. This message had undoubtedly been sanctioned by Washington. "Major André's character and situation seem to demand this of your justice and friendship," the writer admonished Clinton. "Arnold appears to have been the guilty author of the mischief and ought more properly to be the victim."[26]

While Washington put off the execution until noon on October 2, Sir Henry Clinton called together his advisers. Clinton was in no position to countenance a trade. Under British rules, no deserter was ever exchanged; furthermore, Sir Henry had long ago guaranteed Arnold his personal protection if the plot failed. His councillors wanted a conference with Washington so that the British could present "a true state of facts."[27] Clinton wanted to write an angry letter threatening retaliation if Washington touched André. Clinton broke down in tears at the meeting of generals, Loyalist leaders, and royal officials. Clinton was haunted by a letter he had received from André, who claimed that he wanted to

remove from your breast any suspicion that I could imagine I was bound by your Excellency's orders to expose myself to what has

---

* Washington acted under a Continental Congress resolution of 1776 which provided capital punishment for "treason against America." André was one of forty-eight put to death under this law from 1776 to 1783.

*happened. . . . I am perfectly tranquil in mind and prepared for any
fate to which an honest zeal for my King's service may have devoted
me. . . . With all the warmth of my heart I give you thanks for your
Excellency's profuse kindness to me. . . .*[28]

Chief Justice Smith described Clinton at this point as "agonized," ready to avenge André by hanging "many American spies he
had in his power."[29] Clinton's advisers told him this would be impolitic and drafted a toned-down letter to Washington calling for a
meeting to review the evidence. Clinton was not too distraught to
consider a subterfuge. While he signed the conciliatory letter drafted
for him, he asked Benedict Arnold to draft and enclose another letter, signed by Clinton, somewhat firmer in tone:

*If, after this just and candid representation of Major André's
case, the board of general officers adhere to their former opinion,
I shall suppose it dictated by passion and resentment. And if
that gentleman should suffer the severity of their sentence, I
shall think myself bound by every tie of duty and honor to re-
taliate on such unhappy persons of your army as may fall within
my power. . . . I have further to observe that forty of the principal inhabitants of South Carolina have justly forfeited their
lives [for conspiring with Patriots] . . . . [Clinton could not]
in justice extend his mercy to them any longer if Major André
suffers, which in all probability will open a scene of blood at
which humanity will revolt.*

In other words, Arnold, whether or not Clinton had approved his
wording, as his first act as a British general threatened to take forty-
to-one retaliation on hostages if André was executed. Arnold reiterated to make his meaning unmistakable to Washington:

*. . . Suffer not an unjust sentence to touch the life of Major André.
But if this warning should be disregarded, and he should suffer, I
call heaven and earth to witness that your Excellency will be justly
answerable for the torrent of blood that may be spilt in consequence.*[30]

Far from agreeing to Washington's clandestine offer to exchange André for Arnold, Clinton had nominated Arnold as the man who
would avenge anything that was done to André.

While he tried for a week to arrange André's release, Clinton was an emotional wreck, as a letter he began to his sisters at home in England makes clear:

I have been moderate in my correspondence with W[ashington] . . . but have assured him if M[ajor] A[ndre] whom I regard as innocent should suffer, the lives of [forty South Carolinian] delinquents must be forfeited. . . . They treat [André] with great tenderness. . . . As they have delayed it so long, I do not think they will proceed to extremities, but if they do— . . . I wish our poor friend André had not been a little too much off his guard when the militia questioned him . . . Good God, what a coup manqué. . . . To those who do not feel the private losses we have met with, the defection of such a man as Arnold will appear important. . . . I think it is so, and that the ice, once broke, many will follow his example. . . .[31]

It would be five more days before Clinton was in any shape to continue his rambling letter. By then, he had learned that Washington had gone ahead with John André's execution. The twenty-nine-year-old adjutant general of the British army, highest-ranking officer executed in the American Revolution, had only two last requests. He asked Clinton to send out his servant with a fresh British uniform, and he asked Washington that he be allowed to choose the means of his death—a firing squad instead of the gallows. Washington, who always hanged spies and was concerned that any softening on his part would be mistaken as a failing of his resolve that André was indeed a spy and deserved to die like one, refused. According to eyewitnesses, Washington's hand shook as he signed André's death warrant.

In the crowd waiting to witness André's execution was John Paulding, the hulking militiaman who had helped capture André. Paulding later jotted a brief note on a scrap of paper; "I took André the 23 of September 1780 and I seen him hung October 2, 1780 for my children."[32] Also standing near André was young Dr. James Thacher, who had first seen Arnold on Cambridge Common as Washington reviewed the Quebec invasion troops and had next seen Arnold as he lay grievously wounded after Saratoga. Thacher never forgot John André's comportment that day and he recorded the scene:

His breakfast being sent to him from the table of General Washington, which had been done every day of his confinement, he partook of it as usual and, having shaved and dressed himself, he placed his hat on the table and cheerfully said to the general officers, "I am ready at any moment, gentlemen." . . . *A large detachment of troops was paraded and an immense concourse of people assembled. Almost all our general and field officers, excepting his Excellency and his staff, were present on horseback.* . . .

Major André walked from the stone house in which he had been confined between two of our subaltern officers, arm and arm. . . . *He betrayed no want of fortitude, but retained a complacent smile . . . and politely bowed to several gentlemen whom he knew, which was respectfully returned. It was his earnest desire to be shot, the mode of death most conformable to the feelings of a military man.* . . . *At the moment, therefore, when suddenly he came in view of the gallows, he involuntarily started backward and made a pause. "Why this emotion, sir?" said an officer at his side. Instantly recovering his composure, he said, "I am reconciled to my death, but I detest the mode."*

While waiting and standing near the gallows, I observed some degree of trepidation, placing his foot on a stone and rolling it over and choking in his throat, as if attempting to swallow. As soon, however, as he perceived that things were in readiness, he stepped quickly into the wagon and, at this moment, he appeared to shrink, but instantly elevating his head with firmness, he said, "It will be but a momentary pang." . . . *[He took] from his pockets two white handkerchiefs. The provost marshal [Colonel Scammell] with one loosely pinioned his arms and, with the other, [André], taking off his hat and stock, bandaged his own eyes with perfect firmness.* . . . *He slipped the noose over his head and adjusted it to his neck.* . . . *Colonel Scammell now informed him that he had an opportunity to speak. He raised the handkerchief from his eyes and said, "I pray you to bear witness that I meet my fate like a brave man." The wagon being now removed from under him, he was suspended and instantly expired.*[33]

Eyewitnesses said the first great swing of the rope killed him. As thousands wept, his body was lowered to the ground and buried at the foot of the gallows. Forty-one years later, he was disinterred and reburied in Poets' Corner at Westminster Abbey.

Benedict Arnold's letter threatening Washington did not reach Washington before André's execution. Arnold was at the home of Chief Justice William Smith in New York City when the news of André's hanging arrived three days later. Arnold was "vastly disconcerted."[34] He left quickly in a borrowed post chaise. It was four more days before Sir Henry Clinton could compose himself enough to sit down and add a postscript to his long letter recounting the conspiracy for his family in England. "The horrid deed is done," wrote Clinton. "Washington has committed premeditated murder, he must answer for the dreadful consequences. I feel beyond words to describe [André's death] but I cannot reproach myself in the least. . . . Washington is become a murderer and a Jesuit."[35]

A few days after André's death, Squire Smith went on trial for his life. He acted as his own defense counsel and subpoenaed Franks and Varick as witnesses. For lack of evidence after a month-long court-martial, he was able to win acquittal. Freed, he was immediately rearrested by New York State authorities on suspicion of being a Tory. He got his jailers drunk and escaped to New York City disguised as a woman, wearing a red robe. With the help of high-ranking Loyalists he won an allowance from Clinton and fled to England, returning to New York City after the war. The year after Benedict Arnold died, Smith wrote the biography of John André, which included Smith's account of the affair, a best-seller which shaped public opinion of all the participants for half a century.

Franks and Varick also were acquitted by courts-martial after corroborating each other's testimony. Paulding, Williams, and Van Wart were elevated by Hamilton's newspaper prose to national heroes. Invited to have dinner with Washington, they were awarded gold medals by Congress, which also granted each of them lifelong pensions of $200 each in gold. They were also allowed to keep André's boots, watch, horse, and saddle. In 1817, they applied for increased pensions, setting off an uproar on the floor of Congress in which Congressman Benjamin Tallmadge, who had first interviewed them at North Castle and then was in command of John André's guards until his execution, led the fight to turn down their request for more money. Tallmadge, head of Washington's secret service, was a second cousin of Squire Smith's. It was Tallmadge who had guarded Smith as well as André and gathered evidence for Washington. He described Paulding and his two friends as "plundering Cowboys" who were "roving and lurking above the lines, sometimes plundering on one side and sometimes on the other."[36] Their pension petition was denied by Congress.

Peggy Arnold began to find out what it would be like as the wife of a traitor as soon as she left the protection of Washington's sympathetic staff at Beverley on September 27, 1780, and, with Washington's personal pass and the escort of the devoted Major Franks, headed south toward Philadelphia with her six-month-old baby, Neddy, her nurse, and her servant in Arnold's carriage. It was pouring rain and no one along the road would let her buy food for herself, her baby, her servants, or her horses. They went all the way to Kakiat, a distance of sixty-five miles and three days' travel on the northward itinerary, before Franks could persuade someone to take them in late at night. "We got here," Franks wrote to Varick from Kakiat on the twenty-eighth, "I very wet, Mrs. Arnold, thank God, in tolerable spirits." On their way north, they had stopped off at Coe's Tavern at Kakiat: now they were refused. But, Franks said, Peggy was far from the hysterical woman she had been when Varick had last seen her. "I have hopes to get them home without any return of her distress. . . . She expresses her gratitude to you in lively terms and requests you make her acknowledgements to his Excellency, to the Marquis and to Hamilton and indeed to all the gentlemen for their great politeness and humanity."[37]

It was a short, easier drive to Paramus, New Jersey, on the twenty-eighth, and here Franks took her to the home of Theodosia Prevost, the beautiful young widow of a British officer who would herself the next year marry a man who would one day become a famous American traitor, Arnold's onetime aide, Aaron Burr. Peggy must have been infinitely relieved when she reached the relative safety of a Loyalist household. According to Burr, she blurted out the story of her past week, including her own consummate piece of acting at West Point. Many years later, when all of the principals were dead, Aaron Burr's biographer printed the story which he insisted Theodosia Prevost had told him: "As soon as they were alone, Mrs. Arnold became tranquilized and assured Mrs. Prevost that she was heartily tired of the theatricals she was exhibiting." In notes he left for his biographer, Burr averred that Peggy had admitted to Mrs. Prevost "that she had corresponded with the British commander and that she was disgusted with the American cause and those who had the management of public affairs, and that through unceasing perseverance, she had ultimately brought the general into an arrangement to surrender West Point."[38] Both of the Arnolds were dead and unable to confirm or deny Burr's account by the time it was published, but Peggy's family rebutted it and propounded another version, one in which Peggy was all innocent and Burr a lascivious opportunist who made advances to Peggy the next day in her carriage en route to Philadelphia, advances which she angrily resisted before putting Burr out of the carriage and riding on to her father's house. The spurned Burr, the Shippens maintained, spread the story out of spite. There are many unresolvable elements to Peggy Arnold's story, but there is also the possibility that Burr was telling the truth and out of decency waited to publish the story until everyone involved was dead. Whether or not he was a traitor, Burr was not necessarily a liar. There are also two problems with the Shippen version. First, considerable evidence has emerged of Peggy's participation in the plot. Second, Burr was not in the carriage the next day. Franks was.

George Washington had been right about Benedict Arnold when he prophesied that he would not be immediately suffering the pangs of hell for his treason. In fact, Arnold, despite a momentary pang at the news of André's hanging, seems never to have been more himself than in the days and weeks after joining the British army inside New York City. Assured of Peggy's and the baby's protection by Washington, Arnold set about a feverish round of activities, meeting British top brass, writing reports and newspaper proclamations, sketching out proposals for attacks on his old comrades, his old tormentors, pressing Clinton to attack West Point at once, to let him lead the attack, then to siege Congress. His arrival in New York City sent a thrill through many of the thousands of Loyalists who had all but given up on the British taking the initiative in the protracted civil war. Arnold's arrival actually stopped the royal mail to England while British officials hastily wrote out reports of this important development for their superiors at home. "An event has happened that has stopped the packet," wrote the New York royal governor, Major General James Robertson to London:

Arnold, the boldest and most enterprising of the rebel generals, lives with me and sits by me while I write. [It was he who] took Ticonderoga; he conducted the surprising march by Kennebec River to Canada; he collected and conducted into action, almost in spite of Gates, the army that took Burgoyne—and he opposed with almost fatal bravery Mr. Tryon's invasion of Connecticut. He squabbled with a Reed, the Congress sided with the last, and Arnold thought himself ill-used and found means, eighteen months ago, to offer his service to the King.

Robertson, a general who had worked his way up from private, liked Arnold's spirit: "Arnold does nothing by halves." Robertson worked out Arnold's new rank as a brigadier general of provincial troops, with a permanent grade of British cavalry colonel. He firmly expected Lord Amherst, who had turned down André's promotion, to ratify Arnold's. "Arnold is considered as a brigadier in our service," he explained to Amherst, despite Arnold's request

*to have that rank he left in the rebel army continued to him, "not,"
said he, "that I should not be satisfied to act as a [common] soldier
for the King but, because by promoting me, His Majesty's service
will be promoted, as those who are in the state I have left, will be
influenced in their conduct by the reception I meet with." The rank
of brigadier had been offered by André. After conversing with Sir
Henry, I told [Arnold] that a higher rank would offend the brigadiers of our army, that it would be more honorable for him to get
this [higher rank] after performing some service of moment. He
agreed, and longs for an occasion to earn Sir Henry's promise. . . .
Since the year 1777, I have not seen so fair a prospect.*

Brigadier General Arnold had, within a week of his defection,
already outlined for Sir Henry, according to Robertson, a bold plan:
"He proposes driving the Congress from Philadelphia, destroying
the [military] stores there and the ships in the [Delaware] River, and
afterwards, by occupying the ground between the Head of Elk [at
the northern tip of Chesapeake Bay] and Newcastle [Delaware], to
purchase or bring away a sufficient of cattle, forage and provision
for our army."[39] It was the first of many proposals with which Arnold, whose first thought it was to take his revenge on Congress,
would bombard Clinton. Clinton, more melancholy than ever now
without André, said little and sat on his hands. Later, in his memoirs, he claimed the idea as his own.

What Arnold could not have known from the outside was that
most of the British generals and Loyalist leaders he found in New
York City were as contentious, jealous, and indolent as the American officers and politicians who had so exasperated him and driven
him to change sides. But it would be months before he would notice
anything wrong from his point of view, his days were so taken up
with top-level meetings and chores. Living temporarily at the royal
governor's residence at Fort George, at the foot of Manhattan, Arnold wrote to Lord George Germain, secretary of state for the colonies, seeking the king's pardon for his years as a rebellious subject.
The two generals were scribbling away in the same room on October 6 while the packet boat waited. With it, Arnold enclosed a
detailed report, "The Present State of the American Rebel Army,
Navy and Finances." It opened with a familiar Arnold refrain—
"Conscious of the rectitude of my intentions (whatever construction
may have been put on my conduct)"—and explained why he had
waited so long to seek the king's clemency—he had wanted to demonstrate "my zeal by an act which, had it succeeded as intended,
must have immediately terminated the unnatural convulsions that

have so long distracted the Empire." There was a jealousy, Arnold wrote, between the Congress and the army. "Many of the best officers of the army have resigned and others are daily following their example through disgust, necessity and a conviction that the provinces will not be able to establish their independence." By May 1780 the Continental paper dollar had sunk to a 900 exchange rate against silver or gold: "The treasury is entirely empty and the finances are at the lowest ebb."[40] The royal governor had also stopped the city's printing presses while Arnold wrote a proclamation explaining his change of sides, published in an extra edition by Rivington's *Royal Gazette* on October 9, the day Arnold, in his new red uniform, was announced as a British general and congratulated by Clinton, his generals, and ranking Loyalists at a parade at Fort George.

Benedict Arnold's newspaper proclamation "To the Inhabitants of America" was vintage Arnold with an overlay of the Loyalist thinking of Chief Justice Smith, who helped him rewrite two drafts. "When I quitted domestic happiness for the perils of the field," he began, almost word for word repeating the opening speech of his court-martial, "I conceived the rights of my country in danger, and that duty and honor called me to her defense." He had considered the war "a defensive one until the French joined in the combination." Arnold had come to oppose strongly "the insidious offers of France." It was "infinitely wiser and safer to cast my confidence upon [British] justice and generosity than to trust a monarchy too feeble to establish your independency, so perilous to her distant dominions, the enemy of the Protestant faith, and fraudulently avowing an affection for the liberties of mankind while she holds her native sons in vassalage and chains." Arnold's attack on the French, which preceded the French Revolution by less than ten years, came after he had lived and worked at close quarters with aristocratic French officers and diplomats in Philadelphia and after he had seen the French seignorial system at close range during the Quebec invasion of 1775–76.

But Arnold's political prose could not change the nature of his proclamation. He was trying to justify his treason in the eyes of all Americans, his delay in changing sides to the Loyalists now surrounding him. "I affect no disguise," he wrote. "I had determined to retain my arms and command for an opportunity to surrender them to Great Britain. . . . I was only solicitous to accomplish an event of decisive importance and to prevent, as much as possible in the execution of it, the effusion of blood." As a British general, he could assure "my old fellow-soldiers" that Great Britain intended to give

Americans "the rights and privileges of colonies unimpaired together with perpetual exemption from taxation." Arnold argued that it was futile to go on fighting for "much less than the parent country is willing to grant her colonies." He was acutely aware that many Americans were saying that he had quit the American cause too soon. There were some Americans "whom I believe serve blindly but honestly in the cause I left. . . . I pray God to give them all the lights requisite to their own safety before it is too late." Arnold declared that he was now dedicating himself "to the reunion of the British Empire as the best and only means to dry up the streams of misery that have deluged this country." But there would be those who censured him: "They may be assured that, conscious of the rectitude of my intentions, I shall treat their malice and calumnies with contempt and neglect."⁴¹

It was also characteristic of Arnold that as soon as he donned his new uniform and declared himself ready to fight, he presented a bill for his service and then haggled about it. More than ten years later he would still be trying to get Clinton to agree to his original demand: £20,000 if he succeeded, £10,000 if he failed. He admitted that André had assured him at Haverstraw Bay that he would receive only £6,000 indemnity if the plot was discovered. But only two weeks after André's execution, Arnold wrote a letter to the inconsolable Clinton, insisting he still wanted £10,000:

*I have every reason to believe the step which I have taken . . . [will] promote his Majesty's service more effectually than an expenditure of a like sum could possibly have done in any other way. . . . When you consider the sacrifices I have made . . . the sum is a trifling object to the public though of consequence to me, who have a large family that look up to me for support and protection.*⁴²

Clinton refused to allow more than the £6,000 André had promised, plus £350 for "expenses." In 1990 U.S. purchasing power, Arnold was paid, on October 18, 1780, roughly $381,000. As a brigadier, he also received £650 a year, and a £225 annual pension for life, amounting to another $360,000 in 1990 terms, in all $741,000 in modern terms. He had walked away from property worth more than the £6,350 and twice that amount in debts and back pay. But he was alive, a British general, and, to some Loyalists and British officers, a harbinger of hope. His change of allegiance brought him more money than any other American officer earned from the war. And when he went house-hunting in crowded, overpriced Manhattan, he rented one of the finest townhouses in the city at 3 Broadway, op-

posite Bowling Green Park, conspicuously next door to British headquarters.

Peggy Arnold reached her father's house in Philadelphia just in time
for the humiliating, terrifying spectacle of her husband's effigy being
jounced in a wagon over the cobblestones of Second Street to the
cheers and jeers of a mob. Only days later, she and her father would
pore over the wording of her husband's "Address to the Inhabitants
of America" in the *Pennsylvania Packet*. By the time she arrived, her
father's house had already been ransacked in a search for Arnold's
papers: on September 27, the Pennsylvania council, on learning of
Arnold's "having joined the enemy," ordered the city sheriff "to
make a diligent search"[43] for Arnold's papers. One letter was found
which linked Peggy to John André, his August 16, 1779, note to her
offering "to become useful to you here," on the surface an offer to
smuggle to her "capwire, needles and gauze."[44] The letter found its
way to the desk of President Reed, and, on September 30, an anonymous article in Reed's unmistakable style warned about the dangers
of ignoring the importance of women in the city's politics. The
writer urged that women who plotted with the enemy should be
"despised and banished" for "revelling with the murderers and plun-
derers of their countrymen."[45] To the horror of Peggy's family, the
public considered André's note to Peggy "the beginning of a correspondence" leading up to the treason. Peggy's brother-in-law, Neddy
Burd, responded:

*The family say there has been no other letter by her either before or
since, but the letter is an unfortunate one, coming from the very man
who, I will not say corrupted Arnold (because I believe him capable
of the worst actions a man can commit), but who was connected
with him in the horrid plot. The impossibility of so delicate and
timorous a girl as poor Peggy being in the least privy or concerned
in so bold and adventurous a plan is great. . . . It is not possible she
should have engaged in such a wicked one.*

Completely taken in, Colonel Burd misinterpreted Peggy. To him, it
was utterly impossible that "a girl of the most refined feelings, of the
most affectionate disposition," could plot treason. But Burd was
himself sensitive enough to see that Arnold's disgrace had affected
Peggy "in a very extraordinary manner. . . . She keeps her room and
is almost continually on the bed. Her peace of mind seems to me
entirely destroyed." As rumors spread that Peggy was to be banished
from Philadelphia, Burd observed that "if Mrs. Arnold should be

sent off to her base husband, it will be a heart-breaking thing. I am not without hopes she will be permitted to stay."[46] Menacing crowds continued to mill outside Judge Shippen's house as the judge petitioned the council to allow his daughter to stay, promising that Peggy would not write to Arnold and securing her promise in writing. But Reed was adamant. Peggy might try to correspond surreptitiously with Arnold in New York. On October 27, one month after Peggy left West Point, the council passed a resolution banishing her. Peggy Arnold's "residence in this city has become dangerous to the public safety," the council declared, resolving "that the said Margaret Arnold depart this state within fourteen days . . . and that she do not return again during the continuance of the present war."[47]

When the time came for Peggy and her baby to leave, it was Judge Shippen who accompanied them as far as he could, riding glumly across New Jersey with her to the British outpost at Paulus Hook. On November 18, the *Royal Gazette* announced: "On Tuesday last [the 14th] arrived in town the lady and son of Brigadier General Arnold."[48]

As soon as she learned that Peggy was to be banished, Hannah Arnold left Philadelphia, even before Peggy. She took seven-year-old Henry, Arnold's youngest son by his first wife, back to their New Haven house, where the older boys, Benedict, now thirteen, and Richard, ten, were sent to her, not to their father, from Maryland. They would remain with her for the rest of the war. On November 30, 1780, Arnold's oldest son, Benedict was commissioned as an ensign on the muster rolls of the 16th Regiment of the British army, a piece of generosity arranged by Sir Henry Clinton. And in October 1781, Richard, then twelve, and Henry, nine, were also given commissions as lieutenants of cavalry in Arnold's new provincial regiment. All three received not only their salaries during the war— which Arnold transmitted to Hannah to help provide for their support—but lifelong half-pay pensions after the war. Under the British system, they were entitled to their pay from the time of their commissioning, even if they never stepped into British uniforms or served a day with their regiments, on the basis that they would one day take up their positions as officer.

His family provided for, Arnold was, by mid-October, busy recruiting his new Loyalist regiment, the American Legion, its ranks made up entirely of deserters from the Continental Army who answered his "Address to the Inhabitants." Washington categorized Arnold's appeal to the Continental Army an "unparalleled piece of assurance. . . . I am at a loss which to admire most, the confidence

of Arnold in publishing, or the folly of the enemy in supposing that
a production signed by so infamous a character will have any weight
with the people of these states, or any influence upon our affairs
abroad."⁴⁹ Yet, Arnold continued to recruit officers in New York
City and from Loyalist camps on Long Island. More Americans may
have changed sides, but Clinton had so thoroughly fortified New
York City that it was all but impossible to desert to it. Arnold's
recruits included one German baron (Arnold signed him up as a captain of cavalry), one member of the Livingston family (Gilbert R.),
one Connecticut Yankee who had served in both armies, 212 enlisted men, all deserters from the Continental Army (full regimental
strength was 684), and several sergeants, including Sergeant Major
John Champe of the Virginia Light Horse. Arnold's initial success in
setting up a new strike force of cavalry and light horse may have had
some bearing on Washington's decision, suggested by his best cavalry officer, Light Horse Harry Lee, to have Arnold assassinated.

On the moonless night of October 20, 1780, big, powerful Sergeant Major John Champe of Lee's Light Horse Corps rode quickly
past the Continental Army guard post at Totowa, New Jersey, and
headed toward Bergen. He rode all night, narrowly outracing an
American patrol, which hurried back to camp to report his desertion. There, Major Lee stalled them. He had personally chosen the
twenty-three-year-old Champe, a fellow Virginia gentleman, for his
"uncommon taciturnity and inflexible perseverance." He had called
in the dumbfounded sergeant major and told him he was to desert to
the British, enlist in Arnold's American Legion, and "insinuate himself" as close to Arnold as possible. Lee, who was active in Washington's secret service, would put him in touch with American
operatives inside New York City. They would help him kidnap Arnold and bring him by boat to New Jersey, where he would be
hanged by Washington.

Champe hesitated, not at kidnapping Arnold, but at deserting.
Lee offered him a promotion if he succeeded and promised to clear
his name if he failed. Lee wrote Washington that he had undertaken
"the accomplishment of your Excellency's wishes. . . . In my nega-
tion I have said little or nothing concerning your Excellency, as I
presume it would operate disagreeably should the issue prove disastrous." Champe would work with an agent named Baldwin from
Newark, who would be paid "one hundred guineas, five hundred
acres of land, and three Negroes." Champe would also need "a few
guineas" for expenses. Washington quickly approved the plan "with
the express stipulation and printed injunction that he, A——d, is
brought to me alive. No circumstance whatever shall attain my con-

sent to his being put to death. My aim is to make a public example of him." Washington enclosed five gold guineas for Champe, but warned against "appearing with much specie," since it was "too well known to the enemy that we do not abound in that article."[50]

On the morning of October 21, Sergeant Champe struggled through the salt marsh south of Paulus Hook and, a knapsack on his back, plunged into the water as Lee's dragoons overtook his horse. A vigilant British officer offshore, realizing an American was trying to desert, raked the dragoons with buckshot while a boat crew picked up Champe. He arrived in Manhattan on Saturday and was held at the Provost Jail until Monday, when he was taken to head-quarters. He was interrogated for two hours, Sir Henry joining his staff officers toward the end. Champe told them what they wanted to hear: rations were scanty, the soldiers didn't like the French. Clinton tipped the man two gold guineas for his desertion and tried to enlist him in the British army. Champe said it would add to his risk of being hanged as a deserter: he would take his chances finding a job in New York City. In less than an hour, Champe "accidentally" ran into Arnold on the street. The sergeant was still wearing the uniform of his elite unit and was sure to catch Arnold's eye. Arnold liked the soft-spoken, earnest young man, especially after Champe told him that Arnold's desertion had inspired his own. Arnold took Champe to buy him a drink and offered him the same rank, that of highest-ranking noncommissioned officer in his American Legion. Champe signed up.

As Arnold's senior noncom, Champe had access to the Arnolds' handsome townhouse, across from Bowling Green near the city's southern tip. On the north side of Arnold's house was a large, fenced-in garden running all the way down to the rocky Hudson shoreline. Rimming the north side of the garden, just across the fence, was a seldom-used alleyway which also ran down to the water's edge. Over the next several weeks, Champe frequently vis-ited Arnold's house and observed his schedule, his habits. He dis-covered it was Benedict Arnold's invariable habit to end his day by taking a stroll at midnight before going to bed, ending it with a visit to the outhouse before going indoors. As he watched Arnold for several nights from the alley, Champe worked loose three or four fence palings and replaced them. Late at night, he and Baldwin could slip through the fence, down the alley, and around the dark-ened headquarters to a waiting boat. They notified Major Lee that they would kidnap Arnold the night of December 11 and that the dragoons should be ready on the Jersey shore to take him to Wash-ington.

*   *   *

The publication of Arnold's self-justification and recruiting posters also earned him enemies within British ranks. Some officers already despised him for not offering himself in the place of their young friend André, even if Clinton would not permit such an exchange. Others, like retired Captain Archibald Kennedy, whose splendid Georgian mansion was serving as British headquarters, wondered "what benefit has this country derived from the treachery of that wretch—one Arnold—that he should thus triumph and flourish amidst British and American ruin and be caressed by an —— King, while those who have sacrificed so much to real loyalty are rotting in jail or pining in penury?" It offended many career British officers that the erstwhile rebel should even have "superiority over a German corporal." Kennedy spoke for them and for a considerable number of Loyalists when he wrote, "We have lost our honor with an empire, and we have gained—an Arnold!" Kennedy was not the only Loyalist who asked, if not in so many words, "Was it pure zeal of an honest convert or filthy lucre that instigated your savage soul to such horrid unnatural barbarity?"[51]

Not everyone at the full-dress review was cheering for Arnold. There were two major Loyalist factions: the Whig Loyalists, who believed the war could still be settled by political reconciliation; and the High Tory, Anglican, military party, who wanted to win the war first and then work out a political settlement. Arnold joined neither camp deliberately, but by his choice of friends blundered into the Whig Loyalist faction. Like Justice Smith and Sir Henry Clinton, he stopped short of an all-out war that would destroy America. He wanted to destroy its supply bases and its transportation and make it impossible for the radical revolutionaries to go on fighting. Most American soldiers, he believed, remained in the Continental Army only to avoid sacrificing years of back pay, pensions, and land grants from Congress. Almost as soon as he deserted the Americans, Arnold went over Sir Henry's head to London, proposing that Continental soldiers be offered their back pay in gold to join the British standard. This scheme went unanswered, only earning him the displeasure of Clinton for writing secretly to London.

Arnold was bound to encounter enmity, Admiral Rodney wrote from the West Indies to Secretary of State Germain. "Believe me, my Lord, this man Arnold, with whom I had many conferences, will do more towards the suppressing the rebellion than all our generals together." But, added Rodney, "Jealousy, my Lord, unless commands from home signify his Majesty's pleasure, will prevent Arnold being long employed to advantage."[52]

While senior officers were civil to Arnold if not all that friendly, lower-ranking officers shunned him. "General Arnold is a very unpopular character in the British Army," wrote one officer six weeks after Arnold's arrival in New York, "nor can all the patronage he meets with from the commander-in-chief procure him respectability. The subaltern officers have conceived such an aversion to him that they unanimously refused to serve under his command, and the detachment he is to lead was, on this account, officered from the Loyal American Corps [Colonel Beverley Robinson's Loyalist regiment]."

Arnold did not mince words to win friends. He spoke "handsomely" of Washington and many American officers, with the exception of Gates. "He does not scruple to mention the inactivity of our army at certain periods in former campaigns," wrote George Damier to Lord Germain, "and in this he very strongly expressed his astonishment, upon his arrival, at our not having attacked the French upon their disembarking at Rhode Island."[53]

If Arnold could not win the respect of Loyalists and young British officers by defection or proclamation, then he would by his deeds in a British uniform. At first, it appeared that Clinton was more than happy to make Arnold his strong right fist, not only to attack the French, but his rivals. Embroiled in a feud with Lord Cornwallis, whom he had left to command in the South, Clinton rejected Arnold's plan for an attack on Philadelphia and instead ordered him to the South on a diversionary raid. A recent American victory at King's Mountain in the North Carolina highlands had cost one thousand Loyalist troops, forcing Cornwallis to draw back toward his Charleston base and giving fresh hope to the Americans. As Washington sent his trusted second-in-command, Greene, south with a strong Continental detachment, Clinton countered by dispatching Arnold to Virginia. With a select army-navy task force, Arnold was to destroy badly needed American supply bases and thus force Greene to withdraw to Virginia, easing pressure on Cornwallis in the Carolinas. Arnold then was to build up a permanent Loyalist base on the Virginia coast. Along with Arnold's American Legion, he sent the Loyalist Lieutenant Colonel John Graves Simcoe and his elite Virginia-born Queen's Rangers, who had killed or captured twice their number during four years of bitter fighting, with British Lieutenant Colonel Thomas Dundas and his Royal Edinburgh Volunteers and some Hessians. Arnold was in command of the sixteen-hundred-man expeditionary force, but he was ordered to consult Dundas and Simcoe, his subordinates, on "any operation of consequence." Unknown to Arnold, Clinton issued both officers a blank dormant commission in the event of his "death or incapacity. . . .

You are upon no account to make known that you are possessed of such a commission."[54]

On December 11, 1780, the very night of the planned kidnapping of Arnold, Arnold ordered his troops, including Sergeant Major John Champe, aboard ships for the expedition to the James River. Champe had no choice but to go along or be arrested for insubordination; his co-conspirator Baldwin was left behind; Lee's dragoons waited in the cold all night in the Hoboken woods. Champe marched with Arnold as he pillaged Champe's native Virginia and fought Virginia troops, including his own outfit, which was sent to pursue Arnold. It was several weeks before Champe dared to desert again.

Itching to avenge the hanging of ten Loyalists who had surrendered at King's Mountain, Arnold's Loyalist legion arrived off the Chesapeake Capes on January 1, 1781. Fully one-third of the troops were left behind on troop transports scattered by a wild snowstorm at sea. After two weeks at sea, most of the rest of the men were sick, half of the horses were dead. But Arnold was an old hand at winter warfare, and he reasoned, as he had at Quebec, that surprise, not numbers, was all-important. For the three days, Governor Jefferson refused to believe reports of the invasion and delayed calling out the state militia. Meanwhile, Arnold sailed seventy miles up the James River with two ships, the sloop-of-war *Swift* and the transport *Hope,* eluding a "brisk fire" at Hood's Fort, which he paused long enough to capture. Putting his sickest men ashore at Westover at three on the afternoon of January 4 in a heavy rain, he marched the rest of the thirty-three miles overland, pushing them all night. "No time was to be lost," he reported to Clinton.

Reaching Richmond at eleven the morning of January 5 "without opposition," he took the rebel capital by complete surprise. "The militia which had collected fled at our advance." Jefferson and his council fled so quickly that they left behind many of the state records. Establishing headquarters at City Tavern on Main Street, Arnold offered to spare the capital if Jefferson consented to let the British ships remove all the stored goods, especially the valuable tobacco. According to Arnold's report, recently discovered in the British Headquarters Papers, there were "thirty to forty ships full of tobacco, West Indies goods, wines, sailcloth." Arnold said he offered to pay half price for them, especially since many of the ships were owned by Loyalists, but local merchants needed "the approbation of the nominal governor," Jefferson. Arnold gave them "until the next morning to obtain an answer from Mr. Jefferson, who was in the neighborhood." But Jefferson could not be found. "As Mr. Jefferson was so inattentive to the preservation of private property, I found myself under the disagreeable necessity of ordering a large quantity of rum to be [staved in], several warehouses of salt to be destroyed, several public warehouses and smith's shops with their contents consumed by the flames." Arnold insisted that he only set fire to public property—powder magazines, a sailcloth factory—but that a rising wind had spread the fire accidentally: "a printing press and types were purified by the flames." Arnold's legionnaires stripped the tobacco warehouses first, rolling the huge hogsheads to their fleet of ten captured ships and thirty-four open boats. Then Arnold set fire to the warehouses, sparing those that were owned by Loyalists. He also issued passes for Loyalists to escape with shiploads of wine.

Detaching Simcoe's Queen's Rangers seven miles up the James to Westham, Arnold ordered cannon foundry and warehouses of small arms and gunpowder destroyed. "They burnt and destroyed one of the finest foundries for cannon in America," Arnold reported, listing the destruction of twenty-six cannons, 310 barrels of gunpowder, and several warehouses of oats; the gunpowder was rolled down to cliffs and dumped into the river. The nearby town of Chesterfield, its warehouses, mills and clothing depot, also burned that night. The work of plundering exhausted Arnold's troops, who had neither slept nor eaten in two days, but Arnold refused to let them stop. Richmond was still burning when Arnold's legion trudged east toward their ships in the pouring rain. Nine raiders dropped out, fell asleep, were never seen alive again. Arnold force-marched his men thirteen miles before he allowed them to stop. After allowing them six hours' sleep, he led them on to their new base at Portsmouth on Albemarle Sound the next day. He proudly reported that he had marched his men sixty-six miles in three days "with ardor and firmness."[55] Clinton had given him positive orders to go to Portsmouth to reinforce Leslie and avoid any unnecessary risks: the raids on Richmond, Westham, and Chesterfield had been his own idea, giving both sides a taste of the kind of warfare he advocated. Now he reluctantly followed Clinton's orders and dug in at Portsmouth on the coast.

There was a deeper reason for Arnold's discontent at garrison duty. He knew that his raid had stirred a swarm of Virginians, who now joined Baron von Steuben and Lafayette, dispatched by Washington to the South. Arnold was all too aware how isolated and vulnerable he was. One British army historian has said that "Clinton, by setting him down permanently in isolation with a mere handful of men, was giving him as a hostage to fortune."[56]

The American noose slowly closed in around the neck of land

which Arnold was fortifying. Governor Jefferson, as an incentive to sharpshooting Virginians, offered a 5,000-guinea reward in gold for Arnold's capture. Washington wrote orders for Lafayette to hang Arnold summarily when he captured him. The timing of Arnold's invasion of Virginia had been crucial. It came while the Pennsylvania troops of the Continental Line were mutinying about Congress's failure to pay them. They finally agreed to accept $750 in Continental dollars for each dollar in back pay owed them. When New Jersey Continentals mutinied two weeks later, Washington ordered them attacked by loyal troops from West Point. Their camp was taken by surprise and two of their leaders were shot by firing squads. The revolt was smashed, but more than one thousand Continental troops went home. Once again, the British failed to exploit this grave American crisis; once again, Washington, this time with the aid of his French allies, took advantage of Clinton's vacillation. Luck also intervened. The British fleet, half-wrecked by another winter storm, now let the French slip out of the Rhode Island blockade and sail for the Chesapeake. But the French prepared for sea so slowly, not sailing until March 8, that even the lethargic British Admiral Arbuthnot had time to stir, warning Clinton that "the blow meditating against General Arnold is of a deadly aspect."[57] Hanging on coolly with an emaciated force, Arnold waited for reinforcements. Rochambeau, the French commander in chief, wrote Washington that Arnold had told his troops that he would never be taken alive.

Benedict Arnold's last stand did not materialize. The British squadron that intercepted the French on March 16 forced them back to Rhode Island. Ten days later, British transports carrying two thousand redcoats arrived at Portsmouth under the command of Clinton's closest friend, Major General Phillips, who had faced Arnold at Saratoga. Arnold turned over the command to his old enemy.

All that last spring of the war, Arnold was back where he was happiest, fighting and maneuvering in the post of honor, second in command. He got along well with Phillips, as he often did with senior officers, and was at times allowed to command Phillips's army. Phillips died of a fever on May 12. For eight days, Arnold was again in command, despite the grumbling of British officers who hated to serve under him, some of them circulating rumors that Arnold had poisoned Phillips. On May 20, Lord Cornwallis arrived and took over the force. He came just in time: Colonel Dundas wrote to Clinton on the day of Phillips's death that while Arnold's "abilities and inclination" were not in question, "there are many officers who must wish some other general in command."[58] It is one of the more tantalizing questions in history whether the British, had they been willing to serve under a less-than-popular Arnold instead of Cornwallis, would have marched so happily to disaster in Yorktown only a few months later. When Cornwallis and Arnold conferred, Arnold urged him not to fortify the indefensible spit of land at Yorktown but, if he must have a permanent base in Virginia, let it be far up the James River, at Richmond, and out of reach of the French fleet. Cornwallis ignored him.

Arnold was ordered back to New York City in late June 1781 by Clinton, who was once again toying with the idea of sending him to attack West Point. To his new friend, Justice Smith, Arnold confided that he was "disgusted" with Clinton's inactivity. Four days after he landed, Arnold had proposed leading fifteen hundred men to the head of the Chesapeake to link up with Cornwallis and attack Philadelphia. Arnold had argued to Clinton that they should strike now and destroy American supply bases, crippling the rebels' economy, making them sue for peace. Smith recorded that Arnold said that by this time he could have "ousted the Congress at Philadelphia." What Arnold failed to realize was that Clinton's "jealousy is on fire." Clinton, too, was calling at Justice Smith's house to complain about Arnold, who was now on the long list of Clinton's enemies for daring to go over his head to London with a rash of proposals to win the war. On August 1, Arnold rode around the corner to Justice Smith's again. "General Arnold," Smith wrote, "despairs from the defect of a spirit of enterprise and indecision [in Clinton]. He can get nothing done. He is desirous to go Home. . . . Sir Henry is all mystery, seems to approve but changes, and resolves nothing."[59]

Whatever finally persuaded Clinton to do something with his restless brigadier, he approved one of the many raids proposed by Arnold—on the Connecticut naval privateering base at New London, at the mouth of the Thames River Valley, where Benedict Arnold had been born. Since his defection, Arnold had been prodding Clinton to turn him loose with a small joint army-navy task force to raid and destroy American supply and shipping bases along the seacoast from Boston to Philadelphia. It was typical of Clinton's erratic behavior and that of other British generals during the Revolution that he chose this moment to divide his forces and, instead of reinforcing a rival in trouble, sent Arnold north to sack New London, the largest seaport in Connecticut, rather than south to cooperate with the hard-pressed Cornwallis at Yorktown. Arnold's 1,732-man force attacked New London on September 4, the very day that Rochambeau and his French army slipped past Clinton's

main army and marched through Philadelphia on their way to join
Washington's attack at Yorktown.

Arriving off New London Lighthouse shortly after dawn, Arnold's
flotilla sailed up into the Thames estuary. Arnold split his force into
two divisions to attack New London and Groton. For years, New
London had boomed as the main American privateering port. Nearly
five hundred British ships and their cargoes had been towed in and
sold, as rich prizes of war. It had also served as the base for bloody
raids on Loyalist forts and refugee camps across the Sound on Long
Island. Many of the troops Arnold took with him were Connecticut
Loyalist refugees. Under Arnold's personal command on the New
London side of the Thames were one redcoat British regiment, the
38th; Beverley Robinson's Loyal Americans; 120 Loyalist Associators from Long Island; Arnold's American Legion; and 140 German jaegers, who hit the beach first. Arnold had given strict orders
that only military targets were to be attacked: his orders were to
seize and destroy American privateering ships (there were thirty-
three in the harbor at the time) and destroy supply depots, docks,
and the three forts guarding the harbor.

To march up the valley and attack the strongest fort, he had
given the command on the Groton side to Lieutenant Colonel Edmund Eyre, commander of the 40th Regiment, a veteran of five years
of heavy fighting in the Revolution: his troops had stormed and
taken Fort Washington in 1776 and held out against the entire
American army at the Chew House during the Battle of Germantown. Also following Eyre that day was the 3rd Battalion of the
Loyalist New Jersey Volunteers; many of their comrades had been
killed or captured at Kings Mountain. Arnold's attack on his Connecticut neighbors was as savage as any fighting in the American
Revolution. The devastation, the ruthless, total, modern warfare,
that he had once wrought on distant enemies in Canada he now
brought home to the beautiful river valley where he had grown up,
where only a year before one of his own ships had ridden at anchor.
Marching up steep Town Hill Road to the center of New London,
Arnold encountered little resistance. The commander of the local
militia, claiming a violent headache, refused to rally his men, who
mostly stayed out of gunshot range. About one hundred leaderless
Yankees decided to get the best shot at the enemy each man could.
Arnold's main column was guided by Captain Frink, whose sister,
Lucy, lived in the town; he attacked Fort Trumbull, one of two bas-
tions on the New London side, from the rear, while its guns pointed
aimlessly out at the river. Its twenty-three defenders fled after a sin-

gle volley. At the same time, Arnold's force charged Town Hill Fort. From the fort, twelve-pound cannonballs were fired at the British. They fell short, hitting American militia.

It was nearly noon before Arnold worked his way to the top of the town hill and could look out over the valley through his spyglass. Across the river, on a high slope, sat squat Fort Griswold between the fleet of American privateersmen and Norwich Town, upriver. As the Yankee mariners slipped their anchors and set their sails to escape, Arnold, who had no authorization to besiege a strong fort, ordered Colonel Eyre to storm Fort Griswold and turn its guns on the American ships to prevent their escape. Arnold may have been led to believe by Loyalist spies that the fort was only lightly defended, but that is not what he now could see through his spyglass. What he saw was a strong, square fort with bastioned corners that could use its cannon to enfilade assault troops in a deadly crossfire as they approached its abatis of sharpened tree branches and its deep-ditch, which had been picketed with a high stockade fence, even before they reached the fort's high stone walls, which were bustling with twenty-two heavy cannon. Arnold had come to seize ships and destroy supplies. He could see that the privateers were slipping safely past his field pieces, which had been deployed too slowly. He sent a second order to Eyre, a countermand calling off the assault. Expecting his orders to be heeded, he rode back down into New London to personally supervise his torch squads.

But Arnold's countermand did not reach Colonel Eyre in time. With 850 crack troops, Eyre moved quickly up the riverbank, quick-marching three miles to within musket range of the fort. He sent an aide, Captain George Beckwith, to "summon" its surrender. Inside Fort Griswold, Lieutenant Colonel William Ledyard had only 140 men, including fifteen-year-old boys and old men, and only three experienced gunners. His call for trained gunners and crews from the privateering fleet had been largely ignored as the merchant mariners tried to save their own ships. Continental officers home on leave were also inside the fort. They urged Ledyard to abandon it. There were major gaps in the abatis; the gun platforms were rotten; there was little gunpowder. But Ledyard had been promised a regiment of militia in case of attack, and he decided to hold out. He rejected the summons to surrender. Beckwith went back to Eyre, who sent him up once again under a white flag. Unless the fort was surrendered at once, Eyre would invoke martial law and could deny quarter to prisoners. Ledyard again refused.

Attacking Fort Griswold on three sides, British redcoats and Loyalist greens climbed up on their comrades' backs to rip down the picket fencing while the Americans crossfired down on them and poured in cannon fire at close range that sheared their ranks, filling the ditch with 140 dead and wounded British assault troops, including the mortally wounded Colonel Eyre.

Withdrawing with their wounded, the British opened fire with field pieces at long range while they regrouped. One cannon shot cut the lanyard holding the American flag. Thinking the fort had struck its colors, the British ran toward its walls, cheering, only to be cut down again by gunfire. Outraged by what they thought was American duplicity, the British surged through a gap in the picket fence. The first officer through was the second-in-command, Major Montgomery, who was instantly killed by a spear. The British fought hand to hand with sailors wielding boarding pikes in one of the bloodiest and most gruesome episodes of the deteriorating civil war. After forty minutes of fierce fighting, Colonel Ledyard, his garrison outnumbered six to one, half a dozen of his men already dead and a score badly wounded, gave the order to cease firing, but enraged British and Loyalist soldiers ignored their junior officers and kept firing. At that moment, Lieutenant Colonel Abraham Van Buskirk of the New Jersey Loyalist Volunteers demanded, "Who commands this garrison?" "I did, sir, but you do now,"[60] responded Ledyard, turning his sword and presenting its hilt toward Van Buskirk just as British soldiers ran up and bayonetted him. It was several minutes before the British and Loyalists stopped killing. In all, eighty-eight Americans lay dead in the blood and mud, thirty-five more were badly wounded—113 casualties out of 140 men. Preparing to blow up the powder magazine and withdraw, the British piled eight of the worst-wounded revolutionaries into an ammunition wagon. On a steep slope, the wagon got away from them, cascaded two hundred yards down the hillside, and crashed into a tree stump, spilling shrieking wounded onto the ground.

Across the river in New London, having dispatched his order to Eyre but not waiting to learn if it had been carried out, Benedict Arnold was busy destroying all military targets, attempting to enforce his strict order against looting. As he led his column into the center of New London, the streets were thronged with fleeing women and children. In the confusion, a crowd of local ruffians, thirty to forty "shabby looking fellows," as one New Londoner put it, passed by, shouting, "By God, we'll have fine plunder," and headed for waterfront warehouses recently stuffed with goods captured in the West Indies. The eyewitness climbed a fence as the street mob, taking advantage of the pandemonium of the invasion, "loaded themselves with plunder and scamp[ered] off."[61] But not all the invaders followed Arnold's anti-looting order, either: one Hessian so loaded himself down with the plunder of houses, "three small pieces of Holland [linen], a small piece of scarlet broadcloth, a Common Prayer book, a checked linen handkerchief, a comb, a pair of scissors, sundry articles of plate and jewelry and an American flag"[62]—that he was easily overtaken and captured.

Following Connecticut Loyalist guides, Arnold's torch parties set fire to preselected targets. On Post Hill, a party of Association Volunteers torched the house of militia Captain Picket Lattimer. The incendiary squad was led by Yale graduate and former New Haven magistrate Daniel Lyman, whose sister lived in New London and was married to the Connecticut assistant commissary general (whose house also was burned). The Association Volunteers burned the town mill and the printing office, then hurried on to burn all but one house in the Winthrop's Neck section. Moving south along Main Street, the Loyalist torch squads paid calls on the home, two stores, shop, and barn of the revolutionary general Gurdon Saltonstall. Down along Bank and Water streets, Arnold personally gave the orders to burn a dozen ships at their moorings. Unknown to Arnold, one of them contained a large amount of gunpowder. Arnold later reported to Clinton, "The explosion of the powder and change of wind, soon after the stores were fired, communicated the flames to part of the town, which was, notwithstanding every effort to prevent it, unfortunately destroyed."[63]

By the time Arnold and his troops withdrew in midafternoon to catch the tide, half of New London's shipping had been destroyed, along with 151 buildings, including sixty-five houses, thirty-seven stores, eighteen shops, twenty barns, nine public buildings, the Anglican church, and the market wharf and main warehouses. One estimate of damage ran to $485,980. Ninety-seven families were left homeless, and four New Londoners were killed and a dozen wounded, in addition to 113 revolutionaries killed or wounded at Fort Griswold.

When Arnold reported to Sir Henry Clinton back in New York City, Clinton praised him for his "very spirited conduct" but complained about the heavy British losses. Of British and Loyalist troops engaged in the actual fighting at Fort Griswold, one in four was killed or wounded, one of the highest British casualty rates of the war. At this rate, Clinton contended, he could afford few more of Arnold's victories. Criticism of Benedict Arnold's tactics was intermixed with jealousy over his latest conquests in Virginia and Connecticut, which reached a crescendo in late 1781 as rumors spread that the spoils of his raids had made him "rich as a nabob."[64]

Actually, Arnold received £2,000 as the commanding officer's share of the prize money from seizing ten ships and tobacco in Virginia. The award was made after the Royal Navy claimed the prize money, abrogating a verbal agreement with Arnold to split fifty-fifty. An admiralty court eventually awarded half of the spoils to the king and ordered the navy to honor its agreement. The court awarded Arnold one-eighth of the army's half-share. While this was enough to make many British officers jealous, the award was typical of the prize system of the times, where seized goods were auctioned off and the proceeds distributed as a bonus to the low military pay scale.

News now arrived in New York that the king had awarded a £500 pension to Peggy Arnold at Clinton's suggestion. The royal pension was "obtained for her services" in the West Point plot "which were very meritorious."[65]

By October 2, 1781, when Sir Henry belatedly decided to lead a relief force south to Yorktown, Justice Smith, probably at Arnold's instigation, urged Clinton to allow Arnold to lead a diversionary raid on Congress in Philadelphia which would force Washington to back away from the Yorktown siege. On October 7, after being called in by Clinton to discuss the attack, Arnold wrote a convincing memorandum that three thousand troops could be spared to raid Philadelphia without unduly weakening New York City in Clinton's absence. Clinton especially wanted assurance that Arnold could destroy Philadelphia's military depots without burning the city. At first, Clinton seemed to approve, but then he complained to Justice Smith of Arnold's "writing a letter to Lord George Germain with plans of operations unknown to him [Clinton] and subversive of his intentions, and in which Arnold confessed he had done wrong."[66] Clinton never did call in Arnold to discuss any further diversionary raids. By this date in early October, Lord Cornwallis had already abandoned his outer lines at Yorktown. Two weeks later, six days before Clinton finally reached the Chesapeake, Cornwallis surrendered his southern army of nearly eight thousand men and Washington led his victorious army northward to besiege New York City.

Peggy Shippen Arnold spent the last year of the American Revolution with Arnold in New York City. Her last year in her native country was a contradictory time of hope and sadness. The Arnolds, despite all of Benedict's ruthlessness and sporadic lashing out at old and new enemies, were a serene couple. For much of the time, Peggy was pregnant with their second child, which may account for her unaccustomed reluctance to circulate in New York's opulent society, but those who knew her well attested that after André's death, she spent more and more time alone in her room, often spending many hours brooding in bed. Not that she knew many people in Manhattan: there was Becky Franks, also banished from Philadelphia, and there were a handful of other former Society Hill neighbors who kept tabs on her and wrote back news to friends in Philadelphia. Mrs. Samuel Shoemaker wrote that Peggy now "wants animation, sprightliness and fire in her eyes." That Peggy also realized more than most of the banished Loyalist ladies that she might never see her family again was enough to dim her eyes. When she did appear in public, it was as Sir Henry's new favorite at headquarters balls at One Wall Street; the Arnolds were coddled by the commander in chief and his aides. Peggy "appeared a star of the first magnitude, and had every attention paid her as if she had been Lady Clinton."[67]

One week before Arnold had sailed to attack New London, on August 29, 1781, Peggy Arnold delivered a son, James Robertson Arnold, named after Arnold's new friend the royal governor. Gossipy Mrs. Shoemaker was one of the first to spread the news when Peggy and her husband decided to leave New York City to sail to England.

As Sir Henry Clinton, back in New York City from his voyage to the Chesapeake, prepared for the siege he fully expected, Benedict Arnold determined to go to London with Cornwallis to try to win the command of a Loyalist army to fight side by side with British reinforcements under Cornwallis. Together, they wanted to wrest control of the army away from Clinton and vigorously counterattack Washington: Arnold still did not think it was too late. The Loyalists were bitter that British infighting had led to the catastrophe at Yorktown, and many of them now supported Arnold's last ditch efforts. In a series of meetings at the Whitehall Street house of Chief Justice Smith, Arnold and Loyalist leaders worked out a long series of answers to questions that Arnold could give to Parliament in the likely event he was summoned to Westminster to testify about the war. Justice Smith wrote letters of recommendation for Arnold and endorsements of his plan to Lord Amherst, General William Tryon, and Secretary of State Germain, among others. Smith hinted to Tryon, the former military governor of New York whom Arnold had fought in Connecticut, that he should use his influence to have Arnold examined by the king and by Parliament. Smith detailed Arnold's strategy in his diary:

He will concur with Lord Cornwallis in all measures of vigor. He will oppose him in his attachment to the military government. He will concur with Clinton in the call for reinforcements and the retention of New York [but] he will censure his want of enterprise.

Most of all, Arnold supported the Loyalist claims that they could, if given the chance by the army and cooperation by the navy, still "restore the King's interest in this country."[68] Arnold, according to Smith, predicted that unless he was able to stop Washington, Washington would set himself up as king of America. In Arnold's mind, given proper support, he could still suppress the American Revolution and emerge a hero. He would find a house for Peggy and the children in London, then return to America in the spring. That his fire-and-sword style of warfare was only stirring greater American resistance to the British and that the British had grown tired of the war did not deter him. Meanwhile, up the Hudson River at Washington's Newburgh headquarters, troops celebrated the victory at Yorktown by burning Benedict Arnold in effigy.

The 150-ship convoy that transported the Arnolds to England survived a stormy North Atlantic crossing. The *Robuste* sprang a leak: Arnold, Cornwallis, and their suites had to be transferred to a troop transport, the *Edward*. On Tuesday, January 22, 1782, the London *Daily Advertiser* reported the Arnolds' arrival in London on a typically rainy, windy winter day. Some American Loyalists had already gone into exile in England: Arnold's mission coupled with Peggy's beauty set Tory quills wagging. The Arnolds "have taken a house and set up a carriage."[69]

As the Arnolds settled into fashionable Portman Square, near a number of Loyalist friends, there were some discordant notes. "By all accounts," wrote one banker, "she is an amiable woman, and, was her husband dead, would be much noticed."[70] Arnold was, however, alive and noticed favorably in government circles. Secretary of State Germain received him politely at Whitehall and took a look at Clinton's letter of recommendation and at Arnold's plan for ending "the American war" in a year. Lord Amherst welcomed him warmly at the War Office. "I received notice from Lord Amherst." Arnold reported that "his Majesty wished me to return to America." It appears that Amherst was cool to the idea of making him Clinton's replacement, but "it was promised me that I could be promoted."[71] The Arnolds' warmest reception was at the Court of St. James's from King George III and Queen Charlotte. Sir Walter Stirling, a London banker and relative of the Shippens, introduced them at court. Soon, reporters covering the court noticed Benedict Arnold, the king, and the Prince of Wales strolling in St. James's Park, deep in conversation. In Paris, where American negotiators were concluding peace talks with the British, Benjamin Franklin wrote nervously, "We hear much of audiences given to Arnold, and his being present at councils."[72]

Indeed, the king's privy council, after hearing Arnold's report, considered him "a very sensible man." Queen Charlotte was especially taken with Peggy Arnold. According to one London historian, "The queen was so interested in favor of Mrs. Arnold as to desire the ladies of the court to pay much attention to her."[73] The queen supplemented her words and company with generous gifts from her own privy purse: £100 a year annuity for each of Peggy's children for life. Peggy was to raise five children; this piece of largess eventually doubled her pensions from £500 to £1,000 a year, far more than Arnold received from the crown, virtually guaranteeing that Peggy could bring up her children comfortably and with their mother's prestige alone introduce them into society as English gentry.

As the Arnolds' fortunes soared, the *Daily Advertiser* reported on February 4, 1782, that Arnold was "shortly to return back to America and to have command of the Loyalists, a prosecution of the war having been determined upon."[74] The report was erroneous and premature. For months a political crisis had been raging in London, culminating in the resignation of Lord North, Lord Germain, and their prowar party and their replacement by the antiwar Rockingham Whigs. Arnold knew he could expect little from the Whigs, who demanded an end to all offensive operations in North America and a peace treaty which granted independence to the United States. Suddenly, Arnold faced the prospect of being not a major general at the head of a great Loyalist army attacking Washington and Congress but just another British colonel on half-pay pension.

By August 1782, as peace loomed, he proposed his last scheme of the Revolution. Writing to the new secretary of state, the Earl of Shelburne, Arnold petitioned for a grant of £30,000 to build a forty-gun frigate to sail against the Americans under his own command. Now anti-Loyalist sentiment was politically acceptable: in England a torrent of invective was directed at the traitor. *Gentlemen's Magazine* anonymously quoted a peer of the realm who complained about "placing at the King's elbow a man perhaps the most obnoxious to the feelings of the Americans of any in the King's dominions at the moment the House was addressing his Majesty to put an end to the American war."[75] In the House of Commons, Edmund Burke hoped the government would not put Arnold "at the head of a part of a British army"—such a step would "afflict" the "sentiments of true honor which every British officer [holds] dearer than life."[76]

As the now unpopular war ended in British defeat, the Arnolds found themselves hissed at when they attended the theater, attacked in the Whig press. One day, as they escaped for a tranquil stroll in Westminster Abbey, they drifted into shadowy Poets' Corner and were squinting at a new cenotaph, ordered by the king: "Sacred to the memory of Major John André." They could read in the fresh-cut marble how André, "employed in an important but hazardous enterprise, fell a sacrifice to his zeal for his King and Country." No monument would ever immortalize the Arnolds' roles in this conflict. The sight of the Arnolds poring over the inscription was enough to revolt another Loyalist emigrant who was visiting the abbey. As Peter Van Schaack, a New York Loyalist lawyer, wandered down the long aisle, his musings were "interrupted by the entrance of a gentleman accompanied by a lady. It was General Arnold, and the lady was doubtless Mrs. Arnold."[77]

Even old friends publicly spurned him. Silas Deane, who had fled to England from his diplomatic post in Paris during a prolonged investigation by Congress, cut Arnold dead on the day when both turned up at the same time to pay their respects to the royal couple. Later when Arnold paid a call at Deane's boardinghouse, Deane again was icy to him before friends. He still had accounts pending before Congress and could not afford to appear friendly to the traitor. Yet secretly Deane remained Arnold's friend, often dining at the Arnolds'.

Arnold's most serious rebuff came when he applied for a post in India, where he considered joining his friend Lord Cornwallis. But Arnold's stock had sunk so low that when he applied for a post with the East India Company, he was blackballed and his letter of application was frostily returned to him by a director of the company, another Loyalist. Other Loyalists proved hostile as they published unflattering accounts of Arnold's treatment of them before he changed sides. The year 1783 brought the evacuation of 35,000 Loyalists from New York City alone, and some ninety-eight Loyalist regiments were disbanded and offered lands in British Canada. Arnold turned to the task of petitioning for money he had spent to outfit his American Legion. His letters to his old commander Clinton and to Lord Shelburne were echoes of earlier claims for pay, table allowance, and expense advances including back pay for his adolescent son, Lieutenant Henry Arnold. When Parliament approved compensation for Loyalist losses in the war, Arnold filed a voluminous claim, requesting £16,125 above and beyond the £6,365 he had received from Clinton. He claimed £5,000 for his wedding-gift house, Mount Pleasant, long since confiscated, along with two horses, a carriage, and a slave, by Pennsylvania authorities and bought back at auction for Peggy by her father. He claimed as a loss that "in consequence of his loyalty and engagements with Sir Henry Clinton he refused the command of the American Army in South Carolina, offered him by Washington, which was afterwards given to Greene, who [the memorialist is informed] has been rewarded . . . with the sum of 20,000 pounds . . . which would probably have been given to [Arnold] had he accepted the command."[78] Arnold totaled up all that he had lost with his defection and wrote his claim on the heavy, gilt-edged paper of a British general. But then on the same gilt-edged stock he wrote to the Treasury Board in April 1785 to withdraw his Loyalist claim. What Clinton had paid him was "not a full compensation for the loss of my real estate, for risks and services rendered, yet I have, upon duly considering the great expense which I shall probably incur by remaining in London to prosecute a further claim, the loss of time and difficulty attending it, though proper to withdraw my claim."[79]

Arnold spent the summer of 1785 equipping and outfitting his new ship, the brig *Lord Middlebrook,* and testifying at the Loyalist Claims Commission hearings. He helped five petitioners win their claims: Henry Reeves, a ship's captain from Virginia who had escaped from Yorktown; Nicholas Lechmere of New Haven; William Friend of Montreal (whose sloop Arnold had seized after Ethan Allen plundered it); James Tait, assistant quartermaster of the American Legion; and the Reverend William Andrews, an Anglican missionary to Virginia and chaplain at Yorktown. He saw Peggy through the birth, in July, of their daughter Sophia. Then, in October 1785, as late as he thought safe to sail before winter set in, he set his course for Canada.

Arnold sailed away from England a disenchanted man. In the years of controversy and conspiracy before he had deserted the revolutionary army to become a British general, he seems never to have considered the possibility that the American Revolution could succeed without him. Nor in choosing to defect had he con-

sidered the possibility that the British would lose, much less choose
not to go on fighting. He seems never to have imagined a world in
which the United States would win without him, nor what it would
be like to live in England after the Americans won. No longer an
American, Benedict Arnold was never accepted as an Englishman,
either.

20

"THE LAST MAN IN THE WORLD"

General Arnold's
affection for me is
unbounded. He is the
best of husbands.

Peggy Shippen Arnold to her father, February 1786

Twenty-five years old with three children five years or younger, Peggy Shippen Arnold suddenly found herself cut off from her home and family by an ocean. As long as the general was with her, she had felt comfortable, secure. She had found life in London exciting at first, thriving on the crowds, the noise, the stylish swirl at court, the fashionable brick town-houses in the West End, so like Society Hill in Philadelphia. Coddled at home and at court, she was almost always pregnant, babies born to her in 1780, 1781, 1783, 1784, 1785, two dying as infants. But Benedict Arnold's prospects were dwindling year by year in expensive London, and he finally decided he must give up his military pretensions, withdraw his claim for additional indemnification, and emigrate to British Canada, where a new land was being staked out and settled by the American Loyalist refugees and where there would be opportunities for a man of trade like himself. Merchants in British Canada enjoyed a virtual monopoly of the rich Caribbean trade with England now that the government had ordered the Royal

Navy to enforce the Navigation Acts and blockade ships from the United States from its colonial ports. The man who once evaded the British trading laws now hurried to take advantage of them.

Arnold's decision to leave for Canada as quickly as possible meant that Peggy would have to stay behind until she was strong enough to endure an ocean voyage. Arnold left Peggy with a modest income: their net income from pensions was £825 (about $50,000 in 1990 terms) plus the interest from £7,000 in 4 percent consolidated annuities, a total income of roughly £1,100, which made them solidly middle-class. Arnold was able to scrape together the money to buy and outfit his own brigantine, the *Lord Middlebrook,* for the voyage to Canada. Arnold was not content, at forty-five, to live the frugal, indolent life of a retired half-pay colonel.

Life with Benedict Arnold was hard on Peggy's nerves, without him harder. Almost as soon as he left, Peggy was alarmed by rumors that Arnold had been lost at sea. To her father in Philadelphia, Peggy poured out her anxiety:

I am still in the most unhappy state of suspense respecting the General, not having heard from him since the account of his ship's being lost. . . . I assure you, my dear Papa, I find it necessary to summon all my philosophy to my aid to support myself under my present situation. Separate from, and anxious for the fate of the best of husbands, torn from almost everybody that is dear to me, harassed with troublesome and expensive lawsuits, having all the General's business to transact and feeling that I am in a strange country without a creature near me that is really interested in my fate, you will not wonder if I am unhappy.[1]

On November 19, Arnold put into Halifax, Nova Scotia, to visit his friend Justice Smith, who had taken up his new post as chief justice of Nova Scotia. He was not universally welcomed. When it became known Arnold was headed for New Brunswick, Sampson P. Blowers, who had been a Loyalist leader in New York, wrote to his friend Ward Chipman in Saint John, New Brunswick: "Will you believe General Arnold is here? He is bound for your city, which he will of course prefer to Halifax, and settle with you. Give you joy of the acquisition."[2]

As his ship sailed over the reversing tidal falls at the approach to Saint John Harbor with only a pilot and captain aboard, Arnold was in his cabin, bedridden with an attack of gout. He did not see his pilot ignore the course of other vessels in the harbor and head for Marsh River, where the *Lord Middlebrook* ran hard aground. Arnold was furious. The winds had been exactly right, he insisted, and the two crewmen had deliberately wrecked his ship. In a storm of swearing and accusations, Arnold began seven tempestuous years in New Brunswick. As Jonathan Sewall, Jr., wrote to his father, Judge Sewall, on December 5, the wreck of Arnold's brig was, the general believed, "an infamous, preconcerted piece of villainy." The two Halifax mariners had been hired by someone to "injure the credit"[3] of the new port of Saint John. Arnold took an ad in the *Saint John Gazette* on December 20, 1785, offering a reward of ten guineas for the return of "considerable quantities of flour, beef, butter and pork"[4] looted from the ship. By the next spring, he had a new ship built. This time, his arrival in Saint John was smoother. The June 6, 1786, *Gazette* reported that "on Thursday last, came through the falls of the city, now moored, a new and noble ship, the *Lord Sheffield*, belonging to Brigadier General Benedict Arnold, upwards of 300 tons, of white oak." The *Gazette* praised Arnold's "laudable efforts to promote the interests of this infant colony." His first six months of residence had been "very productive of its commercial advantage." Arnold "deserved the praise of every well-wisher to its prosperity."[5]

All that first winter, Arnold had been, in his own word, reconnoitering the colony, sailing up and down the magnificent Saint John River, now strewn with 130 miles of rough new settlements of tents and cabins housing twelve thousand Loyalist veterans and their families. At Maugerville on the Saint John, he staked out a thousand forested acres, the source of timber for a lumberyard he opened on Lower Cove in Saint John, the hilly seaport town with two spreading wings of deepwater harbor opening beneath the protective mantle of Fort Howe. He shopped for town lots, over the next two years buying up waterfront on Broad Street on the west bank of Lower Cove for a wharf, warehouse, and general store which fronted on Main Street at Charlotte. He purchased a house and lot on Broad Street for £63, two lots on Carleton Street for £2 (cash-poor former soldiers who were taking up farming upriver were eager to sell their town lots for hard money). Apparently planning to speculate in Saint John real estate, he bought a waterfront property on Sheffield Street, assembled strips of building lots in Guys Ward, on Prince William Street, and Queen Street (where he bought ten contiguous forty-foot lots), on Germain Street and Smyth Street. On the Nashwaak River, he bought a large farm and leased it to Daniel Lyman, his old New Haven neighbor who had led a torch squad through New London as a captain in Arnold's American Legion. He subscribed generously to civic projects, putting in £10 for a fire company and a like amount for public wells, the largest contributions.

In the provincial capital of Fredericton, where several of his officers and men had settled and where Peggy had cousins, he bought four choice house lots on the south side of the common and built a warehouse at the intersection of present-day Waterloo Row and University Avenue. But he decided, as a trading man, that he must settle in Saint John, close to the sea, where he would gather his family. He wrote to Hannah to come with his three older boys, and he planned to bring Peggy and their three little children in the spring. Forming the business copartnership of Arnold, Hayt, and Arnold with former Connecticut Loyalist quartermaster Munson Hayt and with Arnold's son Richard, now eighteen, Arnold put an ad in the *Gazette* in August 1786: "*Lord Sheffield* will sail August 20th for Campobello, en route to Jamaica."[6] Arnold was willing to take on paying customers and cargo, leaving his son to mind the Saint John store.

By July 1787, Arnold had sailed around the Caribbean and to England and was back in Saint John. He arrived on a new ship, the *Peggy,* with his wife, their children, their friends, Judge Jonathan Sewall and his wife, and a valuable cargo. Only six weeks later, Peggy gave birth to another child, the namesake of King George. For the first time since she left Philadelphia, Peggy was able to make close friends—the Blisses, the Chipmans, the Sewalls—and in warm weather she went riding with them. The gambrel-roofed clapboard house with three big dormers was elegantly decorated with furniture imported from England. There were elegant blue-damask-covered sofas and matching drapes and a mahogany table that seated twelve on blue-damask-covered cabriole chairs that Arnold designed himself. The meals taken by guests at that table were served on Wedgwood giltware. Arnold outfitted chairs, a large terrestrial globe, a solid oak work table, and cases full of books. Upstairs, there were feather beds and mahogany four-poster beds with matching furniture.

The house was opulent and cozy at the same time, an island in a city of deprivation. Nobody in Saint John had any cash, and soon Arnold was involved in a rash of lawsuits as he tried to recover money he had spent and lent. It took cash to buy imported goods, and even though Arnold specialized in importing much-needed food supplies, he had a hard time collecting for them at his stores to pay his deck hands and ship captains. By 1789, Arnold had four trading ships and scores of employees and trading stations in Campobello and Fredericton. He faced frequent decisions to sue, to put men in debtors' prison, or to carry or write off their debts to him. His friend

and lawyer Ward Chipman summed up the problem in a letter concerning another hard-pressed client: "He is now in jail for a very
small sum which he is wholly unable to pay. . . . Really, everybody
is so poor. . . . There is no such thing as money to be had. . . . [A
lawsuit] is the only way to obtain payment."[7] But lawsuits leave
enemies, and soon Arnold had a fresh crop of them. With a warehouse, two stores, a thousand or more acres of land, and twenty-one
house lots, Arnold could find few people who could afford to buy
anything from him. His partner Hayt did little but borrow from Arnold. More and more Arnold turned his business over to his sons,
who mostly had to guard his goods. When tenants reneged on notes,
Arnold could not bring himself to dispossess men with families.

There were some men, too, who remembered Arnold's long-ago
generosity to his troops and, despite his treason, frankly admired the
way he had carried on. One day, Captain John Shackford of Rhode
Island, who had made the march to Quebec with Arnold and was
captured during the assault on the Lower Town, showed up at Arnold's wharf on Campobello and under Arnold's personal direction
loaded one of his ships. "I did not make myself known to him,"
Shackford wrote years later, "but frequently I sat upon the ship's
deck [to] watch the movements of my old commander who had carried us through everything, and for whose skill and courage I retained my former admiration, despite his treason. But when I
thought of what he had been and the despised man he then was,
tears would come, and I could not help it."[8] But as the postwar
depression deepened, there were many people in St. John who resented the distinction between Arnold's conspicuous comfort and
the shabbiness and suffering around him.

As soon as Peggy Arnold arrived in America, her father invited her
to come to Philadelphia for a visit. In some cities, especially in New
York, where large numbers of Loyalists had refused to leave, it was
safe for exiles to return: in 1787, New York State became the first to
remove the bar against Loyalists' voting, serving on juries, practicing
law or medicine. Peggy had hoped to visit her family late in 1788,
but worsening economic conditions in Canada had compelled Arnold to sail to England on a trading voyage that brought him hard
cash. On June 30, Peggy wrote to Judge Shippen that she hoped to
come "in the Fall," but Arnold did not return in time. Peggy had
longed for the visit for eight years, and knew that it could be her
last: there were disturbing signs that Arnold's ventures in Canada
might not take root and they might have to return to England. Peggy
half dreaded a visit to her parents. "My pleasure will not be unac-

companied by pain," Peggy wrote to her parents, "as when I leave you, I shall probably bid you adieu forever. Many disagreeable, and some favorable, circumstances will, I imagine, fix me forever in England upon my return to it."[9] It was another year and a half before Peggy could sail for New York City on her way to Philadelphia. She hesitated to leave the harassed Arnold alone in Saint John: "I feel great regret at leaving the General alone and much perplexed with business but as he strongly urges a measure that will be productive of so much happiness to me I think there can be no impropriety in taking the step."[10] Peggy was also missed by Saint John society; Mrs. Elizabeth Sewall wrote to her son, Jonathan, that her "sociability" made life in the remote provincial port "less irksome" for other Loyalist women. There was fresh cause for anxiety in Saint John and in Philadelphia when a newspaper account said her ship had been wrecked off New York, but Neddy Burd soon was writing relatives in Lancaster that Peggy was safe and had brought her two-year-old son, George, with her. By December 3, 1789, Peggy had arrived on Fourth Street for a five-month sojourn.

The arrival of the traitor's wife in the birthplace of the new nation stirred another controversy. Peggy Arnold had only been banished for the duration of the Revolution, but as old friends, many of them Whigs, called to visit Peggy, there were still former revolutionaries who, in the words of one Loyalist chronicler, treated her with "so much coldness and neglect that her feelings were continually wounded."[11] Others believed "her presence placed her friends in a painful position." She "should have shown more feeling by staying away."[12] Judge Shippen could not be hurt by any more snubs—he had survived revolution and treason and emerged as chief justice of Pennsylvania—but Peggy's mother was ill, and the strain took its toll on her. By the time Peggy left on April 26, 1790, she knew she could never go home again. Back in Saint John she wrote her sister, Betsy, in Philadelphia:

How difficult is it to know what will contribute to our happiness in this life. I had hoped that by paying my beloved friends a last visit, I should insure to myself some portion of it, but I find it far otherwise. The affectionate attention of my friends has greatly increased my love for them, and of course my regret at this cruel dreadful separation. I shall never forget, my dear, my beloved sister, your tender and affectionate behavior to me, and that of my more than brother, Mr. Burd, who has endeared himself extremely to me, and of whom I have as high an opinion as it is possible for me to entertain of any human being.[13]

During his 1788 voyage to England, friends had advised Benedict Arnold to follow a new business practice and insure the contents of his warehouses against fire. Arnold insured his Lower Cove warehouse for £1,000, its stock for £4,000, and the stock in his large new store at Main and Charlotte streets for £1,000. When he returned from England he found that on July 11, 1788, fire had destroyed the Lower Cove warehouse, store, and lumberyard while his sons Richard and Henry were sleeping in the office. They narrowly escaped. When Arnold tried to collect the insurance, however, there were so many rumors that he himself had ordered the fire set that the insurance underwriters tried to evade liability. Two years later, in 1790, shortly after Peggy's return from Philadelphia, Arnold's former business partner Munson Hayt admitted in a legal pleading that he "did speak, assert, publish and proclaim with a loud voice in the hearing of divers of His Majesty's faithful subjects" that "You [Arnold] burnt your own store." The accusation climaxed a stormy partnership with Hayt, and on the day it ended in 1789, Arnold took notes from Hayt for £2,555 Hayt had borrowed from him, a fortune at the time, more than anyone had ever owed him, and still Hayt had not begun to pay him back a year later. As if that didn't hurt enough, to Hayt's accusation that Arnold had torched the store was added an insult Arnold found intolerable. When Arnold demanded a public apology for blackening his reputation, Hayt replied, "It is not in my power to blacken your character, for it is as black as it can be."[14] The insult directly resulted in the refusal of Arnold's insurance company to pay his £5,000 claim.

In the most sensational lawsuit in early New Brunswick history, Arnold hired the two best lawyers in the province, his friends Ward Chipman and Jonathan Bliss, assembled a platoon of thirty witnesses, and sued Hayt for the value of his reputation. The jury trial, at Fredericton, began September 7, 1791, before two supreme court justices with four justices of the peace sitting in as guest justices. Arnold argued that the money Hayt owed him was a motivation. He also produced two eyewitnesses to the fire. One of them, a black Loyalist veteran, testified that he had gone up into the loft of Arnold's warehouse with Arnold's son Henry the night of the fire with a candle to look for some oak to build a boat and had accidentally started the fire. After a two-day trial, the jury voted to convict Hayt of willful slander.

It was up to Justices Joshua Upham and Isaac Allen to put a value on the damage to Arnold's reputation. In effect cleared of the accusation of arson-for-insurance, Arnold would now assuredly collect from the insurance company. Instead of the £5,000 Arnold sought, the judges awarded him only twenty shillings, an unbearable insult. But it was not to be the last. The day after the verdict became known in Saint John, while the Arnolds were still in Fredericton, a mob loyal to Hayt's radical lawyer, Elias Hardy, surged around and into and through the Arnold house on King Street, burning an effigy of Arnold with a one-word sign fastened to its chest: "Traitor." They sacked the house before a justice of the peace could read them the riot act and summon redcoats from Fort Howe.

Six years in New Brunswick had been enough for Benedict Arnold. The September 22, 1791, *Gazette* carried an auction notice listing the contents of Arnold's house as he prepared to move back to England. When the day of the auction came, Arnold's friend and lawyer Ward Chipman bought the set of twelve cabriole chairs from the Arnolds' dining room. Ever since then, Saint John residents have called them the Traitor's Chairs. Five years later, Arnold was still trying to get Chipman to pay for them.

By early 1792, Benedict Arnold was back in London and Peggy was unpacking after their third transatlantic move in ten years. To his friend and lawyer Jonathan Bliss back in Saint John, Arnold wrote an angry letter on February 26. The strain of the last year in Canada had left him ill for nearly the entire winter with "a severe fit of the gout":

We had a very rough and disagreeable voyage Home, but our reception has been very pleasant, and our friends [have been] more than well attentive to us since our arrival. The little property that we have saved from the hands of a lawless ruffian mob *and* more unprincipled judges *in New Brunswick is perfectly safe here, as well as our* persons from insult, *and though we feel and regret the absence of the friends we had there, we find London* full as pleasant*! I cannot help viewing your great city* as a shipwreck *from which I have escaped.*15

Benedict Arnold's last years were filled with his obsessions with his reputation and a long string of business ventures and misadventures. He had left his sons in Saint John to manage his businesses with instructions to his lawyer Jonathan Bliss to turn over to them any money that he collected. He expanded his Caribbean operations, in an eight-year period sending or sailing thirteen different ships on trading voyages to the West Indies. It would take fifty years for his grandchildren to unload the last parcel of Saint John property, and in the meantime Arnold continued to speculate, at the time of his death owning nearly fifteen thousand acres in the Maritimes and in Quebec Province.

For Arnold, there was no distance between his reputation and his credit as a businessman, and as he struggled to expand his shipping interests, he waged a bitter fight to clear his name. As early as 1787, when he had returned alone to England on a trading voyage from Saint John, he seems to have suspected that Sir Henry Clinton contributed to the blackening of his name. As long before as 1781, Clinton had told his confidant Chief Justice Smith that Arnold's desire to lead raids on coastal cities was motivated by his "interest" in money. Such a comment came close to accusing Arnold of selling out West Point only for money, an assertion that many were willing to believe as time went on. By 1787, Arnold was writing to Clinton that he had suffered "much unmerited abuse" for changing sides for "mercenary reasons" rather than motives of "conviction."[16] Clinton reluctantly replied, carefully writing and rewriting three drafts before sending one to Arnold:

I am sorry you should have occasion to think it necessary to ask my opinion of the motives which influenced your choice of being reconciled to the British government and joining the King's army. . . . Had I not been persuaded that the negotiation you opened with me . . . arose solely from principle and a conviction of your error, I certainly should not have paid that regard to it I did.[17]

What had been only a whispering campaign against Arnold became public in June 1792, shortly after Arnold's return to settle in London. As Peggy Arnold explained the affair to her father, a radical Rockingham Whig member of the House of Lords, Lord Lauderdale, while arguing against giving command of antiriot troops to the Duke of Richmond, said that "he did not know of any instance of political apostasy equal to the Duke of Richmond's, except General Arnold's" and that "the intended encampment was designed to overawe the inhabitants of the Kingdom . . . that the Duke of Richmond was the most proper person he knew of to command it, General Arnold first struck off the list."[18] When Arnold demanded an apology for "this unprovoked attack" on his character the Earl half apologized, but not to Arnold's satisfaction. He drew up an apology for Lauderdale, who refused to sign it. When Arnold decided to challenge Lord Lauderdale to a duel, Lord Hawke, "our particular friend," agreed to be his second. Lauderdale's second was Charles James Fox, the former prime minister and head of the radical Rockingham Whig party in Parliament.

In late June, the London newspapers published the shocking news of the duel and reported that Arnold had been killed. Copies were on ships bound for America when Peggy wrote to her father to ignore them. "Friends were flocking to the house to condole with me," Peggy wrote, adding that the episode was giving her "a great deal of pain." In the week before the duel, she had not dared to discuss the matter with the silent general, fearing that would "unman him and prevent him acting himself."[19] The duel took place on July 6, 1792. After Lauderdale refused to fire, Arnold fired and missed. After a conference of the seconds, "his Lordship came forward" and said he was sorry for what he had said. Moreover, Lauderdale had apologized to Peggy in person at their house "that I had been made unhappy." What she had suffered for a week, Peggy told her father, "is not to be described," and it "almost at last proved too much for me, and for some hours, my reason was to be despaired of."[20]

This episode only served to make Arnold more determined than ever to win back his reputation. Once again, he pressed Sir Henry Clinton for written assurances that Clinton, too, believed he had carried out his treason out of conviction, not avarice. His courageous behavior in the face of Lauderdale's public insults won Arnold new friends in the government. Within three weeks of the duel, the prime minister, William Pitt the Younger, ordered the Treasury Board to reexamine Clinton's compensation of Arnold's losses in the American Revolution. Arnold wrote to Clinton that the Treasury Board wanted to talk with him and asked Clinton to put in a word for him, that on the half-pay pension of a colonel, "so far from being able to provide for and educate a numerous family of children, I am not able to support them decently."[21] Would Clinton speak for him to the prime minister, too?

On August 4, 1792, Clinton set down his memories of the painful Arnold-André affair. The Arnolds were out of town for a six-week vacation on the Isle of Wight when Clinton sent Arnold a letter he said could be shown to the prime minister. After meeting with Pitt, Arnold wrote back, "He appeared very much surprised at the small sum I received." According to Arnold, Pitt asked what it would take to restore Arnold to "a situation as good as it *formerly was*." The prime minister asked for "a little time to consider the matter,"[22] but in December 1792, when Arnold wrote Clinton again to thank him for his "very full"[23] endorsement of his claim, Pitt had still done nothing.

* * *

The year 1793 brought the Reign of Terror in France and the first stirrings of a new war with England. With it, Arnold saw a chance to redeem his honor by enlisting in the struggle. When there was no commission forthcoming for him, he outfitted his own privateering ship to attack French shipping and, apparently without being asked, to gather intelligence that would be useful to the British. By February 1794, Arnold had sold off two ships in New Brunswick and bought and armed a new merchantman for a voyage to the West Indies. He would cruise the Caribbean for "five or six months," Arnold wrote Jonathan Bliss in Saint John. "I shall visit the different islands—Barbados, Dominico, Grenada."24

Sailing in late February to avoid French patrols in the English Channel, he had to stop at Falmouth to sit out a violent Channel storm. Among the other ships that put in in mid-March was one carrying exiles from the French Revolution to Philadelphia, where thousands had gathered in the United States capital. One of the exiles waiting restlessly at Falmouth was Prince Talleyrand. As he waited for his ship to be repaired, Talleyrand learned from the innkeeper that there was an American, a general, staying there. Shortly, they were introduced and Talleyrand observed:

After the usual exchange of greetings, I put to him several questions concerning his country but, from the first, it seemed to me that my inquiries annoyed him. Having several times vainly endeavored to renew the conversation, which he always allowed to drop, I ventured to request from him some letters of introduction to his friends in America. "No," he replied and, after a few moments of silence, noticing my surprise, he added, "I am perhaps the only American who cannot give you letters for his own country: all the relations I had there are now broken. I must never return." He dared not tell me his name. It was General Arnold! I must confess that I felt much pity for him, for which political puritans will perhaps blame me, for I witnessed his agony.25

The carnage of the French Revolution convinced Arnold anew that he had made the right choice to turn away from the American revolutionaries. "I am now on my way to the West Indies," Arnold wrote his friend Bliss on March 19, "as the wind is now fair."26 By the time Arnold returned from witnessing the devastation of a year of naval warfare in the Caribbean, he wrote Bliss from Martinique in January 1795 that

*war is carried on now with a brutality unknown to former times,
and very little to the honor of humanity or the cause of freedom. My
situation has often been dangerous and critical. My affairs have
sometimes prospered and sometimes not. I have made and lost a
great deal of money here, but I hope to return to England in April, a
gainer, upon the whole.*[27]

Four months later, Arnold was still straining at the anchor cable in
Martinique: "I expected ere this to have been on my way back to
England but have been detained by the insurrection in some of the
islands, which I am sorry to say is not in a fair way to be quelled."[28]
Once again, Peggy need not have worried: Arnold was thriving as a
ship's captain and trader in the islands he knew so well. To his
friend Ward Chipman in Saint John, Arnold wrote that he was "in
the enjoyment of good health . . . considerably improved in fortune
and infinitely more in health than when I left England, and though I
have experienced the distress of burying two-thirds of my acquaintances in these islands since I came out, I had scarcely an hour's
sickness."[29] When Arnold finally returned to England on August 18,
1795, he met Peggy and the children at Chigwell, outside London,
for a long vacation. From there, his view toward Saint John was
changed, he told Bliss, his opinion that revolution was an evil thing
only deeper:

*In this age of revolution and the consequent horrors and devasta-
tions of War, you are certainly fortunate to be placed in a snug corner, in a great measure out of the reach of them, a happiness which
thousands of the great ones of the earth sigh for in vain, and if we
are disposed to philosophize, there is great consolation to be drawn
from our situations, which are comfortable but not sufficiently elevated to be the objects of envy and distinction. We, therefore, ought
to be content, which is the greatest happiness to be expected in this
world.*[30]

Arnold was many things, but he was no braggart, and he did not tell
his Canadian friends of his latest adventures. In late June of 1794,
having sold his cargo of English goods in Saint Kitts for £5,000
cash, he sailed into Pointe-à-Pitre on the Guadeloupe island of
Grand-Terre, unaware that this West Indian trading station, where
he had been doing business for thirty-five years, had recently been
seized by the British and then retaken by French revolutionaries.
Back in London, Peggy, who had just given birth to her seventh
child, William Fitch Arnold, on June 25, learned of the change of

flags and the danger to Arnold before Arnold did. To Richard Arnold in Saint John, she wrote frantically, "I am now in a state of extreme misery from a report of your father's being a prisoner to the French. . . . Your father's last letter to me, wherein he says he shall set off the next day for Pointe-à-Pitre, makes it but too probable."[31]

As he sailed into Pointe-à-Pitre and realized the ships were French, he decided to land anyway, identifying himself as an American, a merchant. His name—John Anderson. His masquerade failed: he was arrested as a British spy and dragged off to a French prison ship in the harbor. Somehow he managed to conceal his money, and he began to dole it out in small installments to bribe his guards. From them he learned that a British fleet had just arrived offshore to blockade the harbor and that the French revolutionary governor, Victor Hugues was about to have him hanged after learning his identity. More gold pieces changed hands and French guards brought him the equipment that he needed.

On the sultry night of June 29, 1794, Arnold waited for word that the tide had gone out, then placed his money and valuables in a small cask with a letter inside explaining whose property they were and dropped it overboard, then slithered through a cabin window and slid down a rope to a raft that was waiting for him. Paddling quietly with his hands through shark-infested waters, Arnold made his way to a rowboat waiting for him in the harbor, then pulled as hard as he could for the British man-of-war *Boyne,* outrowing a French cutter that hailed him. Aboard the British flagship, he was taken to the commander in chief, General Sir Charles "No Flint" Grey, John André's old commanding officer.

For the next year, Arnold served Grey as a volunteer quartermaster and acted as agent for British planters dealing with the fleet. He also organized the planters into a militia that put down a slave insurrection on Martinique even after Grey refused to make him a senior brigadier on the basis of his rank in the British army during the American Revolution. When the British finally withdrew from Guadeloupe and the other French West Indies they had captured, the British planters and merchants sent a resolution to the ministry in London, praising Arnold for his efforts and requesting that he be sent back as commander of a relief expedition.

In the early years of the Napoleonic Wars, Arnold was his ambitious self again, back in the fight and relishing a hero's praise. He submitted his plan to the ministry for the next year's expedition to the West Indies. While he waited for a reply, he caught up on business and renewed his long correspondence with Bliss. Bliss and his wife and their growing family had moved into the Arnolds' "old habitation"[32] in Saint John and, with Peggy, had handled all the Canadian business in Arnold's absence by mail. It was to Bliss that Peggy sent the news that Arnold and the ministry could not come to terms about a command. The ministry was "fearful of putting him over the heads of so many old general officers," she explained. As Peggy put it to Bliss, "It is universally acknowledged that, had his advice been followed, we should now be in possession of Guadeloupe, and the necessity of sending such a force as is now going, prevented."[33] But for Arnold, the honor of consideration for a command was vindication enough.

Nonetheless, the ministry insisted on rewarding him with land. As a half-pay officer of a former Loyalist regiment, Arnold was entitled to apply for crown lands in the new province of Upper Canada. On April 13, 1798, he applied for five thousand acres for himself, twelve hundred acres each for his wife and five children, and twelve hundred acres for Hannah. (His sons by his first marriage, all British veterans, had already received their own land grants). To receive the 13,400-acre grant, Arnold needed not only a right but interest at court. The Duke of Portland, secretary for the Home Department, granted Arnold's request and issued an order supporting Arnold's petition and exempting him from residence in Upper Canada, as he had requested, "in consequence of his late gallant and meritorious services in Guadeloupe."[34]

His peace was pyrrhic. His oldest son, Benedict VI, had defied him and taken up his commission to fight the French as a captain in the British army. Captured, he spent two years in a French prison and then, when he was released, volunteered over his father's objections for the West Indies campaign that Arnold had wanted to lead. Hannah Arnold wrote that the twenty-eight-year-old firstborn of Arnold's sons "went entirely contrary to the wishes of his father."[35] In February 1796, Sir Grenville Temple rode up Hollis Street to the Arnold residence in the fashionable Portman Square section of London and handed Arnold his dead son's sword. An artillery officer in the Jamaica hills, he had been wounded severely in the leg in a skirmish with maroons. He had refused amputation and died of a gangrenous fever. To his friend Bliss, Arnold wrote, "His death is a heavy stroke on me."[36]

The death of Arnold's oldest son was only the first of a series of family catastrophes. Peggy's health had been declining since their return to England. All through the troubled early years of their marriage, she and Benedict had been extremely close, and no matter how the rest of the world censured him, she was devoted to him. But by December 5, 1795, when she had written the Blisses to congratulate them on the birth of another child, she added, "For my own part, I am *determined* to have no more little plagues, as it is so difficult to provide for them in this country."[37] Arnold's frequent absences at sea seemed the only times, as the years went on, that he was truly content, but the longer he was away, the worse her health became. His long absences may have led to the migraine headaches that became so excruciating that she said she could not write for weeks on end. When he was home, he took her to the baths at Cheltenham and sea bathing off Surrey, and she rallied. After Arnold's oldest son died, he became sick, too; his old gout returned after a respite of six years, worsening each year until he could no longer go to sea again and had to hire other men as his privateering ships' captains, men who took "insignificant prizes" that were "more trouble than profit," as Peggy explained it to her oldest son, Neddy. Arnold suspected that his captains were making handsome profits at sea but not turning them over to him, "but as we have no proof we must sit down quietly with the loss."[38] Peggy began to take more of a hand in his business now even when he was ashore, writing to her father in Philadelphia to invest money she had saved in speculative stocks there. She believed that Arnold's skippers had cheated him out of £50,000, and she now helped him to liquidate assets to raise cash for a large new armed vessel. When it, too, returned after a long cruise with no profits, Arnold grew despondent.

"He is, at present, in the most harassed wretched shape I have ever seen him in," Peggy wrote in January 1801 to twenty-year-old Neddy, who had sailed for India to do his part in the Napoleonic Wars as an aide under the patronage of their friend Lord Cornwallis:

Disappointed in his highly-raised expectations, harassed by the sailors who are loudly demanding their prize-money when in fact their advances have greatly exceeded anything that is due to them, and wishing still to do something [in the war] without the health or power of acting, he knows not which way to turn himself.[39]

He spoke to Peggy little now, only pouring himself out in a rare letter. When Arnold learned that Bliss's wife had died, he wrote that he remembered how, when his first wife had died, all that he could do was to hope someday to meet her in "some happier region."[40] In his last letter to Bliss, Arnold wrote with great pride in his younger sons. Neddy and James were, both of them, engineering officers in the British army, protégés of Cornwallis. Neddy had gone out to

India, where he was serving in Bengal. "It is a great trial to both of us," Arnold told Bliss, "to part with him." War had scattered Arnold's sons, and Peggy only grieved at the distances more audibly. "She has lately been much distressed in parting with her eldest son," he wrote to Bliss, but if Neddy "retains his health"—Arnold did not finish the sentence. "He is much beloved and respected by *all* his acquaintances. . . . Good abilities. . . . Great knowledge. . . . Pleasing manner and strict principles of honor." He was equally proud of James. "Our second son . . . has been at Gibraltar near two years, where the officers speak very highly of him." James had "lately been selected from *all the young officers* there to go to Malta . . . as second officer in conducting the siege." He added news of his little boys, George, twelve, and William, two, "fine boys and coming on well," and Sophia, six, "very tall but very delicate."[41]

Within five months, Arnold was dead, as much a victim of his chronic frustrations and rage at his own impotence as of the combination of severe gout and dropsy that the London doctors diagnosed. In late February 1801, shortly after his sixtieth birthday, his health suddenly broke. He did not seem to want to fight any longer. He had developed a chronic cough in the tropics which no doubt weakened him. His gout flared up and he developed asthma, which kept him from swallowing. Gout in his good leg, pain in his wounded leg, no food, no sleep, no hope of seeing his sons and his sister and their new farms in Canada. His face became wrinkled as his weight fell away until his friends could hardly recognize him except for his intense blue eyes. On June 10, he became delirious. Four days later, at six-thirty the Sunday morning of June 14, 1801, Benedict Arnold died "without a groan"[42] at the age of sixty. "My sister and myself were with Mrs. Arnold when her husband expired," Ann Fitch wrote to Judge Shippen. "She evinces, upon this occasion, as you know she has done upon many trying ones before, that fortitude and resignation which a superior and well-regulated mind only is capable of exerting."[43]

Benedict Arnold's funeral on June 21 was a grim cavalcade made up of four state carriages and seven mourning coaches that rattled slowly from Gloucester Place in the West End to the little copper-spired Church of St. Mary's, Battersea, in an unfashionable district south of the Thames, where he was buried in the crypt next to his Connecticut friend William Fitch, where Peggy was also to be buried. The only monument in the world bearing his name was to be erected at St. Mary's, but the wrong name was entered on the parish records by an oblivious clerk, and when the church was renovated a century later, Arnold's body was disinterred and reburied with hundreds of others in a jumbled unmarked grave. The occasion of his death gave newspapers the opportunity for partisan parting shots. The London *Post* reported, "Poor General Arnold has departed this world without notice, a sorry reflection this for the Pitts and . . . other turncoats."[44] While the state coaches that made up his funeral cortège were filled with notables, Arnold was buried without military honors. No dukedom, no knighthood, no salute of cannons, only an unmarked grave.

Benedict Arnold's widow lived long enough to pay off all his debts "down to the last teaspoon."[45] She was shocked that Arnold had died, shocked again by his will, which left a considerable legacy of land, an education, and an income to one John Sage, age about fourteen. But the existence of an illegitimate son, born the year Arnold had gone out to Canada without Peggy, could not have been a total surprise. When Neddy Burd wrote to her a few months later that he had heard about the legacy, Peggy wrote back: "Years of unhappiness have passed. . . . I had cast my lot, complaints were unavailing, and you and my other friends are ignorant of the many causes of uneasiness I have had."[46] But in a final tribute to Peggy, Arnold had also left her sole power to execute his will and to redistribute his assets as she saw fit. She honored his wishes exactly, proudly, with acumen.

She had been troubled for years by Arnold's activities as a speculator. Ten years earlier, she had confided to her father that worry about the welfare of her children was "a load which has long oppressed me":

The greatest part of our income being dependent on our lives, would make our deaths severely felt by our children. . . . Until I know that, in case of such an event, they would be secured from beggary and absolute dependence, I cannot know tranquility.[47]

When her mother died, Peggy had, on her father's advice, invested her small inheritance in stock in the new Bank of North America, buying more shares with income prudently saved from her royal pension and, as a result, using the wages of her defection to earn money from the treasury of the country she had been forced to leave. Benedict Arnold's death left her with a complicated pile of debts and few liquid assets. The house he had given her as a wedding present turned out to be hopelessly encumbered. She sold off £1,000 in bank stock but left an almost equal amount at interest to augment the £1,000 a year she received for her and her children's royal pension. Enlisting Bliss's aid in disposing of Canadian properties, she moved to a house with rent and taxes that, she proudly told her father, cost only £50 a year, a small fraction of her pensions, but she was not content even with this economizing. To her father, she wrote:

I have been under the necessity of parting with my furniture, wine and many other comforts provided for me by the indulgent hand of affection, and have by these sacrifices paid all ascertained *debts.*[48]

Peggy was proud that despite her wealthy father's refusal to help her by honoring a large debt her insolvent brother owed her, she managed in eighteen months to clear Arnold's enormous debts of £6,000 and emerge with a sufficient income to raise her small children. She was too proud "to describe to you the toil it has been to me, but without vanity add that few women could have effected what I have done." She gave her father the credit for her ability as a businesswoman:

To you, my dear parent, am I indebted for the ability to perform what I have done. . . . You bestowed upon me the most useful and best education that America at that time afforded.[49]

Peggy saw to it that all her children were well educated in schools that prepared them for remunerative professions and entry into British society. She took especial pains with Sophia. Writing to her son Edward in January 1804, when her daughter was eighteen, she described her progress in music, drawing and painting, adding that "she reads a great deal and turns her attention greatly to religious subjects. . . . She will make a most excellent wife to any man who is so fortunate as to get her," even if there was "little chance of her marrying, having but a moderate share of beauty and no money."[50] Sophia soon afterward went to India to live with her brother Neddy, by then a lieutenant in the 6th Bengal Cavalry, and married his best friend and had five children. Neddy became paymaster for his regiment and died in India eight months after his sister's wedding.

For her youngest child, Peggy provided enough money for him to be educated and to take up a commission in the army. Peggy did not want him to turn out exactly like his father. She wanted him to become a soldier—"a soldier may be as pious and excellent in every way as any other man"—but not a speculator: "I hope, my dear William, you will never be tempted to enter into anything like speculation."[51] William followed her advice and became a captain in the

19th Light Dragoons, fighting against the Americans in the War of 1812. Like all of Benedict Arnold's five sons, William was a British officer.

It was to her beloved firstborn, Neddy, that Peggy confided, and her letters to him after his father's death are the strongest expression of her grief in her last years. To Neddy she had written that Arnold's death was caused by "the disappointment of all his pecuniary expectations" that, after all, "the numerous vexations and mortifications he has endured, had broken his spirits and destroyed his nerves." The last blow had been the news that his last privateer, the *Earl Spencer*, had been lost at sea. To Neddy, she proudly confided that while she had sacrificed most of the comforts of her life, "I have not reserved a towel or a tea spoon that I have not paid for."[52]

The years of anxiety and illness had exacted a terrible toll, and Peggy Shippen Arnold's ordeal ended after twenty-five years in the summer of 1804. She had been increasingly ill since Arnold's death. That first summer after he died, she had written to Neddy Burd, "My health is impaired by long anxiety of mind, and my former strength of mind and energy have entirely forsaken me, and indeed I sometimes fear that my reason will give way."[53] But as she cleared away Arnold's debts, her calmness returned, and she wrote of "my returning health and serenity of mind and a degree of contentment that, some time ago, I thought it was impossible for me ever to regain."[54] But she also wrote of "the dreaded evil, a cancer." She had, she told her sister Betsy, "a very large tumor" in her uterus:

I have been indeed very near death, my dear sister, and my complaints are such as to give me very little hope of long continuing an inhabitant of this world. . . . My only chance is from an internal operation which it is at present dangerous to perform. . . . I bear this heavy affliction with great resignation, and I do not suffer my spirits to overcome me.[55]

On July 5, 1804, her brother-in-law, Daniel Coxe, visited her on Bryanston Street. To Peggy's father he wrote of his alarm:

Your daughter now lies on a sick bed, very painful and alarming, not able to partake of the least exercise . . . looking so ill as to shock me. . . . She was not able to write to you or would have done it. . . . She has come to that crisis that must terminate, sooner or later, the existence of one of the finest women I know.[56]

Peggy Shippen Arnold died on August 24, 1804, of cancer of the uterus. She was forty-four. After she died, her children found concealed in her personal possessions a gold locket which contained a snippet of John André's hair. Family tradition holds that Benedict Arnold never saw it.

NOTES

PAH   Papers of Alexander Hamilton
PAPS   Proceedings of the American Philosophical Society
PCC   Papers of the Continental Congress
PCR   Pennsylvania Colonial Records
PHMC   Pennsylvania Historical Museum Commission
PRO   Public Records Office, England
PS   Philip Schuyler
PSA   Peggy Shippen Arnold
PUL   Princeton University Library
RG   Royal Gazette
RM   Richard Montgomery
RUL   Revue de l'Université Laval
RV   Richard Varick
SA   Samuel Adams
SC   Samuel Chase
SD   Silas Deane
WP   Washington Papers
WLCL   William L. Clements Library, University of Michigan
WW   Fitzpatrick, Writings of George Washington

1: "YOU ARE ACCOUNTABLE TO GOD"

GREAT AWAKENING IN CONNECTICUT: Heimert and Miller, *Great Awakening*, 187–363; Bushman, *From Puritan to Yankee*; Zeichner, *Connecticut's Years of Controversy*, 3–29; Goen, *Revivalism and Separatism in New England*; Chauncy, *Seasonable Thoughts on the Present State of Religion in New England*.

NORWICH TOWN IN THE EIGHTEENTH CENTURY: Caulkins, *History of Norwich*, 1845 and 1874 editions; O'Keefe and Doroshevich, *Norwich: Historic Homes and Families*; Sigourney, *Sketch of Connecticut Forty Years Since* and *Letters of Life*, 5–47.

BENEDICT ARNOLD'S BOYHOOD: Decker, *Benedict Arnold: Son of the Havens*, 1–18; W. M. Wallace, *Traitorous Hero*. 5–14, and *Dark Star of the Revolution*, 1–5; I. N. Arnold, *Life of Benedict Arnold*, 15–26; Flexner, *Traitor and the Spy*, 3–18; Haight, *Mrs. Sigourney: The Sweet Singer of Hartford*; Dexter, *Biographical Sketches of the Graduates of Yale College*, 1:701–3; Larned, *History of Windham County*, 1:405–15.

1. "Nathan Cole's Spiritual Travels," in Heimert and Miller, 183–86.
2. Quoted in Caulkins, 1874 ed., 315–16.
3. Quoted in Sprague, *Annals of the American Pulpit*; 1:300.
4. *Boston Post-Boy*, September 28, 1741.
5. Caulkins, 1874 ed., 316.
6. Ibid., 323.
7. Dexter, 1:702.
8. HWA–BA, August 9, 1754, quoted in *Magazine of History*, 3:258.
9. HWA–BA, August 13, 1753, quoted in *Historical Magazine*, 4:18.
10. HWA–BA, August 30, 1753, quoted in Decker, 9–10.
11. Rev. James Cogswell to HWA, quoted in Decker, 10.
12. HWA–BA, April 12, 1754, quoted in Caulkins, 1874 ed., 410.
13. HWA–BA, August 9, 1754, Quoted in *Magazine of History*, 3:258.
14. B. Rush, *Autobiography*, 158.
15. Warrant for arrest, November 4, 1754, MSS., Huntington Library.
16. Dexter, 1:483–84, 741–42.
17. Caulkins, 1874 ed., 412.
18. Arrest warrant signed by Isaac Huntingdon, May 26, 1760, MSS., Misc. Papers, HSP.
19. Mortgage by Daniel Lathrop, MSS., Misc. Papers, HSP.
20. Deed dated October 4, 1763, MSS., Misc. Papers, HSP.

2: "A FAIR PROSPECT OF IMPROVING!"

BENEDICT ARNOLD, SHOPKEEPER: W. M. Wallace, *Traitorous Hero*, 15–30; Flexner, *Traitor and the Spy*, 11–29; Decker, *Benedict Arnold: Son of the Havens*, 19–38; I. N. Arnold, *Life of Benedict Arnold*, 26–35.

SON OF LIBERTY: Gipson, *American Loyalist: Jared Ingersoll;* Collier, *Roger Sherman's Connecticut,* 54–84; Maier, *From Resistance to Revolution,* 3–26; 77–112; Zeichner, *Connecticut's Years of Controversy,* 44–77; Bushman, *From Puritan to Yankee,* 237–58.
1. Original sign in NHCHS.
2. Advertisement in NHCHS.
3. Promissory note, BA to Daniel Lathrop, Misc. Papers, HSP.
4. Advertisement in *Connecticut Gazette,* February 7, 1766.
5. BA to John Remsen, April 21, 1768, MSS., Maryland Historical Society.
6. "An Account of all the Duties collected under the Molasses Act," quoted in Gipson, 112–13n.
7. Quoted in Gipson, 254–57.
8. Quoted in Gipson, 155.
9. Collier, *Roger Sherman's Connecticut,* 365.
10. [BF], *London Chronicle,* November 14–16, 1765.
11. Jared Ingersoll to Thomas Whately, July 6, 1764, quoted in Gipson, 115.
12. William Samuel Johnson to Ezra Stiles, Maier, 12.
13. *Connecticut Gazette,* September 27, 1765.
14. *Connecticut Gazette,* January 30, 1766.
15. Ibid., February 5, 1766.
16. Ibid., February 21, 1766.
17. BA to Remsen, April 21, 1768, MSS., Maryland Historical Society.
18. Benjamin Gale to Jared Ingersoll, August 9, 1762, quoted in Bushman, *From Puritan to Yankee,* 248.
19. Ezra Stiles to Leverett Hubbard, September 21, 1766, MS, NHCHS.
20. Benjamin Gale quoted in Collier, *Roger Sherman's Connecticut,* 52.
21. BA to the Editor, *Connecticut Gazette,* February 21, 1766.
22. New Haven Town Records, 4:489–90.
23. *Connecticut Gazette,* February 21, 1766.
24. Ibid., February 14, 1766.
25. New Haven Town Records, 4:490.
26. BA to the Editor, *Connecticut Gazette,* February 21, 1766.

3: "ARE THE AMERICANS ALL ASLEEP?"

MARRIAGE AND CHILDREN: W. M. Wallace, *Traitorous Hero,* 24–30; Flexner, *Traitor and the Spy,* 15–19; Decker, *Benedict Arnold: Son of the Havens,* 19–38.
MERCHANT SHIPOWNER: W. M. Wallace, *Traitorous Hero,* 15–30, 111–19; Caulkins, *History of Norwich,* 1874 ed.; Calhoon, *Loyalists in Revolutionary America,* 191–94.
1. BA to Margaret Mansfield Arnold, May 28, 1766, MSS., Biddle Coll., HSP.
2. BA–MMA, August 8, 1768, MSS., Dreer Coll., Generals of the Revolution, I, HSP.
3. BA–MMA, August 13, 1768, MSS., Dreer Coll., Generals, I, HSP.
4. BA–MMA, October 5, 1773, MSS., Dreer Coll., Generals I, HSP.
5. BA–MMA, October 7, 1773, MSS., Dreer Coll., Generals I, HSP.
6. BA, *Journal,* NHCHS.
7. BA–MMA, January 21, 1774, *Magazine of History,* 3:259.
8. Ibid.
9. Thomas Longman to Bernard Lintot, July 7, 1766, Dreer Coll., Generals, I, HSP.
10. Deed for wharf, August, 1772, Misc. MSS., N-YHS.
11. BA to Enoch Brown, June 25, 1780, Dreer Coll., Generals, I, HSP.
12. Scrapbook on house in NHCHS.
13. Quoted in W. M. Wallace, *Traitorous Hero,* 27–28.
14. BA to Benjamin Douglas, June 9, 1770, MSS., Dreer Coll., Generals, I, HSP.
15. Calhoon, 191–94.
16. Quoted in Collier, *Roger Sherman's Connecticut,* 88–90.
17. Silas to Elizabeth Deane, [August 31–September 5, 1774], *LDC,* 1:15–19.
18. John Adams's Diary, August 29, 1774, *LDC,* 1:7.
19. Silas to Elizabeth Deane, [August 31–September 5, 1774], *LDC,* 1:20.
20. Quoted in Hatch, *Major John André,* 34–35.
21. Quoted in Collier, *Roger Sherman's Connecticut,* 57n.
22. Rev. Samuel Peters, *General History of Connecticut,* 265.

23. Calhoon, 194.
24. Decker, 44–46.
25. Quoted in French, *First Year of the Revolution*, 14–15, 7.
26. Quoted in Commager and Morris, *Spirit of 'Seventy-six*, 90.
27. Ibid., 91.
28. BA at court-martial, December, 1779, *Proceedings of a Court Martial*, 40.
29. Quoted in Atwater, *New Haven*, 42.

4: "THE GREATEST CONFUSION AND ANARCHY"

TICONDEROGA EXPEDITION: French, *Taking of Ticonderoga;* Commager and Morris, *Spirit of 'Seventy-six*, 97–105; Ward, *War of the Revolution*, 63–72; *Naval Documents of the American Revolution* (hereafter *ND*), Vol. 1; I. N. Arnold, *Life of Benedict Arnold*, 33–48; W. M. Wallace, *Traitorous Hero*, 37–44; J. Pell, *Ethan Allen*, 29–72; B. Arnold, "Regimental Memorandum Book"; E. Allen, "Narrative."
1. Promissory note, BA to James Lockwood, May, 1775, MSS., Copley Library.
2. BA to Mass. Committee of Safety, April 30, 1775, *ND*, 1:250.
3. Minutes of the Mass. Comm. of Safety, May 2, 1775, *ND*, 1:262–63.
4. BA to Albany Comm. of Safety, May 3, 1775, MSS., Copley Library.
5. Thomas Allen to Gen. Seth Pomeroy, May 4, 1775. *FTMB*, 13 (1972), 328.
6. Statement of regimental expenses, BA to Mass. Comm. of Safety, May–June 1775, MSS., André de Coppet Collection, PUL.
7. Edward Mott to Mass. provincial congress, May 11, 1775, *ND*, 1:315.
8. French, *Taking of Ticonderoga*, 47.
9. *Journals of the Continental Congress* (hereafter *JCC*), 2:52.
10. Ibid., 2:56.
11. Ibid., 2:68.
12. Crary, *Price of Loyalty*, 38.
13. Ethan Allen, quoted in Commager and Morris, 102–3.
14. Lt. Jocelyn Feltham to Gen. Thomas Gage, June 11, 1775, *ND*, 1:312–13.
15. BA to Mass. Comm. of Safety, May 11, 1775, *ND*, 1:312–13.
16. Barnabas Deane to Silas Deane, June 1, 1775, *ND*, 1:589.
17. BA to Mass. Comm. of Safety, May 11, 1775, *ND*, 1:313.
18. BA, May 10, 1775, "Memo Book," *FTMB*, 71.
19. BA to Mass. Comm. of Safety, May 11, 1775, *ND*, 1:313.
20. E. Allen to Mass. provincial congress, May 11, 1775, *ND*, 1:313–14.
21. Committee of War of Ticonderoga to Mass. provincial congress, May, 1775, *FTMB*, 13 (1977), 336.
22. E. Allen to Albany Comm. of Safety, May 11, 1775, *ND*, 1:314.
23. BA to Mass. Comm. of Safety, May 14, 1775, *ND*, 1:330.
24. Quoted in Jesse Root to Silas Deane, May 25, 1775, *ND*, 1:528.
25. BA, May 14, 1775, "Memo Book," *FTMB*, 71.
26. BA to Mass. Comm. of Safety, May 14, 1775, *ND*, 1:330.

5: "WE ARE MASTERS OF THE LAKE"

DEFENDING LAKE CHAMPLAIN: *LDC*, 1; *ND*, 1; B. Arnold, "Regimental Memorandum Book"; Van Doren, *Secret History of the American Revolution*, 147–49; W. M. Wallace, *Traitorous Hero*, 48–58; Flexner, *Traitor and the Spy*, 42–54.
1. Eleazar Oswald, *Journal*, in *ND*, 1:330.
2. Ibid., 1:358.
3. BA to Mass. Comm. of Safety, May 19, 1775, MSS., Copley Library.
4. E. Allen, "Narrative," 39.
5. BA to Mass. Comm. of Safety, May 19, 1775, MSS., Copley Library.
6. BA, "Memo Book," *FTMB*, 72.
7. Ibid.
8. Draft, BA to Mass. Comm. of Safety, May 19, 1775, MSS., Fort Ticonderoga Museum.
9. BA, "Memo Book," *FTMB*, 72–73.
10. Ibid., 73.

11. Ibid.
12. Ibid., 74.
13. Ibid.
14. BA to Mass. Comm. of Safety, May 19, 1775, MSS., Copley Library.
15. BA, "Memo Book," *FTMB*, 74.
16. Ibid., 75–76.
17. Lt. John André, quoted in Hatch, *Major John André*, 42.
18. BA, "Memo Book," *FTMB*, 77.
19. *JCC*, 2:55–56.
20. Richard Henry Lee to Francis Lightfoot Lee, May 21, 1775, *LDC*, 1:367.
21. *Journal*, Mass. provincial congress, June 1, 1775, *ND*, 1:586.
22. BA to Continental Congress, May 28, 1775, *ND*, 1:561–67.
23. William Williams to Conn. delegates, May 23, 1775, *ND*, 1:510.
24. Conn. delegates to Williams, May 31, 1775, *LDC*, 1:423.
25. Joseph Henshaw to BA, May 31, 1775, *ND*, 1:579.
26. *Journal*, Mass. provincial congress, May 27, 1775, *ND*, 1:543.
27. Conn. delegates to Williams, May 31, 1775, *LDC*, 1:423.
28. *JCC*, 2:73–74.
29. *Journal*, Mass. provincial congress, June 1, 1775, *ND*, 1:586–87.
30. *New England Chronicle*, May 18, 1775.
31. E. Allen and others to Continental Congress, June 10, 1775, *ND*, 1:647.
32. BA, "Memo Book," *FTMB*, 77.
33. BA to John Holt, printer, *New York Journal*, June 25, 1775, *ND*, 1:753.
34. BA to Continental Congress, June 13, 1775, 1:671–73.
35. BA to Continental Congress, June 15, 1775, MSS., Fort Ticonderoga Museum.
36. Joseph Henshaw to BA, May 31, 1775, *ND*, 1:579.
37. *Journal*, Mass. provincial congress, June 13, 1775, *ND*, 1:668–69.
38. BA, "Memo Book," *FTMB*, 79.
39. Mass. Comm. of Safety to BA, June 23, 1775, *ND*, 1:743.
40. BA to Mass. Comm. of Safety, June 24, 1775, *ND*, 1:748.
41. BA, "Memo Book," *FTMB*, 80; Report of Mass. Comm. of Safety, July 6, 1775, *ND*, 1:825–27.
42. BA to Continental Congress, July 11, 1775, *ND*, 1:862.

6: "THE CANADIANS WILL BE PLEASED"

WASHINGTON'S ARMY: Middlekauff, *Glorious Cause*, 296–304; French, *First Year of the Revolution*, 294–310; *LDC*, 1–2; *Washington, Writings*, Vols. 2–3; Cunliffe, *George Washington, Man and Monument*; Freeman, *George Washington*, Vol. 3; Ward, *War of the Revolution*, 99–124; Commager and Morris, *Spirit of 'Seventy-six*, 118–62.

BENEDICT ARNOLD'S EXPENSE ACCOUNT: Van Doren, *Secret History of the Revolution*, 149–50; W. M. Wallace, *Traitorous Hero*, 56–67; K. Roberts, *March to Quebec*, 715–24; W. M. Wallace, *Dark Star*, 15–17.

PREPARATIONS FOR INVASION: Hatch, *Thrust for Canada*, 63–71; Reynolds, *Guy Carleton*, 59–66; Bird, *Attack on Quebec*, 59–83, 103–22; W. M. Wallace, *Traitorous Hero*, 57–63; *LDC*, 2; *ND*, 2; Justin H. Smith, *Arnold's March*, 56–83; Huston, "Logistics of Arnold's March to Quebec," 110–12; Bush, *Revolutionary Enigma: A Reappraisal of General Philip Schuyler*, 27–55.

QUEBEC ACT: Hatch, *Thrust for Canada*, 1–20; Reynolds, *Guy Carleton*, 34–58; Lanctot, *Canada and the American Revolution*, 15–42; Metzger, *Quebec Act*, 37–91; Neatby, *Quebec*, 125–55; Whitridge, "Canada: The Struggle for the 14th State," 13–17; *Jesuit Relations*, 71:388–92; Burt, *Guy Carleton*, 3–7; Trudel, *La Révolution Américaine*, 87–97; Headley, *Chaplains and Clergy of the Revolution*, 83–97.

1. BA to Captain William Graymont, April 1, 1775, MSS., N-YHS.
2. GW to Philip Schuyler (hereafter PS), August 20, 1775, quoted in Middlekauff, 300–1.
3. Van Doren, *Secret History*, 149–50; BA's Expense Account for the Mass. provincial congress, MSS., de Coppet Coll, PUL.
4. Silas Deane to PS, August 20, 1775, *LDC*, 1:704.
5. GW–PS, August 20, 1775, *ND*, 1:1188.

6. PS–GW, August 27, 1775, *Am. Arch.*, 4th ser., 3:442.
7. Ibid.
8. JA to James Warren, June 7, 1775, *LDC*, 1:452.
9. Quoted in *Jesuit Relations*, 72:391–92.
10. Quoted in Metzger, 102.
11. Ibid.
12. Ibid., 103.
13. James Warren, Suffolk Resolves, in Commager and Morris, 54.
14. Thomas Jefferson, Declaration of Independence, in Commager and Morris, 318.
15. GW, Proclamation to the Inhabitants of Canada, September 25, 1775, in Justin Winsor, *Narrative and Critical History*, 6:159.
16. GW–BA, September 14, 1775, *MSS.*, Copley Library.
17. Guy Carleton to Lord Dartmouth, February 3, 1775, Public Archives of Canada, Q, X, 120.
18. *JCC*, 2:68–70; *JCC*, 1:82–90.
19. Quoted in Lanctot, *Canada and the American Revolution*, 38.
20. Neatby, 148.
21. Quoted in Hatch, *Major John André*, 36.
22. Quoted in Headley, 91.
23. Ibid.
24. Ibid.
25. Quoted in W. M. Wallace, *Traitorous Hero*, 60.
26. William Tudor to JA, September 30, 1775, *ND*, 2:247.
27. Aaron Burr to Sally Burr, September [?], 1775, quoted in Lomask, *Aaron Burr*, 1:39.
28. GW–BA, September 14, 1775, MSS., Copley Library.
29. Roberts, 337.
30. Ibid, 197.
31. Ibid., 653.
32. K. Roberts, 653.
33. Quoted in Headley, 92.
34. K. Roberts, 197.
35. Headley, 93.

7: "BELOVED BY THE SOLDIERY"

ARNOLD'S MARCH TO QUEBEC: K. Roberts, *March to Quebec;* Hendricks, *Journal of the March of a Party of Provincials;* d'Auberteuil, *Essais sur les Américains*, 295–301; Dann, *Revolution Remembered*, 14–19; Leake, *John Lamb*, 123–43; Justin H. Smith, *Arnold's March*, 82–234; Bird, *Attack on Quebec*, 103–22; Mackesy, *War for America*, 76–80; Hatch, *Thrust for Canada*, 72–81, 101–20; W. M. Wallace, *Appeal to Arms*, 72–80, and *Traitorous Hero*, 47–74; Trudel, *La Révolution Américaine*, 101–4; I. N. Arnold, *Life of Benedict Arnold*, 49–82; French, *First Year of the Revolution*, 431–42; Huston, "Logistics of Arnold's March to Quebec"; Coburn, *Passage of the Arnold Expedition Through Skowhegan;* C. J. Nichols, "March of Benedict Arnold"; Greening, "Historic Kennebec Road"; Currier, *History of Newburyport*, 556–61; Ward, *War of the Revolution*, 1:163–80.
1. K. Roberts, 546.
2. Ibid., 131.
3. BA in K. Roberts, 44a.
4. Gage to Admiral Samuel Graves, September 8, 1775, *ND*, 2:47.
5. Gage to Graves, September 27, 1775, *ND*, 2:220.
6. Captain Thomas Bishop to Graves, October 7, 1775, *ND*, 2:331.
7. Governor Francis Legge to Lord Dartmouth, October 17, 1775, *ND*, 2:486–87.
8. *Pennsylvania Packet*, October 23, 1775.
9. Graves to Captain Edward Le Cras, October 18, 1775, *ND*, 2:503.
10. BA–GW, September 25, 1775, *ND*, 2:200.
11. BA to N. Tracy, September 28, 1775, *ND*, 2:225.
12. BA in K. Roberts, 44a.
13. BA–GW, September 25, 1775, *ND*, 2:200.
14. K. Roberts, 511.
15. BA–GW, September 25, 1775, *ND*, 2:201.

16. BA–GW, September 17, 1775, in K. Roberts, 67.
17. BA in K. Roberts, 69.
18. K. Roberts, 301.
19. BA in K. Roberts, 45.
20. K. Roberts, 474.
21. BA–GW, October 13, 1775, *ND*, 2:431–32.
22. Quoted in W. M. Wallace, *Traitorous Hero*, 66.
23. K. Roberts, 549.
24. Ibid., 49.
25. Ibid., 48.
26. Ibid.
27. Ibid., 49.
28. Ibid., 514.
29. Ibid., 205.
30. BA–GW, October 27, 1775, in K. Roberts, 78.
31. BA–PS, October 13, 1775, in K. Roberts, 70–71.
32. BA to John [Mercier], October 13, 1775, in K. Roberts, 69–70.
33. BA to Lt. Steele, October 13, 1775, in K. Roberts, 71.
34. Hendricks, 34.
35. K. Roberts, 51.
36. Hendricks, 36.
37. K. Roberts, 519.
38. BA in K. Roberts, 54–55.
39. K. Roberts, 255.
40. BA–GW, October 17, 1775, in K. Roberts, 78.
41. K. Roberts, 57.
42. Ibid., 210.
43. Ibid., 256.
44. Ibid., 211.
45. Ibid., 137.
46. Ibid., 517.
47. Ibid., 137.
48. BA to R. Enos, October 27, 1775, in K. Roberts, 77–78.
49. BA to Richard Montgomery, November 8, 1775, in K. Roberts, 83.
50. K. Roberts, 628.
51. Ibid., 642–44.
52. BA to GW, October 27, 1775, in K. Roberts, 78.
53. K. Roberts, 79.
54. BA in K. Roberts, 59–60.
55. K. Roberts, 258.
56. Ibid., 335.
57. Hendricks, *Journal*, 39.
58. K. Roberts, 525.
59. Ibid., 554.
60. Ibid., 337.
61. Ibid., 337.
62. Hendricks, 52.
63. K. Roberts, 259.
64. Ibid., 139.
65. Ibid., 338.
66. Ibid., 341.
67. Ibid., 181.
68. Ibid., 261.
69. Ibid., 219.
70. BA, October 31, 1775, in K. Roberts, 80.
71. K. Roberts, 718.
72. Ibid., 219.
73. Ibid., 558.
74. BA–PS, November 27, 1775, quoted in Commager and Morris, *Spirit of 'Seventy-six*, 201.

75. GW–PS, *Am. Arch.*, 4th ser., 3:1703.
76. GW–BA, January 12, 1776, *ND*, 3:110.
77. William Hooper to Samuel Johnston, January 2, 1776, *LDC*, 3:18.
78. Joseph Hewes to Robert Smith, January 8, 1776, *LDC*, 3:58.
79. K. Roberts, 344.
80. Ibid., 522.
81. Ibid., 552.

8: "I KNOW NO FEAR"

DEFENDING QUEBEC PROVINCE: Neatby, *Quebec*, 142–57; French, *First Year of the Revolution*, 595–620; Hatch, *Thrust for Canada*, 82–120; Bird, *Attack on Quebec*, 123–45; W. M. Wallace, *Appeal to Arms*, 67–72; Flexner, *Traitor and the Spy*, 83–100; Pearson, *Those Damned Rebels*, 117–41; Ward, *War of the Revolution*, 1:150–62; Reynolds, *Guy Carleton*, 54–88; Sanguinet, *Journal;* Caron, "Les Canadiens français et l'invasion américaine de 1774–1775," 21–34; Trudel, "L'Invasion du Canada," in *La Révolution Américaine*, 87–121; Lanctot, "When Newfoundland Helped to Save Canada"; Strange, "Notes on the Defence of Quebec in 1775"; Lefebvre, "Les Canadiens français et la révolution américaine"; B. Trumbull, *Journal;* Cohen, "Lieutenant John Starke and the Defence of Quebec."
ATTACKING QUEBEC CITY: Bird, *Attack on Quebec*, 189–218; K. Roberts, *March to Quebec;* Hendricks, *Journal*, 46–51; Ward, *War of the Revolution*, 181–95; Mercier, "Expense Book of the Commissary"; Daly, "Journal of the Siege and Blockade of Quebec"; Lindsay, "Le Siège de Quebec en 1775–1776"; LeMoine, "Arnold's Assault on Sault-au-Matelot Barriers"; Wurtele, *Blockade of Quebec in 1775–1776;* Leake, *John Lamb*, 123–43.
SIEGE AND RETREAT: Bird, *Attack on Quebec*, 221–28; C. H. Jones, *Conquest of Canada*, 16–98; Rumilly, *Histoire de Montreal*, 57–63; S. E. Dawson, "Massacre at the Cedars"; F. Nichols, *Diary;* W. M. Wallace, *Traitorous Hero*, 57–96; H. Livingston, *Journal;* "Documents sur le révolution américaine, 1775–1776; Arnold Papers," *La Revue de L'Université Laval* (hereafter *RUL*) 2 (1947–48), 262–68, 344–49, 454–59, 544–47, 642–48, 742–48, 838–46, 926–34; Haw, *Stormy Patriot*, 58–68; Rowland, *Charles Carroll*, 1:140–76.
1. K. Roberts, 344, 347.
2. Ibid., 220, 222.
3. Ibid., 222.
4. Ibid., 344–45.
5. Ibid., 220–1.
6. Quoted in I. N. Arnold, *Life of Benedict Arnold*, 75.
7. GW, Proclamation, in Winsor, *Narrative and Critical History*, 6:159.
8. BA to Richard Montgomery (hereafter RM), November 8, 1775, in K. Roberts, 83.
9. K. Roberts, 478–9.
10. BA–RM, November 14, 1775, in K. Roberts, 85.
11. Lindsay, *Journal*, 226.
12. BA to Hanchet, November 14, 1775, in K. Roberts, 88.
13. BA to Hector Cramahé, November 14, 1775, in K. Roberts, 89.
14. BA to Cramahé, November 15, 1775, in K. Roberts, 89.
15. BA–RM, November 20, 1775, in K. Roberts, 90.
16. BA–GW, November 20, 1775, in K. Roberts, 93.
17. K. Roberts, 534.
18. RM–PS, December 5, 1775, *ND*, 2:1277.
19. Cramahé to Lord Dartmouth, December 1, 1776, in Shortt and Doughty, 455–56; Carleton to Dartmouth, Provincial Archives of Canada, Q, 9:318.
20. RM–PS, December 5, 1775, *ND*, 2:1277.
21. RM to Carleton, December 6, 1775, *ND*, 3:120.
22. RM to the Quebec merchants, December, 1775, Public Archives of Canada, Q, 12:18–19.
23. Thomas Ainslie, quoted in Cohen, *Canada Preserved*, 28.
24. Ibid., 27.
25. RM–PS, December 5, 1775, *ND*, 2:1228;
26. Col. Samuel Mott to Geo. Trumbull, quoted in *Am. Arch.*, 4th ser. 3:973–4.
27. Benjamin Trumbull, *Journal*, 173.
28. RM–PS, December 26, 1775, Sparks, *Correspondence of the Revolution*, 1:498.

29. RM–PS, November 13, 1775, Sparks, 1:480.
30. Ibid., 481.
31. Ibid., 480.
32. K. Roberts, 147.
33. BA–JH, February 1, 1776, ND, 3:1072.
34. RM–PS, December 26, 1775, Sparks, *Correspondence* 1:497–98.
35. K. Roberts, 701.
36. Ibid.
37. Ibid.
38. BA to Dr. Senter, December 27, 1775, in K. Roberts, 231.
39. Quoted in Flexner, 88.
40. K. Roberts, 535.
41. Ibid., 376.
42. Ibid., 377.
43. Ibid., 235, 233–34.
44. BA to David Wooster, December 31, 1775, ND, 3:314–5.
45. BA to Wooster, January 2, 1776, ND, 3:570.
46. K. Roberts, 234.
47. BA to Hannah Arnold, January 6, 1776, in K. Roberts, 108–9.
48. BA–JH, January 24, 1776, ND, 3:732.
49. BA–JH, February 1, 1776, ND, 3:1073.
50. BA–GW, February 27, 1776, in K. Roberts, 121–23.
51. K. Roberts, 123.
52. Wooster to JH, February 14, 1776, quoted in I. N. Arnold, *Life of Benedict Arnold*, 87.
53. GW to Joseph Reed (hereafter JR), January 31, 1776, Fitzpatrick, *WW*, 4:298.
54. BA–PS, April 20, 1776, *Am. Arch.*, 4th ser., 5:1098–1100.
55. Ibid.
56. Quoted in Haw, 60–61.
57. BA–PS, April 20, 1776, Sparks, *Correspondence*, 1:509.
58. Quoted in Haw, 60.
59. Quoted in Rowland, 153.
60. K. Roberts, 238.
61. BA to Horatio Gates (hereafter HG), *Am. Arch.*, 4th ser., 6:649.
62. BA to Canada Commissioners, May 27, 1776, Sparks, *Correspondence*, 1:521.
63. BA to Canada Commissioners, May 15, 1776, *Am. Arch.*, 4th ser., 6:80–81.
64. Ibid.
65. BA to Canada Commissioners, June 2, 1776, *Am. Arch.*, 5th ser., 1:165.
66. BA–PS, June 6, 1775, *Am. Arch.*, 4th ser., 6:926.
67. BA–PS, June 10, 1775, *Am. Arch.*, 4th ser., 6:977.
68. BA to John Sullivan, June 13, 1776, Sullivan Papers, *NHHSC*, XIII, 1:238.
69. BA–PS, Sullivan Papers, 1:237–38.
70. Lord Germain to General John Burgoyne, August 23, 1776, Stopford-Sackville, MSS., 2:39.

9: "FOR THE HONOR OF AMERICA"

BRITISH INVASION OF 1776: Reynolds, *Guy Carleton*, 99–106; Bowler, *Logistics and the Failure of the British Army in America*, 212–25; Riedesel, "Journal of the Brunswick Corps in America"; Nickerson, *Turning Point of the Revolution*, 65–73; ND, 5–7; Mackesy, *War for America*, 94–96; Stone, *Memoirs of Major General Riedesel*, 1:59–83; Hill, *Lake Champlain*, 100–6; C. H. Jones, *Conquest of Canada*, 99–107; P. D. Nelson, "Guy Carleton versus Benedict Arnold."

CONTROVERSY OVER COMMAND: P. D. Nelson, *General Horatio Gates*, 1–57; Bush, *Revolutionary Enigma*, 56–113; Rossie, *Politics of Command*, 17–77, 96–153.

LAKE CHAMPLAIN NAVAL SQUADRON: Bird, *Navies in the Mountains*, 164–76; Fowler, *Rebels Under Sail*, 187–92; ND, 5; Chapelle, *History of the American Sailing Navy*, 99–110, and *History of American Sailing Ships*, 70–77; Jackson, *Pennsylvania Navy*.

1. JA, *Diary*, 2:231; 3:390–91.
2. HG–JA, April 23, 1776, in Knollenburg, "Correspondence of John Adams and Horatio Gates," 140–41.

3. JA–HG, April 27, 1776, Gates Papers, Box 3, N-YHS.
4. HG–SA, June 8, 1776, Samuel Adams Papers, NYPL.
5. Samuel Chase to HG, June 13, 1776, in Burnett, *Letters,* 1:487.
6. JA–HG, June 18, 1776, Gates Papers, Box 4, N-YHS.
7. HG–JA, July 17, 1776, "Correspondence of John Adams and Horatio Gates," 147.
8. John Trumbull to Jonathan Trumbull, July 12, 1776, *ND,* 5:1035–36.
9. Dr. Lewis Beebe, "Journal," 335.
10. Chapelle, *History of the American Sailing Navy,* 110–11.
11. GW–HG, August 14, 1776, in Fitzpatrick, *Writings of George Washington* 5:433.
12. HG–JH, July 29, 1776, *Am. Arch.,* 5th ser., 1:649.
13. BA–HG, July 10, 1776, *ND,* 5:1008.
14. HG–JH, July 16, 1776, *ND,* 5:1099–1101.
15. HG–BA, July 17, 1776, *ND,* 5:1116.
16. HG–BA, July 13, 1776, *ND,* 5:1057.
17. BA–HG, July 25, 1776, *ND,* 5:1210.
18. BA–HG, July 10, 1776, *ND,* 5:1008.
19. GW–JH, July 10, 1776, *ND,* 5:1010.
20. Nicholas Cooke to JH, July 16, 1776, *ND,* 5:1097–98.
21. Jonathan Trumbull to GW, August 16, 1776, *ND,* 6:203–4.
22. Jonathan Trumbull to PS, August 13, 1776, *ND,* 6:165–66.
23. HG–GW, July 29, 1776, *Am. Arch.,* 5th ser., 1:648.
24. Orderly book of Brigade Major Peter Scull, July 31, 1776, *ND,* 5:1306.
25. BA–HG, September 7, 1776, *ND,* 6:734.
26. BA–PS, July 24, 1776, *ND,* 5:1197–98.
27. BA–HG, September 18, 1776, *ND,* 6:884.
28. HG–BA, September 23, 1776, *ND,* 6:962.
29. HG–PS, September 23, 1776, *ND,* 6:961–62.
30. Captain Richard Varick (hereafter RV) to Captain John Hunn, September 25, 1776, *ND,* 6:986.
31. BA–HG, October 1, 1776, *ND,* 6:1082–84.
32. HG–BA, October 3, 1776, *ND,* 6:1116–17.
33. Quoted in Hammersley, *Lake Champlain Naval Battles,* 3.
34. Hannah Arnold to BA, August 5, 1776, "Documents sur l'invasion américaine." *RUL,* 2 (1948), 644–45, September 1, 1776, 2 (1948), 746–47.
35. Return Jonathan Meigs to BA, July 29, 1776, in *RUL,* 2 (1948), 642–43.
36. Hannah Arnold to BA, August 28, 1776, in *RUL,* 2 (1948), 745–46.
37. Beebe, "Journal," 342.
38. BA–PS, June 10, 1776, *Am. Arch.,* 4th ser., 6:977.
39. Thomas Walker to BA, July 31, 1776, *RUL,* 2 (1948), 643–44.
40. *Am. Arch.,* 5th ser., 1:1273.
41. Ibid., 1:1274.
42. Ibid., 1:1273.
43. Ibid.
44. Ibid, 1:1273–74.
45. HG–JH, September 2, 1776, in *Am. Arch.,* 5th ser., 1:1268.
46. BA–PS, July 30, 1776, *ND,* 5:1282.
47. BA–HG, August 16, 1776, *ND,* 6:205.
48. HG to Jonathan Trumbull, August 11, 1776, *ND,* 6:145.
49. BA–PS, August 8, 1776, *ND,* 6:120.
50. Quoted in Trevelyan, *American Revolution,* 2:223.
51. Gates's Orders to BA, August 7, 1776, *ND,* 6:95–96.
52. *ND,* 6:95–96.
53. BA–HG, August 6, 1776, *ND,* 6:205.
54. BA–PS, August 8, 1776, *ND,* 6:120.
55. Orderly book of Brigade Major Peter Scull, August 10, 1776, *ND,* 6:139.
56. BA to Captains Seamon and Premier, August 17, 1776, *ND,* 6:2155.
57. Jacobus Wynkoop to BA, August 17, 1776, *ND,* 6:215.
58. BA to Wynkoop, August 17, 1776, *ND,* 6:215.
59. BA–HG, August 17, 1776, *ND,* 6:216.

60. HG–BA, August 18, 1776, *ND,* 6:223.
61. HG–PS, August 18, 1776, *ND,* 6:223.
62. BA–HG, August 19, 1776, *ND,* 6:234.

10: "YOUR FRIENDS ARE NOT YOUR COUNTRYMEN"

SKIRMISHING ON LAKE CHAMPLAIN: *ND,* 6; *LDC,* 4; C. H. Jones, *Conquest of Canada;* Bowler, *Logistics and the Failure of the British Army in America;* Riedesel, *Memoirs, Letters and Journals;* Butterfield, "Psychological Warfare in 1776"; *RUL,* 2 (1948).
1. BA–HG, August 31, 1776, *ND,* 6:371.
2. BA–HG, September 7, 1776, *ND,* 6:734–35.
3. BA–HG, September 2, 1776, *ND,* 6:654.
4. BA–HG, September 21, 1776, *ND,* 6:925.
5. Testimony of Thomas Day, August 17, 1776, *RUL* 2 (1948), 647.
6. BA–HG, September 16, 1776, *ND,* 6:857–58.
7. BA–HG, September 18, 1776, *ND,* 6:884.
8. Examination of Sergeant Eli Stiles, September 16, 1776, *ND,* 6:858–59.
9. *JCC,* 5:653–55, 707.
10. BF–BA, August 28, 1776, *PBF,* 22:583.
11. HG–BA, September 12, 1776, *ND,* 6:791.
12. BA–HG, September 15, 1776, *ND,* 6:838.
13. BA–HG, September 21, 1776, *ND,* 6:926.
14. BA–HG, September 28, 1776, *ND,* 6:1032.
15. Examination of Sergeant Eli Stiles, October 1, 1776, *ND,* 6:1084.
16. BA–HG, September 28, 1776, *ND,* 6:1032.
17. J. Wilkinson to RV, August 5, 1776, MSS., André de Coppet Collection, PUL.
18. "Force on the Lake Champlain Tolerably Exact on September 18, 1776," P.R.O., C.O. 5/125, 69c; Serle, *American Journal,* 98.
19. HG to BA, October 3, 1776, *ND,* 5:1117.
20. BA–HG, Supply Requisition, October 1, 1776, *ND,* 6:1082–83.
21. BA–HG, September 21, 1776, *ND,* 6:925–26.
22. HG–BA, October 3, 1776, *ND,* 6:1116–17.
23. HG–PS, September 23, 1776, *ND,* 6:961.
24. BA–HG, September 21, 1776, *ND,* 6:926.
25. HG–BA, October 3, 1776, *ND,* 6:1117.
26. Samuel Chase to HG, May 30, 1776, *LDC,* 4:202.
27. Chase to BA, August 7, 1776, *LDC,* 4:633–34.
28. HG–JA, August 30, 1776, *LDC,* 4:615.
29. JA–HG, August 13, 1776, *LDC,* 4:670.
30. JA–HG, August 13, 1776, *LDC,* 4:670.
31. BA–HG, September 7, 1776, *ND,* 6:735.
32. Ibid.
33. BA–HG, September 15, 1776, *ND,* 6:838.
34. BA–HG, September 18, 1776, *ND,* 6:884.
35. HG–BA, October 12, 1776, *ND,* 6:1237.
36. BA–HG, October 7, 1776, *ND,* 6:1152.
37. BA–HG, October 18, 1776, *ND,* 6:884.

11: "SUCH COOL DETERMINED VALOR"

BATTLE OF VALCOUR BAY: Fowler, *Rebels Under Sail,* 171–211; *ND,* 6; W. M. Wallace, *Traitorous Hero,* 110–19; Hadden, *Journal;* Riedesel, "Journal of the Brunswick Corps" and *Memoirs;* Hammersley, *Lake Champlain Naval Battles,* 1–14; Bird, *Navies in the Mountains,* 196–213; Chapelle, *History of the American Sailing Navy;* Mahan, *Major Operations of the Navies,* 6–28; Millar, *American Ships of the Colonial and Revolutionary Periods;* Enys, *American Journals;* Cohn, "An Incident Not Known to History"; Snyder, "With Benedict Arnold at Valcour Island"; Wells, *Journal;* Bredenberg, "Royal Savage"; Maguire, "Dr. Knox's Account of the Battle of Valcour."

1. BA–HG, September 21, 1776, *ND*, 6:926.
2. Riedesel, *Memoirs, Letters and Journals*, 1:64.
3. Enys, 18–19.
4. Lt. William Digby, *Journal*, in *ND*, 6:1137.
5. Guy Carleton to Hector Cramahé, October 9, 1776, *ND*, 6:1178.
6. Hadden, Orders by General Carleton, October 9, 1776, *Journal*, 17.
7. Pausch, *Journal*, October 11, 1776, in *ND*, 6:1259.
8. Captain John Starke, "An Open Letter to Captain Pringle," MSS., FTM.
9. Riedesel, *Memoirs*, 1:70.
10. Starke, MSS., FTM.
11. Pausch, *ND*, 6:1259.
12. Maguire, "Dr. Knox's Account," 143–44.
13. Lt. Digby, *Journal*, 102, 173.
14. Lt. John Starke, "Open Letter to Captain Pringle," in *FTMB*, 1 (1928), 17.
15. Carleton to Burgoyne, [October 12–15, 1776], *ND*, 6:1272–4.
16. Pausch, *ND*, 6:1259.
17. BA–HG, October 12, 1776, *ND*, 6:1235.
18. Guy Carleton to Captain Charles Douglas, October 14, 1776, *ND*, 6:1257.
19. Starke, MSS., FTM.
20. General David Waterbury to JH, October 24, 1776, *ND*, 7:1295.
21. Pascal DeAngelis, October 13, 1776, quoted in Snyder, 199.
22. BA–PS, October 15, 1776, *ND*, 6:1276.
23. Peter Ferris, quoted in Cohn, 109.
24. BA–PS, October 15, 1776, *ND*, 6:1276.
25. Guy Carleton to William Howe, October 20, 1776, *ND*, 6:1336.
26. Lt. William Digby, *Journal*, November 2, 1776, in *ND*, 7:19.
27. Mahan, 25.

12: "BY HEAVEN, I WILL HAVE JUSTICE"

CONTROVERSY OVER PROMOTION: W. M. Wallace, *Traitorous Hero*, 119–27; Flexner, *Traitor and the Spy*, 161–84; *ND*, 7; Rossie, *Politics of Command*, 135–53; Bush, *Revolutionary Enigma*, 83–133.

DANBURY RAID: East, *Connecticut Loyalists*, 23–26, 30–38; Leake, *John Lamb*, 154–64; Rockwell, *History of Ridgefield*, 103–19; Lossing, *Pictorial Field Book of the Revolution*, 1:407–10; F. Moore, *Diary of the American Revolution*, 1:423–28; G. Jones, "An Early Amphibious Operation."

RETREAT FROM TICONDEROGA: Nickerson, *Turning Point of the Revolution*, 1:129–92; Pancake, *1777: Year of the Hangman*, 114–28.

GATES-ARNOLD DISPUTE: P. D. Nelson, *General Horatio Gates*, 84–156; Bush, *Revolutionary Enigma*, 89–156; I. N. Arnold, *Life of Benedict Arnold*, 163–211; Luzager, "The Arnold-Gates Controversy"; Rossie, *Politics of Command*, 154–73.

RELIEF OF FT. STANWIX: Stone, *Campaign of Burgoyne*, 139–222 ; Holden, "Influence of Jane McCrea on the Burgoyne Campaign"; J. A. Scott, "Joseph Brant at Fort Stanwix and Oriskany"; Pancake, *1777*, 139–45; Nickerson, *Turning Point*, 193–223; W. M. Wallace, *Traitorous Hero*, 137–44.

BATTLES OF SARATOGA: W. M. Wallace, *Traitorous Hero*, 1–4, 145–59; Pancake, *1777*, 114–62; Pearson, *Those Damned Rebels*, 262–91; Flexner, *Traitor and the Spy*, 161–84; Nickerson, *Turning Point*, 298–333, 369–403; Mackesy, *War for America*, 130–44; Bird, *March to Saratoga*, 175–272.

1. BA–PS, October 15, 1776, *ND*, 6:1276.
2. HG to Jonathan Trumbull, October 15, 1776, *Am. Arch.*, 5th ser., 2:1079–80.
3. HG to Jonathan Trumbull, October 22, 1776, *Am. Arch.*, 5th ser., 2:1192.
4. HG, General Orders, October 16, 1776, *Am. Arch.*, 5th ser., 3:527.
5. Lt. James Dacres to Phillip Stephens, *Am. Arch.*, 5th ser., 3:1227.
6. William Maxwell to William Livingston, October 20, 1776, *Am. Arch.*, 5th ser., 2:1143.
7. Richard Henry Lee to Thomas Jefferson, November 3, 1776, *ND*, 7:29.
8. BA–HG, September 2, 1776, *ND*, 6:654.
9. BA–HG, September 7, 1776, *Am. Arch.*, 5th ser., 2:354.

10. Charges listed in full in W. M. Wallace, *Traitorous Hero*, 350–51.
11. *JCC*, 8:382.
12. PS to HG, July 14, 1776, *Am. Arch.*, 4th ser., 6:1038.
13. John Brown to HG, *Am. Arch.*, 5th ser., 2:911.
14. BA to Canada Commissioners, quoted in Hazen Court-Martial Report, December 2, 1776, *Am. Arch.*, 5th ser., 3:1042–43.
15. Samuel Chase to BA, August 7, 1776, *Am. Arch.*, 5th ser., 1:810.
16. HG–JH, November 27, 1776, *Am. Arch.*, 5th ser. 3:875.
17. Leake, *John Lamb*, 149.
18. BA–GW, January 13, 1777, Sparks, *Correspondence*, 1:327.
19. GW–JH, December 14, 1776, 374–75.
20. GW–BA, January 6, 1777, MSS., HSP.
21. Quoted in Forbes, *Paul Revere*, 322–23.
22. Anonymous, *The Motley Assembly*, 1779.
23. BA to Lucy Knox, March 4, 1777, MSS., Copley Library.
24. *JCC*, 7:133.
25. GW–BA, March 3, 1777, Sparks, *Correspondence*, 4:345.
26. GW–R. H. Lee, March 6, 1777, *Am. Arch.*, 5th ser., 7:251–52.
27. BA–PS, March 8, 1777, MSS., Schuyler Papers, NYPL.
28. BA–GW, March 12, 1777, Sparks, *Correspondence*, 4:345.
29. BA–GW, March 26, 1777, Sparks, *Correspondence*, 4:346.
30. GW–BA, April 3, 1777, Fitzpatrick, *Writings of George Washington*, 7:352–53.
31. BA–HG, March 25, 1777, MSS., Gates Papers, N-YHS.
32. Lucy Knox to Henry Knox, April 30, 1777, MSS., Massachusetts Historical Society.
33. GW–BA, April 3, 1777, Fitzpatrick, 7:352.
34. "A British Officer's Account of the Danbury Raid," *ND*, 8:4560.
35. Quoted in W. M. Wallace, *Traitorous Hero*, 129.
36. Ibid., 130.
37. GW–JH, May 12, 1777, Fitzpatrick, 8:47–48.
38. Rush, *Autobiography*, 158.
39. BA–JH, May 20, 1777, *PCC*, Roll 162, 1, f64–65.
40. Burnett, *Continental Congress*, 2:261–63.
41. *JCC*, 8:537.
42. R. H. Lee to Thomas Jefferson, May 20, 1777, *LDC*, 7:95.
43. *JCC*, 7:372–73.
44. JA to Abigail Adams, May 22, 1777, *LDC*, 7:103.
45. BA to Congress, February 2, 1776, *PCC*, Roll 162, L, f64–65.
46. BA to Canada Commissioners, June 2, 1776, *Am. Arch.*, 5th ser., 1:165.
47. *JCC*, 8:382.
48. BA to Board of War, July, 1777, MSS., PUL.
49. BA to Congress, July 11, 1777, *PCC*, roll 162, 1, f106.
50. GW to Congress, July 10, 1777, Fitzpatrick, 8:377.
51. GW to Congress, July 12, 1777, Fitzpatrick, 8:386.
52. *JCC*, 8:623–24.
53. James Lovell to William Whipple, August 11, 1777, *LDC*, 7:458.
54. Lovell to Whipple, August 8, 1777, *LDC*, 7:443.
55. Henry Laurens to John Rutledge, August 12, 1777, *LDC*, 7:469.
56. BA–HG, August 5, 1777, MSS., Gates Papers, N-YHS.
57. Quoted in I. N. Arnold, *Life of Benedict Arnold*, 153–54.
58. GW–PS, July 12, 1777, Fitzpatrick, 9:106.
59. BA–HG, August 21, 1777, MSS., Gates Papers, N-YHS.
60. BA, Proclamation, MSS., Gates Papers, N-YHS.
61. BA–HG, August 23, 1777, MSS., Gates Papers, N-YHS.
62. *JCC*, 8:688.
63. Samuel Adams to James Warren, August 1, 1777, *LDC*, 7:401.
64. Samuel Adams to R. H. Lee, July 15, 1777, MSS., Samuel Adams Papers, NYPL.
65. Samuel Adams to Samuel Freeman, August 5, 1777, *LDC*, 7:414.
66. Henry Marchant to Nicholas Cooke, August 5, 1777, *LDC*, 7:427–28.
67. Henry Laurens to John Rutledge, August 12, 1777, *LDC*, 7:468.

68. See *LDC,* 7:417n, for a useful summary of the charges.
69. PS to Gouverneur Morris, August 19, 1777, quoted in Nickerson, 282.
70. PS–HG, August 20, 1777, quoted in Bush, 133.
71. Quoted in Wilkinson, *Memoirs,* 1:172–73.
72. President of Congress to HG, August 14, 1777, MSS., Gates Papers, N-YHS.
73. BA–HG, September 22, 1777, MSS., Gates Papers, N-YHS.
74. Richard Varick to PS, September 25, 1777, MSS., Schuyler Papers, NYPL.
75. BA–HG, September 23, 1777, MSS., Gates Papers, N-YHS.
76. Varick to PS, September 15, 1777, MSS., Schuyler Papers, NYPL.
77. Quoted in I. N. Arnold, *Life of Benedict Arnold,* 171.
78. Quoted in Wilkinson, 1:245–46.
79. HG–JH, September 22, 1777, MSS., Gates Papers, N-YHS.
80. William Brockhulst Livingston to PS, September 23, 1777, MSS., Schuyler Papers, NYPL.
81. Wilkinson, 1:254.
82. BA–HG, September 22, 1777, MSS., Gates Papers, N-YHS.
83. HG–JH, September 23, 1777, MSS., Gates Papers, N-YHS.
84. BA–HG, September 23, 1777, MSS., Gates Papers, N-YHS.
85. HG–BA, September 23, 1777, MSS., Gates Papers, N-YHS.
86. H. Livingston to PS, September 23, 1777, quoted in P. D. Nelson, *Gates,* 128.
87. Varick to PS, September 24, 1777, quoted in P. D. Nelson, *Gates,* 128.
88. PS to Varick, September 25, 1777, quoted in P. D. Nelson, *Gates,* 128.
89. H. Livingston to PS, September 24, 1777, quoted in I. N. Arnold, *Life of Benedict Arnold,* 178.
90. H. Livingston to PS, September 26, 1777, quoted in I. N. Arnold, *Life of Benedict Arnold,* 180.
91. Varick to PS, September 25, 1777, quoted in I. N. Arnold, *Life of Benedict Arnold,* 184.
92. BA–HG, October 1, 1777, MSS., Gates Papers, N-YHS.
93. Ibid.
94. Burgoyne to Clinton, September 23, 1777, in Wilkinson, 1:251.
95. Council of War Minutes, October 4, 1777, quoted in Burgoyne, *State of the Expedition from Canada,* lxxxviii–lxxxvviv.
96. Wilkinson, 1:254.
97. Ibid., 1:255.
98. Quoted in W. M. Wallace, *Traitorous Hero,* 156.
99. Anburey, *Travels,* 404.
100. Quoted in W. M. Wallace, *Traitorous Hero,* 156.
101. Quoted in Stone, *Campaign of Burgoyne,* 66.
102. Quoted in K. Roberts, *March to Quebec,* 127.

13: "AMERICA HAS SEEN ITS BEST DAYS"

BRITISH-OCCUPIED PHILADELPHIA: Weigley, *Philadelphia,* 132–54; Scharf and Wescott, *History of Philadelphia,* Vol. 1; Jackson, *Pennsylvania Navy,* Weiner, "Military Occupation of Philadelphia in 1777–1778"; Bradford, "Hunger Menaces the Revolution"; and *With the British Army in Philadelphia;* 54–337.
SHIPPEN FAMILY CIRCLE: Walker, "Life of Margaret Shippen," 24:257–67, 401–29; I. N. Arnold, *Life of Benedict Arnold,* 212–29; Tillotson, *Exquisite Exile,* 17–57; Engle, *Women in the American Revolution,* 109–20; Lewis, "Edward Shippen"; R. Klein, "The Shippen Family"; W. M. Wallace, *Traitorous Hero,* 160–79; Flexner, *Traitor and the Spy,* 187–216.
ANDRÉ AND THE MESCHIANZA: Flexner, *Traitor and the Spy,* 202–16; Pollock, *Philadelphia Theatre in the Eighteenth Century;* Scharf and Westcott, Vol. 1; André, "Particulars of the Meschianza," 353–57.
1. Quoted in Weigley, 132.
2. Quoted in Weigley, 133.
3. Thacher, *Military Journal,* 103.
4. HG–JH, October 12, 1777, MSS., Gates Papers, Box 8, N-YHS.
5. GW–BA, January 8, 1778, Fitzpatrick, *WW,* 10:324–25.
6. BA to Betsy DeBlois, April 14, 1778, quoted in Decker, *Benedict Arnold,* 285.
7. BA to Betsy DeBlois, April 28, 1778, quoted in Decker, 287.

8. André to Anna Seward, October 3, 1769, MSS., Houghton Library.
9. André to Marie Louise André, December 17, 1776, quoted in Hatch, *Major John André*, 67.
10. André to Margaret Chew, May, 1779, quoted in Van Doren, *Secret History of the Revolution*, 441.
11. André to Peggy Chew, [May] 1779, MSS., Clinton Papers, WLCL.
12. André to Caleb Cope, October 11, 1776, MSS., PUL.
13. André to Marie Louise André, December 17, 1776, quoted in Hatch, *Major John André*, 71.
14. André, *Journal*, 50.
15. Quoted in Hatch, *Major John André*, 77.
16. André to Marie Louise André, September 28, 1777, quoted in Hatch, *Major John André*, 77.
17. Edward Shippen IV to Edward Shippen III, June 11, 1760, Shippen Papers, 5153, HSP.
18. Walker, 24:258.
19. Tobias Smollett, *History of England*, London, 1828, 3:9.
20. Quoted in Walker, 24:259.
21. Alexander Pope, "First Satire of the Second Book of Horace."
22. Jasper Yeates, quoted in Walker, 24:266.
23. Edward Shippen IV to Edward Shippen III, September 10, 1765, MSS., Shippen Papers, 11:69 HSP.
24. Edward Shippen IV to Edward Shippen, III, April 6, 1766, MSS., Shippen Papers, HSP.
25. Edward Shippen IV to Edward Shippen III, June 23, 1776, MSS., Shippen Papers, HSP.
26. Edward Shippen IV to Edward Shippen III, March 11, 1777, MSS., HSP.
27. Edward Shippen IV to Edward Shippen III, January 18, 1777, MSS., Shippen-Balch Papers, 2:35, HSP.
28. PSA to Edward Shippen III, January 5, 1803, MSS., Shippen Papers, HSP.
29. Quoted in Walker, 24:414.
30. Rebecca Franks to Mrs. William Paca, February 26, 1778, quoted in Jackson, *With the British Army in Philadelphia*, 325.
31. Quoted in Hatch, *Major John André*, 95.
32. Pollock, 34–35.
33. Quoted in Flexner, *Traitor and the Spy*, 202.
34. André, "A German Air," January 1778, MSS., PUL.
35. Quoted in Flexner, *Traitor and the Spy*, 203.
36. Edward Shippen III to Edward Shippen, Jr., December [?], 1778, MSS., Shippen Papers, HSP.
37. William Howe to George Germain, October 10, 1777, quoted in Jackson, *With the British Army in Philadelphia*.
38. Germain to Henry Clinton, March 8, 1778, MSS., Clinton Papers, WLCL.
39. André, "Particulars of the Meschianza," 353.
40. André to PSA, August 16, 1779, MSS., N-YHS.
41. André, "Particulars," 353–57.
42. Lawrence Lewis, Jr., to L. B. Walker, quoted in Walker, 24:428.
43. André, "Particulars," 356–57.
44. Rebecca Franks, quoted in Flexner, *Traitor and the Spy*, 214.
45. "Journal of Mrs. Henry Drinker," *PMHB*, 13 (1889), 306.
46. Charles Stedman, *History of the American War*, 385–86.
47. Serle, *American Journal*, 295–99.

14: "ON YOU ALONE MY HAPPINESS DEPENDS"

CONWAY CABAL: Freeman, *George Washington*, vol. 4, 545–57, 586–611; P. D. Nelson, *General Horatio Gates*, 157–85; Commager and Morris, *Spirit of 'Seventy-six*, 651–56; Ward, *War of the Revolution*, 2:543–55; Royster, *A Revolutionary People at War*, 179–89.

CONVALESCENCE AND REMARRIAGE: Tillotson, *Exquisite Exile*, 41–59; Scharf and Westcott, *History of Philadelphia*, Vol. 1; G. G. Galloway, *Diary*; I. N. Arnold, *Life of Benedict Arnold*, 212–29; Lewis, "Edward Shippen"; Walker, "Margaret Shippen" 25:26–40; Flexner, *Traitor and the Spy*, 217–37.

TROUBLE WITH PENNSYLVANIA: Ousterhout, "Controlling the Opposition in Pennsylvania During the American Revolution"; Van Doren, *Secret History of the Revolution*; Meng, *Despatches and Instructions of Conrad Alexandre Gérard, 1778–1780*; Henderson, "Congressional Factionalism" and "Constitutionalists and Republicans"; Pavlovsky, "Between Hawk and Buzzard"; W. M. Wallace, *Traitorous Hero*, 174–92; Flexner, *Traitor and the Spy*, 237–59; Roche, *Joseph Reed*; Engle, "Esther DeBerdt Reed," in *Women in the Revolutionary War*; Carson, "The Case of the Sloop *Active*"; R. K. Murdock, "Benedict Arnold and the Owners of the *Charming Nancy*"; BA, "Financial Day Book."

1. Dearborn, *Journals*, 118.
2. H. B. Livingston to R. R. Livingston, December 24, 1777, *Sullivan Papers*, 1:598–99.
3. Pierre Etienne du Ponceau to Robert Walsh, June 13, 1836, quoted in *Commager and Morris*, *Spirit of 'Seventy-six*, 648.
4. Dr. Albigence Waldo, *Diary*, in Commager and Morris, 641.
5. JA to Abigail Adams, October 26, 1777, *LDC*, 8:187.
6. J. Sullivan to JA, November 10, 1777, *Sullivan Papers*, 1:577.
7. Conway quoted in Lord Stirling to GW, November 3, 1777, Freeman, 4:550.
8. Ibid.
9. GW to Joseph Reed, December 15, 1775, Fitzpatrick, 4:165.
10. HG–GW, [December] 8, 1777, *MSS.*, Gates Papers, N-YHS.
11. John Laurens to Henry Laurens, January 3, 1778, *LDC*, 8:545–50.
12. Dearborn, *Journals*, 113.
13. Thomas Jefferson to Philip Mazzei, in TJ, *Papers*, 11:95.
14. Silas Deane, quoted in Flexner, *Traitor and the Spy*, 222.
15. *JCC*, 11:571.
16. GW–BA, June 19, 1778, Fitzpatrick, 12:94–95.
17. BA, *Proceedings of a Court Martial*, 10.
18. R. K. Murdock, 23.
19. R. K. Murdock, 26; see also BA "Financial Day Book," October 22–23, 1778, PHMC.
20. Ousterhout, 5.
21. Articles of Agreement, BA, James Mease, and William West, Jr., June 12, 1778, copy, N-YHS.
22. Affidavit by Benjamin Paschall, quoted in PCC, item 69, 2:47; see also *LDC*, 12:266.
23. Van Doren, *Secret History*, 172.
24. BA, "Financial Day Book," p. 9, October 25, 1778, shows Arnold in partnership with Duer, Major Clarkson and Seagrove. Arnold invested £8,000 in the joint venture on that date.
25. R. K. Murdock, 26.
26. John R. Livingston to four New York merchants, July 18, 1778, MSS., HL.
27. BA, *Proceedings of a Court Martial*, 10–12, 26, 43.
28. Quoted in Flexner, *Traitor and the Spy*, 223–24.
29. Carson, 389.
30. Major Franks to GW, July 4, 1778, Fitzpatrick, 12:269–70.
31. Elias Boudinot to GW, June 30, 1778, Fitzpatrick, 12:161.
32. GW–BA, June 19, 1778, Fitzpatrick, 12:94–95.
33. Anthony Wayne, quoted in Stillé, *Anthony Wayne*, 153–54.
34. Josiah Bartlett to Mary Bartlett, August 24, 1778, *LDC*, 10:496.
35. Sarah Franklin Bache to BF, January 8, 1779, quoted in I. N. Arnold, 235.
36. Scharf and Westcott, 1:900.
37. Quoted in Engle, 122.
38. Henry Laurens to BA, August 7, 1778, *LDC*, 10:397.
39. Henry Laurens to Rawlin Lourdes, July 15, 1778, *LDC*, 10:284.
40. Elias Boudinot to Hannah Boudinot, July 14, 1778, *LDC*, 10:276.
41. Conrad Alexandre Gérard to Comte de'Vergennes, July 16, 1778, Meng, 160.
42. BA–GW, July 19, 1778, Fitzpatrick, 12:270n.
43. GW–BA, August 3, 1778, Fitzpatrick, 12:269–70.
44. I. N. Arnold, *Life of Benedict Arnold*, 228.
45. BA to Peggy Shippen, September 25, 1778, in I. N. Arnold, *Life of Benedict Arnold*, 229.
46. BA to Peggy Shippen, September 25, 1778, in I. N. Arnold, *Life of Benedict Arnold*, 229–30.
47. BA to Edward Shippen III, September, 1778, in I. N. Arnold, *Life of Benedict Arnold*, 228.
48. Sally Franklin Bache to BF, September, 1778, quoted in Walker, 25:32.
49. Joseph Reed to Jared Ingersoll, December 15, 1778; W. B. Reed, *Life and Correspondence of Joseph Reed*, 2:39.
50. Ousterhout, 5.
51. Ibid.
52. *Pennsylvania Packet*, November 7, 1778.

53. James Humphreys to Joseph Galloway, November 23, [1778], in James Riker, *Memoria,* vol. 15, NYPL.
54. Isaac Ogden to Joseph Galloway, November 22, 1778, quoted in Crary, *Price of Loyalty,* 237.
55. JR to Nathanael Greene, November 5, 1778, in W. B. Reed, *Life and Correspondence of Joseph Reed,* 2:37.
56. Gen. John Cadwalader to Nathanael Greene, December 5, 1778, MSS., Lee Papers, N-YHS.
57. Mrs. Robert Morris to Elizabeth Tilghman, February 2, 1779, in Walker, 25:35.
58. BA to Robert Howe, September 12, 1780, in Washington Papers, Library of Congress.
59. James Duane to PS, January 3, 1779, *LDC,* 11:405.
60. Col. Edward Burd to Jasper Yeates, in Walker, 25:35–36.
61. Edward Shippen IV to Edward Shippen III, December 21, 1778, in Lewis, 29.
62. JA to Abigail Adams, quoted in Scharf and Westcott, 1:389.
63. Edward Shippen III to Col. Edward Burd, January 2, 1779, in Walker, 25:30.

15: "SELF-PRESERVATION IS THE FIRST PRINCIPLE"

CONTROVERSY WITH PENNSYLVANIA: Brunhouse, *Counter-Revolution in Pennsylvania,* 48–68; *LDC,* Vols. 10–12; W. M. Wallace, *Traitorous Hero,* 170–92; Van Doren, *Secret History of the American Revolution,* 168–93; BA, *Proceedings of a Court Martial;* Walker, "Margaret Shippen," 25:36–40; Flexner, *Traitor and the Spy,* 227–59; Roche, *Joseph Reed;* W. B. Reed, *Life and Correspondence of Joseph Reed,* Vol. 2; S. Cohen, "Hannah Levy and the General."
1. JR to Nathanael Greene, November 4, 1778, MSS., *Lee Papers,* N-YHS Collections, 6 (1887–91), 3:250.
2. Quoted in Flexner, *Traitor and the Spy,* 237.
3. [Timothy Matlack], *Pennsylvania Packet,* November 12, 1778.
4. BA to *Pennsylvania Packet,* November 19, 1778.
5. Brissot de Warville, *Travels,* 2:293.
6. Van Doren, *Secret History of the Revolution,* 178.
7. BA to Timothy Matlack, October 6, 1778, Reed Papers, N-YHS.
8. BA to Matlack, October 12, 1778, Reed Papers, N-YHS.
9. BA, *Proceedings of a Court Martial,* 14.
10. BA to Matlack, October 6, 1778, Reed Papers, N-YHS.
11. BA to Matlack, October 12, 1778, Reed Papers, N-YHS.
12. "Militia Man," *Pennsylvania Packet,* November 13, 1778.
13. "T.G.," *Pennsylvania Packet,* March 6, 1779.
14. "Observator," *Pennsylvania Packet,* December 3, 1778.
15. John Cadwalader to Nathanael Greene, December 5, 1778, *Lee Papers,* N-YHS Collections, 6 (1887–91), 3:270–1.
16. Pennsylvania Council to Continental Congress, January 25, 1779, *JCC,* 13:115.
17. Pennsylvania Council to GW, January 31, 1779, N-YHS.
18. BA–PS, November 30, 1778, Schuyler Papers, NYPL.
19. BA–PS, February 8, 1779, Schuyler Papers, NYPL.
20. John Jay to George Clinton, February 3, 1779, *LDC,* 12:17–18.
21. Proclamation of Pennsylvania Council, *Pennsylvania Packet,* February 9, 1779.
22. Quoted in Van Doren, 189.
23. BA, *Pennsylvania Packet,* February 9, 1779.
24. BA–PS, February 8, 1779, in Walker, 25:38.
25. GW–JR, October 18, 1780, Fitzpatrick, 20:370.
26. BA–PS, February 8, 1779, in Walker, 25:38.
27. Quoted in Flexner, *Traitor and the Spy,* 247.
28. *Pennsylvania Packet,* February 27, 1779.
29. BA, *Pennsylvania Packet,* March 4, 1779.
30. William Paca to Pennsylvania Council, March 4, 1779, *LDC,* 12:152.
31. George Bryan to William Paca, March 5, 1779, MSS., N-YHS.
32. William Paca to the Pennsylvania Council, March 9, 1779, *LDC,* 12:180.
33. *JCC,* 13:412–17.
34. Henry Laurens, March 6, 1779, quoted in Flexner, *Traitor and the Spy,* 251–52.
35. *JCC,* 13:417.
36. W. M. Wallace, *Traitorous Hero,* 188.

37. *Pennsylvania Packet*, September 30, 1778.
38. Edward Shippen III to Edward Shippen IV, February 15, 1779, in Walker, 25:36.
39. Walker, 25:39–40.
40. Elizabeth Tilghman to PSA, April 14, 1779, in Walker, 25:40–41.
41. BA, quoted in W. M. Wallace, *Traitorous Hero*, 197.
42. BA to Congress, April 14, 1779, quoted in *Proceedings*, 53.
43. BA–GW, April 14, 1779, quoted in *Proceedings*, 53.
44. J. R. to Congress, April 24, 1779, *Pennsylvania Archives*, 8:349–50.
45. GW–BA, April 25, 1779, Sparks, *Writings*, 6:518–19.
46. BA–GW, May 5, 1779, Sparks, 6:523.

16: "MY LIFE AND EVERYTHING IS AT STAKE"

OVERTURE OF TREASON: Brunhouse, *Counter-Revolution in Pennsylvania*, 68–76; Van Doren, *Secret History of the American Revolution*, 196–216; Tyler, *Literary History of the American Revolution*, Vol. 2; W. M. Wallace, *Traitorous Hero*, 180–206; Flexner, *Traitor and the Spy*, 275–91; H. H. Peckham, "British Secret Writing."

FORT WILSON RIOT: *Pennsylvania Archives*, 1st ser., 7:732, 735, 744; Brunhouse, *Counter-Revolution in Pennsylvania*, 68–76; Alexander, "The Fort Wilson Incident of 1779"; Scharf and Westcott, *History of Philadelphia*, 1:401–3; W. B. Reed, *Joseph Reed*, 2:149–55, 423–28; Roche, *Joseph Reed;* Walker, "Margaret Shippen," 25:25–27; Samuel Rowland Fisher, *Journal*, 169–97.

1. *Royal Gazette*, February 17, 1779.
2. BA–HG, August 5, 1777, MSS., Gates Papers, N-YHS.
3. BA to Robert Howe, September 12, 1780, MSS., Washington Papers, *LC*.
4. G. G. Galloway, *Diary*, May 5, 1779.
5. Joseph Stansbury, affidavit, March 4, 1784, MSS., Loyalist Claims Commission, P.R.O., AO/13, 96.
6. Sargent, *Loyal Verses*, 103–4.
7. JS, March 4, 1784, P.R.O., AO/13, 96.
8. Tyler, 2:99.
9. W. B. Reed, *Life and Correspondence of Joseph Reed*, 2:170n.
10. Tyler, 2:125.
11. J. Berkenhout, "Dr. Berkenhout's Journal, 1778," *PMHR*, 65 (1941), 79–82.
12. Earl of Carlisle to Lady Carlisle, July 21, 1778, quoted in R. G. Davies, ed., *Transcripts*, 8:131.
13. William Franklin to John André, November 10, 1779, MSS., P.R.O., CO5/85, 52.
14. T. Jones, *History of New York During the Revolutionary War*, 1:319.
15. William Franklin, quoted in Willcox, *Portrait of a General*, 452–53.
16. William Smith, *Diary*, June 21, 1778.
17. André, "Dream," *Royal Gazette*, January 23, 1779.
18. Gen. James Robertson, *Letterbook*, 54.
19. Stephen Kemble, quoted in Hatch, *Major John André*, 129.
20. William Smith, *Diary*, April 24, 1779.
21. André to BA, [May 10, 1779], Van Doren, *Secret History of the Revolution*, 439.
22. Van Doren, *Secret History*, 440.
23. Ibid.
24. JA to Peggy Chew, [May], 1779, MSS., Clinton Papers, WLCL.
25. BA to André, May 21, 1779, MSS., Clinton Papers, WLCL.
26. Odell to André, May 31, 1779, MSS., Clinton Papers, WLCL.
27. Stansbury to Odell, May 26, 1779, MSS., Clinton Papers, WLCL.
28. Stansbury to Odell, June 9, 1779, MSS., Clinton Papers, WLCL.
29. Odell to Stansbury, [June] 9, [1779], MSS., Clinton Papers, WLCL.
30. BA to André, May 23, 1779, MSS., Clinton, WLCL.
31. BA–GW, Sparks, *Writings of Washington*, 6:523.
32. GW–BA, May 15, 1779, Fitzpatrick, *WW*, 14:85–6.
33. Silas Deane to Nathanael Greene, May 29, 1779, MSS., N-YHS.
34. Greene to JR, June 2, 1779, MSS., N-YHS.
35. GW–JR, October 18, 1780, Fitzpatrick, *WW*, 20:370.

36. GW to Robert Howe, April 19, 1779, MSS., LC.
37. GW–JR, May 20, 1779, Fitzpatrick, *WW*, 15:86.
38. GW to Timothy Matlack, June 1, 1779, Fitzpatrick, *WW*, 15:204.
39. BA to André, June 18, 1779, MSS., Clinton Papers, WLCL.
40. *New Jersey Gazette*, December 9, 1779.
41. Clinton to Germain, June 1, 1779, Stevens, *Facsimiles*, 10:999.
42. André to Marie Louise André, quoted in Hatch, *Major John André*, 187.
43. T. Jones, 1:189.
44. Quoted in Hatch, *Major John André*, 129.
45. Van Doren, 207.
46. André to BA, June, 1779, MSS., Clinton Papers, WLCL.
47. BA to André, July 11, 1779, MSS., Clinton Papers, WLCL.
48. Odell to André, July 18, 1779, MSS., Clinton Papers, WLCL.
49. Odell to André, July 21, 1779, MSS., Clinton Papers, WLCL.
50. André to BA, July, 1779, MSS., Clinton Papers, WLCL.
51. André to PSA, August 16, 1779, Van Doren, 454.
52. PSA to André, October 13, 1779, MSS., Clinton Papers, WLCL.
53. BA–GW, July 13, 1779, Sparks, *Writings*, 6:527.
54. GW–JR, December 12, 1778, W. B. Reed, *Joseph Reed*, Fitzpatrick, 12:383.
55. James Read to George Read, August 7, 1779, quoted in Brunhouse, *Counter-Revolution in Pennsylvania*, 71.
56. Peale, extracts from autobiography, Sellers, *Peale*, 203–5.
57. W. B. Reed, *Joseph Reed*, 2:423–28.
58. Peale, 205–8.
59. BA to Congress, October 6, 1779, *PCC*, 162, I, f185.
60. *JCC*, 15:1147.
61. BA to Congress, October 6, 1779, *PCC*, 162, I, f187.

17: "CONSCIOUS OF MY OWN RECTITUDE"

ARNOLD'S COURT MARTIAL: BA, *Proceedings of a Court Martial;* I. N. Arnold, *Life of Benedict Arnold; LDC,* Vol. 12; Fitzpatrick, *Writings of George Washington,* Vol. 19; Van Doren, *Secret History of the American Revolution,* 241–81.
1. Benjamin Paschall, affidavit, *LDC*, 12:266.
2. BA to Congress, April 26, 1779, *LDC*, 12:475n.
3. William Paca to BA, May 15, 1779, *LDC*, 12:475.
4. Gen. William Maxwell to Gov. William Livingston, October 20, 1777, *Am. Arch.*, 5th ser., 2:1143.
5. This excerpt and all others from BA's court-martial are quoted from *Proceedings of a Court Martial*, 40–55.
6. BA to Silas Deane, March 22, 1780, Deane Papers, N-YHS, (1887–91), 4:116.
7. BA–GW, March 6, 1780, Fitzpatrick, *WW*, 18:114.
8. BA–GW, March 20, 1780, Fitzpatrick, *WW*, 18:173.
9. BA to Jeremiah Powell, March 20, 1780, MSS., Copley Library.
10. GW–BA, March 28, 1780, Fitzpatrick, *WW*, 18:174.
11. GW, General Orders, April 6, 1780, Fitzpatrick, *WW*, 18:225.
12. BA to Silas Deane, March 22, 1780, Deane Papers, N-YHSC, 12 (1887–91), 4:116.
13. GW–BA, April 6, 1780, Fitzpatrick, *WW*, 18:225.
14. Lee Papers, *N-YHSC*, 6 (1887–91) 3:442.
15. *JCC*, 14:166.
16. BA to Congress, May 12, 1780, *PCC*, 136, IV. f233–75.
17. Thomas O'Leary, "Arnold at Quebec," *CANJ*, 10 (1913), 45.
18. Quoted in I. N. Arnold, *Life of Benedict Arnold*, 275–77.
19. BA–PS, May 25, 1780, MSS., Schuyler Papers, NYPL.
20. PS–BA, June 2, 1780, MSS., Schuyler Papers, NYPL.
21. "Knyphausen's Notes Regarding Arnold," [May, 1780], Van Doren, *Secret History of the American Revolution*, 458.
22. Van Doren, *Secret History*, 458–59.
23. BA to Captain George Beckwith, June 7, 1780, MSS., Clinton Papers, WLCL.

24. BA to André, June 12–15, 1780, MSS., Clinton Papers, WLCL.
25. BA to André, June 16, 1780, MSS., Clinton Papers, WLCL.
26. BA to Titus Hosmer, August 15, 1780, MSS., Tomlinson Collection, NYPL.
27. BA to Enoch Brown, August 15, 1780, MSS., HSP.
28. Stansbury to Odell, July 7, 1780, MSS., Clinton Papers, WLCL.
29. Joseph Chew to André, June 20, 1780, quoted in Van Doren, Secret History, 271.
30. HC to William Eden, August 18, 1780, Stevens, Facsimiles, 730.
31. BA to André, July 11, 1780, MSS., Clinton Papers, WLCL.
32. BA to André, July 12, 1780, MSS., Clinton Papers, WLCL.
33. André to BA, [July 23], 1780, MSS., Clinton Papers, WLCL.
34. Odell to Stansbury, July 24, 1780, MSS., Clinton Papers, WLCL.
35. André to BA, [July 24], 1780, MSS., Clinton Papers, WLCL.
36. Odell to André, July 29, 1780, MSS., Clinton Papers, WLCL.
37. Stansbury to Odell, August 14, 1780, MSS., Clinton Papers, WLCL.
38. BA–PSA to André, August 14, 1780, MSS., Clinton Papers, WLCL.
39. BA–PSA to André, August 14, 1780, MSS., Clinton Papers, WLCL.
40. GW to Robert Livingston, June 29, 1780, Fitzpatrick, WW, 19:91.
41. GW to John Washington, June 6 [-July 6,], 1780, Fitzpatrick, WW, 19:135–36.
42. BA–PSA, August 5, 1780, MSS., Clinton Papers, WLCL.

18: "I HAVE NO CONFIDANTS"

ARNOLD'S DEFECTION TO BRITISH: Hamilton, Papers, Vol. 2; Van Doren, Secret History of the
American Revolution, 260–344; Flexner, Traitor and the Spy, 275–369; Clinton; American
Rebellion, 209–18; W. M. Wallace, Traitorous Hero, 215–51; Hatch, Major John André,
169–252; Walker, "Margaret Shippen," 24:41–46n; 25:145–49; Barbé-Marbois, Conspiracy
of Arnold and Sir Henry Clinton; Fitzpatrick, Writings of George Washington, Vol. 20;
Davies, Documents of the American Revolution, Vol. 18; W. B. Willcox, Portrait of a General;
Leake, John Lamb, 245–53; Koke, Accomplice in Treason, 33–102; Varick, The Varick Court
of Inquiry.
1. GW, quoted in Winsor, 1:165.
2. GW–JR, October 18, 1780, Fitzpatrick, 20:214.
3. Quoted in W. M. Wallace, Traitorous Hero, 221.
4. GW, General Orders, August 3, 1780, Fitzpatrick, 19:313.
5. Joshua Hett Smith, quoted in Koke, 44.
6. Quoted in Varick, 82.
7. RV–BA, August 7, 1780, quoted in Varick, 82.
8. RV in Varick, 158.
9. William Duer to John Lamb, August 7, 1780, MSS., Lamb Papers, N-YHS.
10. John Lamb to BA, August 9, 1780, MSS., Lamb Papers, N-YHS.
11. William Buirtes, quoted in James Moody, "Narrative," 140.
12. Leake, 247.
13. BA to Lamb, August 11, 1780, MSS., Lamb Papers, N-YHS.
14. Lamb to BA, August 12, 1780, MSS., Lamb Papers, N-YHS.
15. David Franks to BA, August 28, 1780, Walker, "Margaret Arnold," 25:25.
16. BA to Col. Timothy Pickering, August 16, 1780, MSS., de Coppet Coll., PUL.
17. John Lamb to Varick, August 19, 1780, Leake, 253.
18. Varick, 134–35.
19. JCC, 17:772–73.
20. BA to Samuel Holden Parsons, August 27, 1780, Washington Papers, LC.
21. Parsons to BA, August 28, 1780, Washington Papers, LC.
22. Varick, 100–1.
23. BA to André, August 30, 1780, MSS., Clinton Papers, WLCL.
24. Varick, 124.
25. BA to Col. Elisha Sheldon, September 1, 1780, quoted in Varick, 106.
26. Sheldon to BA, September 6, 1780, Washington Papers, LC.
27. BA to Parsons, quoted in Varick, 197–98.
28. Sheldon to BA, September 8, 1780, Sparks, Writings, 7:523.
29. André to Sheldon, September 7, 1780, MSS., Clinton Papers, WLCL.

30. BA to Sheldon, September 10, 1780, Sparks, *Writings*, 7:523–24.
31. BA to André, September 10–15, 1780, MSS., Clinton Papers, WLCL.
32. André to Lord Cathcart, March 11, 1780, quoted in Flexner, *Traitor and the Spy*, 296–97.
33. André to [Clinton], November 13, 1779, MSS., Clinton Papers, WLCL.
34. André, "Activities of Clinton's Aides," MSS., Clinton Papers, WLCL.
35. André to Clinton, November 13, 1779, *MSS.*, Clinton Papers, WLCL.
36. Ibid.
37. André to [John Lewis André], November, 1779, quoted in Hatch, *Major John André*, 187.
38. Amherst to Germain, December 4, 1779, Clinton Papers, WLCL.
39. [André], "The Cow Chace," *Royal Gazette*, September 24, 1780.
40. Willcox, *Portrait of a General*, 337.
41. Clinton, 213.
42. Clinton to André, September 10, 1780, quoted in Van Doren, *Secret History*, 309.
43. BA to John Lamb, September 12, 1780, in Leake, 255.
44. BA to André, September 15, 1780, MSS., Clinton Papers, WLCL.
45. Hannah Arnold to BA, September 4, 1780, Tomlinson Collection, NYPL.
46. GW–BA, September 14, 1760, Fitzpatrick, 20:48.
47. BA–GW, September 14, 1780, Sparks, *Correspondence*, 3:85–87.
48. BA to Nathanael Greene, quoted in Van Doren, 310.
49. Col. Beverly Robinson to BA, September 17, 1780, quoted in Van Doren, *Secret History*, 482–83.
50. John Lamb, testimony at Joshua Hett Smith court-martial, in Dawson, *Record*, 103–4.
51. Joshua Hett Smith, *Authentic Narrative*, 19–20.
52. Alexander Hamilton, *Papers*, 2:463.
53. Varick, 133–34.
54. BA to Robinson, September 18, 1780, Van Doren, *Secret History*, 483.
55. Ibid.
56. Clinton to Germain, October 11, 1780, Van Doren, *Secret History*, 483.
57. André to Clinton, September 21, 1780, MSS., Clinton Papers, WLCL.
58. BA, pass for Smith and André, September 20, 1780, MSS., New York State Library.
59. BA to Maj. Edward Kiers, September 20, 1780, quoted in H. B. Dawson, *Trial of Smith*, 17.
60. H. B. Dawson, *Trial of Smith*, 7–13.
61. Ibid., 25.
62. Col. Robinson to Henry Clinton, September 24, 1780, MSS., Clinton Papers, WLCL.
63. Quoted in Joshua Hett Smith, *Authentic Narrative*, 31–32.
64. H. B. Dawson, *Trial of Smith*, 75–76.
65. BA to Clinton, October 18, 1780, MSS., Clinton Papers, WLCL.
66. Joshua Hett Smith, *Authentic Narrative*, 31–32.
67. H. B. Dawson, *Trial of Smith*, 7.
68. André, "Statement," in Sargent, *André*, 350.
69. Robinson to HC, September 24, 1780, MSS., Clinton Papers, WLCL.
70. *Historical Magazine*, X, Supplement, 33.
71. André, in Sargent, 350.
72. HC, quoted in W. M. Wallace, *Traitorous Hero*, 240.
73. André to GW, September 24, 1780, Sparks, *Writings*, 7:531.
74. Varick, 178–79.
75. André to GW, September 24, 1780, Sparks, *Writings*, 7:531.
76. H. B. Dawson, *Trial of Smith*, 48.
77. Joshua Hett Smith, *Authentic Narrative*, 42–44.
78. Walker, 25:147.
79. Col. John Jameson to BA, September 24, 1780, Sparks, *Writings*, 7:530–31.
80. Quoted in Hatch, *Major John André*, 246.
81. Varick, 190.
82. Dann, *Revolution Remembered*, 58.

19: "THE WORLD SELDOM JUDGES RIGHT"

ANDRÉ'S CAPTIVITY AND DEATH: A. Hamilton, *Papers*, Vol. 2; W. M. Wallace, *Traitorous Hero*, 247–59; Van Doren, *Secret History*, 355–71; Flexner, *Traitor and the Spy*, 360–93; Boynton, *History of West Point*, 139–51; R. H. Lee, *Memoirs*, 2:159–87; Clinton, *American Rebellion*,

209–20; Fitzpatrick, *Writings of George Washington,* Vol. 20; Hatch, *Major John André,* 247–75; Thacher, *Military Journal,* 241; Walker, "Margaret Arnold," 25:148–63.

ARNOLD AS BRITISH GENERAL: Simcoe, *Military Journal,* Frederick MacKenzie, *Diary;* Royster, *Revolutionary People at War,* 255–94; Willcox, *Portrait of a General,* 347–91; W. M. Wallace, *Traitorous Hero,* 260–83; *Twilight of British Rule in America: The New York Letter Book of General James Robertson;* Clinton, *American Rebellion,* 249–58, 272–81, 297–98; Thomas Jefferson, *Papers,* Vol. 4; I. N. Arnold, *Life of Benedict Arnold,* 295–354; Lassiter, "Arnold's Invasion of Virginia"; M. J. Wright, "Lafayette's Campaign in Virginia"; Scheer, "The Sergeant Major's Strange Mission."

1. Walker, "Margaret Arnold," 24:415.
2. GW, quoted in Richard Rush, *Occasional Productions,* 82–83.
3. Quoted in W. M. Wallace, *Traitorous Hero,* 251.
4. Varick, *Court of Inquiry,* 189–93.
5. BA–GW, September 25, 1780, *PAH,* 2:439–40.
6. Leake, *John Lamb,* 264.
7. Joshua Hett Smith, *Narrative,* 52–53.
8. GW to John Laurens, October 13, 1780, Fitzpatrick, 20:173.
9. GW–JR, October 18, 1780, Fitzpatrick, 20:213.
10. GW to William Heath, September 26, 1780, Fitzpatrick, 20:89.
11. AH to John Laurens, October 11, 1780, *PAH,* 2:465.
12. Lafayette to Luzerne, October 12, 1780, *Revue de la Révolution,* 5:546.
13. George Mathew, "Narrative," *Historical Magazine,* April 1857.
14. Gov. William Livingston to GW, October 5, 1780, Sparks, *Correspondence,* 3:111.
15. John Laurens to GW, October 4, 1780, Sparks, *Correspondence,* 3:105.
16. Smith, *Diary,* 335.
17. John Lamb, quoted in Leake, *John Lamb,* 268–70.
18. GW to John Laurens, October 13, 1780, Fitzpatrick, 20:173.
19. BF, Smyth, *Writings of Benjamin Franklin,* 8:251.
20. Andrew Elliott to William Eden, October 4–5, 1780, Stevens, *Facsimiles,* 7:No. 739.
21. AH to John Laurens, October 11, 1780, *PAH,* 2:461.
22. BA–HC, September 26, 1780, MSS., Clinton Papers, WLCL.
23. André, "Statement," in Sargent, *André,* 400.
24. André Court-Martial Board to GW, September 29, 1780, Boynton, 139.
25. GW–HC, September 30, 1780, quoted in Boynton, 141.
26. [AH]–HC, September 30, 1780, quoted in Hatch, *Major John André,* 263.
27. HC–GW, September 30, 1780, MSS., Clinton Papers, WLCL.
28. André to HC, September 29, 1780, MSS., Clinton Papers, WLCL.
29. Smith, *Diary,* 339.
30. BA–GW, October 1, 1780, MSS., Clinton Papers, WLCL.
31. HC to his sisters, October 4–9, 1780, MSS., Clinton Papers, WLCL.
32. J. Paulding, December 3, 1780, MSS., de Coppet Coll., PUL.
33. Thacher, 272–75.
34. W. Smith, *Diary,* 339.
35. HC to his sisters, October 9, 1780, MSS., Clinton Papers, WLCL.
36. Benjamin Tallmadge to Timothy Pickering, March 13, 1817, MSS., de Coppet Coll., PUL.
37. Franks to Varick, September 28, 1780, Tomlinson Collection, NYPL.
38. Parton, *Life of Burr,* 125.
39. Maj. Gen. James Robertson to Lord Amherst, October 6, 1780, *New York Letter Book,* 155–56.
40. BA, "Present State of the American Rebel Army, Navy, and Finances, with Some Remarks," October 7, 1780, MSS., Clinton Papers, WLCL.
41. BA, Gen. Arnold's Address to the Inhabitants of America, October 7, 1780, copy in Clinton Papers, WLCL.
42. BA–HC, October 18, 1780, MSS., Clinton Papers, WLCL.
43. Pennsylvania Colonial Records (PCR), 12:520.
44. André–PSA, August 16, 1779, MSS., Clinton Papers, WLCL.
45. *Pennsylvania Packet,* September 30, 1780.
46. Edward Burd to Jasper Yeates, October 5, 1780, *PMHB,* 40 (1916), 380–81.
47. *PCR,* 12:520.

48. *New York Royal Gazette*, November 18, 1780.
49. GW to Congress, October 29, 1780, Fitzpatrick 264, 289.
50. L. H. Lee, *Memoirs*, 2:165–66.
51. [Archibald Kennedy], "Queries to a Renegade Rebel," MSS., Clinton Papers, WLCL.
52. Admiral Rodney to Germain, December 22, 1780, in Historical Manuscript Commission Report, Stopford-Sackville MSS., 2:193.
53. George Damier to Germain, October 13, 1780, in Historical Manuscript Commission Report, Stopford-Sackville MSS., 2:184.
54. HC to Simcoe and Dundos, December 14, 1780, MSS., Clinton Papers, WLCL.
55. BA–HC, January 23, 1781, MSS., Clinton Papers, WLCL.
56. Fortescue, *History of the British Army*, 3:359.
57. Arbuthnot to Robertson, March 3, 1781, MSS., Clinton Papers, WLCL.
58. Dundas to HC, May 12, 1781, MSS., Clinton Papers, WLCL.
59. W. Smith, *Diary*, 428–9.
60. BA–HC, September 8, 1781, MSS., Clinton Papers, WLCL.
61. Jonathan Brooks's narrative in Harris, *Groton Heights*, 79.
62. *Connecticut Gazette*, September 14, 1781.
63. BA–HC, September 11, 1781, Report, in F. MacKenzie, *Diary*, 2:624, MSS., Clinton Papers, WLCL.
64. W. Smith, *Diary*, 440.
65. HC, Notes of conversation with William Pitt, November 14, 1792, MSS., Clinton Papers, WLCL.
66. W. Smith, *Diary*, 428.
67. Mrs. Samuel Shoemaker to Anna Rawle, November, 1780, quoted in Walker, 25:162–3.
68. W. Smith, *Diary*, 469.
69. London *Daily Advertiser*, January 22, 1782.
70. Sir Walter Stirling, quoted in Flexner, *Traitor and the Spy*, 399.
71. BA to William Smith, June, 1782, in Flexner, *Traitor and the Spy*, 399.
72. BF to Robert R. Livingston, March 4, 1782, quoted in I. N. Arnold, *Life of Arnold*, 359.
73. S. A. Drake, *Historic Fields and Mansions of Middlesex*, 258.
74. London *Daily Advertiser*, February 4, 1782.
75. *Gentlemen's Magazine*, March 1782.
76. Edmund Burke, quoted in Lomask, *"Benedict Arnold: The Aftermath of Treason,"* 86.
77. Peter Van Schaack, quoted in Van Schaack, *Life of Peter Van Schaack*, 147n.
78. BA, Loyalist Claim Petition, P.R.O., AO13/96, No. 799.
79. BA to Commission for American Claims, April 26, 1785, PRO, AO13/96, No. 799.

20: "THE LAST MAN IN THE WORLD"

ARNOLDS IN CANADA: Condon, *Envy of the American States: The Loyalist Dream for New Brunswick;* Bell, *Early Loyalist St. John;* E. C. Wright, *Loyalists of New Brunswick;* Teed, "Foot-Prints of Benedict Arnold;" Lawrence, *Judges of New Brunswick and Their Times;* Blakely and Grant, *Eleven Exiles;* Decker, *Benedict Arnold, Son of the Havens,* 439–50; G. A. Rawlyk, "Federalist-Loyalist Alliance in New Brunswick, 1784–1815"; Walker, "Margaret Shippen," 25:452–60, 26:71–80, 224–44. 322–334, 464–68; W. M. Wallace, *Traitorous Hero,* 284–309; I. N. Arnold, *Life of Benedict Arnold,* 2–74; Sereisky "Benedict Arnold in New Brunswick;" Robinson, "Pioneers on King Street;"
LAST YEARS AND DEATH: Willyams, *Expedition Against the French West India Islands in the Year 1794;* W. M. Wallace, *Traitorous Hero,* 297–309; Walker, "Margaret Shippen," 26:71–80, 224–44; Ward Chipman Papers, Odell Collection, NBM.
1. PSA to Judge Shippen, March 6, 1786, in Walker, 25:453.
2. Sampson Salter Blowers to Ward Chipman, November 22, 1785, quoted in Decker, 439–40.
3. Jonathan Sewall, Jr., to Judge Jonathan Sewall, Sewall Papers, PAC, M.G.23, G.10, Vol. 2.
4. *Saint John Gazette,* December 20, 1785.
5. *Saint John Gazette,* June 6, 1786.
6. *Saint John Gazette,* August [?], 1786.
7. Ward Chipman to E. White, May 25, 1786, MSS., Chipman Coll., NBM.
8. Capt. John Shackford, quoted in Wells, *Campobello,* 446.
9. PSA to Judge Shippen, June 30, 1788, Walker, 25:168.

10. PSA to Betsy Burd, August, 1788, quoted in Sereisky, 41.
11. L. Sabine, *Sketches of the Loyalists,* 2:179.
12. Edward Burd to Jasper Yeates, November 15, 1789, Walker, 25:168.
13. PSA to Elizabeth Tilghman, July 5, 1790, Walker, 25:169.
14. Munson Hayt, affidavit, May 7, 1790, MSS., Arnold-Hayt Papers, Library Archives, University of New Brunswick.
15. BA to Jonathan Bliss, February 16, 1792, MSS., Odell Coll., NBM.
16. BA–HC, May, 1787, MSS., Clinton Papers, WLCL.
17. HC–BA, May 26, 1787, MSS., Clinton Papers, WLCL.
18. Cobbett, *Parliamentary History,* 29:1518–19.
19. PSA to Judge Shippen, June 26, 1792, Walker, 25:170.
20. PSA to Judge Shippen, July 6, 1792, Walker, 25:173–74.
21. BA–HC, October 17, 1792, MSS., Clinton Papers, WLCL.
22. Ibid.
23. BA–HC, December 3, 1792, MSS., Clinton Papers, WLCL.
24. BA to Jonathan Bliss, February 10, 1794, MSS., Odell Coll., NBM.
25. Talleyrand, *Memoirs,* 1:174.
26. BA to Bliss, March 19, 1794, MSS., Odell Coll., NBM.
27. BA to Bliss, January 3, 1795, MSS., Odell Coll., NBM.
28. BA to Bliss, May 4, 1795, MSS., Odell Coll., NBM.
29. BA to Ward Chipman, January 14, 1795, MSS., Chipman Coll., NBM.
30. BA to Bliss, August 15, 1795, MSS., Odell Coll., NBM.
31. PSA to Richard Arnold, August, 1794, Walker, 25:464.
32. BA to Bliss, September 5, 1795, MSS., Odell Coll., NBM.
33. PSA to Bliss, December 5, 1795, MSS., Odell Coll., NBM.
34. Duke of Portland, order, PRO, C.O. 42/88 f. 871.
35. Hannah Arnold, quoted in Sparks, *Benedict Arnold,* 10–11.
36. BA to Bliss, February 20, 1796, MSS., Odell Coll., NBM.
37. PSA to Bliss, December 5, 1795, MSS., Odell Coll., NBM.
38. PSA to Edward Arnold, August 15, 1800, Walker, 25:473.
39. PSA to Edward Arnold, January 14, 1801, Walker, 25:482.
40. BA to Bliss, December 20, 1799, MSS., Odell Coll., NBM.
41. BA to Bliss, September 19, 1800, MSS., Odell Coll., NBM.
42. PSA to Edward Arnold, July 1, 1801, in Taylor, *Some New Light,* 59–60.
43. Ann Fitch to Judge Shippen, June 29, 1801, in Walker, 25:472.3.
44. Taylor, 27.
45. PSA to Edward Arnold, January 17, 1804, in Taylor, 66.
46. PSA to Edward Burd, August 15, 1801, Walker, 25:177.
47. PSA to [Walter Stirling], June 20, 1792, Walker, 25:165.
48. PSA to Edward Arnold, November 5, 1802, Walker, 25:173.
49. PSA to Judge Shippen, January 5, 1803, Walker, 25:173.
50. PSA to Edward Arnold, January 11, 1804, Taylor, 65.
51. PSA to William Fitch Arnold, quoted in Taylor, 33*n.*
52. PSA to Edward Arnold, January, 1804, Taylor, 33.
53. PSA to Edward Burd, August 15, 1801, Walker, 25:174.
54. PSA, Fall, 1801, in Walker, 25:174.
55. PSA to Elizabeth Tilghman, May 14, 1804, Walker, 25:175.
56. Daniel Coxe to Judge Shippen, July 5, 1804, Walker, 25:175.

BIBLIOGRAPHY

KEY TO ABBREVIATIONS IN BIBLIOGRAPHY

AH	*American Heritage*
AHR	American Historical Review
BRH	Bulletin des Recherches Historiques
BSHFA	Bulletin de la Societé d'Histoire Franco-Américaine
CANJ	Canadian Antiquities & Numismatic Journal
CDQ	Canadian Defence Quarterly
CHR	Canadian Historical Review
CHSC	Connecticut Historical Society Collections
CM	Canadian Magazine
CMNR	Canadian Monthly and National Review
FTMB	Fort Ticonderoga Museum Bulletin
HT	History Today
LC	Library of Congress
LDC	*Letters to Delegates of Congress*
LHSQ	Literary and Historical Society Quarterly
MAQR	Michigan Alumnus Quarterly Review
MHM	Maryland Historical Magazine
MSRC	Mémoires de la Societé royale du Canada
NEQ	New England Quarterly
NHCHS	New Haven County Historical Society
NJH	*New Jersey History*
NYH	New York History
NYHAP	New York Historical Association Proceedings
N-YHS	New-York Historical Society
NYPL	New York Public Library
PA	*Pennsylvania Archives*
PAPS	Proceedings of the American Philosophical Society
PCR	Pennsylvania Colonial Records
PH	Pennsylvania History
PMHB	Pennsylvania Magazine of History and Biography
PNJHS	Proceedings of the New Jersey Historical Society
QHSD	Quebec Historical Society Documents
RUL	Revue de l'Université Laval
SAHRJ	Society for Army Historical Research Journal
UNB	University of New Brunswick
VH	*Vermont History*
WLCL	William L. Clements Library, University of Michigan
WMQ	*William & Mary Quarterly*

Abbatt, William C. *New York in the American Revolution*. New York, 1929.

Adams, John. *Diary and Autobiography*. Edited by L. H. Butterfield et al. 4 vols. Cambridge, Mass., 1961.

Adams, Randolph G. *Political Ideas of the American Revolution*. Rev. ed. Introduction by Merrill Jensen. New York, 1958.

Adams, Samuel. *Papers*, NYPL.

Ainslie, Thomas. *Canada Preserved: A Journal*. Quebec, 1905.

Alexander, John K. "The Fort Wilson Incident of 1779." *WMQ*, 3d ser., 31 (1974), 589–612.

Allen, Ethan. "A Narrative of the Captivity of Colonel Ethan." In Richard M. Dorson. *American Rebels*. New York, 1953.

——. "Mr. James Morrison and the Montreal Merchants at the time of the American Invasion," *CANJ*, 3 (1847), 13–15.

Allen, Gardner W. *Naval History of the American Revolution*. 2 vols. New York, 1962.

Allen, Robert S., ed. *The Loyal Americans: Military Role of the Loyalist Provincial Corps*. St. John, N.B., 1983.

Almon, John, ed. *The Remembrancer, or Impartial Repository of Public Events . . .* 17 vols. London, 1775–84.

"The American Fleet on Lake Champlain, 1776." *FTMB*, 5:5–6 (1940), 138–39.

Anburey, Thomas. *Travels Through the Interior Parts of America*. 2 vols. London, 1789.

——. *With Burgoyne from Quebec*. Toronto, 1963.

André, Major John. *Journal of Operations of the British Army, June, 1777 to November, 1778*. New York, 1904. Repr. 1930.

——. *Poems . . . to Which Are Added Letters . . . to her . . . by Major André . . . in 1769*. London, 1781.

——. "Particulars of the Meschianza." *Gentlemen's Magazine*, 48(1778), 353–57.

——. "The Meschianza, Humbly Inscribed to Miss Peggy Chew." *Annual Register*, 1780. London, 1758–.

Anonymous. *The Motley Assembly*. Boston, 1779.

Archevêché du Québec. *Lettres*. Quebec, 1888.

Archibald, E.H.H. *The Wooden Fighting Ship in the Royal Navy, 897–1860*. London, 1968.

Arnold, Benedict. *Daybook of Financial Transactions, 1777–1779*. Revolutionary Government Papers. Division of Archives and Manuscripts. Pennsylvania Historical and Museum Commission. Harrisburg, Pa.

——. *Expense and Pay Accountings*. MSS. André de Coppet Collection, PUL.

——. *Journal of His Expedition to Canada*. In Kenneth Roberts, ed., *March to Quebec*. New York, 1938.

——. *Minute Book*, June–August 1768. NHCHS.

——. *Proceedings of a General Court Martial of the Line . . . for the Trial of Major General Arnold*. Philadelphia, 1780.

——. "Regimental Memorandum Book," *FTMB*, 14 (1981), 71–80.

——. "Letters Written While on an Expedition Across the State of Maine to Attack Quebec in 1775." *Maine State Historical Society Collection*, 1 (1831), 341–87.

——. "Present State of the American Rebel Army, Navy, and Finances, with Some Remarks," Clinton Papers, WLCL.

——. *Waste Book*, April 1773–March 1780. New Haven Colony Historical Society.

Arnold Correspondence and Lieutenant George Mathew's Narrative, *Historical Magazine*, 1 (1905).

"Arnold Letters." *Magazine of History*, 3 (1906).

Arnold Papers. N-YHS.

Arnold-Hayt Papers. Library Archives, UNB.

"Arnold's March to Quebec: 11th September to 14th November, 1775." *CDQ*, 7 (1929–30), 63–77.

"Arnold's Investment of the British Subsidy." *Magazine of American History*, II, Pt. I (1878).

Arnold, E. S. *The Arnold Memorial, William Arnold of Providence and Pawtuxet, and a Genealogy of His Descendants*. Rutland, Vt., 1935.

Arnold, Isaac N. *The Life of Benedict Arnold: His Patriotism and Treason*. Chicago, 1880.

——. "Benedict Arnold at Saratoga." *United Service Magazine* (1890).

Arnold, S. G. *History of the State of Rhode Island*. 2 vols. New York, 1860.

Aspinall, A. *The Later Correspondence of George III.* Cambridge, 1962.
Atkinson, C. T. "British Forces in North America, 1774–1781: Their Distribution and Strength."
     Journal of the Society for Army Historical Research, 14–15 (1936–37), 136–46; 16 (1937),
     3–23; 19 (1940), 163–66.
———. "Some Evidence for Burgoyne's Expedition." *Journal of the Society for Army Historical
     Research,* 26 (1948), 132–42.
Atwater, E. E. *History of the City of New Haven.* New York, 1887.
Atwood, Rodney. *The Hessians.* Cambridge, England, 1980.
Augur, Helen. *Secret War of Independence.* New York, 1955.
Baby, François, Gabriel Taschereau, and Jenkin Williams. *Journaux.* Quebec, 1927–28.
Badeaux, Jean-Baptiste. "Journal des opérations de l'armée américaine lors de l'invasion du Can-
     ada en 1775–1776." *QHSD,* 3rd ser., 6 (1871), 1–43.
Bailyn, Bernard. *Ideological Origins of the American Revolution,* Cambridge, Mass., 1967.
———. *The Ordeals of Thomas Hutchinson,* Cambridge, Mass., 1974.
Bain, James, Jr. "Journal of the Most Remarkable Occurrences in Quebec Since Arnold Appear'd
     Before the Town on November 4, 1775." *QHSD,* 7th ser., 10 (1905), 93–154.
Bakeless, John. *Turncoats, Traitors and Heroes.* Philadelphia, 1959.
Baker, William A. *Colonial Vessels.* Barre, Mass., 1962.
Balch, Thomas Willing. *The Pennsylvania Assemblies.* Philadelphia, 1916.
———, ed. *The Examination of Joseph Galloway, Esq., by a Committee of the House of Com-
     mons.* Philadelphia, 1855.
Balderston, Marion. "Lord Howe Clears the Delaware." *PMHB,* 96 (1972), 326–46.
Baldwin, Jeduthan. "Diary." *FTMB,* 4:6 (1937–38), 10–40.
Barbé-Marbois, François de. *Conspiracy of Arnold and Sir Henry Clinton.* Paris, 1816. Repr. New
     York, 1972.
Barber, J. W., and Henry Howe. *Historical Collections of the State of New York.* New York,
     1841.
Barch, Oscar T. *New York City During the War for Independence.* New York, 1931.
Baxter, James Phinney. *The British Invasion from the North.* Albany, 1887.
Beebe, Lewis, Dr. "Journal of a Physician on the Expedition Against Canada, 1776." *PMHB,* 49
     (1935), 321–61.
Bell, D. G. *Early Loyalist St. John: The Origins of New Brunswick Politics, 1783–1786.* Frederic-
     ton, n.b., 1983.
Bemis, Samuel Flagg. "The British Secret Service and the French-American Alliance." *AHR,* 29
     (1924), 474–95.
"Benedict Arnold." *CANJ,* 12 (1885), 53–94.
"Benedict Arnold's Address to the Inhabitants of Quebec." *CANJ,* 2 (1873–74), 79–80.
Benoit, Pierre. *Lord Dorchester.* Quebec, 1961.
Benson, Egbert. *Vindication of the Captors of Major André.* Boston, 1972.
Berkenhout, John. "Dr. Berkenhout's Journal, 1778." *PMHB,* 65 (1961), 79–82.
Billias, George Allan, ed. *George Washington's Opponents.* New York, 1969.
Bird, Harrison. *Attack on Quebec.* New York, 1968.
———. *March to Saratoga: General Burgoyne and the American Campaign, 1777.* New York,
     1963.
———. *Navies in the Mountains.* New York, 1971.
Bishop, Morris. "You are Invited to a Meschianza." *American Heritage,* 25 (1974), 69–75.
Blake, J. B. "The Inoculation Controversy in Boston," *NEQ,* 25 (1952), 489–506.
Blakely, Phyllis R., and John N. Grant, eds. *Eleven Exiles: Accounts of Loyalists of the American
     Revolution.* Toronto, 1982.
Blanchard, Claude. *The Journal of Claude Blanchard, Commisary of the French Auxiliary Army
     Sent to the United States During the American Revolution, 1780–1783.* Translated by William
     Duane. Albany, 1876.
Bliven, Bruce. *Battle for Manhattan.* New York, 1956.
Boissonnault, Charles-Marie. "Revolution en Amérique (1775)." *RUL,* 3:3 (1948–49), 256–69.
Boldt, David R., and Willard Sterne Randall, eds. *The Founding City.* Philadelphia, 1976.
Bolton, C. K. *Private Soldier Under Washington.* New York, 1902.
Bonomi, Patricia U. *A Factious People: Politics and Society in Colonial New York.* New York,
     1971.
Bonsal, Stephen. *When the French Were Here.* New York, 1945.

Bowler, R. Arthur. *Logistics and the Failure of the British Army in America, 1775–1783.* Princeton, 1975.

Boyd, Julian P. "Silas Deane: Death by a Kindly Teacher of Treason?" *WMQ,* 3rd ser., 16 (1959), 319–42.

Boynton, Edward C. *History of West Point.* New York, 1863. Repr. Freeport, N.Y., 1970.

Bradford, S. S. "Hunger Menaces the Revolution." *MHM;* 61 (1966), 1–23.

Bradley, A. G. *Sir Guy Carleton.* Toronto, 1966.

Brault, Lucien. "Anglo-Canadians pro-rebelles pendant la Révolution Américaine." *BRH,* 44 (1938), 343–44.

Bredenberg, Oscar R. "Royal Savage." *FTMB,* 12 (1966), 128–49.

———. "The American Champlain Fleet, 1775–1777." *FTMB,* 12 (1968), 249–63.

Brinton, Ellen Star. "The Rogerenes." *NEQ,* March 1943.

Brissot de Warville, J. P. *New Travels in the United States of America, 1792.* Translated by M. S. Vamos and Duranc Echeverria. Cambridge, Mass., 1964.

British Headquarters Papers, MSS., WLCL, University of Michigan, Ann Arbor, Mich. Referred to as BHQP.

Broglie, Duc de. *Memoirs of the Prince de Talleyrand.* 5 vols. New York, 1891.

Brown, Gerald Saxon. *American Secretary: The Colonial Policy of Lord George Germain, 1775–1778.* Ann Arbor, Mich., 1963.

Brown, Wallace. *The Good Americans: Loyalists in the American Revolution.* New York, 1969.

———. *The King's Friends: The Composition and Motives of the American Loyalist Claimants.* Providence, 1966.

Brunhouse, Robert L. *The Counter-Revolution in Pennsylvania, 1776–1790.* Harrisburg, Pa., 1942.

Buel, Richard. *Dear Liberty: Connecticut Mobilization for the Revolutionary War.* New York, 1980.

Burgoyne, John. *Orderly Book of Lieutenant-General John Burgoyne.* Edited by E. B. O'Callaghan. Albany, 1860.

———. *State of the Expedition from Canada.* London, 1780. Repr. New York, 1969.

Burnaby, Andrew. *Travels Through the Middle Settlements in North America, 1759–1760.* London, 1775.

Burnett, Edmund C., ed. *Letters of the Members of the Continental Congress.* 8 vols. Washington, D.C., 1921–36.

———. "Ciphers of the Revolutionary Period." *AHR,* 22 (1917), 329–74.

Burt, Alfred L. *The Old Province of Canada.* New York, 1970.

———. *Guy Carleton, Lord Dorchester, 1724–1808.* CHR booklet, 1968.

———. "Sir Guy Carleton and His First Council." *CHR,* December 1923.

Bush, Martin H. *Revolutionary Enigma: A Reappraisal of General Philip Schuyler of New York.* Port Washington, N.Y., 1969.

Bushman, Richard L. *From Puritan to Yankee: Character and the Social Order in Connecticut, 1690–1765.* Cambridge, Mass., 1967.

———. "Corruption and Power in Provincial America." Library of Congress, *Symposium on Development of a Revolutionary Mentality,* Washington, D.C., 1972, 63–91.

"A Calculation of Ordnance and Ordnance Stores Wanted for the Army of the Northern Department, Made by Order of the Honorable Major-General Schuyler." *FTMB,* 3 (1934), 190–91.

Butterfield, Lyman H. "Psychological Warfare in 1776: The Jefferson-Franklin Plan to Cause Hessian Desertions." *PAPS,* 94 (1950), 233–41.

Calhoon, R. M. *The Loyalists in Revolutionary America, 1760–1781.* New York, 1973.

Callahan, North. *Flight from the Republic: The Tories of the American Revolution.* New York, 1967.

Caron, Ivanhoe. "Les Canadiens français et l'invasion américaine de 1774–1775." *MSRC,* 3rd ser., 23 (1929), 21–34.

Carp, E. Wayne. *To Starve the Army at Pleasure.* Chapel Hill, N.C., 1984.

Carrington, Henry B. *Battles of the American Revolution.* New York, 1876. Repr. New York, 1961.

Carson, Hampton L. "The Case of the Sloop *Active.*" *PMHB,* 16 (1893), 385–98.

Case, James R., ed. *Tryon's Raid on Danbury.* Danbury, Conn., 1927.

Caulkins, Frances M. *History of New London.* New London, Conn., 1852.

———. *History of Norwich.* Norwich, Conn., 1845 and 1874 editions.

Cavendish, Sir Henry. *Debates of the House of Commons.* London, 1792.

Cecil, Robert. "When Canada Did Not Choose Freedom." *HT,* 13 (1963), 511–19.

Chalmers, George. "Journal of the Siege from 1st December, 1775." *QHSD,* 8th ser., 11 (1906), 11–53.

Champe, John. "Sergeant Champe's Adventure." Edited by Wilbur C. Hall. *WMQ.* 2d ser., 18 (1938), 322–42.

Chapelle, Howard I. *History of American Sailing Ships.* London, 1936.

———. *History of the American Sailing Navy.* New York, 1949.

Chauncy, Charles. *Enthusiasm Described.* Boston, 1742.

———. *Seasonable Thoughts on the Present State of Religion in New England.* Boston, 1743.

Clark, George Ramsey. *A Short History of the United States Navy.* Philadelphia, 1910.

Clark, Jane. "The Command of the Canadian Army for the Campaign of 1777." *CHR,* 10 (1929), 129–35.

Clark, William Bell. *George Washington's Navy.* Baton Rouge, La., 1960.

———, ed. *Naval Documents of the American Revolution.* 10 vols. Washington, D.C., 1964–73.

———. "American Naval Policy, 1775–76." *American Neptune,* 1 (1941), 26–41.

Claus, Daniel. "Memorandum of the Rebel Invasion of Canada in 1775." *QHSD,* 8th ser., 11 (1906), 105–11.

Clinton, Sir Henry. *The American Rebellion: A Narrative of His Campaigns, 1775–1782.* New York, 1949.

———. Papers, WLCL.

Clowes, William Laird. *The Royal Navy: A History from the Earliest Times to the Present.* 5 vols. London, 1898.

Cobbett, William. *Parliamentary History of England.* 36 vols. London, 1806–20.

Coburn, L. H. *Passage of the Arnold Expedition Through Skowhegan.* Skowhegan, Me., 1912.

Coffin, Robert P. T. *Kennebec: Cradle of Americans.* New York, 1937.

Coffin, Victor. *The Province of Quebec and the Early American Revolution.* Madison, Wis., 1896.

———. "The Province of Quebec and the Early American Revolution: A Reply." *CM,* 9 (1897), 56–67.

Coggins, Jack. *Ships and Seamen of the American Revolution.* Harrisburg, Pa., 1969.

Cohen, Sheldon S. "Hannah Levy and the General." *Mid-America,* 68 (1968), 5–13.

———. "Lieutenant John Starke and the Defence of Quebec." *Dalhousie Review,* 47 (1967–68), 56–64.

———, ed. *Canada Preserved: The Journal of Captain Thomas Ainslie.* Toronto, 1968.

Cohn, Art. "An Incident Not Known to History: Squire Ferris and Benedict Arnold at Ferris Bay." *VH,* 55 (1987), 97–112.

Coke, Daniel P. *The Royal Commission on the Losses and the Services of the American Loyalists.* Hugh E. Egerton, ed. Oxford, 1915.

Colledge, J. J. *Ships of the Royal Navy: An Historical Index.* Vol. 1, Devon, England, 1969.

Collier, Christopher. *Roger Sherman's Connecticut.* Middletown, Conn., 1971.

———. *Roger Sherman and the New Hampshire Grants.* Montpelier, Vt., 1962.

Commager, Henry Steele, and Richard B. Morris. *The Spirit of 'Seventy-six.* New York, 1967.

Condon, Ann G. *The Envy of the American States: The Loyalist Dream for New Brunswick.* Fredericton, N.B., 1984.

Connecticut (colony). *The Public Records of the Colony of Connecticut, 1636–1776.* Edited by J. H. Trumbull et al. 15 vols. Hartford, Conn., 1850–90.

Connecticut Historical Society. *Collections.* Hartford, Conn., 1860–.

Connecticut, State of. *Public Records, 1634–1776.* 15 vols. Hartford, Conn., 1850–90.

———. *Public Records, 1776–1919.* 17 vols. Hartford, Conn., 1894–1919.

Continental Congress. *Journals.* Edited by Worthington C. Ford and others. 34 vols. 1904–37.

Cooper, Duff. *Talleyrand.* London, 1932.

Crary, Catherine. *The Price of Loyalty.* New York, 1973.

Cunliffe, Marcus. *George Washington, Man and Monument.* Boston, 1958.

Cunningham, Peter, ed. *The Letters of Horace Walpole.* 9 vols. London, 1858.

Currier, John J. *History of Newburyport, Mass., 1764–1905.* Newburyport, Mass., 1906.

Curtis, Edward E. *The Organization of the British Army Revolution.* New Haven, Conn., 1936.

d'Auberteuil, Hilliard. *Essais sur les Américains.* 2 vols. Paris, 1785.

Dann, John C., ed. *The Revolution Remembered: Eyewitness Accounts of the War of Independence.* Chicago, 1980.

Davies, K. G., ed. *Documents of the American Revolution, 1770–1783.* Colonial Office Series. 21 vols. Dublin, 1972–81.

Davis, Joseph S. *Essays in the Earlier History of American Corporations.* New York, 1965.

Dawson, Henry B. *The Sons of Liberty in New York.* New York, 1969.

———. *Record of the Trial of Joshua Hett Smith.* Morrisania, N.Y., 1866.

Dawson, Samuel E. "The Massacre at the Cedars." *CMNR,* 5 (1874), 305–23.

Deane, J. W., H. T. Drowne, and E. Hubbard. *Genealogy of the Family Arnold.* Boston, 1849.

Deane, Silas. *Papers.* 5 vols. N-YHS. New York, 1887–91.

Dearborn, Henry. "A Narrative of the Saratoga Campaign." *FTMB,* 1 (1928–29), 3–12.

———. *Revolutionary War Journals.* Edited by Lloyd A. Brown and Howard H. Peckham. Chicago, 1939.

Decker, Malcolm. *Benedict Arnold: Son of the Havens.* New York, 1961.

Dexter, F. B. *Biographical Sketches of the Graduates of Yale College.* 4 vols. New York, 1885–1919.

Digby, William. *Journal.* In *The British Invasion from the North.* Edited by James Phinney Baxter. Albany, N.Y., 1887. Repr. New York, 1970.

Dionne, Narcisse-E. "L'Invasion de 1775–76." *BRH,* 6 (1900), 132–40.

Dix, Morgan, ed. *A History of the Parish of Trinity College in the City of New York.* New York, 1898.

"Documents relatifs à la révolution américaine de 1775." *RUL,* 1 (1946–47), 65–69, 142–47, 299–303, 469–73, 670–76, 888–90; 2 (1947–48), 262–68, 344–49, 454–59, 544–642, 742–48, 838–48, 926–34.

Documents Relative to the Colonial History of the State of New York. Edited by E. B. O'Callaghan. 15 vols. Albany, 1853–87.

Doerflinger, Thomas M. *A Vigorous Spirit of Enterprise: Merchants and Economic Development in Revolutionary Philadelphia.* Chapel Hill, N.C., 1986.

Doniol, Henri. *Histoire de la Participation de la France à l'Etablissement des Etats-Unis d'Amérique: Correspondance Diplomatique et Documents.* 5 vols. Paris, 1886–92.

Drake, S. A. *Historic Fields and Mansions of Middlesex.* Boston, 1874.

Drinker, Elizabeth. *Journal.* Edited by Henry Drinker Biddle. Philadelphia, 1889.

Duane, James. *Papers.* MSS., N-YHS.

Duncan, Henry. *Journals of Henry Duncan, Captain, Royal Navy, 1776–1782.* Edited by J. K. Laughton. London, 1902.

Dunn, Mary Maples. "Saints and Sisters: Congregational and Quaker Women in the Early Colonial Period." *Atlantic Quarterly,* 30 (1978), 582–601.

Dupuy, Trevor N. *The Military History of Revolutionary War Naval Battles.* New York, 1970.

Eardley-Wilmot, John. *Historical View of the Commission for Enquiring into the Losses, Services and Claims of the American Loyalists.* 1815. Repr. Boston, 1972.

East, Robert A. *Business Enterprise in the American Revolutionary Era.* New York, 1938.

———. *Connecticut Loyalists.* Chester, Conn., 1974.

East, Robert A., and Jacob Judd, eds. *The Loyalist Americans: A Focus on Greater New York.* Tarrytown, N.Y., 1975.

Eelking, Max von, ed. *Memoirs and Letters and Journals of Major General Riedesel During His Residence in America.* 2 vols. Albany, 1868.

Egnal, Marc. "The Changing Structure of Philadelphia's Trade with the British West Indies." *PMHB,* 99 (1975), 156–79.

Ehrman, John. *The Younger Pitt.* New York, 1969.

Einstein, Lewis. *Divided Loyalties: Americans in England During the War of Independence.* London, 1933.

Elliott, Emory. *Power and the Pulpit in New England.* Princeton, 1975.

Engle, Paul. *Women in the American Revolution.* New York, 1976.

Enys, John, Lt. *American Journals.* Edited by Elizabeth Cometti. Blue Mountain Lake, N.Y., 1976.

Evans, Elizabeth. *Weathering the Storm: Women of the American Revolution.* New York, 1975.

Ferguson, E. Jameson. "Business, Government and Congressional Investigation in the Revolution." *WMQ,* 16 (1959), 293–318.

Ferling, J. E. *The Loyalist Mind: Joseph Galloway and the American Revolution.* University Park, Pa., 1977.

[Finlay, Hugh.] "Journal of the Siege and Blockade of Quebec by the American Rebels in Autumn 1775 and Winter 1776." *QHSD,* 4th ser., 7 (1875), 3–25.

Fisher, Samuel Rowland. "Journal, 1779–1781." *PMHB*, 41 (1917), 145–87, 274–333, 399–457.

Fitzpatrick, John C., ed. *Writings of George Washington*. 38 vols. Washington, D.C., 1931–44.

Fleming, Thomas. *1776: Year of Illusions*. New York, 1975.

Flexner, James Thomas. *George Washington: The Forge of Experience (1732–1775)*. Boston, 1965.

———. *The Traitor and the Spy: Benedict Arnold and John André*. Rev. ed., Boston, 1975.

Flick, Alexander C. *Loyalism in New York During the American Revolution*. New York, 1901.

Forbes, Esther. *Paul Revere and the World He Lived In*. Boston, 1942.

Force, Peter, ed. *American Archives: Consisting of a Collection of Authentic Records, State Papers, Debates, and Letters* . . . 4th ser.: Mar. 7, 1774–July 4, 1776; 6 vols. 5th ser.: July 4, 1776–Sept. 3, 1783; 3 vols. Washington, D.C., 1837–46 and 1848–53. Referred to as *Am. Arch.*

Ford, Corey. *A Peculiar Service*. Boston, 1965.

Fortescue, Sir John W. *A History of the British Army*. London, 1899–1930.

Fort Ticonderoga Museum. *Bulletin*. Fort Ticonderoga, N.Y., 1927–.

Fowler, William M., Jr. *Rebels Under Sail: The American Navy During the Revolution*. New York, 1976.

Franklin, Benjamin. *The Papers of Benjamin Franklin*. Edited by Leonard W. Labaree et al. 25 vols. to date. New Haven, Conn., 1959–83. Referred to as *PBF*.

Freeman, Douglas Southall. *George Washington: A Biography*. 7 vols. New York, 1951.

French, Allen. *The First Year of the Revolution*. Boston, 1934.

———. *The Taking of Ticonderoga*. Cambridge, Mass., 1928.

Galloway, Grace Growden. *Diary*. Edited by R. C. Werner. New York, 1971.

Galloway, Joseph. "Letters of Joseph Galloway from Leading Tories in America." *Historical Review*, 5 (1961), 271–301.

Gates, Horatio. *Papers*. N-YHS.

Gerlach, Don. *Philip Schuyler and the American Revolution in New York, 1733–1777*. Lincoln, Neb., 1964.

Gerlach, Larry R. *The American Revolution: New York as a Case Study*. Belmont, Calif., 1972.

Gipson, L. H. *American Loyalist: Jared Ingersoll*. New Haven, Conn., 1971.

———. *The British Empire Before the American Revolution*. 15 vols. New York, 1966–70.

Goen, C. C. *Revivalism and Separatism in New England (1740–1800)*. New Haven, Conn., 1972.

Graham, Gerald S. *The Royal Navy in the War of American Independence*. London, 1976.

Graymont, Barbara. *The Iroquois in the American Revolution*. Syracuse, N.Y., 1972.

Greening, W. E. "Historic Kennebec Road." *Canadian Geographical Journal*, 75 (1967), 162–67.

Greenman, Jeremiah. *Diary*. Edited by R. C. Bray and P. E. Bushnell. DeKalb, Ill., 1978.

Greven, Philip. *The Protestant Temperament: Patterns of Child-Rearing, Religious Experience, and the Self in Early America*. New York, 1977.

Gruber, Ira D. *The Howe Brothers and the American Revolution*. Chapel Hill, N.C., 1972.

Glover, Michael. *General Burgoyne in Canada and America*. London, 1978.

Hadden, Lt. James M. *A Journal Kept in Canada and upon Burgoyne's Campaign in 1776 and 1777*. Albany, 1884.

Haight, Gordon S. *Mrs. Sigourney: The Sweet Singer of Hartford*. New Haven, Conn., 1930.

Hall, Hiland. *The Battle of Bennington*. Milford, Conn., 1877.

Halleck, Henry W. "Military Espionage." *American Journal of International Law*, 5 (1911), 590–603.

Hamelin, Jean, ed. *Histoire du Québec*. Montreal, 1977.

Hamilton, Alexander. *The Papers of Alexander Hamilton*. Edited by Harold C. Syrett. Vols. 1–4. New York, 1961–62.

Hammersley, Sydney Ernest. *The Lake Champlain Naval Battles of 1776–1814*. Waterford, N.Y., 1959.

Hannay, James. *History of New Brunswick*. St. John, N.B., 1909.

Harris, W. W. *Battle of Groton Heights* (Revised and enlarged by C. Allyn, New London, 1882.

Hatch, Robert McConnell. *Major John André: A Gallant in Spy's Clothing*. Boston, 1986.

———. *Thrust for Canada*. Boston, 1979.

Haw, James. *Stormy Patriot: Life of Samuel Chase*. Baltimore, 1980.

Headley, Joel Tyler. *Chaplains and Clergy of the Revolution*. New York, 1864.

Heimert, Alan, and Perry Miller, eds. *The Great Awakening*. Indianapolis, 1967.

Henderson, Herbert James. *Party Politics in the Continental Congress*. New York, 1974.

————. "Congressional Factionalism and the Attempt to Recall Benjamin Franklin." *WMB*, 38 ser., 27 (1970), 246–67.

————. "Constitutionalists and Republicans in the Continental Congress, 1778–86," *Pennsylvania History*, 36 (1969), 119–44.

Hendricks, Captain William. *Journal of the March of a Party of Provincials*. Glasgow, 1776.

Higgenbotham, Don. *The War for American Independence: Military Attitudes, Policies, and Practice, 1763–1789*. New York, 1971.

————, ed. *Reconsiderations on the Revolutionary War: Selected Essays*. Contributions in Military History No. 12. Westport, Conn., 1978.

Hill, Ralph Nading. *Lake Champlain: Key to Liberty*. Montpelier, Vt., 1976.

The Historical Magazine. Boston, 1857–75.

Historical Manuscripts Commission. *The Manuscripts of the Earls of Dartmouth*. Eleventh Report, Part 5; Fourteenth Report, Part 10; Fifteenth Report, Part 1. 3 vols. London, 1887–96. Referred to as *Dartmouth MSS;*

Hoadley, Charles J. *Public Records of the Colony of Connecticut*. 15 vols. Hartford, Conn., 1890.

Hoadley, Charles J., and L. W. Labaree, eds. *Public Records of the State of Connecticut*. 4 vols. Hartford, conn., 1894–1942.

Holden, James A. "The Influence of Jane McCrea on the Burgoyne Campaign." *NYHAP*, 12 (1913), 249–310.

Hubbard, Timothy W. "Battle at Valcour Island: Benedict Arnold as Hero." *AH*, 17 (1966), 8–11, 87–91.

Huddleston, F. J. *Gentleman Johnny Burgoyne: Misadventure of an English General in the Revolution*. Indianapolis, 1927.

Howson, Gerald. *Burgoyne of Saratoga*. New York, 1979.

Humphrey, William. "William Humphrey Marches with Arnold to Quebec." In Henry S. Commager and A. Nevins, eds., *Heritage of America*, 161–65. Boston, 1949.

Huston, James A. "Logistics of Arnold's March to Quebec." *Military Affairs*, 32 (1969), 110–24.

Jackson, John W. *The Pennsylvania Navy, 1775–1781: The Defense of the Delaware*. New Brunswick, N.J., 1974.

————. *With the British Army in Philadelphia*.

James, William, M. *The British Navy in Adversity*. London, 1926.

Jefferson, Thomas. *Papers*. Edited by Julian Boyd. 15 vols. Princeton, 1950.

————. *Writings*. Edited by Paul Leicester Ford. 20 vols. Washington, D.C., 1903–4.

Jellison, Charles A. *Ethan Allen: Frontier Rebel*. Syracuse, N.Y., 1983.

Jenkins, Kathleen. *Montreal, Island City of the St. Lawrence*. New York, 1966.

Jensen, Arthur L. *Maritime Commerce of Colonial Philadelphia*. Madison, Wis., 1963.

Jensen, Merrill. *Tracts of the American Revolution, 1763–1776*. Indianapolis, 1967.

Jesuit Relations. Edited by R. G. Thwaites, Vol. 71. Cleveland, 1901.

Johnson, David R. "Benedict Arnold: The Traitor as Hero in American Literature." Unpublished doctoral dissertation, Pennsylvania State University, 1975.

Jones, Charles Henry. *History of the Campaign for the Conquest of Canada in 1776*. Philadelphia, 1882.

Jones, Gwynfor. "An Early Amphibious Operation: Danbury, 1777." *SAHRJ*, 46 (1968), 129–31.

Jones, Thomas. *History of New York During the Revolutionary War*. 2 vols. New York, 1879.

Jordan, John W. *Colonial Families of Philadelphia*. 2 vols. New York, 1911.

Katchen, P. *The American Provincial Corps, 1775–1784*. Reading, Pa., 1973.

Keith, C. P. *The Provincial Councillors of Pennsylvania*. Philadelphia, 1883.

Kirkland, Frederick R., ed. "Journal of a Physician on the Expedition Against Canada, 1776." *PMHB*, 59 (1935), 321–61.

Klein, Milton, and R. W. Howard. *Twilight of British Rule in Revolutionary America: The New York Letter Book of General James Robertson, 1780–1783*. Cooperstown, N.Y., 1983.

Klein, Randolph S. "*The Shippen Family: A Generational Study in Colonial and Revolutionary Pennsylvania*. PhD. dissertation, Rutgers University, 1972.

Knollenburg, Bernhard. *Growth of the American Revolution*. New York, 1975.

————. *Origin of the American Revolution*. New York, 1960.

————. "Correspondence of John Adams and Horatio Gates." *Proceedings of the Massachusetts Historical Society*, Vol. 67. Boston, 1945.

Knox, Captain John. *Account of the Battle of Quebec*. Old South Leaflets. Vol. 3. Boston, 1896.

Koke, Richard J. *Accomplice in Treason: Joshua Hett Smith and the Arnold Conspiracy*. New York, 1973.

Konkle, Burton. *Benjamin Chew, 1722–1810.* Philadelphia, 1932.

Kyte, George M. "A Projected British Attack Upon Philadelphia in 1781." *PMHB,* 76 (1952), 379–98.

———. "Some Plans for a Loyalist Stronghold in the Middle Colonies." *PH,* 16 (1949), 177–90.

Labaree, B. W. *Patriots and Partisans: The Merchants of Newburyport, 1760–1815.* Cambridge, Mass., 1962.

Labaree, Leonard. "Nature of American Loyalism." American Antiquarian Society, *Proceedings.* 54 (1944), 15–58.

Lafayette, Marquis de. *Memoirs, Correspondence and Manuscripts of General Lafayette.* 3 vols. London, 1837.

Lanctot, Gustave. *Canada and the American Revolution, 1774–1783.* Toronto, 1967.

———. "Le Quebec et la révolution américaine," *MSRC,* 3e série, 35 (1941), sec 1: 91–111.

———. "When Newfoundland Helped to Save Canada," *MSRC,* 3rd ser., 45 (1951), 41–52.

Larned, E. D. *History of Windham County.* 2 vols. Worcester, Mass., 1874–80.

LaRoche, John F. *Joseph Reed.* New York, 1957.

Larter, Harry C., Jr. "German Troops with Burgoyne, 1776–1777." *FTMB,* 9 (1952), 13–24.

Lassiter, Francis R. "Arnold's Invasion of Virginia." *Sewanee Review,* 9 (1901), 78–93, 185–203.

Lawrence, J. W. *The Judges of New Brunswick and Their Times.* Edited by Alfred A. Stockton. St. John, N.B., 1907.

Leake, Isaac Q. *Memoir of the Life and Times of General John Lamb.* Albany, 1850.

Lee, Henry. *Memoirs.* Edited by Robert E. Lee. 2 vols. Philadelphia, 1825. Repr. New York, 1969.

Lefebvre, J. J. "Les Canadiens français et la révolution américaine." *BSHFA,* 47 (1946), 150–76.

———. "Officiers et miliciens du district de Québec en 1776." *BRH,* 59 (1953), 225–27.

Leiby, Adrian C. *Revolutionary War in the Hackensack Valley.* New Brunswick, N.J., 1962.

LeMoine, James M. "Arnold's Assault on Sault au Matelot Barriers." *QHSD,* 4th ser., 7 (1875), 46–70.

———. "The Assaults of Brigadier-General Richard Montgomery and Colonel Benedict Arnold on Quebec in 1775." *TRSC,* 2nd ser., 5 (1899), 457–66.

Lewis, Lawrence, Jr. "Edward Shippen, Chief Justice of Pennsylvania." *PMHB,* 7 (1883), 11–34.

Lindsay, William. "Extracts from Journal of the Proceedings at Quebec Commencing at the Time the British Militia Were Embodied 17 September 1775 Until May 1776." *BRH,* 45 (1939), 225–48.

———. "Le Siège de Quebec en 1775–1776." *BRH,* 45 (1919), 225–47.

Livingston, Major Henry. *Journal.* In *PMHB,* 22 (1898), 9–33.

Livingston, William. *The Independent Reflector.* Edited by Milton Klein. Cambridge, Mass., 1963.

Lomask, Milton. *Aaron Burr.* 2 vols. New York, 1979.

———. "Benedict Arnold: The Aftermath of Treason." *American Heritage.* 18 (1967), 16–17, 84–92.

Lossing, Benjamin Franklin. *Pictorial Field Book of the Revolution.* 2 vols. New York, 1851–52.

Louis-Philippe, Comte de Ségur. *Mémoires ou souvenirs et anecdotes.* 3 vols. Paris, 1824–26.

Lundberg, Philip K. *The Continental Gunboat "Philadelphia" and the Northern Campaign of 1776.* Washington, D.C., 1966.

Luzager, John F. "The Arnold-Gates Controversy." *West Virginia History,* 27 (1966), 75–84.

McClelland, William S. *Smuggling in the American Colonies at the Outbreak of the Revolution.* New York, 1912.

MacKenzie, Frederick. *Diary.* 2 vols. Cambridge, Mass., 1930.

Mackesy, Piers. *The War for America, 1775–1783.* Cambridge, Mass., 1964.

MacNutt, Wallace S. *New Brunswick: A History, 1784–1867.* Toronto, 1963.

Magazine of American History. 30 vols. New York and Chicago, 1877–93.

Maguire, J. Robert. "Dr. Robert Knox's Account of the Battle of Valcour, October 11–13, 1776." *VH* (1977), 141–50.

———. "Hand's Cove: Rendezvous of Ethan Allen and the Green Mountain Boys for the Capture of Fort Ticonderoga," *VH,* 33 (1965), 463–68.

Mahan, Alfred Thayer. *Major Operations of the Navies in the War of American Independence.* London, 1913.

———. *Types of Naval Officers.* Boston, 1901.

Maier, Pauline. *From Resistance to Revolution: Colonial Radicals and the Development of American Opposition to Britain, 1765–1776.* New York, 1972.

Mandements des Evêques du Quebec. Quebec, 1888.

Mann, Bruce. *Parishes, Law and Community in Connecticut, 1700–1760.*

Marshall, Douglas, and Howard H. Peckham. *Campaigns of the American Revolution.* Maplewood, N.J., 1976.

Mather, Frederic G. *Refugees of 1776 from Long Island to Connecticut.* Albany, 1913.

Meng, John J., ed. *Despatches and Instructions of Conrad Alexandre Gérard, 1778–1780,* Baltimore, 1939.

Meredith, R. B. "The Siege of Quebec, 1775–1776." *CDQ,* 6 (1928–29), 88–95.

Metzger, C. H. *The Quebec Act: A Primary Cause of the American Revolution.* New York, 1936.

Middlebrook, Louis F. *History of Maritime Connecticut during the American Revolution, 1775–1783.* 2 vols. Salem, Mass., 1935.

Middlekauff, Robert. *The Glorious Cause: The American Revolution, 1763–1789.* New York, 1982.

Mika, Nick, and Helma Mika. *United Empire Loyalists: Pioneers of Upper Canada.* Belleville, Ont., 1976.

Millar, John F. *American Ships of the Colonial and Revolutionary Periods.* New York, 1978.

Miller, Nathan. *Sea of Glory: The Continental Navy Fights for Independence, 1775–1783.* New York, 1974.

Mingay, G. E. *Georgian London.* London, 1975.

Monaghan, Frank, and Marvin Lowenthal. *This Was New York.* Garden City, N.Y., 1943.

Moody, James. "Narrative." In Dorson, Richard M., *America Rebels: Narratives of the Patriots.* New York, 1953.

Moore, Christopher. *The Loyalists: Revolution, Exile, Settlement.* Toronto, 1984.

Moore, Frank. *Diary of the American Revolution from Newspapers and Original Documents.* 2 vols. New York, 1860.

Morgan, Edmund S., and Helen M. Morgan. *The Stamp Act Crisis: Prologue to Revolution.* Rev. ed. New York, 1962.

Morison, George. "Account of the Battle of Quebec, 1776." *PMHB,* 14 (1890), 434–39.

Murdock, David H., ed. *Rebellion in America: A Contemporary British Viewpoint.* Oxford, 1979.

Murdock, Richard K. "Benedict Arnold and the Owners of the *Charming Nancy.*" *PMHB,* 84 (1960), 22–26.

Murray, Eleanor M. "Résumé of the Court Martial of General Arthur St. Clair Resulting from the Evacuation of Fort Ticonderoga and Mount Independence, July 6, 1777." *FTMB,* 7 (1946–47), 3–20.

Murray, James. *Letters from America, 1773 to 1780.* Edited by Eric Robson. New York, 1951.

Naval Documents of the American Revolution. Edited by William Ball Clark. Washington, D.C., 1964–73. Referred to as ND.

Neatby, Hilda. *Quebec: The Revolutionary Age, 1760–1791.* Toronto, 1966.

Neilson, Charles. *An Original, Compiled, and Corrected Account of Burgoyne's Campaign, and the Memorable Battles of Bemis's Heights.* Albany, 1844.

Nelson, Paul David. *General Horatio Gates: A Biography.* Baton Rouge, La., 1976.

——. "Guy Carleton versus Benedict Arnold: The Campaign of 1776 in Canada and on Lake Champlain." *NYH,* 7 (1976),

Nelson, William H. *The American Tory.* Boston, 1961.

——. "New York in the Strategy of the Revolution," in Alexander C. Flick, ed., *History of the State of New York.* 10 vols. New York, 1933. Vol. 4, 78–83.

Nichols, C. J. "March of Benedict Arnold Through the District of Maine." *Sprague's Journal of Maine History,* 11 (1923), 144–150, 195–208; 13 (1923), 69–78.

Nichols, Lieutenant Francis. *Diary.* In *PMHB,* 20 (1897), 504–14.

Nickerson, Hoffman. *Turning Point of the Revolution.* Boston, 1928.

Nolan, James Bennett. *Neddie Burd's Reading Letters.* Reading, Pa., 1927.

Norwich. *Vital Records.* 2 vols. Hartford, Conn., 1913.

Oaks, Robert F. "Philadelphia in Exile: The Problem of Loyalty During the American Revolution." *PMHB,* 96 (1972), 298–325.

O'Callaghan, E. B., ed. *Documents Relative to the Colonial History of the State of New York.* 14 vols. Albany, 1856–83.

O'Keefe, Marian K., and Catherine S. Doroshevich. *Norwich: Historic Homes and Families.* Stonington, Conn., 1967.

O'Leary, Thomas. "Arnold at Quebec." *CANJ,* 3rd ser., 10 (1913), 45–58.

Ousterhout, Anne M. "Controlling the Opposition in Pennsylvania During the American Revolution." *PMHB,* 105 (1981), 3–35.

Paltsits, Victor Hugo. "The Use of Invisible Ink for Secret Writing During the American Revolution." *New York Public Library Bulletin,* 39 (1985), 361–64.

Pancake, John S. *1777: Year of the Hangman.* University, Ala., 1977.

Park, Edwards. "Could Canada Have Ever Been Our Fourteenth Colony?" *Smithsonian Magazine,* 12 (1987), 41–49.

Parton, James. *Life and Times of Aaron Burr.* 2 vols. Boston, 1892.

Paullin, Charles O. *The Navy of the American Revolution.* Cleveland, 1906.

Pausch, Georg. *Journal of Captain Pausch, Chief of the Hanau Artillery During the Burgoyne Campaign.* Albany, 1886.

Pavlovsky, Arnold M. "Between Hawk and Buzzard: Congress as Perceived by Its Members, 1775–1783," *WMQ,* 3d ser., 349–64.

Pearson, Michael. *Those Damned Rebels: The American Revolution as Seen Through British Eyes.* New York, 1972.

Peckham, H. H. "British Secret Writing in the Revolution." *Michigan Alumnus Quarterly Review,* 44 (1938), 126–31.

————, ed. *Sources of American Independence.* 2 vols. Chicago, 1978.

————. *The Toll of Independence: Engagements and Battle Casualties of the American Revolution.* Chicago, 1974.

————. *The War for Independence: A Military History.* Chicago, 1958.

Pell, John. *Ethan Allen.* Lake George, N.Y., 1929.

————. "The Montgomery Expedition." *NYH,* 15 (1934), 184–89.

Pell, S.H.P. *Fort Ticonderoga.* Pamphlet. Ticonderoga, N.Y., 1975.

Penn, William. *Papers.* Vol. 4. Edited by Richard S. and Mary Maples Dunn. Philadelphia, 1987.

Pennsylvania, State of. *Colonial Records.* 16 vols. Harrisburg, 1938–53. Includes *Minutes of the Provincial Council of Pennsylvania; Minutes of the Council of Safety; Minutes of the Supreme Executive Council.* Referred to as *PCR.*

Pennsylvania Archives. Edited by Samuel Hazard and others. 9 series. Philadelphia and Harrisburg, 1852–1935. Referred to as *PA.*

The Pennsylvania Magazine of History and Biography. Philadelphia, 1877–.

Pennypacker, Morton. *General Washington's Spies.* Brooklyn, 1939.

Peters, Samuel A. *General History of Connecticut.* London, 1781.

————. *Works.* Edited by Kenneth W. Cameron. Hartford, Conn., 1967.

————. "Account of Major General Benedict Arnold." *Political Magazine,* 1 (1780), 690, 746–48.

Pettengill, Ray W., ed. *Letters from America, 1776–1779: Being Letters of Brunswick, Hessian and Waldeck Officers with the British Armies.* Boston, 1924.

Pollock, Thomas C. *Philadelphia Theatre in the Eighteenth Century.* Philadelphia, 1933.

Potter, Janice. *The Liberty We Seek: Loyalist Ideology in Colonial New York and Massachusetts.* Cambridge, Mass., 1983.

Powell, Walter Louis. "New London." Unpublished doctoral dissertation, Kent State University, 1978.

Preston, Anthony, et al. *Navies of the American Revolution.* Englewood Cliffs, N.J., 1975.

Quebec Archives. *Documents relatifs à la révolution américaine de 1775.* Quebec, 1946.

Raddall, Thomas H. *The Path of Destiny: Canada from the British Conquest to Home Rule.* New York, 1957.

Randall, Willard Sterne. *A Little Revenge: Benjamin Franklin and His Son.* Boston, 1984.

————. "The War." In David Boldt and Willard S. Randall, eds., *The Founding City.* Philadelphia, 1976.

Rawlyk, George A. *Revolution Rejected: 1776–1776.* Toronto, 1968.

————. "The Federalist-Loyalist Alliance in New Brunswick, 1784–1815." *Humanities Association Review,* 27 (1976), 142.

Raymond, W. D. *Kingston and the Loyalists of the "Spring Fleet" of 1783.* Saint John, N.B., 1889.

————. *The River St. John.* Saint John, N.B., 1910.

————, ed. *Winslow Papers.* Saint John, N.B., 1901. Repr. Boston, 1972.

————. "The Loyalists in Arms," *Collections of the New Brunswick Historical Society,* 5 (1904), 189–223.

————. "Roll of Officers of the British American Loyalist Corps." *Collections of the New Brunswick Historical Society,* 2 (1898–99), 224–72.

Reed, Joseph. *Papers.* N-YHS.

Reed, William B. *Life and Correspondence of Joseph Reed.* 2 vols. Philadelphia, 1847.

———, ed. *Original Letters from George Washington to Joseph Reed.* Philadelphia, 1852.

Reid, Marjorie G. "The Quebec Fur Traders and Western Policy, 1763–1774." *CHR,* 6 (1925), 15–32.

Reynolds, Paul R. *Guy Carleton: A Biography.* New York, 1980.

Ricord, Frederick W., and William Nelson, eds. *Documents Relating to the Colonial History of the State of New Jersey.* Newark, N.J., 1886.

Riedesel, Major General Baron von. *Memoirs, Letters and Journals.* 2 vols. Albany, 1868.

———. "Journal of the Brunswick Corps in America." In H. H. Peckham, *Sources of American Independence,* 1:226–39. 2 vols. Chicago, 1978.

Riker, James. *Memoirs.*

Risch, Erna. *Supplying Washington's Army.* Washington, D.C., 1981.

Rivis, R.G.L. "Sir William Grant and the Blockade of Quebec, November 1775 to May 1776." *Journal of the Society of Army Historical Research,* 10 (1941), 101–4.

Roberts, Kenneth. *March to Quebec: Journal of the Members of Arnold's Expedition.* New York, 1938.

Roberts, Robert B. *New York's Forts in the Revolution.* Rutherford, N.J., 1980.

Roche, John F. *Joseph Reed.* New York, 1954.

———. "Quebec Under Siege, 1775–1776: The 'Memorandums' of Jacob Danford." *CHR,* 50 (1969), 68–85.

Rockwell, George L. *History of Ridgefield, Conn.* Ridgefield, 1927.

Rommel, John G. *Richard Varick: New York Aristocrat.* PhD. dissertation, Columbia University, 1966.

Rossie, Jonathan Gregory. *The Politics of Command in the American Revolution.* Syracuse, N.Y., 1975.

Roth, David M. *Connecticut: A Bicentennial History.* New York, 1979.

Rowland, Kate M. *Life of Charles Carroll.* 2 vols. New York, 1898.

Royster, Charles. *A Revolutionary People at War: the Continental Army and American Character, 1775–1783.* Chapel Hill, N.C., 1979.

———. "The Nature of Treason: Revolutionary Virtue and American Reactions to Benedict Arnold." *WMQ,* 3rd ser., 36 (1979), 163–93.

Rumilly, Robert. *Histoire de Montréal.* 2 vols. Montreal, 1970.

Rush, Benjamin. *Autobiography.* Edited by George W. Corner. Philadelphia, 1948.

Rush, Richard. *Occasional Productions, Political, Diplomatic and Miscellaneous.* New York, 1860.

Ryerson, Richard A. *The Revolution Is Now Begun.* Philadelphia, 1978.

Sabine, Lorenzo. *Biographical Sketches of the Loyalists of the American Revolution.* 2 vols. Boston, 1864.

Sabine, William H. W. *Historical Memoirs from 26 August 1778 to 12 November 1783 of William Smith.* New York, 1971.

Sanguinet, M. *Journal.* Quebec, 1975.

Sargent, Winthrop. *Life and Career of Major John André.* Boston, 1861.

———, ed. *Loyal Verses of Joseph Stansbury and Jonathan Odell.* New York, 1860.

Scharf, John T., and Thompson Wescott. *History of Philadelphia.* 3 vols. 1884. Vol. 1.

Scheer, George. "The Sergeant Major's Strange Mission." *AH,* 8 (1957), 26–29, 98.

Scheer, George F., and Hugh F. Rankin. *Rebels and Redcoats.* Cleveland, 1957.

Schuyler, George L. *Correspondence and Remarks upon Bancroft's History of the Northern Campaign of 1777, and the Character of Major-General Philip Schuyler.* New York, 1867.

Schuyler, Philip. *Papers.* NYPL.

———. "A Winter's Campaign Against Canada." *CANJ,* 3 (1947), 7–12.

Scott, Duncan Campbell. *John Graves Simcoe.* Quebec, 1926.

Scott, John A. "Joseph Brant at Fort Stanwix and Oriskany." *NYH,* 19 (1938), 399–406.

Scott, Kenneth. "The Tory Associators of Portsmouth." *WMQ,* 3rd ser., 17 (1960), 507–15.

———, ed. *Rivington's New York Newspaper: Excerpts from a Loyalist Press, 1773–1783.* New York, 1973.

Seabury, Samuel. *The Congress Canvassed.* New York, 1774.

See, Geoffrey. "A British Spy in Philadelphia, 1775–1777." *PMHB,* 85 (1961), 3–37.

Sellers, Charles Coleman. *Charles Wilson Peale.* 2 vol. Philadelphia, 1947.

Sereisky, Jean E. "Benedict Arnold in New Brunswick." *Atlantic Advocate.* 8 (1963), 33–43.

Serle, Ambrose, *The American Journal of Ambrose Serle, 1776–1778.* Edited by E. H. Tatum, Jr. San Marino, Calif., 1940.

Sheppard, John H. *The Life of Samuel Tucker, Commodore in the American Revolution.* Boston, 1868.

Shippen, Edward IV. *Papers.* HSP.

Short, W.T.P., ed. "Journal of the Principal Occurrences During the Siege of Quebec by the American Revolutionists Under Generals Montgomery and Arnold in 1775–76." *QHSD,* 8th ser., 11 (1906), 57–101.

Shortt, Adam and Arthur G. Doughty, eds. *Documents Relating to the Constitutional History of Canada, 1759–91.* Ottawa, 1918.

Shy, John. *A People Numerous and Armed.* New York, 1976.

———. "A New Look at Colonial Militia." *WMQ,* 3rd ser., 20 (1963), 175–85.

———. "Quartering His Majesty's Forces in New Jersey." *PNJHS,* 78 (1960), 82–94.

Sigourney, Lydia Huntley. *Sketch of Connecticut Forty Years Since.* Hartford, Conn., 1824.

———. *Letters of Life.* New York, 1866.

Simcoe, John Graves. *Military Journal.* New York, 1844.

Sims, J. P., ed. *The Philadelphia Assemblies, 1748–1948.* Philadelphia, 1948.

Smith, Joshua Hett. *An Authentic Narrative of the Causes Which Led to the Death of Major André.* New York, 1808.

Smith, Justin H. *Arnold's March from Cambridge to Quebec.* New York, 1907. Repr. 1982.

Smith, Paul H. *Loyalists and Redcoats: A Study in British Revolutionary Policy.* Chapel Hill, N.C., 1964.

———. "The American Loyalists: Notes on Their Organization and Numerical Strength." *WMQ,* 3rd ser., 25 (1968), 259–77.

———. "New Jersey Loyalists and the British 'Provincial' Corps in the War for Independence." *NJH,* 87 (1969), 69–78.

———, et al., eds. *Letters of Delegates to Congress.* 12 vols. to date. Washington, D.C., 1976–. Referred to as *LDC.*

Smith, William. *Historical Memoirs from 12 July 1776 to 25 July 1778.* Edited by W.H.W. Sabine. 2 vols. New York, 1956.

———. *Historical Memoirs of William Smith 1778–1783.* Edited by W.H.W. Sabine. New York, 1971.

Smyth, Albert H. *Writings of Benjamin Franklin.* 10 vols. New York, 1905–07.

Snyder, Charles M. "With Benedict Arnold at Valcour Island: The Diary of Pascal DeAngelis," *VH,* 42 (1974), 195–200.

Spargo, John. *The Bennington Battle Monument.* Rutland, Vt., 1925.

Sparks, Jared, ed. *Correspondence of the American Revolution.* 4 vols. Boston, 1853.

———, ed. *Writings of George Washington.* 12 vols. Boston, 1837.

———. *Life and Treason of Benedict Arnold.* Boston, 1835.

Sprague, William B., ed. *Annals of the American Pulpit.* 9 vols. Philadelphia, 1858.

Stedman, Charles. *History of the Origin, Progress and Termination of the American War.* London, 1794.

Stember, Sol. *Bicentennial Guide to the American Revolution.* 3 vols. New York, 1974.

Stevens, Benjamin F., ed. *Facsimiles of Manuscripts in European Archives Relating to America 1773–1783 . . .* 25 vols. London, 1889–98.

Stewart, Gordon, and George A. Rawlyk. *A People Highly Favored of God.* Toronto, 1972.

Stewart, Walter, *True Blue: The Loyalist Legend.* Toronto, 1985.

Stiles, Ezra. *The Literary Diary of Ezra Stiles.* Edited by Franklin B. Dexter. 3 vols. New York, 1901.

Stillé, Charles J. *Major General Anthony Wayne.* Philadelphia, 1893.

Stinchcombe, William C. *The American Revolution and the French Alliance.* Syracuse, N.Y., 1969.

Stone, William Leete, ed. *Ballads and Poems Relating to the Burgoyne Campaign.* Albany, 1893.

———. *The Campaign of Lieutenant General John Burgoyne and the Expedition of Lieutenant Colonel Barry St. Leger.* Albany, 1877.

———. *Memoirs of Major General Riedesel.* 2 vols. Albany, 1868.

Stopford-Sackville MSS. Historical MSS. Commission Reports.

Strange, Thomas B. "Notes on the Defence of Quebec in 1775." *Transactions of the Literary and Historical Society of Quebec,* New Ser., 12 (1876), 11–45.

Sullivan, John. *Letters and Papers of Major-General John Sullivan, Continental Army.* Edited by Otis G. Hammond. 2 vols. Concord, N.H.

Taylor, J. G. *Some New Light on the Later Life and Last Resting Place of Benedict Arnold.* London, 1931.

Tebbenhoff, Edward H. "The Associated Loyalists: An Aspect of Militant Loyalism." *NYHSQ*, 63 (1979), 115–44.

Teed, Eric L. "Footprints of Benedict Arnold." *New Brunswick Historical Society Collections.* 73 (1971), 57–97.

Tesser, Charles H., ed. *The Sinews of Independence: Monthly Strength Reports of the Continental Army.* Chicago, 1976.

Thacher, James. *Military Journal.* Boston, 1823.

[Thompson, James.] "Journal of the Siege from 1st December, 1775." In *Blockade of Quebec.* Edited by Frederick C. Wurtele. Quebec, 1906. Repr. New York, 1970.

Tillotson, Harry S. *The Beloved Spy.* Caldwell, Idaho, 1948.

———. *The Exquisite Exile: Life and Fortunes of Mrs. Benedict Arnold.* Boston, 1932.

Todd, Charles Burr. *The Real Benedict Arnold.* New York, 1903.

Trevelyan, George O. M. *The American Revolution.* 6 vols. London, 1895.

Trudel, Marcel. *La Révolution Américaine.* Quebec, 1976.

Trumbull, Benjamin. "Benjamin Trumbull's Journal of the Expedition Against Canada, 1775." *CHSC*, 7 (1899), 137–73.

Trumbull, Jonathan. *Papers.* Connecticut State Archives. Hartford, Conn., 1860.

———. *The Trumbull Papers.* Massachusetts Historical Society Collections, ser. 5, vols. 9 and 10; ser. 7, vols. 2 and 3. Boston, 1885–1902.

———. Letter Books, 1775–1779. MSS., Library of Congress.

Tyler, Moses Coit. *Literary History of the American Revolution.* 2 vols. New York, 1897.

Uhlendorf, Bernhard A., ed. *Revolution in America: Confidential Letters and Journals 1776–1784 of Adjutant Major General Baurmeister of the Hessian Forces.* New Brunswick, N.J., 1957.

U.S. Continental Congress. *Journals, 1774–89.* Edited by Worthington C. Ford et al. 34 vols. Washington, D.C., 1904–37.

———. *Letters of Delegates to Congress.* Edited by Paul H. Smith et al. 15 vols. to date. Washington, D.C. 1976–.

United States. *Proceedings of a General Court Martial . . . For the Trial of Major General Arnold . . .* Philadelphia, 1780.

Upton, L.F.S. *The Loyal Whig: William Smith of New York and Quebec.* Toronto, 1969.

Van Closen, Ludwig. *The Revolutionary Journal of Ludwig Van Closen.* Translated by Evelyn M. Acomb. Chapel Hill, N.C., 1958.

Van Doren, Carl. *Benjamin Franklin.* New York, 1938.

———. *Secret History of the American Revolution.* New York, 1941.

Van Dusen, Albert E. *Connecticut.* New York, 1961.

Van Powell, W. Howland. *The American Navies of the Revolutionary War.* New York, 1974.

Van Schaack, Henry C. *Life of Peter Van Schaack.* New York, 1842.

Van Tyne, Claude H. *The Loyalists in the American Revolution.* New York, 1902.

Varick, Richard. *Varick's Court of Inquiry.* Edited by Albert Bushnell Hart. New York, 1907.

Vialer, Anthony. "Orderly Book of the Siege of Quebec by Montgomery." *QHSD*, 7th ser., 10 (1905), 155–265.

Vidal, Gore. *Burr.* New York, 1973.

Walker, Lewis Burd. "Life of Margaret Shippen." *PMHB*, 24 (1900), 257–67, 401–29; 25 (1901), 20–46, 145–90, 289–302, 452–97; 26 (1902), 71–80, 224–44, 322–34, 464–68.

Wallace, W. Stewart. "Brigadier-General Montgomery at Quebec." *CM* 36 (1910–11), 590–93.

Wallace, Willard M. *Appeal to Arms: A Military History of the American Revolution.* Chicago, 1951.

———. *Dark Star of the Revolution.* Hartford, Conn., 1976.

———. *Traitorous Hero: The Hero and Fortunes of Benedict Arnold.* New York, 1954.

Walpole, Horace. *Journal of the Reign of King George the Third.* 2 vols. London, 1859.

———. *The Last Journals of Horace Walpole.* Edited by A. F. Steuart. 2 vols. London, 1858.

———. *Letters.* Edited by Peter Cunningham. 8 vols. London, 1963.

———. *Memoirs of the Last Ten Years of the Reign of King George the Second, 1751–1761.* 2 vols. London, 1822.

Ward, Christopher. *The War of the Revolution.* 2 vols. New York, 1952.

Washington, George. *Writings, 1745–99.* Edited by John C. Fitzpatrick, 38 vols. Washington, D.C., 1931–44.

Waterman, Edgar F. *The Waterman Family*. 2 vols. New Haven, Conn., 1939. Vol. 1.
Watson, John F. *Annals of Philadelphia and Pennsylvania*. 3 vols. Philadelphia, 1844.
Waugh, Albert E. *Samuel Huntingdon and His Family*. Stonington, Conn., 1968.
Webb, J. Watson. *Reminiscences of Gen'l Samuel B. Webb, of the Revolutionary Army . . . by his Son, J. Watson Webb*. New York, 1882.
Webb, Samuel Blachley. *Correspondence and Journals of Samuel Blachley Webb*. Edited by Worthington C. Ford. 3 vols. New York and Lancaster, Pa., 1893.
Weigley, Russell F., ed. *Philadelphia: A 300-Year History*. New York, 1982.
Weiner, Frederick B. *Civilians Under Military Justice*. Chicago, 1967.
———. "Military Occupation of Philadelphia in 1777–1778." *PAPS*, 111 (1967), 310–13.
Wells, Bayze. *Journal*. In *Connecticut Historical Society Collections*, 7 (1899), 241–96.
Wells, K. G. *Campobello*. Boston, 1893.
Wertenbaker, Thomas J. *Father Knickerbocker Rebels: New York City During the Revolution*. New York, 1948.
Westcott, Thompson. *Historical Mansions of Philadelphia*. Philadelphia, 1877.
Wheatley, Henry B. *London Past and Present*. 3 vols. London, 1891.
Whitefield, George. *Journals*. London, 1960.
Whitridge, Arnold. "Canada: The Struggle for the 14th State." *HT*, 17 (1967), 13–21.
Wilkinson, James. *Memoirs of My Own Times*. 3 vols. Philadelphia, 1816. Vol. 1.
Willcox, William B. *Portrait of a General: Sir Henry Clinton in the War of Independence*. New York, 1964.
———. "The British Road to Yorktown: A Study in Divided Command." *AHR*, 52 (1945), 1–35.
———. "British Strategy in America, 1778," *Journal of Modern History*, 19 (1947), 97–121.
———, ed. *The American Rebellion: Sir Henry Clinton's Narrative of His Campaign, 1775–1782*. New Haven, Conn., 1954.
———. "Why Did the British Lose the American Revolution?" *Michigan Alumnus Quarterly Review*, 62 (1956), 317–24.
Wilson, Samuel Knox. "Bishop Briand and the American Revolution." *Catholic History Review*, 19 (1933–34), 133–47.
Winsor, Justin. *Narrative and Critical History of America*. 6 vols. Cambridge, Mass., 1888. Vol. 6.
———. "Virginia and the Quebec Bill." *AHR*, 1 (1895–96), 436–43.
Wood, Gordon S. "A Note on Mobs." *WMQ*, 3rd ser., 23 (1966), 635–42.
Wright, Esmond, ed. *Red, White and True Blue: The Loyalists in the Revolution*. New York, 1976.
Wright, Esther C. *The Loyalists of New Brunswick*. Moncton, N.B., 1955.
Wright, M. J., "Lafayette's Campaign in Virginia." *Southern Historical Association Publications*. 9 (1905), 234–40, 261–71.
Wrong, George M. *Canada and the American Revolution*. Toronto, 1935.
Wurtele, Fred C. *Blockade of Quebec in 1775–1776*. Port Washington, N.Y., 1970.
Young, Henry J. "The Treatment of Loyalists in Pennsylvania." Unpublished doctoral dissertation, Johns Hopkins University, 1955.
Zeichner, Oscar. *Connecticut's Years of Controversy, 1750–1776*. Chapel Hill, N.C., 1949.

INDEX

About the Author

Willard Sterne Randall has won numerous awards, among them the National Magazine Award from the Columbia School of Journalism for his articles on political corruption in Philadelphia. As a historian, his book *A Little Revenge: Benjamin Franklin and His Son* was awarded a Frank Luther Mott Prize from the University of Missouri School of Journalism. Randall lives in Winooski, Vermont, where he lectures on British and American history at the University of Vermont.